Vatican II As I Saw It

Letters, Journal, Diary and Papers of Lawrence Leslie McReavy

Cuthbert Peter Johnson OSB

British Library Cataloguing in Publication data

A catalogue record for this book is available from the British Library

ISBN 978-0-907077-67-1

First published in 2015 by St Michael's Abbey Press
Farnborough Abbey,
Farnborough, Hampshire GU14 7NQ

www.farnboroughabbey.org
www.theabbeyshop.com

St Michael's Abbey Press is a division of
St Michael's Abbey Press Ltd (reg. no. 326241)

Printed and bound in Slovakia

To the memory of Lawrence L. McReavy
one of the "Grand Old Men" of Ushaw
a *Peritus* at the Second Vatican Council
recording events for his Alma Mater

Contents

Acknowledgements

This work was begun, it might be said, by accident. While searching for material on the Constitution on the Liturgy *Sacrosanctum Concilium* of the Second Vatican Council I came across a reference to the Archives at Ushaw College and the papers of Monsignor Lawrence Leslie McReavy. I decided to pay a visit and examine the material in the dossier. It is, therefore, necessary to thank Dr Jonathan Bush, the Archivist, who received me kindly and showed me the material that had stirred my interest. Throughout subsequent visits Dr Bush showed the same concern and kindness. Two other Archivists deserve a mention. Again for help and assistance the Reverend Dr John Sharp, Archivist of the Archdiocese of Birmingham and the Reverend Father Nicholas Schofield, Archivist of the Archdiocese of Westminster.

A word of thanks to the Trustees of Ushaw College, particularly the Right Reverend Terence Patrick Drainey, Bishop of Middlesborough and the Right Reverend Seamus Cunningham, Bishop of Hexham and Newcastle who also kindly accepted to present this volume. The copyright for the material from the Ushaw Archives remains with the above mentioned Trustees.

Thanks to some of Monsignor McReavy's former students particularly, Canon Robert Spence, the Reverend Fathers Stephen Johnson, Alan Macknight and Joseph Parkes and others who have expressed their interest in this work and offered encouragement.

C.J.

Presentation

Generations of Priests not only from our Diocese but in the whole of the Northern Province were indebted to the work and teaching of Monsignor Lawrence Leslie McReavy, Professor of Canon Law at Ushaw College, Durham, for nearly fifty years. His regular series of Canonical Questions and Answers which he contributed to the *Clergy Review* for over thirty years made him a household name in the Church in Great Britain and Ireland. Although not involved directly in pastoral parochial ministry, he was very active in promoting the ecumenical movement and the lay apostolate.

As the fiftieth anniversary of the conclusion of the Second Vatican Council and the solemn promulgation of its Constitutions and Decrees draws near, it is indeed fitting that we should honour one of our own men who played a discreet but not insignificant part in its work both at the level of the Preparatory Commissions and during the course of the Council from 1962 to 1965.

Monsignor McReavy's experience of the Council and his zeal for its implementation was to remain with him for the rest of his life. In a letter to Monsignor Paul Grant, the President of Ushaw, my predecessor, Bishop James Cunningham, caught something of McReavy's enthusiasm when he wrote, "The opening of the Council was a really wonderful experience with the Holy Father there with all his bishops. It will take Monsignor McReavy years to describe it! He is, as you surely know, at the Venerabile and working hard but enjoying himself as you can imagine".

Many of those who were influenced by Monsignor McReavy's example at Ushaw College of faithfulness to duty and love of the Church, have also gone before us marked with the sign of faith. However, I am sure that the image of Lawrence Leslie McReavy, the devoted Priest, Professor and faithful son of the Church which emerges from these pages will be an inspiration to all who are seeking the Lord and putting their diverse gifts at the service of the Church.

+ Seamus Cunningham
Bishop of Hexham and Newcastle
Feast of the Translation of Saint Cuthbert, September 4th 2014

Introduction

Since the Second Vatican Council closed on December 8th 1965 not a single decade has gone by without there being a celebration to commemorate that great event in the life of the Church.[1] During the past half century there has been a continuous flow of publications assessing and commenting upon the Council, its work and the documents it promulgated.[2] The fiftieth anniversary of the opening of the Second Vatican Council in 2012 opened with the celebration of the Year of Faith and commemorative events are planned to continue to mark each of the Council's four Sessions.[3]

While recognising that it is appropriate to commemorate the Council, which he described as "a beautiful work of the Holy Spirit", Pope Francis has reminded the Church of the Council's call for a transformation of mind and heart: "After 50 years have we done everything the Holy Spirit was asking us to do during the Council? No. We celebrate this anniversary, we put up a monument but we don't want it to upset us. We don't want to change and what's more there are those who wish to turn the clock back."[4]

The Council Fathers understood that renewal is the work of the Holy Spirit and that "in its pilgrimage on earth, Christ summons the Church to continual reformation of which it is always in need in so far as it is an

---

[1] For example: "on this tenth anniversary of the closing of the Second Vatican Council" Pope Paul VI issued the Apostolic Exhortation *Evangelii Nuntiandi* (December 8, 1975). The Congregation for Divine Worship held a Congress for the Presidents and Secretaries of national Liturgical Commissions to assess twenty years of liturgical renewal, 23-28 October 1984. The Second Extraordinary Synod of 1985 marked the twentieth anniversary of the conclusion of the Second Vatican Council: "The end for which this Synod was convoked was the celebration, verification and promotion of Vatican Council II". On December 4th, 1988 Pope John Paul II issued an Apostolic Letter to mark the occasion of the twenty-fifth anniversary of the promulgation of the Constitution *Sacrosanctum Concilium* on the Sacred Liturgy. The thirtieth anniversary of the opening of the Council was chosen as the date for the promulgation of the Catechism of the Catholic Church. The commemoration of the anniversaries of the promulgation of various texts of the Council have taken place at intervals during the past twenty years.

[2] For an extensive bibliography: Philippe J. Roy, *Bibliographie du Concile Vatican II* (Libreria Editrice Vaticana 2013).

[3] The proclamation of a Year of Faith was timed "to coincide with the fiftieth anniversary of the opening of the Second Vatican Council" and was a call to return to the study of "the texts bequeathed by the Council Fathers ... to be read, known and taken to heart as important and normative texts of the Magisterium, within the Church's Tradition"". Benedict XVI, Motu Proprio: *Porta Fidei* n. 5.

[4] Homily. April 16, 2013.

institution of human beings here on earth" and that "every renewal of the Church is essentially grounded in an increase of fidelity to her own calling".[5]

In what Pope Francis has called "a memorable text which continues to challenge us"[6] Blessed Pope Paul VI developed the theme of renewal in his Encyclical Letter on the Church *Ecclesiam Suam*: "The Church must look with penetrating eyes within herself, ponder the mystery of her own being... This vivid and lively self-awareness inevitably leads to a comparison between the ideal image of the Church as Christ envisaged her and loved her as his holy and spotless bride (cf. Eph 5:27), and the actual image which the Church presents to the world today... This is the source of the Church's heroic and impatient struggle for renewal: the struggle to correct those flaws introduced by her members which her own self-examination, mirroring her exemplar, Christ, points out to her and condemns".[7]

Many faithful Catholics are not only challenged but also troubled by the image of the Church today as fragmented and dysfunctional. They want renewal and are not prepared to accept any attempt to disguise the flaws and weaknesses of what was once thought to be a mighty stronghold. A Church which is perceived as an authoritative structure that has shown itself incompetent in the welfare of its members, devious in some of its undertakings and defective in its mission to sanctify, must heed the Council's call to holiness if it is to undergo that "purification and renewal so that the sign of Christ may shine more brightly over the face of the earth".[8]

The sign posts pointing the way to renewal can be found in the teaching of the Second Vatican Council and the Magisterium and not in the theories of those who want to "turn back the clock". Pope Francis understands that by responding to the Council's call for holiness, service and solidarity with the poor and the most vulnerable in society, the process of healing the wounds of the scandals that have shamed the Church in recent years can begin. "The Council was a beautiful work of the Holy Spirit" and the Church, heeding the words of Saint Paul, needs to stir up the Spirit that was given to us.

Even as the preparations for the Council were drawing to a close and the day of its opening drawing near, some concern was expressed as to whether the Council would succeed in its purpose: "To question the Second Vatican Council's chances for success on the eve of its opening may seem to be inappropriate, at the very least, — if not misguided or even disloyal.

---

[5] Decree on Ecumenism No. 6.

[6] Pope Francis, *Evangelii Gaudium* : Apostolic Exhortation on the Proclamation of the Gospel in Today's World (24 November 2013) n. 26.

[7] Paul VI, Encyclical Letter *Ecclesiam Suam* (6 August 1964), 9, 10, 11: AAS 56 (1964), 611-612.

[8] Dogmatic Constitution on the Church *Lumen Gentium* n. 15.

Yet the subject deserves airing precisely because it continues to be raised, for a variety of reasons, in some circles".[9]

While the Church teaches that the Holy Spirit guides and preserves a Council from error, the Holy Spirit does not guarantee that its outcome will be successful. The Council was not a failure but as Pope Francis has said we must examine our consciences and ask whether we have failed the Council: "have we done everything the Holy Spirit was asking us to do during the Council?".

Abbot Christopher Butler wrote from Rome to his sister two months before the end of the Council: "The Roman Catholic people in England have, so far, only a very shadowy and imperfect idea of what it all means. They are preoccupied with little changes in Mass ceremonies etc. To me, the Council is potentially one of the biggest things that have happened in the Church since 1054. But so many people even if they have been members of the Council don't seem to see it".

These words still ring true today. There are those who still do not realise that the Council was "one of the biggest things that have happened in the Church" and that the teaching of the Council, while being in continuity with Tradition, brought about change that was without parallel in the history of the Church.

Alongside the many studies that have been published about the Council there has arisen an interest in the work of the Council as it was experienced by those who were present and participated in its work. This has given rise to the publication of a number of private journals, memoirs and diaries of the Council. Among the most significant to date are the Journals of Yves Congar, Henri de Lubac and Hélder Câmara.[10]

It was during the course of research on the Second Vatican Council, that I came across a reference to the Council papers of Monsignor Lawrence L. McReavy in the Archives of Ushaw College, Durham. There are, of course, Council papers in many diocesan archives, but the name McReavy

---

[9] From an Article in the Jesuit magazine *America* October 6, 1962. As the work of preparation proceeded many began to realise how daunting the task was that lay before the Church. An unprecedented gathering both in numbers and material for discussion, the weaknesses in organisation and the lack of clarity in the lines of procedures, all combined to give rise to justifiable concern for the success of the undertaking.

[10] Congar, Yves. *My Journal of the Council*, Translated by Sr. Mary John Ronayne, OP, and Mary Cecily Boulding, OP Liturgical Press 2012; Lubac, Henri de. *Carnets du Concile*. Paris: Cerf, 2007 2. volumes; Câmara, Hélder. *Lettres Conciliares, 1962-1965*. Paris: Cerf, 2006. 2 volumes. Philips, Gérard. *Carnets conciliaires de Msgr. Gérard Philips, Decrétaire adjoint de la Commission doctrinale*. Edited by Karim Schelkens. Leuven: Maurits Sabbebiliotheek; *Faculteit Godgeleerheid*; Peeters, 2006; Tromp, Sebastian. *Konzilstagebuch: mit Erlätegungen und Akten aus der Arbeit der Theologischen Kommission, II Vatikanisches Konzil*. Roma: Editrice Pontificia Universita, 2006- 2 volumes; *The Second Vatican Council Diaries of Met. Maxim Hermaniuk, C.Ss.R. (1960-1965)* Translated by by J.Z. Skira, annotated by Karin Schelkens, Peeters, Leuven 2012.

was of particular interest to me. My first meeting with Monsignor McReavy took place three days before his departure to participate in the Fourth Session of the Second Vatican Council in 1965 and I was to meet him several times during the following years.[11] So the personal element was an added incentive to visit the Ushaw Archives.

Even a brief examination of the McReavy material, was sufficient to show that his day by day account of the unfolding of the work of the Council deserved a place alongside other published Journals and Collections of Letters from the Council. The McReavy papers present a unique view of the work of the Second Vatican Council from its convocation in 1959 until its conclusion in December 1965.

The publication over the last decade of collections of private papers and texts are providing a valuable, even if unofficial, source for understanding the work of the Second Vatican Council. Letters, Journals and Diaries often show that despite the diversity and sometimes conflicting views expressed both in the debates of the Council as well as behind the scenes, there was, nevertheless, an overall desire on the part of the Council Fathers to work harmoniously in the cause of unity and the common good. They provide insight into the strengths and weaknesses of the personalities who played an important role in the work of the Council. Moments of elation, frustration and displeasure are recorded with honesty and criticisms made with sincerity.

Monsignor Lawrence L. McReavy is not as well known nor of such scholarly repute as Congar, de Lubac, Joseph Ratzinger and many others who like himself were "Periti", that is expert advisors, at the Second Vatican Council. This, however, does not diminish the value of his observations, insights and record of the Council as he saw it unfold before his eyes.

The note books, papers and letters of Monsignor McReavy manifest the determination and meticulous care with which he is remembered as having approached every task that was set before him. Those who knew him, especially his students at Ushaw College, will readily recognise his characteristic thoroughness. Whether in the classroom or working in the College grounds McReavy gave himself totally and unstintingly. Even when he admits to moments of weariness and boredom which occurred during the period of the four Sessions of the Council, this did not dampen his enthusiasm nor diminish his efforts to keep an accurate record of these important moments in the life of the Church.

On the eve of the funeral of Monsignor McReavy, Sunday February 4th 1990, the community of Ushaw College gathered for a Vigil Service,

---

[11] In his Diary entry for Wednesday, September 8, 1965, Monsignor Lawrence Leslie McReavy records: "Heavy rain. Breakfasted at our digs and then in a taxi with mother to the Abbey where I concelebrated at the solemn Mass at which Leo made his *Solemn Profession*. Lunch with the monks. Tea in the parlour." It was on the occasion of the Solemn Profession of Brother Leo Avery at Quarr Abbey that I was introduced to "Uncle Leslie" by his nephew and my fellow monk Brother Leo.

during which the then President of Ushaw, Peter Walton, paid tribute to the memory of the deceased: "the crowning experience of his life and work was the Second Vatican Council. For Lawrence Leslie it came when he was at the height of his powers just 60, with his confidence and expertise in full flood. We should remember too that he has left us his Diaries of the Vatican Council — a fascinating record for some future monograph."

The Ushaw Archives

The Lawrence Leslie McReavy collection in the Archives of Ushaw College contains both printed material and personal papers. The printed material consists of two sets of official documentation. The first set are the Draft texts and proposals which McReavy received as a Consultor of the Preparatory Commission for the Discipline of the Clergy and Christian People (1960-1962). The second set is a collection of the Schemata, Relationes, Acta, and Decreta from each of the Conciliar Commissions, which were distributed to those who participated directly in the work of the Council either by right or by appointment. Monsignor McReavy received this material in his capacity as a "Peritus" that is an appointed "Expert" to the Council (1962-1965). The personal papers for the whole period 1960-1965 contain his letters, diaries, lectures and Council notebook.[12]

---

[12] Lawrence McReavy Papers 1920-1989 5 files Held by Ushaw College Archives. Reference code: GB-0298-UC/P41. Contents of Archive: Photographs of Liturgical celebrations, portrait and group photographs, synod papers, seminary papers, obituaries, personal correspondence, diplomas and certificates, transcripts of speeches, and printed material. The catalogue was created by Jonathan Bush from the Ushaw Personal Papers series created by Fr. Michael Sharratt in 1990. For the material relevant to this present study the following information is taken from the Official Catalogue of the Collection:
Papal appointments for McReavy in connection with the Second Vatican Council: UC/P41/C2/1 8 August 1960 Consultor for the Preparatory Commission for Vatican II UC/P41/C2/2 25 November 1961 Domestic Prelate. UC/P41/C2/3 24 September 1962 Periti Conciliarium. UC/P41/C2/4 30 November 1962 Consultor of the Conciliar Commission "De Disciplina Cleri Et Populi Christiani". UC/P41/C3 1960-1962 Papers relating to the Preparatory Commission for Vatican II. UC/P41/C4 9 October 1962 — 5 December 1965 Correspondence between McReavy and President Grant relating to the progress of the Second Vatican Council. UC/P41/C5 1962 Un-named "Commentary on the *Prima Series* of the *Schemata Constitutionum et Decretorum de Quibus Disceptabitur in Concilii Sessionibus*". UC/P41/C6 1962-1965 Speeches delivered by McReavy mostly to the Lancashire clergy and relating to the progress of the Vatican II sessions. UC/P41/C7 1962-1965 Papers, notices and programmes of the Second Vatican Council. UC/P41/F5 1934-1987 Diary notes containing very brief entries concerning Masses celebrated, meetings and social engagements attended, and journeys made. 9 notebooks. Photographs: Reference: UC/P41/G, UC/P41/G1 1933 — [1989] Photographs of McReavy.

This present study is designed to present that "fascinating record of the Second Vatican Council" which Lawrence Leslie McReavy has left for posterity.

The title given to this study: "Vatican II as I saw it" are the words which Monsignor McReavy wrote at the beginning of his Journal of the Council, the day to day summary of the debates and events.

Every effort has been made to present the picture of the Council as L.L. McReavy "saw it". The notes and annotations that have been added are few and are intended to help the reader understand certain points that would have been evident to McReavy's original readers but may not be so clear fifty years later.

Monsignor McReavy signed his letters L.L. McReavy and so I have decided to use this signature form when referring to him throughout the text, rather than constantly use his name in full or use his title, it also avoids simply calling him "McReavy" which does not seem appropriate.

+ Cuthbert Johnson OSB

CHAPTER I

Ushaw was his Life

In October 1793, following upon the outbreak of the French Revolution, the English College at Douai in northern France, founded in 1568 by William, later Cardinal, Allen, was suppressed and its buildings confiscated.[1] It had the distinction of being the first Seminary instituted in accord with the Decrees and Directives of the Council of Trent. For just over two hundred years, Priests trained at Douai were sent to England where they endured great hardships, persecution and some were called to witness their faith by martyrdom.

Following their expulsion from Douai, the Staff and students, after undergoing many dangers, including imprisonment, made their way to England. They divided into two groups, one settled at Old Hall, Ware, and those who had been destined for work in the Northern Vicariate found temporary residence in the Durham area at Pontop and Tudhoe.[2]

In October 1794 the College of Douai was formally re-established at Crook Hall, about eleven miles from the city of Durham. To underline the continuity between Douai and Crook Hall, the President of Douai at the time of its suppression, John Daniel, was installed as President. Since this was a symbolic gesture, his tenure of Office lasted only a few days and he was succeeded as President by Thomas Eyre.[3] Among the professors at

[1] William Allen was born in 1532, at Rossall, Lancashire. Educated at the University of Oxford, he became Principal of St Mary's Hall in 1556. He died in Rome October 16, 1594.
M. Haile, An Elizabethan cardinal, William Allen (1914); Eamon Duffy, "Allen, William (1532–1594)", *Oxford Dictionary of National Biography*, Oxford University Press, 2004.
On Saturday, October 12, 1793, a decree, ordering the arrest of all British subjects, was posted on the walls of Douai, the students who did not escape were imprisoned at Doullens. J.P. Marmion, "Douay, A Tale of two Cardinals" in *Ushaw Magazine* December 260 (1982) 2-18

[2] D. Milburn, "Journey to the promised land: from Douai to Durham", *Ushaw Magazine*, 274 (1993–4), 12–26; Leo Gooch, "Gibson, William (1738–1821)", *Oxford Dictionary of National Biography*, Oxford University Press, 2004.

[3] Thomas Eyre (1748–1810) entered English College at Douai in 1762. From 1775 he ministered in the mission area between Newcastle and Hexham. In 1794 Bishop William Gibson (1738–1821), vicar apostolic of the northern district, asked him to take charge of the Northern students from Douai. Mr. Eyre assembled the students first at Pontop Hall and in October 1794, at Crook Hall, where he became President of the new college. Cf. Burton, Edwin. "Thomas Eyre." *The Catholic Encyclopaedia.* Vol. 5. New York: Robert Appleton Company, 1909; B. Ward, *The dawn of the Catholic revival in England*, 1781–1803, 2 vols. (1909); D. Milburn, "Eyre, Thomas (1748–1810)", *Oxford Dictionary of National Biography*, Oxford University Press, 2004.

Crook Hall was the illustrious historian John Lingard.[4]

The decade following their arrival at Crook Hall saw a significant growth in the number of candidates for the priesthood. Consequently Bishop William Gibson, recognising the limitations of Crook Hall, decided that a suitable permanent home for the students was necessary.

In 1804 a property was acquired and the building of Saint Cuthbert's College at Ushaw Moor began. After only four years an imposing building in a magnificent setting, four miles west of Durham City, was ready to receive the students.[5]

The memory of Crook Hall is integral to the history of Ushaw as it is the connecting link between Ushaw and Douai.[6] Everything at Crook Hall was a reflection of Douai. To any suggestion of change or modification the ready answer was always, "that is how it was done at Douai". This mentality, very common in religious institutions, was to pass from Crook Hall to Ushaw College.

In 1837 Charles Newsham was appointed the fourth President of Ushaw. The thirty years since the College's foundation had been a period of consolidation and development for the Seminary.

Recognising the needs of a growing community, Newsham arranged for the finest architects of the Gothic revival, Augustus Charles Pugin and his son, Augustus Welby Northmore Pugin, as well as Charles and Joseph Hansom to undertake the designs and construction of a second church, library, infirmary and other academic and domestic facilities required by a growing community.[7]

Douai and Ushaw have always reverenced the memory of the Martyrs and saintly men who dedicated themselves to the preparation of candidates for the priesthood. Whatever its limitations or excesses that formation was perfectly coherent with the circumstances of the various moments of its history. Both in outlook and in the life led within its walls, Ushaw College, like many other such institutes and Religious Houses in the nineteenth and early twentieth century, was conditioned by a certain fortress and defensive mentality. If the strictness of discipline was sometimes almost military in its

---

[4] S. Gilley, "John Lingard and the Catholic revival", *Renaissance and renewal in Christian history*, ed. D. Baker, Studies in Church History, 14 (1977); J. P. Chinnici, *The English Catholic Enlightenment: John Lingard and the Cisalpine movement, 1780–1850* (1980); E. Jones, *John Lingard and the pursuit of historical truth* (2001); P. Phillips, ed., John Lingard remembered (2003).

[5] For further information see: Milburn, David, *A history of Ushaw College: a study of the origin, foundation and development of an English Catholic seminary, with an epilogue 1908-1962* (Durham 1964).

[6] Laing, Robert C, *Ushaw College, A Centenary Memorial* (Newcastle, 1894); Butler, *Records and Recollections of Ushaw* (Durham, 1885). "The Crook Hall Centenary at Ushaw" in *The Tablet* October 20, 1894.

[7] "Monsignor Charles Newsham, D.D. President of Ushaw, 1837-1863", *Ushaw Magazine* 47, (July 1937), p. 97-118.

rigidity this was because it was believed to be the best way to form a strong character in those who would have to proclaim the Faith and exercise their priesthood in a very hostile environment.

When the celebration of the centenary of Ushaw College took place in 1908 the northern Seminary was no longer considered to be a foreign implant, it had taken root in the affection of Catholics and was held in esteem by all who came in contact with it.[8] This was in part due to the qualified Staff and the hard working priests who had been trained at Ushaw and whose example of dedication won the respect of the Protestant populace. Among the illustrious alumni, ecclesiastical and lay, were 30 bishops, 5 archbishops, and 4 cardinals.[9] Among lay students trained at Ushaw were the Royal Academician Charles Napier Hemy, the architects George and Edward Goldie and Peter Paul Pugin, the writer Wilfred Ward and the poet Francis Thompson and many others who achieved important positions in government and public life.

The atmosphere of the centenary was captured in the report which appeared in the *Tablet*: "Bands of old students from Lancashire and Yorkshire had started upon the journey to their old home on Saturday and Sunday, and, forgathering in York, Darlington, and other places, thronged into Durham by train and motor ... it seemed in the North of England on Monday morning as if all roads led to Ushaw. The trains dropped large parties of Ushaw men at Durham. There was a heavy claim upon the means available to traverse the four miles that lie between the cathedral city and the hilltop on which Ushaw stands. From afar, as we journeyed thither, the Union Jack could be seen fluttering in the sunshine, and at the college gates was a triumphal arch by which Ushaw proudly told the passers by that she dated back to Douai in 1568. The avenue was gay with flags and bunting, and two more triumphal arches told of the sojourn of the College at Crook Hall, and finally her coming to Ushaw. The great doors stood wide open in welcome to the children she had called from afar to share her joy at a hundred years of growth and fruitful work".[10]

Lawrence L. McReavy at Ushaw

It was only four years after those triumphant centenary celebrations, in September 1912 that the young Laurence McReavy entered the junior Seminary: "Ushaw first received me as a somewhat apprehensive

---

[8] For an account of the celebrations see *The Tablet* August 1, 1908.

[9] Cardinal Wiseman, first archbishop of Westminster 1850-1865, Cardinal Merry del Val, Secretary of State to Pope Pius X, Cardinal Bourne, archbishop of Westminster 1903-1935, Cardinal de la Puente, archbishop of Burgos 1857-1867.

[10] *The Tablet*, August 1, 1908.

ten-year-old into her capacious if rather abstract embrace".[11] It was an embrace from which he was never to be released and from which he never sought to be free. In order to understand something of the life and work of Lawrence Leslie McReavy it is necessary to keep in mind his deep love and devotion to Ushaw College. This dedication and loyalty was such that those who knew him would readily agree that L.L. McReavy and Ushaw, if not quite synonymous, are certainly indissolubly linked. Apart from the four years spent studying at the University of Louvain, (1929-1930 and 1931-1934) his life at Ushaw College spanned seventy eight years.

Lawrence Leslie McReavy was born in Southwick, Sunderland, County Durham, in the parish of Saint Hilda, on July 2nd 1902, the son of Catherine and Henry Wyne McReavy. He was the second of four children and brought up in a devout Catholic household. It is not surprising that a vocation to the priesthood was nurtured in such a setting but what is unusual is that Lawrence McReavy was ten years old when accepted for Ushaw two years under the minimum age of twelve required for admission to a Seminary.

In an Article for the *Ushaw Magazine*, "Recollections of an Earlier Ushaw", L.L. McReavy recalls the day of his arrival at Ushaw in late September 1912: "I rode with excited anticipation in the taxi which our parish priest (later Provost William Smith) had hired to bring my parents and me from Durham station to the College, and which was the first horse-less carriage I had ever set foot in, a vehicle of battleship-like structure and height such as one sees nowadays only on table-mats."[12] The McReavy family were welcomed by the recently appointed President, Monsignor W. H. Brown, an honour which L.L. McReavy attributes to the esteem in which the President held his parish priest.[13] The arrival at Ushaw of Lawrence McReavy coincided

---

11 L.L. McReavy, "Recollections of an Earlier Ushaw", *Ushaw Magazine* 88, no. 249 (June 1977), p. 3; "In response to an editorial suggestion" McReavy recorded for the *Ushaw Magazine* his "reminiscences of an Ushaw that is now long gone and likely to be little known". What he described as "jottings (that) have been compiled (by) ...simply let my memory range freely over the distant past" resulted in the publication of two Articles about his first years and life at Ushaw: *Recollections of an Earlier Ushaw* in *Ushaw Magazine* 88 249 (June 1977), pp. 3-20 and *Recollections of Ushaw Life in Two World Wars* in *Ushaw Magazine* 96, no. 265 (1984-5), pp. 22-33

12 L.L. McReavy, "Recollections of an Earlier Ushaw", *Ushaw Magazine* 88 249 (June 1977) 3.

13 "Monsignor William Henry Canon Brown", *Ushaw Magazine*, Vol. 44 (1934) 173-198. McReavy wrote: "Chief among the (Professors) was the extremely dignified President. His full and correct title was the Right Reverend William Henry Brown, but he was universally known to us as "Bob" or "Mons Bob", never, needless to say, to his face. Indeed, even when I became a Professor under him I never knew anyone treat or address him familiarly. One could scarcely fail to respect him, so complete was his dedication to his job. Apart from a brief stroll after lunch, his day seemed to consist almost entirely of prayer and work". L.L. McReavy, "Recollections of an Earlier Ushaw", *Ushaw Magazine*, v. 88, no. 249 (June 1977), p. 6.

with the beginning of the building of new lecture halls under the direction of Pugin Powell, a nephew of the renowned A.W. Pugin.

Another new undertaking which began shortly before the young McReavy arrived at Ushaw was President Brown's reorganisation of studies, both secular and ecclesiastical which would have an effect upon Lawrence McReavy's future. Brown reintroduced the London Intermediate Arts examination that would enable the students to take the London BA. From his very first years in the junior Seminary L.L. McReavy began to show his academic ability. While his name does not appear in the sporting section of the College Notes in the *Ushaw Magazine*, from 1915 until 1925 his name appears every year in the academic section of the Magazine among the list of Prize winners, in one year alone he won six prizes.[14] In 1925 L.L. McReavy took his London MA, one of the examiners was the Biblical scholar Professor Charles Harold Dodd who showed him particular kindness and encouragement.[15]

Beginning life at Ushaw as a ten year old would not have been easy, especially as the clouds of the first world war were gathering on the horizon. Life at Ushaw in 1912 was still marked by the pattern and social mores of late Victorian and early Edwardian England. If not altogether austere, life was nevertheless spartan for both students and Staff: "the general rigour of life in those days, bearing in mind that life outside was not all that soft or enervating. By modern standards, I suppose, the general pattern of our College life would be reckoned pretty tough".[16]

The young McReavy was aware of the political situation and the rise of German militarism, he recalls: "I have a distinct recollection of saying to

---

14 1915 First Prize in Classics; 1916: First Prize Classics; Greek history first division; 1917 Examination for Honours Silver Medal and First Prize Roman history; 1918 Examination for Honours First Prize; for Apologetics First Prize; 1919 Examination for Honours First Prize; Classics First Prize; Logic and English second prize; Scripture history First Prize; first class in matriculation £5; special prize week recitation £2; 1920 Examination for Honours First Prize; Classics First Prize; Logic and English First Prize; Scripture history First Prize; 1921 First-year Philosophy Second Prize £5; Church History First Prize £5; Prize awarded for first class honours in Latin and Greek in Intermediate Arts £10; 1922 Metaphysics First Prize £7; Church History First Prize £5; 1923 London BA; 1924 Second Class honours in Classics £5; 1925 London BA prize £10; 1926 Latin Essay "De Ordinationibus Anglicanis" Jubilee Fund prize £20; Sacred Scripture Second Prize £8; Sermon Writing First Prize £6.

15 F. W. Dillistone, *C. H. Dodd* (1977); G. B. Caird, *Charles Harold Dodd, 1884–1973*, PBA, 60 (1974), 497–510; R. W. Graham, *Charles Harold Dodd, 1884–1973: a bibliography of his published writings*, Lexington Theological Library Occasional Studies (1974).

16 L.L. McReavy, "Recollections of an Earlier Ushaw", *Ushaw Magazine* 249 (June 1977) 9.

a Minor Professor at the top of the Junior House stairs, some-time in 1913, "Please Sir, when are we going to fight the Germans?"".[17]

Within a year war broke out and its effects were soon to be seen and felt at Ushaw. The impact of the call to arms was clearly visible in the places vacated by those students who were eligible to join up and leave for the Front and in the war time rations for those left behind.

Like everyone else, the students and Staff of Ushaw, experienced the effects of rationing: "The abundant supply of beef produced by our home farm was suspended when rationing was introduced during the 1914-18 war, and we had to depend on obtaining our meagre and uncertain ration from the local butcher at Auton Style. Since he did not always receive it himself, we depended in effect on what the Procurator could procure. The war also put an end to the daily and copious supply of beer, a light ale served in readily replenishable jugs at dinner, which we children had not learned to appreciate before it was snatched from our lips for ever".[18]

The austere regime continued throughout the duration of the war and beyond. Monsignor John McHugh recalls that L.L. McReavy described to him a somewhat sad Christmas Day six weeks after the end of the war: "Food was terribly short by the end, but somehow or other, my mother had managed to get some fruit to make a Christmas cake in December 1918, and she sent me a piece. I was in Poetry [Lower Sixth] and had a room on the back of Top Gallery, towards the west. We had sung Matins, Midnight Mass and Lauds, in the gaslight, with St Cuthbert's half-empty, for there were very few Philosophers or Divines. Then High Mass of the Day at ten o'clock. Readings Up at twelve, a dreadful dinner, and later Vespers. I went back to my room at half-past four, and fetched myself a glass of cold water. Then I settled down beneath the gas jet (only professors had mantles) with the piece of cake and the glass of water to celebrate, and spent two or three hours reading one of the duller novels of R.L. Stevenson."[19]

After the First World War life at Ushaw gradually returned to normality except that a number of students who had gone to the front never returned and those who did like many of their comrades bore the scars, both physical and mental, of the war. "There had, of course, been wide differences in the length, nature and severity of their experiences. A few had starved in harsh prison camps. Some had been badly wounded and bore the tell-tale scars for the rest of their, infrequently shortened lives. Some had slogged it in the bestial conditions of the Flanders mud, or had nearly died of thirst or malaria in the Mesopotamian desert. One of these latter shared a room with

---

[17] L.L. McReavy, "Recollections of Ushaw Life in Two World Wars", *Ushaw Magazine* 265 (1984-5) 22.

[18] L.L. McReavy, "Recollections of an Earlier Ushaw", *Ushaw Magazine* 249 (June 1977) 10.

[19] John McHugh, "The Right Reverend Monsignor Lawrence Leslie McReavy", *Ushaw Magazine* 270 (1989-90) 100.

me on his return and told me some of his experiences; he dropped dead about three years after his ordination. ... If the returned heroes, or "fought-and-bleds" as they called themselves, occasionally took a liberty with the rigid discipline of those days, the president, William Henry Brown, held the reins loosely enough not to choke the deviants".[20]

Life at Ushaw until the middle of the twentieth century shared in many respects the characteristics of Religious and monastic Houses. There were strict limits to the movements of students on the property and trips outside of the College were strictly limited. Until 1921 the summer holiday was the only period away from the College. Strict limitations were also placed on information coming into the College from outside, this included family contacts, newspapers and other forms of communication.[21] Even the privileges to students as they came closer to the completion of their years of formation were not extensive.[22]

Lawrence Leslie McReavy was ordained to the priesthood at Ushaw by Bishop Joseph Thorman on Sunday, July 21st 1929. It was presumed that L.L. McReavy would join the Staff and teach Classics, a subject in which he had always excelled. He was, however sent to the university of Louvain later that year with a view to obtaining a Degree in Moral Theology. Professor Dr Alphonse Van Hove advised L.L. McReavy to inscribe himself in the Faculty of Canon Law as he believed that this would give him a better grounding for teaching Moral Theology. The four years that L.L. McReavy spent at Louvain prepared him for what was to be his life's work: the study of Canon Law. Upon his return to Ushaw in 1934 Lawrence McReavy began his lectures on Fundamental Moral Theology and which, apart from a few interruptions, he gave until 1979. He was Professor of Canon Law and lectured in this subject until 1972.

It was in 1954 that Lawrence McReavy took responsibility for the "Questions and Answers" section in the Clergy Review. His replies were

---

20 L.L. McReavy, "Recollections of Ushaw Life in Two World Wars", *Ushaw Magazine* 265 (1984-5). 27-28.

21 "Wireless had been invented but, in 1912, the amateur set which had already been erected on Tip-Top, with an aerial on the roof, received only Morse (it received some exciting messages at the outbreak of war in 1914, but thereafter had to be dismantled by government order). Broadcasting did not begin until the Autumn of 1923, and though a number of Divines immediately made themselves primitive crystal sets, using their spring-mattresses for an aerial and their gas-pipe for an earth, the President ordered that they were all to be taken home at Christmas and not brought back. The cinematograph was still in its infancy and gramophone records rare and primitive by present standards". Ibid.

22 Entry from the *Senior Student's Diary* for Thursday, 21 January 1958: Vice-President sent for Secretary... "I have something strange to tell you". He sure had – DIVINES MAY HAVE DAILY PAPERS AND THE WIRELESS. The reason – give Divines more responsibility, and further, "Rome has urged this type of thing for some time now." Radio committee will select programs we shall listen to. They select to cater for every taste.

precise and to the point but always inspired by a pastoral concern for the well being of the questioner.

It came as no surprise that L.L McReavy was appointed in 1960 a member of the Preparatory Commission for the Second Vatican Council. Shortly before the opening of the Council he was appointed a Domestic Prelate and named a "Peritus" and member of the Commission for the Life and Ministry of Priests. A fellow member of that Commission was the Dominican Father (later cardinal) Yves Congar, another "Diarist" of the Council.

Formative influences

One of the characteristics of Ushaw College which should not be underestimated in importance as a formative influence upon L.L. McReavy is stability. This stability was most clearly evident in the lives and dedication of many members of the Ushaw Staff. There were Professors and Officials whose whole life was dedicated to the formation of students at Ushaw. Indeed, for many of them, as it was to be for Lawrence McReavy himself, Ushaw was their life. Perhaps the significance of this stability is little understood in society today where a job for life is hardly possible and not always seen as desirable.

For Professor McReavy it was perfectly normal that his whole life was spent at Ushaw, for him and many others, tradition and continuity were not regarded as extraordinary. John McHugh was absolutely right when he made a comparison with monastic life when he wrote of L.L. McReavy that "Like that other child from Monkwearmouth, Bede, he was to give the rest of his life to study, teaching, prayer and priesthood, all in the same community".[23]

When Lawrence McReavy entered Ushaw in 1912 the Head of Junior House was George Esmond Phillips who was born in 1842. He was Master of Low Figures from 1869 until 1882 and Rector of Junior House for thirty years until his death in 1918.[24] He was for the young boys of Ushaw a living link with the great (now Blessed) John Henry Cardinal Newman. L.L. McReavy recalls his first meeting: "The following day, Sunday, I was taken to see the Seminary Rector, the Rev. George Phillips, known to generations of Ushawmen as Swippy, from the "swipes' (bread and milk) which had been the College breakfast before such exotic infusions as tea became acceptable. To us he seemed as old as the yew tree in the Sem bounds had

[23] John McHugh "The Right Reverend Monsignor Lawrence Leslie McReavy" *Ushaw Magazine* 270 (1989-1990) 99.

[24] Edward Towers "The Rev. G.E. Phillips: A Panegyric" *Ushaw Magazine* 28 (March 1918) 1-9; "In Memoriam: Rev. G.E. Phillips" *Ushaw Magazine* 28 (March 1918) 98-112.

seemed to Francis Thompson, and we understood that his mother had followed Newman into the Catholic Church".[25]

The President of Ushaw during L.L. McReavy's years as a student and his first years as a member of Staff was William Henry Brown who was born in 1852. He was educated at Ushaw, and taught as a minor professor before his ordination to the priesthood in 1881. (A Minor Professor was a senior student selected to teach in the junior house for a period between the philosophy course and that of theology, a post which L.L. McReavy occupied for three years). Regarded as a highly qualified Professor and Prefect of Studies, William Henry Brown was appointed President in 1910, a post which he occupied for almost quarter of a century until his death in 1934. L.L. McReavy wrote of him, "One could scarcely fail to respect him, so complete was his dedication to his job. Apart from a brief stroll after lunch, his day seemed to consist almost entirely of prayer and work. Yet he was far from being a hard man to others, and during the first World War he kept in constant touch by letter with his many conscripted students at the front. He had not left the College since his arrival in 1865 as a boy of twelve. Made President in 1910, he held that office until his death in 1934".[26] The admiring phrase "He had not left the College since his arrival" is almost amusing coming from L.L. McReavy whose life at Ushaw was to exceed Brown's by a decade and be the longest-serving member of Staff in the history of the College! The Spring issue of the *Ushaw Magazine* for 1924 drew attention to the lengthy terms of Office and asked: "we wonder if any other college in England can rival the claims of Ushaw? ... Monsignor Broadhead is not the first Procurator to spend 50 years at Ushaw. Monsignor C. Gillow was here for upward of 57 years and the Rev. T. Croskell had just completed his half-century when he left. Monsignor Wrennall, 51 years elapsed between his coming to Ushaw and his leaving ... The Rev. T. Tatlock fell a few weeks short of 50 years."

Lawrence McReavy was fully aware of the value and significance of such life long dedication. For example in his Recollections he wrote about "the Rev. Dr. Gabriel Coulston who had first come to the College in 1838 as a boy of eight, travelling in a stagecoach which took three days to bring him from Lancashire to the Three Tuns in Durham, where he stayed the night before being brought up to the College in a cab. There used to be a group photo on the wall of the north ambulacrum showing him as a young Professor in the eighteen-fifties. We understood that, after a while, he had gone to Rome to acquire a doctorate in theology but that having found life there little to his liking he had bought a doctor's diploma at one of the less reputable seats of learning and returned to the polite life of the Professors' Parlour after a total absence of six months. He remained here until his death in 1915. The only memory I retain of him was of his occasional stroll past our

[25] L.L. McReavy, "Recollections of an Earlier Ushaw", *Ushaw Magazine* 249 (1977) 4.

[26] L.L. McReavy, "Recollections of an Earlier Ushaw", *Ushaw Magazine* 249 (1977) 6.

football field; but it is interesting to reflect that he could have transmitted to us memories of Douai at second hand."[27] In a tribute to "the Grand Old Man of Ushaw" published in the *Ushaw Magazine* it is recorded that "for almost 77 years the life of Dr Coulston was bound up with the life of Ushaw. He saw her in sunshine and in gloom, in poverty and in prosperity; he knew her beginnings, he watched her growth, he gloried in her triumph; and we who loved him regarded him as being in some way the embodiment of the past".[28] These words could, in some respects, be applied to Lawrence Leslie McReavy.

Such lengthy tenures of members of Staff were not exceptions and they continued to be characteristic of Ushaw during Monsignor McReavy's own seventy-eight years of life at Ushaw. The recipients of the letters which he sent during the Council were dedicated and life long members of the Staff: Paul Grant, Laurence Hollis, Bernard Payne, Philip Loftus and Robert Gowland.

From the time of his entrance to Ushaw in 1912 until the retirement of Paul Grant in 1967, a period of fifty five years, Lawrence McReavy had known only three Ushaw Presidents. This is in marked contrast with the subsequent forty four years leading up to the closure of Ushaw in 2011 when there were seven Presidents. Stability, almost monastic in character, was certainly a defining element in the life of pre-Conciliar Ushaw and of Lawrence McReavy.

* * *

There are those who might consider a life within the narrow confines of College walls as something of a limitation. Surprisingly it was an Alumnus of Ushaw, Archbishop John Carmel Heenan, who publicly espoused this view. In a speech at the Council on October 22nd, 1964, he severely criticised the work of certain experts "periti" whom he considered had exceeded the bounds of their mandate. The Archbishop made the offensive remark that the blame for this lay in the fact that some of them had led far too sheltered lives in their monasteries, seminaries or houses of study. Lawrence McReavy humbly remarked: "I myself must be numbered among those who have spent their lives sequestered from the world in seminariis, in domibus religionis, in accademiis". *(Letter 25)*

However, for all of the years which he spent at Ushaw, his vision and outlook were far from narrow. It was another Archbishop, Derek Worlock of Liverpool, who fittingly remarked in the Sermon which he preached at L.L. McReavy's funeral: "in such a learned and wise priest, there was, in some sense, a holy and child-like simplicity lying at the heart of his spirituality. How else can we explain the commonly accepted fact that more than 77 years at Ushaw had failed to produce an institutionalised eccentric,

[27] L.L. McReavy, "Recollections of an Earlier Ushaw", *Ushaw Magazine* 249 (1977) 6.

[28] "The Rev. Gabriel Coulston, D.D." *Ushaw Magazine* (July 1915) 101-110.

narrow-minded, perhaps self-opinionated, ready to be classified amongst the "opiniones" in the card-index of the traditionalist moral theologian? How else can we explain that he had become instead a humble, open, and much-loved member of the College community?".

His opened mindedness could even shock as John Butters recalls: "nobody could doubt Bomb's utter loyalty to the Church and the papacy — all those articles, talks, addresses explaining and defending. By intellect he could be a radical thinker, but emotionally he tended to be traditional. The radical thinker would never lead him into unorthodoxy, but he wasn't narrow-minded, in fact quite independent — he caused considerable surprise to about half-a-dozen of the Staff in the parlour at dinner one Saturday evening a few weeks before his death. The subject of women priests came up; he exclaimed with some vehemence, "of course you can have women priests. I have always thought you could. I have always thought how stupid it was that a Reverend Mother still had to get a priest in to say Mass in her convent for her community'. This positive explosion astonished all of us."[29]

At the end of the First Session of the Council in December 1962 in answer to a newsman's question during a Press Conference: "How do you tell a conservative from a progressive?" Father Francis J. McCool, S.J., professor at the Pontifical Biblical Institute of Rome replied: "A progressive looks to the future and sees the promise in it. A conservative looks to the future and sees a threat to the past."

Lawrence McReavy looked to the future with hope and because he was imbued with a sense of tradition he never felt threatened by change. The fact that he was proud to have been appointed a Prelate and often remarks in his letters that he wore his robes when he attended ceremonies and other ecclesiastical events, does not mean that he set great store by such things. He was not over-enamoured of clerical ceremonial dress speaking as he did of: "copes and mitres and all that lark". *(Letter 20)*

At the same time he was able to comment that "the scene in Saint Peter's Square never fails to thrill me, when the cars and coaches disgorge their purple load (there are about 35 coach loads) and the whole front of Saint Peter's steps is splashed with purple" and again "At 8.45 the great purple tide began to flow into Saint Peter's". Such almost poetical outpourings as these can surely be attributed to his refined artistic sense and led him to capture the scene in a splendid watercolour.

The artistic ability of Lawrence Leslie McReavy was well known. All who have seen his work cannot but fail to admire his ability as a watercolourist. Wherever he went his sketch book, paper and watercolour paints accompanied him. When on holiday at Maidstone he painted local scenes and historical monuments. When visiting his nephew at Quarr Abbey the gardens and the imposing church were favourite subjects. His beloved north east, its wild landscapes, its majestic cathedral at Durham,

---

[29] John Butters, "Further Memories" *Ushaw Magazine* 270 (1989-1990) 118.

the Roman Wall were all subjects to which he returned. He was generous in giving a gift of a painting to those who admired his work. His output over the years was quite phenomenal. When he sold some of his watercolours in aid of the charitable work of Blessed Mother Teresa of Calcutta he raised a considerable sum of money which is not only a credit to his generosity but also an indication of the pleasing quality of his work. L.L. McReavy was a cultivated man in many respects, he "was excellent company, a very talented wide reader of classics, history, art, and literature; again and again working through Jane Austen, Dickens, Shakespeare. Together with his retentive memory this made him a great conversationalist".[30]

There was a weakness in Lawrence Leslie McReavy's character which manifested itself even in early childhood. John McHugh remembered that "he amused a group of us by recalling a childhood story: My grandfather had a ferocious temper, and I remember standing up to him once when he was remonstrating with me — I must have been about nine or ten — and saying, "I'd have you know that the same blood flows in my veins as in yours!"". L.L. McReavy was quite right in affirming that the same blood flowed in the veins of grandfather and grandson. The similarity did not end there since Lawrence Leslie was his grandfather's equal in having "a ferocious temper", especially in his youth. This weakness gave rise to the nickname "Bomb" which he was given by the Staff. John McHugh makes no apology for describing L.L. McReavy's flaw in temperament: "not for nothing was he known as Bomb. One might even have added: "High Explosive — Short Fuse". Any obituary which overlooked this trait would be a lie. It would also detract from his spiritual stature. Students who knew him only in his last years find it almost impossible to believe the stories of long ago; but those who lived with him for many years were all too conscious of the long and heroic struggle to overcome his impatience and to bring that volatile temper under control. As more than one professor has said, "If there is one thing worse than being the target, it's waiting for the apology!" It always came, often at the end of a meeting, and in public; it was so humbly given, and so sincere, that one felt very small".[31]

Another insight into L.L. McReavy's character is found in the Memories compiled by Father John Butters in the *Ushaw Magazine*: "Bomb was a grateful man; especially grateful for the ordinary blessings of life. More than once he said, "Very few could say that they had a lovely room to work in, with magnificent view, centrally heated and, if desired, a coal fire, three meals a day at regular times, and attractive grounds in which to exercise. He was amazed at kindness shown to him by domestic staff and students ("Why are they so kind to me?"). And even close to his death he had tears in his eyes remembering a student just days before feeding him

---

[30] John Butters, "Further Memories" *Ushaw Magazine* 270 (1989-1990) 119.

[31] John McHugh "The Right Reverend Monsignor Lawrence Leslie McReavy" *Ushaw Magazine* 270 (1989-1990) 102.

with soup. That affection and esteem ran very deep amongst the students — they enjoyed looking after him, doing anything that might relieve the growing burdens of the last months of his life. ... His true greatness, the one he worked at most, was his priestly example — a consistent example as a confessor, spiritual director, his obvious love for the Mass, and deep affection for our Lady. As so many have said, it can he summed up in the fact that he was always there — his presence became so much more eloquent than even his words, his many words! ".[32]

John McHugh in the conclusion of his tribute to Lawrence McReavy in the *Ushaw Magazine* wrote: "The main part of his life must, of course, go unchronicled, for it was hidden with Christ in God. No one will ever forget his presence, early every morning, in St Cuthbert's, for his meditation, of his punctilious attendance at all Church services. For over fifty years he had been a regular confessor; and many former professors could testify to his prudence, wisdom and moderation at tense moments in meetings concerning admission to Holy Orders. Lawrence McReavy was from first to last a priest, and when he reached the Diamond Jubilee of his ordination on 21 July 1989, I am sure he felt it was time to go. He had enjoyed a long and full life, though not without suffering, almost to the end. And if there is one phrase which sums up both his life's work and the inspiration which guided him throughout it, it is there in the final words of the new Code of Canon Law: "the salvation of souls, which must always be the supreme law in the Church, is to be kept before one's eyes" (c.1752). Lawrence McReavy never thought of Canon Law or of the priesthood in any other way".[33]

A significant part of his life which goes unchronicled in this present study is Lawrence McReavy's involvement in various ways in the subject of Canon Law. Not only was he an able Professor, he was for many years an advisor to members of the hierarchy, and through his "Questions and Answers" page in the Clergy Review, he resolved the difficulties of many. To go into this dimension of his life would fall outside the scope of this present volume. It would, however, be unpardonable not to recall that Lawrence McReavy made an important contribution to the revision of the 1983 Code of Canon Law especially in the area of Book V on the Temporal Goods of the Church. In recognition of his life long service of the Church in the field of Canon Law, he was appointed Protonotary Apostolic in December 1989.[34]

There is no doubt that Lawrence Leslie McReavy, who died on the afternoon of Saturday January 27th 1990, should be listed among the "Grand Old Men" of Ushaw. His funeral took place on February 5th and Archbishop

[32] John Butters, "Further Memories" *Ushaw Magazine* 270 (1989-1990) 120.

[33] John McHugh "The Right Reverend Monsignor Lawrence Leslie McReavy" *Ushaw Magazine* 270 (1989-1990) 113.

[34] L.L. McReavy was appointed a Consultor of the Pontifical Commission for the Revision of the Code of Canon Law on March 29th 1967, a position which was extended for a further two five year periods in 1973 and 1978. See Ushaw Archives UC/P41/C2/5-10.

Worlock in his homily paid the following tribute: "He was truly a great lover of the Church: to him to be such was part of his faith – not just to believe in the Church and its teachings but to love them, with a whole-hearted and at times self-sacrificing love". Describing his love for Ushaw the Archbishop remarked that "he had become part of the fabric of the place ... He begrudged no day he ever spent here. These warm, good-natured qualities of consistent commitment and devotion brought confidence to the Common Room, humanity to the Canon Lawyer, and gave to the moral theologian the requisite sense of humour, as relevant and highly delicate as the occasion of demanded."

Monsignor Lawrence Leslie McReavy was laid to rest in the cemetery at Ushaw alongside his many friends, colleagues and spiritual forebears who had dedicated their lives to the service of the Church and Ushaw.

Conclusion

Lawrence Leslie McReavy was almost sixty years old when he was called to contribute to the preparatory work of the Second Vatican Council and to participate in it as an expert. Fifty of those sixty years had been spent at Ushaw which embodied much of the ethos and mentality that prevailed in the Post-Tridentine Church with all its strengths and weaknesses. As a Professor and member of the Ushaw Staff, he had contributed to the preservation and handing on of that tradition to many of the Clergy of the dioceses which make up the northern Province.

While he loved and respected the heritage of Ushaw, he was not limited by it nor frozen within in it. There were some aspects of the developments and changes brought about by the Second Vatican Council that disturbed him. This did not in any way diminish his commitment to the implementation of the teaching of the Council. He would have agreed with Pope Francis' words "We celebrate this anniversary, we put up a monument but we don't want it to upset us. We don't want to change and what's more there are those who wish to turn the clock back." Lawrence McReavy recognised that he was conditioned by his upbringing. However, he understood the living character of tradition and to a degree he embodied tradition and therefore would have had little sympathy for those who appeal to tradition to justify their personal preferences.

During the third Session of the Council in 1964 he wrote to the President of Ushaw, Monsignor Paul Grant: "I admit that I am an old "square", so mentally conditioned by an inordinate attention to a misconceived magisterium as to be unable to tune in to the new theological wavelength, but I reflect that pendulums have a back-swing and feel sure that when this one swings back, I shan't be quite so far "out on a limb"." *(Letter 26)*

During the opening ceremony of the Second Vatican Council, McReavy looked down from one of the Tribunes allocated to the Council "Periti" on the 2500 Council Fathers from all parts of the world. They had been brought up in much the same way and in the same ecclesiastical climate as himself but some of whom were more limited in their outlook and lacked the theological and canonical background that he had acquired at Ushaw.

Already during the period of the preparatory work for the Council L.L. McReavy was aware that there were subjects to be treated in the Council that would give rise to anxiety and possibly even conflict. A changed world and ever rapidly new developments called for an examination of the Church in the world. Such moments of reflection occur at regular intervals in the course of history. Change was already in the air when L.L. McReavy entered Ushaw half a century before.

For example, in an address at the 1908 centenary celebrations, the Bishop of Newport, John Cuthbert Hedley posed the question of the need for change: "Will the needs, the aspirations, the achievements of the world and of the Catholic Church call for the same training, the same culture, the same endeavour that have been so successful in the days that are gone ? .... there will be interesting changes ... The coming century, besides its material progress, will be marked by two features: scientific method and fundamental inquiry. ... Will Ushaw students and superiors, of every grade, become more grave, more anxious, more preoccupied with life's problems and life's conflicts? It cannot be doubted that there is a tendency in this direction — a tendency which will become more pronounced as the century goes on, and the modern spirit of unrest asserts itself. As generations succeed each other, the young seem to become less simple and less reverential, the student less content with his text-book and his discipline, the teacher more unsatisfied with his official task, the whole community more alive to doubt and to danger. This is a spirit not wholly bad. If it leads to a bracing reaction — to diligence, to accuracy, to clear views, and to a more intelligent grasp of the truth — then it is good and wholesome. ...Those who are in charge of our colleges and seminaries have serious work before them. On them depends in great measure whether our coming generation will be prepared to make Catholicism and the genuine Christian spirit felt in the modern world".[35]

Fifty years later, Lawrence McReavy on the occasion of the 150th anniversary of the opening of Ushaw in 1808 stated: "To those who ask whether Ushaw is still the same as it always was, the answer is: Thank God it isn't, and please God it never will be. It is no compliment to say that Ushaw never changes; "Stillness is an attribute of death, change a mark of life and growth. All things flow,' said the Greek philosopher."[36] Within a few months of this declaration, the newly elected Pope John XXIII announced the calling of a Council, bringing about change for the Church, Ushaw and Lawrence McReavy.

---

[35] *Ushaw Magazine* 18 (1918) 282-283. The text was also published in *The Tablet*, 1st August 1908.

[36] *The Tablet*, July 26, 1958 p. 11.

Ushaw College still stands, an elegant and impressive example of the best in neo-gothic architecture, situated within an area of 400 acres of pasture and woodland. In June 2011, after 200 years as the Catholic Seminary for the dioceses of the North of England, the formation of students for the priesthood at Ushaw came to an end. In 1908 Bishop Hedley had remarked "Conceivably, means might fail, her sons might emigrate, and strangers might occupy her courts" For the Bishop of Newport and his contemporaries this was unthinkable: "This is not likely". Nevertheless, elements in the centenary discourse of the Benedictine Bishop of Newport, John Cuthbert Hedley, sound notes of warning: "there are considerations which must not be lost sight of — considerations which are almost entirely beyond the control of Ushaw herself". Hedley was born in the Diocese of Hexham and Newcastle, a bishop for over a quarter of a century and a man of considerable experience whose remarks would not have been taken lightly by his listeners.

"Whatever be the fate of these buildings there can be no doubt as to what Ushaw will be as long as a Catholic College is housed within them". Hedley's words have already found fulfilment, if not in the way that he expected, it is hoped that a Catholic College may still be housed within its buildings. Ushaw College provides a perfect setting for academic training and ecclesiastical studies and it is to be hoped that plans to ensure its continuance as a Catholic College and centre of learning and research will prove successful.

CHAPTER II

Lawrence Leslie McReavy and the Second Vatican Council

Lawrence Leslie McReavy was a man of the Council and as Archbishop Derek Worlock in his homily at L.L. McReavy's funeral stated: "For Lawrence McReavy the Second Vatican Council was to a great extent the peak of his academic career".

The President of Ushaw Peter Walton declared that the "crowning experience of his life and work was the Second Vatican Council. For Lawrence Leslie it came when he was at the height of his powers – just 60, with his confidence and expertise in full flood. He always maintained that this was the highlight of his life".[1]

His participation in the work of the Council marked a turning point in his life. As his Ushaw colleague John McHugh remarked the Council was for Lawrence McReavy "a fresh stimulus" which enabled him "to listen to a very different presentation of doctrine from the one he had heard as a student at Ushaw more than 30 years before".[2] This was acknowledged by Archbishop Worlock, in his funeral tribute, when he admitted that for both himself and for L.L. McReavy the Council helped "to open our minds to new insights and from which we had returned with the good news to help in the renewal of the Church".

Monsignor McReavy was both humanly and spiritually, nourished and enriched by his participation in the work of the Second Vatican Council. When he returned from the Council "with the good news" he became a zealous apostle for the implementation of its teaching: "Lawrence McReavy did much to spread the word by his own acceptance of the conciliar teaching – within Ushaw as well as without".[3]

L.L. McReavy readily welcomed every invitation to speak about the Council to Priests, Religious and Laity. It was for him a duty to share with others the privilege he had received in sharing in the life of the Church at an important moment of its history. For some, however, Lawrence McReavy's zeal for the Council could be a little too much: "When he returned from the Council, Lawrence would hold forth at breakfast, lunch and dinner on what the Council wanted and which way the "Church" was going, and

---

[1] From the Homily of the President of Ushaw Peter Walton at the Service held on Sunday February 4th the eve of L.L. McReavy's Funeral.

[2] McHugh, J., "The Right Reverend Monsignor Lawrence Leslie McReavy", *Ushaw Magazine*, 270 (1989-90) 111.

[3] Butters, J., "Further Memories" *Ushaw Magazine* 270 (1989-1990) 119.

Monsignor Grant would look down at his food and look more and more worried".[4]

* * *

Already while participating in the preparatory work during the two years leading up to the Council, L.L. McReavy was conscious of the fact that he was taking part in a momentous event: "I felt that I was assisting at something unique in the history of Church. Never before had such a large representative body of experts been gathered from all over the globe to prepare a General Council". He was immensely proud to have been among those experts from all parts of the world: "No Council in the history of the Church has ever been so ecumenical in its preparation. The resources of the whole Catholic world have been harnessed and used. No Council in the history of the church will have been anything like as geographically universal in its membership."[5]

The Lecture on the Preparation for the Council which he gave to the Philosophers and Divines at Ushaw in February 1961 already reveals something of his growing enthusiasm for the great undertaking that had been set in motion. He understood the historical significance of what was about to take place: "The great work is on the move and promises to make of the second Council of the Vatican one of the greatest assemblies in the history of Christendom." He already grasped something of the momentous undertaking that the Council represented: "Never before has the agenda of a Council been so wide and varied. Previous Councils have normally had to settle a point of dispute. The Second Vatican will seek to review the whole function of the Church in the modern world, to give new vigour to Catholic faith and morals, to retrieve the common potentialities of the Church, to adapt religious practice to the needs of modern life."

As the days grew closer for the opening of the second Vatican Council many were wondering how long the work of the Council would take. Bishops from large dioceses with great responsibilities were anxious not to be absent from their Sees for what might turn out to be indefinitely long periods. L.L. McReavy had already broached this question in his 1961 Lecture: "How long it will take no one can say. The thorough preparation should make prolonged discussion less necessary, but some of the proposals are also novel and far-reaching in effect that one can expect a marked difference of opinion about them among the bishops. But, here again, air travel should make it possible for the Council to be paroled from time to time to enable the bishops to return to their dioceses. Most of them can get home in a day and return as quickly. No reason, therefore, why it should not last for years".

[4] From a two page unpublished *Recollections of Lawrence McReavy* by Cuthbert Rand in the Ushaw Archives.

[5] Ushaw Archives: Green Note Book dated November 1961.

* * *

Despite his zeal for the Council and its work Monsignor Lawrence McReavy was not blind to its short comings and limitations. He recognised that there were flaws in both the organisation and procedure of the Council. He saw the danger that the Council might have dragged on indefinitely, or more probably ground to a halt owing to the impracticability of reassembling the bishops year after year for apparently endless discussions. Consequently, like many others, he welcomed the remedial modifications that were introduced during the course of the Council.

He was also critical of some of the Council Fathers who wasted time because they were nothing other than useless "blatherers" and that there were "too many speakers who took too long to make a few pettyfogging points". He had little time for pious platitudes which he dismissed with "etc. etc."

He was not alone in suffering boredom patiently for he records: "There is one Spaniard who has already intervened five times without throwing a spark of light on anything, and has been more than once shot down in flames without apparently becoming depressed. We know he'll come back undismayed, though he can hardly appreciate the dismay which the reading out of his name creates in the assembly. It is no use rushing out for coffee, because the bars are filled to overflowing as soon as a bore gets underway, and some of the Fathers can smell a bore in advance. I have already compiled a mental black-list of names, and if some of them are due to perform after 11.15, I get my coffee; otherwise not". *(Letter 20)*

He was also aware of the negative feeling on the part of some members of the Roman Curia: "If one were to ask them: why then should we be having a General Council at all, I feel sure that their answer explicit or implicit would be that they never wanted one, and worked perfectly content with everything as it was, i.e. everything as it was being run by the Roman Curia. One gets the impression that the Curial Cardinals regard a General Council as an unwanted or at least unwelcome intrusion by outsiders into their domestic affairs". *(Letter 20)*

* * *

The work of renewal in the Church was already in action when Pope John XXIII announced the calling of an Ecumenical Council in January 1959. Pope Benedict XVI was at pains to point out that the Second Vatican Council was not a rupture in the history of the Church and should be read in the optic of a hermeneutic of continuity. The principle of continuity is simply a recognition of the historical fact that the Council was a moment of intensification in a programme of renewal begun by Pope Pius X and strengthened and enhanced by Pope Pius XII.

The developments within the Church during the first six decades of the twentieth century show clearly that not only had the ground been prepared but that the seeds of renewal which had been sown had taken root and were beginning to bear fruit even before Pope John XXIII called the Council.

Nevertheless not everyone who attended the Council arrived with a clear idea of what was being asked of them. The various episcopates came to the Council with different ideas. Some of them arrived rather with an attitude of expectation regarding the programme that was to be developed. His four years in Louvain had contributed to L.L. McReavy's awareness that the episcopates of Central Europe — Belgium, France and Germany — came with the clearest ideas. In matters of detail, they stressed completely different aspects, yet they had common priorities.

In one of his lectures L.L. McReavy noted: "To judge from initial reactions, many had come to the Council unconvinced of the need of a wholesale pastoral review, or with little realization of what changes it might entail". A considerable majority of the Council Fathers were of L.L. McReavy's generation or older. They had received a similar formation and had experienced the tragedies of two world wars and yet, as he remarked, they seem to have forgotten what they learnt. While Monsignor McReavy held the Episcopal Order in respect he was not blind to their limitations and narrow perspectives on life and its problems.

It is interesting to note in his Journal how much space he gives to an intervention on the possibility of allowing an abandoned innocent spouse to re-marry. His acceptance in later life of the possibility of admitting women to the priesthood is disturbing to those who rightly see in L.L. McReavy, a man who was a staunch upholder of doctrine and the magisterium.

Remote preparation for the Council

The formation of Lawrence McReavy for the priesthood and his subsequent academic career took place during the years of progressive renewal within the Church which led up to the Second Vatican Council. The importance of this period was touched upon in a Lecture to the participants of the Pastoral Congress of the Diocese of Aversa in Italy in September 2001, by the then Prefect of the Congregation for the Doctrine of the Faith, Cardinal Joseph Ratzinger who stated: "Just after the First World War, Romano Guardini coined an expression that quickly became a slogan for German Catholics: An event of enormous importance is taking place: *the Church is awakening within souls*. The result of this awakening was ultimately the Second Vatican Council. Through its various documents it expressed and made part of the patrimony of the whole Church something that, during four decades full of ferment and hope (1920 to 1960), had been maturing in knowledge gained through faith. To understand Vatican II one must look back on this period and seek to discern, at least in outline, the currents and tendencies that came together in the Council".

The "currents and tendencies" were not only the "awakening" of scholarly research in the study of the Scriptures, the Liturgy and the History of the Church but is also found in the teaching of the popes of that period, above all in the magisterial teaching of Pope Pius XII. His great encyclicals on the Church, the Liturgy and Sacred Scripture were to have a profound effect upon the Second Vatican Council.

In a celebration to mark the twenty-fifth anniversary of the death of Pope Pius XII, the then archbishop of Genoa, Cardinal Siri, said: "If we study the indices of Vatican II, we can easily see that after those taken from Holy Scripture, the most numerous quotations are those derived from the writings of this Pope".

The documents of the Second Vatican Council contain 201 quotations from the discourses and writings of Pope Pius XII. In the Dogmatic Constitution on the Church *Lumen Gentium* there are 58 citations from the teaching of Pope Pius XII.

Cardinal Fiorenzo Angelini who attended all the sessions of the Second Vatican Council, stated "after having had the honour and responsibility under Pope Pius XII of work that led me to have contact with him, the link between the Magisterium of Pius XII and the documents approved by Vatican II has always seemed beyond dispute, confirming a clear magisterial continuity".

Pope Pius XII considered the possibility of convoking a Council and to this end a series of preparatory studies were undertaken. It soon became evident, however, that an undertaking of such immense proportions was beyond the means of the Holy See in the difficult years following the Second World War.

A Timeline of the Awakening Church

The "awakening of the Church in souls", those "decades full of ferment and hope" which led "ultimately to the Second Vatican Council" began just over a year after the birth of Lawrence McReavy. In 1903 Pope Saint Pius X issued a Motu Proprio calling for a renewal of liturgical music and to this end he established the first of a series of Pontifical Commissions to oversee a reform of the Liturgy. The first meeting of Pius X's Commission took place in England, on the Isle of Wight in 1904 at Appuldurcombe House where the monks of the Abbey of Solesmes were living in exile. Experts from Rome and other parts of Europe crossed the English Channel and the Solent to begin a work which was to have far-reaching repercussions throughout the world.

Pius X stated in December 1903 in his Motu Proprio *Tra le sollecitudine* that the primary and indispensable source of the true Christian spirit is participation in the most holy mysteries and in the public, official prayer of the Church. This principle was to be developed during the subsequent six decades culminating in the promulgation of the Constitution on the Liturgy *Sacrosanctum Concilium* in December 1963.

In 1905, Pope Pius X issued the Encyclical Letter *Acerbo Nimis* in which he called for the setting up of the Confraternity of Christian Doctrine which would ensure that the catechism would be taught in parishes throughout the world. The Catechism of Saint Pius X was issued in 1908 and an English translation appeared shortly afterwards. Like many Popes before and since his time Pope Pius X set out to organise the Roman Curia and to this end he issued the Constitution *Sapienti Consilio* in 1908. In 1910, Pius X issued the decree *Quam Singulari*, which involved an important change in the lives of Catholic children. The age for the reception of Holy Communion was set at 7 years old, the age of discretion.

In 1909 with the Apostolic Letter, *Vinea Electa* Pope Pius X founded the Pontifical Biblical Institute to promote the study of Sacred Scripture.

The reformed Roman Breviary of Pope Pius X was introduced the year after Lawrence McReavy entered Ushaw. Although, as an eleven year old school boy, it would have affected him very little, nevertheless it was a significant change for the Professorial Staff and the Senior Students of the College.

Pope Pius X declared in his Motu Proprio *Abhinc duos annos* published in 1913 that the programme of reform which he had begun would continue: "according to the views of the experts, a work both detailed and extensive; and therefore it is necessary that many years should pass, before this, so to speak, liturgical edifice... reappears in new splendour in its dignity and harmony, once the marks of old age have been cleared away".

In 1917 the Code of Canon Law, begun by Pius X and completed by Benedict XV, was promulgated, it was to play an important part in the life and work of Lawrence McReavy.

In 1925 Pope Pius XI founded the Institute of Christian Archeology to promote the study of both archeology and liturgy. As Librarian of the Ambrosian Library of Milan, Pius XI had admired the work of the Farnborough monks Fernand Cabrol and Henri Leclerc, and as the title of their great work indicates *Dictionnaire d'archéologie chrétienne et de liturgie*, first published in 1907, the two subjects were not considered to be unrelated. It is not surprising, therefore, that three years after the foundation of the institute Pius XI issued the Encyclical *Divini cultus* on the Sacred Liturgy. Of the Encyclicals of Pope Pius XI the one which was to play a significant part in Lawrence McReavy's role as a Canonist and in the debates of the Council was *Casti Connubii* on Christian marriage issued in 1930.

In 1943, during the Second World War, Pope Pius XII issued two important Encyclical Letters, the first *Mystici Corporis Christi* on June 29, and *Divino afflante spiritu* on September 30. The implications for the development of Biblical studies with the publication of the encyclical *Divino afflante spiritu* was so far-reaching that some scholars in France were anxious that the document might not be genuine, and that it was part of the German propaganda regime to confuse Catholics. After the war, in November 1947 Pope Pius XII issued one of his most influential encyclicals *Mediator Dei*. The Reform of the Liturgy of Holy Week followed not long afterwards in 1951 and 1955.

These three Encyclicals, *Mystici Corporis Christi, Divino afflante spiritu* and *Mediator Dei* had a direct bearing both upon the preparatory work for the Second Vatican Council and upon the documents which it published.

It would be an incomplete picture that did not show Pope John XXIII's own contribution to the preparation for the Council.

While the work of preparation for the Council was in progress, Pope John XXIII went about fulfilling his duties as Bishop of Rome and Successor of Saint Peter. There was the usual series of audiences with pilgrims, with various members of Religious Orders and lay movements, bishops, nuncios and Heads of State. Such occasions were not only opportunities for words of appreciation and encouragement from the Pope but also an opportunity to speak about the forthcoming Council.

During this preparatory period Pope John XXIII issued eight Encyclical Letters. The significance of Pope John's Encyclicals for reading the Council has not yet been sufficiently examined. Even when they do not explicitly treat of the Council, many of the subjects were to find a place and be developed in the Documents of the Second Vatican Council.

For example the Priesthood is discussed in *Sacerdotii Nostri Primordia* (August 1, 1959). The missionary activity of the Church is the subject of *Princeps Pastorum* (November 28, 1959). The Encyclical *Mater et Magistra* on Christianity and social progress (May 15, 1961) not only commemorated the great social Encyclical of Pope Leo XIII *Rerum novarum* but was intended to encourage "all who would seek appropriate solutions to the many social problems of our times. Our purpose, therefore, is not merely to commemorate in a fitting manner the Leonine encyclical, but also to confirm and make more specific the teaching of Our predecessors, and to determine clearly the mind of the Church on the new and important problems of the day".

It is in the opening paragraphs of his first Encyclical *Ad Petri cathedram* (June 29, 1959), that Pope John makes explicit mention of the Council whose announcement had already "received widespread approval and bolstered the universal hope that the hearts of all would be stirred to a fuller and deeper recognition of truth, a renewal of Christian morals, and a restoration of unity, harmony, and peace". Already before a clear line had emerged regarding the work of the Council, Pope John outlined his own vision of the Council: "Bishops from every part of the world will gather there to discuss serious religious topics. They will consider, in particular, the growth of the Catholic faith, the restoration of sound morals among the Christian flock, and appropriate adaptation of Church discipline to the needs and conditions of our times. This event will be a wonderful spectacle of truth, unity, and charity. For those who behold it but are not one with this Apostolic See, We hope that it will be a gentle invitation to seek and find that unity for which Jesus Christ prayed so ardently to His Father in heaven. (*Ad cathedram Petri* 61-62).

In this first Encyclical the Pope's words concerning theological discussion have particular significance for England: "The Catholic Church, of course, leaves many questions open to the discussion of theologians. She does this to the extent that matters are not absolutely certain. Far from jeopardizing the Church's unity, controversies, as a noted English author, John Henry Cardinal Newman, has remarked, can actually pave the way for its attainment. For discussion can lead to fuller and deeper understanding of religious truths; when one idea strikes against another, there may be a spark. But the common saying, expressed in various ways and attributed to various authors, must be recalled with approval: in essentials, unity; in doubtful matters, liberty; in all things, charity." (nn. 71-72).

The Encyclical to mark the fifteenth centenary of the death of Pope St Leo the Great, *Aeterna Dei sapientia*, published just less than a year before the opening of the Council, presented an apt occasion for highlighting his hopes and aspirations for the Council: "the time is drawing near for the Second General Council of the Vatican. Surrounding the Roman Pontiff and in close communion with him, you, the Bishops, will present to the world a wonderful spectacle of Catholic unity. Meanwhile We, for Our part, will seek to give instruction and comfort by briefly recalling to mind St Leo's high ideals regarding the Church's unity. Our intention in so doing is indeed to honour the memory of a most wise Pope, but at the same time to give the faithful profitable food for thought on the eve of this great event". (n. 35) "It is to render the Church better able to fulfill this high mission of hers that We have resolved to summon the Second General Council of the Vatican. We are fully confident that this solemn assembly of the Catholic Hierarchy will not only reinforce that unity in faith, worship and discipline which is a distinguishing mark of Christ's true Church, but will also attract the gaze of the great majority of Christians of every denomination, and induce them to gather around "the great Pastor of the sheep" who entrusted His flock to the unfailing guardianship of Peter and his successors". (n. 62).

In his last Encyclical before the opening of the Council, *Paenitentiam agere* on the need for the practice of interior and exterior penance (July 1, 1962) Pope John declared that the "renewal of Christian life is one of the principal aims of the coming Council ... and to render more effective that divine work which our Redeemer accomplished".

Greeting the bishops who were preparing to leave for Rome Pope John expressed his hope "to see the dawning of a new and fairer age for the Catholic Church throughout the world".

Not only the participants of the Council but everyone has a part to play: "in making this Second Ecumenical Vatican Council, which is especially concerned with the refurbishing of Christian morality, an outstanding success".

Louvain and its influence

According to John McHugh the four years that L.L. McReavy spent in Louvain "were to him golden years".[6] The friends which he made during that period, especially his class mate Willy Onclin were to be significant during his time at the Council and afterwards in the work of revision of the Code of Canon Law. L.L. McReavy frequently visited the Belgian College in Rome during his time at the Council. The day after his arrival both for the First and Second Sessions he went to visit his Belgian friends: "In the evening, called on Anné at the Belgian College and met Bishop Calewaert of Bruges. Momentary encounter with Cardinal Suenens at entrance".

While L.L. McReavy was in Louvain he could not have been unaware of the various movements that were developing in that country. The Liturgical Movement in Belgium had its centre in the Benedictine monastery in Louvain, Mont César whose great liturgical scholar Dom Bernard Capelle was abbot during L.L. McReavy's years in Louvain. In 1925 the young Christian Workers Movement was founded by the Belgian Father (later Cardinal) Cardijn.

The English scene

The Society of St Gregory was founded in 1929 and the Centre de Pastorale Liturgique in 1943. Father S.J. Gosling founded in 1942 the society for the Use of English in the Liturgy.

As is already evident it was Ushaw itself which was a prime formative influence upon Lawrence McReavy. The highly competent Professorial Staff, with such members as Leonard Johnston, John McHugh, Aidan Pickering to name but a few, would keep the members of the Ushaw Parlour up to date with developments in their own areas of competence and interest.

An insight into the thought of Lawrence McReavy

Twenty years before the announcement of the calling of the Council, Lawrence McReavy gave a talk in Wallsend (April 30, 1939) on the Lay Priesthood. This provides a valuable insight into his thought and gives an indication of how well he was informed of the then current areas of interest. The following text, edited by John Butters was published in the *Ushaw Magazine* for the Academic Year 1992-93, pp. 35-36.

---

[6] *Ushaw Magazine* 270 (1989-1990) 106.

There is a general tendency today to regard the Church of Christ as composed of two radically distinct bodies, the clergy and the laity. According to this misconception the clergy alone are the active element, responsible to Christ not only for the government and administration of the Church, but for all the active steps towards its spread and development.

The laity, on the other hand, are relegated to the status of a purely passive element, whose only function is to be moulded as the Potter moulds the clay and to provide, when required, the material resources necessary for the church's many activities.

It is true that this doctrine has no official support or approval, and can only be said to be widespread insofar as it represents a common attitude of mind but the fact remains that it is as pernicious in practice as it is wrong in theory, and until it is eradicated they can be no full Christian life.

The truth is that the church is one single living organism, consisting, like the human body, of many members, and though these members differ in dignity and function, nevertheless they are intimately linked and coordinated by a common vital principle and the common action, "for as the body is one", says Saint Paul, "and has many members, and all the members of the body, so also is Christ. For in one spirit we were all baptised into one body, whether Jews or Gentiles, whether bond or free; and in one spirit we have all been made to drink" (1 Cor 12, 12-13). It follows, therefore, that since Christ is "a priest forever", we who are in Christ, we are the Mystical Body of Christ, share all alike in his eternal priesthood. "You are a chosen generation", said Saint Peter to his disciples, "a kingly priesthood, a holy nation, a purchased people" (1 Pet 2,9), and so he exhorted them: "be you also as living stones built up, a spiritual house, holy priesthood, to offer up spiritual sacrifices acceptable to God by Jesus Christ" (ibid. v.5).

We can distinguish, therefore, in the Church, a twofold priesthood. There is an official, ordained priesthood which belongs only to those who have received the full sacrament of Holy Orders, and which enables them, and them alone, to renew on our altars the unique sacrifice of the New Testament.

But at the same time there is an unofficial or common priesthood, shared by all who are made one in Christ, our great High Priest, by baptism, and consecrated by the fullness of his Spirit in Confirmation. That is why Confirmation is so much in need of emphasis today. It is, as it were, the layman's ordination. In Confirmation as in Holy Orders, there is a laying on of hands, there is an infusion of the Holy Spirit there is an anointing with chrism, and there is the conferment of a special character. Don't mistake me. Confirmation is not a lesser form of Holy Orders: it does not make you sacrificing priests in the unique Christian sense of that word. But, by completing the work of

> baptism, it consecrates you as Saint Peter says, "to offer up spiritual sacrifices, acceptable to God by Jesus Christ".
>
> You were not anointed as disciples, but as apostles, and it is your mission to preach your faith, to bear witness to it, to "let your light so shine before men, that they may see your good works, and glorify your Father who is in heaven" (Mt. 5, 16). Listen to the words of the heroic Cardinal champion of the persecuted Church in Germany, "through Baptism we become children of God, through Confirmation we become apostles of Christ; through Baptism we become stones in the city of God, through Confirmation we receive the summons to be workers and builders in that city. It is not enough for us to be fishes in the net of the apostles, we must be fishers and apostles ourselves. You have had your Pentecost. You have been strengthened from on high by the gift of the Holy Ghost in Confirmation, and equipped with the graces and gifts you need for your work. You are ready to start'.

This text could easily be taken as a reflection upon the teaching of the Constitution on the Church, *Lumen gentium* and the Council's teaching on the lay apostolate if it was not for the fact that it was written almost twenty five years before the Council.

A canonist at the Council

It is fortunate that L.L. McReavy himself reflected upon his role as a canonist at the Council: "it has to be admitted that Canon Law had a somewhat dusty image at Vatican II. In the mouths of many Fathers the term "juridical" became almost a dirty word. Modest canonists listening to the speeches felt as though they ought to blush for having shamelessly introduced so improper an element into a community of the spirit that lived only by charity, never by law. On the part of some of the anti-juridical Fathers, the note of hostility or suspicion may have been due to irritation at having had some fond project of their own scotched or curbed by the cold hand of law; in others it may have been mere bandwagonism (or, more politely, following what seemed to be a movement of the Spirit); but it would be a purblind canonist who would dismiss the widespread critical attitude to the existing juridical discipline of the Church as quite unfounded. Indeed, much of the criticism had already been initiated by canonists."

A Comparison of Witnesses

It is a fair question to ask how Monsignor McReavy's account of the Council compares with those of other Fathers and experts who were present at its discussions. It is not possible to provide an extensive comparison and even the following example cannot be considered fully satisfactory. It does however illustrate something of the character and the content of L.L. McReavy's observations in relation to other similar material.

The following comparison is drawn from the diary entries of the recently published journals of Archbishop Maxim Hermaniuk, the first Metropolitan for Ukrainian Catholics in Canada and the Dominican Father Yves Congar.

The day chosen is the one on which Archbishop Heenan criticised the schema that was eventually to become the Constitution on the Church in the Modern World.

The diary entry of Metropolitan Hermaniuk is concise as well as precise: "Today the Archbishop of Westminster, Heenan (from England) very sharply criticized the schema *De ecclesia in mundo huius temporis* and its authors, and more concretely, the "experts" who, as he said, have no contact with the world since they abide in monasteries or universities. (He as some say, had in mind Father Häring, the Redemptorist who criticized him last year)."[7]

The Journal entry of Yves Congar is more complete but as in many of his entries manifests his frequent personal irritation of events as they unfolded: "I caught the end of an intervention by Msgr Heenan; extremely violent. For him schema XIII would be the disgrace of the Council. What is said about the family cannot go through. The evil comes from experts who pick and choose among pontifical teachings. But they are not infallible (implying: for all that they seem to believe that they are!). Heenan would have in mind, particularly Küng and Häring who had intervened in the English situation. Häring had spoken about birth control. There had also been the intervention of Msgr Roberts. In short, the English bishops do not want to hear mention at the Council of either the pill or the bomb. Heenan was strongly applauded. By some perhaps, because of the humour of his speech; by many, especially at the top of the assembly, because they saw in his speech a savage attack on schema XIII, which they do not want. From the experts' tribune, one saw that it was Felici who, if he did not actually start the applause, at least encouraged it as soon as it started."[8]

Lawrence McReavy's description of the same event is given in his Letter to Monsignor Paul Grant (n. 25): "Thursday was a big day for us English. Heenan began the morning with the finest speech he has yet made, judged purely from the oratorical point of view. Indeed, many round me were of the opinion that it was the best speech yet delivered at the Council, and it was clear from the next day's papers that many journalists shared this opinion. It had all the tricks of the public speaker's trade, several times moving the Fathers to laughter, and receiving at the end a loud burst of applause. But there was by no means the same agreement as to its content.

---

[7] *The Second Vatican Council Diaries of Met. Maxim Hermaniuk, C.Ss.R.*, (Eastern Christian Studies 15, Leuven 2012).

[8] Yves Congar, *My Journal of the Council* (2012).

Most of those who knew about the Häring-Heenan clash in the newspapers after the Hierarchy's response to Roberts, interpreted his remarks about a few *Periti* usurping the functions of the episcopate as prompted by personal animosity to Häring, architect of this schema, and felt that this should not be done in a Conciliar speech to which Häring could not reply. (Incidentally, Häring was sitting in the tribune opposite me, next to Claude Leetham, who said to him: "He means you"; to which Häring replied: "Don't I know it"). Others who perhaps were ignorant of the earlier clash felt that an attack on certain unnamed Periti, even though Heenan insisted that they were few, inevitably discredited all. Others, especially Periti, rallied to the defence of what they conceived to be the function of theologians in the evolution of the Church's doctrine." *(Letter 25)*

The following day (October 23rd) the following observations describing the reaction to Heenan's speech appear in each of the three accounts of the General Congregation from the same sources.

Metropolitan Maxim Hermaniuk wrote: "Abbot B. Reetz, Superior General of the Benedictine Congregation in Beuron, Germany, admirably responded to Archbishop Heenan from Westminster (England) concerning his speech yesterday against the "experts" from monasteries and universities."

Yves Congar briefly observed that there was a "very funny intervention by Dom Reetz, (Beuron), who took Heenan up, point by point."

The account by L.L. McReavy is not only more informative but it contains a personal observation which is also autobiographical: "B. Reetz, Abbot General of the Beuron Congregation, made a witty come-back, evidently written overnight, to the Heenan speech. He spent the first part of his speech explaining why, after certain remarks made yesterday, he was afraid to speak. We had been told that it was a waste of time to seek any expert advice on world problems from people like him who had led a cloistered life, and who, if as simple as doves, were certainly not as cute as serpents. "Sum simplex columba". But he remembered that Gregory the Great had sent Saint Augustine and 40 other monks to turn the Angles into Angels. "Forsitan ii quoque mundum vix cognoverunt". Then he went on to discuss the general merits of the schema in terms which, some thought, added weight to the charge that monks were somewhat remote from the hard realities of life. On this I pass no judgement, since I myself must be numbered among those who have spent their lives sequestered from the world "in seminariis, in domibus religionis, in accademiis" ... The following morning, Friday, everyone was still talking about the Heenan speech, and the Italian dailies gave it an unusual prominence and full-length treatment, characterizing it as brilliant and commenting on the touches of "humour inglese" which had punctuated it."

Reflections of Monsignor McReavy on the Council

Concerning the Liturgy Monsignor McReavy wrote: "Ever since the beginning of the century, with the full support of the Popes, a liturgical movement had been working for a reform of the liturgy which, by devising more appropriate forms and making greater use of the vernacular would promote more active and meaningful participation by the laity in the daily worship of the Church. This essentially pastoral object and inspired the draft document on liturgy. The discussion was long-winded, and much time and labour were required to get the eventual constitution through the various stages of revision and amendment, but when it was finally approved and promulgated on December 4, 1963, there were only four dissentients. It was the first, and one of the chief fruits of the Council, one which, in my opinion, helps us to bring us closer to our fellow Christians. Certainly it does not widen the gulf".

Commenting on the Constitution on the Church *Lumen Gentium*, L.L. McReavy stated: "The key document of the whole council was the dogmatic Constitution on the Church. To my mind, it marks a notable step forward. Instead of concentrating on the external framework of the Church, it probes into its inner reality, presenting it primarily as the sacrament or sign and instrument of man's union with God in Christ and of the unity of the whole human race, and mystery which the Bible itself can only convey in symbols and images, such as the kingdom of God, the one fold, God's field, house, family, Temple, spouse, the mystical body of Christ, the people of God".

When *Lumen Gentium* was put to the vote: "the final verdict was 2151 to 5, a clear guarantee that the seal of the Holy Spirit is on the new look which the Council has given to the old Church, and an assurance that it remains the same Church. In my non-expert opinion, it is a magnificent document."

As regards ecumenism: "the ground-work had therefore been well laid long before the Council was even thought of, and doubtless for this reason the document had a relatively easy passage through the ordeal of conciliar debate. There were, of course, differences of opinion as to the right means to the goal, but no dispute about the need for a more positive and active approach to the problem of Christian reunion."

Concerning the Pastoral Constitution on *The Church in the Modern World*: "I feel, this is of ecumenical value, because in it the Church, for the first time in Council history, addresses herself not just to her own members, or even to Christians generally, but to mankind as a whole and seeks to enter into dialogue with all who will genuinely respond beginning with a survey of the modern situation, it reflects on the vocation of man and human society as seen in the light of Christian faith, and points the way to the solution of some of the grave of modern problems. As a first essay of its kind, it naturally had its teething troubles, and it remains far from perfect; but at least it bears witness to the outward looking which characterised this council, it's ready appreciation of positive values wherever found, and its willingness to collaborate with all men of goodwill".

Lawrence McReavy never lost sight of the aims of the Council. On his return from the first Session of the Council he wrote: "The declared purpose of the Pope in calling this Council was to restate the Church's doctrine, without compromise or watering down, but in a way which would commend it to modern man and, in particular, to our separated brethren".

While assisting at the closing ceremony of the Council, L.L. McReavy reflected that the Second Vatican Council could well be the last such great event in the life of the Church and developing this thought he wrote: "Pope Paul VI brought to a close what may prove to have been the last ecumenical Council in the history of the Church. I suggest this, not because of any presentiment of imminent doom, or because the number of bishops is increasing at a rate which must soon make it impossible to assemble them all in what could meaningfully be called a Council, but because the Church appears to have found what may prove to be an adequate substitute. I refer to the "Synod of Bishops" which the Holy Father set up ... as a permanent central institution representative of all the bishops of the world and a practical expression of their collegiality. By convoking this synod in general assembly, the Pope will henceforth be able to seek and discover the mind and will of the whole episcopal college through the accredited and duly briefed representatives of the various episcopal conferences. The synod could therefore well serve all the purposes for which it has hitherto been necessary or useful to call a General Council. Nor would the consequent change from an institution in which every bishop was theoretically entitled to speak his mind *coram Ecclesia* to one in which he could only intervene through chosen spokesmen be an altogether novel development. It was substantially introduced in the first session of Vatican II, when the Fathers decided that a topic could be closed to further discussion by majority vote and that thereafter the right to speak should be limited to those who spoke on behalf of at least seventy other Fathers, a restriction that was in fact frequently applied in later periods of pressure".

L.L. McReavy was aware that certain ideas that had arisen since the closure of the Council were not always a true reflection of the mind of the Council. For example speaking as a canonist he wrote: "these are truths as old as the gospel itself. They have been parentally taught and yet have been constantly overlooked. But of churchmen and faithful alike have regularly attended in practice to visualise the Church more according to its external juridical structure than according to its inner reality, the remedy surely is to correct the imbalance of the mental picture, not to create a contrary imbalance by undervaluing the external juridical structure. Yet that is what the more starry-eyed visionaries have been doing since Vatican II. Not merely have they tended to overemphasise the spiritual nature of the Church and the charismatic activity of the Spirit with in it (a certain amount of overemphasis of a neglected truth is understandable), but they have sought to create a false antithesis between the Church of the Spirit and the Church of Law. Properly understood, however, these two aspects of the Church are not in conflict. The Church is both spiritual and temporal, both internal and external, both guided by the Spirit and yet structured and regulated by law, but as a single living organism, no more divided or divisible than the Body of Christ. As an external society of imperfect and often very unspiritual members, the Church needs law to direct their social relationships and activities, no less than it needs to provide for such charisms as they may receive; but, in God's design for the Church, law and charism are meant to work in harmony for the same end. This is certainly the mind of Vatican II".[9]

A hand-written note of Lawrence McReavy provides a fitting conclusion to this Chapter and a fitting introduction to his Letters, Journal and other papers.

> History will give its verdict. It will take many years before the changes bear fruit and much depends on how earnestly bishops, priests and faithful cooperate.
>
> Unique in many respects. In sheer size of the assembly, in the number and variety of themes discussed, in benefiting from the presence and cooperative criticism of delegate observers from other Christian churches, in the breadth and universality of the Council's outlook and address.
>
> It has certainly sharpened the Church's sense of involvement in the problems that vex the modern world, war, hunger, illiteracy, over population and pledged her to active cooperation with all men of good will. It has charted the path of the Church perhaps for centuries to come.

---

9 "The Place of Canon Law in the Church" in *Ushaw Magazine* 244 (1974) 11-12.

Chapter III

The Letters

General Introduction

The letters which Monsignor Lawrence Leslie McReavy wrote from Rome to the President of Ushaw, Monsignor Paul Grant, and to members of the Staff form an important part of the McReavy Archive. They present a vibrant, narrative account of the Council. Even those who did not know Lawrence McReavy personally will still be able to grasp something of his personality and his *joie de vivre* as he shares with his seminary family and friends his experience of the Council. He knew that his letters to the President would be made available for the Staff (called the Parlour) to read and so he aimed to be as informative as possible about the events as they unfolded before his eyes and the rumours that came to his ears.

If the letters to Monsignor Paul Grant appear to have a certain air of formality, this is not only because L.L. McReavy knew that members of Staff would be reading his letters but also because at that time such formality would be expected in the correspondence of a member of Staff to the President of the College. Paul Grant and Lawrence McReavy had known each other since 1915 when Grant entered Junior House. In the homily which Monsignor McReavy gave at the Requiem Mass for Monsignor Grant he describes their relationship as "an acquaintance lasting over sixty years". L.L. McReavy's respect for Grant can be detected in the following tribute: "from the time when he first came to Ushaw in 1915, as a boy of 12, till the day he left it, in 1967, I never knew him decline or avoid the jobs that need doing because it meant hard work ... Steady application to the task assigned to him, or to work that called for his attention, remained throughout his life perhaps his most striking characteristic. ... As a Superior, his natural bent was more towards old-fashioned discipline than towards modern dialogue, but to no one under his authority was he harder than to himself. Well or ill, he drove himself unsparingly."

The letters designed to describe the unfolding of the Council contain nevertheless many personal touches, humourous comments and remarks. For example L.L. McReavy readily shares his moments of relaxation and enjoyment of the outings to the Castelli and surrounding area of Rome. He is careful, however, to point out to his readers that there is only one free day a week, "lest my appreciation of the occasional treat convey a false impression, let me emphasize that this sort of thing occurs at most one day in seven." *(L = Letter: L32)*

While in Rome Ushaw was never far from his mind and in the chill of a Roman evening he writes: "I think fondly of my fire" at Ushaw *(L6)*. He especially enjoyed meeting and entertaining the Ushaw students who were studying in Rome: "I have promised to take the Ushaw lads out to dinner tomorrow. I find that there are twelve of them, so that, adding my server, we shall be fourteen in all! A visit to the bank is indicated." *(L26)* He did not stint at these events and on one occasion he records that the meal "was gargantuan but very enjoyable, and we needed to walk all the way back from the Via Merulana to work it off." *(L19)*

The English College Villa at Pallazola in the hills outside of Rome was used by the English and Welsh Bishops as a place of rest and relaxation on their free days. L.L. McReavy mentions his visits there, but "sitting about" was not easy for him: "I haven't yet decided what to do with my weekend. Most seem to be going out to the villa, but I soon get tired of sitting about, even in beautiful surroundings, and there is not much else for men of our age to do. I might even stay here and work." *(L29)*

The letters also reveal that Monsignor McReavy made a substantial contribution to the participation of the English and Welsh Bishops in the debates of the Council. Even before the main work of the Council got under way he was already at their service. He wrote on October 20th 1962: "I worked from 8 a.m. to 1 p.m. drafting a summary of the schema *De Liturgia* which Monsignor Worlock multicopied for all the bishops. Several, including the Cardinal, expressed appreciation". *(L3)* A few weeks later he told Monsignor Philip Loftus: "I have spent the All Saints-All Souls break analysing the debate on chapter I for the benefit of our bishops, re-editing a manuscript of notes to 6 pages of typescript which Worlock is going to roneo." *(L6)*

He was also kept busy providing a commentary on the interventions and debates in the Aula of Saint Peter's Basilica: "Saturday and Sunday I spent working on a combination of the weeks' debates with comments for the benefit of our Bishops: it is being poly-copied at this moment by our secretariate. I could not even spare the time to attend the Papal Taking-Possession ceremony at the Lateran. *(L17)*

L.L. McReavy did not just miss events such as the newly elected Pope Paul VI taking possession of his Cathedral, he even had to forego the short holiday breaks in order to provide the Bishops with help and information: "Friday to Monday inclusive was declared a mid-term break and most of the bishops went off on various 3 to 4 day jaunts, I had been given the job of preparing comments on *De Episcopis*, so that kept me busy for three of the four days." *(L16)* In his diary entry for Thursday, November 22nd 1962 he notes: "Worked from 8 to 1.15 on a summary of the 50 page schema on the Means of Social Communication".

These are not isolated examples of his dedication and generous use of his time and show the considerable extent of his work for the Bishops. He even helped Bishop Dwyer in liturgical matters: "Most of my evenings have been spent trying to work out a suitable English version of the Ordination of Priests on the basis of the comments sent in to Dwyer by about ten experts regarding three previous versions — a complicated job, as you can imagine." *(L32)* On occasions he was called upon to give a Lecture: "Wednesday 4 p.m. to 5.30. Discussion in our Bishops Common Room, at which I presented and expounded a votum which I had prepared *De Communicatione in sacris. (L19)*

He was not afraid to admit that at times he felt the burden and pressure of work: "I am always tired out at the end of the General Congregation day, and when we have eight in ten days, as we have had up to All Saints, I feel as if I had been put through the wringer". *(L6)*

Over and above his considerable work for the Bishops, Lawrence McReavy had his own Commission work. Since the meetings of these Commissions required the presence of some of the Council Fathers, they always took place in the afternoon, thus adding to his burden of work: "just returned from a Sub-commission meeting which lasted from 4.30 to 7pm" *(L12)*

The letters show that Lawrence McReavy was realistic and down to earth in his view of the Council and so could write: "I sit in my Tribune, scribbling everything down for three hours on end, as though there was bound to be gold in them there hills, only to find, when I have spent another couple of hours in the evening perusing my notes, that there is precious little but sand." *(L6)* He was, nevertheless, conscientious and diligent in recording the debates and happenings in the daily General Congregations "I took over 54 pages of close-written notes at the five General Congregations of the week." *(L35)*

L.L. McReavy was also called upon to participate in some of the Press Conferences given by the English Bishops: "On Friday evening, I participated in a press conference on the Liturgical changes with Archbishop Grimshaw, and Canon O'Connell. I was asked to join the panel in case any other question, about which I might know something, came up." *(L14)* On November 19th 1964 he himself gave the Press Conference.

The many and various services that L.L. McReavy provided for the Bishops of England and Wales continued throughout the Four Sessions of the Council. While he was immensely helpful to the Bishops, it must not be forgotten that he was present at the Second Vatican Council in his own right by virtue of his nomination on September 24th 1962 as a *Peritus*, (an expert advisor), and as Member of the Commission for the Discipline of Clergy and People.

Nevertheless, his worth was recognised by the Bishops because even if he had not received a Papal nomination to the Council, L.L. McReavy would have been in Rome as an advisor: "Monsignor Frank Davis has just told me that, in any case, our hierarchy had decided to have the pair of us in tow as their tame Theologians." *(L1)*

His final letter from the Council reveals a touch of sadness as he realised that an important chapter in his life was drawing to a close: "I used to think that I should be glad when the Council was over and I could say goodbye to

Rome. I am not so sure now. It will be goodbye to many good friends whose company I have enjoyed and to a whole way of life". *(L40)*

Often L.L.McReavy gives some information about his activities during the period following his previous letter. In those instances where he fails to do this and where it may prove useful, relevant information has been taken from his Diary notes.

The First Session

October 11th – December 8th 1962

On September 22nd 1962 Monsignor Lawrence McReavy returned to Ushaw after his summer holiday which included his customary stay with his family at Maidstone and a visit to his nephew at Quarr Abbey on the Isle of Wight. The following day he began his annual Retreat. Both holiday and Retreat were to prove a fitting preparation for the reception of some unexpected news. He records in his Diary: "I had assumed that my extremely modest contribution to the Council had ended with the group photo which celebrated the completion of the work of our Preparatory Commission, and that the Bishops of the world would now take over, with the assistance, no doubt, of a small panel of eminent theologians of worldwide repute. It was with considerable surprise therefore that, on Tuesday, 2 October 1962, I received a Brief from the Cardinal Secretary of State (Cardinal Cicognani), with an enclosed card from Archbishop Felici, Secretary General of the Council, notifying me that I had been appointed a "Peritus Conciliaris".

His diary entry for that day records that after lunch he rang Bishop James Cunningham "who said I should treat it as a command". Characteristically L.L. McReavy lost no time in making his preparations. His Diary entry informs us that immediately after his phone call to the Bishop he began to make his preparations: "I rang Norman Richardson (travel agent) and by 3.30 was booked for the Alitalia flight (Monday 8th 12.45)". His next step was to find somewhere to stay: "I wired the Vice-Rector of the English College asking him to fix accommodation for me somewhere".

The few days left to him at Ushaw were "spent in clearing up *Clergy Review* work and preparing for departure". On October 7th after an early morning Mass and breakfast he "departed Durham at 10.58, arrived King's Cross for 4.39 p.m." And so began what Father Peter Walton, President of Ushaw described as: "the crowning experience of his life and work: his participation in the second Vatican Council. For Lawrence Leslie it came when he was at the height of his powers – just 60, with his confidence and expertise in full flood. He always maintained that this was the highlight of his life."

Letter 1

The English College, Rome
Tuesday, October 9th 1962

Dear Monsignor,

All went well on the first part of my journey. Mr Hollis took me to Durham and even put me on the train. I was met at King's Cross by Father Peter Anglin who took me by car to Clitherow House where, as usual, I was most hospitably housed, and from whence, on Monday morning, I was transported to the airport.[1] There I was immediately pounced on by the Public Relations Officer-ess of Alitalia, herded temporarily with some English and Commonwealth bishops and their secretaries and then ushered in advance to the plane.

The prospect was not so bright at Rome airport. Monsignor Alan Clark met the plane and regretted to tell me that the English College was full up and that he had to book a room for me at a nearby pensionat off the Piazza Navona. On arrival at the College, I was taken by car to this supposed pensionat and found that it was nothing of the kind.

Yes, they said, a room had been prepared, and I was taken up to see it. It consisted of four walls, a marble floor, a wash-basin and literally nothing else. They had been wondering when the new occupant was going to bring his furniture! So back I went to the English College, where I was given the room of Bishop Parker (not yet arrived) for the night, and the problem was shelved. I did not get to sleep until 3 a.m., wondering where I would sleep the next night.

After breakfast this morning, however, the problem was solved by a student who informed the Rector of his intention to leave on Friday. They decided that they could bed me down somewhere until then, though, in fact, it is Peter Cookson who has generously moved to some attic and given me three days tenancy of his room.[2] I can now relax. Nearly all the bishops and the number of secretaries have now arrived and the "House Full" notice is definitive.

This morning, I went to the Secretariate of the Council to pick up some information about when, how and where we late-comers are to profess our faith and emit our oaths. The others did it yesterday evening in Saint Peter's, just about the time I reached Rome. I also discovered that the Periti do not walk in Thursday's procession but proceed directly in choir-robes to their Tribune in Saint Peter's. It is a pity, because I should like to have seen the procession in the piazza. I shall see it only as it proceeds up the nave of the basilica.

I then went to lunch at Monsignor Lefebvre's flat (Auditor of the Rota) and learned that, as far as he can discover, the Periti were named by the

[1] Peter Anglin was a Cathedral chaplain at Westminster.

[2] Peter Cookson was to become President of Ushaw 1977-1984.

Cardinal Presidents of the Preparatory Commissions at the suggestion of the Secretaries. If so, it was Berutti OP who named me, and it can only be because I did my homework to the bitter end. Monsignor Frank Davis has just told me that, in any case, our hierarchy had decided to have the pair of us in tow as their tame Theologians.[3] Meanwhile, it may be quite a while before there is any real work for us to do. The mills of Rome grind slowly. Everybody is questing for gaff, the bishops included, but the general impression is that no one has any idea.[4]

Yours sincerely.
L.LMcR

* * *

The day after his first letter to Monsignor Paul Grant, Wednesday, October 10th L.L. McReavy along with many other Periti went to obtain his identity card. Among them was Father Yves Congar who records in his diary that he "went to the Secretariate bringing two photographs in order to be given an expert's identity card". On Thursday October 11th there was the solemn opening of the Council about which Bishop James Cunningham wrote "It will take Monsignor McReavy years to describe it!".

Letter 2

The English College, Rome
Saturday, October 13th 1962

Dear Monsignor,

You will want to hear about the Great Day (11th October). I rose at 5.45, but postponed my Mass to the evening, making use of the privilege we have been granted. At 7.20, vested in choir robes, I set out for Saint Peter's in a car shared with Bishop Grasar and Monsignor Davis. The rain which had fallen in torrents all night stopped quite suddenly on the way, and as we walked across the piazza from our car park the sun broke through.

A great crowd was milling around the prelates' entrance in the Colonnade, but I got in easily on the strength of my choir robes without having to show my papers, which may account for the large number who gate-crashed. I am pretty certain there were some phonies in our Tribune

[3] Harry Frank Davis, (1903-1986) Priest of Archdiocese of Birmingham, Professor at Oscott College for 28 years. During the Council one of his tasks was to assist in explaining procedures to non-Catholic Observers.

[4] The widespread sense of confusion is recorded in most Journals and accounts of these first days: "there was a lot of unpreparedness" (Yves Congar). "There was great confusion everywhere with bishops practically trampling on each other to register and collect their bundle of documents." (L.L. McReavy).

who had collected whatever robes they could lay hands on. There were certainly some strange mixtures.

We "Periti" did not walk in the procession but went straight to the tribunes, between the pillars of the nave, that had been assigned to us. In a way, it was a blessing, because I had a comfortable seat during the hour that the bishops spent assembling outside.

When eventually the head of the procession appeared at the great West door, I had a splendid view of the whole scene. Some of our bishops who found seats between me and the door and spotted me, told me afterwards that I had a better view than they. It took about half an hour for the 2500 plus to file into their seats.

The scene was magnificent beyond words and much more colourful (white copes and mitres notwithstanding) than I had expected. All the space between the pillars was completely sealed off with red damask, trimmed and tasselled with gold, and the backcloth of every Tribune was hung up with a superb Tapestry. There was a great splash of scarlet where the 80 Cardinals were seated, at the front end of the gospel side, and the green upholstery of the rank upon rank of Bishops' seats set off their embroidered white copes. There was an impressive sprinkling of black faces from Africa and of gorgeous robes and headgear from the East. Some of the Coptic bishops wore golden crowns.

Not all the bishops could be accommodated in the nave, about 40 had to come up into the Tribunes (including Heenan and Grimshaw). I had to yield my front corner seat to an Abyssinian Ordinary in a golden vestment and silk cap, and move one place back. The Pope descended from his gestatorial chair halfway up the nave and walked the rest of the way to the throne erected for him in front of the Papal altar.

After the High Mass, sung by Tisserant, the Pope made his profession of Faith, and then the Secretary General led the bishops in theirs. The Pope gave us a long Latin allocution, during which I nodded off several times (I learned afterwards that several of the bishops had done the same), and, after the Papal Blessing and Plenary, we scrambled out in any order about 1.30 p.m.

In the evening there was a torchlight procession in Saint Peter's Square and most of the public buildings of Rome were illuminated, — Hadrian's Mausoleum and the Capitol with *live* torches. I went out in a car with the Vice-Rector and Monsignor Worlock and saw the Capitol, but the traffic jam prevented us from reaching Saint Peter's Square.

On Friday, I got my Vatican passport, and on Saturday I attended the first General Congregation at 9 a.m.. After the dialogued Mass (very impressive), the President called upon the bishops to elect 16 of their number to each Commission. Liénart protested that it was impossible to do so without some idea of who were considered "magis apti" and time was needed to meditate. Frings supported him, and after a pause the session was prorogued till Tuesday next. We were out by 10.15.

The Cardinal and seventeen other English bishops, are in residence here, and the half a dozen others come here regularly for meetings and stay for meals. We eat at a different time from the students, and rather well. I have consumed more "hooch", wine and brandy in a week than in any normal year. I have the room occupied by John McHugh from 1950 to 1954. The weather is warm and humid, with frequent showers; so I prefer to stay in and study the schemata and brush up my theology.

Kind regards to all.
All the best
L.LMcR

* * *

Two days after the opening of the Council, Saturday October 13th the first General Congregation took place. L.L. McReavy recalls in one of his Lectures that the Council "ran into its first snag which might have been foreseen. The President called on the Bishops to nominate sixteen of their number to be members of each of ten Commissions. Time was needed to consult. The Congregation was brought to a close and we were out of the Basilica by 10.15". "Sunday October 14th and Monday 15th were spent in seeking names". On Tuesday October 16th at the second General Congregation the votes were taken. The following three days (while the votes were being counted) were free. On Friday he made a preliminary pencil sketch of the Theatre of Marcellus and painted it on the Saturday afternoon. The third General Congregation took place on Saturday, October 20th, the voting results were made known and a message to the peoples of the world calling for peace and social justice was issued by the Fathers of the Ecumenical Council.

Letter 3

The English College, Rome
Saturday, October 20th 6 p.m.

Dear Monsignor,

Not a great deal has been achieved since I wrote to you last Saturday. I have spent most of my time studying Volume I of the Schemata, and the English Bishops have been busy holding their October week meeting and compiling their lists of names to vote for in the composition of the Commissions. Each of them had to name in all 160 bishops, 16 for each of the 10 Commissions. There was much going to and fro between the Episcopal Conferences of the various countries.

Sunday was a feast. We celebrated Saint Edward the Confessor with a first class "do".

Tuesday dawned bright and sunny. The scirocco was at last over. We drove to Saint Peter's for the second General Congregation at 9 a.m. and after dialogue Mass, Cardinal Ottaviani was the first to speak. To save time in the voting for Commissions, he proposed that a relative majority of votes should suffice. Cardinal Roberti observed that this was an excellent idea but *contra ius*. Cardinal Rufini, for the Presidency, pointed out that the Pope could change the law, and that it would be best to proceed with the voting and ask the Pope to dispense. This was done, except that those who had not yet completed their list or wished to change it, and preferred to do so at their leisure at home, might do so, provided they handed in their lists at the General Secretariate by 6 p.m. that evening. It was then announced that there would be no further General Congregation until Saturday (presumably to allow time for the collation and counting of all the 2500x160 names), and that the first topic to be dealt with next week would be *De Liturgia*.

I am violating no secrets. The official hand-outs in the *Osservatore Romano* were more restricted, but all the above and more appeared in Wednesday's *Il Tempo* and *Messagero*. It may be possible to maintain secrecy about what happens in the Commissions, but no one seems to expect to keep the General Congregations secret, even though, after the Mass, the President cries: *Exeant omnes! Nemo rimanere potest nisi Patres Conciliares, Periti, Officiales et Observatores*, after all, the *nisi* covers about 3000, and if a journalist cannot get a full account from one or other of them, he is not trying.

Incidentally, though all the discussion is in Latin (except for one or two Orientals who use French) the announcements and propositions, put to the vote, are translated into Spanish, French, English, German and Arabic.

There was great disappointment felt and expressed that the preliminaries were taking up so much time. Everyone wants to get to work as promptly and effectively as possible.

Wednesday. After studying the Schemata, I went to Herder's bookshop, where I met Robert Spence. They are staying at their Villa and it takes them over an hour to reach the University, and have nowhere to go in between lectures.[5]

Thursday. All the English College guests took the day off. A few went to Assisi, the rest of us to Palazzola. It was a perfect day, and I went in Bishop Dwyer's car with Bishop Foley. We did a tour of the Castelli (Frascati, Monte Porzio etc) and had a magnificent lunch at a new Albergo just below the Villa, where the rest of the bishops joined us. After lunch, we drove up to the Villa and wandered around or lazed in deck chairs in midsummer weather.

[5] "The Collegio Scozzese was originally in the Via Quattro Fontane opposite the Palazzo Barberini. Austin McElhaton and I were there for our first year 1960-61, but then it was sold and while the new building was going up on the Via Cassia we lived at the Villa in Marino and were bused in and out to the Greg., which was very tedious". (Canon Robert Spence)

Friday. I worked from 8 a.m. to 1 p.m. drafting a summary of the schema *De Liturgia* which Monsignor Worlock multicopied for all the bishops. Several, including the Cardinal, expressed appreciation. It helped me to feel that I was doing something useful.

Saturday. Third General Congregation.

At 8.45 the great purple tide began to flow into Saint Peter's. I made for my usual tribune. After Mass, the result of Tuesdays voting was announced and the 16 members of seven Commissions (plus the 8 nominated by the Pope for the Liturgy Commission) were read out.

Bishop Dwyer came high among those chosen for the *Bishops and the Government of Dioceses*, Grimshaw was elected to the Liturgy and Petit to the Apostolate. Heenan, of course, is on the Unity Secretariate which remains in being. The other three Commissions are to be announced next week, when presumably the Periti will be told where they have to work.

The rest of the morning was spent in the discussion of a message to the world to be issued by the Council. Forty Fathers spoke, including Heenan, and the text with amendments was accepted by a large majority. I was the second to emerge from Saint Peter's door onto the square; it was 12.45 and after nearly 4 hours I was dying for a smoke. I began to make my way towards the door (fortunately the door of the Tribunes open on to the aisles) as soon as the votes had been collected. Even so, a Bishop beat me to it. There was the usual crowd waiting in the Piazza, and when we reached the barrier, there were cries of "finito? "Finito", I replied in my best Italian.

Sunday morning. Two of the Anglicans (Pawley and De Sousa) are coming to lunch here today. Ripon cannot manage it until tomorrow. We have another General Congregation tomorrow, Monday, when, at long last, the real work of the Council will begin.

Sorry to hear about your domestic upsets. I hope you do not have to set up soup kitchens.

All the best,
Bomb.

* * *

On Sunday and Monday afternoon (October 21/22) L.L. McReavy sketched and painted the Fabrician Bridge built in 62 B.C. and spans the Tiber River in Rome. On Monday, October 22nd, the fourth General Congregation began at 9 a.m., with a Mass celebrated by Archbishop Lorenz Jaeger of Paderborn, Germany. The President of the day's session was Norman Cardinal Gilroy, Archbishop of Sydney, Australia. The first draft project, *De Liturgia* consisting of a preface and eight chapters, was presented to the assembly for discussion by Arcadio Cardinal Larraona, President of the Commission on Sacred Liturgy, and Father Ferdinando Antonelli, O.F.M., secretary of the commission. At the sixth General Congregation on Wednesday, October 24th, Mass was celebrated in the Byzantine Rite, sung in Greek and Arabic, thus bringing home to the Fathers the fact that while the Church is catholic, there existed liturgical diversity.

On Tuesday afternoon, October 23rd he went with Bishop Dwyer to visit the archeological remains of the Baths of Caracalla.

The following four letters to members of the Staff at Ushaw present an account of the first working days of the Council.

Letter 4

Letter to Monsignor Laurence Hollis

Laurence Hollis (1918-1997) entered Ushaw in 1932 as a student, he was for a time a minor Professor. He was a much respected music director and choirmaster and Vice-President until he left Ushaw for parish ministry in 1967.

The English College, Rome
Thursday, October 25th 1962

Dear Laurence,

Thank you very much for forwarding the correspondence. I can answer your letter without difficulty, because today is our day off. The first three days of this week were pretty tiring, with a General Congregation every morning, and last night I felt really whacked.

The program is the same on all such days. Mass at seven (though we can postpone it to the evening if we like, and some do), breakfast 7.45, and then at 8.20 Monsignor Davis and I set off to walk to Saint Peter's. The Bishops still have to wear choir dress and therefore travel by car, but, since the first day, most of us Periti have formed the custom of turning up at our tribunes in black cassock and sash, and a car would be unwarranted expense. Besides, on these lovely mornings it is a very pleasant walk.

The scene in Saint Peter's Square never fails to thrill me, when the cars and coaches disgorge their purple load (there are about 35 coach loads) and the whole front of Saint Peter's steps is splashed with purple.

The Mass begins promptly at nine (yesterday, Wednesday, it was in the Byzantine Rite) and the debates last till about 12.15, without any break. To get a proper picture of the discussion, one has to take notes at full speed for the whole three hours. I emerge limp from the Basilica, with 2500 to 3000 others, and arrive back in time for the pre-prandial snifters before lunch, and the long desired smoke. No work is even thinkable before tea, and then, after tea, it usually takes all the time available before supper to make out a fair copy of my pencil scribble, say Office, etc. Supper from 8 to 8.45, October Devotions from 9.15 to 9.50, and then after a rendezvous in the new smoke room, bed about 11. That will again be my programme tomorrow

(Friday) and Saturday. But today (Thursday) has been our free day, and an excellent institution it is indeed.

Like every day for more than ten days now, it has been a windless day of unbroken sunshine. At 10.30, I went out with Bishop Dwyer, in his car, for the Alban Hills. We drove out along the Via Appia Antica, past the tomb of Caecilia Metella, to Albano and visited the ancient church of San Pietro. Then to the shrine of Our Lady of Galloro. From there, by glorious mountain roads, with immense vistas, to Nemi, where we had lunch on the upper terrace of the Trattoria De Sanctis, overlooking the lake. During lunch, in came two Canadian bishops, one of whom, Malcolm MacEachern, was with me for three years at Louvain. A small world! Then by more mountain roads to Velletri and so through the Latin Vale to Palazzola for tea, where a half a dozen of the bishops had foregathered. Back here by 6.15. A lovely day.

It would seem from the programme that we get a much longer break next week, from Thursday to Sunday inclusive, because of All Saints and All Souls, with the Saturday thrown in for good measure. I will be ready for it. No Commission work yet, except for the Liturgy chaps. When that comes it will be all work and no time for anything else except meals and sleep.

All the best,
Yours sincerely
L.LMcR

Letter 5

Letter to Monsignor Bernard Paine

Bernard Edwin Payne was born in 1899 and educated at Ushaw which he entered at the age of 12. He was an Honours graduate there in Classics and, following ordination in 1927, he taught English and elocution, Church History and Catechetics. He was for many years Librarian. He died in 1983. Monsignor McReavy described him in a Panegyric as "tall, rather thin, gentle and benign; he was a fixture at Ushaw – we always thought that he would be unable to survive in the outside world".

In this letter L.L. McReavy conveys something of the atmosphere of the Council beginning its work and setting out on unchartered territory.

The English College, Rome
Thursday, October 25th 1962

Dear Barney,

As a former Professor of Church History, you will no doubt be glad to have a glimpse into the workings of the Church assembled in all her might.

A brief description of the three General Congregations we have had so far this week (Monday to Wednesday) should suffice.

Monday 22 October

Cardinal Gilroy presided and was the best President we have had yet. A clear voice and quite authoritative. The first Bishop to exceed his ten minutes was brought to an abrupt halt with an imperious "SATIS". The discussion of the schema *De Liturgia* was opened, then various Fathers who had notified the Secretariate of their desire to speak being summoned to the microphone in order of dignity.

Cardinal Frings was good, Cardinal Lercaro rather disappointing. Montini excellent, Spellman not so good, Döpfner too brief and bitty (partly because he agreed with Frings and didn't want to speak unnecessarily (O si sic omnes!). Dante detailed but in a frail husky voice, difficult to decipher. Twenty two speakers in all.

Tuesday, 23 October

Felici began by begging the Fathers to speak clearly, distinctly and slowly, keeping within the subject matter and the allotted time. The only one universally obeyed is the time-limit and that is because the chair is firm.

Ottaviani was almost as rigid as we anticipated, but not quite. Ritter of St Louis very practical. Volk of Linz very earnest, almost emotional. Ruffini picked holes. Cardinal McIntyre read (rather badly), from a script prepared evidently by someone else, a paean of praise for Latin, which two Americans sitting next to me assured me he barely knows (he was a Wall Street Runner who became a priest in his thirties). Cardinal Léger was clear and to the point. Cardinal Godfrey, by general consent, gave the best debating speech we have had up-to-date, taking the line everybody expected but not as rigidly as expected.

Wednesday 24 October

Began with a triste nuntium that Bishop Aston Chichester SJ, had collapsed on the steps of Saint Peter's and died. We all said the De Profundis.

The best speech of the morning was by Cardinal Gracias, comprehensive, orderly, well reasoned, with a touch of humour, and delivered in a clear ringing voice. Cardinal Bacci uttered a false quantity which he quickly withdrew (illorum tempórum). Parente was delightfully fluent.

And now to supper!

All the best.
Yours truly,
Bomb

* * *

On Friday afternoon, October 26th, L.L. McReavy made a preliminary sketch of the Castel Sant Angelo. The long free weekend was spent in summarising and collating the debate on the Preface and chapter I of *De Liturgia*.

L.L. McReavy described this period as follows "most speakers were merely repeating what others had said, and in spite of constant appeals from the Presidential Bench, they persisted in doing so. Those of us who had to listen for three hours every morning to this sort of thing were becoming more and more depressed. It was like being in a tunnel with no visible end to it. When one asked why it was allowed to go on, the only answer forthcoming was that every Bishop had a right to speak his mind on every point submitted to the Council. The Presidential Bench had no authority to gag their fellow bishops, etc." On All Souls day Friday, November 2 in the company of Monsignor Frank Davis he visited the Cemetery of San Lorenzo.

Letter 6

Letter to Monsignor Philip Loftus

Philip Loftus a priest of the diocese of Salford joined the Staff at Ushaw in 1950 and was Prefect of Studies from 1961 until appointed President of Ushaw 1967-1977.

The English College, Rome
Saturday, November 3rd 1962

Dear Pippy,

Having just had tea with the English, Irish and Scots hierarchies in a room just comfortably large enough to contain our own, it is something of a relief to escape to my fourth floor room and write you an overdue letter. Since, as I gather, my previous chronicles have gone the rounds, it will be enough to take up the story where I left off, a week last Thursday.

The 7th and 8th General Congregations of Friday and Saturday (26th- 27th October) ploughed away along the interminable furrow of the Proemium and Caput I of the schema *De Liturgia*. Most of the speakers had nothing fresh to say, and usually spent the first minutes of their ten minute allowance admitting it, but it did not prevent their reading their script to the bitter end, with the flowery little flourishes which may have seemed decorative or impressive in their college or hotel rooms, but which inevitably sounded hollow in *hac sacra Aula*, as Saint Peter's is called.

Yet there I still sit in my tribune, scribbling everything down for three hours on end, as though there was bound to be gold in them there hills, only to find, when I have spent another couple of hours in the evening panning my notes, that there is precious little but sand. I am always tired out at the end of a General Congregation day, and when we have eight in ten days, as we had up to All Saints, I feel as if I had been put through the wringer.

It was a great relief when, twenty-five minutes before the end of the ninth General Congregation (Monday October 29th) we moved on to chapter

II (there are five in all). It is shorter and there appears to be only three points of dispute in it. Even so, we have already been subjected to an argy-bargy lasting over six hours on these three points.

These last three days, I have weakened to the extent of taking ten minutes off, about 11am, to fight my way through massed bishops, and even cardinals, to the counter of one or other of the two bars where free coffee (espresso) and biscuits are dispensed by the Holy See. It is an amazing sight, and the crush is such that some bishops do not hesitate to ease out into the adjacent side-chapel and finish their fags there. Others walk up and down the aisles (screened from the Aula) chatting volubly or flogging their breves, while all the time the loud speakers carry the voice of the latest "repetitore" of some well-worn theme.

Meanwhile, there are lots of behind-the-scenes efforts (as yet abortive) to devise ways and means of shortening the debates. The Presidential Bench has been approached, but none of them is willing to intervene, lest he be accused of restricting the liberty of the bishops. All they do is to call the next speaker and shut him up with "Satis!" or "Excellentissime Pater, iam per decem momenta locutus es", if he runs on too long (though Ottaviani got away with fifteen minutes before he was called to a halt).

Suenens is trying hard to devise a method of abbreviation, and Smedt of Bruges, who came here to lunch today, outlined a scheme whereby all the European groups might get together (through representatives), find out how many divergent points of view there were, and agree as to who should put each point of view. If it would work, we might eventually see an end, however distant, to the Council. But so far it is only an idea.

I have spent the All Saints-All Souls break analysing the debate on chapter I for the benefit of our bishops, reducing a manuscript of notes to six pages of typescript which Worlock is going to roneo. Tomorrow (Sunday), we have a Capella Papale at 9.30 in Saint Peter's.

I hope the "Teasmade" is helping you to bear up.

All the best.

Bomb.

PS. My room is turning cold, I think fondly of my fire.

* * *

On Sunday, November 4, L.L. McReavy records in his Diary "Attended, in choir robes, the Capella Papale in St Peter's, for the fourth anniversary of Pope John's coronation. Solemn Mass in Ambrosian rite by Cardinal Montini. The week was taken up with General Congregations, except for Thursday when he worked on writing up summaries of the debates. It was recognised that some means would have to be found to draw the debates to a close and avoid numerous unprofitable repetitions.

On Sunday (November 11) he admitted: "Feeling exhausted. Long siesta in afternoon."

Letter 7

To Monsignor Robert Gowland

Robert Gowland (1903-1973) joined the staff at Ushaw College in 1931 where he spent the rest of his life. He was a professor of Philosophy and Procurator of Ushaw College.

The English College, Rome
November 11th 1962

Dear Bob,

Since the last issue of my chronicle of the Council on November 1st, we have had a strenuous but valuable week of debates on the Sacred Liturgy schemata.

But first, let me record that on Saturday, November 3rd, the Scots and Irish hierarchies joined our own here at the English College for tea, followed by a meeting in the College Library. There were over fifty Bishops present, including Cardinals Godfrey, D'Albion and Heard, which must be a record for the College. I, of course, was not at the meeting, but I gathered afterwards that one of the topics was how to abbreviate the apparently endless debate which had still not got beyond chapter II of the schemata. They were not alone in their solicitude. Visitors from other hierarchies had raised the same point in our Common Room and we knew that several individual approaches had already been made to the Presidential Council, though in vain, because the Presidents were afraid of seeming to limit the freedom of the Bishops, and the Pope was said to be equally chary about intervening. It was felt, however, that a corporate approach might have more effect.

Whether or not it was due to the approach of our joint hierarchies that action was eventually taken, I cannot say, but, after another day and a half of repetitive speeches on the same old subjects, concluding with an entirely irrelevant harangue from a Spaniard on bad wages, excessive hours, undernourishment and world famine, which was cut short by the President of the day, (Cardinal Tappouni), the Secretary General (Felici) intervened to announce that the Pope had granted the Presidential Council the faculty to propose to the vote of the Fathers the closure of the debate, when it judged that the topics had been adequately expounded and argued. If the vote were for closure, those Fathers who still wanted to say something could do so in writing, and send it to the Secretariate.

Even before Felici had finished calling upon those in favour of the closure of the debate on chapter II to indicate their pleasure by standing up, the whole assembly (2211 present that day) had leapt to its collective feet. When they had resumed their seats, and Felici had called: "Nunc surgant qui nolunt", one solitary bishop, a Franciscan, rose to his feet. The whole assembly hummed as though vivified by a fresh wind (was it Pentecostal?), and everyone felt (and most expressed) an immense sense of relief.

Until that moment (about 10.15 a.m., Thursday, November 6th) there was no glimmer of light visible at the end of the tunnel.

An American Anglican observer (here for lunch one day) had quoted a current story to the effect that all the relevant information had been fed into the computer (number of chapters in all the schemata, number of speakers who had already intervened on the first two of Liturgy, amount of time they had taken, etc) and, in answer to the question how long the Council would last, it had spat out "300 years". Now, at least, we have hope.

We started immediately on chapter III (Sacraments and Sacramentals), and were treated by one bishop to an elementary catechism on the difference between the two, which made the Periti in our tribune squirm with exasperation, and finished it (without applied closure) at 11.45 a.m. on Thursday (November 8th), and yesterday (Saturday 10th, 11.45 a.m.) Ruffini, with unanimous approval of the Fathers, closed the debate on chapter IV.

As we are discussing the remaining four chapters *together*, we ought to be through with Liturgy next week, and get on to the explosive subject of *De Fontibus Revelationis*, on which, I gather, there is much lobbying and ganging-up behind the scenes. I can't wait for it to start.

On this same happy Tuesday, Felici announced that the Holy Father had decided to close this session with a Capella Papale on December 8th. Two hours later, I had booked my return flight for that same afternoon.

It is a pity I haven't found time to record all the scraps of "gaff" which I pick up here and there, but it takes me two to three hours in the evening to write out a fair copy of my scribbled notes of the morning's debate, and I have spent the last two free days, (Thursdays) composing for our bishops an analysis which Worlock's typists duplicate. It is a chore which it was perhaps unwise to undertake, because last night I felt almost completely exhausted by this week's incessant work.

But here are two snippets. I believe that the Italian bishops have begun to refer to the main bar in Saint Peter's as Bar-Jonah. And yesterday, after Ruffini had intervened to defend the Roman curial officials from what he felt to be undeserved criticisms, one Spanish Bishop remarked to his neighbour (Dwyer): "Nolite tangere christos meos".

Ruffini himself is pretty ruthless. As President, he interrupted a sermon from an Italian Bishop with: "Excellentissime Pater, omnes Episcopi sunt ipsi praedicatores; et praedicantibus non est praedicandum!". Godfrey afterwards, to me, deprecated it as too harsh a rebuke. Certainly the victim must have found it somewhat deflating. He collapsed like a pricked balloon.

I keep making interesting contacts in our tribune. The other day, I found myself sitting next to Dr Hubert Jedin, the historian of Trent. He asked me where I came from, and when I said "Ushaw", he told me that, in 1938, he had visited the College hoping to be taken on as a professor of Church History. One thing that had attracted him was our library, and especially the Mann additions to it. However, he said, it was already after Munich, and Corbishley was loth to take on another German, so he came out to Rome and got a job at the Lateran.[6]

Other neighbours these last few days have been Monsignor Arthur Ryan, formerly professor of scholastic philosophy at Queens, Belfast (his successor, Dr Daly, called at the College to see me, the other day), Dr Cremin, the Maynooth moralist, Fr Kerrigan OFM of the Antonianum and the Biblical Commission.

There must be lots of other bits of gaff that I have forgotten, but it is time for lunch. There are nearly always visitors from the other hierarchies.

Kindest regards to all the brethren.
Yours sincerely.
L.LMcReavy

* * *

The permission given by Pope John XXIII to close a debate by a vote had an immediate effect. The closure of the debate *De Liturgia* was proposed and voted on Tuesday November 13th at the 18th General Congregation. It was then announced that Pope John XXIII had ordered that St Joseph be honoured in the Roman Rite by having his name included in the Canon of the Mass.

On Wednesday, November 14th Cardinal Ottaviani introduced the schema *De Fontibus*, L.L. McReavy wrote in his Diary "it came immediately under attack". Three positions emerged regarding the schema. Some of the Fathers asked that it be rewritten in its entirety. Others considered it to be acceptable and should be debated and modified as necessary. The remainder wanted the project to be put aside.

Letter 8

The English College, Rome
Saturday, November 18th 1962

Dear Monsignor,

C'é bruto tempo! The Tiber has broken its banks at Viterbo, and I had to leap out of bed at 12.30 a.m. last night to prevent the water pouring into my room.

We have had a full and tiring, but more interesting week since we moved on to *De Fontibus Revelationis*, which has brought a clash of personalities and a sharp division between northern and southern Europe as to the

---

6 The Very Rev. Horace K. Mann, D.D., of St Cuthbert's Grammar School, Newcastle-on-Tyne was a historian who specialised in the history of the papacy. On his death his specialist library of 5000 volumes was given to Ushaw.

appropriate way of presenting the Gospel to our age, and controlling error without suppressing scholarly research.

The north i.e. France, Belgium, Holland, Germany and Austria, is practically unanimous in calling for the total rejection of the schema prepared by the Theological Commission (under Ottaviani) and the substitution of another, written from an entirely different (more pastoral and ecumenical) viewpoint.

The south (or, more exactly, Italy, Spain and *some* of the Latin Americans) is less unanimous in praise of the schema, but more or less agreed that it provides an adequate basis for discussion, and must be accepted with such emendations as are found to be necessary.

It is an awkward problem which, I noticed, is exercising our English bishops considerably. Some of them clearly do not like the steam-roller tactics which are being used to get the schema accepted, and are inclined to believe the charges, already made in Aula, that the same tactics were used in the Preparatory Theological Commission and the Central Commission.

We have been warned, in Aula, that it would be improper, disrespectful, discourteous, "iudicam illicitum" (said one), to reject a schema passed by majority vote and approved by the Pope for discussion. But yesterday, the President was asked by a written note from one of the Assembly to read out Article 33, paragraph 1, which says that any Father is free to propose the acceptance, *rejection*, or emendation of any schema. So perhaps we shall hear less of this big-stick argument.

On the other hand, if this schema is rejected, how, where and when do we get another? I feel certain therefore that, when it comes to a vote, many who are sympathetic to the northern point of view will vote for the acceptance of the schema and hope to change both its content and its tone, *radicitus*, in the debate and subsequent voting on emendations. In any case, if the "south" votes at all solidly, it can swamp the "north" by sheer weight of numbers.

Meanwhile, it is certainly not boring. No skull-caps have been thrown, but there is more of a debate developing, with speakers taking up points that have been made on the previous day, or even on the same day (though this latter is only possible to Cardinals, who can poke their oar in at any moment by application to the President).

Thanks for the local news. It helps to cure my home-sickness.

Only three more weeks!

Yours sincerely.
Bomb.

* * *

On Monday evening, November 19th, L.L. McReavy went to the North American College to hear a lecture on Form-criticism by Father Barnabas Aherne, C.P., and declared it to be "a first-class performance".

Monsignor McReavy considered the presentation of the draft document on the *Sources of Revelation* as the turning point of the Council. The text was considered unsatisfactory in that it favoured the view that revelation is contained partly in Scripture, partly in tradition, thereby implicitly excluding the equally tenable view that it is contained in Scripture as understood and expounded by tradition.

Letter 9

The English College, Rome
Monday 8 a.m.
(Post mark November 27th 1962)
From internal evidence Monday November 26th

Dear Monsignor,

I doubt whether I'll be able to finish this letter before I leave for Saint Peter's in 20 minutes time (a cloudless crisp, sunny morning), but I have to make use of odd moments.

Yesterday (Sunday) evening, I was at the Vatican but failed to see the Pope. Our Hierarchy was due to be received in audience at 6 p.m., and Heenan and Grimshaw and others were insistent that Monsignor Davis and I should go along with them, confident that they would get us into the audience. I went in the Cardinal's car with Worlock, but as we were advancing along that painted gallery we saw on the TV show of the Queen's reception, we encountered Nasali Rocca who said to the Cardinal "soli vescovi". The Cardinal did not argue the point, so we "Periti" and a couple of secretaries stayed behind in the throne room where the Pope normally receives visiting Heads of State, while the bishops went on to their audience chamber. It was disappointing, but gave me time to study the magnificent appointments of the throne-room, especially the rows of tapestries and the superb ceiling.

From the point of view of the debate in Saint Peter's, it has been an exciting week.

(1 p.m. just back from Saint Peter's).

Monday (November 19th) was the highlight, a really constructive debate which held our attention so much that I, and even some of our bishops, missed their usual visit to Bar Jonah or Bar Abbas (choir Bar Sinister) for morning coffee. It contained the best speech yet delivered, by Bishop Smedt of Bruges, who sought to prove that many of the bishops who described the schema *De Fontibus Revelationis* as "ecumenical" had not yet grasped the meaning of the word in its modern context.

The result was that on Tuesday (November 20th), after a few blatherers (five in all) had been given their ten minutes, the Presidency interrupted the debate to seek a vote on the proposition: "An disceptatio de schemata interumpenda sit" (i.e. That it should be sent back for thorough revision before discussion was resumed). The form in which this question was put created a stir in our tribune, because it meant that those who want the schema sent back (*placet*) would have to win two thirds of the votes. Even so, they nearly managed it. Out of 2209 present (required majority = 1473) there were 1368 *placet* to 822 *non placet* (19 null).

The press-handout that evening was less than frank. It announced that a vote had been taken and that the effect was that discussion of the schema would continue. It was not very good sense when, because, as anyone could have forecast, the evening papers had got the figures and published them.

That night (as I learned when I reached our tribune next morning) Tisserant and Cicognani had a meeting with the Pope, and the Wednesday session began with a declaration that the Pope had decided to send the schema to a special Commission (Theological and Unity mixed) for revision. Yet, because we were not ready to begin immediately on another subject, we wasted the rest of the morning listening to speeches on the old one. Abbot Butler was admired for altering his speech on the spot and talking more or less off the cuff, but most of the others just plugged away through their script as though it was still relevant. The bars were never so busy as that morning.

Thursday being a free day, I spent the whole morning (8 to 1.15 without a break) doing a marginal summary of the 50 page schema on *Means of Social Communication*, which we were to begin discussing on the Friday. After tea, I dictated it to one of the Grail-girls, who had it polycopied that night, and delivered early next morning.

There was not a great deal of meat, or at least bones to pick, in this schema, and, after two and a half days debate, the President intervened this morning to ask the Fathers to indicate "surgendo" whether they had had enough. There was the usual mass uprising, and they will have an opportunity tomorrow to determine by vote what is to be done with the document.

We moved on immediately to a schema prepared by the Oriental Commission on *Reunion with the Oriental dissidents*. We had been warned of this, so I stayed up till 11.30 on Saturday night doing a marginal summary which was dictated and polycopied on Sunday, ready for today's debate. It is a much more interesting subject and I think it is a good schema, though several have already objected to its placing. They say it should have come after the Theological Commission's schema *De Ecclesia* (which incidentally is the next subject). The old guard have already shown signs of wanting to torpedo any approach to the Orientals that is not couched in exactly the same terms as we have fruitlessly used these past ten centuries.

If one were to ask them why then should we be having a General Council at all, I feel sure that their answer (explicit or implicit) would be that they never wanted one, and were perfectly content with everything as it was, i.e. everything as it was being run by the Roman Curia. One gets the impression that the Curial Cardinals regard a General Council as an unwanted or at least unwelcome intrusion by outsiders into their domestic affairs. I suppose after all, that it is a perfectly natural and understandable reaction.

Our own bishops have exactly the same attitude to a Plenary Council, and I have noticed that they view with alarm any suggestion that the Bishops' meeting should have any legislative power over their respective dioceses. I am tempted to drop the hint (though I have so far resisted the temptation) that Ottaviani is not alone in seeking to keep intruders "off his mat". When we get round to the subject of Sacramentality of mats (*De Episcopis et De Diocesiosis regimine*) an astute Curial defender could hardly be blamed if he introduced the "tu quoque" theme.

Not that it would have any effect on some of the regular participants, who intervene on every topic with a strictly irrelevant speech and rattle through it at machine-gun speed to make sure of getting it all said before the Presidential voice breaks their flow with: "Excellentissime Domine, tempus tibi concessum iam expletum est", or (when Gilroy is in the chair) an abrupt and ringing "Satis".

There is one Spaniard who has already intervened five times without throwing a spark of light on anything, and has been more than once shot down in flames without apparently becoming depressed. We know he'll come back undismayed, though he can hardly appreciate the dismay which the reading out of his name creates in the assembly. It is no use rushing out for coffee, because the bars are filled to overflowing as soon as a bore gets underway, and some of the Fathers can smell a bore in advance. I have already compiled a mental black-list of names, and if some of them are due to perform after 11.15, I get my coffee; otherwise not.

All good wishes to the brethren.
I shall be with them a fortnight tonight.

Yours sincerely,
Bomb

* * *

On Thursday, November 29th Bishop Cunningham of Hexham and Newcastle invited Monsignor McReavy to join the diocesan students for lunch at Tre Scalini in the Piazza Navona. In the evening L.L. McReavy attended an "At Home" at the residence of Mr Cape, First Secretary to Legation to Holy See. On Sunday December 2nd L.L. McReavy joined a group of English bishops in a visit to the excavations under St Peter's Basilica. The British Minister to the Holy See, Sir Peter Scarlett held a reception at his residence on Monday, December 3 and it was there that L.L. McReavy first met Hans Küng.

Letter 10

The English College, Rome
Tuesday, December 4th 1962, 7 p.m.

Dear Monsignor,

D. V., I shall catch the 1 p.m. train from King's Cross next Monday, December 10th, due to arrive in Durham at (I think) 5.50. I shall spend the weekend resting at Maidstone.

I delayed this notification because I was not sure about my liberty until an hour ago. Last Friday, a stranger came to me in my tribune in Saint Peter's and told me that I had been nominated to the Conciliar Commission on Discipline of Clergy and People, and that I was to attend a meeting this evening (Tuesday) at the Congregation of the Council Offices.

Since several of the Fathers have been urging that the Conciliar Commissions should continue in between the sessions revising the schemata for September next, I was afraid we might be told to stay on, or at least to return shortly. It is not as bad as that. Our schemata (reduced in number by coordination with other Commissions) are to be issued promptly to the Bishops and they are to send in their comments by January 15th. Subcommissions of the members (Bishops) of our Commission will then study the various questions in the light of these comments. They will be able to call upon the services of the Periti attached to the Commission, and could summon us to Rome, but it is probable that we shall be able to render our services in writing, without personal presence. Anyway, I got a diplomatic negative to my question (or rather assertion) "minime necesse est Romae manere?"

The staff of Periti, like the corps of Episcopal members, has been entirely reconstituted. Only about six of us remain from the former Preparatory Commission. We have a new Secretary, a Spaniard, who unfortunately prefers to talk in Italian rather than Latin, but the same President, Ciriaci, who addressed us in his usual emphatic Latin. He told us that the list of Periti on our Commission was not yet complete. We, about 25, from 17 nations, were his first choice from the list of Conciliar Periti approved by the Pope, but he hoped to bring in representatives of other nations. Inside the Commission, there would be no distinction between Patres and Periti, as in Saint Peter's. "Hic omnes fratres sumus" et alia humus modi in his usual blarneying manner. But he apparently has a good memory for faces or names, as behoves a "frater", because, when I shook hands with him at the end of the meeting, he said (in English) "Ah yes, from Ushaw", which was pretty good, considering that he never attended a single one of our preparatory Commission meetings, except the first, in November 1960, and a reception after our last meeting in April.

It has been another hectic week. Last Friday we finished discussing the Reunion with Orientals *Ut unum sint*, and on Saturday began the explosive schema *De Ecclesia*. Ottaviani, its creator, introduced it, but perhaps learning from the chill reception given to the big-stick manner in which he had introduced *De Fontibus Revelationis*, he adopted an entirely different approach, sardonic and almost jocular. This did not prevent the opposition from weighing in immediately with adverse comments which commonly take the line "multa et quidem optima invenio in hoc schemata, tanto labore atque peritia elaborato. ATTAMEN – and then the conclusion: Remittatur ad Commissionem mixtam ut peritus recognoscatur et funditus redigatur". We have now had three days debate on *De Ecclesia* and I think the majority (certainly the big shots) have taken this line.

We have three more General Congregations, and it will be interesting to see if there is any strong come-back. The only violent reaction so far came from an Italian Bishop who suspected a concerted plot to wreck the Church and practically accused those who wanted the schema to be written in a different tone, of heresy. He provoked an outburst of laughter.

Well, it is nearly time for supper and I haven't finished my Office, so you will have to wait for the rest of the gaff until I get back.

All the best to all my regular readers
Yours sincerely
Bomb.

* * *

For the days following the last letter of the first Session Monsignor McReavy's Diary provides the following information:

On Wednesday, December 5th the General Congregation concluded at 11.55 to enable the Council Fathers to assemble in Piazza for Pope John XXIII's blessing at midday. The following day L.L. McReavy records that he felt dizzy during his Coffee break in St Peter's. On returning to the College he felt "definitely unwell" and so "took a Beecham's powder and went early to bed". The following day he did not feel fit enough to attend last General Congregation of the Session. He was still not well enough on Saturday, December 8th "to go to St Peter's for the closing Mass and Pope's Blessing". After lunch with students Monsignor Clark drove him to the airport. He reached London airport shortly after 4 p.m. in heavy rain: "caught the 5.50 train to Maidstone. Called at the Presbytery and Father Twomey drove me home. Feeling very much under the weather". On Sunday morning, December 9th he was able to celebrate the "10 o'clock Mass and rested at home for remainder of day".

His return to Ushaw was arranged for Monday, December 10th. After celebrating Mass at 8 a.m. he "took a Beechams just before leaving for 11am train from Maidstone. Caught the 1 p.m. from King's Cross and at 5.50 arrived into Durham. I was met by A. Smith with College car. Warm welcome, but everyone disturbed by my wan appearance. Early to bed".

The Second Session

September 29th – December 4th 1963

In the period between the First and Second Sessions of the Council Pope John XXIII died and Cardinal Montini was elected taking the name of Paul.

In a letter to Eugene Cardinal Tisserant on the resumption of the Second Vatican Council dated September 12, 1963, Pope Paul VI declared: "The labours of the ecumenical Council will be resumed and continued. As for us, we shall use all our efforts for this work, confident that the help of the council Fathers and of the Holy Spirit, which gives assurance to our hope, will not be lacking". The schemata were reduced to seventeen "revised in a briefer form ... and with "the pre-eminence of the pastoral nature of this Council is kept in mind".

Eleven laymen were invited to attend the second Session of the Council. Sixty-three non-Catholic religious leaders attended the second session of the Council, an increase of 18 over the number of observers at the first session of the Council. The rule of secrecy was lifted in regard to discussions in the Aula.

Concerning the Second Session of the Council Monsignor McReavy wrote in an Article for the *Ushaw Magazine* (March 1964 n. 220 p. 1): "There were fewer sensational developments in the second session of the Second Ecumenical Council of the Vatican, largely because the schemata discussed had been revised during the interval to suit the pastoral and ecumenical viewpoint which the majority of the Fathers felt to be proper to the general purpose of the Council, and for lack of which the first session had thrown out the schemata submitted on the Sources of Revelation and on the Church. The structure of the Council had also been revised with a view to greater efficiency. At the first session, the General Congregations in St Peter's were controlled, more or less, by a presidential bench of ten cardinals They still sit impressively at a long, scarlet-draped table at the head of the nave and their number has been increased to twelve, but their only real function now is to see that the rules are observed. Effective direction of the debates has been transferred by Pope Paul to a new group of four "Moderators," who sit at a small table in front of the Presidents and take control by turns. They are Cardinals Agagianian, Lercaro, Döpfner and Suenens, and they were probably chosen, not only because they are rather more dynamic, but also because they had identified themselves more openly at the first session with the pastoral and ecumenical aims of the Council".

* * *

After a short family visit to Maidstone Monsignor Lawrence McReavy flew to Rome on Friday, September 27th. The following evening he visited his friend Monsignor Anné at the Belgian College where he met Bishop

Calewaert of Ghent and Cardinal Suenens. On Sunday, September 29th he attended the Inaugural Public Session of the Council in St Peter's.

Letter 11

The English College, Rome
September 30th 1963

Dear Monsignor,

Once again we are in full swing and most of us find it difficult to realise that we have been away for more than a brief break, so familiar does this whole routine and the environment seem.

I had a pleasant journey with Bishops Cunningham, Brunner, Parker and Grasar as fellow passengers. The stewardess produced a document assuring us that we were dispensed from the Friday abstinence and this enabled us to enjoy a very nice meal. Two cars met us at the Rome airport (V.I.P. lounge at both airports) and I travelled up to the College with Bishop Grasar, who seemed under the weather and had a temperature of 103 the following morning. He is improving but not yet around.

The weather was, and has remained hot, sunny, around 75° but very sweat-making. One perspires with the least expenditure of energy.

I am very comfortably housed in a recently recovered mezzanine flat on the opposite side of the cortile, which has been completely modernised during the holiday: 4 rooms (Petit, Frank Davis, Birmingham's secretary and self) and two bathrooms. My room looks out onto the Montoro, at present a cul-de-sac and therefore less noisy than of old.

The opening ceremony, yesterday (Sunday) was, of course, very impressive, but very tiring. Our tribune was full when I reached it, but, having fortunately taken the trouble to vest in choir robes, Worlock and I were able to obtain seats in the special place reserved to Prelates, Rotal Auditors and others, just to the right of the Papal Altar. The Pope was about a half an hour late in arriving and his speech, at the end of a long ceremony, took a little over an hour. Most of us fell asleep from time to time. We had lunch at 2 p.m.!

At the 37th General Congregation, today Monday, the Fathers were reminded that the obligation of secrecy still remained in regard to the content of the schemata and discussions, and that they should observe the utmost prudence. I must therefore measure my words. Suffice to say that, so far at least, the schema *De Ecclesia* has been favourably received, at least as a suitable basis for discussion. Owing to the lengthy preliminaries, there was time only for about a half a dozen speakers, but, though most of them thought the schema could be improved in various ways, no one was really hostile.

The Secretary of our Commission buttonholed me in the bar-Jonah this morning about some work he wanted me to do, and several Bishops have been expressing hopes that I would produce a summary of the present debate at the end of this week; so it is not going to be easy to take things easy. At present, however, I am held in check by the condition of my eyes. I am sleeping, eating and drinking well.

All the best to all.

L.LMcR

* * *

The General Congregations from Monday September 30th to Friday October 4th were devoted to the debate on the schema *De Ecclesia* which was opened by Joseph Cardinal Frings, Archbishop of Cologne and by Giuseppe Cardinal Siri, Archbishop of Genoa. As the discussion unfolded during the course of the week it emerged that the general consensus towards the schema was favourable with recognition of the need for improvement in certain areas.

Letter 12

The English College, Rome
October 4th 1963

Dear Monsignor,

Bishop C. Calewaert of Ghent asked me the other day if I could obtain for him a copy of the Ushaw rules and regulations. I told him that we were governed largely by unwritten law, but would ask you to send whatever you have in written form. To save me a journey to the Belgian College, perhaps you would be so kind as to send it direct to him there. It is in the street that runs along the back of the Quirinale.

I forgot to mention in my earlier letter that Patsy Redmond is among the guests here. He came out with Bishop Dwyer on holiday, and his theological knowledge has been quite useful in the formal discussions which we have been having in the Common Room (Hierarchy and Periti) on dogmatic questions arising out of the schema *De Ecclesia*. I am quite out of my depth, or rather, I sit in as a disciple, and have found the discussions very helpful. The chief expert participants have been Bishops Wall and Dwyer, Abbot Butler and Davis and Redmond. This is a new development, under Heenan's leadership, which enables our bishops to go to the General Congregations with some idea of the more difficult points at issue, and to plan interventions in Aula in the name of our whole hierarchy. The first such intervention, by Heenan, was well planned, well prepared and written, and well received (to judge by reactions in our tribune). Beck's name is down for a second such intervention, which was planned, drafted and generally accepted in last night's Common Room meeting.

We have had a heavy week, with a General Congregation every morning from Monday to today (Friday). Under the new system, we get Saturday and Sunday off, instead of Thursday and Sunday. The debates have been pretty good with a larger measure of really worthwhile speeches than in the First Session. Possibly it is the result of the appeal of the Moderators that, as far as possible, Episcopal Conferences should arrange that, where a number of their members hold the same view, they shall choose a spokesman to represent them. There are still a few lone horses airing their private views, but the schema *De Ecclesia* offers far less opportunity for crankish or extreme views than did *De Liturgia*.

By the same token, there are fewer occasions for amusement. It is all hard graft. The Moderators are determined to press on, and so far they have been very successful. We are already on to chapter II of *De Ecclesia*. Ruffini is getting his own back. The original schema which he defended was rejected because it was too scholastic and juridical. The new one proceeds from Sacred Scripture. Ruffini is industriously picking holes in the alleged scriptural foundations, with no little skill and appeal to the original Greek. He is a doughty fighter.

All the best to all the brethren.
L.LMcR.

* * *

Monsignor McReavy spent the first weekend of October working on a summary of the debate of the first week for the benefit of the English and Welsh bishops. The American Press Office had begun to produce a full and accurate daily summary of the debates, and arrangements had been made to supply copies to other English speaking hierarchies. These daily reports and the notes on points of dogma arising from the debates supplied by Dr Patsy Redmond meant that L.L. McReavy: "felt much less under pressure than at the first Session".

The debate on *De Ecclesia* continued during the second week of the Session dealing with the Hierarchical Constitution of Church and on Collegiality and the Pope and the proposed restoration of the diaconate.

The entry in L.L. McReavy's Diary for Tuesday, October 15 reads: "First meeting of Subcommission of Commission on Discipline, to which I had been appointed some days earlier. Our job, to revise *De Clericis* chapter II, *De Studio et activita pastorali* in line with emendations sent in by the Fathers during the interval between the Sessions. Four members (Bishop Janssens of Hildersheim (Chairman), Bishop of Luxembourg, Bishop of Liège and an Italian Bishop) and four Periti (self, Nabuco, an Italian, and Father Heston who did not turn up). Secretary, Father Sigmond OP, Rector of the Angelicum. We made excellent progress, with the minimum of fuss."

Letter 13

The English College, Rome
Tuesday, October 15th 1963

Dear Monsignor,

Having just returned from a Subcommission meeting which lasted from 4.30 to 7pm, I can find time to write a letter, "recreationis causa".

The weather has been perfect these past four or five days, cloudless blue sky, no wind, with an autumnal freshness in the shade, but hot in the sunshine.

Last Saturday, having worked through the previous weekend, I decided to have a day off and took the underground from the Colisseum to Ostia Antica. At the entrance to the ruins, I was met by Bishop Dwyer and Patsy Redmond, who had decided, after my departure, to join me by car. We found the ruins fascinating and worked up a nice hunger and thirst for a fancy meal at a restaurant facing the Castello (outside the ruined town), which we also visited after lunch. Then we drove to the Lido and down the coast, before returning alia via to Rome. A very enjoyable outing.

Sunday was the Feast of Saint Edward so that my Subcommission work was more or less terminated by the College "do" at 1 p.m. onwards. Since then non-stop work. Fortunately, however, the Subcommissions are small in number (four Bishops and four Periti), and tonight, for example, we made really good progress during our two and a half hour meeting.

The General Congregations are less controversial, and therefore less liable to produce "sensational" developments, than in last year's session, because the schemata have been revised to assure a greater measure of agreement. There is a lot of repetition, because the Moderators consider the schema *De Ecclesia* to be the key document and do not want to apply the closure too speedily. They proposed it, however, this morning on chapter II and the Fathers arose almost to a man. It is still possible for Fathers who speak for five or more Bishops to demand their say on chapter II, but we all hope that tomorrow it may be possible to proceed with chapter III. Meanwhile, the Fathers have voted on the amendment of *De Liturgia* chapter II, and after 700 had voted iuxta modum (all these modi have to be re-examined), they have begun to deal with the emendations of chapter III. At this rate, the Council seems likely to last for years. (I must break off now to go to supper).

Wednesday, 8 a.m., in the half hour between breakfast and leaving for Saint Peter's.

The cost of hired cars has risen so steeply that the Bishops decided over the weekend to hire a coach every morning and travel together. I go with them. The coach is labelled Collegio Inglese, which, in the light of the present debate, can be taken to mean the English College of Bishops. About 60% of the speeches are, or have been for over a fortnight, on the Collegiality of the Bishops, about 25% on the restored diaconate, and the rest on sundry subjects. The English (Beck), South African (Hurley) and Irish (Conway) hierarchies have voted for the priesthood (the P.B.I.) almost alone.

The outstanding speech so far was delivered the other day by the Auxiliary of Bologna (Bettazzi), who wasn't even consecrated when this session began. It was a masterly refutation of those of his fellow Italian bishops who tend to suggest that support for Episcopal Collegiality is a veiled attack on the Primacy. It was full of quotations from some of the most ardent supporters of the Primacy, and nicely laced with irony. The Bishops have more or less stopped applauding, in response to frequent appeals of the Moderators, but they broke into a round of applause when Bettazzi stepped down.

They were very sorry here when the Doctor decided that Ormston must return to England. All liked him.

Kindest regards to all the Parlour.

Yours sincerely,

L.LMcReavy

P.S. Thank you for the rules. I gave them to the Bishop of Ghent this morning in the middle of Saint Peter's main aisle, coram 2000 Episcopi...

* * *

On October 15th the debate on the hierarchical structure of the Church was closed and the debate on the laity was opened.

In his Diary entry for Sunday, October 20th L.L. McReavy noted that he was "suffering from bad eyestrain which had begun before I left England". Instead of going to the Epsicopal Ordination at St Peter's of Monsignor Igino Cardinale, L.L. McReavy preferred to do some sight seeing: "visited Castel Sant Angelo and climbed to roof and in the evening, made a holy hour at S. Lorenzo in Damaso".

Letter 14

The English College, Rome
Sunday, October 20th 1963
8:30 a.m.

Dear Monsignor,

The perfect weather, clear sky, warm sun and no wind or rain, has continued all week, though there are some slight wisps of cloud this morning which perhaps portent a change.

The Bishops have all gone off to Saint Peter's to attend the consecration of Monsignor Igino Cardinale, the new Delegate, and thirteen others. They had to leave at 7.30, which meant saying Mass at an ungodly hour, so I decided to give the ceremony a miss. Some of them expressed surprise, or was it perhaps envy, that I wasn't coming. I pointed out that a Delegate is a representative of the Pope *Apud Hierarchiam* and has no special relationship to the clergy and people, and promised that if ever a representative of the Hierarchy to us ordinary clergy ("secundi ordinis" as the schema says) were consecrated, I should not fail to attend, whatever the hour.

We had another full week of important but not very exciting debates in Saint Peter's. (Incidentally one of the speakers deplored the existence of Apostolic Delegates). We've moved on from the collegiality of the bishops to the universal priesthood of the Populus Dei, which has given some of the Fathers opportunity for sermonising. Before the move from chapter II to chapter III, Bishop Holland was able to make a valuable suggestion (planned at one of our Common Room meetings) of which you will surely read in *The Times*.

It was well received. I get the impression that we pull more weight than our modest numbers would suppose likely. (Interruption for High Mass! Redmond and I, the only visitors present, have just put the kettle on for elevenses, though at 10 a.m.).

We had our first Subcommission meeting on Tuesday evening (4 bishops – Hildesheim, Liège, Luxembourg and an Italian; 3 Periti – Nabuco (the Pontificale pundit), Ceriani of Milan and self; and our secretary, Sigmond OP (Rector of the Angelicum), a nice manageable number). We worked for two and a half hours and made about three times the progress that is possible in the large unwieldy Commission of over forty members. Unfortunately (or perhaps fortunately) the Episcopal members have so many other engagements that we could not arrange another meeting until next Tuesday.

On Friday evening, I participated in a press conference on the Liturgical changes with Archbishop Grimshaw, and Canon O'Connell. I was asked to join the panel in case any other question, about which I might know something, came up. The journalists were mainly from Catholic newspapers and agencies, but questions were put by Kaiser (of *Time*, whose book on the first session achieved notoriety) and Reuters' man. It was an interesting experience, but somewhat sedate.

Our English Bishops are exercised at the moment, not so much by what is going on in the Council, but rather by the Bekker's effusion and the Dutch Hierarchy's statement that nothing can be said for or against the Pill until the Council pronounces, as reported in *Herder Correspondenz.* Bekker's explanation of his TV performance seemed like a pure Situation-Ethics.

Yesterday, (Saturday) Davis and I went with Pearson, in a car hired by him, to Fuigi-Fonte, forty miles east of Rome, stopping at Palestrina and Genazzano on the way out, and at Agnani on the way back. We passed through Frosinone, where the memory of Bob Gowland's felony and imprisonment is still fresh among the local old lags.

A very successful day off.

Best wishes to all the parlour.

Yours sincerely,

L.LMcReavy

* * *

On Monday, October 21st L.L. McReavy records that he "caught a chill in the evening and went to bed early after taking a Beechams".

On the following afternoon he "attended the second meeting of our Subcommission, at which we completed the task assigned to us. Returned to English College in time to attend the reception of the East African Bishops at the College".

Letter 15

The English College, Rome
Sunday, October 27th 1963

Dear Monsignor,

I passed on your joint letter to the three Ushaw men (Sharrat, Tully and Cookson) who were well and truly ordained by Cardinal Heard in the College Chapel this morning. Afterwards, I went with Peter Cookson and his family to their "do" at the convent of the Sisters of the Atonement on the Janiculum — and very nice too. They were still at it when I came away at 3:30 and caught a taxi back to the College to put on robes and accompany the bishops, in motor-coach, to Saint Peter's for the second part of the Beatification Ceremony of the Blessed Dominic Barberi. Encouraged by their Lordships, I advanced with them to the special bench reserved for the English Hierarchy just to the right (about five or six yards) from the Pope's priedieu, and squeezed in. We couldn't have had a better place. The Pope's speech was relatively brief, fervent, and included a very warm tribute to the great Newman. Unable to find our bus in the crush outside, we (most of us) walked home; a fine night with a fresh autumn breeze.

Yesterday, Saturday morning (Day off), I was working quietly in the College library at 11 a.m., when who should walk in, shepherded by Patsy Redmond, but Leo and Barney Shag. I packed up work and went with them on a tour of Saint Peter's and they came back with us to lunch at the College. Patsy went to the Shag ordination dinner today at the Pallottini place where I believe Bishop Cunningham joined him.

It has been a dullish week in Saint Peter's. Everything that could be said on chapter III *De Ecclesia* (*De Populo Dei et speciatim de laicis*) had been said by last Tuesday (5th day on chapter III), when Suenens made a well applauded speech on the continued existence of charismata (contra Ruffini), and we had to put up with two more days of repetition and sermonising before the closure was unanimously voted towards the end of Thursday's session, and the last half hour was devoted to the question whether the schema *De B.M.V.* should remain separate or be joined to the schema *De Ecclesia*. Cardinal Santos put the case for keeping it separate and Cardinal Konig for attaching it to *De Ecclesia*. There is to be a vote on the question on Tuesday morning, and it is to be settled by a simple majority. Our English Hierarchy have been pressing, ever since we arrived, for joining it to *De Ecclesia* and our secretariate has circularised 600 copies of an alternate form (suitable for inclusion in *De Ecclesia*), sponsored by Abbot Butler, to the various hierarchies, Butler and Davis gave a press conference about it last Friday. I doubt whether the motion would have won a two thirds support, but it may well get by on a single majority vote. We are negotiating with the Chilean Hierarchy, who also have an alternative draft ready for the same purpose, to see if the two can be fused into one. I hope it comes off. If there had been a Christological Schema, B.M.V. would, I suppose, have been ideally attached to that. As it is, it is best that She should be dealt with in the context of the Church. Two Latin-American bishops (to my surprise) have said in Saint Peter's that there is too much of a tendency among their people to treat Mary and the Saints as a *Corpus Theologicum a se*. We don't want that. It is not even ecumenical (blessed word).

Monday 8.15 a.m.

Yesterday, for the first time since our arrival, there was a slight wind, and it had an autumnal nip in it, so that it seems likely that we can expect no more Indian summer weather. The heating has not gone on yet in the College, but it would not come amiss in the evenings.

This morning, in place of the usual General Congregation, we are to have a Mass celebrated by the Holy Father and an address by Cardinal Suenens to commemorate the anniversary of Pope John's election. "Postea" said Felici, "omnes Patres discedant". It is like being let out of school early.

Good wishes to all the brethren.
Yours sincerely,
L.LMcReavy

* * *

Monsignor McReavy's Diary entries for the following days are unusually ample and therefore merit to be reproduced in their entirety:

> **Tuesday, October 29.** The vote was taken on BMV, the Fathers deciding by a bare majority of 40 (1114 to 1074) to attach it to *De Ecclesia*. There had been considerable activity over the weekend by the opponents and several statements of the case for separate BMV

had been circulated. *Il Tempo* accused English bishops of seeking to attenuate defined doctrines such as the Assumption and Immaculate Conception. Msgr Worlock made a protest at *Il Tempo* Offices and finally obtained a printed "dementi" which withdrew the charge in response to a "prezziossima chiarificazioni" from the English Bishops! *The long awaited propositions of the Moderators* on chapter II *De Ecclesia* were distributed during the Congregation. A small informal meeting was held in our Common Room at teatime to discuss how the Bishops should vote. A small informal meeting in Common Room at teatime discussed what vote should be given on the five propositions. Some doubts were expressed whether Episcopus = summus gradus Sacramenti Ordinis. 7 p.m. Redmond and I entertained the two Fathers Sharratt (Bernard and Leo) to dinner at the Trattoria da Pancrazio, an underground vault in the ruins of the Theatre of Pompey.

Wednesday, October 30. 58th General Congregation. The five propositions were carried, all by large majorities. 1. 2123 *placet* to 34 *non placet*. 2. 2049 to 104. 3. 1808 to 336. 4. 1717 to 408 5. 1588 to 525 (diaconate). At the end of the General Congregation the Fathers voted to close the discussion *De Ecclesia*, subject to right of those who invoked article 57; and it was announced that the next subject would be *De Episcopis*. A very satisfactory morning's work. Rumour has been circulating that the long delay in putting the above five propositions (said to be wanted by those members of the Theology Commission who were being blocked by the Ottaviani faction) was due to doubts raised by the Presidents Bench whether the Moderators were competent to discuss this; and that the issue was finally settled at a joint meeting by a majority of one vote. The Bishop of Coutances (apparently) confirmed this at lunch today. In the evening most of the Bishops and 30 students went to Saints John and Paul for a Pontifical High Mass (Heenan) and Sermon (Alfred Wilson CP) in honour of the Beatification of Dominic Barberi. The Pope has written a letter to Archbishop of Westminster, for general release, on the same subject. I spent the evening studying the schema *De Episcopis*.

Thursday, October 31. 59th General Congregation. The relatio on chapters VI and VII *De Liturgia* was made and the Fathers were asked by Moderator Döpfner if, instead of voting on the individual emendations, they were content to vote on the chapter as a whole. They indicated their affirmative "surgendo" and at the end of the Congregation it was announced as passed by large majority.

Döpfner observed that there had been constant complaints about the protracted debates, yet, despite yesterday's vote to end debate *De Ecclesia*, more than 25 still wanted to speak vi art. 57. He begged them to keep strictly within the limits of the subject, to avoid all repetition; notified them that they would be warned at 6 mins and gonged at eight, and reminded them that written observations would be given the same attention as spoken. We just managed to get through by the end of morning. Archbishop Roberts came to supper. He is staying with "Bob Kaiser". Worlock went to *Il Tempo* to protest against the charge that the British draft *De BMV* sought to "attenuate" Immaculate Conception and Assumption. The editor agreed to see Abbot Butler.

Friday, November 1. All Saints. Raining. House is half empty. Bishops Dwyer, Beck, Rudderham and Petit are in England. Bishops Restieaux and Pearson at Nice. Bishops Grasar and Foley at Assisi. Archbishop Grimshaw and secretary at Villa above Palazzola. Bishop Holland on Retreat at Frascati. Heenan and Brunner have colds. *Il Tempo* this morning prints an implicit retraction which it calls a "preziossima chiarificazione" of the English draft on BMV, both as regards its intention and contents.

Saturday, November 2. All Souls. Dry but scirocco. Worked on schema *De Episcopis.*

Letter 16

The English College, Rome
Monday, November 4th 1963

Dear Monsignor,

You will have learned from the daily Press that the proposal to add the schema *De B.M.V.* to *De Ecclesia* was carried by a mere 40 votes (1114 to 1074), and that the long awaited "Propositions" of the Moderators on chapter II *De Ecclesia* were finally agreed upon, put to the assembly, and all confirmed. They are not final, and are indeed merely meant to give the Theological Commission some idea of the general opinion of the Fathers on the principal issues that emerged during the debate on chapter II; but if the same could be done on every schema, a great deal of time could be saved. The rumour has been circulating that the delay was due to doubts raised by some members of the Commission who did not want to have their hands forced by an expression of the assembly's will and by the Presidential Board, as to whether it was within the competence of the Moderators to put such questions to the vote, and then the question was eventually settled at a plenary meeting by a single vote. The Bishop of Coutances later assured me that this was true.

Last Tuesday (29th October) Patsy Redmond and I entertained the two Shags (Bernard and Leo) to dinner (7-9pm) at the Trattoria de Pancrazio in the ruins of Pompey's theatre (underground). Leo Sharratt did not seem his usual bright self, or, should I say, his former bright self.

On Wednesday, 30th October, the Fathers voted to end the debate on *De Ecclesia*, but the following day, over 25 claimed the right to speak, as representing more than five other Fathers. Döpfner, Moderator for the day, drew their attention to the illogicality of constantly complaining to the Moderators about the slowness of the debate and then hamstringing their efforts to abbreviate it in this way; and he warned the 25 speakers that they would have a maximum of eight minutes instead of ten, and would be stopped if they wandered off the subject or merely repeated what had been frequently said. We got through the 25 speakers in the morning and hope to start *De Episcopis* tomorrow, Tuesday.

Friday to Monday inclusive was declared a mid-term break and most of the bishops went off on various 3 to 4 day jaunts, I had been given the job of preparing comments on *De Episcopis*, so that kept me busy for three of the four days. However, on Sunday, I gladly accepted an invitation to accompany Cashman, Redmond and Ashdowne (driver) on a car trip to Cassino. It was a perfect summer day, warm and sunny, with a pleasant breeze. We drove down through the Campania and Pontine Marshes to Terracina and along the magnificent coast to Formio, where we had an excellent (not too heavy lunch) in a restaurant overlooking the picture postcard blue bay. We then cut through the Aurunci mountains to Cassino, drove up to the Abbey (9 kilometres of winding road) and returned via the monotonous autostrada at 75 mph. A most successful day.

Today, I worked like a black from 8.30 to 1 and again in the afternoon. Tomorrow we resume the daily grind in Saint Peter's and if we get 25% of good speeches among the general current of hot air, we shan't do badly. Tonight, many of the bishops have been dining on a liner off Cività Vecchia (firms invitation). Patsy Redmond is returning home this week, because Dogma has had its day for the moment. Bishop Dwyer is back. Foley has "Roman pot" but still hopes to get back for his VG's funeral.

All the best,
L.LMcReavy

* * *

The following entries in Monsignor McReavy's Diary supplement the information given in the letters.

Tuesday, November 5. 60th General Congregation began *De Episcopis* in genere. Some good speeches, especially from the French Bishops who complained that the schema failed to give practical expression to the theological principles enunciated in *De Ecclesia*. Hot sticky scirocco, oppressive even in St Peter's.

Wednesday, November 6. Still hot scirocco. Death of Archbishop Mannix. Exhausting weather. Dragged my steps throughout a 20 minute walk to the far end of the Piazza Navona and back.

Thursday, November 7. Heavy rain during the night. Sunny with scirocco.

Friday, November 8. 63rd General Congregation. Felici announced presence of Archbishop Carinci (aged 101) who wished to thank Fathers for their messages of previous day, and to wish them as long a life as his and even longer.

Saturday, November 9. Weather still very warm. Worked all day on a collation of last week's debates about expressions of Episcopal Collegiality in a representative central Council assisting the Pope in government of Church, and on question whether episcopal faculties are regularly regarded as concessions.

Sunday, November 10. Weather still very warm. No rain. After lunch, watched the Italy v Russia match on TV. Evening, worked until 7pm on Collation of Debates with comments.

Monday, November 11. Warm and sunny, like a summer's day. After lunch, went for a long walk with Bishop Dwyer round the centre of Rome.

Letter 17

The English College, Rome
Monday, November 11th 1963

Dear Monsignor,

It is a warm summer's day. Murphy and Ellis left this morning for England, the former because he has suffered constantly from stomach trouble ever since he came out; the latter largely in sympathy (they are bosom pals).

The Council has spent the week debating the first two chapters of *De Episcopis*, and on the whole the debate has been interesting.

On Tuesday, we learned at lunch-time that "Jock" Tickle had been nominated Bishop to the Forces (he is to be consecrated in the College Chapel on, I think, December 1st). At 4 p.m., we had a conciliar meeting of the Hierarchy, and which I had to present and expound a votum on *De Episcopis*, followed by a reception for the Canadian Hierarchy.

On Wednesday Maximus IV Saigh of the Melchites of Antioch delivered another harangue in French, demanding that the Roman Curia should be replaced by an Episcopal Council in which only those Cardinals who are residential Bishops should have a place.

Fulton Sheen, the Bishops of Lourdes and Quimper, Agnellus Andrew, et alii, came to lunch. Tom Driberg MP came to supper and started a long theological discussion in the Bishops Common Room afterwards by posing a question on Anglican Orders.

Thursday: Bishop Foley and Patsy Redmond left for England.

His Beatitude Ignatius XVII Batanian astonished the General Congregation with a most glowing tribute to the virtues of the Roman

Curia (and was warmly thanked the next day by Ruffini who revealed that Batanian was a former pupil of his!).

Friday: Frings (in a very mild voice) called for a change in the Holy Office procedure which would ensure that no one was judged or condemned without being given a hearing and a chance to correct himself or his book: and was subsequently told (in an angry and passionate protest) by Ottaviani that the insinuation was based on "nescience" in regard to Holy Office procedures. There was quite a "to do" about it at the American Bishops' Press Conference that afternoon at 3 p.m.

I went to our Bishops' Press Conference at 5 p.m. (Dwyer on *De Episcopis*), but ours was mildness itself, "no comment!", much to the disappointment of the few journalists who had come to us from the American. I must sample the Americans next time there is a sensation "in Aula". I understand that it consists of a whole bench of Bishops and a raft of Periti, and that they really let their hair down, on the principle that everything gets out almost immediately in any case, and that it is better to be frank and try to put things in their proper context and perspective.

The most constructive speeches of the Friday General Congregation were made by Lercaro and Rugambwa who, while approving of the suggested Central Council of Bishops, observed that it could not simply be plonked into the existing structure of universal Church government without creating all sorts of practical problems concerning the existing Papal organs (Cardinals and Curia) which could not be ironed out in a three day debate, or without the intervention of the Pope, and therefore that a special Commission should work out proposals to be submitted to the Fathers for their approval and then presented to the Pope in their name as a petition.

Saturday and Sunday I spent working on a combination of the week's debates with comments for the benefit of our bishops: it is being poly-copied at this moment by our secretariate. I could not even spare the time to attend the Papal Taking-Possession ceremony at the Lateran.

This morning (*Monday*) we had an impassioned speech from the Bishop of Lucknow protesting against any suggestion that aged or incapacitated Bishops should be asked or advised to resign. A Bishop was wedded for life to his diocese. It was worse than divorce (I reflected that Archbishop Heenan has been twice divorced on his way to Westminster) and the condition of those who had been so imprudent as to resign was "miserrima" (I reflected on the pitiful condition of Archbishop Roberts). Rumour is that the next schema is to be on Ecumenism, because the Pope wants something to publish pronto.

Well there's the picture! Only three weeks more to go and we shall all be very glad to pack up and make for cold and foggy England.

All the best to all the Parlour.
L.LMcReavy

PS. We all got a medal this morning in Saint Peter's.

* * *

Once again the Diary entries provide a much ampler background to the following letter:

Tuesday, November 12. Still warm and sunny. At the 65th General Congregation Cardinal Suenens made a strong plea for a prescription regarding resignation by aged and infirm Bishops; a law is required, salvo iudicio in casiis particularibus. Hervas proposed abolition of Coadjutors cum iure. Some wanted less Titulars, less Auxiliaries, others wanted them to be given a clearer juridical status. Some want to solve the problem of aged bishops by appointing Coadjutors with all the power of an Administrator Apostolic, so that the old man retains role and honours, but all responsibility and rights pass to Administrator. 4 p.m. Hierarchy Conciliar meeting on Liturgy and on Ecumenism. 5.30 to 7 p.m. Reception at College for French, Belgian and Dutch Hierarchies, plus the one Bishop of Denmark. At supper, Van Vilsen, a Dutch Dominican Bishop (Kronstadt, South Africa), defended the Pill and claimed that good Dutch Catholics were using it without scruple.

Wednesday, November 13. Still equally warm and sunny. The 66th General Congregation began with a magnificent Mass in the Byzantine Russian Rite (Liturgy of St John Chrysostom), beautifully sung, especially the Deacon who had a magnificent bass voice. Debate all the morning on Episcopal Conferences. Afternoon, booked my return flight for Thursday, December 5, 1.15 p.m. and ordered two copies of photo of Bishop Cunningham and self on steps of St Peter's (November 12th).

Thursday, November 14. "Rain during the night, and still falling lightly when we left for St Peter's. There we received copies of Paul VI's Apostolic Letter *Summi Dei Verbum* commemorating fourth centenary since establishment of Seminaries by Trent.

Friday, November 15. "Mild, some cloud, but no rain. I devoted the evening to a votum on the relation of *De Oecumenismo* to the crushing law of Canon 1258 re *Communio in sacris.*

Sunday, November 17. "Some rain. Still warm. The bishops met at 10 a.m. to discuss what immediate steps might be taken in implementing the liturgical reforms and concerns especially regarding the vernacular. Grimshaw is anxious to keep the lead among the English speaking nations.

Letter 18

The English College, Rome
Sunday, November 17th 1963

Dear Monsignor,

The marvellous weather continues, except that during the past three or four days it has changed from summer to early autumn, or rather to late spring. There is a freshness in the warm sunshine that makes it a pleasure to walk, or would do so, were not Rome's streets such a bedlam of wheeled traffic.

On the whole it was a dull week in the Aula, and the debate on *De Episcopis et De Dioecesis Regimine* eventually petered out on Friday for lack of enough speakers to fill the morning Congregation, an unprecedented event. We were actually let out of school half an hour early, with the announcement that we would resume on Monday with *De Oecumenismo*. It was not that the Bishops were uninterested in Bishops and Government of Dioceses, but that they were uninterestingly uniform in their views. When a conservative like Cardinal Siri got up and said he fully agreed with Frings et alii that Episcopal Conferences should not normally be able to impose a juridical obligation on their members, even by a two third majority, it was evident that on one point at least there is no left wing or right wing: all bishops are monarchs at heart, however much some of them may trumpet their collegiality when it is the central government of the Church (and the Roman Curia) that is in question.

On Tuesday (12th November) we had a very successful reception here at the College for the French, Belgian and Dutch hierarchies (5.30 to 7 p.m.). There was a very good turn-up and the gallery and salone were very crowded. These receptions can be very interesting, though they are tiring on the feet, and a series of "bits and pieces" and drinks ruins one's supper at eight. The students carry around the trays, but I noticed Bishop Cowderoy carrying one around quite evidently to avoid being caught in French conversation with any of the visitors. Next Wednesday, I believe, we are to receive the American Hierarchy (US) we have already had the Canadians, and the "gate" is likely to be a record. Among lunch visitors, Oscar Cullmann and Professor Skydsgaard were very agreeable and interesting company.

On Friday, Archbishop Heenan, Monsignor Frank Davis and Father Charles Davis gave an interesting and well attended Press Conference on Ecumenism.

On Saturday we had the Hexham and Newcastle binge at the Tre Scalini restaurant in the Piazza Navona, which must have cost Bishop Cunningham at least £20, but was very enjoyable and shocked my stomach out of the heaviness that had been affecting it for some time. That same day, all Rome was buzzing with rumours about a top level meeting then being held in the Vatican, coram Papa, to resolve differences between the

Presidents, the Moderators and other leading figures. No further news has yet emerged as to what happened.

(Resumed, Monday 1 p.m.).

We have just returned from the first debate on Oecumenism. Most of the morning was taken up with "Relationes" on the schema and on the final version of chapter I *De Liturgia* (now definitively passed), so that we had room for only nine speeches from Cardinals and Patriarchs. The Orientals (Tappouni, Stefanos I and Maximos IV) were very critical of the last minute addition of a chapter *De Iudaeis* and Arreby y Castro (Spain) was critical of nearly everything in the schema. Indeed, all in all, the schema had a good morning, but the defenders have yet to speak, and I expect them to show up in force tomorrow or the next day. It is largely hazard that determines the order of speakers. I am thinking of doing without my siesta this afternoon and going to the American Press Conference at 3 p.m. They should have some interesting questions to meet from correspondents who want the low-down on the attitude of the Fathers to the Jews, and they may have picked up some gaff about yesterday's meeting in the Vatican.

5 p.m. I should have had my siesta. Nothing newsworthy emerged at the American Press Conference, and some of the off-the-cuff answers given to correspondents were open to misinterpretation. Yes, there is a definite nip in the air and this afternoon I was tempted to wear my raincoat over my lounge-suit for warmth. In the end I didn't, nor did I feel the need of it.

Best of wishes to all the brethren in a truly ecumenical spirit.

Yours

L.LMcReavy

* * *

The Diary entries provide background information to the following letter.

Tuesday, November 19. Sharp but pleasant. Most of the 70th General Congregation was taken up by Malabar Mass, and three Relationes on *De Oecumenismo.* (Bukatko on *De Orientalibus*, Bea on *De Judaeis*, and De Smedt on *De Libertate Religiosa*). After lunch, with Dwyer in car to Aventine, where we visited Santa Sabina and strolled around. Tickle and Foley back from England. Evening. Gonzi of Malta came to talk to our Bishops.

Monday, November 25. Cardinal Tisserant intervened to complain that leaflets had been distributed, bearing names of Fathers who invited other Fathers to join with them in voting *non placet* to the Decree *De Communicationibus*, which had already been approved by a large majority in Aula. He deplored it as contrary to the dignity of the Council. He said leaflets were distributed to us as we got out of our buses, and before we went through the barrier below the steps of St Peter's.

Letter 19

The English College, Rome
November 25th 1963

Dear Monsignor,

I was very glad to get your reassuring news about Dick Bell's operation. Proficiat! The poor weather continues, sharp at times, but not cold.

A mixed week at the Council. The English Hierarchy met on Sunday November 17th to discuss what immediate steps they might take in implementing the schema *De Liturgia*, and they resumed the subject with the Irish hierarchy when we went to the Irish College for tea on Friday, 22nd of November. The chief difficulty seems to be in getting a worthy and agreed translation for those parts in which Vernacular may be allowed.

The debate in Saint Peter's became much more interesting when, on Monday November 18th, we began the discussion of *De Ecumenismo*. Some apparently still have no idea what Ecumenism really means, imagining that it is enough to tell heretics the truth with charity; or else that is their discreet way of saying that they disapprove of the whole notion.

Some, especially the Arabs, object strongly to the inclusion of a special chapter on the Jews, and some, especially the Spaniards, see felonious intent in the addition of a fifth and final chapter on Religious Liberty. The Moderators therefore, after the debate in genere, merely asked the Fathers to approve of chapters I to III as a basis of discussion, and left the question of chapters IV and V to be decided "at a later date". It seems unlikely that there will be time to settle this question before the end of the session, and a rumour came from the bar into our tribune this morning that the Pope had decided to omit IV and V from the schema, and have these topics dealt with elsewhere.

Wednesday, 20th November (temperature 72 F in Piazza at midday).

Archbishop Heenan made what all agreed was the speech of the morning, the only one that drew applause. You will have read about it in *The Times*. It was very carefully prepared and appeared in two preliminary drafts before the final version was settled. Cardinal Bacci caused a minor stir by claiming that he had been refused leave to speak when the famous five propositions were announced as about to be put to the vote. Later in the debate, the Moderator, Agaganian, explained that Bacci had come to the table seeking an opportunity to suggest to the Fathers that the clause safeguarding the "ius primatiale" of the Pope should read "ius primatus" and that the Moderators have decided there was no reason to hold up the proceedings, when the meaning of this phrase was evident from text and context.

Wednesday 4 p.m. to 5.30. Discussion in our Bishops' Common Room, at which I presented and expounded a votum which I had prepared *De Communicatione in sacris*.

5.30-7. A reception for the US hierarchy in the Salone; well attended, and there would have been more, if there hadn't been a day's strike of all public transport. Tom Burns (of B.O.W, Universe, *Tablet*) came to supper and there was a warm discussion afterwards about some of the recent indiscretions (to put it mildly) of *The Universe*. Burns admitted that, ever since he had come to Rome, he hadn't realised how fanciful was the Universe's picture of the Council.

Thursday, November 21st. We moved on to discussion of chapter I, even though over 27 bishops still had their names down to speak on the schema in genere. In the evening, I attended an international group meeting at the Spanish College, vice Heenan, to discuss Ecumenism with some non-Catholic observers. Lukas Fischer said that, to judge from the schema we'd have to begin by having a dialogue on the dialogue.

Friday, November 22nd was memorable in that it saw the final acceptance of *De Liturgia*, The first complete and amended document to get through (*placet* 2158; non pl. 19; null 1).

Yves Nolet came to lunch as my guest.

4.30 Tea at the Irish College.

Supper was dramatically interrupted by news of the death of Kennedy. We had some journalists to supper and one of them, Patrick Smith (BBC Rome correspondent) was called to the phone and came back for a moment with the news. Kaiser (*Time*) and Nichol (*Times*) had to leave at once. (note: the heating came on for the first time that night, and tonight I wish it was off.)

Saturday and Sunday, I worked at a moderate pace on a collation of the week's debates, and on Sunday we had a "do" in honour of the new Apostolic Delegate attended by Sir Peter Scarlett, Cape, the whole Hierarchy, and various odd-bods.

Monday, November 25th. This morning we moved on to chapter II *De Oecumenismo*. This evening I went in robes to the Solemn Requiem for Kennedy celebrated at the papal altar at the Lateran by Cardinal Spellman, attended by 35 Cardinals and about 1000 Bishops. The Americans were very touched by the turn up. They need some consolation.

Tonight, the Phils are giving their annual concert, in which I believe even I get a carnal and innocuous mention.

All the best. Only a week and three days to go!

Yours sincerely,
L.LMcReavy

* * *

From the Diary:

Thursday, November 28. Damp but warm. Nothing very threatening in the morning's debate.

Friday, November 29. Bright and breezy. Springlike. With Dwyer by car to the Janiculum, where we had a very pleasant walk, with lovely views of Rome.

Letter 20

The English College, Rome
Friday, November 29th 1963. 12.45 p.m.

Dear Monsignor,

Please thank Laurence for sending the packet of correspondence; on examining which I decided that I'd answer the questions more easily when I get within reach of my book and files, which may be an indication that I am tired, as I find are all the others. This will probably be my last bulletin. I have just returned from the last General Congregation of this week and there is unlikely to be much progress made on Monday to Wednesday, next week.

When I arrive in England, next Thursday afternoon, fog permitting, I plan to go down to Maidstone for the weekend in order to rest and acclimatise myself. If so, I shall return to Ushaw on Monday, 9th December, by the 1 p.m. train from King's Cross, which unless recently changed is due into Durham at 5:50.

It has not been a very exciting week in Saint Peter's. The Fathers have simply plodded through chapters II and III *De Oecumenismo* with scarcely a flare-up and few memorable speeches to empty the bars or prevent their being overcrowded. Wednesday's debate was not bad, at least from the point of view of hustle by the Moderators. When only seven of the 41 announced speeches on chapter II had said their piece, Moderator Döpfner intervened to say that, judging from the number of repetitions, meditations and examinations of conscience, the Moderators were satisfied that the subject was exhausted, and proposed that the debate pass to chapter III. This gave Dwyer the opportunity to make a rousing and realistic speech. Needless to say, the Fathers agreed "surgendo" almost to a man, but, also needless to say, 15 of the disappointed speakers exercised their right to re-examine chapter II the following day. Among them was Frings who, while insisting strongly on the present discipline regarding mixed marriages and the "gravissima obligatio" of all the children being brought up as Catholics, wanted mixed marriages outside the Catholic Church declared valid, as they were before *Ne Temere* was imposed on Germany.

The main interest of the week lay in activities *extra Aulam*. On Monday night, we had the Phils' concert (much better than last year). Earlier in the evening, I went with most of the bishops to the Requiem by Spellman at the Lateran.

On Tuesday, I was summoned to attend a meeting of our Commission, but exercised my liberty to come away once the material of our Sub-commission had been dealt with. They had moved on to another chapter, and had spent ten minutes arguing over a word of no theological significance, several speaking together (the Bishop of Liège meanwhile giving me a large wink). When Nabuco and I decided we'd had enough, we stood up, bowed politely to Cardinal Castaldo of Naples and made our escape. I arrived back at the college to find the Salone and approaches crowded with about 100 bishops (including five Cardinals) from Germany, Austria, Poland and Eastern Europe, all standing about in vivacious groups, drinking, nibbling and smoking, and mostly able to talk enough English to make contact with our Hierarchy. Our receptions this year have been a great success and this was about the best of them.

Yesterday, Thursday, I took nine Ushawmen (eight Venerabili and Spence from the Scots) to lunch at the Scoglio De Frisio. It happened to be American Thanksgiving Day and they had prepared our table on the assumption that we were Americans and would want the traditional Thanksgiving menu. Seven of us liked the look of the menu and took it. The main dish, turkey and all the trimmings, was gargantuan but very enjoyable, and we needed to walk all the way back from the Via Merulana to work it off.[7]

We have had some thunder showers this week, but today it is bright and breezy again and this afternoon, on the Janiculum, where I went with Dwyer for a walk, it was springlike, the leaves still on the trees and mainly green, people sitting on the park benches etc. We have been extraordinarily lucky with the weather, by comparison with last year.

About half an hour of this morning's session (Friday) was taken up by announcements from Felici regarding next Wednesday's Sessio Publica. The Fathers were warned that they would not be defining any doctrine of faith and morals in giving their solemn approval to the Constitution on Liturgy and the Decree on Social Communications, and were notified (subject to the Pope's eventual decision) that the next session would be from September 14th to November 20th. Among the extra members elected to the various Commissions (for what practical purpose it is difficult to say) were Abbot Butler (Faith and Morals) and Wall (Seminaries).

---

7 "The Scoglio da Frisio was a much frequented restaurant by Scots College students particularly. It belonged to the family of the Vignerolo at the Scozzese Villa at Marino. L.L. McReavy enjoyed being serenaded at the table!" (Canon Robert Spence).

A busy weekend ahead. Tomorrow (Saturday) morning, consecration of Jock Tickle in the College Chapel by Heard, followed by a reception and luncheon. In the evening, a papal audience for Periti. Sunday, some other reception (my memory is getting as wonky as my handwriting). Tuesday, a commemorative ceremony in Saint Peter's for the fourth centenary of Seminaries, and, of course, the Sessio Publica (copes and mitres and all that lark) on Wednesday next. Further details when I get back to the calm and ordinary round of life in Alma Mater.

All the best to all readers.
Yours sincerely
L.LMcReavy

* * *

The following information concerning the period following this letter until Monsignor McReavy's return to Ushaw is taken from his Diary.

Saturday, November 30. 9-11am. Attended, in choir robes, the Episcopal Consecration of Monsignor Tickle (Ordinary of the Forces) in the College Chapel, by Cardinal Heard, assisted by Archbishop Heenan and Bishop Grasar, in the presence of the British Hierarchy and many other celebrities. Reception afterwards in the Salone and Gallery (champagne and sandwiches). 6.45 To the Vatican, with Msgrs Clark and Worlock in the College car, for the Papal Audience to Periti (7.15) in the Sala Clementina. Monsignor Colombo read an address to the Holy Father, who then read an address to us (over 200) stressing the volume of work for the Council. He then walked along the front row, giving his ring to as many as could get near him.

Sunday, December 1. Weather still fine. Hierarchy met 10.15-12.30 to discuss liturgical changes. 1.30 Consecration Dinner with Cardinal Cicognani as chief guest. Afterwards, drove with Bishop Dwyer to the Pincian Gardens for a stroll. Lovely weather. No need of an overcoat. Visited the Sacred Heart convent next to San'Trinità dei Monti to see their picture of Our Lady (1840) and bought copies. The Americans are said to be annoyed at the apparent unwillingness of the Council authorities to let the Fathers vote as to whether chapter IV (De Judaeis) and chapter V (De Libertate Religiosa) are to be kept in the schema *De Oecumenismo*. Rumours that Cardinals Meyer and Ritter had decided to raise the subject but had received a hint that it would not be welcomed.

Monday, December 2. Bright and sunny. Feast of the College Martyrs.

79th and last General Congregation of the Session. Mass by Archbishop Ngô-Dinh-Thuc, brother of late President Diem of

Vietnam, who offered it for his 2 dead brothers, on the 30th day after their murder.

Felici explained the inter-Session work. The Commissions will work hard on the *Animadversiones Patrum*, and the Fathers can send in fresh ones up to January 30th. Owing to the large number of *Animadversiones* (over 600) sent in regarding the proposed *Nuntius* from Council, it would be impossible to send it out now; and therefore must be postponed. Only 15 speakers were announced and one of them withdrew. When the debate finished, Bea summed up, and then Bishop Hengsbach gave a relatio *De Apostolatu Laicorum*, which it had been hoped to discuss in this Session. The Moderator then thanked everyone and the Session ended.

1 p.m. Photo in Cortile of Hierarchy, visitors and students, followed by feast in refectory and coffee and liqueurs in the gallery. 6 p.m. Reception at the Legation. 8 p.m. Film: "The World of Harold Lloyd".

Tuesday, December 3. Solemn Commemoration of Fourth Centenary of the Council of Trent. Dialogued Low Mass coram Papa by Cardinal Secretary of State, a long Latin discourse on Trent and its effects by Cardinal Urbani, Patriarch of Venice, a French address to the Holy Father (mainly on Ecumenism) by Jean Guitton, and a short Italian speech by Signor Veronese. Then Felici read out the list of Faculties granted, as from December 8, to the Bishops, Resident and Titular. All rather boring. Weather fine and warm. 12.30 with Bishop Brunner, Msgr O'Mahoney and Father B. Loftus to the Ristorante Da Pancrazio for lunch. Drowsy afterwards.

Wednesday, December 4. Solemn Public Session to close second Session of the Council. 8.30 a.m. In robes, with the Bishops, by coach to St Peter's. Walked up the nave and found a good seat, next to Msgr Worlock, in the benches reserved to Prelates at the right of the Papal throne. An impressive and not too prolonged ceremony. Dialogued Low Mass. Solemn voting on the Constitution *De Sacra Liturgia* (passed with only four dissentients) and on the Decree on Means of Social Communications (164 *non placet*). At the end of the Pope's address, he announced his intention of paying a visit to the Holy Land early in the New Year. (Applause). Out into the sunshine a little after 12.30. After tea, went to Gammarrelli's to buy sash, piping and buttons. Raining. Started to sort out my papers etc. Father Hoersy SJ and Father Molinari SJ came to supper and afterwards, in the Common Room, they were challenged about indisciplined Jesuits, notably Rahner. They admitted that the General had been too unwell these last two or three years to exercise effective control. Molinari said of Rahner that he posed more questions (in an obscure way,) than he attempted to answer.

Thursday, December 5. Packed until 10.30. Then discovered that my plane ticket was made out for BEA 1.15 p.m. November 5 instead of Alitalia 1.15 December 5. Temporary panic. Fortunately Bishop Tickle rang up the airline offices and discovered that my name was on the passenger list correctly. 11.45. In car, driven by Msgr Clark, with Bishop of Middlesborough, to Beda to pick up Bishop Cunningham. Near Ostia Antica, found Bishops Grasar, Parker and Restieaux standing by the side of the road, their hired car having broken down. An American in a C.D. car was returning from taking Bishop McDevitt to the airport came to their aid. I transferred to his car with Bishop Parker and we arrived in good time. No excess baggage was charged to our party. The plane took off at 1.20 but when it had climbed over the Mediterranean, with sundry things that, we thought, indicated trouble with the landing gear, the captain announced that, owing to a mechanical fault, we were returning to Rome airport. Rather tense for a while, but the trouble cannot have been landing gear, because we made a smooth landing and a number of cars with technicians came out and tinkered with various things in the pilot's cabin, and again taking on fresh fuel, we took off at 2.15 and reached London about 3.40, English time. Caught the 5.20 to Maidstone and arrived home by taxi about 6.30.

Friday, December 6. Received letter from Monsignor Grant informing me of the sudden death of Reverend Leo Sharratt, in sleep, in night of Wednesday to Thursday.

Saturday, December 7. Assisted at reception into Church, at St Francis' Maidstone, of Tony Brown, Kate's fiancé.

Monday, December 9. Returned to Ushaw, to learn that Leo Sharratt had been buried that morning.

December 10-25. This time (unlike First Session) I was fit enough to resume duties at once. I also prepared a talk on the second Session of the Council and gave it on different nights, first to Divines and then to Philosophers.

The Third Session

September 14th – November 21st 1964

The following information regarding the period between Monsignor McReavy's departure from England and his arrival in Rome has been taken from his Diary.

On Tuesday, September 1, L.L. McReavy arrived at Dover: "Nearly strained my arms carrying my heavy case and sack from taxi to the boat. Ceinture at Paris to Gare de Lyon, where I had to lump my bags along a very long platform to change trains. A good dinner on the train and dozed fitfully through the night in a first-class carriage with six occupants".

The following morning he arrived at Pisa and "booked a room in Hotel Nettuno on the Arno and drove there in a carrozza. Lunch, siesta then visited the Campo dei Miracoli".

He spent Thursday painting "a sketch of the leaning Tower, with Cathedral in background". On the following day he took a coach to Lucca, where he painted the church of San Frediano.

On Saturday L.L.McReavy took a long walk in search of subject to paint but his search was interrupted by a shower of rain. In late afternoon he made a sketch of an old tower on the Lungarno. The scirocco which had begun on the previous day continued, he painted a view in the Piazza dei Cavalieri until hindered by showers of rain in the afternoon.

On Monday, September 7 he records that he "read and packed until 11.45 when the taxi to the train station arrived. He took the 12.10 train to Empoli where he changed train for Siena and arrived there at 2.15 p.m. "An Italian with whom I talked on the train gave me a lift in his car and booked me into the Hotel Italia, just outside the gates".

Tuesday, September 8. The weather in Siena was "perfect" and he spent the morning making a sketch of the Duomo and in the afternoon he made a rough sketch of the tower in the Campo. During the remaining three days in Siena he records in his Diary that he made sketches of San Domenico; of the surrounding landscape from the walls; the Porta Romana and the parish church where he celebrated Mass.

On Saturday, September 12 he took the "12.20 train to Rome, via Chiusi. The train from Chiusi was packed even in the first-class and it was only by kindness of a traveller that I had a seat for part of the journey. Arrived Rome 4:30 p.m. and got a taxi to the College. Tea, a bath, and then unpacked in my old room in the Mezzanine flat".

The Sunday was spent relaxing. He went for a walk both in the morning and the afternoon with Bishop Dwyer.

Letter 21

The English College, Rome
September 18th 1964

Dear Monsignor,

It is one p.m., Friday, and we have just returned from the last General Congregation of the week. A week's work, and you have still a day before you re-assemble. I enjoyed my ten days painting holiday, five at Pisa (with a visit to Lucca) and five at Siena, and I had good accommodation in both places at very reasonable prices. I reached Rome, last Saturday afternoon and moved into the same room as last year, in the mezzanine flat; very nice except that I always have to use artificial light, because the palazzo on the other side of the Montoro cuts out all view of the sky. Ever since I arrived in

Italy, seventeen days ago, the sun has shone almost continuously every day and it has been really hot, with too much humidity for my liking, though perhaps most of the humidity comes from my constant perspiration which continues more or less day and night. I sleep under a single sheet, but my pyjamas and pillow bear evidence of night-long perspiration when my alarm breaks my too brief sleep at six a.m. or earlier.

From the conciliar point of view it has been a heavy, expeditious, but not very exciting week. The opening ceremony was the most enjoyable yet, though not perhaps the most splendiferous. The Bishops were excused from wearing cope and mitre and came in choir dress. As usual, we Monsignori had better places than their Lordships in the special benches reserved for us about twenty yards to the right of the papal altar. We had a perfect view of the *Missa dialogata* concelebrated by the Pope and twenty four bishops. It was a very impressive rite, without any of the fussy and oriental-despot ceremonial that characterizes a papal high Mass. There was full participation by the whole assembly, clergy and laity. There was only one detail that I would prefer to see changed. At the Communion of the concelebrants, the paten and the chalice remained in front of the Pope and the others had to process right round the enlarged altar table twice in order to pick up their large particle (a triangular section) of the host and again in order to dip their spoon in the Precious Blood (consumed on the spot). It would seem to be more appropriate to the nature of a meal that the paten and chalice should circulate round the table, rather than that the participants should do so themselves.

In the afternoon, Archbishop Grimshaw offered me a lift in his car out to the villa at Palazzola where most of the students still are, and I began a sketch of the cortile. My schemata, which I posted before leaving England had not yet arrived, and, with the best will in the world, there was not much work I could do.

The first General Congregation was on Tuesday; everything as usual, except that the bar does not open until 11 a.m. (formerly 10.30), and the debate goes on until 12.30 (formerly 12.15). I am told that there was a minor scene outside one of the bars when Felici intervened to prevent some hungry or thirsty Fathers from jumping the gun.

To revert to more serious matters, we were assured once again by the Cardinal Dean that we were not called upon to settle *nova doctrinae capita*, but many of the Fathers have difficulty in seeing how they can fail to do so when they vote on the controversial sections dealing with the sacramentality of the episcopate and collegiality. The Pope himself, in his opening address, said once again that it was for this Council to settle the position of the episcopate as Vatican I had settled the position of the Supreme Pontiff, and unless my ears deceived me, he used the expression *dirimere controversias*. Meanwhile, we Periti have been solemnly warned, in a printed instruction (in Latin and the four main European languages, in case we are unused to Latin) to avoid forming cliques, or denigrating the Council.

One good feature of the session is that fewer Fathers are claiming the right to speak on the various chapters; perhaps because, under the new rule, they have to apply (with a typed copy of the proposed speech) five days in advance, or else produce evidence that seventy Fathers support their claim, Anyway, the debate on the new chapter VII *De Ecclesia, De indole eschatologica vocationis nostrae ac de nostra unione cum Ecclesia coelesti* was completed early in the second General Congregation (Wednesday) and the debate on chapter VIII, *De Beata Maria Virgine Deipara in mysterio Christi et Ecclesiae* had used up the listed speakers by the end of Thursday morning.

This morning (Friday) Frings claimed the seventy-backers right to speak on chapter VII, and Alfrink and Castan did the same in regard to chapter VIII, but we were then able to move on to the new schema *De Pastorali Episcoporum munere in Ecclesia*, which is the revised version of *De Episcopis et Dioecesium regimine* and incorporates the schema *De cura animarum* and has to be debated in respect of the new material, but only that.

Bishop Foley made his maiden speech on *De cura animarum*. Butler had spoken earlier in the week on *De Ecclesia*. At the present rate, we might well finish the present schema at next Monday's Congregation. But there is a great deal of voting to be done on *De Ecclesia*, especially chapter III, for which no less than thirty-nine revised sections have to be voted. The voting itself does not hold up things much (a minute or two to announce each vote and less than that to publish the result), but whenever there is a complicated issue to be voted, someone has to read out a "relatio", and the printed relationes on chapter III, distributed this morning and to be read out on Monday, run to thirty-two pages of print, large pages at that. So, on second thoughts, we are perhaps not likely to finish with *De Pastorali Episcoporum munere* on Monday; there will be little time left for speeches.

On Tuesday afternoon, I went out again to Palazzola with Archbishop Grimshaw (he lives in our flat and has given me a more or less permanent invitation). My mailed schemata arrived on Wednesday, so I stayed at home on the next two afternoons to do some homework; but this afternoon (Friday) I had another trip to the villa. We went out at 3 p.m. and were back at 6.15, which leaves a fair amount of time for work before supper at 8 p.m. Tomorrow is our day off, and many of us are going out to the villa for lunch. It is the only way of getting some really fresh air. One oozes continually in Urbe.

That, I think is about all there is to record for this first week of the session. The authorities still hope that it may be possible to finish the Council this session, and we are certainly making much faster progress. But there might well be a protracted debate on *De Revelatione*, and especially on *De Ecclesia in Mundo huius Temporis*, which would not give time enough to revise such documents and vote them through in their revised form.

All good wishes to all the brethren,
Yours sincerely,
L.LMcReavy

Saturday morning.

It is difficult to realize that I have been away. My window is only about 20 feet above the Montoro street level and life down below is exactly as I left it, people, sounds and activities. The kids are still playing cowboys and Indians, there are constant calls for "Claudio!", and the deaf-mute from the house over the way keeps making the same animal noises.

Hans Küng sat next to me in our tribune the other morning and seemed more subdued. I asked him whether his summer break had been as hectic as last year. He said he still had too much work, but had managed to have a holiday at his Swiss home, Lucerne. He had a wry look when the announcement was made about Periti refraining from forming cliques among the Fathers, and airing their views about the Council to the Press.

P.S. Please ask Laurence to deal with my correspondence as he did last year.

* * *

On Sunday, September 20 L.L. McReavy spent the morning working on conciliar texts. In the afternoon he went to the Villa Pamphili to watch cricket between touring Australian amateurs and the Roman Sports Association. News arrived of the death in England of Monsignor Lamb, Vice-Rector of the Beda College.

After lunch, on Monday he did a preliminary sketch of the church of San Giorgio in Velabro which he finished the next day.

In the afternoon of Wednesday, September 23 he made a preliminary sketch of triumph of Apollo Sostenes which he completed the following afternoon.

Letter 22

The English College, Rome
September 26th 1964

Dear Monsignor,

Today is Saturday, end of the second week of the session, and our day off when we all feel like kids who have been let out of school. In a few moments, at 11 a.m., I shall be going out to the Villa for lunch, and returning about 5 p.m. when I hope to be able to finish this letter.

The pace of the Council is hotting up considerably. On Monday, while the debate on the Pastoral Function of Bishops continued, the Fathers began voting on the famous chapter III of *De Ecclesia,* on which there are thirty-nine sections to be individually voted, and there were frequent and urgent invitations to them to stay in their seats, which, in general, have been well obeyed, at least until the morning's quota of votes have been taken, when there is a general exodus towards the bars and the aisles.

In view of the importance of the issues to be decided, there were four long "Relationes", 32 pages in all, given by Franic (Zagreb), Konig (Vienna) and Parente (Holy Office, but speaking, so he insisted, as Titular Archbishop of Thebais). Franic put the case against collegiality and Parente the case for it. Henriquez explained the proposals concerning priests and deacons, especially deacons. The result was that there was only time for six speakers on the schema being debated.

On the Tuesday, however, we got through the remainder of those who had given due notice, and, apart from two Fathers who invoked the seventy-backers rule next day, that was the end of the *disceptatio De Episcopis*. We also had time for De Smedt's *relatio* (a carefully prepared effort) on the *Declaratio de Libertate Religiosa*, originally a chapter of the Constitution *De Ecclesia*, which, like the chapter *De Iudaeis*, had been left undebated at the end of last session. (I am wrong it was given on the Wednesday morning).

Wednesday's debate on Religious Freedom was easily the best of the present session. Nearly all the big guns were in action, Ruffini (captiously critical), Quiroga (almost unintelligible in his enunciation), Léger (gravely earnest and firmly pro), Cushing (a market-place oration which at first amused many by its unusual tone but eventually captured attention by its patent sincerity), Bueno of Seville (cautiously favourable), Meyer of Chicago, "nomine fere omnium episcoporum Statuum Foederatorum" (declaratio ut tota accipienda, and necessary if any good is to come from the Council), Ritter of St Louis (cut out the controversial reasons and simply publish the declaration), Henriquez of Venezuela, for 58 Latin American Bishops, warmly favourable, as long as it is not taken as approval of improper proselytism, Ottaviani (critical of the reasoning), Cekada of Skoplje (mindful of the consequences of the religious intolerance of Nazism and Communism).

I should also have mentioned that the morning began with a unique ceremony. The Pope walked humbly up Saint Peter's carrying in his own hands the heavy reliquary containing the head of Saint Andrew which, as Cardinal Konig explained in his address, was to be restored to the Orthodox Church of Patras in fulfilment of a promise made by Pius II when it was brought from Patras for safe-keeping, and which Cardinal Bea is at this moment taking to Patras (I went to the airport this morning with Bishop Dwyer, homing for the weekend to bury Mgr Dinn, and noticed that the papal flag was flying next to the Italian).

Thursday was not nearly so interesting, though there were a few good speeches; too many took too long to make a few pettyfogging points. The main interest was in the results of the voting on chapter III *De Ecclesia*. We had already had the really important votes on the Tuesday and Wednesday mornings, when the sections establishing the principle of collegiality had been voted by a large majority. Vote n. 13, that the Ordo Episcoporum, which succeeds to the college of Apostles, "una cum Capite suo Romano Pontifice, et numquam sine hoc capite, subiectum quoque supremae ac plenae potestatis in universam Ecclesiam existit, quae quidem potestas independenter a Romano Pontifice exerceri nequit", was carried by 1927 to 292, and the subsequent votes on the consequences of this principle followed more or less the same pattern.

What amused me was that when, on Friday, they came to vote on certain sections about the infallibility of the Pope and the Church, which were more or less verbatim quotations from the de fide definitions of Vatican I, there were still anything up to 40 who were voting *non placet*. It could mean that they did not think the wording was strong enough but I wondered whether they realised that they were dealing with defined doctrine. And in practically every ballot, there was one Bishop who voted *placet iuxta modum*, notwithstanding constant warnings from the Secretary General that a vote iuxta modum was invalid except in a vote "de integro capite". On the few occasions when he did not have to end his reading of the results with "Placet iuxta modum, ergo nullum, unum", we could only conclude that the modist was in the bar or saying his office in the aisle.

On Friday, Bishop Dwyer was due to speak for England on Religious Liberty (we had had the speech at our domestic conciliar meeting on the Thursday evening at the college and it promised well), but they had to curtail the debate at the end of Friday morning to enable Cardinal Bea to give his relatio on *De Iudaeis* before leaving for Patras, and Dwyer was among the few who were axed when the Moderators proposed the closure (which, as always, was approved "surgendo" by the vast majority). However, the present plan is that Heenan will give the speech on Monday, by invoking the 70-backer rule. I fancy that Peter Simple's "Rentacrowd" must be operating in Rome, because there seems to be no difficulty in finding the required number of backers.

Anyway, we ought to spend most of Monday morning on *De Iudaeis* and, at the present rate, finish it on Wednesday at the latest. We then pass on to *De Divina Revelatione*, the first complete new schema of this session. To judge from the dates fixed by the Moderators for the sending in of summaries of intended speeches on this and the other remaining schemata, they have allotted a maximum of 5 days to *De Revelatione*, which is to be followed by *De Apostolatu Laicorum* (3 days) , *De Ecclesia in Mundo Hodierno* (5 days), and then one day each for the schemata which have been reduced to propositions, in the following order: *De Ecclesiis Orientalibus, De Activitate Missionali, De Sacerdotibus, De Religiosis, De Matrimonii Sacramento, De Institutione Sacerdotali, De Scholis Catholicis.*

If they propose the closure (hitherto always abundantly approved by the Fathers) in time to keep every debate to this schedule, the last of the schemata should have been debated by October 21st at the latest.

Meanwhile, each schema, after being debated, will be going back to the appropriate Commission for revision in line with the suggestions of the Fathers and being returned to the Aula for approval by the vote of the Fathers. In the final vote on each revised schema, they can vote *placet, non placet*, or *placet iuxta modum*. If in no case the sum of *non placets* and *placets iuxta modum* exceeds one third of the total, it should be possible to conclude the Council by the date assigned for the end of the session; so too, if only one or two of the schemata fail to secure a two-thirds majority at the first voting. Hitherto the *non placets* have never amounted to much, so it would seem that everything depends on how many of the Fathers append modi to their final vote on the various schemata when they are returned in revised form by the Commissions. However, it begins to seem really possible that the Pope's declared desire to finish the Council this session will be fulfilled.

Apart from my day off at the villa (depart 11 a.m., return 6 p.m.) I have had no time this week for la dolce vita. I have taken time off after lunch to do a couple of sketches in the vicinity of the College, but only by foregoing the siesta. Every evening is required in order to keep abreast of the constantly changing schemata, and by "keeping abreast" I do not mean thorough study. I cannot see how anyone can find time for that. And the pressure is more likely to be increased than relaxed.

Two Bishops died the other day, Gawlina (formerly with the Poles in exile), and De Nigris of Propaganda. Gawlina had spoken a couple of days before in Saint Peter's. It is to be hoped that the pressure does not increase the mortality rate.

Best wishes to all the brethren,
Yours sincerely,
L.LMcReavy

* * *

On Monday, September 28, heavy rain caused a traffic jam after the General Congregation so that the coach did not reach the College until 1.25 p.m. The following afternoon L.L. McReavy made a preliminary sketch of the church of San Nicola in Carcere which he completed the following afternoon. On Saturday and Sunday afternoon he went to the Villa Pamphili to watch cricket knock-out competition.

Letter 23

The English College, Rome
October 4th 1964

Dear Monsignor,

It is Sunday morning, 8.30 a.m., and I have just had a brief chat with McConnell, Martin and Cookson, who arrived yesterday afternoon: I also spotted McAndrew. The house has now filled up, the students at the Villa having returned on Friday. The weather remains hot, yesterday cloudy with scirocco and occasional drops of rain, today back to the unbroken blue.

At the Council, the pace continues to be hot. Last Monday morning, before we could begin the debate on the Declaration on Jews and non-Christians, we had to listen to four speakers who claimed the right (seventy supporters) to resume Religious Liberty, including Archbishop Heenan. He spoke very well, pragmatically rather than theologically, as is his wont, but with a clear ringing voice and in short staccato sentences which all could easily follow. He summarized our religious history since the Reformation, showed how much better the present regime of religious liberty worked, admitted the risks, but preferred them to the *sequelae funestae* that almost inevitably follow any form of State interference in religious matters. He received one of the few bursts of applause that have occurred so far in this sober session.

The rest of the morning was devoted to *De Iudaeis* and the level of the speeches was in general high, Lienart leading off with an approving but constructively critical speech. But then immediately came the Arab Cardinal Tappouni with a flat negative in the name of all the Oriental Patriarchs. Their opposition, he said, was not in any way against the Jewish religion, or even the Jewish race; they themselves were Semites, but this declaration would raise grave obstacles to their pastoral work, and he begged "ut simpliciter ab actis deleatur".

Frings wanted the earlier text restored. Ruffini said he wouldn't dare to say no to this panegyric, or blame the Jews for the crucifixion, but "obtusi sunt sensus eorum usque nunc", their Talmud is pretty beastly about us, they support the Freemasons, and it is about time they were as charitable to us as we propose to be to them, and as some of us were to them during the war.

For Lercaro the declaration was the fruit of the fuller knowledge which the Church today had of herself; for Léger it was a necessary act of the renovated Church which has begun to enter into dialogue with the world. The American Cardinals were of course warmly in favour, Cushing, in another market-place harangue, wanting the declaration to be less timid, Meyer preferring the earlier text, Ritter wanting more stress on our common patrimony and no reference to conversion of the Jews in particular. The debate continued right through the long Tuesday morning, but was less interesting because of the inevitable repetition, though one Father came close to anti-Chalcedonian heresy by suggesting that the term "deicide" could not be used theologically of the crucifixion. Heenan wanted the earlier text; all the world had read it and changes were likely to be interpreted as a change of heart for the worse. A lonely voice from Syria (Tawil) wanted neither; what about the millions of Arabs who had been driven from their homes in Palestine by those who were here being addressed with honour.

On Wednesday we moved on to the Constitution *De Divina Revelatione*, a revised version of the *De Fontibus Revelationis* which was thrown out in the first session. Franic began with a Relatio on behalf of the minority of the Commission, claiming that the Church had committed herself since Trent to the doctrine that Tradition was a fons constitutivus (not merely *interpretativus*) of divine revelation, distinct from and independent of Scripture, and therefore that the schema could not leave it an open question. He received a fair amount of support in the ensuing debate, notably from Ruffini ("plane consentio cum minoritati"), and from others who urged that at least the words of Vatican I, quoting Trent, "in libris scriptis et sine scripto traditis" should be repeated. The debate continued through the Thursday without any intervention from our Hierarchy. Indeed, it was not until the Thursday evening that the subject was even raised in our private Conciliar meeting at the College, when Charles Davis was called upon to explain the schema to us and what all the shindy was about. He did it very well, but it was apparently not felt that we had any worthwhile contribution to make, because no intervention was planned.[8]

Our Bishops are much more interested in the schema *De Ecclesia in Mundo Hodierno* which is looming up and is likely to lead to a head-on clash, especially in regard to the way in which Häring (Secretary of the Commission) has dealt, or failed to deal, with the hot question of contraception. Since this schema has never previously been presented in Aula, it will first have to undergo a debate in genere, after which there will be a vote as to whether it is acceptable as a basis for detailed discussion. It seems at the moment quite possible that it will be rejected as unacceptable. In which case, the Pope's dream of finishing the Council this session is unlikely to be realized.

On Friday, the debate continued on chapters I and II of *De Revelatione*, and Butler intervened (a solitary English voice, and very English at that) with a typical speech, most of it off-the-cuff and referring expressly to what had been said that morning, in which he pointed out that it is only in recent years that scriptural exegesis has become dynamic, as distinct from static, and has begun to find evidence in Scripture for much that was formerly thought to be known only from unwritten tradition. Hence the Magisterium need not be taken to mean that certain revealed truths were not contained in Scripture, but only that they were not clearly contained in Scripture as then understood.

We then moved on to chapter III and had time for the usual critical speech from Ruffini and one from Konig, claiming that modern Oriental research had proved conclusively that the historical knowledge of the sacred writers was sometimes limited and defective. A frank admission of

[8] A fuller account of this meeting is given in his Diary: "Thursday, October 1. Conciliar meeting of Hierarchy. Father Davis reported on the revised schema *De Revelatione*. Monsignor Worlock on the schema *De Ecclesia in Mundo Huius Temporis*. Bishop Pearson on the reaction of National Board of Catholic Women to reports of change in Church's doctrine on Contraception. According to Worlock, the final vote of the Commission was that the schema should include the Church's doctrine on Contraception. It is not in the schema".

this would overcome many difficulties and enable the authority of Scripture to be better defended.

That is the position up to date. Yesterday, Saturday, I worked all the morning, but went up to Villa Pamphili in the afternoon to watch a cricket match between an embassy team (which eliminated the College team in the last round) and the Roman Australians. It was worth it, if only because the air up there was so different from hot-humid atmosphere down here. It was positively cool. I am tempted to go up there again this afternoon (Sunday) for the final, after which Bishop Tickle is to present the cup, but may go out instead to the Coelian to finish a sketch of Saints John and Paul, of which I did the pencil outline the other day. This has become my common practice in the afternoons. Instead of having a siesta, or even going up to the Common Room for coffee and liqueurs, I go out immediately after dinner. One day, it will be to find a suitable subject for a water-colour and to do the pencil outline, and the next day to do the painting. So far, I have done about six, which accounts for 12 of my afternoons. I get back in time for tea, more or less, and feel much fresher for work in the evening than if I had snoozed. Moreover, I sleep better at night. What with the racket in the Montoro, sleep is quite a problem. There is a gambling den in the Monserrato, opposite the College, and some of the patrons park their cars in the Montoro. They break up between 2 and 2.30 in the morning, hold a post-mortem under my window "alta voce", practise banging their car doors to make sure that the final big bang will rouse everyone in the vicinity, rev-up a few times to ensure that they will be able to race off at full throttle. This is a change from last year, when Archbishop Murphy maintained that a lorry used to dump outside his window, at 2 a.m, a load of gravel which had always mysteriously disappeared by the time he rose at six.

Omnia faustissima omnibus
L.LMcReavy

P.S. The other day, during the debate *De Iudaeis*, Felici intervened to make an announcement "omnibus Patribus, non tantum iis qui sedibus suis permanserunt, sed etiam iis qui sunt in diaspora."

* * *

After lunch on Wednesday October 9 L.L. McReavy made a sketch of the church of Saints John and Paul. As he mentions in his letter the change in weather meant that he was unable to make his afternoon painting excursions.

On Thursday evening he attended a Conciliar meeting of Hierarchy in the College about the schema *De Ecclesia in Mundo Huius Temporis*.

Letter 24

The English College, Rome
Friday, October 9th 1964, 1 p.m.

Dear Monsignor,

We have just returned from the last General Congregation of the fourth week. There is a scirocco, cloudy with sunny periods and occasional rain. Not much opportunity for painting excursions in the afternoons.

The interest this week has been more in the rumours as to what is happening in the background than in the debate in Saint Peter's. Keeping rigidly to the schedule *implied* in the list of dates given earlier in the session for the sending in of summaries of intended speeches (I say *implied*, because we have never been officially informed of any schedule), the debate on Divine Revelation was allowed to run on until a quarter of an hour from the end of Tuesday's General Congregation, when Cardinal Cento was called upon to introduce the schema *De Apostolatu Laicorum*.

At the beginning of that morning, Felici had announced that the Pope wanted some Patres "partem habere" in the short discussion which will precede the voting on *De Sacerdotibus*, when that Series of Proposition comes up. If mere presence at the discussion is meant, it would seem a mere gesture.

Nevertheless, there must have been such a rush of Bishops to the secretariate table to suggest names, that Felici had to intervene again and declare the list closed, "otherwise even this vast basilica would be inundated". Butler, in one of the last speeches of the morning, made a plea for a distinction to be drawn between an exegete's duty "sub luce fidei", certain in his own mind of the divine inspiration of the Sacred Books, with all that this entails, and his duty as a scholar to investigate all questions " ex praeambulo fidei", in which he should be free to discuss all possibilities, e.g. allowing for Midrashim in the New as well as in the Old Testament: some would abuse this liberty, but the risk must be taken.

The rest of the week, Wednesday to Friday, has been devoted to *De Apostolatu Laicorum*. The motion as to whether the Fathers accepted the schema as a basis for further discussion was put to the vote after only four had discussed its merits in genere, a good example of the hustle that has characterized all this session.

The motion was carried quasi-unanimously "surgendo", but we had to spend the rest of the morning listening to general judgements, because all who had got their names down for that morning had assumed that it would be entirely taken up by the general debate. By the end of the Thursday morning, all the worthwhile points had already been made and underlined, but on we plugged this morning to the bitter end, presumably because a minimum of three days had been allotted to this schema and no arrangements had been made for the introduction of the next. Of this, more below.

The next, according to the "summaries" schedule, is *De Ecclesia in Mundo Huius Temporis*, the only remaining schema entitled to a full-scale debate, and it is largely this much-awaited event that has been responsible for most of the week's gossip. The text has had a poor reception at least from the Fathers and Periti whom I regularly meet. The first three chapters (*De integra hominis vocatione; Ecclesia Dei hominumque servitio dedita; De ratione christianorum se gerendi in mundo in quo vivunt*) lay down some fine, or fine-sounding, principles about which there is not likely to be much dispute.

It is the fourth chapter (*De praecipuis muneribus a christianis nostrae aetatis implendis*), or rather those sections of it which purport to deal with the main questions on which the world is expecting the Council to pronounce (birth-control, the Pill and the Bomb) that have caused dismay. On nuclear war, it says little more than that it is a wicked thing which should never be allowed to happen; which, in the sense in which all would accept it, is a platitude, and, in the sense in which the unilateralists will interpret it, is an unproved assertion.

On marriage it says that it is not a mere instrument of procreation, but should be a union of love; this love, however, is of such a kind that marriage is of its nature ordinated to the procreation and education of offspring. These are unexceptionable statements. The trouble is that they can be accepted, not only by those who hold to the doctrine solemnly proclaimed in *Casti connubii*, but also by those who, like Janssens and Häring (in their reported private statements) are prepared to allow any form of contraception (pills, condoms, diaphragms) which is compatible with conjugal love and a *general* orientation of married life to procreation and education. Indeed, it is generally held to have been drafted by Häring (Secretary of the Commission) in this form, precisely in order to bring the Church's doctrine into line with Lambeth, or at least to enable the Lambeth line to be followed, tutta conscientia, by such Catholics as want it. Incidentally, there is not a word about the Pill; a silence which can be defended on the ground that the Fathers lack the factual information necessary to a comprehensive judgement, but which is likely to be interpreted as the green light for any of its uses. However, the rumour is still current in fairly reliable circles that the Pope intends to deal with the Pill in a pontifical document.

I do not know what proportion of the Fathers would be willing to accept the schema as a basis for detailed discussion, but I know of quite a number who are opposed to its being brought into the Aula even for general debate, because the Robertsites might leap into action and their advanced views would be headlined in the world's press as representative of the feeling of the Council. These Fathers are therefore hoping that it will not even be introduced until it has been completely re-written.

If certain reports are true, it does not represent the mind of the Commission on the controversial points, but was railroaded by Häring, notwithstanding certain instructions given to him by majority vote of the Commission. What is certain is that it is a boiled down version of a longer document which spoke briefly but without ambiguity on contraception and nuclear weapons. Last week, a brochure of 63 pages, entitled "Adnexa", but in fact a fuller and more explicit version of the points made in the schema (43 pp), was distributed to us in the Aula. At first, Felici described it as a purely private document, but he corrected himself later at the request of the Moderators, explaining that it had been prepared by the joint-commission under instructions from the Coordinating Commission, and therefore could not be described as a private document, even though it was not to be debated in the Aula. It was meant, he said, to be a key to the minds of the joint-commission responsible for the schema. The significant thing is that, on the subject of contraception, it summarizes the doctrine of Casti connubii, to which it gives a footnote reference, and says that such a manner of acting cannot be reconciled with the integrity of conjugal love. The whole passage, while taking a positive view of marriage and conjugal love, is significantly different from the ambiguous final version. If the former represents the mind of the joint-commission, the question is bound to be asked how the latter emerged as the authentic text for debate.

On Thursday morning, I was told that *De Mundo Hodierno* had been the main issue the previous evening at a Vatican meeting called by the Pope to decide whether the Council could be finished this session, or whether it would be necessary to have a short session sometime next year. Apparently some were opposed to its being even introduced until it had been completely rewritten, whereas some wanted it introduced, though they would agree to the withdrawal of the sections on married life and on peace and war.

This morning, I learnt in our tribune that, according to the Superior General of the La Salette Congregation, the schema was being hurriedly rewritten and the Moderators had been instructed to keep the Lay Apostolate debate going until it was ready. This report gained verisimilitude at the end of the morning when the Moderators failed to propose the closure of the Lay Apostolate debate, which had not only exhausted the three days allotted (?) to it, but had patently run out of fresh ideas, and, according to all precedents, should have been brought to a close. Certainly, if the debate is allowed to drag on next Monday, it will be clear evidence that something is being done to *De Mundo Hodierno*.

Incidentally, Bishop Carli of Segni, indefatigable and voluble opponent of episcopal collegiality, has apparently not yet given up hope. He is said to have lodged a formal charge of nullity against the overwhelming vote of the Fathers, on the ground that the vote on chapter III, *De Ecclesia*, was taken in two parts (by consent of the Fathers), whereas, according to the rules, there should have been a vote "de integro capite". There should be a sorting office for behind-the-scenes rumours. It is difficult to keep abreast of them. A rumour which I was able to confirm is that the Pope has decided himself to settle the extra-Conciliar controversy as to whether and how far the Church should modify her requirements in regard to mixed marriages. He ordered Felici to set up a small Commission to report on it and Felici named my old Louvain pal, Willy Onclin, to act as Secretary. I met Onclin in the bar and he told me it was true. He admitted that Jeger of Paderborn and Fulton Sheen were among the few members so far named, but that he had no one from Great Britain. He agreed with me that our Bishops should be represented, but it was not for him to choose the members. Our Bishops are certainly anxious to have a say. They don't trust the Dutch.

Had I time, this sort of Chronicle could go on indefinitely. But there is always a pile of work to do.

With good wishes to all my faithful readers.
Yours sincerely,
L.LMcReavy

* * *

The weather in the interval between letters was unsettled with periods of heavy rain. L.L.McReavy records that he was reduced to making a "sketch of the Via Appia Antica from a photo". He spent the wet weekend of October 24-25 working: "Wrote animadversions on *De Ministerio et Vita Sacerdotalis* and delivered them by hand at Congregation of Council. Felt giddy on way up to tea, and again on Monday at Mass. Exhausted".

Letter 25

The English College, Rome
Sunday, October 25th 1964

Dear Monsignor,

It has been an exciting week, relatively speaking, largely because on Tuesday the Fathers moved on from *De Ecclesiis Orientalibus* to *De Ecclesia in Mundo Huius Temporis*, which, from the moral point of view, is as controversial a document as *De Fontibus* and *De Ecclesia* from the dogmatic.

Over the weekend, all the Fathers had received a brochure through the post, signed by notable laymen of various countries, in French and English, urging them to take the liberal line on contraception. If, as seems likely from the wording, it had been written by a theologian, and that theologian were one of the Periti, it was a cute way round the prohibition that the Periti must refrain from lobbying. It is not however certain now that the Fathers will be called to pronounce on this question, for a reason that emerged later in the week.

The schema was introduced with considerable adroitness by Bishop Guano of Leghorn, clearly a coming man. He admitted its deficiencies, but pleaded that the Commission had done its best in the relatively brief time available, bearing in mind that it was an entirely new kind of Conciliar document. It could be perfected by the animadversions of the Fathers, but should at least be accepted as a basis of discussion.

Our English Bishops, on the whole, were not of this opinion, feeling that it ought first to be re-drafted by a new team, well briefed on all points of fact by the best available experts. But, when the debate "in genere" (to decide acceptability) began, it soon became evident that the majority, however critical of certain features of the schema, preferred to accept it as a basis for discussion rather than postpone it to the Greek Kalends. When the list of speakers was read out on the first day, there was such a tally of big names (Lienart, Spellman, Ruffini, Lercaro, Léger, Döpfner, Meyer, Silva Henriquez, Suenens, Ottaviani, Bea, Maximus IV) that there was a general and audible stir all round the Aula; so much so that Felici interrupted his reading of the list to say in a tone of feigned puzzlement: "Quare "I rumori', Venerabiles Fratres?" (There is a municipal campaign in Rome at the moment against "rumori", sc. noises of every kind). Of the first eight in the above list (which was all we had time for on the first morning), all except Ruffini indicated that they were satisfied with the schema as a basis for discussion. Ruffini, who is so querulous and niggling as to be worth votes to the other side, found it repetitious, ambiguous and full of "sententiae quae aut non sunt rectae, aut eas non intelligo" (with all which criticisms I tend to agree); but when he proceeded to give examples, he was ruled out of order by Moderator Döpfner and couldn't recover his balance. The following day, Ottaviani did not turn up, but the three cardinals who opened the debate (Landazzuri-Ricketts, Suenens and Bea) all accepted the schema in genere; so too the majority of the less empurpled Fathers who followed them. Conway of Armagh made a weighty speech, criticizing the timidity and ambivalence of the schema, and expressing the hope that, after it had been discussed in detail, it would be thoroughly revised.

Thursday was a big day for us English. Heenan began the morning with the finest speech he has yet made, judged purely from the oratorical point of view. Indeed, many round me were of the opinion that it was the best speech yet delivered at the Council, and it was clear from the next day's papers that many journalists shared this opinion. It had all the tricks of the public speaker's trade, several times moving the Fathers to laughter, and receiving at the end a loud burst of applause. But there was by no means the same agreement as to its content. Most of those who knew about the Häring-Heenan clash in the newspapers after the Hierarchy's response to Roberts, interpreted his remarks about a few Periti usurping the functions of the episcopate as prompted by personal animosity to Häring, architect of this schema, and felt that this should not be done in a Conciliar speech to which Häring could not reply. (Incidentally, Häring was sitting in the tribune opposite me, next to Claude Leetham, who said to him: "He means you"; to which Häring replied: "Don't I know it"). Others who perhaps were ignorant of the earlier clash felt that an attack on certain unnamed Periti, even though Heenan insisted that they were few, inevitably discredited all.

Others, especially Periti, rallied to the defence of what they conceived to be the function of theologians in the evolution of the Church's doctrine.[9]

A few speeches later, Charue of Namur inserted a brief impromptu rejoinder at the end of his speech and expressed his belief that the Commission had "optimos peritos". At the end of the morning Archbishop Beck's turn came and he used it very well, avoiding personalities, accepting the schema for discussion, but nevertheless alerting the Fathers to the undoubted fact that chapter IV, as it stands, and particularly as it is capable of being interpreted, raises the whole issue of the magisterium, as exercised in *Castii Connubii*. Father Francis Connel CSSR, retired professor of moral theology at Catholic University Washington, was sitting next to me and immediately scribbled a note of congratulation which he asked me to give to Beck.

The following morning, Friday, everyone was still talking about the Heenan speech, and the Italian dailies gave it an unusual prominence and full-length treatment, characterizing it as brilliant and commenting on the touches of "humour inglese" which had punctuated it. To our (the Periti's) astonishment, even Felici, who usually refers to us in a tone which implies schoolmasterish disdain, went out of his way to give us a boost.

Announcing that the Commissions were hard at work in order to ensure that some documents would be ready for papal approval in a "Sessio Publica" before we went home, he qualified a reference to the Periti with the clause – "quorum haud pauci bene meriti sunt", which was received with applause. As to the further session for which Heenan had called, he remarked: "alia sessio habebitur cum SS. Dominus eam constituerit". More applause, for which Moderator Döpfner promptly rebuked the assembly. A little later, B. Reetz, Abbot General of the Beuron Congregation, made

[9] The following letter from Father Bernard Häring was sent to Archbishop Heenan at the English College and is dated October 24, 1964:
Your Grace, May I take the liberty of addressing a few lines to you on the subject of your intervention some days ago in the Council debate on schema 13? You spoke your mind firmly and frankly on the schema itself and, as I think I am justified in assuming, on my personal contribution to it. You spoke with some severity. I absolutely recognise your Grace's right to have spoken thus, even on the personal issues involved. You did so from a sense of obligation to the Church, whose humble children and servants we all are. The fact that you expressed sentiments and opinions contrary to mine, the fact that you in a sense took a personal stand against me, is quite secondary. I harbour no resentment or bitterness whatever on that score. In my work for the Council and for the schema 13 in particular I have tried to serve the Church to the best of my abilities. Your Grace, as Archbishop of Westminster and as a Father of the Council, deemed it your duty to criticise my work in no uncertain terms. So be it. It is the service of the Church that counts, and it is the common task of serving her that unites us in the peace of Christ beyond and above our differences, which will, I trust, prove to be of the transient nature. Assuring your Grace of my sincerest goodwill and humbly begging your Grace's blessing, if not as Jacob, then as Esau begged it of Isaac (Gen. 27, 36). I remain, Your Grace's obedient servant in Christ, Bernard Häring.

a witty come-back, evidently written overnight, to the Heenan speech. He spent the first part of his speech explaining why, after certain remarks made yesterday, he was afraid to speak. We had been told that it was a waste of time to seek any expert advice on world problems from people like him who had led a cloistered life, and who, if as simple as doves, were certainly not as cute as serpents. "Sum simplex columba". But he remembered that Gregory the Great had sent Saint Augustine and 40 other monks to turn the Angles into Angels. "Forsitan ii quoque mundum vix cognoverunt". Then he went on to discuss the general merits of the schema in terms which, some thought, added weight to the charge that monks were somewhat remote from the hard realities of life. On this I pass no judgement, since I myself must be numbered among those who have spent their lives sequestered from the world "in seminariis, in domibus religionis, in accademiis".

Half way through the Friday morning, the Moderators called upon the Fathers to vote the closure of the debate in genere, which they promptly did "surgendo", and then, after the Relator (Guano) had had his say, they voted, per schedulas, 1579 to 296, in favour of accepting the schema for detailed discussion. Guano, after defending the Commission and claiming that many expert laymen had been consulted, gave us an interesting and important bit of news, confirming a report made earlier in the summer about which little had been heard since. He said that the Commission had deliberately refrained from going into detail on the more delicate points, because the Holy Father had instituted a study by "docti viri in omni scientia" on these points, "de quibus iudicium sibi reservavit". This has raised some speculation as to whether, when we come to chapter IV, the Fathers will be allowed to debate the question of contraception, and one English Bishop whose intended speech I have had to recast and latinize more than once is beginning to wonder whether all his and my labour will be wasted. Guano also remarked that it would be impossible for the schema to reach definitive approval in this session, and indicated that the Council might issue an interim declaration on peace, hunger, poverty, etc. Some have since commented that, if this is done, the schema may never see the light of day. However, no doubt we shall be wiser by the end of the coming week. Meanwhile, we are grinding along with a somewhat "airy-fairy" discussion of the obscurely pretentious proemium and chapter I.

The weather has been definitely autumnal these last 10 days, with occasional spells of very heavy rain, and yesterday the heating went on in our part of the house. Six of the college students were ordained priest today, none from Ushaw.

I have led a very cloistered life for a few weeks. Last Wednesday evening, I had a very pleasant dinner at the Grand Hotel, with Bishops Grant and Wheeler, as guests of Father Brian Houghton, but otherwise life has been an unbroken round of work. Even so, it is impossible to keep pace with the Council. Six weeks completed and four to go. I shall be relieved when it is all over, provided of course, that the Holy Ghost saves the Church from any grave imprudence. As far as I know, that is not necessarily included in the guarantee of infallibility, especially when it is constantly being asserted that the Fathers are not being asked to define anything infallibly.

All the best to all the brethren, Auguri.
Yours sincerely,
L.LMcReavy

* * *

In his Diary entry for Monday, October 26, L.L.McReavy recorded: "Evening collected my Third Session medal at Santa Marta and booked my return flight to London for Friday, November 20th, 14.25. Still feeling physically and mentally exhausted, and rather wobbly on my feet".

Letter 26

The English College, Rome
October 31st 1964

Dear Monsignor,

Please thank L. Hollis for the latest packet of correspondence, safely received. As you will have gathered from the newspapers, the tension created in the Council by the introduction of the schema *De Ecclesia in Mundo huius Temporis* has been maintained and even increased by this week's debate. It should however be remembered that the journalists tend to concentrate on attacks on established positions, as being more newsworthy, and that there is another side to the picture. Nor should it be imagined that the excitement of a debate of this kind is maintained right through the three hours of each General Congregation.

Indeed, on Monday and Tuesday, when the debate was limited to chapters I to III, it was definitely dull. Speakers were mainly concerned with the schema's imprecise and ambivalent concept of the "world" with which it was seeking to open a dialogue, and with the sense in which the world could be said to have been"consecrated" by the Incarnation. To some the text smacked of platonism or false irenism.

A more concrete and controversial issue was raised by two or three speakers who felt it to be out of keeping with the mind and practice of modern man that ecclesiastical positive laws should be made binding *sub gravi*. The Church must foster true liberty and eschew any compulsion contrary to human dignity. *Plenitudo legis est dilectio*, etc. (O.K., but they had better remember the sharp drop that would probably occur in the Sunday Mass collections.).

Maximus IV extended his strictures even to the common interpretation of divine moral laws. The Commandments should be regarded as ways of beatitude rather than of condemnation, not so much as orders under pain of sin but as counsels of love. (The amount of love pervading this debate is almost embarrassing).

It was on Wednesday that we moved to chapter IV, where all the meat is; but even then, we had to wait for the controversial n. 21, on conjugal fecundity, because the Moderators decided to divide the chapter into parts. Moreover, it seemed at first as though there was to be no debate on n. 21, because Agaganian, in introducing the chapter, said that it was widely felt that a public discussion of certain matters in it would be unseemly and that the Fathers were therefore asked to send their animadversions, cum omni libertate, but in scriptis. The relator (Wright of Pittsburgh) pleaded that it was not the purpose of the chapter to be exhaustive or definitive, but merely to say the first word in the new dialogue with the world.

Wednesday was devoted to the preliminary section on the dignity of the human person and evoked a series of denunciations from India, Africa and the USA against any form of discrimination, colour bar, apartheid, or failure to uphold the dignity and proper function of women in society.

Then, on Thursday, the Relator for the Commission (Dearden of Detroit) introduced n. 21. He emphasized once again that the schema, here as elsewhere, was not meant to lay down detailed rules, but merely to state the general position of the Church on conjugal fecundity. In saying that it was for the spouses themselves to decide, according to their conscience, how many children they should have, did not mean to imply that the method was left entirely to them. They must form their conscience correctly according to the mind of the Church, and refrain therefore from any intervention which interferes with the natural order or is contrary to conjugal love; hence there was no room for subjectivism. The text had avoided all reference to the Pill, because the Pope had wisely reserved judgement on that matter to himself.

The debate on n. 21 was then opened, and, thus far at least, I must confess that the case for the traditional position has been very ineffectively presented. The reason, I think, is largely that the initiative lay with those who questioned it and they had very carefully prepared their attack, whereas the defenders gave the impression of having been taken by surprise.

Ruffini, first speaker, wasted most of his ten minutes in his usual querulous criticisms about defects of clarity and accuracy in the text, and only at the end appealed to *Casti Connubii* and Pius XII's address to midwives as "magisterii vivi et ordinarii Ecclesiae monumenta".

(This surely is the major issue, which no one so far, on either side, has really faced; i.e. whether the absolute condemnation of any directly contraceptive intervention, constantly maintained in the unbroken Christian tradition to which *Casti Connubii* appealed, and "proclaimed anew," by Pius XI "as spokesman for the divine ambassadorship of the Church" in the field of Christian morals, is part of the ordinary and universal magisterium of the Church, and, as such, divinely guaranteed.

If I remember rightly, not one of those who have called for a re-examination of the traditional doctrine or for its revision have so much as mentioned *Casti Connubii* or the unbroken tradition which it claimed to declare, much less confronted frankly the difficulty which it raises; their tactic is apparently to sidestep it. Nor has any of the defenders of the traditional position challenged its critics to meet and answer this difficulty. Unprepared perhaps for the evasive tactic, they have done no more than appeal, per transennam, to the magisterium).

But to continue. The attack was opened by Léger, of Montreal, who followed after Ruffini. He began by referring to the universal anxieties and doubts among the faithful, the difficulties they face and their dissatisfaction with the answers hitherto given. Many hold, he said, that the difficulties are due to insufficiency of the traditional doctrine, influenced by a pessimistic philosophy of sex. They (the tactic of reported opinions is favoured by the attackers) want the *fines matrimonii* revised. This could opportunely be done by declaring that the fecundity-end belongs to the whole course of married life rather than to each individual act of intercourse. Human love should be recognized as a true *finis constitutivus*, good and holy in itself, with its own exigencies and *its own proper laws*, and that it remains a *finis ipsius operis* even when the act is not ordered to procreation. (This of course is familiar stuff; but the odd thing is the shyness shown in drawing the conclusion, admitted in private by adherents of this school of thought, that love justifies condomistic intercourse when the parties have a sufficient reason for evading procreation. The tactic seems to be to get the fine-sounding premisses accepted, and leave the conclusion to emerge gradually and without shock).

Then came the adroit Suenens, anxious to have a foot with the progressives on the far bank, but careful not to burn his bridges. The first job of the special Commission, in collaboration with the conciliar Commission, should be to enquire whether all aspects have been sufficiently considered. The Church could never withdraw a doctrine which she has authentically taught, but she sought continually to bring forth *nova et vetera*. We may not yet have achieved the perfect equilibrium between "crescite etc" and "sint duo in carne una". The Council must have regard to the interpersonal communion and the population explosion, must be faithful to the doctrine of the Church and also to the exigencies of conjugal love, must examine whether the classic doctrine has taken enough account of modern discoveries about the complexity of nature, must follow the progress of science, avoid a new Galileo, pursue truth and submit to the judgement of the magisterium; finally, (with a ringing voice) "veritas tota et vitalis liberabit vos".

Maximus IV was less cautious, though even he tended to proceed by way of question rather than statement. Did God really will the impasse in which the population explosion condemns millions to misery? Should not the official line be revised in the light of modern findings? The "finalité du marriage" (he speaks always in French) should not be split into primary and secondary. Is not the official position due in part to outdated ideas of manicheistic celibates? Is the biological correctness of acts the only rule? etc.

Botero of Columbia stood up for tradition. We cannot deny the practical difficulties entailed by the Church's doctrine. But it is not enough simply to refer the problem to experts, much less leave it to the consciences of spouses, when we already have such an abundant doctrine from recent Popes (*Casti Connubii*, and the Midwives); and it is regrettable that many proceed on the principle that sexual appetite cannot be controlled (cf. e contra S. Paul). A completely new text should replace n. 21.

Staverman (a Dutch Vicar Apostolic in Indonesia) was the most outspoken of the progressives. The text is good and liberating. Love is rightly given first place as the command that should direct all things, and "maximi momenti sunt etiam quae *non* dicuntur". It is rightly silent about Natural Law and about the biological end of the conjugal act. But it is defective in beginning with marriage as an immutable institution. All human reality is historical and evolving. Marriage belongs to the historicity of the human race and is evolving to an ever more authentic form. The Church should rejoice in this evolution and should be grateful for the wise counsel contained in the brochure signed by laymen of many countries and recently mailed to all the Fathers.

Friday began with Alfrink, à la Suenens: As all priests know, many well intentioned Catholics are alienated from the Church by the difficulties arising from the traditional doctrine which they cannot obey without detriment to the *bona matrimonii*. The Church cannot change the divine law of which she has custody. Nor can social changes alter it. Nor can she yield to situational ethics. She must always hold that sacrifice is of the essence of the Christian life. *Attamen*, it is not only Cross but also resurrection.

Conflicts often arise between the *valor procreationis* and the *valor educationis*, when conjugal love needs to be fostered by carnal congress and the choice is limited to continence, or "exclusio proles in hoc concreto actu". If the latter is intrinsically evil, the Church must forbid it. But in view of the growing distinction between biological sex and human sex, an honest doubt arises about the arguments advanced. Too premature a solution must be avoided. The Church must be solicitous for the divine law, but also for the human values.

Ottaviani was then called and confessed that he had not expected to be called until the following day and could only offer a few off-the-cuff comments. The scriptural command "crescite" is not contradicted by "duo in carne una", as other texts show. He himself was the 11th of 12 children of a worker and they had never had occasion to doubt divine providence. Lilies of the field, etc. (All true and very touching, but not a very complete answer). He ended with the remark "Nunc in dubium vocatur quod Ecclesia per saecula docuit".

Cardinal Browne, in his usual mournful tone, was more comprehensive but had no bite. It is certain from the magisterium that the *finis primarius operis* is procreation and education of offspring, and that the secondary end is etc. As to this love business, we must distinguish between amor amicitiae (disinterested) and amor concupiscentiae (self-interested). The love that is required for the bona matrimonii is amor coniugalis amicitiae ad invicem. (Some more unexciting textbook stuff, and then —). There can be no doubt about all these points because they belong to the treasury of all theologians and are clearly contained in Leo's XIII's *Arcanum*, Pius XI's *Casti Connubii* and Pius XII's Midwives etc.

Reuss (Germany) then resumed the attack, claiming the support of 140 Fathers. Human sexuality differs not merely biologically from all non-human sexuality. It connotes a specific community of persons and as such not merely demands conjugal love, but has it for foundation. In this path, spouses must realise that they are called ad prolem and must not avoid it egoistically. (Note once again, that the conclusion is not drawn). The schema is to be praised for speaking cautiously.

Del Campo (Spain) seemed not to have realised the tactic. He remarked, somewhat ingenuously, that, in n. 21, the value of conjugal love is so extolled that the simple reader will be led to think it the primum bonum, et cardo, to which all else in marriage is subject. A beautiful idea (he exclaimed) but is it true? Love is important, but we must keep the correct hierarchy of values. It is the ordinary motive of matrimonium in fieri, but it is not the end or sole good of matrimonial life. The text is too generic and can give rise to confusion and subjectivism. It says nothing about the objective end derived from the natural ordination of the generative faculty. The traditional doctrine should be reaffirmed, and *Casti Connubii* quoted.

Hervas from Spain made a balanced plea for a more positive approach to fecundity, less stress on the obstacles and more on faith in divine providence, on the merits of those who unselfishly devote themselves to raising a large family, etc; and then abruptly the debate was brought to an end, prematurely, in the opinion of many Fathers who remained seated when the assembly was asked to indicate "surgendo" whether they had had enough (a majority always have had enough). Two or three English Bishops who had put their names in were thus prevented from speaking, but I was glad to learn in the bus on the way home that Monsignor Worlock (indefatigable and efficient secretary to the Hierarchy) had already collected the seventy names required to enable two of them make their intervention when the Council resumes on Wednesday. I hope others are busy elsewhere engaging the services of "Rentacrowd".

The attack has had a pretty full run, but the case for the defence has hardly been stated. Unless it is effectively presented, there is a real possibility that n. 21 (which says nothing clearly false but which could be signed by any Lambeth supporter) will get a *placet.*

This is a *placet* Council in the sense that a majority of the Fathers seem ready to vote *placet* to any text which the appropriate Commission finally recommends for their approval. It is of course possible, and perhaps probable that the Commission itself will amend the text satisfactorily before bringing it back for voting.

My apprehensions are not of course shared by all. The brilliant and indefatigable Charles Davis (who finds time to sit daily on the American Press panel at 3 p.m., when I am fit for nothing except sleep) is exhilarated by every fresh evidence of the freedom of theologians to evolve the magisterium. (He flew to Edinburgh for this long weekend).

His interest is, of course, in dogmatic theology rather than in moral doctrine, and being thus one stage further removed from "agenda", he is less concerned than I about practical consequences. As a moralist I have to draw the line between what is objectively right and wrong. I don't want to be 1iberated from a constricting magisterium. I need every bit of guidance it can give me and shudder to think of the vague waffling to which I would be reduced if I had to rely on the meditations of avant-garde theologians on the data of Sacred Scripture. I could complete my course in one lecture: Integrate the Ten Commandments with the law of love and respect for human personality, integrally considered in its psycho-somatic and sociological relations, and act sincerely according to your honest conscience, and, for the rest, your guess is as good as mine. Finis!

The arrival in Rome of the symposium "Contraception and Holiness" (Herder and Herder, Introduction by Roberts) provoked the forecast that Burns and Oates would soon be on the market with neat little boxes of condoms bearing a picture of the Holy Family on the lid; that a new *Benedictio condomorum* would have to be added to the Ritual, and that special indulgences would appropriately be granted to those who piously use them "cum vero amore coniugali" as a means of growing in holiness. And why not?

Incidentally, I don't think I can even teach canon law on the basis of the Léger premisses: Matrimonial consent could no loner be defined as giving and receiving a "ius in corpus, *perpetuum* et exclusivum, in ordine ad actus *per se aptos* ad prolis generationem" (c.1681), and those who have had their marriage annulled "ob exclusum bonum prolis" would have be told to get back into it.

Ah well, it is good to remember that most of the Fathers have not yet spoken, that there is a Pope who yet has to sign, and that divine providence is not outdated. I admit that I am an old "square", so mentally conditioned by an inordinate attention to a misconceived magisterium as to be unable to tune in to the new theological wavelength, but I reflect that pendulums have a back-swing and feel sure that when this one swings back, I shan't be quite so far "out on a limb".

Apart from a bit of Commission Work *De Sacerdotibus*, I have taken things easily this week, and hope to profit by these few days of rest. Last Sunday I felt exhausted. It is not difficult for me to avoid extra work. Exponents of the traditional line are not in demand. Extra-conciliar meetings are crowded only when tradition is under attack.

I have promised to take the Ushaw lads out to dinner tomorrow. I find that there are twelve of them, so that, adding my server, we shall be fourteen in all! A visit to the bank is indicated.

Only three more weeks!

All good wishes,
Yours sincerely,
L.LMcReavy

Letter 27

The English College, Rome
Sunday, November 8th 1964

Dear Monsignor,

It has been an odd sort of week. We had a long weekend, Saturday to Tuesday incl., but the weather was too changeable. On Monday I went out with Archbishop Grimshaw and his secretary to the little villetta above Palazzola and spent the day indoors in front of a wood fire, except for driving over to De Sanctis restaurant at Nemi for lunch; otherwise I stayed at home and did a modest amount of work.

When the Council resumed on Wednesday, we took it for granted that the two English Bishops who had applied under the"rentacrowd" rule to say their piece on the closured n. 21 (about use of marriage) of *De Ecclesia in Mundo Huius Temporis* would be called to speak, but to our surprise their names were not read out, nor were the names of any others who had collected seventy supporters, and I feel sure there must have been some. It was the first time that this had happened and no explanation was forthcoming. One could only conclude that the Moderators had decided to ignore the rule and prevent any further discussion of the matter. So we spent the morning instead in a rather cloudy discussion of the Church's attitude to culture (n. 22), and then moved on to "Economic and Social Life" (n. 23).

There was further evidence of ruthless stopping of mouths on Thursday. Felici read out the names of eight Fathers who had applied to speak on n. 23, including Bishop Gordon Wheeler, and a further four who had taken the precaution of getting seventy backers; but before the debate had even begun, Moderator Lercaro proposed to the Congregation that only these latter four should be allowed to speak (equivalently a vote of closure, followed by application of the seventy backer rule) and as usual the majority of the Fathers stood up in assent. Oddly enough, one of the favoured four, Bishop Alba of Mexico, started speaking about usus matrimonii, (quoting *Casti Connubii*, emphasizing its magisterial authority) coupled with the consonant doctrine of the universal episcopate, and had just got to the point of claiming that it was irreversible when he was sharply interrupted by

Lercaro and told to confine his remarks to n. 23. After protesting that he had put his name down for n. 21, he returned to his seat. Rummy, eh?

Before n. 24, we had an address in Latin by an American layman, James Norris, on the problem of world poverty. Frings made a very solid and concrete contribution, Alfrink begged the Council not to produce yet another "simplex damnatio communismi", ignoring the equally widespread atheism of non-marxist materialists, and Rupp of Monaco entertained us with a typical harangue, quoting an Armenian who had said ruefully to him that if the Armenians had not been Christians they would have received more ready aid from the Christian West.

Friday's Congregation was unique in that the Pope came for the first part of it. We began with an interminable Ethiopian Mass ("the natives are restless tonight"), and then, the debate on *De Ecclesia In Mundo Huius Temporis* having been interrupted, the schema of propositions on the Church's Missionary Activity was introduced (I assume that this was to suit the timetable of the Pope, who had previously arranged to be present when this particular schema was introduced and couldn't very well just hang around in the wings until it happened).

Incidentally, the Pope simply walked up the centre aisle with four attendants, knelt at a prie-dieu in front of the Conciliar altar, and then, after the Mass, sat in the middle of the presidential table, where Tisserant normally sits, but on a chair that had been slightly raised for the occasion.

After his own opening address, he remained for the two introductory "relationes", and then departed as briskly and informally as he had come. It was just on 11 a.m. when the coffee bars open, and when I nipped down to the bar sinister; I was disappointed not to find him leaning against the counter and supping a cappucino.

Because we had had our two days vacation at the beginning of the week, the Moderators, stopped our usual Saturday off, — dirty trick!

There was a much thinner attendance than usual, but, contrary to our expectations, the debate proved most interesting. The main reason was the strong feeling for which it served as an outlet. The great body of missionary Bishops had apparently been champing at the bit waiting for a chance to say what they thought of the coordinating Commission's reduction of their beloved schema to a few measly propositions. We had had this reaction to the Propositions *De Sacerdotibus*, which our Commission is now busy rewriting as a full-length schema, but the missionaries added a tropical heat to their protests.

Lamont of Umtali, Rhodesia, a Northern-Irishman and an orator of undoubted talent, made the speech of the morning, comparing the propositions to the dry bones of Ezechiel's vision and asking the Fathers: "Thinkest thou that these dry bones will live". They had expected the Council to light a beacon and had been offered a candle. To equip them for the war against worldwide paganism they were given bows and arrows. And much more to the same effect. But perhaps the most talked-of event of the morning was the dementi which Suenens added to his speech, and which was perhaps the main reason for his intervention. After giving a boost to the Missions, he said that he would like to take this opportunity of correcting a false impression of his earlier speech on n. 21 (conjugal fecundity) which certain newspapers had spread abroad. It had never been his intention to suggest that the Church should withdraw what she had taught on this subject "authentice et definitive". He had called merely for a fresh synthesis of the Church's doctrine, taking account of modern scientific findings. Moreover, the Pope had the last word. I regret that I haven't yet seen a verbatim report of this passage of his speech, but it is clear that he doesn't want to be classed with Léger and Maximus IV. I hope that the Catholic Herald will make this clear in its next issue.

Tomorrow, Monday, we expect to finish Missions and get back to the Church in the Modern World, when perhaps the nuclear bomb will warm things up. Beck (who has had the use of my pamphlet) is expected to speak and has been gathering supporters from Rentacrowd to make sure that he does.

(I interrupted this letter to go for a walk after tea with Bishop Dwyer, and who should we run into (and in a little back alley like the Giubonnari) but Leo Edgar! Along with other lay apostles he had been received in audience this morning by the Holy Father and was feeling very bucked.)

I have booked my return flight on the 14.25 plane of Friday, November 30th. The session ends officially with two Marian functions, coram Papa, on Saturday, November 21st, morning and afternoon, but, if there is a solemn session to promulgate *De Ecclesia*, as we hope, it will be on the Friday morning. I could attend it and still catch the afternoon plane. That will give me a restful weekend at Maidstone before returning to Ushaw on Monday, November 23rd (1 p.m. from King's Cross due into Durham about 5.50?).

I shall gladly leave to others the privilege of sitting near the Papal altar through two long papal ceremonies. Time was...!

All the best,

L.LMcReavy

P.S. Bishop Dwyer takes repeated comfort from the constantly renewed assurances of Felici and others that the Fathers of this Council are not being asked to define anything infallibly.

Letter 28

The English College, Rome
Saturday, November 14th 1964

Dear Monsignor,

I do not know whether this will reach you before my return, because the stop-go strikes have now spread to the Post Office and everything, according to the press, is in a state of chaos. It is a Saturday morning, 8.15, and I should be looking forward to a free day, but once again our free day has been cancelled, this time so that the progress of the Council will not suffer from yesterday's ceremony in Saint Peter's when, instead of a General Congregation, we had a full-length Byzantine Mass, concelebrated by Maximus IV with sundry other patriarchs, at which, as you will have read, the Pope embraced Maximus and gave up his tiara for the relief of world poverty. It was the tiara that the Milanese gave him and there has been no little speculation as to whether it was meant to indicate that the Pope was finished with tiaras, or simply to stimulate a much more active international campaign for the relief of world hunger. (Time to leave for Saint Peter's!)

The debate this morning was about Seminary training (*De Institutione Sacerdotali*). Once again the bombshell came from the bold Léger and this time it was Saint Thomas that was clobbered. Ruffini had complained that the section on the study of philosophy made no mention of Saint Thomas. Léger complained that it did this implicitly by requiring philosophy to be taught in such manner "ut alumni perennis philosophiae principia clare perspiciant eiusque cohaerentem synthesim acquirant". He wanted this out. The expression "philosophia perennis" was ambiguous. If it meant scholastic philosophy, he did not see how it was reconcilable with the general purpose of the schema, adaptation of seminary training to modern conditions. (Incidentally, the schema goes on to require a knowledge of other systems that exercise a major influence in propria natione). Nor, said Léger, was it reconcilable with the very nature of philosophy, which proceeded not from authority but from inquiry and asked not what authors say but what things are.

The section on theology, after requiring that students be taught the "mysteria salutis" from Scripture and the Fathers, modestly adds that they must learn to penetrate them and see their connection "ope speculationis, S.Thoma magistro". Léger wanted the Phrase "S.Thoma magistro" to be deleted and a clause to be added explaining that it is not the system of Saint Thomas that the Church proposes, but the manner in which he probed into things. He ended by taking a belt at moral theology, as out of touch with modern times and not fully Christian.

Döpfner, who followed, inserted a sentence in his prepared speech to the effect that he agreed with Léger about Saint Thomas. Then came Suenens who began by remarking that he adhered to Léger and Döpfner.

I went out to coffee, because Dino Staffa was next on the list and I could guess what line he would take. I got back in time to hear him protesting that what mattered was not what century or part of the world Saint Thomas spoke for, but whether what he said about the nature of man etc. was true or false; and reminding the Fathers that, according to all recent Popes, his essential doctrine "sancte est servanda". It would have been better for Saint Thomas if someone less openly committed to the party line, had stood up in his defence. As it is (if the debates are a reliable key to the future of the Church – on this there is room for doubt), Saint Thomas has had it. Out he goes with all the rest of the impedimenta which interfere with the streamlining of the Church to the modern world. The "nova figura", if some have their way, will be so renovated as to be no longer recognisable.

The morning's work began with the announcement that it would probably be necessary to have Congregations in the afternoon, as well as morning, next week (audible groans!), and that there would be a Sessio Publica on the Saturday morning. The earlier announcement on October 23rd had not made this clear. It had said that there would be two solemn celebrations on the final Saturday, a concelebration by the Pope with twenty four Fathers in whose dioceses were the chief Marian sanctuaries, and, in the afternoon a further solemn celebration, coram S.P., at St Mary Major's.

I had concluded that, if there were to be a Sessio Publica for the promulgation of completed documents, it would be on the Friday morning, and consequently I booked my return for the Friday afternoon. I think I shall stick to my booking. I shall be sorry to miss the Sessio Publica (even though I can learn the outcome from the newspapers), but I should be even more sorry to miss my long weekend.

The week began, as you will have read, with the rejection of the Propositions on the Missionary Activity of the Church. The Pope had personally introduced them on the Friday (the only instance of this in the whole Council so far), and had apparently been advised that they were generally acceptable and only needed a little polishing. I hope he reprimanded his advisers. They apparently knew nothing about the form. Even the Relator spent much of his time admitting that they were quite insufficient and that the Commission would never have reduced their original schema to such tenuous form, had it not been bullied into doing so by the Coordinating Commission.

We then resumed the Church in the Modern World, n. 25, on Peace. There was a certain amount of fine sounding but unrealistic condemnation of nuclear war, to which even Kruschev, when in power, could have subscribed, but which got us nowhere, and then again, on Tuesday, after Maximus IV had blown his top to the same vain effect, two sober and realistic speeches from Hannan and Beck, which were well reported in *The Times*. The debate expired about coffee time (11 a.m.), and after a Spanish speaking layman had addressed the Fathers on World Hunger, and Guano had summed up, we passed to the schema *Propositionum de Accomodatione*

Vitae Religiosae. There was only time for Spellman, and I hadn't time even for him because I had arranged to entertain fourteen students to lunch at the Soglio di Frisio. I hadn't realized how many there would be when I made the offer and, as you may imagine, paid heavily for my lack of foresight. My bill was exactly double what it was last year.

There was less dissatisfaction with the Religious schema and, on Thursday, it was passed for detailed voting by 1155 to 882. Then came *De Institutione Sacerdotali*, about which see above.

All good wishes,
L.LMcReavy

* * *

The following information for the period after this letter until his return to Ushaw is taken from his Diary:

> **Sunday, November 15.** Did a sarcastic cartoon about recent pronouncements in the Council debate on *De Ecclesia in Mundo huius Tempore*. Supper at the Columban Fathers.
>
> **Wednesday, November 18.** Tisserant announced that many Fathers had asked for congruum tempus to study the revised schema *De Libertate Religiosa* (discussed previous day, Tuesday, November 17), because it is a new text which, vi art. 35, should first be examined. The Presidency had decided that there should be a vote tomorrow (Thursday).
>
> **Thursday, November 19.** *De Ecclesia* Final Vote. Only 10 dissidents. Tisserant announced that the Presidential Council had reviewed their decision and ruled that, after the Fathers had heard the Relatio of de Smedt on religious liberty, they would not proceed to vote on it in this session. Their comments should be sent in to the Commission before January 31, 1965.
>
> *Sensation*. Cardinals Meyer and Ritter and other American bishops immediately organised a counter-petition to Pope and had gathered over 800 names before the end of the Congregation. After the Congregation they sought audience with the Pope, who that evening called a meeting of the Cardinals and decided that he could not reverse the Presidents' decision, since it was according to the rulebook.
>
> **Friday, November 20.** Last General Congregation of this Session. Final votes on *De Oecumenismo* and *De Ecclesiis Orientalibus*. Tisserant — Many Fathers "magno dolore afflicti sunt" by yesterday's decision not to proceed to voting on Religious Liberty. Announced Pope's decision, as above. I came away at 12, as Heenan finished speaking on mixed-marriages, caught a bus to the College, had early lunch 12.42-1.10 with the Vice-Rector (J. Brewer) who then drove me to the airport where I caught the 2.25 plane. Reached London on time and

caught the 5.22 to Maidstone, reaching home by 6.30. Kate's new baby – Damian.

Monday, November 23. Returned to Ushaw.

The Fourth Session

September 14th – December 8th 1965

The following information concerning the period immediately before his departure for Rome is taken from Monsignor McReavy's Diary:

> **Wednesday, September 8.** Heavy rain. Breakfasted at our digs and then in a taxi with mother to the Abbey where I concelebrated at the solemn Mass at which Leo made his *Solemn Profession*. Lunch with the monks. Tea in the parlour. Taxi back to digs, where the landlady made supper for us. Kathleen and Alban called later.
>
> **Thursday, September 9.** Bright and sunny. Sat in deckchairs and had a picnic lunch on promenade and then got the 1 p.m. boat and 1.40 boat train. Packed train for Waterloo. Back to Maidstone about 6 p.m. Mother bore up splendidly.
>
> **Monday, September 13.** Dennis Dockery drove me in his car to London airport.

Letter 29

There is no date on this letter but internal evidence shows that it was started on Thursday September 16th and completed the following day Friday September 17th 1965. The postmark on the envelope was dated 18th September 1965.

The English College, Rome

Dear Monsignor,

The fourth and certainly final session is now well under way. I flew out on Monday September 13th by the 1 p.m. Alitalia plane and, being in the company of Archbishops Beck and Gray, I shared their VIP treatment (free drinks in the departure lounge and a private car over the tarmac to the plane.) We were met at Rome airport by the Rector and, at 4.30, were sitting down to tea in the Bishops' Parlour at the College. It was a lovely evening and I thoroughly enjoyed my stroll up the Via della Conciliazione to collect my set of schemata at the Secretariate, meeting various acquaintances on the way. It is now Thursday evening and the weather has remained set, fair, constant sunshine, but with a temperate breeze to take the edge off the heat.

On Tuesday, we set off in the motorcoach at 8.30, and, as on previous occasions, the Rector, Monsignor Worlock and I made straight for the benches reserved to the papal household immediately to the right of the papal altar, where we had as good a view of the concelebrated Mass and inaugural address of the Pope as one could ask for, far better than that of any of the conciliar Fathers. The Holy Father dispensed with all triumphalism. Dressed merely in Mass vestments and precious mitre, he walked up the nave at the rear of the procession of concelebrating bishops, and, after the ceremony, when his servants brought the sedia gestatoria, he signalled that he did not want it and departed as he had come.

His address, mainly on charity, was rather long-winded (40 minutes), but we were out in the piazza before noon. In the afternoon, at 4.40, we set off by coach for Santa Croce, where, after standing until 6 p.m. on the steps of the basilica, we moved off in a slow and immensely long procession, flanked by dense crowds, to Saint John Lateran. The head of the procession must have reached the Lateran before the Pope, carrying a cross-shaped silver reliquary of the Holy Cross, had left Santa Croce. The whole route was covered by loud-speakers and we sang all the way in response to an invisible choir. The procession was well organized and very impressive. There must have been about 2000 bishops walking, not to mention hundreds of others such as myself. It was very tiring, especially when Cardinal Traglia treated us to a longish sermon on the steps of the Lateran, but the Pope set the example of Penance (object of the procession) by walking the whole way, carrying the heavy reliquary, and refusing the throne they brought out to him during Traglia's sermon. We were on our feet for three solid hours and it was a delicious relief to get back into the coach for our return to the College, which we reached at 8.30.

Wednesday, September 15th, 8.20 coach to Saint Peter's for the first General Congregation of the session (128th of the Council – of which I have missed so far only one).

To our surprise, the Holy Father came for the first part, to assist at the solemn reading and promulgation of his long-awaited Motu Proprio on the *Synodus Episcoporum* which is to give concrete expression to the collegiality defined in the constitution *De Ecclesia*. Never can a Pope have entered or left Saint Peter's more modestly. He appeared suddenly, with two attendants from the right-hand transept and walked briskly to a faldstool near the conciliar altar. After the conciliar Mass, he walked round to the slightly raised chair set for him in the middle of the Presidential Bench, between Tisserant and Lienart, and after the reading of the Motu Proprio, departed as he had come, with a brief bow to the Fathers in the nave and to the observers in the tribune at the corner of the right transept.

That left time only for a few of the cardinals to express their mind about the "re-emended text" of Religious Liberty (first of the four schemata which remain to be discussed): Spellman, Frings, Urbani, Cushing and Alfrink spoke in favour, Ruffini, Siri, Arriba y Castro against. The same arguments and counter-arguments all through Thursday and now Friday morning (I have just got back from the last Congregation of the week, a lovely feeling).

From the strictly logical point of view, or perhaps I should say, at the level of theory, the opponents or critics of the schema make a better show. Most of them are ready to admit that a large measure of religious liberty has to be conceded in practice, but find flaws in any attempt to base it on irrefragable principles. The defenders appeal almost exclusively to the dignity of the human person and are content to declare their conviction that Religious Liberty is a good thing and works better than its opposite. It gets rather dull after the same two records have been played over and over again for hours on end. We expect the debate to end on Monday morning, and discussion of *The Church in the Modern World* to begin.

The programme issued yesterday provides as follows:

I. Four schemata to get the full treatment, discussion, voting, approvement of modi: Religious Liberty, Church in Modern World, Missionary Activity, Ministry and Life of Priests (in that order).

II. Two schemata to be voted on, *placet, non placet,* or *placet iuxta modum* (and later vote on the Commission's treatment of the modi): Divine Revelation (voting to begin on Monday next) and Apostolate of the Laity.

III. Five schemata to be voted quoad modos tantum (they got through the first stage of voting during the last session): Pastoral Office of Bishops, Adaptation of Religious Life, Christian Education, Training of Priests, Relation to non-Christian Religions.

I see no reason to change my forecast that the debates should not last more than five weeks. How quickly the voting is completed depends largely on how fast the Commissions work.

I haven't yet decided what to do with my weekend. Most seem to be going out to the villa, but I soon get tired of sitting about, even in beautiful surroundings, and there is not much else for men of our age to do. I might even stay here and work.

All good wishes to the returning brethren.
Yours sincerely,
L.LMcReavy

Letter 30

The English College, Rome
Friday, September 24th 1965

Dear Monsignor,

It is 1 p.m. and we have just returned from the last Congregation of the second week, a moment which we greedily look forward to all through the week. This was, I think, the moment at which I began last week's letter, when I had no plans for the weekend except perhaps some desultory work. It turned out better. Bishop Cleary invited me to accompany him and his secretary, in the latter's car, on a trip down the coast. We made the mistake of going first down to Ostia, which is dull and interminable, but eventually reached a part of the coast quiet enough for the Bishop to have a bathe, and for me to wade. Then a very pleasant lunch at a good roadside trattoria. Then on to Anzio, where we walked round the great bay of the allied landings, inspected the sumptuous yachts, chatted to some New Zealand Bishops. On to Nettuno and beyond to visit the house where Saint Maria Gorretti was murdered, back to Nettuno to visit the church where her body lies, out onto the pier to inhale the sea breezes, a pause for caffe latte and then the 40-mile drive home. The day, like every day since we arrived, was one of unbroken sunshine with a pleasant breeze. (Excuse the bad typing. The spacer of this machine works intermittently). Sunday, I stayed at home; most of the bishops went to the villa.

Monday, September 20th, we continued the debate on Religious Liberty, while the Fathers plugged ahead with the voting on *De Revelatione*. There was an impressive phalanx of cardinals among the speakers, including Beran and Cardijn, but we had already reached the point at which it was difficult for anyone to say anything really new; and there was some disappointment at the failure of the Moderators to propose the closure. However, they proposed it next day, Tuesday, at 10.40, just when Bishop Holland was due to speak next, and, as always the Fathers supported them almost unanimously. Sixty two Fathers had had their say, and, as Agaganian remarked in proposing the motion, "videtur satis".

According to the normal procedure, the schema should have gone back to Commission for revision in line with the debate before any vote was taken. It came as a surprise therefore when Agaganian put a further motion: "Utrum textus re-emendatus de Libertate Religiosa placeat Patribus tamquam basis definitivae declarationis ulterius perficiendae iuxta doctrinam Catholicam de vera religione et emendationes a Patribus in disceptatione propositas et approbandas ad normam ordinis Concilii". The vote was taken "per schedulas" and the result, announced to an attentive aula a little later was: Voting 2222; *placet* 1997, *non placet* 224, null 1.

Rumour has it that the Coordinating Commission had decided by 16 to 9 against taking a vote at this stage, but that the Pope himself had overruled them and imposed the form of the question so as to have something concrete to take to New York with him.

Certainly, Tisserant and Agaganian did not come in that morning until after the Mass. In a sense, it complied with the rule that, after a schema has been debated in genere, the Fathers should declare by vote whether they accept it as a basis for detailed discussion. The point was that the four-days debate had not been divided into debate in genere and then in specie. Why, I do not know. It had been praised or criticised in genere and specie throughout the sixty two speeches, so that there had been no moment at which the Moderators could close the debate in genere and ask for a vote on the general acceptability of the document. If therefore the schema had gone back to the Commission without further ado, the Commission would have had to do its revision with little idea of the general mind of the Fathers. It may well be therefore that the pressure for a vote on the general acceptability of the schema came from the Commission and was supported by the Pope rather than originated by him. Anyway, there was general satisfaction, especially among the Americans, that a vote had at last been taken and that the great majority of the Fathers favoured the declaration or at least its general tenor. That was the one high spot of the week.

We moved on immediately to discussion of the revised schema on The Church in the Modern World. It has been upgraded to the dignity of a "Pastoral Constitution", which some Fathers have already stigmatized as a contradiction in terms. The debate has not been very exciting. The revised version has won more compliments than last year's effort, but there are still plenty of criticisms. Bea found the Latin very obscure. Ruffini (next day, Wednesday) found it "tam inepta ut latina generatim dici nequeat". His own Latin is a joy to hear, virile, without pedantry, fluent and clear.

We've had quite a few good speeches, but I doubt whether the Commission will find them very helpful; so often they cancel each other out, or else ask for something which experience has shown to be beyond the capacity of the Commission. They've got to speak to the world, Christian and non-Christian, in a language that all can understand and yet not descend to the mere level of natural reason, or forget that we preach Christ crucified, etc. etc.

On Wednesday, we had a Hierarchy Meeting in the College Library and I can say without breach of secret that we did not come up with a magic formula that would overcome all the difficulties. After the meeting, Fr Vin Lang arrived with his mother, and, after drinks in my room, Bishop Holland entertained us to dinner at the Pancrazio.

On Thursday, the debate in genere on the Church in the Modern World was brought to an end by form of vote which committed no one to anything except moving on: "Placetne Patribus ut exacta disceptatione de Ecclesia in Mundo Huius Temporis in genere, transitus fiat ad disceptationem circa singulas partes". The result, of course, was the same. Anyone who voted *placet* thereby approved the document as providing a suitable basis for detailed discussion and amendment, without actually saying so.

Judging from Friday's performance, I cannot see the debate in specie lasting longer than it did last year, though it may hot up when we come to the chapters on concrete problems, especially fecundity and nuclear war.

The Secretariate expects the debates to be over by October 15th, i.e. end of the 5th week (which has been my estimate all along). Fast though the voting on past documents is going at the moment, there is bound to be a considerable amount remaining after the last schema (our Commission's effort on Priests) has been discussed. No one knows yet how it will be timed. Perhaps three days a week. All depends on how fast the Commissions can work.

It is now Saturday morning, 9 a.m.. At 10.30, I am leaving for Anzio with the same two companions as last week. It is fresher by the sea in this weather than at the villa, where most of the Bishops seem to be going.

Greetings to all the Parlour,
Yours sincerely,
L.LMcReavy

Letter 31

The English College, Rome
Saturday, October 2nd 1965

Dear Monsignor,

End of the third week, and within sight of the end of it all. A very pleasant trip to Anzio last Saturday, where I painted a sketch of the harbour, while Bishop Cleary bathed. Then the weather broke temporarily. We awoke to torrential thunder showers last Sunday and the weather remained unsettled until Tuesday. Since then it has been perfect again and today (Saturday) it promises very well for my third trip to the coast.

Ten days ago, Bishop Dwyer invited Bishops Holland and Cleary and Monsignor Davis and me to concelebrate with him on the anniversary of his consecration. We liked it and it suited the College (half of them still at the villa), so we have made it a daily arrangement at 7 a.m. in the martyrs chapel.

The debate on the Church in the Modern World has plugged along with few highlights. In order to ensure that no Father, however eminent, will be able to speak more than twice, the schema has been divided for purposes of debate into its two parts, instead of being taken chapter by chapter.

Monday and Tuesday were mainly devoted to examination of the problem of atheism in its modern forms, and then, since at the end of Tuesday morning we had run out of speakers on Part One (or at least out of those who had given the required week's notice and thus established a right to speak), we passed on to Part Two, which deals with concrete problems.

Chapter I deals with matrimony, and since the Moderators are calling speakers on Part Two according to the chapter with which their intervention deals, all the speeches for the next two and a half days (till mid-morning on Friday) were concerned with the controversial section on marriage which, because the Pope has not yet spoken, has nothing to say on the hot subject of birth control, or at least on what means, if any, are immoral. Ruffini was understandably querulous on this point. Léger and Suenens evaded it, confining their criticisms to other points.

Colombo of Milan was excellent. He praised what was positive in the schema, but pointed out that, since the Church and all its theologians has hitherto insisted on the grave obligation of respecting the integrity of the sexual act, failure to make this clear would be taken to imply a substantial change of doctrine on this point. Zogbhi of Egypt intervened with a plea that the Church should line up with the Orientals (schismatic) in allowing a second marriage to the innocent party of a broken marriage. He was answered the following day in a learned speech from Cardinal Journet.

On Thursday also, there were two excellent speeches from Heenan and Conway. Heenan observed that the Commission could not be blamed for saying nothing on the hot point because it had been reserved to the Pope, but added that, unless and until the Pope's ruling could be incorporated in the conciliar document, it would be better to omit the whole chapter on marriage; it would be absurd to condemn abortion, as the schema does, and have nothing to say on contraception and sterilisation. Conway noted that the schema did not correspond to the mind of the Commission which had required a clear statement of the media illicita. Pending the papal ruling, it should at least insist that birth regulation could only be "mediis legi Dei consentaneis".

Perhaps the most interesting speech of the week was Felici's opening announcement, on Friday morning, of the calendar of the Council as far as it could be foreseen. General Congregations will continue to be held until Friday 15th October, and, if necessary, on Saturday 16th. By then, it is confidently expected that the debates will be completed, and meanwhile, of course, the voting will continue on such documents as are ready for it.

During the week 17th to 23rd October, there will be a vacatio from Congregations but, he hastened to add, not from work. The Commissions will be working full-time, getting documents ready for voting, and the Holy Father has a job for all the other Conciliar Fathers to do. He wants their advice "on certain topics about which he himself is to issue instructions" (which presumably include contraception and mixed marriages). The Presidents of the various episcopal conferences will be given topics to discuss with their members "iuxta dies et rationes indicatas".

By the 23rd of October, it is expected that some schemata will be ready for voting and the Congregations will be resumed for that purpose. Towards the end of the month, it is hoped that it will be possible to have a Sessio Publica for the promulgation of such decrees as have by then been finally approved.

Then comes the short All Saints-All Souls break. No one can give a firm estimate of the number of days in November that will be required to complete the voting. It depends, of course, on how quickly the Commissions and the printers work. My guess is three weeks at the outside. But it is only a guess.

On Monday, when the Pope leaves for Rome, we are having the Congregation Mass for his intention, and on Tuesday, when he returns, we are to receive him in Saint Peter's around about noon, and hear an address from him. Then, I suppose, he will go to bed.

Sunday morning. A very enjoyable visit to the coast near Anzio, yesterday, and a nice meal at a friendly Trattoria which we discovered on our first visit. Yesterday, the students returned from the villa, so that we now have a fairly full house. A considerable contingent has yet to arrive from England, including the largest first-year intake which anyone can recall, over twenty. Bishop Cashman also arrived yesterday, having been delayed by the many problems involved in taking possession of a newly-constituted diocese. He has acquired a house near Storrington. He contemplates changing his motto, because his previous one was chosen as proper to an Auxiliary "Coram eo ministravi". Someone has suggested that he change to: "I'm all right now, Jack".

All good wishes to all the Parlour,
Yours sincerely,
L.LMcReavy

Letter 32

The English College, Rome
Sunday, October 10th 1965
End of Fourth Week.

Dear Monsignor,

I've just had another enjoyable Saturday. Last session, you may remember, they made us meet even on Saturdays. The difference is remarkable. I was due to go to the sea again, this time with Bishop Foley taking the place of Bishop Cleary (temporarily back in England), but was pressed by John Brewer to accompany him and the Rector and a couple of others to the vineyard of Enzo (the College's winegrower) to see the end of the harvest. Enzo showed us the intricacies and tricks of picking etc., and then entertained us to a gargantuan meal on the roof of his vineyard house, itself on the top of one of the Alban hills. The air itself was a wonderful appetizer and I cannot remember ever before eating and drinking so much with so little effect. Then we drove to his establishment in Albano for coffee and licks before watching the process of extracting the stalks and the first yield of juice from the grapes. I was in no mood for work when we got home and instead went for a walk up the Corso.

But, lest my appreciation of the occasional treat convey a false impression, let me emphasize that this sort of thing occurs at most one day in seven. It has in other respects been a busy week. Most of my evenings have been spent trying to work out a suitable English version of the Ordination of Priests on the basis of the comments sent in to Dwyer by about ten experts regarding three previous versions — a complicated job, as you can imagine.

Also, I find, I took over fifty four pages of close-written notes at the five General Congregations of the week.

The week began, of course, with the excitement of the Pope's visit to UNO, which preoccupied our thoughts when the debate on The Church in the Modern World (Part II, chapters II-III) was resumed last Monday — Culture and Economic and Social life being the topics. After we had listened to hours of worthy but unexciting speeches, we hurried home to an early lunch and then watched the TV non-stop presentation of the Pope's arrival at New York and drive into the city from 2 p.m. to 4.45, when we had a Holy Hour (requested by the Council).

In the evening, we watched the UNO speech, (next evening a recording of Yankee stadium, World's Fair and drive to the airport). The following morning, Tuesday, we dragged on the debate until about 12.50, when the great doors of Saint Peter's were thrown open, and the apparently tireless Pope, followed doggedly by the group that had gone with him, walked briskly up Saint Peter's amid great applause (which drowned the *Tu es Petrus* we were supposed to sing), took his place at the centre of the presidential bench and, standing, gave us an address to the effect that the *vox verbi* for world peace must now be followed by the *vox actionis* on the part of all the episcopate. It was a historic moment and I imagine we all felt vividly conscious of it.

Meanwhile, we were making fast progress with the schemata and voting. On the Tuesday morning, after a few speeches on chapter III (including a fine one from the Mill Hill General, Fr G. Mahon, on the need of a special secretariate to coordinate all aid-schemes for the underfed half of the world), we moved on to chapter IV (Church and State) which attracted only four speakers, and then to chapter V on Peace and war. We continued this all through Wednesday and most of Thursday. On Wednesday we had three English participations in close succession, by Butler, Wheeler and Grant, though not, of course, *in* English.

On Thursday, Archbishop Beck just breasted the tape in time. The closure of the debate on *The Church in the Modern World*, was proposed and accepted immediately after he had finished his speech. His main point was even though possession of the nuclear deterrent can be justified for the time being as a necessary proximate occasion of grave sin, i.e. until the individual states can be protected from aggression by an effective world authority, no states or nations had yet shown any readiness for that diminution of national sovereignty without which a world authority with real power could never be brought into being; in other words they were not making any real effort to escape from the occasion of sin, as they were morally bound to do, and it was this moral obligation that the Council should stress in its message to the world.

It is nowadays extremely rare for the Fathers to break the rule forbidding applause of speeches, but they broke it for old Ottaviani who, in his most eloquent Latin, pleaded for constant action in favour of a federated world (with sovereign authority as in US and Brazil), as being the only alternative to the present Balance of Terror. Veniamus tandem ad rempublicam universalem in qua omnes habent nonnisi unam patriam, ipsum mundum (my notes, rather than his exact words).

With the closure of this debate, the Council passed on to the discussion of the second-last schema, *De Activitate Missionali*. It was interrupted at the beginning of the Friday Congregation to allow the intervention, on the Church in the Modern World, of five Fathers who had meanwhile collected the necessary support of seventy Fathers. One of them was Philbin of Down and Connor who made a most eloquent criticism of the whole schema. The trouble with the modern world, as with man throughout his history, was not that it did not know what was good and what was evil, but that, like Saint Paul, — "perficere autem non invenio", — it was incapable, without the grace of Christ, of doing the good and avoiding the evil. The one solution which the Church had to offer the world was the Gospel truth — sine me nihil potestis facere. Whether or not modern man is in the mood to accept it, it is the only answer to modern man's despair. A dialogue at the Pelagian level would get us nowhere and would reveal us as no more competent to solve the world's problems than men of the world.

Most of the speeches on Missions seem to find the revised schema substantially satisfactory and it looks like having an easy passage. I should not be surprised to see the Council move on, on Monday, to the final schema, that of our Commission, on The ministry and Life of Priests; in which case, there should be no difficulty in bringing the discussion-part of the Council's work to an end, next Friday (which will be the 150th General Congregation), as planned.

The Fathers are also due to complete during this week the voting on *De Institutione Sacerdotali*, *De Educatione Christiana*, and *De Habitudine Ecclesiae ad Religiones non-Christianos*. Many are dissatisfied with *De Educatione Christiana*, so there may be a slight hold-up there. But the main question is: how long will it take the joint-Commission to revise the Church in the Modern World to the satisfaction of the Fathers and get it through the two stages of voting. The answer at the moment is anybody's guess. The pessimists (or perhaps realists) suggest seven weeks, which would carry us to the end of November. I still think that, if they work efficiently in sub-commissions, they should be able to do it in five weeks. But this is not a prophecy.

I had almost forgotten. Archbishop Dwyer's translation to Birmingham was divulged at noon on Thursday. I gather that the Consistory had informed him little more than a day before (needless to say, he kept mum when we went for a walk together the previous afternoon). He and Bishop Cleary left for England the following morning, to arrange things in Birmingham and

Leeds. He agreed to my suggestion that I should give him a brief summary of his present position and powers and regretted later that he had.

All the best to all,
L.LMcReavy

Letter 33

The English College, Rome
Sunday, October 17th 1965

Dear Monsignor,

This record of the fifth week will have to be brief. I have a job to do which will keep me fully occupied for a day or two. The debates went more or less according to plan, but though the debate on the Missionary Activity of the Church was closured by the usual massive majority at the end of Tuesday morning, so many missionary speakers raked up seventy supporters as to occupy the whole of the Wednesday Congregation. That meant, of course, the loss of our Saturday off, because the debate on the Ministry and Life of Priests could not decently be given less than three days. It was closured towards the end of yesterday (Saturday) morning. I did not however completely lose my Saturday. J. Brewer met Worden and me in Saint Peter's square at 12.30 and drove us out to Albano to see the final stage of the wine-making — the filtering — at Enzo's. We then ate and drank more than was good for us and arrived back at the College at 5 p.m. I was in no mood for the work I had planned to do and instead had a long siesta.

The schema on Priests, prepared by our Commission, has had a very favourable reception on the whole, and yesterday, after the closure, when the vote was taken on its acceptability "as a basis for elaboration according to the animadversions of the Fathers", the result was 1507 for, 12 against, 2 null. (You will notice from the total how many of the Fathers had taken their Saturday morning off).

The cardinals seemed particularly anxious to say their piece. We had seven on Thursday, seven on Friday, and eight on Saturday. Heenan received applause (a very rare thing nowadays) for a typically practical contribution, and even had a word of commendation for priests golfing together. His advice was promptly acted upon by Cardiff and Nottingham who left before the end of the debate to have a round together.

On Friday, Felici outlined the future course of the Council, as far as he could do so without the gift of prophecy. There are to be no Congregations next week. They will be resumed on Monday October 25th for the voting through of Religious Liberty (first stage) and for approval of the treatment of modi on *De Revelatione* and *De Apostolatu Laicorum* (final stage).

On October 28th, there is to be a Sessio Publica for the promulgation of schemata which have been finally approved already in General

Congregation, i.e. *De Pastorali Episcoporum Munere, De Accomodata Vitae Religionis Renovatione, De Institutione Sacerdotali* and *De Educatione Christiana.*

There may be a further Congregation on October 29th, but then there will a break for "Feriae Mortuorum seu Aestas S. Martini" until November 8th, during which only the Commissions (including our own) will be hard at work. The rest of the Fathers are already planning their trips. Congregations will resume for voting from November 9th and continue as long as there is material on which to vote. There may be another Sessio Publica on November 18th, for Promulgation of schemata which have meanwhile been finally approved in Congregation. The rest, as Felici added, is prophecy, but there may be a further week of vacation during the second half of November. It all depends on the Commission responsible for the revision of *The Church in the Modern World.* I still think it may all be over before the end of November. I am posting this in an envelope bearing the stamps commemorative of the Pope's UNO visit, franked on the day of his departure, and distributed last week to the Fathers.

Final note. I spent all last week studying the Birth Control Commission's Report to the Pope (of which the Cardinal had secured a copy) with a view to presenting a compte-rendu to our Hierarchy next week. After I had done about 12 hours work on it, I was told that the Pope had scrubbed it as quite inadequate. My own verdict on it would be that it was a complete waste of time; yards of highfalutin waffling on points about which there is no dispute and a complete breakdown when it came to the crunch.

Since the Commission consisted largely of men who had hit the headlines through the public expression of their novel views (various), it was expecting a lot that they should prove impartial judges. What happens now is anybody's guess.

Omnia optima omnibus
L.LMcReavy

Letter 34

The English College, Rome
Sunday, October 24th 1965, 7 p.m.

Dear Monsignor,

The sixth week of the session, in which there has been a "vacatio" from General Congregations has been for me the busiest week yet. The Cardinal had told me that he would want me to give a lecture to our hierarchy on the Birth-Control controversy some time during the week, and the preparation of that took me several days, morning to night. He fixed it finally for Friday morning, 10 to 12, allowing ample time for questions. They were very appreciative in their comments and it is to be multi-copied for their further study. I was relieved to get it off my chest and went out after it to Alfredo's for lunch (opposite S. Maria in Trastevere), with Monsignor Anné (Belgian Auditor of the Rota and old Louvain pal) and Yves Nolet (out here as a secretary to Cardinal Suenens) who called for me in the latter's car. The Cardinal had also handed on to me a 93-page report on the revision of the present system of indulgences, prepared by an extra-conciliar pontifical Commission. I have put in about four days of work on that, reducing it to about six pages of typescript, so that our hierarchy will more easily be able to answer the questions which it puts to them.

I have had no Saturday off this week, or even Sunday. I finished my summary a few minutes ago, 7 p.m. Sunday evening, after a full day's servile work. I shall be glad to get back to General Congregations tomorrow, when the last few speeches of the Second Vatican Council will be made by those Fathers (there are sure to be some) who have collected seventy supporters, on the schema on Priests, debate on which was closured at the last General Congregation. Thereafter, there will merely be voting, and of course, the few Commissions which have yet to get their schemata through the Council will be hard at work. The latest news is that the mixed Commission responsible for *The Church in the Modern World* has completed the revision of the schema in line with the comments of the Fathers and will have it printed and ready for submission to the vote by the end of October.

Since, however, there is to be a break from the end of October to 8 November, and the revised schema on Religious Liberty (already to hand) precedes it in the voting order, it is not likely to be presented for voting until November 11th and will take several days.

I am convinced that, as far as the Commissions are concerned, it ought to be possible to get all the schemata through all the stages of voting before the end of November. But there was that mention of a possible week of vacation in the second half of November, and I believe that the Coordinating Commission's time-table has set December 4th as a deadline for the final voting of the Church in the Modern World. The Cardinal thinks that, whatever happens, December 8th is the probable closing date. He said that, however the voting goes, the Pope will not let the Bishops disperse until they have given him the replies he wants on certain "argumenta", on which he is eventually to issue instructions. That may be so, but I doubt whether he will want me around that long.

Meanwhile, my Commission still has quite a bit of work to do. The autumn nip came two days ago and I have at last dispensed with my thin summer suit.

Auguri to all the brethren.
Yours sincerely,
L.LMcReavy

Letter 35

The English College, Rome
October 30th 1965

Dear Monsignor,

The seventh week has been both busy and eventful. On the first two days, we had further interventions on *De Ministerio et Vita Presbyterorum* from Fathers who had collected seventy backers during the previous "vacant week". The Moderators were glad to have them, because now that the last of the schemata has been debated, they are finding it something of a problem to fill up the time between the votes. We finished before noon on both days. On the Tuesday, Bishop Foley made an earnest and widely appreciated speech on the importance of house-to-house visiting in the care of souls.

When we got back to our flat (shared by Worlock, Clark, O'Brien and self), Worlock was able to reveal to us his appointment as Bishop of Portsmouth. He had known for 10 days but had been under secret until noon of that day. We promptly drank his health in our little kitchenette, where the fridge is kept adequately supplied with vermouth, etc. I had noticed that he had been sleeping badly of late, for whenever I rose during the night, there was nearly always a sliver of light below his door. I have grown to like him very much and think he will make a good bishop. He is certainly a tireless worker. I don't know anyone who has had as little time-off during the sessions of the Council.

I had my first Commission meeting that same afternoon; we have been the last to get busy, because our schema was the last debated, and, of course, it could not be revised "iuxta animadversiones Patrum" (as it had to be before being put to the vote) until all their comments, spoken and written, had been collated and digested.

After two hours, I left the meeting in order to go to supper at the Cape's (First Secretary of the British Legation to the Holy See) with Bishop Holland. Not till I got there could I work out why I had been invited. In fact, I did not really tumble to it until afterwards. One of the ten guests was the Bishop of Indore (a gaunt Dutchman) who had made a markedly "liberal" speech on the subject of conjugal morality. I fancy that Mrs Cape herself has advanced views, because she had previously told me at a reception that she did not share those which I had expressed in the Clergy Review. She must have thought that we would make suitable opposition, and perhaps provide an entertaining collision, but the plan did not work. I was seated between Princess Aurietta Doria-Pamphili and her husband Frank Doria (né Pogson) and immediately opposite Agnellus Andrew, and my conversation was almost entirely limited to them. I gathered afterwards that Mrs Cape had immediately drawn Bishop Simons of Indore onto his conciliar theme and then endeavoured to get Bishop Holland's reaction. He, (Holland), wasn't having any. It was only later, when he told me of the manoeuvre, that I guessed why I had been among those invited. This, I suppose, is what is presumably called "hostess womanship". In the event, I enjoyed a pleasant dinner, and the Doria-Pamphilis drove us home to the College in their Rover.

Wednesday's Congregation was mere voting, except for a speech (rather good) by an American Parish Priest invited to comment on *De Ministerio et Vita Presbyterorum;* and again we got home early. Nevertheless, these were hectic days. Tuesday, Wednesday, Thursday, Friday, after a brief siesta, I had to hare off to the Congregation of the Council in Saint Peter' s square for a Commission meeting which lasted from 4.30 to 7.30, and on Friday from 4 to 8.

The President and Secretaries seemed determined to get the text revised before the *Feriae Mortuorum,* and, at five to eight last night (Friday 29 October) we made it. I got back the College (having jumped a bus) just as they were finishing supper, and, after stuffing a couple of eggs hurriedly fried for me I relaxed in the Common Room listening to a talk by Malcolm Muggeridge (out here to do a feature TV programme on Heenan). He is obsessed, almost to a Manichean degree, by the caducity and insufficiency of all things earthly and temporal, and argued that if the Church were ever to associate itself with the world's endeavour to build a heaven on earth, it would follow the world down the gadarene precipice. He has even turned Puritan and no longer smokes or drinks, but was good company in the Salone afterwards.

But I find that I have passed over Thursday (28 October), when, as you know, there was a Sessio Publica at which the Pope promulgated five more conciliar documents. As usual, it was a magnificent scene, with full lights and the bishops all in cope and mitre (2328 voted), and, as usual, the Rector, Worlock and I had no difficulty in securing a seat in the benches reserved to Rotal Auditors and Monsignori, just to the right of the papal altar, a closer and better viewing position than even the Cardinals enjoyed. But what a full day it was for me. As soon as I got back to the College from Saint Peter's and changed from robes into borghese, I had to set off with J. Brewer, Vice-Rector, for a trattoria in Trastevere where the Ushaw students had arranged to entertain me to dinner. I had taken them out these last two years, and last year, though I was unaware of it, they had not failed to note that my bill came to about £25. This year, they insisted that it was to be their turn and they had it all arranged with the Rector. They would not even let me pay for the drinks. With their usual acumen in matters of this kind, they had ferreted out a nice family trattoria where the cooking was excellent and the prices (so they said) were reasonable, and we had a long alcove table to seat the 18 of us. It was a long and leisurely meal and I had to leave them after gulping my liqueur, at 3.40, to get back to the College and from there straight to Saint Peter's Square for our Commission meeting (4.30 to 7.30). Fortunately they serve lemon tea in the middle of our meetings, else I might have had great difficulty in keeping awake.

On Friday, at the General Congregation, a choir had been engaged to fill up the intervals between the taking of the seven votes on the treatment of the amendments (modi) to *De Divina Revelatione*. We didn't get the results of all the votes, but of those we did get, the highest negative total was 55, and the *placets* exceeded 2100. Florit's *relatio* on how the Commission had reconciled the doctrine of Vatican II with that of Trent and Vatican I, sounded very convincing to me and yet represented real progress.

Felici announced the programme for November, as far as it could be forecast. The Congregations will resume on November 9th, dealing first with the amendments on *De Apostolatu Laicorum*. It is expected that the revised texts on Missions and on Priests will then be ready for distribution (as I have indicated, ours certainly will) and that on the *Church in the Modern World* about November 11th. All three will be taken through the first stage of voting during these days, and the Fathers will be called upon to vote on the treatment given to amendments on Religious Liberty.

Another Sessio Publica on November 18th, followed by General Congregations to 22nd or 23rd. "Praevidetur" a further break until November 30th. Then resumption of voting, on treatment of amendments to *Church in the Modern World, Ministerio et Vita Presbyterorum*, and *Missions*, "et in finem properabitur" (probably December 8th). If they keep to this timetable (which I think could be abridged), our Commission will not be absolved until about December 4th; in which case I might as well stay for the final Sessio Publica.

(Sunday morning.)

The house (our part of it) is nearly empty. Most of the bishops have either returned to England for this eight-day break or gone to some delectable part of Italy. I might have planned a trip elsewhere myself, had I known in advance that our Commission would finish its first revision on Friday night. Actually I expected that we would have to resume our meetings on November 3rd. However, I think I shall enjoy myself just as well here. I have already cleared up a lot of delayed correspondence, and can always find relaxation in painting, for which I have had hardly any time so far this session.

This morning, Christ the King, eight of us concelebrated in a High Mass in the College chapel with Bishop Grasar as principal. The chanting of the canon, and especially of the words of consecration, was very impressive and even Cardinal Dante would, I think, have nodded approval to our carrying out of the ceremonies. Even Archbishop Beck, who constantly emphasizes that he has no ear for music and who attended the Mass; said afterwards that he had been deeply moved.

I am sure that I must have passed over any other interesting snippets of news, but the above will have to do. The bitterest comment that I have heard yet in this Council, is that the Dutch Church seems to favour substantial change in everything concerning faith and morals, except in the bread and wine. Unjust and uncharitable, of course, but I gather that the

Dutch Bishops have begun to be concerned about their public image and are anxious to redress it.

Omnia optima omnibus,
L.LMcReavy

Letter 36

The English College, Rome
Saturday, November 6th 1965

Dear Monsignor,

If last week was for me the toughest of the session, this, the eighth week, has been by far the easiest. And not for me alone. Some of the bishops left as early as Friday afternoon, October 9th, whether to attend to business in England, or to recreation in other parts of Europe (the Cardinal indeed suddenly decided to fly off to Palestine for a ten-day pilgrimage), and by Tuesday there were only four of us guests left in the College, Restieaux, Grasar, Worden and self. There proved to be advantages in not transporting oneself elsewhere for the week. One could attend at leisure to correspondence that had accumulated during the days of pressure, and then choose the moment to relax.

We began the week piously enough with a sung concelebration on each of the first three days, Christ the King, All Saints and All Souls. On Tuesday, I had a day out with Restieaux and Grasar at Palazzola and Nemi, and yesterday, Friday, the three of us had a thoroughly enjoyable trip to Brazziano, roughly from 11 a.m. to 5 p.m. in each case.

Dwyer, back in England for the moment, had given Restieaux the use of his Roman car, a second-hand Fiat which has proved very reliable. Brazziano, which I had never seen, was my suggestion and my two fellow-trippers agreed that it was an inspired one. The Via Cassia, along which we drove most of the way, is much more agreeable than the roads going south from Rome, and, at this time of the year, the trees which line it and the winding by-road which turns off to Brazziano were a blaze of gold and russet and red. We inspected the Odescalchi Castle from outside (it was not a visitors' day) and the Church (cluttered and garish, with a makeshift extra altar — facing people) from inside, and then drove down to the lakeside, where we ate a pleasant lunch at a trattoria right on the water's edge. The air was balmy and, after lunch, we took a brief siesta in cafe-chairs a yard or two back from the lapping waves. Then we drove round the lake, and, after passing through Vicarello, we parked the car and went for a goodish walk along the lakeside. Back in the car, we completed the circuit, through Trevignano, and so back to Rome.

Four of the bishops returned from their week's holiday in time for supper. The weather is still mainly good. We had torrential rainstorms during two nights, but in both cases it cleared up before ten in the morning.

The Council resumes its General Congregations on Tuesday, when we shall be able to estimate how far the Mixed Commission has progressed in the revision of *The Church in the Modern World*, still referred to commonly as Schema XIII.

They have had plenty of time to prepare a text more acceptable to the Fathers, but I have no inside knowledge. Indeed, I haven't heard a word of news or rumour about the Council since the last Congregation; but the general opinion seems to be that the Pope and Coordinating Commission, having plumped for December 8th as a suitable Feast on which to bring the Council to a close, will keep to it, whether it means marking time or proceeding at the double. The intervals between speeches are to be partly filled by reports from Presidents of Episcopal Conferences on the views of their members concerning the *Positio de Indulgentiis*. Our conference will not be the first to report. They have my summary of the *Positio*, but cannot hold a meeting to discuss it, until the Cardinal returns from the Holy Land.

Did you get my letter in the special envelope franked with the series of stamps commemorating the Pope's visit to UNO? I meant it for the College collection, but feared that a collector might snitch it en route.

Yours sincerely,
L.LMcReavy

Letter 37

The English College, Rome
November 14th 1965

Dear Monsignor,

The story of the ninth week is easily told. We began a day late (Tuesday) but had to turn up on Saturday and so did our normal stint. Tuesday was devoted to voting on the treatment of *modi* submitted on *De Apostolatu Laicorum;* it was approved and is to be promulgated at next Thursday's Sessio Publica. To fill in the time between the taking of votes, it was decided to call upon the Presidents of Episcopal Conferences to report orally, if they so chose, on the non-conciliar *Positio de Indulgentiis.*

On Tuesday, we merely had the reading of the introductory relationes of Cardinal Cento and Monsignor Sessolo of the Sacred Penitentiary. But, on Wednesday, old firebrand Maximos IV Saigh, who tends to look with a frigid eye on anything in the Latin Church which the Orthodox haven't got (except perhaps the Pope), opened the bowling with some nasty bouncers. The Orient does not know indulgences. They were introduced into the West on premisses which do not justify the conclusions. If the Church won't suppress indulgences purely and simply, let it at least make them acceptable by etc. etc.

Sidarous of Egypt, on the contrary, while admitting that indulgences were an obstacle to reunion with the Orthodox, said that his faithful believe and practise the Catholic doctrine and that he approved of the proposed reforms. So too, in general, did Wysczinski, speaking on Thursday for the Polish Bishops, though his main desire was that the reform should not be delayed. Alfrink, for the Dutch, complained (his lugubrious voice would add a note of complaint even to a greeting) that the *Positio* did nothing to remove the discrepancy between the practice hitherto and modern theology.

The two most thoughtful speeches were those of Konig and Döpfner, both reporting on the joint meeting of the Austrian and German Bishops. I fancy that the latter's speech must have been written for him by Karl Rahner, because it summarized the Poschmann-Rahner position, as expounded by Courtney in the *Clergy Review*, 1959, p. 464 ff. I read Courtney's article the same evening and it sounded like an echo of the morning's speech. Anyway, Döpfner concluded by asking that the *Position* should not be promulgated in its existing form, that the Commission which prepared it should be notably augmented with dogmatic theologians of the various schools, and that the theological section should be re-written. Not all the speeches took this line, but Döpfner received loud applause, and it would seem that the Sacred Penitentiary developed cold feet.

Anyway, there were no further speeches on Friday or Saturday. The Fathers were told that all their time would be taken up with voting, as indeed it was, and that any further reactions of Conferences should be sent in "in scriptis".

For two whole Congregations we had to listen to Felici and his four henchmen reading, section by section, our Commission's revised version of *De Ministerio et Vita Presbyterorum*. As soon as one of them finished reading a section, he called upon the Fathers to mark their voting card, and the next reader began the next section. It was a relief when, as happened occasionally, Felici intervened to communicate some information to the Fathers. But one of his interventions was less happy. He said: The Secretariate has been asked whether the Conferences which are being given in the Domus Mariae this month have official status or have at least been authorized by the Secretariate. The answer to both parts is (fortissimo) "NEGATIVE." The question was either naive in the extreme, or disingenuous. I had heard that Schillebeeckx had given a conference at the Domus Mariae and that there were to be others. But no one with any knowledge of the Council could suppose for a moment that they were official or authorized. One doesn't need authorization of the Council Secretariate to give a lecture outside of the Council. The question was formulated evidently to elicit a public rebuff. I did not like the devious Latin method adopted, and I was surprised and sorry that Felici had fallen for it. Perhaps he wasn't a free agent.

L.L. McReavy at Louvain in 1930.
From left: Rev. John Flynn, L.L. McReavy, Harry McNeill, Rev. J.D. Simmons (later archbishop of Melbourne), Rev. James O'Connell, Rev. John Finnegan.

School days at Ushaw – 1915.
(L.L. Mc Reavy marked X.)

School days at Ushaw – 1918.

L.L. McReavy (marked X) during the First World War.

L.L. McReavy in 1934.

L.L. McReavy in about 1966.

L.L. McReavy sketching.

Monsignor Paul Grant,
President of Ushaw 1950-1967.

L.L. McReavy in the monsignorial garments.

L.L. McReavy in old age.

Ushaw College as painted by L.L. McReavy (below) and today (above).

Ushaw today – the Staff dining room known as "the Parlour" (above) and the Library (below).

L.L. McReavy teaching at Ushaw.

On Saturday (the next day), he began "Aliqui conqueruntur quod Secretarius Generalis nimis loquatur". Believe me, I would possess my soul in silence, if it rested with me, but silence is not always an effective method of communicating things. The Secretary General almost never speaks on his own authority. I was expecting that this was leading up to an explanation of the previous day's question and answer, but he then went on to deal with other matters. Verb. sap.?

At a reception the other night, Heenan told Suenens of a Reverend Mother in England who had only one desire; the head of Suenens in a dish. Suenens replied with a bit of hot information about the two Public Sessions to be held on the last two days of the Council. They are to be marked by two outstanding ceremonies. At the first, there is to be a solemn public baptism of Ottaviani into the new Catholic Church; at the second Bea is to be circumcised. Typical Roman humour, I believe, but in this case without venom. Both men are generally liked and admired. The last time that Ottaviani spoke (on War), he was warmly applauded. One got the impression that many Fathers who do not share his conservative views had been waiting for an opportunity of showing him that they like him personally. He is reported to have said of himself that he had been appointed head of the corps of watchmen and had tried be a good watchman. I doubt whether he is altogether out of a job.

The Pope's *Adhortatio Apostolica* distributed to us on Saturday, which calls upon the Bishops to organize worldwide supplications coincident with the ending of the Council, and which reminds the Bishops of the tasks they will face on their return home, has the following significant passage: "Scilicet opus erit praesertim christifidelium prudenter componere animos ad novas excipiendas normas; eorum inertiam excitare, qui novo rerum cursui se accommodare renuant; compescere aliorum intemperantiam, qui plus aequo privatis novitatibus indulgeant, atque adeo incepto renovationis operi haud parum nocere possint; disciplinae immutationem intra fines continere a legitima auctoritate praescriptos; in omnium denique animis fiduciam erga sacros Pastores inculcare plenamque suadere oboedientiam, quae veri amoris erga Ecclesiam testimonium est, ac simul unitatis felicisque exitus tutissimum pignus".

Tailpiece: an ingenuous student of the Venerabile confided to Cardinal Heard, the other day, how much he admired Archbishop Roberts! It is not reliably reported what Heard said, if anything. I imagine he spat vitriol and made another hole in the carpet. Incidentally, Heard may need to be "roused out of his inertia to accommodate himself to the new course of things". He is reported to have declared that he has no intention of ever himself using the vernacular in the Mass.

I have had no rest this weekend. A very difficult problem from the C.M.A.C. kept me busy until tonight (Sunday). I have booked my return flight for the afternoon of December 9th.

The weather is stormy and decidedly cool. We could do with the heating on.

All good wishes to all,
Yours sincerely,
L.LMcReavy

Letter 38

The English College, Rome
Sunday, November 21st 1965

Dear Monsignor,

The final definitive calendarium of the Council was announced the other day. There are only four General Congregations yet to come, plus two Public Sessions. The Fathers had their last opportunity of proposing "modi" last Wednesday, when the voting on the revised version of *De Ecclesia in Mundo Huius Temporis* was completed. All that remains now is the approval of the *expensio modorum* affecting Missionary Activity, (at the General Congregation of Tuesday November 30th), Ministry and Life of Priests (Wednesday December 2nd) and Church in the Modern World (Saturday December 4th, and, if need be, Monday December 6th).

All these documents are as good as through and will be re-voted and promulgated at the Public Session of December 7, along with Religious Liberty. This had its final voting last Friday (November 19th) with the following result: present voting 2216, *placet* 1954, *non placet* 249, *placet iuxta modum*, ergo invalid 7, null 6.

The Carli-Sigaud-Lefebvre group had circularized all the Fathers during the previous days, arguing that the necessary modifications had not been incorporated and that the only recourse now of those who had wanted them was to secure a massive *non placet*, big enough to enable the Pope to intervene. They did not do badly, but clearly failed by a considerable margin to rally the full weight of the Italo-Iberian Fathers.

At the Public Session last Thursday (November 18th), I had no difficulty in getting my usual privileged seat just to the right of the Papal Altar, and gratified Monsignor R.L. Smith (out here on a visit) by taking him along with me. Most of us were very pleased with the Pope's Address. As you will be able to read in the *Osservatore Romano*, after dealing with the reform of the curia (beginning with the Holy Office — and here he gestured towards Cardinal Ottaviani, seated at his right), he warned those who have taken the occasion of the Council to question nearly every doctrine and practice that, once the Council has said its final word, they will have to conform to the lines it has laid down.

You will already have read the massive approval of the two documents promulgated: *De Divina Revelatione* — 2344 *placet*, 6 *non placet*; *De Apostolatu*

Laicorum — 2305 *placet*, 2 *non placet*. I was puzzled by the difference in the total number voting, 2350 at the first vote, 2307 at the second, until I learned later from the Cardinal that the coffee bars had opened as usual, despite the solemnity of the Public Session. Or was it that the calls of nature had meanwhile become urgent for the 47 absentees? Otherwise it was a dull week.

At the General Congregations each day, we simply had to listen while the Secretary and his five subs who took turns in reading through *De Ecclesia in Mundo Huius Tempore*, section by section, and then calling on the Fathers to vote. One morning, the Vienna Boys' Choir enlivened the intervals with pieces from Palestrina and Bach.

On Friday, at midday, we broke up for another ten-day interval, though our English Fathers do not seen to be treating it as another holiday. Not so far, at least. Bishop Rudderham has gone back temporarily to his diocese (I miss him, because we do the *Times* crossword together every night), and it may be that others have sundry trips in mind, but at the moment we have a full house.

So far it has been no rest for me. Our Commission has to expend 10,000 modes (fortunately not all different). We were hard at it from 4.30 to 7.30 on Friday night, and from 9 to 12 yesterday morning, Saturday. We meet again tomorrow, Monday. But at the rate we are going, I expect to get most of the week off. To be quite frank we are going through the "modes" with an expedition that amounts to steam rollering. I gather from a Japanese Bishop who sits next to me and serves also on the mixed Commission dealing with *De Ecclesia in Mundo Huius Tempore* that the exact contrary occurs at its plenary sessions; people actually make speeches. Thank God, we have been spared that.

All good wishes to all,
Yours sincerely,
L.LMcReavy

There goes the midday-gun. It is warm and moist. The central heating is on, and I have a single blanket at night.

The Vice Rector (J. Brewer) was proclaimed a Privy-Chamberlain yesterday evening at supper.

Yes, I have at last gone out and bought a new ribbon.

Letter 39

The English College, Rome
November 28th 1965

Dear Monsignor,

This has been an easy week, not only for the Fathers in general who have had no General Congregations to attend, but even for the few who still had Commission work, for all, in fact, except the unfortunate members of the mixed Commission who have been busy all week, morning and evening, wrangling over the 40,000 "modes" that were sent in by the Fathers regarding the schema of *The Church in the Modern World*.

Our Commission dealt very expeditiously (a little too expeditiously, I feel) with the 10,000 "modes" we received on *Life and Ministry of Priests*. We breasted the tape on Tuesday evening, after four sessions of roughly 3¼ hours each. It was tough going, but worth it. I found it hard to realize, as I gathered up my papers, that this was the end of a series of pre-conciliar and conciliar meetings, in this same room looking out over Saint Peter's Piazza, that began in November 1960.

In theory, of course, we are not absolved until the Fathers, in General Congregation, next Thursday (December 2nd), vote affirmatively to the motion; "An placeat Patribus expensio facta de modis respicientibus schema De Ministerio et Vita Presbyterorum". But there is no chance of a negative vote. Indeed, our "relator", Archbishop Marty of Rheims, will end his relatio by asking for a "quasi-unanimous" vote of approval; and at our final meeting some wanted to omit the "quasi".

I spent Wednesday morning gathering together in leisurely fashion and parcelling into three bundles the heap of conciliar documents accumulated during this session of which I shall have no further need here.

In the afternoon, I went with Archbishops Beck and Dwyer to the Villa Miani (the superb residence, on top of Monte Mario, of some friend of Cardinal Suenens) to hear a talk given by the Rector of a new kind of seminary, highly experimental, established at Louvain by Suenens. Yves Nolet had rung me up to say that Suenens was very proud of his new venture and eager for some of our Bishops to hear about it. The Bishop of Liège told Dwyer that the other Belgian Bishops were content to wait and learn from Suenens' mistakes. It is a three year course for Philosophers, of which the first is a kind of noviciate year. The other two years, they attend University courses (all of which, at Louvain, include some of the faculty of Philosophie et Lettres) alongside the lay undergraduates. (At question-time, the Rector admitted that the Catholic character of the University made a difference. And to the question whether they would get a diploma for the two years, which would count, if they left the seminary, Suenens intervened to say that this would shortly be seen to. As Chancellor, he had every reason for his apparent confidence).

Inside, it is very much a liberty-hall. They are divided into "equipes", of about eight or nine. Each "equipe" has a room of its own, where the members make and wash-up their own breakfast and afternoon tea, budgeting from a fixed allowance. This is meant to teach them the value of money. There is a chaplain to each team (though, when I suggested that this meant a large number of chaplains, it transpired that one chaplain may serve as many as three teams). He occasionally has breakfast or tea with them and always assists at their weekly "revision de vie", which appeared to me to be a sort of Buchmanite affair. Anyway, they are expected to use it to correct their own mistakes, as well as in planning when and how they will fulfil the round of duties (if that is the word) — prayer, study, silence, going to bed and getting up, which they have been told to regard as normal. Incidentally, they are all vetted by a psychiatrist before being admitted. Beck was interested, if not impressed. Dwyer was sceptical.

On Friday, I went with Bishop Grasar to hear a lecture on the history of the Christian attitude to contraception by an American Catholic layman who has made a very thorough and objective study of it, J. Noonan, now of Notre Dame. It was recently published in England. So, you see, I improve the shining hour, though I must confess that I had been specially rung up by the chairman of the meeting, and could not very well avoid it.

Talking of contraception, the chapter of schema XIII that deals with family regulation seeks to avoid the controverted issues (on the ground that the Pope has reserved them to his own judgement), and limits itself to saying that, in regulating their families, spouses must not use means condemned by the Magisterium. Now, twice above in the same chapter, a statement is supported by a footnote reference to *Casti connubii*, but not this statement. When therefore I was asked by one of our Bishops to suggest any "modi" that might be appropriate, I composed one to the effect that omission of any reference to the most solemn condemnation ever issued by the Magisterium (the passage in *Casti connubii* condemning onanism) would be taken as implying a substantial change in the Church's doctrine. Arrangements were made to have about 50 copies run off by the Grail secretariate, to accommodate other Fathers who agreed with the "modus". But, on the day when the "modi" had to be handed in, the Grail, for the first time, bungled their job and put the wrong wax sheet in the machine. Result, only the two or three bishops to whom I had given my carbon copies sent in my "modus". It would appear, however, from a report in the *Avvenire d'Italia*, that the Pope himself has sent a similar "modus" down to the Mixed Commission, suggesting that, to show the doctrinal continuity of the Church, a reference should be included to *Casti connubii* and Pius XII's Midwives Address of 1951. I gather that Léger and others are resisting this suggestion, on the ground that it would hamstring the special Pontifical Commission set up by the Pope to help him in reaching the decision which he has reserved to himself. I enclose the cutting from *L'Avvenire*.

You may remember that, when the Pope set up the special Commission, he said that so far he saw no reason to change the norms given by Pius XII and made no reference to Pius XI's solemn pronouncement. I concluded at the time that he regarded the latter as outside the field of discussion and viewed the problem as limited to the Pill, on the development and working of which he felt that up-to-date and expert advice was needed. His latest intervention would seem to confirm this assessment of his mind. It is not shared by a considerable bloc in the Schema XIII Commission, who feel that the whole issue is under review and that it is not for them to settle it either way. In that case, I feel, they should not deal with family regulation at all. To deal with it and omit reference to *Casti connubii* is implicitly to support the group who want to scrub *Casti connubii*.

It turned sharp at the beginning of the week and there was talk of some snow on Monte Cavo, but on Friday we were back to a humid scirocco. Today it is betwixt and between. It is difficult to decide what to wear.

All good wishes to all,
Yours sincerely,
L.LMcReavy

Letter 40

The English College, Rome
December 5th 1965

Dear Monsignor,

I told you last week how, owing to a slip-up at our Grail secretariate, the "modus" which I had planned (calling for footnote reference to the relative passage in *Casti connubii* at the point in the schema which bans the use of means of birth-control which have been reprobated by the magisterium) was not multicopied and we had to set out for Saint Peter's with only my two carbon copies. Two of the Bishops sent them in, however, at the General Congregation, and they are duly recorded in the volume of "expensio modorum" which we received on Friday, p. 39, thus: "107, h) Duo denique suggerunt ut in nota citetur Enc. Casti Connubii: Denz. 3176-3177."

As I also told you, quoting from newspaper reports which I have had confirmed by a member of the mixed Commission, though the volume does not (of course) mention it, the Pope made the same request in the modi which he sent to the Commission through Cicognani. In fact, he wanted more, and there was prolonged resistance in the Commission by those who objected that they were being asked to settle in the Council an issue which had been withdrawn from the Council and reserved to a special Commission. A compromise was eventually reached. The text was slightly strengthened and a note was added.

The text now reads (italics indicate the additions): "Moralis igitur indoles rationis agendi, ubi de componendo amore coniugali cum responsabili vitae transmissione agitur, non a sola sincera intentione et aestimatione motivorum pendet, sed obiectivis criteriis, *ex personae eiusdemque actuum natura desumptis,* determinari debet, quae integrum sensum mutuae donationis ac humanae procreationis in contextu veri amoris observant; *quod fieri nequit nisi virtus castitatis coniugalis sincero animo colatur.* Fili*is* Ecclesiae, *his* principiis *innixis,* in procreatione regulanda, vias *inire non licet,* quae a Magisterio, *in lege divina explicanda,* improbantur." (Footnote) "Cf. Pius XI, Litt. Encycl. *Casti connubii*: AAS (22) 1930: Denz. Schon. 3716-3718; Pius XII, *Allocutio Conventui Unionis Italicae inter obstetrices,* 29 Oct.1951: AAS 43 (1951), pp. 835-854: Paulus VI, *Allocutio ad E.mos Patres Purpuratos,* 23 Junii 1964: AAS 56 (1964), pp. 581-589. Quaedam quaestiones quae aliis ac diligentioribus investigationibus indigent, iussu Summi Pontificis, Commissioni pro studio populationis familiae et natalitatis traditae sunt, ut postquam illa munus suum expleverit, S. Pontifex iudicium ferat. *Sic stante doctrina Magisterii* (my italics), S. Synodus solutiones concretas immediate proponere non intendit."

I doubt if my modest "modus" would have received such attention (the volume of *expensio modorum,* making no mention of the Pope, presents its footnote as the answer to the "duo" who sent in my suggestion), if the Pope had not happened to be thinking along the same lines. But it is a comfort to know that he was.

From the point of view of Council work, it was an easy enough week; only three General Congregations, Tuesday (*expensio modorum* on Missionary Activity), Thursday (ditto on Ministry and Life of Priests – approved by 2243 to 11), Saturday (ditto on Church in the Modern World). I was kept busy in between summarizing and assessing for Cardinal Heenan a 60-page document on the revision of the Code, and I attended two important lectures, but there was no sense of strain.

Last night, the Pope and Fathers attended a "sacra celebratio" for reunion, at Saint Paul's, in which non-Catholic Observers participated actively, reading lessons etc. Our Bishops feel that it will scarcely be possible now to retain their rule that joint services should be limited to public halls.

I shall follow hot on the heels of this last report, my present intention being to catch the 1 p.m. train from Kings Cross next Saturday. I used to think that I should be glad when the Council was over and I could say goodbye to Rome. I am not so sure now. It will be goodbye to many good friends whose company I have enjoyed and to a whole way of life. Some of the bishops are beginning to experience the same kind of ambivalent feeling. E.g. I have just come in (12 noon) from a visit, with Dwyer, to the inside of the Farnese Palace, round the corner from here, an artistic treat. It's goodbye to all that!

Auguri to all.
Yours sincerely,
L.LMcReavy

* * *

The information from the time of the last letter until Monsignor McReavy's return to Ushaw is taken from his Diary:

Monday, December 6. *168th and Last General Congregation.* Vote *De Ecclesia in Mundo Huius Temporis.*

Tuesday, December 7. Public Session. Promulgation of *De Libertate Religiosa; De Activitate Missionali; De Ministerio et Vita Presbyterorum; De Ecclesia in Mundo Huius Temporis.* 7.30 Papal audience to Periti. Supper with secretaries at trattoria near Piazza Navona.

Wednesday, December 8. Public session of closure in St Peter's Piazza. Good seat about 20 yards to side of Pope's throne. Lovely warm day. Packed in evening.

Thursday, December 9. 1.10 Alitalia plane to London. Reached Maidstone at 6 p.m.

Saturday, December 11. Tony drove me to station. 1 p.m. from King's Cross. President and Vice-President met me at Durham. Ushaw 6 p.m. Reception with drinks in front parlour 6-6.30.

End of the Fourth and Final Session

Chapter IV

The Journal

Introduction

A record of the General Congregations of the Second Vatican Council is to be found in a collection of thirteen notebooks in which Monsignor Lawrence McReavy wrote down what might be described as the "minutes" of each meeting: "I sit in my Tribune, scribbling everything down for three hours on end". *(L6)*

The notebooks which he himself described as his "scribbled notes" *(L7)* contain copious information and are a tribute to his attentiveness. The pencil script is not always easy to read and after fifty years some degree of fading is evident. Fortunately, McReavy recognised that it would be a daunting task for anyone to transcribe his notes and undertook to do the work himself. On the last page of the typed manuscript is written: "I completed this typescript copy of the notes which I had scribbled during the Council, in November 1975".

On the first page of this manuscript Lawrence McReavy has given a title to his notes "Vatican II As I saw It". There could be no other suitable title for this present collection of his papers.

In two ring binders, this Journal numbers 210 pages. Although a fuller version of the information contained in this "Journal" can be found in the official printed Acta of the Council and in the various published reports and Press releases of the time, Lawrence McReavy's notes have the vividness of an eye witness account of the Council. These "scribbled" notes give not just factual information but convey something of the atmosphere of the Aula in Saint Peter's Basilica and the writer's own enjoyment of the occasion.

Vatican II As I Saw It

An account based on my defective
and probably inaccurate notebooks

L.L.McReavy

The Second Vatican Council which ended its labours on December 8th, 1965, after 168 General Congregations (of which I missed only the concluding one of the first Session) and 10 Public Sessions (for solemn promulgation of documents etc), spread over 4 years, was very different from any other of the 20 Ecumenical Councils which had preceded it, from Nimes in 325 to Vatican I in 1870. Not merely was it more "ecumenical" in the etymological sense of the word, i.e. representative of the whole inhabited world, attended by 2500 bishops from every country, as against 700 mainly European bishops at Vatican I, but it was also unique in its object and general approach.

Most previous Councils were called to define doctrines or settle disciplinary disputes. Not Vatican II. It was no internal difference that moved Pope John to call a Council, but rather the difference between the world of his youth and that of his old age. The world had indeed changed more radically in the previous 100 years than in any earlier century. In some ways it had come closer together; one could have lunch in London and supper in Los Angeles. One could not only talk from continent to continent, but watch events as they happened on the other side of the globe by live television.

In other ways, the world was split as never before, politically and ideologically by the Iron Curtain, spiritually and religiously by the rapid spread of atheism, not merely of the practical kind, but militantly defended as the only rational attitude. Pope John felt that the time had come for the Church to take a good look at herself, to re-examine her institutions, her methods of acting, her way of presenting herself and her doctrines to the world, primarily from the point of view of pastoral effectiveness and then to decide what adaptations were needed to meet the changed and still changing situation. He summed it all up in the word "aggiornamento" — "updating". Ultimately and indirectly he hoped that this might pave the way to the eventual reunion of Christians, a cause which had been close to his heart especially since his days as papal representative in the Near East.

There were two initial phases in the furtherance of the project. In the first or antepreparatory phase, all the bishops of the world, over 3000 of them, were circularized for suggestions, and the thousands of suggestions that were received were collated and digested by the Roman curia into a series of questions covering every aspect of Church life.

The Preparatory phase began with the setting up of 10 Commissions and 2 Secretariates. I was appointed as a Consultor in August 1960 to a Commission "On the discipline of clergy and people" and we were all assembled in Rome in November 1960 to begin the task of drafting schemata for discussion by the Fathers of the Council. During the next two years, our Commission held 12 sessions of a week each, with continual homework in between.

(I attended only three because I found that they were unwieldy in the number of members and consultors and that I could say what I wanted to say just as well or indeed better by written submission on the agenda of each meeting).

Looking back, it seems clear that the Preparatory Commissions which worked from 1960-1962 in the preparation of 73 draft documents for the Council to discuss, failed to keep the Pope's objectives clearly in mind or at least to realize their practical implications. In the main, they did not really take a fresh look at their respective topics, or start from the firm ground of Scripture and Tradition in order to rethink their approach to the problems arising. They tended rather to take the doctrine and discipline as it was to be found in the received authors and ask what modifications of matter or presentation, if any, were called for; in other words, they rehashed accepted positions and perhaps tinkered with them. Even when the Council assembled in 1962, many of the Fathers, to judge from their initial attitudes and reactions, thought that this was all that was needed. Only a minority, I think, came convinced that Pope John's objectives of pastoral renewal and updating and eventual reunion of Christians could not be attained without a complete rethinking of received positions or had clear ideas of what this involved; though the speed with which the majority were converted indicated that they were ripe for conversion.

The turning point or confrontation which awakened the uncommitted came, as I saw it, half way through the first session when a schema on the "Sources of Revelation" was submitted for discussion. But of that more later.

The First Session

October 11th – December 8th 1962

I had assumed that my extremely modest contribution to the Council had ended with the group photo which celebrated the completion of the work of our preparatory commission, and that the bishops of the world would now take over, with the assistance, no doubt, of a small panel of eminent theologians of worldwide repute.

It was with considerable surprise therefore that, on Tuesday, 2 October 1962, I received a Brief from the Cardinal Secretary of State (Cicognani), with an enclosed card from Archbishop Felici, Secretary General of the Council, notifying me that I had been appointed a "Peritus Conciliaris", whatever that might be. (I learned later that there were just 198 short of 200 in this first list, and that we would be notified if and when we were needed to serve as consultor of a Conciliar Commission.)

Six days later, 8 October 1962, I flew to Rome and found accommodation at the English College, with difficulty and only because a student had decided that night to leave. Most of the English and Welsh Bishops were accommodated in rooms newly-prepared for them in the College.

Tuesday, 9 October, I visited the Secretariate of the Council to seek information about the profession of faith and oath I was to make and which the rest of the periti had made in a common ceremony in St Peter's the night of my arrival. They told me that I would be informed in due course; I was never summoned.

Wednesday, 10 October, I went with Mgr Frank Davis to obtain a photo for my Council passport (*tessera*). My passport was not yet ready and I was told that in the meanwhile my Brief of appointment would do. There was great confusion everywhere with bishops practically trampling on each other to register and collect their bundle of documents. All bishops and periti had been given the privilege of an antimension and evening Mass on any Congregation day. On this evening, the eve of the Council, the warm oppressive weather of the past few days had at last resolved itself into a thunderstorm with heavy rain, but car transport had been arranged by the College for all of us on the morrow and we would be able to vest in the college before leaving.

* * *

At this point in the Manuscript the following note is inserted:

> Several bishops are anxious to learn how exactly the members of the various Commissions will be chosen. According to the Ordo Celebrandi, one third of the 24 episcopal members of each Commission will be nominated by the Pope and the other two-thirds will be elected by the General Congregation of Fathers; but how will the names be proposed for election? Heenan seems to be concerned lest well-organized hierarchies, like the Germans, who are alleged, to have arrived with a determined policy may succeed in staffing the Commissions with men favourable to their designs. I said (knowing little or nothing about it) that I did not think there was need to worry, since it seemed likely that at least some names would be proposed by the President or General Secretary, and that, in any case the Commissions could not displace the General Congregations which would always have the final vote. The function of the Commissions was simply to revise the various documents according to the expressed will of the Fathers assembled in General Congregation, incorporating all amendments (modi) which had been voted there.
>
> The prescribed secrecy in regard to the deliberations of the General Congregations seems unlikely to be preserved; there are too many loopholes. E.g. the Observers, though bound like all others admitted to the General Congregations to secrecy, are said to be free to communicate matters discussed to their respective "communities", and it seams unlikely that there will be no leakages to the Press at this point. Cardinal Godfrey was saying today that some pressmen are complaining that they cannot find out anything definite, but neither for the moment can anyone else. But once there is something definite to get hold of, it is morally certain that the Press will ferret it out someway or other.

(*Note.* This anticipation was soon verified. one morning as I was returning home from a General Congregation, I was met by Douglas Woodruff who asked me what had happened. When I reminded him that I was bound to secrecy, and that, in any case, he could get a better report than mine in *Il Tempo*, he smiled and said: "Le Monde is even better". The story was told of a journalist who asked a bishop to get him in to a General Congregation, saying that he merely wanted to see how it worked and would guarantee not to report what was said. The bishop managed to get him past the doorman. Later the "journalist" met the bishop and said he felt he owed him an apology; he was not a journalist, merely curious. The "Bishop" replied: "That's all right; I'm not a bishop".)

My general impression gathered in these days of idle conversation before the opening of the Council, is that most of our bishops are, as expected, conservative. Some of them seem to fear that the Germans will abandon the line of resistance to the Protestants which they have hitherto held, and that the French will introduce all manner of liturgical novelties which would not suit our English taste, at least as their Lordships interpret it.

* * *

The Solemn Inauguration of the Council, Thursday 11 October 1962, was of course an impressive affair but very tiring. Having postponed our individual celebration of Mass to the evening we breakfasted at 6.30 and, at 7.20, vested in choir robes, I set out for St Peter's in a hired car shared with Bishop Grasar and Mgr Davis. The rain which had continued all night long, ceased while we were on our way and we walked across the piazza in brilliant sunshine. A large crowd was milling around the prelates's entrance at the foot of the steps leading up from the colonnade on the right, and it was evident that many unauthorized persons were getting past the guards. For example, when I reached the tribune on the left of St Peter's nave to which I was directed, there were three "clerics?" next to me in the front row who seemed to have shared out between them certain items of bishop's dress. We had comfortable chairs and a superb view, but we had to wait over an hour before the head of the procession of more than 2500 bishops came through the main west door and advanced six-deep up the nave, filing into the banks of seats on either side, beginning from the west end.

There was a considerable admixture of oriental headgear (black plant-pot hats, bulbous mitres and even a few gorgeous golden crowns), and there must certainly have been more black faces than at any previous gathering in the history of the Church.

The seating banked on either side of the nave could not contain all the bishops who had arrived and some had to be directed up into the tribunes. When after the ceremony had begun, I had to move back one place to make way for an Abyssinian bishop in a sort of baker's white cap, so distinctive that I was always able to identify myself subsequently on panoramic photos of the ceremony. It was much more vividly colourful than I had anticipated, the red damask and gold tassels and edgings of the tribunes, which completely filled the spaces between the pillars of the nave, making a magnificent backcloth to the rank upon rank of white mitres and ornamented copes.

After the High Mass (old style and stuffed with grandiose papal ceremonial), the Pope, seated on his throne above the Confessio S. Petri, made his solemn profession of faith. The Secretary General then led the bishops and other Fathers in their profession and asked them to sign their individual copies and present them to the ushers (*assignatores locorum*) before leaving. The Pope then gave his allocution, followed by the papal blessing. I gathered later from Cardinal Godfrey that as Cardinal Ciriaci rose from his seat, he pointed over to the statue of St Peter, robed in a cope for the occasion, and said "it is all right for him; he's made of bronze".

It was now nearly 1.30 p.m., and, having been in the basilica since 7.45 a.m., I did not wait for the procession out, but made my way out into the piazza and sank into our hired car. I gather later that the bishops themselves broke loose as soon as the Pope had gone and scrambled out in any order. We had a sumptuous lunch at 2.20 and I said Mass at 6.30. There was a torchlight procession, but I was too tired to participate.

A word or two on the general setup and working of the Council.

A General Congregation consisted of a gathering of all the Fathers, Periti and Observers (invited non-Catholics) in St Peter's. There was one held five days a week, from 9 to roughly 14.15. The Fathers wore choir dress and the Congregation began with a Mass, usually a Latin dialogue Mass, but occasionally one of the Eastern rites. To emphasize the evangelical function of the Council, there was a solemn inthronization of the book of the Gospels, a magnificently illuminated early manuscript copy being used; in the first session, this ceremony followed the Mass, later it preceded it. On one occasion, after an Ethiopian rite, I think, there was a minatory rolling of drums behind the scenes before the procession began and one English bishop was later reported to have whispered to his American neighbour: "The natives are restless tonight!".

To meet our fleshly needs there were two bars behind the scenes, one on either side, one known as the Bar-Jona, the other as the Bar-Abbas, where coffee, tea and soft drinks were dispensed gratis for about an hour in the mid-morning.

Procedure

After a schema (preliminary draft) had been introduced by the Relator of the Commission responsible for it, there was an initial debate in genere, i.e. as to whether it provided an acceptable basis from which to elaborate the final document: "An placet tamquam basis disceptationis?". If it was accepted, it was then debated chapter by chapter, or perhaps even section by section. When the Fathers decided that it had been sufficiently discussed, it was sent back to the responsible Commission to be revised according to the views expressed by the Fathers in their spoken or written submissions (which, as I can testify from my experience in the Commission to which I was attached, received equal attention).

Some time later, perhaps even at a later session, the amended version was explained by the Commission's Relator and then in General Congregation voted upon section by section.

In the debates every speaker was limited to 10 minutes, and to avoid delay, his successor was called to the microphone when he himself was announced, thus: "Loquatur A.B., et accedat ad microphonium C.D." if a speaker exceeded his time limit, he was interrupted with "Satis!" (Enough!) from the President, the speaker usually concluded his speech with "dixi!" ("I have had my say!").

* * *

Saturday, 13 October, we assembled at Saint Peter's in heavy rain for the First Congregation. It was something of an anticlimax. After the Mass, Cardinal Tisserant. seated at the presidential table of 10 cardinals who took turns in directing the proceedings during the First Session, announced that the Council would now proceed to elect 16 members to every Commission.

The Fathers had already received or were now given:

1) a complete list of all bishops attending the Council;

2) a list of those bishops who had already served as members or consultors of the preparatory Commissions;

3) 10 sheets on which every bishop was asked to write 16 names for every one of the 10 Commissions.

Cardinal Liénart of Lille rose immediately and protested that it would be quite impossible to do so then and there, since the various episcopal conferences needed time and opportunity to study the lists provided, consult each other, and decide on the "magis apti" ("most suitable").

Cardinal Frings of Cologne seconded this protest, saying that Cardinals Alfrink (Utrecht), Koenig (Vienna) and, I think, Döpfner (Dutch) agreed.

After a short pause, the President (Cardinal Tisserant) announced that the request was accepted and that the election would be postponed until the next General Congregation, to be held on Tuesday, 16 October (3 days later).

The Congregation thus closed prematurely at 10 a.m.

* * *

Next day, Sunday, our bishops held a meeting in the College library to discuss candidates for election, and established contacts with other episcopal conferences, each supplying to the other lists of men whom they regarded as "magis apti" (best suited) for this or that Commission, though the American Episcopal Conference list was not available until 7 p.m. on the Monday evening. All day Monday, our bishops were busy compiling their ten lists with the aid of these lists of "magis apti". A Spanish Bishop who called at the College as envoy of his Conference expressed apprehension (not justified in the event) about the effect of any bloc voting by the Italian Episcopal Conference.

* * *

Tuesday 16 October, at the Second General Congregation, Cardinal Ottaviani was the first to speak. To save time, he proposed that the votes of the bishops should be valid for any Commission so that none would be wasted, and that a relative majority should suffice, otherwise they might go on voting until December.

Cardinal Roberti said that that would be fine if it were not contrary to the law of the Code. Cardinal Ruffini, from the Presidential Bench, observed however that the Pope might authorize such a derogation from the law, and therefore they could proceed to the collection of the votes, and the method of counting them could later be referred to the Pope. The Secretary General then asked those Fathers who had already completed their lists to hand them to the ushers, and those who wanted some time to amend or fill up their lists, to ensure that they were delivered by hand to the General Secretariate before 6 p.m. that evening. He than informed the Fathers that the first matter to be debated next week would be the schema *De Sacra Liturgia*, and that those who wished to speak should supply written copies of what they proposed to say 3 days in advance to the General Secretariate. It was then announced that the Holy Father had nominated four Under-Secretaries: Archbishop Gonzalez of Saragossa, Jean Villot (Coadjutor of Lyons), Archbishop Kroll of Philadelphia, Bishop W. Kemp of Limburg.

As the Fathers began to disperse, Felici boomed out: "Proxima Congregatio Generalis locum habebit Sabbato proximo, hora 9, non feria V" (The next Session will take place at 9am on Saturday, not on Thursday. In the first Session Thursday was the free day).

The following day, Wednesday, *Il Tempo* had a complete account of what happened at Tuesday's General Congregation. It also described in detail the negotiations between the chief Episcopal Conferences which had preceded it, and gave the French the credit for negotiating an understanding between the main blocs (Italians, USA, Latin America) which would ensure a fair degree of regional representation.

(I spent the Friday doing a summary of the schema *De Liturgia* which was multicopied by our Grail secretariate for the benefit of our Bishops. Until the Commissions started working, I felt it necessary to justify my presence by work of this kind, but eventually found it very exhausting).

At the beginning of the third General Congregation, Saturday 20 October, Archbishop Felici announced that, in view of the great number of votes obtained by many bishops who had nevertheless failed to obtain an absolute majority, the Pope, not wanting to delay the work of the Council any further, had agreed to the necessary dispensations and declared elected the 16 Fathers who had obtained most votes on the list of each Commission.

The first seven lists were then read out (the remaining 3 to be published next week). Bishop Dwyer was 5th among those elected to the Commission "On bishops and government of dioceses", with 1582 votes. Bishop Petit was elected to the Commission on the Apostolate, and Archbishop Grimshaw to the Commission on the Sacred Liturgy. To enable this last to get busy immediately, the Pope's 8 nominees to it were then read out.

The rest of the morning was devoted to discussion of a Message to the World which the Presidential Bench, with the Pope's approval, proposed to send out. There were about 40 speakers. Archbishop Heenan of Liverpool expressed disappointment that the first message of the Council should be so long and vague. At the end of the morning the Fathers who approved were asked to express their *placet* (acceptance, literally "It pleases") by standing. The vast majority stood, the ushers counted the few dozen who remained seated, and the amended version was declared carried by a large majority. It was 12.45 when I emerged (second out of the door), 9 days after the solemn opening and the real work of the Council had not yet begun. The Message seems to have been a damp squib, at least in the English speaking world.

Monday 22nd October – 4th General Congregation.

The members elected to the three remaining Commissions were announced. Bishop Beck of Salford had been elected to the Commission on Religious. It was announced also that the Pope had granted Commission status to the already existing Secretariate for Christian Unity.

Then, at long last, the schema *De Liturgia* was introduced. It was the fruit of a movement which had been gaining ground over the past fifty years and more, and the initial reactions were so favourable that the debate *in genere* i.e. whether the schema provided a suitable basis for detailed discussion and amendment was completed by 10.45 of the following fifth General Congregation on Tuesday October 23rd when discussion "in specie" of the Proemium and chapter I was introduced.

At that time, the rule-book made no provision for applying the closure to any debate, other than exhaustion of the list of intending speakers. Discussion of this first section accordingly dragged on until the 9th General Congregation on Monday 29 Oct., when, almost at the end of the morning (11.52), it moved on, for lack of speakers, to chapter II. There were enough speakers to keep this discussion going until the 13th General Congregation, Tues. 6 November, and many of us became more and more depressed.

One of our bishops said he had heard me quoted as having estimated that at this rate, with 73 schemata to deal with, the Council would last at least 20 years. I think I had made some such remark though without careful reckoning; but it could well have been a fair estimate.

Then, during the 13th General Congregation (happy day!) Archbishop Felici intervened after the first four speakers of the day to announce that the Pope had empowered the Presidential Bench to propose to the Fathers the closure of any discussion when they judged that the matter had been adequately aired and argued. The Fathers would be asked to vote by raising their hands or rising to their feet, and if the vote were for closure those who still wanted to contribute something could do so equally effectively by sending their script to the Secretariate. Those in favour of the closure of the discussion of chapter II were then asked to rise to their feet. The whole assembly rose as a man. When Felici, then asked: "num surgant qui nolunt"; one humourist rose with a broad grin; he was alone. It was as refreshing as a cool bath on a hot day.

The discussion of chapter III lasted only from the 13th to the 14th General Congregation That on chapter IV (On the divine office) from late on the 14th General Congregation to the 16th, when, at 11.45, with 11 speakers still to come, the President proposed closure again with universal agreement.

Chapters V-VIII were completed by the 18th General Congregation, when, at the end of the morning, the President proposed the closure of *De Liturgia* as a whole and the Fathers agreed *fere nem. con.* (Almost no one against).

At the 16th General Congregation, an Italian Bishop had begun to preach a sermon on devotion to Mary, when Ruffini, who was presiding that day, intervened brusquely with the remark: "Omnes episcopi sunt praedicatores, et praedicatoribus non est praedicandum". (All the bishops are preachers and preachers are not to be preached to).

At the 19th General Congregation 14 November, Felici called for a provisional vote on *De Liturgia*, explaining that when in due course the Liturgy Commission had examined and attended to all the emendations proposed by the Fathers in their spoken or merely written submissions, their more specific votes would be sought. Voting from now on was to be "per schedulas" (voting slips). Those in favour of a motion or text were to make a mark, e.g. a cross, with their magnetic pencil over the word *placet* on the voting slip, those against, over *non placet*. This was to enable the votes to be counted rapidly by an electronic machine in one of the transepts.

* * *

The next schema, entitled *De Fontibus Revelationis* was then introduced with the remark that, in a matter of such moment, the Fathers ought to be ready to listen fraternally to all opinions, even adverse, and ponder them *coram Deo*. Sparks were evidently expected and they were quick in coming. Cardinal Ottaviani who presented the schema on behalf of the Theological Commission which had prepared it was bellicose rather than diplomatic. He complained that substitute schemata of no authority were already being circulated, an action grossly disrespectful to the Pope who had approved this official schema for discussion, and, where necessary, amendment. He was followed immediately by Cardinal Liénart who declared his dissatisfaction with the schema: it was inadequate, frigidly scholastic and in need of thorough revision. Frings of Cologne took the same line: the schema would repel by its tone (he mentioned that in Vatican I, a schema by Franzelin had been rejected as too professorial), and the doctrine of two sources which it presented was a 19th century invention. Ruffini begged to differ from Cardinals Liénart and Frings, and held that the Council was bound to accept the schema as a basis for discussion. Cardinals Siri of Genoa and Quiroga (Spain) were content to accept it as such. Then the pendulum swung the other way. The next seven big guns, Cardinals Léger of Montréal, Koenig of Vienna, Alfrink of Utrecht, Suenens of Malines-Brussels, Ritter of St Louis, Bea of the Unity Secretariate and the imposing Maximus IV Saigh of Antioch, for various reasons, did not like it. It simply repeated an opinion to be found in all the modern manuals, and there was no need to call a Council just to do that. In any case, it sided with one side in a dispute among the theologians which the Council had not been called to settle. It lacked the pastoral approach and was unecumenical. Archbishop Manek, for all the bishops of Indonesia, was likewise hostile, though Morcillo of Saragossa, claiming to speak for many Spanish bishops, favoured it.

At the 20th General Congregation, (16 November), the supporters rallied. Among the Cardinals (who had the right to speak first at every Congregation), Cerejeira of Lisbon, Camara of Rio di Janeiro, McIntyre of Los Angeles, Caggiano of Buenos Aires, Santos of Manila, Urbani of Venice, and Cardinal Browne O.P. of the Curia were all satisfied to accept it as a basis. Indeed, only two Cardinals that morning, Lefebvre of Bourges and Silva Henriques of Chile declared themselves opposed, though of the other Fathers who followed them five were in favour and five (including Abbot Butler) against.

At the 21st General Congregation, (17 November), the battle swayed more or less evenly, until Cardinal Bacci, the Curia's chief Latinist, imprudently exposed his chin. In a plaintive voice he told the Fathers that it would be in opportune, not to say elicit (ne dicam illicitum) to reject it. After two further speeches had been given, the President of the day, Cardinal Gilroy, intervened to say that he had been asked to call attention to article 33, paragraph 1 of the Rule-book "any Father may speak on any schema proposed, either to accept it, or reject it, or emend it". It created quite a hubbub in St Peter's. The majority had either not read the rule or had forgotten it, and felt that an attempt had been made to rob them of their rights, and were the more inclined thereafter to assert them, if given the chance.

The debate was, however, allowed to drag on for two further days, and then, during the 23rd General Congregation, 20 November, the President proposed a peculiar form of vote, viz: "Is discussion of this schema to be interrupted?".

It was explained that a *placet* would mean interruption *sine die* and therefore a new schema would have to be prepared. There were 2209 who cast their vote, hence the two-thirds majority required to reject the schema was 1473. In the vote, those against rejecting it amounted to 822; those in favour of rejecting it were 1368, not quite the necessary two-thirds.

I am sure that I was not alone in feeling depressed the rest of that day, because it seemed as though the Fathers were going to have to continue discussing a draft which the great majority did not want. The following morning, however, when I turned up for the 24th General Congregation, 21 November, Fr Barbabas Ahearne, C.P., the eminent American Scripture scholar, told me that he had it on good authority that Cicognani and two other Cardinals of the Presidential Bench had been to see the Pope overnight about the impasse and that there was to be an announcement. There was, and to my mind it changed the character of the Council. It was announced that Pope John had decided that, as some of the opponents of the schema had proposed, the subject should be referred to a joint Commission, made up of the Theological Commission and the Secretariate of Unity, to rework it completely. (Nevertheless the rest of the morning was wasted to allow those who had their names down to speak on chapter I to say their piece. Much more time than usual was spent in the bars).

The new-look Fathers who wanted the Council to be pastorally effective and ecumenical had not only won the first battle, they now knew their numerical strength. The uncommitted began to swing in their direction. It was the decisive turning point in the Council.

* * *

At the 25th General Congregation, 23 November, the schema on *The Media of Social Communication* was presented. It came under immediate criticism on the ground that it was not proper for an Ecumenical Council to go into such detail on such a matter. Even Bishop Beck of Salford who was a member of the responsible Commission found it too long, diffuse, didactic and hortatory, and proposed that the Fathers should simply vote as to whether they agreed with the general project, and that, if they did, the matter should be referred to a special Office of experts to be set up by the Holy See to work out the details. The discussion dragged on for two days, and then, at the 27th General Congregation, 26 November, the Fathers voted by rising to bring it to a close. A motion was then circulated, to be voted upon at the next General Congregation, to the effect that the substance of the schema was worthy of a General Council, should be revised in the light of the debate by the competent Commission, and that the practical details should be issued in a pastoral Instruction by the Holy See. It was approved by 2138 to 15.

* * *

Cicognani then (in the same 27th General Congregation) presented the first of the ecumenical schemata *De Ecclesiae Unitate – Ut Unum Sint*. It referred only to union with the Oriental Churches, but as Bishop Dwyer of Leeds said in his speech, it was not clear whether it was talking to them or to us. If to them, it was inept, because it offended against a primary principle of education, that we must begin where they are in order to bring them where we wanted them to be; it was useless to begin as the schema did, with the Primacy of Peter.

At the end of the 30th General Congregation, the Fathers decided that the schema had been discussed enough for the time being. In any case, in this last week of the session, it was essential at least to introduce the key document of the whole Council, *De Ecclesia*, and sample the general reaction of the Fathers.

* * *

When Ottaviani presented the schema *De Ecclesia* at the 31st General Congregation, December 1st, he was clearly on the defensive from the start. It had been prepared with great care by the 70 members of the Theological Commission, examined and passed by the Central Commission and approved by the Pope for discussion by the Fathers. It was pastoral, biblical etc., so he hoped to be spared litanies of charges to the contrary. Yet, he said, he felt that he was wasting his time and that some were all ready to shout "Tolle, tolle", and had had a substitute schema prepared even before the official one was distributed.

Once again, it was Liénart who led the attack. The schema did well to begin with the concept of the Church as the Mystical Body of Christ, but it should not imply that our baptized separated brethren do not belong to that Mystical Body. He was supported by Konig, Alfrink (who proposed that a fresh draft be made by a new and mixed Commission nominated by the Pope), and Ritter who criticized the schema's closed and limited concept of the Church.

But the main speech, or at least the most eloquent speech of the whole debate came from Bishop De Smedt of Bruges. The schema he said lacked the ecumenical spirit and suffered from a certain "triumphalismus" (this, it would seem, was the origin of the word, at least in its modern sense), "clericalismus; and "iuridicismus". It was time to put an end to the triumphalism of, e.g., the Osservatore Romano, whereby the Church's progress was presented as a series of triumphs, a picture quite foreign to the real state of the People of God who, in the experience of most pastoral bishops, always remained the "pusillus grex".

Clericalism: presentation of the Church as a pyramid with the Pope, Bishops and Priests at the top and the Christian people at the bottom in a secondary and receptive role. Power in the Church was essentially transitory, peculiar to the *status viae* in which the Church now was. What was permanent was the People of God to which we all belong, (and the Pope was one of the faithful), in which we were all conjoined, all sharing in Christ's priesthood, all approaching the same sacraments, sharing the same Bread. Hierarchical power is a service.

Juridicism: the Church is primarily our Mother. All the baptized are her children and always remain so; even those who were separated from us are our brothers. The juridical language of the schema was not that of a mother.

* * *

The debate continued right through the final week of the Session, from the 32nd General Congregation (Monday 3 December) to 35th (Thursday 6 December), more or less the same points being made on either side.

On the Tuesday, Cardinal Frings observed that the schema took account only of the last 100 years of theological writing and ignored the tradition of the Greek Church and the theology of the place of the laity.

Cardinal Suenens while endorsing the criticisms already made, sought to ensure that the Second Session would be centred round "Ecclesia Christi, lumen gentium" as a main theme, and deal first with the Church in herself, and secondly the Church in dialogue with the world about the pressing problems of the day. He asked that the Council should itself determine its future programme in this sense, that the various schemata should be forthwith revised in line with it, and that a vote be taken on the opportuneness of a secretariate for modern problems.

The following day (Wednesday, 5 December), Ruffini – for the opposition, so to speak, welcomed the proposal to deal separately with the Church *ad intra* and *ad extra.*

Cardinal Montini of Milan (now Paul VI), in a major speech, held that the two cardinal aspects of the Church to be treated distinctly were what she is and what she does. The document needed to develop the concept of the mystery of the Church as the Body of Christ, not simply a society founded by Him, but an instrument of His Incarnation. It must complement Vatican I's doctrine of the papal primacy with a full and clear doctrine of the Episcopate, on lines similar to those followed in Pastor Aeternus, i.e.;

1) Institution of the College of Apostles;
2) Succession to it of the Bishops;
3) Functions and powers of Bishops.

Finally, it must adopt a more ecumenical approach. He proposed therefore that the schema should be revised by the Theological Commission and Secretariate of Unity in a way more easily intelligible to our separated brethren.

Things were evidently on the move behind the scenes, because already at the beginning of this 34th General Congregation (Wednesday 5 December), the Secretary General had announced that a large number of the existing schemata were to be reduced to general principles and co-ordinated so as to cut out overlapping.

The following day, Thursday, 6 December (35th General Congregation), he made a number of further announcements, approved by Pope John:

1) before the next Session, all schemata were to be re-examined and perfected by the responsible Commissions, aided by sub-commissions and mixed commissions;

2) their guiding principle was to get the work of the Council finished, and to bear in mind that a General Council is not called simply to repeat accepted Christian doctrines, but to present them in a way adapted to contemporary man, pastorally;

3) the first need was to select certain more general principles, especially those concerning the Church as a whole and avoid verbosity and repetition (reform of the Code of Canon Law was to be referred to a special Commission established for that purpose);

4) new Commission under the Secretary of State was to co-ordinate and direct the work of the existing Commissions;

5) the individual schemata were to be sent out to the Bishops (or Presidents of Episcopal Conferences) so that they might examine them and express their views without undue delay. We were informed that so far there had been 1110 contributions from the Fathers, of which 587 had been delivered viva voce in St Peter's. It felt like it.

The following day, having contracted a chill, I was absent from a General Congregation for the first and only time. I gathered that nothing significant had happened, except that the Council had been prorogued.

* * *

Before it re-assembled on 29th September 1963, the 73 schemata had been reduced to about 16, and the future course of things had become to some extent predictable. No document presented to the Fathers could hope to satisfy the majority of them, unless it was biblically based, pastoral in tone and approach, and helpful or at least not harmful to Christian reunion.

The Second Session

September 29th – December 4th 1963

The Second Session of the Council was inevitably less sensational than the first, if only because the schemata had been revised during the interval mainly with a view to eliminating the kind of unproductive confrontation which had held up the work of the first.

The structure of the Council had also been revised with a view to greater efficiency.

The presidential bench of 10 mainly very elderly cardinals had been increased to 12 and still sat at a long scarlet-draped table at the head of the nave, but they no longer had control of the debates, their only function being to see to the observance of the rule-book. The real direction had been transferred by the new Pope to a group of four younger and more dynamic cardinals, called Moderators, who sat at a smaller table in front of the Presidential table and took control by turns. They were Agaganian of Armenia, Lercaro of Bologna, Döpfner of Munich and Suenens of Malines-Brussels, and they had been presumably chosen not only because they were younger and more active, but because they had shown themselves at the first Session to be in full sympathy with the pastoral and ecumenical aims of the Council, as defined by Pope John and now confirmed by Pope Paul VI.

According to the programme of this Session, the plan was to complete the discussion of five schemata: The Church, The Blessed Virgin, Bishops and Government of Dioceses, Ecumenism, and the Lay Apostolate.

In fact, there was time only for full discussion of the Church, Bishops and Government of Dioceses and the first 3 chapters of Ecumenism. Of the 43 General Congregations in this Session (as against 36 in the first), 23 were devoted to the Church, 9 to the Bishops and 11 to Ecumenism.

The revised schema *De Ecclesia*, prepared by a mixed Commission (Theology and Christian Unity), had been issued by the Pope for transmission to the Fathers on 22 April 1963, and many emendations submitted by them in writing were already available in print when the first General Congregation of the Session (37th of the Council) assembled on 10 September 1963.

It consisted of four chapters only:

I. On the Mystery of the Church.

II. On the Hierarchical Constitution of the Church, and, in particular, On the Episcopate.

III. On the People of God, and, in particular, On the Laity.

IV. On the Vocation to Sanctity in the Church.

But a new arrangement of chapters had already been proposed by Cardinal Suenens, and was printed on the flyleaf of the second fascicle of proposed emendations issued at this first Congregation. It anticipated the evident criticism that the People of God embraced Pope, Bishops, Clergy,

Religious and Laity, and therefore should be dealt with before treatment of its constituent elements.

The new plan therefore was to be: I. The Mystery of the Church. II. The People of God in General. III. The Hierarchical Constitution uf the Church. IV. The Laity in particular. V. The Vocation to sanctity in the Church.

The revised text, the discussion of which was to be allowed to run its full length because of the key importance of the document, was received with general approval as providing a satisfactory basis. Frings for the German hierarchy and Silva Henriquez for 84 Latin American Bishops proposed that the separate schema on the Blessed Virgin would be better attached to that on The Church as a final (already contained in a footnote) chapter, but when the Moderators promised to attend to this proposal, the schema was accepted as suitable for discussion by 2231 votes to 43,

The main point of discussion in chapter I, On the Mystery of the Church, was which of the many images or symbols of the Church presented should receive the principal emphasis. The underlying implication, that no definition or image could completely convey the mystery was scarcely questioned — a marked development on the rejected schema. Cardinal Bea wanted the texts quoted from Scripture and Tradition re-examined. Not all were used in their correct sense.

At the 5th General Congregation, (41st) the debate passed on to chapter II, On the Hierarchical Constitution of the Church. This was regarded by many as the key chapter of the chief document of the Council, because a clarification of the status of the Episcopate in relation to the Papal Primacy had been awaited ever since Vatican I had been prevented by the invasion of the Papal States from providing this necessary complement to its doctrine. The discussion of the chapter was therefore given free rein and lasted for nearly nine General Congregations.

Most of the speeches were concerned with the question of Episcopal Collegiality. No one could doubt that the bishops form a College with the Pope when they were assembled by him in an Ecumenical Council, (cf. Canon 228) and few seemed to doubt that this collegiality with the Pope applied equally to the episcopate dispersed throughout the world. Pope Paul had already shown that he favoured the doctrine and simply wanted it elucidated. The main preoccupation of the speakers who dealt with it was to reconcile it with the defined doctrine of the primacy of the Pope. Some Cardinals were on the defensive. Siri of Genoa, for example, while admitting that the collegiality of the Bishops was not a creation of the Pope, stressed that it could only exist in communion with him. Cardinal Léger of Montreal, from the opposite point of view, saw it as strengthening rather than weakening the Papal Primacy, because the more the Bishops acted collegially, the more the centre of unity was reinforced. Cardinal Konig of Vienna was to show that, far from being a modern novelty, Episcopal collegiality was an ancient tradition, defended at Vatican I by the protagonists of the Primacy; the aim of this Council was not to prove it, but to determine the method of its exercise.

The same point was made at the 10th General Congregation by a young Auxiliary of Bologna, Bettazzi by name, who had been consecrated only 8 days before, in a most eloquent speech that held the attention of the whole assembly. I was later told that it had been the subject of his doctoral dissertation.

In the 42nd General Congregation, once again, De Smedt of Bruges captured the attention of all by a typically powerful speech on this topic. His object was to show that a clearer doctrine on collegiality, which he defined as active cooperation of the whole episcopate with the Pope, corresponded to contemporary pastoral needs. Collegiality, he said was necessary for two reasons. First in order that Peter might confirm his brethren. For this a central organ was needed, by means of which active communion among Bishops might flourish. The task and responsibilities of the Pope had been greatly increased. The more he could be helped, the more effectively could he fulfil his central function. The second reason was in order that the highest degree of union in the Priesthood of Christ might be attained. In Christ the hierarchy was one College. Ontologically and sacramentally all bishops formed one organ in Christ. It depended on them whether they lived as such. In the past, the wider the Church spread, the more had communication been hindered. Now for the first time the obstacles had been overcome and constant intercommunication was possible. Now for the first time the Successor of St Peter could work together with the successors of the Apostles for the salvation of the world. Christ the one and only Priest was no longer separated in Peter and the Apostles. Those Bishops who had lived in close proximity to the Pope, e.g. in Italy, had devotedly collaborated with him. This was now the desire of the whole Episcopal College.

Speaking for 63 French Bishops, Cardinal Liénart developed the scriptural evidence for episcopal collegiality. Christ established a college of 12 apostles, of which Peter was made the head without ceasing to be a member. He, Peter, was to confirm the others, but as his "brethren", not his servants. So, after the Ascension, we find them acting as a College under Peter. The Papal power would be more readily accepted, if it were always exercised in the light of the Gospel saying: "whoever would be first among you, let him be your servant". Cardinal Frings, accepting a point made by several critics that Pope and Bishops did not constitute a College in the strict juridical sense of a society of men of equal status, but only in one of the broader senses later explained by Cardinal Browne O.P. at the end of the debate, sought to complement Liénart by showing how episcopal collegiality existed and operated in ancient tradition. Just as the universal Church consisted of many local churches in union with Rome, so also this truth was expressed in the union of the Bishops with the successor of Peter. It was as clear as the primacy itself and even the word "College" was used to express it.

There were inevitably a number of speakers whose fear of the abuse of the concept outweighed their appreciation of its value, but few were bold enough to deny it outright, not even Carli, a great traditionalist from a tiny Italian see, though he asked that the word "college" be avoided, and "corpus" or "coetus" be used instead. (For the finally approved teaching, cf. *Lumen Gentium* nn. 18-20).

A closely related subject in this chapter of the schema was the sacramental character of episcopal consecration. It received relatively little attention, perhaps because the schema, in n. 14, completely ignored the mediaeval view that episcopal consecration was a mere sacramental and firmly declared that "no one should doubt that the Episcopate is truly and properly the supreme grade of the sacrament of Order". Of the few who did deal at some length with the topic, most were concerned to emphasize that episcopal "ordination", as it has since come to be called, conferred not only the order but also the powers, and that canonical mission by the Pope was required merely in order to direct and coordinate the exercise of those powers.

Bishop Beck of Salford was the first to criticize the skimpy treatment which the schema gave to priests, lumped with deacons in a single section (n. 15) concerned merely to point out that they are "true priests of secondary dignity and provident cooperators of the Episcopal order". His point was subsequently taken up by Archbishop Conway of Armagh, Archbishop Hurley of Durban, a German Bishop Schick speaking for the German and Scandinavian hierarchies, and Bishop Bernard of Versailles. Conway pointed out that the schema devoted nine pages to bishops, 7 to the laity, and half a page to priests, a grave imbalance in his view. Hurley was almost cynical. It was all right, he said, to ascribe to the Bishop the job of teaching, sanctifying and ruling. But in practice what did it amount to? The real ministry of teaching and sanctifying was done rather by the priests. The Bishop was an unknown person to 99% of his flock. The priests were his ears, his hands, his eyes and his very voice. It was his job to lead, but he couldn't do it without his priests.

In explanation of this strong criticism, it should be remembered that a special schema on the Ministry and Life of priests had not yet even been proposed, let alone drafted. The Commission which was eventually charged with producing it (of which I was a member) had nothing more at this stage than a series of propositions on clerical discipline, to which its previous output had been reduced by order during the interval between the first and second Sessions. Even so the final promulgated version of *Lumen Gentium* 28 clearly benefited from the criticism directed at the original draft. It is fuller and more positive.

Rather more attention was paid to a brief proposal in n. 15 of the schema, that in future it should be possible for the diaconate to be exercised as a permanent grade of the hierarchy, where the Church deemed it necessary for the care of souls, either in certain regions or in all; in which case it should be for the rulers of the Church to decide whether such deacons were to be bound by celibacy or not. Some reacted against it as undermining the firmness of clerical celibacy, and would only approve of permanent deacons if they were subject to the same law as those proceeding to the priesthood. Cardinal Döpfner, on the other hand, pointed out that the text of the schema was more cautious and limited than that of Trent, merely opens the way to Pastors of the Church that wanted to use it, and constituted no threat to celibacy unless it were indiscriminately introduced. Many missionary bishops, with a few exceptions, welcomed it as a practical necessity in their areas, for not only were the pagan populations increasing more rapidly than the Christians, but the number of priestly vocations was dropping. An Argentinian Bishop (Camara?), claiming to speak for Latin America, said that in theory they should have 1 priest per 6000, but in practice it worked out at 1 per 10, 20 or 30 thousand. (For the final result, cf. *Lumen Gentium* 29).

Notwithstanding the originally declared intention of the Moderators to let the debate on this important chapter run to the bitter end, they were induced to put the closure to the vote at the 12th (48th) General Congregation, Tuesday 15 October, when, as they said, there were still enough intending speakers to last 3 more days. The vote was morally unanimous. However, at the request of some Fathers, the main propositions on the episcopate were to be put to a vote, the text to be distributed on the morrow (13th General Congregation) and the vote to be taken the next day (14th General Congregation). Meanwhile, those for 3 or more Fathers who were waiting to speak would be allowed to do so, vi Art. 57.

It was fortunate that they were, because Bishop Holland just managed to get in the door with what proved in the event to be an important proposition. In England, he said, we had a legal adage to the effect that it was not enough for justice to be done; it must be seen to be done. So with this schema: it was not enough to declare that there would in future be some sort of cooperation of the Bishops with the Pope, it was necessary that this be made evident to the eyes of the world. Thererfore an organ should be set up, composed of Bishops representative of their respective Conferences, to help in the government of the Church and perpetuate the spirit of the Council. It would be a practical demonstration of a union not visible hitherto. As is evident, the Synod of Bishops does precisely what Bishop Holland asked for.

* * *

Discussion of chapter III, then entitled: "On the People of God and in particular on the Laity", began during the 13th (49th) General Congregation (Wednesday 16 October), with the assurance already given that, in the amended version, those sections dealing with the People of God in general would form the new chapter II (between Mystery and Hierarchy) and those on the laity would form chap. IV. But since the Fathers were free to speak on any topic in the amalgamated chapter III of the schema in front of them, the People of God and the Laity were constantly intermingled in the discussion. Bishop Muldoon, an Auxiliary of Sydney, had a point when he urged that in a dogmatic treatise on the Church we should not be talking of the laity at all, but of the faithful (christifideles) defined as members of the body of Christ, incorporated in Him by baptism. The Apostolic vocation of the laity as such could well have been left to the document to be issued "On the Apostolate of the Laity".

The three main topics were the universal Priesthood of the People of God (often wrongly presented, as Bacci complained, as the universal priesthood of the Laity), the concept of the laity and its apostolate, and the continued existence in the Church of charismata. The best speech on the first theme was by De Smedt of Bruges. Speaking in the name of 60 other Bishops, he urged that the schema's doctrine about the universal priesthood of the laity be applied to the christian life of layfolk. Christ still lived and exercised His priesthood in all the baptized who offered their whole lives in Him. So too they exercised their prophetic mission in Christ, bearing witness to His truth, and were called to share in his royal function. Cardinal Gracias of Bombay asked that the apostolic mission of the laity should not be confused with that of the hierarchy; each in its own order was distinct.

Cardinal Ruffini, while conceding that charismata were abundant at first, claimed that history showed that they had ceased and now were not even granted to the most worthy. Cardinal Suenens answered that this was to take charismata in too narrow a sense. It was important to revive the concept, lest the Church be regarded as a mere administrative apparatus. The Pilgrim Church was the Church of the Holy Spirit who was given to all. St Paul speaks not only of the extraordinary charismata of his day, but of those of faith, of teaching, of discernment of spirits, etc. The Church still needs them and it is for her pastors to detect, promote and foster them. We must not "extinguish the Spirit". True, said Florit of Florence, but that is not what "charism" meant nowadays; it was ambiguous, for we did not talk of a theologian exercising his charism, but his function.

None of these issues, compared with what had gone before, aroused much keen controversy and the debate dragged its dull length along for six days. Finally, during the 19th (55th) General Congregation (Thursday 24 Oct), Cardinal Döpfner intervened to say that he and his fellow Moderators felt that we had had enough "iam satis", and if the Fathers felt the same, would they please vote with their feet. The vast majority, as usual, stood up. Those who had had their names down to speak were told by Döpfner that "if they wanted to use their right (i.e. to speak for 3 or more Fathers), *quod minime est obligatio*, they should give in their names again on the morrow". Meanwhile, Cardinal Browne O.P. would sum up on behalf of the Commission. He did so and then Döpfner made the announcement all had been waiting for. Many Fathers had requested that the separate schema on the B.V.M. should be attached to *De Ecclesia*. To ensure a well-informed vote, Cardinal Santos of Manila would put the case for keeping it separate, and Cardinal Konig for integrating it. The text would be available the next day and the vote would be taken the following week.

Our own Hierarchy of England and Wales was intimately involved in this project. They had studied the question at a Westminster meeting and had come to Rome determined to press for the integration of the two schemata on theological as well as ecumenical grounds. In fact, they had brought with them an alternative draft on Our Lady, drafted by Abbot Butler, which would fit easily into the context of *De Ecclesia*, and from the day of their arrival they had sought support from other Episcopal Conferences. They were by no means alone in their desire and indeed the Moderators had promised at the very beginning of the Session that there would be a vote on the proposal in due course. But their activity during that weekend was noted and a writer in *Il Tempo* who was opposed to the motion accused our Hierarchy of wanting to play down the Marian doctrines of the Immaculate Conception and Assumption. Since, as the text of their alternative draft showed, this charge was patently untrue, a strong protest was made to *Il Tempo* and it eventually withdrew the charge in response to what it called a "precious clarification" of the English point of view.

The vote was taken on the Tuesday, 29 October, at the 21st (57th) General Congregation It was fortunate from our point of view that the Moderators had announced beforehand that a simple majority (51%.) would do, because that was practically the margin by which the motion was passed.

The Fathers voted by 1114 to 1074 to attach the schema on BVM to that on the Church as a final chapter, a majority of 40. It may well be that the pressure exerted by our Bishops was decisive. But no doubt the Holy Spirit had providentially ensured that so it would be. Mary is first and foremost the Mother of Christ, God made man, and the Church is His Mystical Body. The two are inseparably connected in Christ.

* * *

The long-awaited propositions about the chapter on the Hierarchy (then II) were distributed that same day. Rumour had it that the fortnight's delay in producing them was due to determined opposition by some of the Presidential Council who had supported Cardinal Ottaviani's contention that only the Commission which had produced the schema and of which he was president had the right to propose texts for the discussion and vote of the Fathers. The issue was said to have been finally settled at a plenary meeting of the Presidential Council, the Moderators and the Secretariate, and I was assured by a French Bishop that the right of the Moderator to put the proposed questions was carried by a single vote. It was also rumoured that the Pope had intervened on their side.

In these questions, on which the Fathers voted the next day, 30 Oct., 22nd (58th) General Congregation, they were asked whether they wanted the schema to be drafted in such manner as to make the following five statements:

1) that Episcopal Consecration constitutes the supreme grade of the Sacrament of Order (carried by 2123 to 34);

2) that every Bishop legitimately consecrated in the communion of the Bishops and of the Roman Pontiff who is their Head and principle of unity, is a member of the Body of Bishops (carried by 2049 to 104);

3) that the Body or College of Bishops succeeds to the College of Apostles in the office of evangelizing, sanctifying and pasturing, and that it, along with the Roman Pontiff its head and never without this head (whose primatial right over all pastors and faithful remains safe and sound), possesses full and supreme power over the whole Church (carried by 1808 to 336);

4) that the said power belongs by divine law to the College of Bishops united to their Head (carried by 1717 to 408);

5) that consideration be given to the opportuneness of restoring the diaconate as a distinct and permanent grade of the sacred ministry, according as it may be useful to the Church in various regions (carried by 1588 to 525).

The announcement of these results was greeted with loud applause (notwithstanding the frequent admonition: "abstineant Patres a plausu"), indicating that the great majority of the Fathers regarded this as an excellent method of discovering the real balance of opinion on these issues without an indefinite debate. The Congregation dispersed in good humour to enjoy the long weekend occasioned by All Saints and All Souls; it is to be hoped that even the defeated found comfort in it.

* * *

During these latter Congregations, in between the taking of votes, the Fathers had been discussing the chapter (then IV) on the Vocation to Sanctity in the Church. There was no dispute on the reality of this vocation and most speakers were pleased or at least satisfied in the main by the manner in which the schema presented it. No objection was raised when the debate on it was concluded at the for the time being end of the 23rd (59th) General Congregation, Thursday 31 October, and with it the debate on *De Ecclesia*.

When the Council reassembled on Tuesday 5 November for the 24th (60th) General Congregation, the related schema on Bishops and Government of Dioceses was introduced. To judge from the general "day-after" atmosphere in St Peter's and the reactions or lack of them at Press conferences held outside the Council, the 9-days debate on this schema stirred little interest, at least by comparison with what had preceded it. The same points of difference kept recurring.

But even if it was something of an anticlimax, it had its moments. After a day and a half of general discussion, during the 25th (61st) General

Congregation (6 November), the Fathers were asked whether they were satisfied with the schema as a basis on which to work. They accepted it, but with a large dissentient vote: 2100 for, 477 against, probably because it failed to take account of the doctrine of episcopal collegiality, on which they had recently voted that it be given expression in the schema *De Ecclesia*. Earlier in this same Congregation, Cardinal Ruffini had anticipated this objection by observing that, according to the declaration of the Moderators themselves, that vote was merely a "straw" vote meant to provide occasion for subsequent issue debate and had by no means settled the issue.

He was right in one sense, but two days later, at the 27th (63rd) General Congregation, Cardinal Frings took up Ruffini's point. He agreed with those who wanted a chapter on the College of Bishops in the present schema. Was the almost unanimous consensus of the Fathers to count for nothing? It was not for Conciliar Commissions to deal again with things already settled by the Fathers. Their job was simply to give expression to the will of the Fathers. He then went on, in his mild voice, to observe that the distinction made between administrative and judicial power should be extended to all the Roman Curial Congregations, not excluding the Holy Office, "whose way of acting", he said,"is not adapted to modern conditions. Even in the Holy Office no one should be judged or condemned unless he had previously been heard and given occasion to correct himself or his book". There were inevitably two intervening speakers before Cardinal Ottaviani, Prefect of the Holy Office, could get to the miicrophone, but when he did, his voice was far from mild. "Allow me to protest altissime", he said, against the charges made against the Holy Office. They proceed, I will not say from ignorance, but from nescience". Only those in the Holy Office, he said, knew how many were consulted, how many heard.

On a more conciliatory note, Cardinal Lercaro, speaking between Frings and Ottaviani, pointed out that, although there was nothing in principle to prevent the regular exercise of episcopal collegiality through a representative central organ of Bishops (this was what Bishop Holland had proposed), only the Pope could integrate it in the existing structure of the central government of the Church Universal. Proposals to this effect, which Pope Paul had already said he hoped to receive from the Council, could not be worked out in a few days debate, and therefore they should be left to a special Commission to elaborate in the interval between this and the next session. (Actually, the *Ordo Synodi Episcoporum Celebrandae* was issued by the Secretariate of State, 8 Dec.1966, and has since been revised).

When the discussion passed to the function of the National Conferences of Bishops in chapter III of the schema, most speakers seemed anxious to avoid giving them any more power over their individual members than was absolutely necessary. As one Bishop remarked outside the Council, they were keen enough on having a collegial share in the government of the universal Church, but did not like the idea of anyone else sharing in the government of their own dioceses. Nor was their much vocal support for the proposal in the schema that Bishops should be obliged to resign at a fixed age, though it got through in a slightly amended form eventually (cf. *Christus Dominus*, n. 21) and was implemented by Paul VI in *Ecclesiae Sanctae*, n. 11, as an urgent request that they should offer their resignation to the Pope not later than the age of 75.

In the same chapter, it was proposed that Coadjutors and Auxiliaries, who, under the law of the Code (c.350-5) had only such power as might be given to them in their papal brief of appointment or delegated to them by their Bishop, which might be very limited indeed, should be given a status corresponding to their episcopal dignity. Germany is outstanding for the size of its dioceses, and it was fitting therefore that one of its many Auxiliaries, Reuss (of Mainz, I think), should make the most impressive speech on their behalf. Theologically, he argued, even Residential Bishops obtained the substance of their power by virtue of their consecration, and the same applied to Coadjutors and Auxiliaries. They too became by consecration members of the College of Bishops which, in union with the Roman Pontiff, had by divine law supreme power over the universal Church, and they too, on the same ground, shared in the divinely assigned office of evangelizing, pasturing and ruling. He, therefore, supported the proposal of the schema that they should at least have all the powers and faculties enjoyed by Vicars General and should be consulted by the Bishop in all major matters. (For the final result, cf. *Christus Dominus*, nn. 25-26).

Chapter IV, on the suitable size of dioceses and provinces, evoked no major controversy, and at the 32nd (68th) General Congregation (15 November), discussion of the schema petered out at 11.45 for want of speakers (an unprecedented event) and we were let out of school a half-an-hour early.

* * *

Monday, 18 November, 33rd (69th) General Congregation saw the introduction of the eagerly-awaited schema on Ecumenism which contained five chapters (I. The Principles; II. The Practice; III. Christians separated from the Catholic Church; IV. Jews; V. Religious Liberty). To forestall captious criticism, the Moderators had arranged that three explanatory reports ("relationes") should first be given by chosen speakers: Bishop Bukatko on the Oriental Churches, Cardinal Bea on the Jews, and Bishop De Smedt on Religious Liberty. They were very impressive performances but they did not prevent strong criticism being made, especially by Bishops from Arab countries, of the inclusion of the Jews, and by some who held that Religious Liberty was a separate question altogether from Ecumenism. To avoid delay, therefore, the Moderators proposed that the question of these two disputed chapters should be left to a later date, and that the Fathers should vote simply on the acceptability of the first 3 chapters as a basis. They accepted them after the usual general discussion and the detailed discussion of each chapter in turn began. (During the general discussion, Archbishop Heenan made a rousing speech on the readiness of the English and Welsh Hierarchy to carry out the recommendations of the Council, but urged that they rather than foreigners should conduct the dialogue with separated brethren in their own country. His speech won the only applause (illicit) of that particular morning).

Once the discussion in detail had been begun, the hustle was manifestly on. At the 41st (77th) General Congregation (27 November), when 41 announced speakers were still awaiting their turn to speak on chapter II, Cardinal Döpfner, Moderator that day, persuaded the Fathers that, to judge by the number of repetitions, meditations and examinations of conscience to which they were being subjected, it was time to pass on to chapter III. This gave Bishop Dwyer, formerly of the Catholic Missionary Society, the opportunity to deliver a realistic speech on the problems to be encountered in dialogue with non-Catholics. It was not enough, as some seemed to imagine, to expound the truth with wide charity (a constant phrase of some speakers). The Anglican Archbishop of Wales had recently declared that Anglicans rejected Catholic doctrines not because they did not understand them, but because they did. Moreover, all sorts of contradictory positions and moral doctrines were held even by members of the same non-Catholic denomination, and there would therefore be need for endless patience.

Three days later, at the 43rd (79th) General Congregation of the Session (Monday 2 December), the discussion was closed without the Fathers having been given the promised opportunity to decide on the acceptability of the last two chapters, on the Jews and on Religious Liberty. There must have been some complaints about this, because Cardinal Bea, President of the Ecumenical Commission, intervened to assure the Fathers that the only reason was lack of time. The Council was due to be prorogued by the Pope in a solemn Public Session on the Wednesday, 4 December, and that left only one free day, the Tuesday (3 December). It was not enough for adequate discussion of the acceptability of two such controversial chapters and was devoted instead to a solemn celebration of the Fourth Centenary of Trent. He guaranteed that the opportunity would be provided when the Council reassembled the following September.

The Third Session

September 14th – November 21st 1964

(The opening and closing dates were brought forward to enable Fathers to attend the Eucharistic Congress at Bombay).

The distinctive feature of the Third Session of the Council was the sheer volume and variety of the subjects presented to the Fathers for discussion and voting. The Co-ordinating Commission had decided in the interval that it was possible as well as desirable to complete the work of the Council in this Session, and, with this in view, they had arranged for all the remaining schemata, not yet presented, except The Church in the Modern World and The Lay Apostolate, to be reduced by their respective Commissions to series of brief propositions on which the Fathers were to be asked to vote after a summary discussion. To expedite the debates, a rule was made that intending speakers must give five days notice, along with a summary of what they intended to say, and to judge from the list of dates issued to the Fathers for the presentation of their summaries on the various schemata, an unofficial time-table appeared to be in operation, which, had it been kept to, would have completed the debates by about the 23rd October, leaving the remaining month for amendments and voting.

For the first five weeks, the debates were kept to schedule through hard driving by the Moderators and the cooperation of the great majority of the Fathers who never failed to vote the closure of a discussion when it was proposed by the Moderators. The plan began to creak when the discussion of The Lay Apostolate schema was allowed to run on for four days. It was evident that the plan had broken down (though this was never officially admitted) when the first of the sets of Propositions, i.e. the set On Priests (*De Sacerdotibus*) was rejected as utterly inadequate. The Fathers had devoted so much time and space to the functions and duties of Bishops that they hadn't the nerve to deal with priests in a few mainly juridical propositions, and after a two-day debate they called for a full-length theological document.

The responsible Commission, of which I was a member, and which had originally been concerned solely with the "Discipline of the Christian Clergy and People", promptly co-opted some competent theologians (Lécuyer, Congar, etc.) and produced the desired theological document in less than three weeks, but it was clear to all that it would be impossible to get it discussed, amended and voted in the rest of the crowded four weeks which were all that remained after the rejection of its predecessor.

The Co-ordinating Commission then devised a new plan to ensure that all the remaining schemata would at least be presented and discussed sufficiently to enable the Commissions to gauge the general mind of the Fathers and introduce such revisions as would make the documents basically acceptable in the Fourth Session.

Let us return to the debates of the Third Session.

It had been agreed at the Second Session that a chapter be added to the Constitution on the Church dealing with the Eschatological Nature of the Pilgrim Church and that the schema *De B.M.V.* be added also.

The former was presented and adequately discussed at the First General Congregation (80th), on 15 September and was in general found satisfactory. Discussion of the latter began at the Second General Congregation (81st) and was completed at the beginning of the Fourth (83rd).

Cardinal Ruffini felt that it did less than justice to Mary's association with our Redeemer, and urged that the firm foundation of Mary's universally accepted title of Mediatrix of graces should be made clear. He received strong support from Bishop Randeiro of Portugal, who, speaking for 82 other Bishops, begged that at least what the schema said about Mary's mediation should remain intact, otherwise there would be *admiratio* caused among the faithful who believed that all graces came to us through Mary. Bishop Ancel of France, however, would personally have preferred reference to Mary Mediatrix to be avoided, and accepted it only for the sake of unanimity and provided it was presented as a conclusion from the accepted doctrine of Mary's Maternity in the economy of grace, involving no derogation from Christ's unique mediation. Cardinal Léger, intervening next but one after Ruffini, wanted the title "Mediatrix" omitted, because it was differently understood and not easy to explain accurately. Cardinal Bea's position was more or less the same; the title was open to misunderstanding by Catholics and created difficulties for non-Catholics. Cardinal Alfrink, who had waited till the second day of the debate, also urged caution. The object of the schema was to state accepted doctrine, not opinions. Certainly Mary had a special function, but it was necessary to distinguish between the title of "Mediatrix" and the doctrine behind it, because Mary was called "Mediatrix" in a sense absolutely different from that in which Christ was called our Mediator, indeed Our sole Mediator. It was therefore better to avoid the title.

Cardinal Wyszynski of Warsaw, speaking for the Bishops of Poland, wanted the schema to proclaim Mary "Mother of the Church". Bishop Hervas of Spain went further: the chapter should be entitled *De B.M.V. Mater Ecclesiae*. That, he claimed, was why many of the Fathers had wanted the schema inserted into the Constitution on The Church. It was a solidly grounded doctrine, recently confirmed by Pope Paul, and its omission would seem like an implicit denial. The General of the Servite Order, Father Monta, held that it should not hesitate to call Mary, in imitation of St Augustine: "Mother of the members of Christ".

Cardinal Suenens seemed to feel his way to a midway position. The schema, he said, suffered from a certain minimalism; it tended to present Mary too much as a figure of the past and was not explicit enough about her present association with Christ in the work of salvation, as taught by the Magisterium and believed by the faithful. This applied especially to the intimate link between her motherhood and the active apostolate.

* * *

Certain sections from the suppressed schema *De Cura Animarum* were then presented for discussion with a view to incorporation in the already discussed document on Bishops and Government of Dioceses, thenceforth to be entitled: *De Pastorali Munere Episcoporum*. Since the original schema *De Cura Animarum*, had been prepared by the Preparatory Commission on Discipline of the Christian Clergy and People, (to which I had belonged) it had contained many points of canon law. These had since been reserved to the Commission which was to revise the Code, to the regret of one of the first speakers, Cardinal Richaud of Bordeaux, who had been hoping for a discussion of the law on the removal of Parish Priests which he found unsatisfactory.

Bishop Foley of Lancaster, on the other hand, had been waiting for this moment to plead for a renewal of the pastoral life and work of Priests, which, he maintained, required intimate contact between priest and people, after the example set by Christ Himself. (It may well have been his own outstanding devotion to that kind of pastoral care as a Parish Priest in the Brentwood diocese that had brought about his promotion to the diocese of Lancaster).

Given the importance of this topic in relation to the main purpose of the Council, pastoral renewal, the debate on it was disappointing. It flipped from one relatively minor point to another and, apart from Cardinal Léger, most of the big guns remained silent. Léger's main point was the essential need for pastors to get to know modern man, a very different creature, still changing fast, and to speak to him humbly and intelligibly in modern terms. Bishops needed to establish dialogue with their people, and for that they must change their own external aspect. Several other speakers called for a change in the life-style of bishops, among them Bishop Staverman from Indonesia. The "figura episcopi", he said, was antiquated. A bishop should indeed be a "good shepherd", but must remember that his flock were not literally "sheep".

Bishop Renard of Versailles, among others, stressed the union of a bishop with his priests. He formed one presbytery with them by the very nature of the priesthood, and he should value their experience and advice. Archbishop Guerry of Cambrai wanted attention drawn to a new way in which bishops could and should exercise their teaching function, namely, by making public pronouncements on social events of moral or religious significance, after the manner of Pius XII. It manifested the presence of the Church in the world and her solicitude, but its fruitful exercise required accurate knowledge of the facts, supernatural prudence and impartiality, ardent charity, humility and courage, and clarity of exposition.

* * *

When the discussion ended early in the Seventh General Congregation (86th 23 September), after little more than two General Congregations, the thoroughly revised and keenly awaited schema on Religious Liberty, which had begin life as a mere chapter of the schema on Ecumenism, was presented for consideration. This time there was no lack of big guns from the College of Cardinals (who, be it noted, had the right to speak first at the beginning of any General Congregation, and also when a new subject was introduced for discussion during a General Congregation; and who therefore, if enough of them used their right, almost inevitably covered most of the important points worth making).

Cardinal Ruffini opened the debate with a statement of what could fairly be described as having been up to then the more common position. Quoting John 8,32, "veritas liberabit vos – the truth shall make you free", he drew the conclusion that religious liberty was proper to religious truth and therefore only the one true religion had a right to it, though the common good required tolerance to those in honest error.

Understandably, others in due course took much the same line. Cardinal Bueno of Seville, while admitting that the schema contained much that was useful and true, insisted that account must be taken nevertheless of the objective truth that only the Catholic Church had the God-given right to propagate itself. Cardinal Ottaviani admitted that no one may justly be forced into a religion, but held that the erring were not "honore digni – deserving of honour", but only of tolerance. According to Bishop Nicodemo of Bari, since only truth had an objective right to liberty, the religious liberty of the erring could only be based on their subjective right to follow their own certain conscience within the limits allowed by the common good. Bishop Granados of Spain objected that a right to propagate error was a novelty in the Church. Forgetting, as many had done before him (myself included, at least before the Council), that rights could only be predicated of persons, he based his position on the alleged principle that only truth had rights.

There was probably much less difference of opinion at the purely pragmatic level than the speeches of the Fathers seemed to imply. Most, I think, would have agreed substantially with Bishop Carlo Colombo of Italy that, at least in the modern situation, the State would be wise to allow as much religious liberty as was compatible with the common good and public order. And all would presumably have agreed that every man had at least a *subjective* right to follow his honest certain conscience in his religious faith and practice. The real question at issue was whether every man had an *objective* right to do so, both in his private and in his social life, a right therefore which should be guaranteed to him by civil law.

Bishop de Smedt, the Relator, had made it clear in his preliminary *Relatio* that the revised schema now presented to the Fathers was not calling simply for religious tolerance by civil authorities everywhere, but was asserting an objective right "based on the nature of the human person as created by God". It was appealing to the fact that man, as made by God, could only seek to conform his will to God's by following his own honestly formed certain conscience, because that was how God's will reached him in the final issue. Every man therefore had not only a divinely imposed duty but also a corresponding God-given right to worship God as his honest certain conscience prescribed or permitted, correctly or mistakenly, and to do so as a social person, because that also was how God made him. This very fine distinction had seldom if ever been worked out in such detail before, and many even of those who wholeheartedly supported the practical conclusion of the schema either overlooked or avoided the argument on which it was firmly based, some of them deliberately. Cardinal Ritter of St Louis, for example, although a convinced defender of religious liberty, like the American hierarchy almost to a man (after all, it has always been a key point of the American Constitution), thought it would be wiser to omit any disputed reasons. Cardinal Cushing, stridently claiming to speak for most of the US hierarchy, urged that the declaration be made, if anything, stronger, so as to present the Church as the protagonist of religious freedom; she had always had to fight for it for herself and now wanted it for all. More surprisingly, Cardinal Silva Henriquez of Chile claiming to speak for 58 Latin American bishops, declared his and their full support of the schema. Religious liberty was supremely important for the world as a whole and especially for Latin America in this pluralistic age. Before they could approach others for recognition, they needed to convince them that they conceded to others what they claimed for themselves.

Criticisms and reservations were expressed mainly by European Spaniards and Italians; the declaration was said to be ambiguous, open to misinterpretation, neglectful of due distinction between truth and error. Firm support however came from all parts of the world, notably from behind the Iron Curtain, where it tended to be based especially on harsh experience. Religion, said the Bishop of Skoplje in Jugoslavia, must be intolerant dogmatically, but if every religion took that attitude in practice, life would be impossible. Bishop Klepacz, speaking for the Polish Hierarchy relied rather on the principle that every man had a right to be guided by his conscience in his choice and practice of religion, a right which no human authority could deny to him in theory or in practice without injustice.

The closure was voted when the debate had lasted nearly three General Congregations, but at the succeeding General Congregation (10th, on 28 September), a few more speakers who had obtained 70 supporters claimed their right. Among them was Archbishop Heenan who, as usual, took the pragmatic line. English experience had shown that full religious liberty was the only way to peace and progress. It had now become necessary to the common good of the whole world. There were real dangers involved, but they were worth risking. The reasons would have to be stated, otherwise the Council's sincerity would be doubted, in the opinion of the last speaker, also, (Bishop Zola from East Africa) appeal to experience was not enough. A merely pragmatical declaration would make the Council's internal belief suspect. Its doctrine must be based on the nature of man.

The declaration still had quite a way to go. Indeed, it was not finally promulgated until the last day of the Council, 7 December 1965. But its supporters must have begun to feel optimistic. Of the speakers who made their position quite clear, fourteen in my reckoning were critical, seventeen ready to vote for the declaration more or less as it stood.

* * *

It was immediately followed in that 10th (89th) General Congregation (Monday 28 September) by discussion of a document on the Jews (*De Iudaeis*) which had originally been a chapter in the schema on Ecumenism and was now offered as part of a Declaration on the relation of the Church to Non-Christian Religions. Its destination at this stage, however, was still in dispute. Cardinal Liénart maintained that, in spite of the Arab opposition to its inclusion in the decree on Ecumenism, it was still necessary to ecumenism. We Christians too were children of Abraham according to the faith and shared the same inspired books. Christ, Mary and the Apostles were all Jews. It was right for the Church to acknowledge these truths openly, but neither necessary nor right to speak of the Jews as reprobate or as guilty of deicide, neither of which charge was true. Cardinal Tappouni of Syria, however, speaking for the other Eastern Patriarchs, while maintaining that they were not anti-Semites or hostile to Judaism, claimed that the proposed declaration would cause grave pastoral difficulties for them, and asked therefore on their behalf that it be simply deleted from the Acts of the Council.

There may have been some sympathy for the Arab Bishops' predicament, but they elicited little support for their proposition. The declaration, said Cardinal Lercaro, was necessary for reasons which had nothing to do with politics or racial distinction. It was a natural fruit of the Church's fuller awareness of her ontological plenitude and origins. Cardinal Léger regarded it as a necessary stage towards renewal of the Church's dialogue with the non-Christian world. A similar line was taken by Cardinal Bueno of Seville. Jews and non-Christians could not be left out of ecumenism in the broad sense. The Church's dialogue must extend to all the children of the common Father. All reference to reprobation of the Jews must be omitted. No one now held it and mere mention of it opened an old sore. Bishop Mendez of Mexico called for explicit rejection of the false interpretation of certain texts which historically had led to persecution of Jews.

Archbishop Heenan found the new text to be in some ways less friendly to the Jews than the old and said they would want to know the reasons for the change. The Pauline text about their ultimate conversion should be omitted. Ecumenism was not directly concerned with conversion, but with better knowledge and understanding. The previous text had exculpated them from the charge of deicide, if the new text did not, false implications might follow. The exculpation should be explicitly renewed. Bishop Leven from Texas and Archbishop O'Boyle of Washington took much the same line.

A Lebanese bishop delivered a eulogy of the Moslems who, he said, would be justly offended by the ampler treatment given to the Jews. A bishop from Turkey, Descuffi, spoke of the devotion of the Moslems to Our Lady. One Indian bishop, Antipetti, presumably from the Hindu area, declared the preference shown to the Moslems to be odious. Another, Paracattil, sought recognition of the obligation of Christians to acknowledge what was good in Hindu culture. Though their sacred books did not know Christ, they yet sought Him. A bishop from Syria, Tawil, wanted to know what about the millions of Arabs excluded from Palestine by those whom the Council was proposing to treat with special honour. It was inopportune, to say the least.

Those who had to steer the document through the Council, Cardinal Bea in particular, might well have felt that it could more correctly be called impossible. The debate was allowed to run for about two General Congregations, and then, at the 12th General Congregation (30 Sept), the document on divine revelation which, under its original title of *De Fontibus Revelationis* had provoked such controversy in the first session and, after a momentous but inconclusive vote confirmed by John XXIII, had been sent back for complete revision, returned at long last into St Peter's under the non-committal title of *De Divina Revelatione*.

Cardinal Döpfner, speaking in the name of 79 German and Scandinavian bishops welcomed the revised text as an improvement on the old, notably inasmuch as it avoided the controversial theory of two sources. Next day, at the 13th General Congregation, Cardinal Léger of Montreal and Cardinal Landazzuri of Peru praised it for the same reason, and others expressed their satisfaction on similar grounds. But there were quite a few critics who made it clear that the supporters of the two sources theory had not given up. Bishop Compagnone of Anagni insisted that Tradition covered a wider field of revealed truth than Scripture, which itself was only known through Tradition as a source of revelation. He urged that the schema should therefore repeat the Tridentine phrase, itself a compromise: "in libris scriptis et sine scripto traditionibus". Similarly Bishop Antipetty from India: for four centuries Tradition had been a constitutive source of revelation not contained in Scripture, and indeed it was on this ground that dogmas such as the Assumption were defined; it would be fatal to abandon that position.

* * *

At the 14th (93rd) General Congregation, the debate moved on to the discussion in particular of chapters I and II, though many speakers continued to indicate their opinion of the schema in general, usually in laudatory terms, but not always. Bishop Beras of Santo Domingo, for example, was severely critical. The Commission had claimed to have avoided controversial statements and kept to what was accepted doctrine. But if this had been the general intention of the Council, it would have kept silent about episcopal collegiality, the sacramentality of episcopal ordination, the mediation of the BVM., etc. They had all been taught in their catechism that not all the faith was contained in Scripture, as could be seen from the statement of the Catechism of the Council of Trent: "partim in Scriptura, partim in traditionibus adest". To say that revelation was contained in both was not the same as saying that it was contained partly in the one and partly in the other. A Bishop Baldassare was critical of the suggestion that the time had not yet come to settle the question whether or not all revealed truths were contained in Scripture at least fundamentally. Councils postponed decisions as premature only when the questions concerned were of second rank. That could hardly be said of this question. Was the dogma regarding the canon of Scripture fundamentally contained in Scripture, or only in Tradition? To judge however from the number of speakers who did not clamour for a settlement of the question but chose rather to offer constructive criticisms on less basic issues, the non-alignment of the schema was regarded more commonly as a virtue, or at least as a reasonable omission.

* * *

The debate then passed on to chapter III. Cardinal Ruffini, learned but very conservative, was unhappy about the concession made to "genera litteraria". It could not be admitted that the Christian people had hitherto been ignorant of the "genus litterarium" of the Scriptures, and thereby unable to understand their message.

When, at the 15th (94th) General Congregation, chapters IV-VI were open for discussion the prestigious Cardinal Bea, scripture scholar and ecumenist-in-chief, took the opportunity to express his general satisfaction with the document. He rejoiced over its positive approach, the best way to deal with errors, its avoidance of disputed questions, its biblical language. It was not perfect, and he suggested some points in which it might be improved. Bishop Weber of Strasbourg called it "excellent in every respect". Bishop Philbin of Down and Connor, speaking in the name of over 30 bishops, praised the text in general but complained of certain ambiguities, in particular in regard to the historicity of the gospels, and urged that their historicity be clearly asserted in the proper sense of the word.

At the 16th (95th) General Congregation (6 October), Abbot Butler used his turn at the microphone to make a plea for the necessary freedom of exegetes. They needed to be free to speak intelligibly to other scholars. While accepting the inspired truth by the light of faith, they had also to view questions "ex praeambulo fidei", take account of *genera litteraria*, common even to the evangelists, and allowing for midrashim in the NT as in the OT. Some would turn liberty into license, but that was a risk that must be taken for the greater good. After two more speeches, the debate was concluded.

* * *

The document *De Apostolatu Laicorum* was presented for discussion at the beginning of the 17th (96th) General Congregation (7 October). Since, in general, it was well received, it should suffice to summarize the main points made during the debate which lasted from the 17th (96th) to the 20th (99th) General Congregation.

All Christians, it was said, had a twofold vocation: first, as men, to subdue the earth (Genesis 1,28), secondly, as Christians, to cooperate for the restoration of all things in Christ by proclaiming His kingdom, each according to his proper mode of life. Hence the proper and unique way of the laity called to work as only laymen can for the renewal of the universe. The implication which one speaker detected in the document, that laymen were needed in the apostolate merely to supply for lack of clergy, must be corrected.

They had their own proper function as baptised members of the Mystical Body of Christ, and as the leaven in the lump, in helping to make the Church incarnate in the world which had to be redeemed. It should be made clear that they were exercising their apostolate whenever they fulfilled their proper function well.

An Indian Bishop, D'Souza, was critical of the phrase "Nil sine Episcopo". It had led to many abuses. Admittedly "Nil contra vel praeter episcopum", but the Church was not a totalitarian State. He was not alone in wanting it made explicit that Catholic Action was merely one form of the lay apostolate. As Archbishop Heenan observed later, at the 20th (99th) General Congregation, the name had a political flavour in England and we sought to avoid it. Bishop De Smedt of Bruges wondered whether it was made sufficiently clear that Catholic laymen should respect the religious liberty of others; apostolic laymen had been known to use force when they could, at least moral force. True they should imitate the zeal of Christ, but also His humility and patience. The point was made that the *missio ad intra* must precede the *missio ad extra*, and Archbishop Conway of Armagh developed it in his speech. The schema should insist more firmly and explicitly that a fruitful apostolate was rooted in personal holiness. The more complex the structure, the more danger there was of "professional" apostles, stimulators of activism rather than of true apostolic action. Priority should be given to spiritual formation. It was also urged that since the layman's vocation was a consequence of the priestly character he derived from his baptism and confirmation, the lay apostolate was no less proper even where there were plenty of clergy; it consecrated the layman's life.

The maturity and responsibility of the laity must be acknowledged and trusted. There was no place for clericalism. Priests should be ready to help lay apostles, but not seek to substitute for them. Bishops had the right to direct the lay apostolate, but not to cripple it. There should be a consultative senate of laity from which the Bishop could learn their mind. The principle of subsidiarity needed to be applied, so that individual laymen and intermediate societies might be free to do what they were competent to do. The notion of Catholic Action needed to be more clearly defined, because the text as it stood seemed to grant a privileged state to certain forms, whereas there should be no discrimination based simply on the juridical status of a movement. Either Catholic Action should have a generic meaning, or some other term should be devised to cover all legitimate forms of the Lay Apostolate.

The Lay Apostolate, it was also said, was too restrictively defined in terms of evangelising. Any activity undertaken for Christ was a form of apostolate, a form to which all were called, whereas not all were called to evangelize. A distinction should be drawn between the apostolate in the strict sense which needs a mandate and the apostolate in the broad sense which does not. The formation of lay apostles should be truly lay, suited to their effective insertion in the contemporary world. They needed theological formation even if they were outstanding in the profane sciences. The proposed Secretariate ought to seek lay advice and not be organized like a curial Congregation. Its members should be mainly laymen.

At the end of the 20th (99th) General Congregation (Monday 12 October), the Fathers voted the closure of the debate. The following day, however, at the 21st (100th) General Congregation, three more speeches were admitted on the 70-Backers rule, and then "clarissimus vir" Pat Keegan (ex-Wigan Young Christian Workers) was called to the microphone to speak (in English) for the Catholic layman of the world. He called for more adaptation of the schema to the Constitution *De Ecclesia*, a clear distinction between the basis and the object of the lay apostolate, and a clarification of the relation between the apostolate of laymen and their role as animators in the temporal order. The Relator of the Commission, Bishop Hengsbach, welcomed his useful comments and added some of his own in regard to the criticisms made during the debate. The object of the Commission had been to leave as much liberty as possible to bishops and layfolk.

A schema prepared by the Commission *De Disciplina Cleri et Populi Christiani* and which had begun life as a disciplinary piece *De Clericis*, and had been reduced by order to a series of ten (later twelve) brief propositions *De Sacerdotibus*, was then presented to the Fathers under the title *De Vita et Ministerio Sacerdotali*. Since the Commission itself was very dissatisfied with the end product of such chopping and changing, — as a member of the Commission I speak from personal knowledge and had expressed my own dissatisfaction, — it was not surprising that the Fathers gave a cool reception to the document. Having spent so much time and devoted so many words to the image of bishops, they must have felt uncomfortable at the thought of presenting their clergy with twelve jejune and mainly canonical propositions. Bishops, it was observed, depended principally on their priests both for their own apostolate and for stimulating and aiding the lay apostolate. In practice, "nil sine presbyteris" was more true than "nil sine episcopo". A complete theological document was needed and it should not be limited to the canonical obligations of priests. It should comfort and strengthen them in their task. Rural priests in particular needed help. It should promote community life among them. There should be a "spiritual Father" for the clergy of every diocese.

At the 22nd (101st) General Congregation, Archbishop F. Gomes of Goiânia, Brazil speaking in the name of 100 other Bishops and to frequent applause, urged the Fathers not to vote on the text as it stood, but to ask that a new text be prepared for their votes in a Fourth Session (the Coordinating Commission was still keeping up the pretence that a Fourth Session might not be necessary). The priesthood was too great and too holy to be dismissed in a brief discussion.

As the debate continued, this plea received more and more support. Cardinal Alfrink, at the 23rd (102nd) General Congregation, observed that though the emended text (the schema gave a textus prior and a textus emendatus) marked a laudable improvement, it still failed to meet the just expectations of priests, because the image of the priest was far from clearly depicted. Bishop Jenny, Auxiliary of Cambrai, hoped that if it were delayed, though not "to the Greek Kalends", it might be made more fruitful. Bishop Sartre of the Cameroons asked that the Propositions be replaced by a substantial document, freshly drafted.

The Moderators took the hint and, with the consent of the Fathers (conveyed by rising to their feet), brought the debate to a close in the 23rd (102nd) General Congregation (15 October), except for Cardinal Lefebvre who spoke for 70 Fathers, and observed that the very brevity of the schema, in a matter of such moment, was regrettable. It failed to do justice to the importance of the ministerial priesthood, an essential point in view of the current wide interest in the common priesthood.

Archbishop Marty of Rheims summed up as Relator for the responsible Commission. The schema did not pretend to deal fully with the priesthood, but only with certain aspects of the life and ministry of priests. That indeed was why the title had been changed from *De Sacerdotibus* to *De Vita et Ministerio Sacerdotali*. The theology of the priesthood belonged to the Constitution *De Ecclesia* (where incidentally it was covered in a single, admittedly lengthy, section, n. 28). However, the Commission shared the desire expressed by some Fathers that the Council should direct to priests an extended set of Propositions or some other more formal document.

(At the next General Congregation, the 24th (103rd), a decision of the Coordinating Commission, made in response to representations from many Fathers, was communicated to the following effect. After each schema of Propositions had been briefly discussed in general, the Fathers would vote as to whether they wanted to proceed to vote on it in detail. If an absolute majority voted in the negative, the whole matter would be sent back to the responsible Commission to be revised by it in accord with the comments of the Fathers. The vote on *De Vita et Ministerio Sacerdotali* was taken at the 25th (102nd) General Congregation, (Monday 19 October) It was referred back for revision by 1199 to 930. It was negative. Our Commission immediately co-opted some distinguished theologians, Lécuyer, Congar, etc, who got busy on a completely new theological document, but though it was ready within three weeks, it was now clear that the Council could not finish in this third session).

* * *

Immediately after Marty's Relatio at the 23rd (102nd) General Congregation, the Propositions *De Ecclesiis Orientalibus* had been introduced. They received a much more favourable assessment, even from the Oriental Bishops, than the Propositions on Priests. It was rumoured that since it enabled the Oriental Bishops to get busy settling and organizing their own affairs, which was what they mainly wanted, their chief object was to get it through the Council as quickly as possible and they were not disposed to delay that achievement by petty criticisms. Sidarous of Alexandria, Egypt, began by assuring the Council that this schema was the fruit of prolonged labour, contained all the essentials and should be given a large majority vote. For Maximus IV Patriarch of Antioch it constituted in general a step forward, though it was weak, indeed inadmissible, on Patriarchs, and he devoted the rest of his speech to enlightening the Fathers on the history, status and juridical role of Patriarchs.

The vote as to the general acceptability of the schema was taken at the 26th (105th) General Congregation, and resulted in 1911 *placet* to 265 *non placet*. A promise was made that the particular voting (*placet, non placet*, or *placet iuxta modum*) would begin on the following day. (*Placet iuxta modum* meant Yes, but with an amendment, the text of which had to be given in with the vote).

* * *

Meanwhile, at the same 26th (105th) General Congregation, the schema *De Ecclesia in Mundo Huius Temporis* had been introduced. Cardinal Liénart damned it with faint praise. It was an excellent synthesis which contained all the essential elements in a few pages. But two things needed to be corrected. Its general form must be revised; in place of a continual exhortation, it must provide a full explanation of our principles, so that the world could know whether the Church was in a position to help it. Secondly, it ought to distinguish better between the natural order and the supernatural. Admittedly they were united, but "gratia non tollit naturam sed perficit", and since each was the work of God, it was permissible to deal separately with the natural order, instead of flipping from one to the other as did the schema.

Cardinal Spellman, on the other hand, seemed to think it just fine. This undoubtedly, in his opinion, was what the Council had been hoping for. In this new text the Commission had done a wonderful piece of work which ought not to be weakened. It was a public, solemn and simple rededication of the Church to the betterment of the world, a more abundant life for all, even though the Church cannot definitely solve all human problems. Cardinal Ruffini had begun to make detailed criticisms when he was reminded by the Moderator (Döpfner) that general opinions only were in order at this stage, whereas he proposed that the schema be fundamentally revised with more attention being shown to the Papal Encyclicals since Leo

XIII. Cardinal Lercaro urged the necessity of discussion at some length. If the text presented were forthwith returned to the Commission, substantial progress would not be possible. An equilibrium between the opposing tensions had not yet been achieved, but that also showed the need for continuing the discussion. Cardinal Léger thought the schema provided an excellent basis for a fruitful discussion. So too did Cardinal Döpfner, speaking for 83 German and Scandinavian Fathers, and he was in favour of it being discussed as fully as was necessary to its perfection, which could not be achieved in the five days allotted. It had been objected that some topics were inopportune for public discussion and that was certainly true if the Fathers descended to details, but he trusted to their discretion.

Cardinal Meyer of Chicago agreed with those who wanted a more thorough discussion. The schema hadn't made its mind up as to why Christians must cooperate in the building up of the earthly city. It was too afraid of the danger of abuse, which no one questioned. It failed to explain the principle by which dualism was avoided viz the Pauline principle: "In ipso condita sunt universa... Omnia in ipso constant... reconciliare omnia in ipso, sive, quae in terris sive quae in caelis sunt". It was, however, only eschatologically that we could understand the total extension of this cosmic Christ. Our labour belonged to the perennial order and had its consummation only in the new earth and the new heaven. This compenetration of the Church and the World needed to be explained.

The same line was taken by Cardinal Silva Henriquez of Chile. The Council must present the World with a Christian cosmology, showing that the new creation did not involve the destruction of the old. Cardinal Landazzuri of Peru welcomed a thorough discussion of the schema because it was the one in which the world was chiefly interested; it wanted to know how the Church would face the modern problems. But the Council must clarify what precisely it means by "the World", and always use the term "Church" in the same sense. And the principles governing the tension between the temporal and the spiritual must be more accurately stated than in the past. The religious life which used to be presented as a flight from the world was now seen as a service of the world.

For Cardinal Suenens, it was above all necessary to stress that the Church's reply to the World's problems was ecclesial, i.e. derived from her own mission and treasury, and that her perspective was religious and moral. It was also important to explain the relation between humanization and evangelization; the Church civilized by evangelizing, and not vice versa. More consideration must be given to the modern phenomenon of militant atheism and how to conduct dialogue with atheists. Cardinal Bea praised the schema as an excellent collection of very difficult material, but more proof should be offered of the principles proposed, especially scriptural proof, because the document was primarily directed to the faithful. The difference between the sons of light and the sons of this world lay in the motive from which they laboured; for Christians it was the glory of God and eternal life.

The Maronite Patriarch of the Lebanon, Meouchi, was more critical. He accepted the schema as a basis for discussion but wanted more and sounder theology. It seemed to imply that the Church had been instituted for social welfare and made little allowance for divine providence. An Indian bishop, M. Alfonso, wanted a simpler form and a more dynamic total vision of the world, with stress on God as "pater providentissimus" of the world and Christ as the Light of the world, and more emphasis of the Natural Law principles of justice, as in the papal encyclicals.

Archbishop Morcillo of Madrid did not like the schema at all, though he admitted that it had some good points. It needed to decide whether it was addressing Christians or non-Christians, because different language was necessary. To Christians the Church spoke as authoritative preacher of the Gospel and as bound to preach it. With non-Christians she could only invoke the Natural law, and this was lacking in the schema. Archbishop Conway of Armagh thought that something worthwhile might yet be made of it, but there were grave difficulties to be overcome. It must be made crystal clear what it intended to do and what it did not. Many were expecting it to contain what the Church had to say to the modern world, but in fact it could only do so in a very small degree. The Church talked to the World, not just in a single Council, but in all her preaching and by her very existence. The schema was timid in regard to the errors of the World; it had little to say about the persecuted Church, nothing to say about the commercialization of sex which was doing such harm to youth. And it laid too much stress in moral matters on the individual's decisions as if it were the norm, and neglected the objective divine.

Bishop L. Elchinger, Coadjutor of Strasbourg, however, wanted less moralizing. The schema must show Christians to be lovers of life, of that "more abundant life" which Christ came to bring, and it must treat the problems with the prophetic spirit and flair, not in professorial terms.

Bishop Woityla, on behalf of the Bishops of Poland, called attention to the fact, so far overlooked, that there was more than one World, a World which wants the presence of the Church and a World which did not. The Council was talking in effect not to "the World", but to men who lived in different worlds.

Archbishop Heenan created something of a stir when he intervened at the beginning of the 28th (107th) General Congregation (22 October) He was sorry not to be able to join in the general applause. The document was unworthy of a General Council. If the Fathers wanted to address the World, it should do so in clear and simple terms. The World had long awaited their advice on its problems and would read this document with greedy expectation. What would its judgement be? In a matter of this kind it was better to say nothing than utter empty platitudes. They would be laughed at if, after long discussions on theology, they rushed into statements on war, etc. Christians must be prepared to talk to all, even those who are not of good will, and not just in terms of pious exhortation. The schema's treatment of the major problems was obscure and ambiguous, and indeed, without the Supplement (to which at that time detailed treatment of some major problems was relegated), dangerous. And if the supplement were not discussed in the Council (as was then proposed), the mind of the Council would be learnt by the World through the periti, and God forbid that! He feared Periti when it was left to them to explain what the bishops meant. The Church had suffered much from them; it was their voice, rather than that of the bishops that was heard everywhere, even the teaching of the Popes was ignored on the ground that their encyclicals were not infallible. The authority of the bishops must be vindicated; the Church had not so far defined the infallibility of periti.

Real periti were lacking on the Commission that produced the schema, i.e. men who lived in the real world, as distinct from the simple doves who lived in religious houses, seminaries, etc. He proposed therefore that the whole schema along with the Supplement ("Adnexa") be handed over to a new Commission consisting of learned and experienced men, married persons, more pastoral priests, etc, and then, after they had worked on it for 3 or 4 years, a fourth and final session of the Council be called to discuss all the social problems. It would be scandalous if the job were rushed.

(Fr Benedict Reetz, Superior General of the Benedictines of Beuron, defended the periti at the following 108th General Congregation, saying that he hesitated to speak because he too was a "simple dove who lived in a religious house and his opinion was therefore presumably worth nothing. But the periti in question had been nominated by the Pope and had laboured praiseworthily, especially in the supplement, from which much should be transferred to the schema itself.)

Archbishop Roy of Quebec wanted the document drafted in a simple pastoral style which could be read by the ordinary man in the newspapers, and the teaching based on principles and facts evident to all. Similarly Bishop Stümpfle of Augsburg called for a more realistic vision of the world and a solid theological foundation. The problem of militant atheism must be frankly and courageously confronted. This problem in its Marxist form was understandably prominent in the mind of Bishop Franic of Jugoslavia. Marxists, he said, were convinced that faith in God alienated, man from the problems of the modern world. The purpose of the document was to show that was this was not so, but this purpose had not been made clear.

Archbishop Hurley of Durban likewise complained that the purpose of the document was not made clear. Bishop Charue of Namur, in a preliminary statement which he had apparently inserted in answer to Archbishop Heenan, thanked the Fathers and the periti who had collaborated with them in the preparation of the document, and declared that they could not wait four years to get it out to an expectant world. He admitted however that its birth had been hastened now it needed much development. But it should be possible to publish it the following year. The Commission had excellent periti and could be given others.

Archbishop Sheehan of Baltimore suggested that the image of the Church could be made more realistic in the schema if it made more use of the encyclical *Ecclesiam Suam* which contained a more solid and clear doctrine. Bishop Duval of Algiers observed that before the Council could talk intelligibly to the World, it must itself understand the World. It should begin from the desires and anxieties of men and then deal with their problems, not all, but only the major ones. Archbishop Beck of Liverpool, (unlike Archbishop Heenan) felt that the schema in general deserved full discussion. But if it was to obtain its full effect, it must capture attention from the first sentence. The present introduction was obscure and would not be read. Like Pope John's *Pacem in terris,* it should begin with men's real problems. It must touch the real world. Otherwise, it might end as a soliloquy. It must not present the Church as primarily a good-time society, mainly concerned with philanthropy, or imply that it was what one did rather than what one believed that mattered. But it must firmly assert that the foundation of all social life as reverence for justice – rendering to each his due, and that man is meaningless except in the light of eternity.

* * *

At the beginning of the 29th (108th) General Congregation (23 October), it was announced that the Session was to end on 21 November with a solemn Mass concelebrated by the Pope along with 24 Fathers in whose dioceses were the chief Marian sanctuaries (The date of the next Session would be announced when the Holy Father decided it). And in clear reference to Heenan's controversial speech, the Secretary General, in a reference to work being done by periti, added: "quorum haud pauci bene meriti sint". Then the apparently endless preliminary debate on *The Church in the Modern World* was resumed.

Bishop Tchidimbo of Conakry, Guinea, wanted the schema to be profoundly modified with the aid of bishops from the third world. The Church was the mother of the poor. The condition of the poor was a grave question affecting the solidarity of the human race. According to St Thomas a fair share in the goods of the earth was due to the poorer nations in natural justice, not simply in charity. Racial discrimination and apartheid were a disgrace to our age. Bishop Paul Yupin, exiled Bishop of Nanking, wanted a whole chapter devoted to atheistic communism, the major feature of our age, the sum of all heresies. Similarly, Bishop Bolatti of Rosario, Argentina.

Bishop Gonsalez Moralejo, for 60 Spanish-speaking Bishops, had a more fundamental criticism to make. The two hinges of the Council were: What the Church was, and What the Church did. The schema replied to the second question only, forgetting that more than 2000 million people do not know what the Church was to them, what their own true nature was. Even among Christians, the majority saw things only from the outside. Properly presented, the document could constitute a real "praeambula fidei" for millions.

At this point Döpfner asked the Fathers to vote the closure of the debate "in genere" by rising. The majority as usual rose, but because of the considerable number who remained seated, he asked that a written vote be taken. Meanwhile, the Relator, Bishop Guano, summed up. In clear reference to Heenan's attack, he assured the Fathers that many and learned laymen as well as priests of pastoral experience and bishops had already been consulted. The Commission was grateful to the periti for their work. Decision lay with the Conciliar Fathers. In the interval before the next session, the major problems (peace, famine, poverty, atheism) would be further studied.

The debate on chapter I was then introduced. Bishop Guyon of France said that the schema's vision of the world was not sufficiently comprehensive, global and coherent, and, on the other hand, its tone was unduly emotional, as of men far removed from real life. There were scandals today which called for the voice of a John the Baptist, burning and bold. In the view of Bishop Schmitt of Metz, the schema did not sufficiently bring out the novelty of the complex civilization evolved in the last four centuries of the world's history; that was the world to which it should be addressed, for, if the Church was to be missionary, she must exist in the historically progressing world. Bishop Romero (Spain) felt that, the preface lacked any clear explanation of the basis of dialogue between Church and World.

What was lacking, according to Bishop De Wet, speaking for the Bishops of Holland, was a satisfactory definition of the world. In so far as it was defined, it appeared to be something extraneous. The wickedness of the world certainly needed to be made clear, but one clear statement was enough; there was no need for six. The first three chapters were not governed by the Christian vision of the world, or at least that vision was not made explicit.

Bishop Del Rosario urged that chapter I should clearly state what it sought to achieve, how, and why. The idea of the resurrection should be the foundation of the whole chapter. Christ had come to overcome evil and win for Himself a new People. The purpose of man's domination of the earth was to overcome evil and promote good. The Church had a part to play in this struggle. She did not exist simply to save souls.

The difficulty, according to Bishop Schoiswohl of Graz, Austria, was that modern man no longer believed in the immortality of the soul, and without a firm hope no amount of eloquence could succeed; dialogue must begin at that point.

On Monday 26 October, I was feeling very exhausted when I attended the 30th (109th) General Congregation.

Cardinal Léger opened. The primacy of man's supernatural end must be made more clear in the first chapter, he said. And in dealing with the fulfilment of man's vocation, more attention must be paid to the complexity of the human condition which was radically good and yet subject to sin. Dualism had falsified Christian life. Christians must be induced to be more solicitous about their earthly duties. As for those who were tempted to abandon their religious duties, it was not enough to propose liturgical participation as a cure.

Bishop Pietraszko of Poland, omitting much of what he had meant to say, because it had already been said by others (O, si sic omnes!), limited himself to a plea for a clear and simple clarification of the notion of the World: a) as created by God, b) as redeemed by Christ, and c) as developed by man in the material order according to or contrary to the mind of the Creator. Abbot Prou, O.S.B., of Solesmes in France, wanted it made clear what precisely was the consecration of the world by Christ and the consecration of the world by the members of Christ. Some modern theologians were maintaining that the whole creation was consecrated and elevated to the supernatural order from its beginning intuitu Incarnationis, a beautiful idea perhaps, but one which appeared to conflict with the faith and should not therefore be favoured by the schema in any way. Only the human soul could be intrinsically and immediately elevated to the supernatural order.

Bishop J. Guerra, of Spain, asked that the schema, in dealing with atheism, should bear in mind that some Marxists were agnostics, whereas others combined their Marxism with religious elements. Denial of religion was not properly speaking an act of renunciation on the part of Marxists. For Bishop J. Pogacnik, of Jugoslavia, the ultimate reason why Divine Providence had permitted the great modern apostasy which atheism represented in East and West alike, was our correction and complete conversion of the world to God (Perhaps he meant that the grim experience of a Godless world would bring men back to Him; or else I missed his point).

Bishop Tenhumberg (Germany) suggested that the remedy lay in a renewed theology of the Holy Spirit in the Church on biblical and patristic lines, such as would favour a right understanding of authority in the Church which did not extinguish the Spirit.

The Spirit of Christ, said Bishop de Roo (Victoria, Canada), was not one that condemned or despised the world, but one of love, incarnation and communion. The faithful must learn that their whole vocation was realized when they fully entered into the life of the world, and that no one worked for Christianity unless he played his part in perfecting the human community.

* * *

When the debate passed on to chapters II and III, Bishop Ancel (Auxiliary of Lyons) called for an explanation of the manner in which the Church integrates temporal affairs in her mission, in order to obviate widespread errors about the nature and object of the Church, e.g. the idea that the Church had renounced her spiritual and eternal mission and sought to adapt to the modern mentality of materialism. The Church was concerned with the terrestrial order, not because the State was not doing its job well enough, but because it was an integral part of her eternal mission. Bishop Hacault (Canada) called for a candid statement that the Church (not merely the Hierarchy) could not produce a solution for all man's problems, but that her service of the world united her with all men in the quest of solutions.

There was need, according to Bishop Spülbeck (Germany), for lively dialogue with the modern scientific world, but for that we must be able to speak its language, as did Teilhard de Chardin, for whom it had a healthy respect. Most theologians were too timid to engage in dialogue with it. Bishop Klepacz of Lodz, Poland, was also concerned about fruitful dialogue with the world, but at the leve1 of social doctrine. The Church could and must put her doctrine across, but it was necessary to remember that her formal authority counted for little or nothing with most modern men.

Bishop H. Golland (Brazil) had perhaps the same point in mind when he said that bishops must come down out of their palaces and cease to be ornamental; and Bishop Fourrey of Belley (France), whose main point was that the message must be put across in deeds rather than words, and the schema should insist that the spirit of poverty be manifested in that way.

At the 31st (110th) General Congregation (27 October), there was a return of the scarlet. Cardinal Frings, unable to read his speech because of bad sight, called upon his secretary to read it for him. He wholeheartedly agreed with those who had detected Platonism in the document. God became man to redeem the whole man, body as well as soul, and the whole world. But earthly progess did not lead immediately to the kingdom of God. Heaven and earth would first pass away. True and absolute progress consisted in the increase of faith, hope and charity. The Church and the World remained divided; neither could be resolved into the other. Three revealed truths must always be borne in mind: Creation (God loves His creatures); the Incarnation (that all men might be consecrated to God); the Cross and Passion (abstinence in regard to worldly things).

Cardinal Caggiano of Buenos Aires wanted to know why only the spirit of poverty was commended. The "spirit" was unintelligible to most men of today. They wanted justice, for the sense of justice is primary in the natural order, and most of them lived in conditions that were unjust. The Church must proclaim justice for all men, everywhere. Cardinal Silva Henriquez of Chile, after distinguishing between evangelical poverty (a way of life freely chosen) and human poverty (a consequence of human servitude and imperfection which debased the heart of man and militated against the exercise of virtue), proposed that the Council should set up an international organization to foster aid to the poor everywhere and press for justice, should ensure that it eventually became inter-Christian, and organize an annual worldwide collection.

Maximus IV Saigh, Melchite Patriarch of Antioch, maintained that, if the Church wanted to contribute to the terrestrial City, the faithful must first be formed in the basic moral principles of the law of Christ. Modern men had grown out of the childhood of the Middle Ages. Obligations had to be proved to them, not simply asserted. The commandments must be ways of happiness rather than of condemnation, counsels of love rather than orders under pain of sin.

Fourteen more speakers succeeded to the Patriarch that morning, but nothing new of major significance was said. Bishop Himmer of Tournai wanted a clearer explanation of the intrinsic value of christian poverty, as christian, i.e. a supernatural virtue impossible without grace, and insistence on its witness-value. Bishop Cleven (Germany) said that it was commonly believed that the Church was still opposed to science, as in the days of Galileo. The Church must show her esteem for scientific labour, must acknowledge full scientific liberty, and urge the faithful to collaborate responsibly in scientific work, while making it clear that salvation did not come from science but from charity. Bishop Nicodemo of Bari regarded it as a prime necessity to expound the complete christian vocation in relation to the world. It was always evangelical, apostolic and eschatological, looking forward to the recapitulation of all things in Christ. So it was that the Church was not extraneous to the world, even to the non-christian world. A similar point was made by Bishop Pourchet of Saint-Flour, France. The people of God was inserted in the whole human race as a leaven, and therefore lived in complete solidarity with all men.

Bishop Mendez Arceo of Ceuernavaca, Mexico, taking up a point made by Maximus IV, agreed with him on the need to recognize the personal dignity and responsibility of modern man. The Church must foster true liberty and refrain from any compulsion contrary to human dignity. Many positive laws of the Church were said by moralists to bind under pain of grave sin. They should all be expressed in terms charity, for in that lay the fulness of the law. A similar point was made by Bishop Huyghe of Arras. The Church was supposed to be the "congregation of charity", but often appeared rather as an administrative institution which, as soon as a group was formed, intervened to load it with heavy rules. There could be no dialogue with non-Christians, until there was dialogue between the different classes in the Church.

* * *

With the 32nd (111th) General Congregation (28 October), the discussion passed to chapter IV of the schema which dealt with concrete moral problems.

Cardinal Agaganian, introducing the Relator, Bishop Wright of Pittsburg, warned the Fathers that certain matters in the chapter were not suitable for public discussion, and begged them to offer their comments to the Commission with full liberty but in writing; they would be given due consideration in the drafting of the definitive text. The Relator, while admitting that the chapter contained key questions, suggested that it was not for the Fathers to give slick replies on points of detail. It would need years of work and would be better done by experts than in Council. Moreover, the chapter was not meant to be exhaustive or definitive, but simply the first word in a new dialogue. A small group had already been set up to receive and study comments from the bishops of the world, especially the Third World.

To secure a more orderly debate, those who proposed to speak on the section dealing with marriage (n. 21) were kept waiting, and priority was accorded to speeches on nn. 9-20, which dealt mainly with the dignity of the human person. Cardinal Ritter was pleased with the priority given to recognition of the dignity of the human person, which was the necessary foundation of all human life, but critical of the way it was treated.

Bishop Athaide of Agra, India, in the name of many other bishops warmly subscribed to the statement in n. 23 on racial segregation, colour bar, apartheid.

For Bishop Bejot (France), it was not enough to give first place to the dignity of the human person; an explicit statement was necessary that this truth must be seen in the light of the faith, for it was in Christ that man attained to his full dignity as a person. Bishop Goutka of Gary, U.S.A. complained that the schema was not strong enough in its condemnation of racial discrimination and segregation. But the most complete and forceful statement on this subject came from Archbishop O'Boyle of Washington, speaking in the name of all the bishops of the U.S.A. Racial discrimination, he said, was found in various forms all over the world, but it was primarily a religious and moral problem. The text of the schema dealt with it only in passing. They, the Bishops of the USA, asked that it be dealt with formally as a distinct subject, under its moral and religious aspect. The Council should not attempt particular solutions, but it ought to issue a definitive condemnation of it in all its forms and seek the cooperation of all men of good will. It was one of the gravest problems of our time.

Bishop Coderre from Canada, speaking in the name of 40 others, called for a clear recognition that woman received her own personality from God and had her own specific function to fulfil. Woman's awareness of her dignity and function was one of the signs of our times. Now that she was in a better position to fulfil her role, it was time for the Church to spell it out and help her to fulfil it. Without the woman's contribution the civil society was imperfect.

Bishop Bauerlain of Jugoslavia wanted to know why, if they should talk about "race", they should not also talk about the class-struggle. For "social condition" the schema should read "social class".

Bishop de la Chanonie (Clermont, France) called attention to the problem of "unadapted" youth. As a result of this failure to adapt, due to various causes, many — as many as 40% in his area — did not achieve an ordered life.

Bishop Malula of Leopoldville, Belgian Congo, reverted to the dignity of the human person. It must be acknowledged in every man, everywhere and by all. He was not satisfied that the text enunciated this truth clearly enough. It had to be proclaimed not because modern man tended to admit it, but because it was true. The Council should openly condemn not only discrimination for reasons of race or colour, but also tribalism (which he did not define, but declared to be a grave sin against charity).

Bishop Laszlo of Eisenstadt in Austria spoke of the ambivalence of the word "liberty". Parental indulgence, pornography, dolce vita, etc. were all justified in its name. They diminished rather than increased true personal liberty.

A German bishop, on the other hand, J.S. Stümpfle of Augsburg, extolled the benefits of liberty when the debate was resumed at the 33rd (112th) General Congregation (29 October). Where the true liberty of the sons of God was to be found, there the dignity of the human person was fostered. There should therefore be great liberty in, e.g., the field of education, so as to avoid the danger of legalism, full liberty too in scientific investigation, the greatest degree of liberty of spirit in the administrative field.

Bishop Quadri (Italy) wanted the insertion in the document of a summary of the social teaching of the Church. It extended more widely than economic life. It was not a system merely of the temporal order but supplied principles of the natural and supernatural order which were not tied to any system, yet touched upon all systems.

Bishop Frotz (Germany) brought the debate back to the subject of the dignity of womankind. It was a new problem of worldwide extension which as yet had hardly been realized. A balance between woman's family ties and her social involvements and duties had not yet been discovered, so that many women were in a state of crisis. The Church must point the way to a just solution of the problem, foster the movement towards it, recognize women as adult daughters of the Church, and give explicit expression to the Church's desire that women should assert and exercise their personality in public life.

* * *

At this point the discussion of the first part of chapter IV was brought to a close, thus ensuring, indirectly at least, that woman had the last word. Archbishop Dearden of Detroit then rose (as Relator for the responsible Commission) to introduce the controversial n. 21. He began by stressing that the Commission did not mean to give a detailed exposition of the Church's doctrine on marriage and married life, but merely some general guidelines. In saying that spouses could and should form their conscience in regard to their vocation to parenthood, it meant a rightly formed conscience, i.e. one formed according to the mind of the Church. It did not therefore follow that they could adopt whatever methods they chose. No intervention which interfered with the natural order or excludes conjugal love could be lawful. There was no room for subjectivism. The text, he added, had avoided all reference to the Pill, because the Pope had wisely reserved the question to himself, as one which could not be settled in the Council Hall.

The first to his feet was the veteran conservative, Cardinal Ruffini, Archbishop of Palermo. It was, he said, a very grave question which had been neither clearly nor sufficiently cautiously put in the text. One could only wonder at its silence about the nobility of Christian marriage, image of the union of Christ and His Church, basis of its unity and indissolubility, by which also conjugal love was fostered. It was no answer to say that the document was addressed to all men. The Church was seeking to show her true face to the world. Without a full exposition of the Church's doctrine it was impossible to persuade mankind that divorce, adultery, etc. were evil. As for the statement that it was for the spouses to decide the number of their children, this indeed was a hard saying, and obscure as well. Like St Augustine, they must not be afraid to condemn contemporary abuses. They should turn to *Casti Connubii* and to the address given by Pius XII to midwives; there they would find everything excellently compressed in regard to the loving acceptance of offspring and the unfailing observance of chastity in marriage; these were the documents of the living and ordinary magisterium of the Church.

In complete contrast was the speech that followed, that of Cardinal Léger of Montreal. Outstanding among modern problems, he said, were those of marriage. They were the cause of anxiety and doubt everywhere. The faithful, burdened by daily difficulties, were seeking solutions and were not satisfied with the answers hitherto given. Confessors did not know what to answer. Theologians were seeking a full investigation and were begging the Church to proceed to conduct it with the greatest of care. From the theological point of view some feared that a revised doctrine was likely to be opportunist; but the object was only to get at the truth. Many held that the difficulties were due to an inadequate doctrine based on a false and pessimistic philosophy of sex. They wanted a revision of the ends of marriage. In his view, fecundity as an end was well enough presented in the schema, but it could be opportunely said to be an end of marriage as a whole, rather than of each act of marriage. And human love should be presented as a true end, good and holy in itself, with its own exigences and its own laws, an intrinsic end (finis operis) of the marriage act, even when this was not ordered to procreation.

After this somewhat sensational speech, Cardinal Suenens spoke with rather more circumspection, keeping his options open, as was not infrequently his wont. On this crucial question of the common good, he said, it was necessary to complete the text with points drawn from the Supplement ("Adnexa"). It was also necessary that the Commission responsible for the text should collaborate with the special Pontifical Commission charged with the study of these problems, and that this latter should know the mind of the Council. The first task was to enquire whether all aspects had hitherto been sufficiently highlighted. The Church would never withdraw a doctrine which she had authentically taught, but she had always sought to bring out of her treasure "new things and old". Perhaps a perfect balance had not yet been established between the two truths of Genesis: "Increase and multiply" and "two in one flesh" too little account having been taken of marriage as an interpersonal communion. The Council must have regard to the population explosion. It was no answer to say that there lay the open road to moral laxism. Fidelity to the doctrine of the Church must be matched by fidelity to the exigences of conjugal love. At the scientific level also, it was necessary to examine whether the classical doctrine had taken enough account of modern discoveries concerning the complexity of nature. They had learnt a thing or two since Aristotle, and must follow the progress of science, if they were to avoid another Galileo case. In a word, they must pursue the truth and then submit to the judgement of the Magisterium. He ended on a ringing note; "Veritas tota et vitalis liberabit vos" — "The truth, total and vital, will set you free".

Maximus IV, Patriarch of the Melchites of Antioch, speaking as usual in French (because Latin was the language of the Latin Church only), followed rather the Léger trail. The common good, he said, required that they face the situation with courage. There was a contradiction between the doctrine of the Church and the practice of the great majority of the faithful. The population explosion condemned millions to misery. The Council must find a workable solution and decide whether God really willed the existing impasse. Ought not the official position of the Church to be revised in the light of modern findings? The ends of marriage should not be divided into primary and secondary. Were not the official positions due to out-dated ideas, due possibly to celibates and tainted with Manicheism? Was the biological rectitude of acts the only rule? Modern exegesis had shown that many long-held interpretations of S. Scripture were false. With Léger and Suenens, he said, he demanded that the question be studied by theologians, scientists, etc. etc. and that other religions be consulted. He did not want to minimize the difficulty, but was it not the duty of the Church to educate the moral sense of its children rather than to wrap them up in a series of prescriptions and prohibitions.

After the big guns, Bishop Botero of Columbia must have doubted whether many of the Fathers would give him their full attention. The difficulty of reconciling the Church's doctrine with practical difficulties, he said, had to be admitted. But it was not therefore sufficient simply to refer the problem to the study of experts and much less to leave it to the consciences of spouses. Such an omission could not be justified in view of the abundance of papal doctrine. It was regrettable that many proceeded on the principle that sexual appetite could not be controlled. That was not St Paul's attitude. He proposed therefore that parish priests be urged to instruct parties to marriage on the sanctity of their undertaking, that the

Christian family movement be commended, and that a completely new text be substituted for n. 21 of the schema.

After a diversion by Bishop Busch of Innsbruck on the problem of divorce, a Dutch missionary bishop from Indonesia, Staverman, returned to the endless problem of contraception (though it was noticeable how seldom this word was used). He said he felt he had to speak on a problem of such weight as that of marriage and the family. The manner in which the schema spoke on it was very good and liberating. It rightly put love in the forefront as the commandment which directed all things. It was a matter of great importance also what it did not say. It was rightly silent about the Natural Law and about the biological purpose of the conjugal act. Where it failed was in beginning from marriage as an immutable institution. Every human reality was historical and evolving. Marriage belonged to the historicity of the human race and was evolving to an ever more authentic form. The Church should rejoice in this evolution, and not simply apply past doctrine.

The following day, 30 October, at the 34th (112th) General Congregation, three Cardinals opened the batting. The first was Alfrink of Utrecht. All priests, he said, regularly met with matrimonial difficulties even among faithful of good will. Not infrequently they led to estrangement from the Church, or a spiritual struggle which could not be borne without detriment to the goods of marriage. The Church was the guardian of the divine law and could not change it. Nor could social changes alter the divine law. Nor could the Church yield to Situation ethics. She must always hold that sacrifice was of the essence of the Christian life. On the other hand, it was not all cross, but also resurrection. The difficulties were not seldom such that anxious conflicts arose between the value of procreation and that of education, when spouses were united by a love which was fostered by conjugal intercourse. Here lay the moral conflict. Respect for the biological end did harm to the goods of union and education; otherwise continence was the only remedy. The only solution of the problem lay in preventing concrete acts from resulting in conception. If it were intrinsically evil, the Church must forbid it, but the growing distinction between biological sex and human sex had raised honest doubts about the arguments hitherto accepted as valid. The Church must be solicitous about the divine law, but also about values.

Cardinal Ottaviani bluntly declared himself dissatisfied with the statement in n. 21 about birth control. Had they forgotten the scriptural command "Increase and multiply" which did not in any way contradict "Two in one flesh"? And there were other texts . He himself was the 11th of 12 children of a working man and he never had reason to doubt divine Providence. "Consider the lilies of the field". Doubt was now being cast on what the Church had taught through the ages.

Cardinal Browne began by remarking that it had not been his intention to speak, because he had been a member of the mixed Commission which had worked on the schema and he had been hoping to derive further light from the discussion. If he spoke now, his motive was simply to supply evidence in regard to points that could usefully be discussed. Some things were already certain, either from the Magisterium or from theology, viz: that the primary end of marriage was the generation and education of children, and that the secondary ends were mutual aid and the remedy of concupiscence. As for love, a distinction must be drawn between *amor amicitiae* (unselfish love) and *amor concupiscentiae* (self-interested love). In married life, mutual love of the former kind was to be desired as conducing best to the goods of marriage. Its physical expression produced a pleasure which was honest in so far as it is related to the honest conjugal act. The more the parties were drawn together by *amor concupiscentiae*, the less became their conjugal *amor amicitiae*. The conjugal act did not need to be limited to the fertile period; fidelity was a sufficient reason for rendering the marriage debt. At this point, the Cardinal seemed to feel that he was labouring the obvious, for he added that there was no doubt on all these points; they belonged to the store of all theologians and were to be found in *Arcanum*, *Casti Connubii* and Pius XII's allocutions to Midwives and Doctors. Difficulties remained about the use of the infertile period; they had been partly solved by doctors, but others were still being studied and the theologian could only wait for the end of their labours. He would say nothing on these matters; they were in the Pope's care. (Presumably he believed that many of the Fathers had long since forgotten the main elements of their moral theology. Perhaps he was right).

He was followed by Bishop Reuss, a mere Auxiliary of Mainz, but influential enough to have found 140 backers. He began by praising n. 21 for attaching such great importance to conjugal love. But it needed strengthening still. Human sexuality differed from all non-human sexuality, and not merely biologically. It involved a specific communion of persons. Consequently, marriage not merely demanded conjugal love, but was based on it. It should extend to the whole of daily life. It constituted the dignity and difficulty of marriage. It needed to be cultivated. Often it was difficult to have all the main "goods" of marriage together. Spouses should realize that they were called to have children and should not avoid them egotistically. The schema was to be praised for speaking so cautiously on this point. It said no more than could be said nowadays. Further investigation was not superfluous. A comprehensive group of experts was needed to examine these questions.

Bishop Del Campo of Calahorra, Spain, was more realistic or, perhaps, pessimistic. No. 21 had a lot to say about conjugal love, he began; indeed, its value was so extolled that it might seem to the simple reader to be preached as the primary "good", the hinge on which all the rest depended. A most beautiful idea! But was it true, he asked. Love was very important, yes, but they should beware of exaggeration. It was necessary to maintain the right hierarchy of values. Love would always be a principal motive for getting married, but it was neither the end of marriage nor the constitutive good of the whole of married life. In describing its intimate nature the text used a too generic phrase which could give occasion to confusion and subjectivism. It was not calculated to avoid equivocation. In regard to the objective ends of marriage which were derived from the natural ordination of the generative faculty, the text was silent. He suggested therefore that a clearer explanation be given of the ends of marriage, that *Casti Connubii* be cited, that the text be less absolute about it resting with the spouses to determine the number of their children; — for, after all, there were objective norms, and that there were other ways of preserving conjugal love besides conjugal intercourse.

Another Spanish bishop, Hervas, took a similar line. The text emphasized "Christian prudence". Well and good. But it had very ltttle to say on supernatural faith in divine Providence towards those who take up the cross. Its whole approach it was was too negative; it was dominated by consideration of the obstacles, whereas it should begin by praising virtue, especially the virtue of those who, disregarding their own convenience, accepted the children God gave them.

After Bishop B. Yago, Abidjan, Ivory Coast, had criticized the western outlook of the schema and its neglect of such third-world problems as polygamy, the abuse of marriage dowries, etc. which the Church should fight, the Fathers agreed to terminate the discussion of n. 21 and to pass on to the less controversial n. 22, on the proper promotion of culture.

* * *

A less provocative subject, it drew only 13 speakers, of whom only one was a cardinal. Their themes were very varied. The first speaker, J. Ferreira, a Vicar Apostolic from Africa, was not satisfied with the schema's approach to the topic. It should have had something to say about the kind of humanism which was nowadays identified with atheism, and it should have indicated the norms to be followed in cultural dialogue. Nor should it have confused civilization and culture; they were different things.

Bishop R. Johan of Agen, France, spoke of the value of contemplation in the whole cultural order and hoped to see the establishment of cultural centres in which the faith animated everything. In the same line, Bishop Bejza of Poland extolled the essential and most humanizing influence exerted by the saints in the promotion of culture, and called for the beatification of John XXIII; but he complained that nothing was said about Christian philosophy.

The General of the Dominicans, A. Fernandez, wanted a tidier explanation of the right order of values which put the spiritual above the material and the supernatural above the natural, and mention of the cultural role of philosophy and theology. Bishop Munoz Vega of Ecuador wanted to know how hostility between the Church and secular culture could be healed. A rift which had developed at university level after the Reformation had now spread to the practical level. His query was destined to remain unanswered, because the Fathers then dispersed for the All Saints – All Souls midterm break, four welcome days (Sat. Sun. Mon. Tues.)

* * *

When the 35th (114th) General Congregation assembled on Wednesday, 4 November, Cardinal Lercaro said he regarded n. 22 as the nodal point of the whole schema, the point of distinction and of union of Church and World. The Church must tend more and more everyday towards poverty, getting rid of riches which were unseemly today. She must renounce them or at least not glory in them. A merely negative poverty was not enough. Moreover, the Church should separate herself more than ever from any particular cultural organ. She must develop a new course of ecclesiastical culture otherwise there would be no dialogue. Bishops must become theological doctors as of old. (Since the Cardinal's name had only appeared on the list of speakers about n. 22 over the weekend, it would seem that these reflections were the fruit of his weekend meditation).

Archbishop de Provenchères, of France, was anxious lest anyone should be excluded from culture for racial reasons now that the means of making it open to all were available. Bishop J. Zoa of the Cameroons was more concerned with the problem of the encounter of different cultures. The schema had acknowledged its existence, but had not sufficiently indicated the fundamental principle involved. If different cultures were to contribute to true progress, each must present its principles. Whatever was truly human was neither thine nor mine but ours. Western culture was lacking in a sense of causality and tended to atheism, whereas African culture had a religious sense towards society and towards the supreme being. Africa's crisis was that it lacked a Christian culture; she needed a synthesis of the true values of the West with those of Africa.

Bishop Elchinger, Auxiliary of Strasbourg, began by remarking that among the leaders of modern culture who directed its course there were many outstanding people who had abandoned Christianity or were even opposed to it. Among Christians devoted to culture there were many who felt themselves insufficiently supported by the Church. The Church's struggle with Modernism had left an open wound which was, however unfairly, a cause of suspicion. There was some ground for it. We cultivated a dogmatic imperialism, as if the faith made us universally competent and there were nothing of value in other branches of knowledge. The Galileo case was regarded as typical of us. No reparation was ever made and it was time it was made. The Church should pay due regard to the cultural fact in all its aspects, with an open mind, with confidence and no prejudices. She could confer much, but must avoid paternalism and freely receive the rich fruits of deep culture.

After Bishop Proano of Ecuador, speaking for 70 other Fathers, had described the situation in Latin America where, despite many good efforts, the greater part of the population remained illiterate, the debate moved on automatically to no. 23, on economic and social life.

* * *

Cardinal Wyszynski of Warsaw, speaking in the name of the bishops of Poland, said that they wanted the text of the Supplement (Adnexa) substituted at this point; it was more up-to-date and practical. The whole chapter IV and especially no. 23 failed to meet the expectations of those who looked to the Church for help. The schema should commend all the great social encyclicals in which the authentic social doctrine of the Church was contained, and should foster their study. The Church could not accept all economical systems; some had grave defects.

Cardinal Richaud of Bordeaux, on the other hand, was more concerned to make the principles of the Church concrete, for there could be no dialogue otherwise. The text must therefore deal with the grave obligation of employers of labour to do their best to avoid the misery of unemployment. Some share in management and some prudent measure of information should be given to workers. Principles should be stated in regard to associations of labour. Means of meeting the inevitable modern mobility of labour must be suggested. There must be something about just price, and against inordinate speculation and gains made from mere gambling. If the Council remained silent on these concrete issues, its voice would not be listened to by workers.

Bishop Harrera of Malaga, Spain, was disappointed in the schema. In his view, it should have begun by acknowledging the basic fact that wealth was not justly distributed and that this was a danger to internal and external peace. Innumerable workers had left the Church as being indifferent to their fate. It must be made clear to them that the Church was concerned about their economic welfare and development. The Council should address grave words to employers and statesmen, that their first obligation was to ensure a just distribution. Similarly Bishop Zambrano was concerned about fair shares. Unless the Council was clear and explicit in regard to just prices and profits, it would be presumed to consecrate the rule of supply and demand.

* * *

When the 36th (115th) General Congregation assembled on 5 November, there were still 12 speakers waiting to give their view of n. 23, but the Fathers predictably approved a preliminary suggestion of the Moderators that only the four who had each obtained 70 backers should be allowed to make their points *summatim* before the debate passed to n. 24. Bishop Wheeler was one of those who were gagged in this way. And only two of the four used their right. Bishop Benitez of Paraguay spoke of the economic and political aspects of the population explosion in Latin America where, owing to the low level of productivity, the average annual income was not more than 200 dollars. Bishop J. Alba of Mexico used his microphone time to revert to the subject of the use of marriage (no. 21) and, not being called to order, was able to make a plea in defence of the doctrine of *Casti Connubii.*

When the discussion moved on to n. 24, on promoting the solidarity of the family of peoples, the first speaker was Cardinal Frings. He had, he said, two objects: that the Church should show herself to be a mother and that the episcopate should give a sign of its collegiality. To these ends, all national Episcopal Conferences should set up episcopal "works" (opera) to raise the standard of living of the poorer nations. These works should be social rather than charitable, i.e. designed to help them help themselves. They should be universal, i.e. without racial discrimination, though giving priority to "those of the household of the faith". They should be religious, i.e. motivated solely by the desire to serve Christ in one's brethren, and supported by collections taken at Mass in the penitential seasons of Advent and Lent, simultaneously with non-Catholics, if that could be done. Finally, they should be well ordered. To this end, there should be an episcopal commission in every nation to distribute the collection with the aid of lay experts, meeting at least once a year to coordinate the work and collaborate with the Holy See. A Secretariate should be set up by the Holy See to coordinate the work throughout the year all over the world in cooperation with the World Council of Churches or some other such organization, e.g. U.N.O.

Cardinal Alfrink began by saying that he adhered most readily to what Cardinal Frings had said. For several years the Dutch Hierarchy had had a "work" for relief of the poor of the world. As to the solidarity of peoples, many judged this from the point of view of communism and atheism but it would serve no purpose merely to repeat the condemnation of communism already rightly made by the Holy See and by individual bishops. That would leave the other form of atheism untouched. Dialogue with individual men of good will was still fruitful. As for atheistic communism, the Council should invoke whatever was necessary to dialogue with individuals, separate the good from the bad in their tenets, urge the need to work for social justice and to practise charity to the individual poor. In that way the Church would repudiate whatever ought to be repudiated and yet avoid closing the way to dialogue.

Bishop Rupp of Monaco was critical of the obscure style of n. 24. It said very little in very many words. In dealing with the demographic problem it had nothing to say about the universal and necessary right to emigrate, and yet the crowded East was denied access to great empty territories. It ought to have dealt with the lack of solidarity among Christians of different confessions which did great harm in the world. Bishop Pildain of the Canaries complained of the silence of the schema in regard to the basic principle, ignored by all liberal capitalists, that "in case of extreme necessity all things are common". Bishop Swanstrom of the U.S.A. wanted mention of the great responsibility of bishops and priests to participate actively in relief work.

At the 37th (116th) General Congregation (6 November), over which the Holy Father presided in person, the schema on *Missionary Activity* was presented for discussion at his special request, the debate on the *Church in the Modern World* being suspended. In his preliminary address Pope Paul explained that, having decided to accede to the invitation of the Council to attend at one of its Congregations, he had chosen this particular subject because of its importance. He had found much in the schema deserving of praise and believed that with a certain amount of polishing it would prove acceptable to the Fathers. (It would seem probable that he had been misinformed, at least in regard to the probable reaction of the missionary Fathers). Father Schütte, Superior General of the Society of the Divine Word, had already composed a letter to the Moderators claiming that the brief series of thirteen propositions to which the original schema on the Missions had been reduced was utterly unacceptable in view of the importance of the missionary aspect of the Church, and he was actively collecting signatures. Even I knew that a rebellion was brewing, and I find it difficult to believe that the Moderators did not. It seems more probable that the Pope's advisers hoped that his words of commendation would induce a majority to accept the schema of propositions as the basis of the final document. They were destined to be disappointed. (Cf. *The Rhine Flows into the Tiber*, by Ralph M. Wiltgen, S.V.D., pp. 193-198).

Cardinal Léger opened the bowling. The Council had not only admitted the principle of legitimate diversity in the Church but had rendered it possible. Nowhere more than in the Missions was this new liberty of bishops to adapt the message of the Gospel to the various peoples needed. The schema should expand its treatment of this liberty. It should also have more to say about the initiating of dialogue with non-Christians, about which the Church had hitherto been too timid. He was glad it fostered greater cooperation of the religious institutes with each other and with the bishops, but this too needed expanding. The proposed central council could be an apt means. Cardinal Tatsui-Doi of Japan found the schema ambiguous about its precise object; it would be better limited to missionary activity strictly so called. Cardinal Rugambwa of Africa called attention to St Paul's missionary principle to the Corinthians: "Hold on to what is good". The necessity of adaptation needed to be developed at greater length in a distinct chapter. The Church flourished where she adapted, suffered where she failed to adapt and simply "colonized". Adaptation required that local religious and moral values be acknowledged by foreign and native clergy alike and that only those elements which were opposed to man's true end be suppressed.

Cardinal Bea, speaking in the name of all the bishops of Africa and many of those of Asia, said that the schema ought to suggest remedies for the dangers arising from the decline in religious vocations. It should further clarify the scope of activity, viz, to further the great design of God for the whole human race, to restore all things in Christ and create one family of God. This presented missionaries in their proper light, not as apostles of the white race, but as ministers of Christ.

When the debate was resumed at the 38th (117th) General Congregation (7 November), Cardinal Frings, who had already been canvassed by Father Schütte, S.V.D. declared bluntly that missionary activity was too important to be dealt with in a few propositions. It needed a full theological and practical schema, and it was the fervent desire of the missionary bishops and Fathers General that this be proposed to the General Congregation. He then added his comments on some of the propositions.

Cardinal Alfrink also confessed that he had been asked to speak on behalf of many Dutch missionary bishops. The propositions scarcely dealt with the question of missionary vocations except to say that bishops should willingly favour them. After enlarging on the magnitude of the problem to be solved, he "made bold to ask" that special attention be devoted to it, and concluded by saying that it could not be treated adequately in a few propositions.

Cardinal Suenens announced that he was speaking in the name of the bishops of the whole of Africa. Some of the propositions needed to be redrafted. The primordial importance of missionary activity was not sufficiently expounded. It was of the very essence of the Church and must be asserted more firmly. All must collaborate directly in the preaching of the Gospel. Converts must themselves become converters. (He ended with a personal statement designed to correct, what he claimed were misinterpretations of his speech on the use of marriage).

A series of speeches from missionary bishops followed, all of them inclined to be critical of the schema. An Indonesian bishop, Geise, claimed that all the bishops of Indonesia wanted a full new schema drawn up and that their petition had the support of 25 Episcopal Conferences and of many Fathers General. The President of the Commission had expressed the desire that the whole Church should be missionary. Would these propositions show that the Council really felt itself to be missionary? Bishop Donal Lamont of Umtali, Rhodesia, said they had all been expecting a document of solid doctrine. The Propositions were good, but they were like a machine without its motor. They resembled Ezechiel's dry bones. "Thinkest thou that these dry bones will live?" he cried. Had this document moved a single one of them to new missionary effort. All it had kindled was a candle. (This outburst drew a round of loud applause, followed by a rebuke from the Moderator, Döpfner: "Cut out the rhetorical orations and get down to details!").

Bishop Moors of Roermond, Holland, speaking for the Dutch Episcopal Conference, called for a magna charta of missiology, with a theological vision, an explanation in biblical fashion of the basic reason of Christ's command, "Go ye and teach all nations". It should deal with the great problems which arose from the Church's encounter with alien cultures, and with her relation to the "third World". Bishop G. Riobe of Orleans implicitly supported this plea. The Commission responsible for the schema had wavered between the theological and the juridical concept of mission. It should be recast. Bishop J. Moynagh of Calabar, Nigeria, in likewise demanding a complete reworking of the schema, insisted on the need to preserve the traditional distinction between missionary activity, i.e. the first preaching, and the subsequent care of the converted.

Before the subject was resumed at the 39th (118th) General Congregation, (9 November) the Moderator, Cardinal Döpfner, reminded the Fathers that four schemata, in addition to the rest of that on the *Church in the Modern World*, still needed to be briefly discussed, if they were to be amended in line with their views during the interval before the next Session. It would help if they readily voted the closure when it was proposed. When six more speakers had had their say on the Mission schema, adding little of substance to what had already been said, the closure was promptly approved, and discussion of n. 24 of the *Church in the Modern World* was resumed.

Fr G. Mahon, Superior General of the Mill Hill Fathers (now Auxiliary of Westminster) had been patiently waiting his chance to show the connection between the solidarity of the human family and the work of the Missions, especially in the hungry Third World. He recalled that the Industrial Revolution took place long before 1870, yet Vatican I had had nothing to say about proletarianism. The depressed masses could hardly have been expected to be thrilled by the definition of Papal Infallibility. Here again in Vatican II most of the time had been devoted to internal affairs, but now the Council faced the world. The disparity between nations was no less than that which had existed formerly between the classes. The proletarian nations were now awaiting the implementation of international justice. Missionaries had to work in this Third World in which 400 million actually suffered hunger. Some people regarded socio-economic action as secondary for the missionary, but that was not the lesson of Christ's parable of the Good Samaritan. The whole of the Gospel was to be preached, not just the spiritual part. The Good Samaritan must operate on a worldwide scale. It followed, he said, that the campaign against hunger must, by reason of its gravity and urgency, be one of their first concerns. All Christians must be educated to regard themselves as responsible towards the needy of the world. Coordinated ecumenical action of Christians was needed. He agreed with Cardinal Frings that a special Secretariate should be set up to organize the efficacious conduct of this campaign.

(At this point, the result of the vote taken after the closure of discussion of the missionary schema, on the proposal that "it should be revised again by the competent Commission", was announced. 1601 Fathers said Yes (i.e. 83%) 311 said No. One wondered how the Pope's advisers felt).

Cardinal Richaud, in the name of 70 Fathers and especially of Cardinal Silva Henriquez, President of *Caritas Internationalis*, begged leave to say a word on the special obligation of international charity. C.I., he said, comprised 70 (?) national and international organizations devoted to works of mercy. Occasional help was not enough. It was necessary to co-ordinate the operations proper to the various nations, saving their independence.

* * *

The discussion then moved on to n. 25, on the *strengthening of Peace*. Cardinal Alfrink began by remarking that the Council could not ask less than *Pacem in Terris*. On the reduction of armaments the encyclical spoke more positively than the schema; the schema should follow suit. In regard to ABC weapons, the schema was inexact in implying that their effect was always incapable of being estimated or controlled; there now existed "clean" bombs whose effect could be computed. But it did not follow that there could be a war in which they could be used justly. That however was not the chief question, but rather how to ensure that they were never used. *Pacem in terris* rightly said that justice and right reason required that atomic weapons be forbidden. As President Kennedy had said, unless we destroyed them, they would destroy us.

Bishop Ancel (France) found n. 25 to be self-contradictory. It condemned wars, especially nuclear wars and yet affirmed the lawfulness of forcibly resisting unjust aggression, and since effective resistance was impossible without use of the same weapons as those of the enemy, it implicitly legitimated the use of nuclear weapons. That was why the mad armament race went on unchecked. Somehow this apparent contradiction must be overcome. It was not for the Council to discover technical means, but to say to the world what were the morally true demands of the common good, and promote conditions in which even a defensive war could not be justified. J. Guilhem, Bishop of Laval in France, would not admit any qualification. The use of atomic weapons could not be justified by any moral principle and should be absolutely prohibited.

Maximus IV took the same line when the debate was resumed in the 40th (119th) General Congregation (10 November), with impassioned rhetoric (in French) rather than with sober reasoning. The world was threatened by a cataclysm of worldwide extent which no reason could justify. Ought not the doctrine of just war of self defence be revised? The Council should speak bravely as did *Pacem in terris*. The schema was too platonic. There was need of a declaration *urbi et orbi*, "nette et précis". It could snowball. A solemn condemnation of all ABC warfare should be issued.

Bishop Hengsbach of Essen claimed that the schema went no further than Pius XII and *Pacem in terris* in regard to the limits of defensive war, and he asked whether the Council could not advance further.

Bishop P. Hannan of the U.S.A., on the other hand, said it was necessary to distinguish between what the Church sought for and what moral theology required, and to use experts (peritissimi) who knew what they were talking about. They wanted peace but with justice. War was always odious, but it was necessary to say what was not allowed in a just defensive war. The schema was misleading in its reference to nuclear weapons whose effect could not be estimated. There were some noble ones whose effect was very circumscribed. Nor was it correct to say that all nations have attempted "pariter" to promote peace. They all knew the source of aggression.

Archbishop Beck of Liverpool also called for more clarity and accuracy, especially in regard to nuclear weapons. Certainly the Council must firmly condemn the direct killing of innocent people by indiscriminate weapons as being intrinsically evil, but it was important to make it clear that this condemnation did not include all arms, e.g. those designed to attack hostile satellites in space. The Council therefore should not condemn all use of nuclear weapons as necessarily evil. The decision lay with governments and the Council should show its regard for those who carried this burden. They had a duty to protect their country and its way of life. They must indeed do this by peaceful means, as far as possible, but it could happen that they could only deter unjust aggression by a balance of terror. The Council ought not to demand of governments that they disarm unilaterally merely because of abuse. It should however emphasize even more the obligation of working for an international order which would make possible nuclear disarmament "hinc inde per idemque tempus", as *Pacem in terris* proposed.

After three more speeches on a variety of topics, discussion of the *Church in the Modern World* expired, a Spanish layman addressed the Council on World Famine, Bishop Guano summed up as Relator for the responsible Commission, and the next schema, *On the Renewal and Adaptation of Religious Life* was introduced.

* * *

This too had suffered major amputations. In the period of drastic pruning that followed the First Session, the original schema comprising 201 articles in 32 chapters and covering 110 pages had been reduced to 19 Propositions in four pages. Nevertheless, the Roman Union of Superiors General had decided that it might be wiser to improve the Propositions by qualified affirmative votes rather than reject the schema outright by a massive negative vote (cf. Wiltgen, op.cit. p. 216).

Cardinal Spellman was the first commentator. He expressed general satisfaction with the text. Granted some major amendments, it could serve as a basis for a prudent renewal of religious life. He was more concerned about certain attempts currently being made to change the nature of religious life radically.

* * *

When the topic was resumed at the 41st (120th) General Congregation, (11 November), Cardinal de Barros Camara of Rio di Janeiro said it was in general acceptable to the 163 Brazilian Bishops in whose name he spoke. It prudently left the details to be worked out in a post-Conciliar Commission. Cardinal Ruffini, while admitting that necessity knew no laws, regretted the fragmentary appearance of the Propositions which could have been avoided in a complete schema, and also certain things that had been over-looked. Cardinal Richaud of Bordeaux had found many good things in it, but indicated certain defects which needed correction. It was too juridical; for example the preamble contained not the slightest reference to the Holy Spirit.

Cardinal Döpfner, on the other hand, called for a complete revision. The schema had to be examined in the light of the renewal promoted by the Council. In that light it was revealed as poor. It did not get to the heart of the difficulties. Its chief defect was the lack of cardinal points. Things of major importance were mixed up with those of minor importance. The primary need was a spiritual renewal, but all the schema offered was outward forms. It was necessary to get back to the sources, to true spiritual theology. The piety of many institutes smacked too much of the nineteenth century. The second need was adaptation to our times. Religious must feel that they belonged to this world. How could they recognize the signs of the times unless they were open to them? How else could their poverty become a meaningful witness to the world? Their obedience must be that of a contemporary adult. Above all, the members must receive a better, more theological instruction than in the past.

Cardinal Landazzuri of Lima, however, was satisfied that the Propositions, when complemented by the theological aspects contained in the Constitution *De Ecclesia*, contained sufficient material for their purpose. Cardinal Suenens agreed rather with Döpfner. The schema was unacceptable because it failed to provide adequately for the desired renewal.

In Congregations of active sisters, it must conduce to the integral promotion of adult womanhood. Pastors and theologians must elaborate a spirituality more adapted to modern life and define the apostolate in its full sense. A twofold danger had to be avoided, excessive maternalism in superiors and passivism or infantilism in inferiors. Antiquated customs and too radical separation from the world of their apostolate must be altered.

What troubled Cardinal Bea was the almost complete lack of principles in the schema. It was these rather than juridical norms that were needed. It was true that they were to be found in *De Ecclesia*, but not expressed from the practical viewpoint. It was for each Order to safeguard the values received from its founders, but in full collaboration with other Orders.

Bishop Pacificus Perantoni of Lanciano, Italy, claimed to speak in the name of 370 Fathers from various nations, and, though he did not say so, almost certainly spoke for the opposition that had been building up against the Döpfner-Suenens line. The schema was basically satisfactory and should be retained. True, not all questions were treated, but with good reason. The doctrinal side was already treated in chapter VI of *De Ecclesia*, and the external apostolate in the decree on the Pastoral Office of Bishops. The present schema was concerned only with the adaptation of religious life. The details were best left to post-Conciliar Commissions. But the schema needed completing on one or two points, in particular, on the necessity of the religious life in the Church of today, on the protection of variety as an expression of different charisms, on the proper fostering of religious vocations, on the gratitude due especially to the non-clerical religious institutes.

For Bishop R. Guilly of Georgetown, British Guiana, the schema restricted the term "apostolate" unduly to the external apostolate, whereas it should denote any activity which helped to spread the kingdom of God, e.g. interior life, etc.

Far too little was said about the contemplatives who by their prayers and sacrifices contributed more than others to the apostolate, even on the missions. That was why Pius XI made St Thérèse of Lisieux patroness of the missions. There should be a distinct proposition extolling the contemplative life.

Fr J. Buckley, Superior General of the Marists, who claimed to speak for 130 Fathers, tended rather to the Döpfner-Suenens position. The schema was not acceptable. It had too many lacunae. It made no gesture of friendship towards the secular clergy. Religious needed to appreciate the antipathy they created by speaking as though they alone were in the way of perfection. The diocesan clergy had much in common with them, common life, celibacy, obedience, and often poverty. Religious priests devoted to active apostolate were closer to diocesan clergy than to contemplative religious. The schema did nothing towards removal of the difference between orders and congregations; the latter should not be regarded as of "second rank". It applied a monastic concept of religious obedience. The crisis was one of superiors rather than subjects, and yet nothing was said about the obligation of the former to consult the latter. The adaptation of obedience consisted in the reform of Superiors.

* * *

At the 42nd (121st) General Congregation, (12 November), Bishop Huyghe of Arras, France, also rallied to the Döpfner-Suenens line. The schema was too juridical, western, out of touch with the Council. A new one should be drafted which would duly situate the religious life in the life of the whole Church, internal and external. Religious should exemplify and promote unity in the Church. They ought not therefore to segregate themselves from other members of the Church which was perfected only by union in charity. They should create bonds and collaborate fraternally for concord. Ecumenism was of the very nature of their life. Externally, in the pagan and post-Christian areas where the Church was missionary, religious should be the Church's soldiers, her first missionaries, whether or not they belonged to a so-called missionary institute. New forms of religious, more poor and humble, should be instituted, new forms of enclosure, even for *moniales*, for they belonged to the 20th C., not to the Middle Ages. On the missions, they should adapt their life to the situation and not transport rules and customs made for Europe to an entirely different setting. A new schema was needed, because the present one was incurable. Superioresses should be taken into consultation to ensure that women religious become fully adult in the Church, like laywomen.

P. Hoffer of the Marianists spoke in the name of religious teaching brothers and asked that something be said of their kind of religious life. Their personal religious status was complete without the priesthood; they had made the triple sacrifice. Having dedicated themselves to the training of youth they should be encouraged to make themselves fully suited to their sacred task. Their dedication to God involved no contempt of the world, but helped them the better to influence it for good. Their labour was a true apostolate, and therefore it was very desirable that the Council should highlight the spirituality proper to teaching brothers.

In the opinion of Fr G. Lalande, C.S.C., supported by 140 Fathers and 143 Fathers General, the schema was useful but very insufficient. It seemed exclusively juridical and lacked "pastoral sap". It should show the link between the renewal of the Church and that of religious life, and therefore should be revised according to the spiritual and pastoral norms of the Council.

To Bishop Carroll of Australia, who spoke in the name of forty Fathers, it was acceptable as a basis for discussion, but needed a paragraph on the vocation of teaching brothers and sisters, acknowledging that the vocation of a teaching brother had its own value as a complete and proper form of religious life, independently of the priesthood.

After four more speeches which added little not already said, the Congregation readily voted on closure of the discussion, to be followed by a Yes or No vote.

* * *

The schema *De Institutione Sacerdotali* was then introduced. A draft of 19 propositions had been sent out to the Fathers in May 1964 and had been amended in line with their comments and slightly enlarged, so as now to comprise 22 propositions.

Cardinal Buono y Monreal of Seville, who claimed 20 years experience in the business, found not a few things in it worthy of praise. However, the first necessity was to get students, and to that end a clearer description of priestly vocation was needed, especially in view of the various senses in which the word "vocation" was used nowadays, even in the Church. A vocation was a grace of God given to those who had the required endowments and freely offered themselves. Spontaneous generation should not be expected, the ground had to be cultivated. The priesthood should be held up to young men as an ideal; many of them never thought of it until it was presented to them. In many cases, the best indication of the seed was a good family life plus spiritual direction.

(The result of the vote on the general acceptability of the Propositions on the *Adaptation and Renewal of Religious Life* was announced at this point. 1155 had voted *placet*, as against 882 *non placet*. Voting on the schema by sections, *placet*, *non placet* or *placet iuxta modum*, was to begin two days later).

Cardinal Meyer of Chicago was pleased that a *ratio studiorum* was to be drawn up for each nation by its Episcopal Conference, because this ensured a real possibility of keeping in touch with the local pastoral situation. He doubted however whether the principles common to all nations could be clearly enough presented in the schema in a few propositions. Bishop Drzazga (Yes!) doubted whether the schema made it clear that the model was Christ. Its principles were so universal and indeterminate as to seem insufficient. It needed to be redrafted.

Bishop Colombo of Milan was very pleased with it on the whole, but noted two defects. It lacked organic unity and it failed to provide for the human formation of the students. Most of them did not come to sufficient maturity as men; they were too passive, too cut off from society.

The following day, Friday 13 November, was devoted to a Byzantine Mass concelebrated by Maximus IV with other Patriarchs, *coram Summo Pontifice*. At the end of the long ritual, the Pope gave to the relief of world hunger the tiara which had been presented to him by his former diocese of Milan, and then, after embracing Maximus on both cheeks, processed out on foot.

* * *

At the 43rd (122nd) General Congregation, (14 November), after a warning that there would probably be afternoon as well as morning meetings the following week (which fortunately was never implemented), discussion of the schema on priestly training was resumed.

Cardinal De Barros Camara of Brazil said he agreed with Colombo. The schema provided an excellent basis on which the present structure could be revised in the light of the ecclesiastical, liturgical and biblical renewal. Details were wisely left to the local episcopal conferences. Confidence in their pastoral prudence was due to them. They should not have to look to the Council or to Rome for everything.

Cardinal Ruffini, speaking from 30 years experience of Seminary life and 17 as Secretary of the Congregation of Seminaries, lamented the lack of any mention of St Thomas in the proposition on the study of philosophy, and begged that he be restored to his due place. Was not Leo XIII's testimony adapted to contemporary needs?

Cardinal Léger, on the other hand, while pleased with the general inspiration of the new redaction, objected even to the mention of the "philosophia perennis". It was ambiguous. If it meant scholastic philosophy, he could not see how the purpose of the proposition could be attained. Philosophy, of its very nature, depended not on authority but on investigation, not on what authors said but on what things were. In the section on theology, the references to St Thomas as the "Magister" should be omitted, and it should be made clear that it was the method rather than the system of St Thomas that was commended as a model.

Seminarists must not be cloistered from the world. The moral theology traditionally taught to them needed revising. It did not meet modern needs, was too casuistic and not fully Christian. The schema should deal explicitly with it and insist that the link with dogmatic and biblical theology be restored.

Cardinal Döpfner liked the moderation of the propositions and agreed with Léger about St Thomas; the schema was just right about his due place. It should however deal at greater depth with the nature of vocation, with due attention to the biblical evidence; and deal more fully and directly with collaboration with clerics, for the isolation of the clerical state (good in itself) demanded that seminarists be specially trained to meet the world.

Cardinal Suenens said he agreed with Léger and Döpfner, but he also, wanted the institution of a special Commission. A mere text was not enough for pastoral renewal in which the seminaries must be integrated; there were some perennial principles to be preserved, but there was need of prudent revision to meet changing circumstances. Spiritual formation remained essential, but its modality was to be determined by the final object of the diocesan clergy, not from monastic life. The intellectual formation should begin with a biblical and liturgical initiation; philosophy was too hard an introduction for youths. Their pastoral formation should envisage the priest as "laicatus animator", and for that he needed a practical pastoral initiation. It was not enough to add a 7th pastoral year; the whole course should be pastorally orientated.

Archbishop Dino Staffa of the Curia then came to the defence of St Thomas. It was a matter of no importance when thomistic philosophy began; the question was whether or not it was true. Truth was always truth, whether in East or West. Human nature was the same everywhere. And according to the teaching of the Popes, the doctrine of St Thomas was to be religiously preserved not only in theology but also in philosophy.

Little fresh was said in the half-dozen more speeches of the morning, though Bishop Botero of Colombia was kind enough to suggest that a word of praise might be added for those who devoted their lives to teaching in seminaries.

At the 44th (123rd) General Congregation, Monday 16 Nov., it was announced to loud applause that the threatened afternoon Congregations would not take place, because the afternoon hours were needed for the study of the propositions that had to be voted, which were many and difficult.

Then Cardinal Caggiano of Buenos Aires resumed the subject of priestly training. The schema very rightly required it to be adapted to its pastoral end, but the renewal must be both new and traditional, not a radical revolution. A Christian philosophy was needed and that was above all the philosophy of St Thomas, the principles of which were especially concordant with revealed truth. In Paul VI's words, it "expresses the very essences of things" for East and West, past and present. Vitoria held that St Thomas' doctrines were to be abandoned only if there were clearly stronger arguments to the contrary. There must also be a return to the integrity of theology; there was too much dissection today.

Cardinal Bacci said he had been perturbed by what was said at the previous General Congregation about the *philosophia perennis*. He thought none of the Fathers would wish to reject the teaching of St Thomas which had been extolled with high praise by 80 Supreme Pontiffs from the 13th Century down to modern times. That would set the Council not above but against the Supreme Pontiff. He would admit of course that philosophy progressed and the *philosophia perennis* with it. He would propose that it be clearly stated that the perennial or thomistic philosophy be held in high honour, though other authors were not therefore to be neglected.

Bishop J. Komba of Tanganyika raised what seemed to me a reasonable objection to the change of the title from *De Sacrorum Alumnis Formandis* to *De Institutione Sacerdotali*. Instruction was given in class; formation included it, but much more. And they were not instructing priests but *prospective* priests.

Archbishop Hurley of Durban called for an introductory course which directed the minds of the students to the mystery of Christ. He agreed with Suenens that the placing of the philosophy course needed reviewing, but neo-scholasticism should not be undervalued today; there was danger of opening the door to systems incompatible with Christian faith. Truth was not twofold.

Bishop Charue of Namur said that there was need more than ever before of a deep and austere spiritual formation for future priests. They must be kept free from all infantilism and fully adult, and be initiated to the apostolate and the various forms of ministry. But exaggerations must be avoided. All the talk nowadays was of efficiency and the spirituality of action. He readily agreed, provided it was rightly understood. The schema excellently kept to the middle way and he hoped it would be widely accepted.

Bishop Weber of Strasbourg, with 25 years of experience, also praised the schema, brief as it was, for its moderation and balance. In his view, a seminary was worth what its superiors were worth. They should therefore be well prepared, devout and with some pastoral experience.

At the end of this Congregation, the Moderators proposed the closure of the discussion and the Fathers agreed. But, at the next, the 45th, (124th) 17 Nov., three Fathers claimed the right to speak in the name of 70 Fathers.

The first was Archbishop Garrone of Toulouse (destined later to become head of the Congregation of Seminaries). He liked the schema, especially for leaving the local episcopal conference to decide the *ratio studiorum*. This changed the work of the Congregation of Seminaries, but relative autonomy did not mean independence but collaboration. It was to be hoped that the Congregation would be restructured, for its new task. In order to perceive the needs, it must transcend the timeless field in which it had hitherto been labouring and be linked with the Congregation of priests, aided by experts from everywhere. It must also keep abreast of progress in theology and philosophy and their relation with the profane sciences. He hoped it would be reformed in such a way as to be able to cooperate continually ("iugiter") with the local episcopal conferences. (One can see why Paul VI, after the Council, pulled him out of his diocese and gave him the job he had outlined).

Bishop S. Mendez of Mexico criticized the negative presentation of celibacy in the schema. So too Bishop Reuss, Auxiliary of Mainz.

The result of the vote on the general acceptability of the schema was: *placet* 2076, *non placet* 41. Which meant that the detailed vote, section by section, with room for amendments, could then begin.

* * *

The *Declaration on Christian Education* was then presented. Cardinal Spellman, perhaps with an eye to the American press, used the occasion to press for fair subsidies from the State as the only way to ensure parental liberty in regard to the education of their children. Cardinal Ritter kept to the document. It contained many good things. In particular it wisely kept within the limits of present possibility, for the Council could not go into detail in a matter of such complication and diversity. The two things necessary were: a special post-Conciliar Commission, and freedom for episcopal conferences to determine particular matters. It should declare the parental rights in regard to the administration of schools. Schools and universities should be examples of liberty.

Bishop Elchinger of France, on the contrary, wanted the schema thoroughly recast. It must reflect the spirit of the Council in regard to the end of education, i.e that the Church be missionary; it must introduce the spirit of service, and it must uphold the principle of respective competence. The parents were the primary educators, but no one possessed the children.

The first speaker at the 46th (125th) General Congregation, 18 Nov., was Cardinal Léger. He suggested that it would be better to remit the schema to the Commission until next session. They had neither the time nor the energy to examine it with care, and it would be unseemly to approve with undue haste a text destined to be a *magna carta* for many years. It had some excellent points but lacked inspiration and either omitted some grave problems or treated them superficially. It contributed nothing to the solution of the problem of coordination and cooperation in higher studies. It had nothing to say on the question of liberty of scientific investigation, on which many Fathers and scientists had expected a declaration from the Council. It should be proclaimed in regard to all sacred sciences.

Bishop J. Malone of Youngstown, U.S.A., speaking in the name of 80 Fathers, suggested three improvements to an otherwise acceptable schema. It should be amplified so as to include the reasons for the various rights and duties asserted. The distinction between society (i.e. the united people) and the State, its instrument, should be stressed. It should provide a clearer view of the relations between those who participated in education, as in Pius XI's *Divini illius Magistri*.

Bishop J. L. Henriquez of Venezuela did not like the schema. It was too conservative and avoided the difficulties. In his country, only 10% were in Catholic schools; other means of education must be found for the rest. The Church was almost absent in the State schools.

Archbishop Beck of Liverpool, speaking in the name of several episcopal conferences and 30 Fathers, regretted the reduction of the previous document to a brief declaration. 1) The text should speak more clearly and strongly about the natural right of parents to educate their children according to their own conscience. It was first mentioned in n. 4, whereas it should, in view of its great importance, figure at the very beginning of the declaration; for the Church should be the defender of the natural rights of all, not just of Catholics; and therefore if circumstances make it practicable, the State should aid parents to exercise their right (Catholic parents included, since they too are citizens) without any discrimination, as already happened in several countries. 2) The schema rightly mentioned the Church's right to build schools, but failed to explain the basic reason, namely: "Go and teach all nations", a major defect in a conciliar document. (Applause).

There followed two speeches from missionary bishops on the importance of Catholic schools in their countries, and one from an Ecuadorian bishop on the tendency of the modern state to monopolize education and of the modern world to divorce science from revealed truth and so dechristianize culture, problems which were not dealt with by the inadequate schema.

At the 126th General Congregation (47th) 19 November, Bishop Pohlschneider of Aachen said he agreed with Archbishop Beck, on the need of a clearer statement that the State was bound in distributive justice to give equal treatment to schools. The laicist concept of education was the great heresy of our time. It was not enough that the Catholic religion be taught in the school; the school must be Catholic.

After three further speeches, two from Nigeria and one from the Lebanon, the closure was proposed and voted. The General of the Dominicans, Fernandez, asserted his claim to speak in the name of 73

Fathers and plugged the philosophy of St Thomas. Then the Fathers voted by 1457 to 419 to accept the schema and proceed with the detailed voting in 4 section-ballots, which they completed in fact during that same Congregation.

Meanwhile Cardinal Tisserant introduced a *Relatio* on the *Declaration on Religious Liberty*. He said that, in the opinion of the Council Presidency there was not enough time for due reflection on the revised version of the Declaration, and it had therefore decided that, after the Fathers had heard the *Relatio*, the voting would be postponed until the next Session. Bishop De Smedt then delivered his *Relatio* with oratorical emphasis, emotion and to constant applause, which was renewed in several waves for some minutes afterwards. He admitted that the structure of the schema had been considerably changed, but said it contained the same doctrine more accurately and prudently expressed. The postponement caused considerable displeasure among the Americans, some of whom regarded religious liberty as their special gift to the world, and a group of them, including Mgrs Quinn of Chicago and Fred McManus of Washington, periti, from the tribune in which I was sitting, immediately began to organize a melodramatic petition to the Pope begging him "instanter, instantius, instantissime" that the vote be allowed to take place before the end of that session of the Council, "lest the confidence of the Christian and non-Christian world be lost"!! There was quite a hubbub in the aisles where a number of American bishops and periti speedily congregated and began lobbying in what one presumed was the approved American convention style. There was talk of a massive revolt, and the U.S. Bishops news agency quoted an unnamed US Bishop as saying that "perhaps 1000 signatures from Bishops from all over the world had been collected". The exact number was later found to be 441. [The following day, the last General Congregation of the session, Cardinal Tisserant announced that the Pope had authorized him to tell the Fathers that the postponement of the vote, requested by an international group of Fathers, had been granted by the Presidency because the Rule Book required it, and out of respect for the liberty of other Fathers who wanted a proper, profound and careful examination of a document of such great importance. (Cf. Wiltgen, op.cit., p. 235-238)].

In the midst of all this Brouhaha, a schema *De Matrimonii Sacramento* was produced. Cardinal Gilroy conceded that it contained some practical rules to prevent too easy invalidity, but suggested some improvements. The promise to be demanded only of the Catholic and the notification to be made to the non-Catholic should have to take place before the Parish Priest or his delegate, so that it could be established in the external forum. (End of a crowded and stormy General Congregation).

* * *

The 127th (48th) and final General Congregation of the Third Session (Friday 20th November) had a crowded programme, so crowded as to be scarcely serious. Four documents were distributed: the schema on Ecumenism on which the Fathers were to be presently asked to vote; a Pontifical Rescript in regard to certain faculties; the amended schema (actually completely rewritten) on the Life and Ministry of Priests, and the amended schema on Divine Revelation (which had started its journey in the middle of the first Session). In regard to these latter two, Felici observed it would be impossible to vote them through, but that the Fathers could submit their comments up to January 31, 1965. A number of other documents which had been partly voted would also have to be completed in the next Session.

As to the *Votum de Matrimonii Sacramento,* discussion would have to be completed that morning. The Moderators therefore proposed the following motion: "Was it the pleasure of the Fathers that, after the discussion, the whole matter concerning this Votum, along with the comments of the Fathers, be referred to the Supreme Pontiff in order that he may provide through the competent organs". If they had further comments to make, they could likewise send them before 31 January 1965. The Fathers voted affirmatively. The morning was spent mainly in criticisms of particular points. Ruffini and Bueno went into detail. Döpfner (Moderator for that General Congregation) said that for brevity's sake, he would omit what he had prepared, except to say that the schema respected the demands of the divine law and of ecumenism in regard to mixed marriages, and to beg that the Pope would deal with these latter as soon as possible in a *motu proprio*. Ritter of St Louis liked the new dispositions both in regard to the promises and in regard to the form. On the other hand, Bishop J. Fearns, speaking for Spellman and in the name of over 100 US bishops, feared that some of the changes would do grave harm in the US, and they needed time to consult their Parish Priests, especially, in the most pluralist areas. Krol of Philadelphia noted that more than 60 million in the US went to no Church, and yet the schema made no distinction between them and sincere non-Catholic Christians.

Renard of Versailles, in the name of 100 French bishops, raised the French problem of the baptized *non-pratiquants* who sought a Church marriage though did not regard it as a sacrament. Charrière, in the name of the Swiss hierarchy, said they must consider how they were to put across the new attitudes and rules to the faithful.

Archbishop Heenan of Westminster warmly welcomed the religious celebration of mixed marriages. Hitherto they had been so denuded of sacred rites as to be more like funerals. If they married them at all, it should be a happy day, blessed by the Church. The chief difficulty lay in regard to the religious education of the children. The first reality to be borne in mind was that the vast majority of mixed marriages were between Catholics and persons who belonged to no Church and hardly ever objected to the promises. Special rules should be provided for sincere Protestants, though even they did not often refuse Catholic education, because it was not necessarily against their conscience, since they seldom regarded their Church as the only true one. If the text wanted to be really ecumenical, it ought to make provision for sincere non-Catholics. There was no reason why after a Catholic marriage they should not seek a blessing in their own Church.

I came away at this point, caught a bus to the English College, had an early lunch with the Vice-Rector who then drove me to the airport to catch the 2.25 plane for England. I was home in Maidstone by 6.30 for a long weekend.

The Saturday 21st November 1964 was devoted to a solemn Public Session for promulgation of certain documents, to wit: *Lumen Gentium* (The Church), *Orientalium Ecclesiarum* (Eastern Catholic Churches), and *Unitatis Redintegratio* (Ecumenism).

The Fourth Session

September 14th – December 8th 1965

Tuesday, 14th September, 1965, Solemn Opening.

8.30 to St Peter's in prelate's robes which secured us our usual privileged seats, just to the right of the papal altar. The Pope's address which lasted 40 minutes was mainly about charity, but included mention of the new Synod of Bishops to be promulgated on the morrow.

At 4.40 p.m. we assembled outside Santa Croce for the Penitential Procession for which the Pope had asked. Our part of the crowd did not get moving until about 6 p.m., and when we reached the Lateran we had to remain standing throughout a long sermon by Cardinal Traglia, the Pope's vicar. A large throne-like arm chair was brought out of the basilica for the Pope but, no doubt out of solidarity with all the elderly ecclesiastics around him, he refrained from using it. The huge crowd was blessed with a relic of the True Cross which the Pope had carried from Santa Croce, and after extricating our coach from a traffic jam, we got back to the English College at 8.30, ready for supper!

Wednesday 15th September, 1st (128th) General Congregation began with a somewhat revised liturgy in which the enthronement of the Gospel was now part of the Introit procession.

The Motu Proprio *Apostolica solicitudo* constituting the new *Synodus Episcoporum* was first introduced by Cardinal Marella, President of the Commission on Bishops, and then read by the Secretary General, Archbishop Felici. The Pope left at 10.40.

Cardinal Tisserant welcomed the Fathers on the part of the Presidency, begging them to avoid vain repetition and abstain from applause, and then Cardinal Agaganian, Moderator for that day added his greetings. In fulfilment of the solemn promise given at the somewhat stormy end of the Third Session, the revised schema *De Libertate Religiosa* was then promptly introduced by its Relator, Bishop De Smedt of Bruges.

The first speaker, Cardinal Spellman of New fork found it "omnino pergratum". Religious Liberty was always and everywhere acknowledged. The schema wisely avoided the term "liberty of conscience" which was ambiguous. He feared lest any change should be a cause of suspicion. It should be accepted as it stood.

To Cardinal Frings of Cologne also it was in general pleasing. It breathed the Spirit of the Lord who willed the gospel to be spread without force, as was clear from the parable of the cockle which was to be allowed to grow with the good seed until the harvest. He suggested a few verbal amendments.

Cardinal Ruffini grudgingly admitted that it contained several excellent points, e.g. in regard to the dignity of the human person. But, it needed to distinguish at the very outset between physical and moral liberty."Veritas liberabit vos". Agnostic indifferentism was to be avoided. The State could not licitly behave as though there were no God, but ought always to favour religion. He feared lest the result would be complete separation of Church and State which Popes have described as an error, and lest it would undermine conventions between Church and State, eg. the Italian, which recognized the Catholic religion as that of the State. As it stood the schema was liable to have the gravest consequences, and ought to be amended.

Cardinal Siri of Genoa stressed that he was not speaking against liberty, but against its abuse. Liberty was a faculty of action. The faculty to sin was not liberty but toleration; God tolerated the fact. We could not embrace, but at most only tolerate, anything contrary to God's will. The schema, on the other hand, defended all liberty; and though liberty was in general to be defended, even more to be defended was the divine law.

Cardinal Arriba y Castro of Tarragona said he would briefly offer a few very simple points. He doubted whether the Council had dealt with anything more fundamental. Only the Catholic Church had the right and duty to preach the Gospel. Others should be prevented from doing so not only by the Church but even by the civil power. The norm of toleration was determined by the common good. The solution should be left to the local episcopal conference, because it had to be adapted to circumstances of time and place. The worship of non-Catholics ought to be free, and no religion could be imposed by force on anyone.

Cardinal Urbani of Venice, in the name of 30 Italian bishops, found the schema substantially satisfactory on various grounds. Men of different religions had to live together in the same region, and it was therefore necessary to declare the rights and functions of citizens in religious matters. The question at issue was in some sense a new one which could not be solved simply by quoting the Magisterium. Religious liberty was one aspect of civil rights, a question of relations between persons, the State and the common good. There had been a clear development in the doctrine of recent Popes from Gregory XVI onwards, However, there should be a clearer declaration in the preamble of the kind of liberty meant, i.e. *civil* liberty in religious life. A distinction ought also to be made between the juridical and the moral aspect, since only religious truth had a moral right. The schema insisted too much on the obligation of obeying the declarations of conscience, and too little on the right and duty to seek the truth.

Cardinal Cushing had no difficulties or doubts. Religious liberty as asserted in the schema was solidly based in Catholic doctrine and also a pastoral necessity of the first order throughout the world. He admitted that he was not a philosopher of great repute, but he knew that every right had to be based on some truth and have some good for its object, and the whole of the schema was about these two things. The truth was that the dignity of the human person lay in acting according to one's own decision and responsibility, not under external compulsion. This dignity was fundamental not only to all human rights, but to the whole social order, even in religious matters. The good of maximum importance to man in society, was that he be not coerced against his conscience even by the public authority. Hence, he concluded, religious liberty was based on the objective, not the subjective order.

Cardinal Alfrink agreed that in general the schema was very praiseworthy. Religious liberty was not a negative thing, liberty from, but rather a positive right to choose.

There were still two cardinals waiting their turn to speak when the debate was resumed at the 129th (2nd) General Congregation. But before they were called, Felici announced the programme of work for the Session:

1) 4 schemata which were substantially new still had to be discussed, viz: *De Libertate Religiosa, De Ecclesia in Mundo Huius Temporis, De Activitate Missionali Ecclesiae,* and *De Ministerio et Vita Presbyterorum.*

2) 2 schemata had to be subjected to the triple vote of the amendment stage (*placet, non placet,* or *placet juxta modum* (i.e. with modus, a.v. amendment attached), viz: *De Divina Revelatione,* and *De Apostolatu Laicorum.*

3) 5 schemata were to be voted simply in regard to the treatment given to the suggested amendments by the Commission, *placet* or *non placet*: *De Pastorali Episcoporum Munere in Ecclesia, De Accomodata Renovationis Vitae Religiosae, De Educatione Christiana, De Institutione Sacerdotali, De Habitudine Ecclesiae ad Religiones non-Christianos.*

Cardinal Ritter then rose to express his great joy over the schema on Religious Liberty. In his view, it merely remained to approve and promulgate it. The whole world was waiting for it, and therefore "caritas Christi urget nos" to approve it. Many were suffering persecution. The Fathers could bring them peace. The decree on Ecumenism was useless without this.

Cardinal Silva Henriquez of Chile was satisfied with the order, arguments and restricted object of the schema. It did not lead to relativism or favour it. It did however invite us to re-examine our own apostolic activity, so as to ensure that we abstained from any kind of political coercion or proselytism, even in regard to perseverance in the faith.

Patriarch Paul Maouchi of the Maronites observed that the Council was dealing with the same problem as had Pius IX a century before, but in different historical circumstances. Now that Christians and pagans were proclaiming the same things but without the same meaning, it was vitally important not to use the world's different vocabulary without taking account of the mentality of the modern world. The schema should be vetted from this point of view. Nor should it seek to argue from theology or philosophy, but from experience based on the concrete human situation. Neither the dignity of the human person nor the image of God was patent to human reason. Religious liberty was based on the very nature of faith.

Archbishop Slipyj, speaking in the name of the Ukrainian Episcopal Conference, while fully supporting the main theme of the schema, urged that it needed to be more explicit in regard to the cases in which the State could justifiably limit precisely religious freedom in the interests of public order. It was precisely on this ground that religious freedom was practically denied in his part of the world. It was an offence against liberty if the State prevented parents from exercising their right to educate their children in the faith.

Archbishop L. Jaeger of Paderborn, speaking in tha name of the German Episcopal Conference, said that though all were agreed that the Christian State of the Middle Ages had altogether disappeared, there were still uni-confessional States. The schema did not exclude such a regime, but insisted that there must be real freedom for the minority. It was not enough to refrain from forcing them into the Church, or merely to allow them to have private worship. The schema avoided religious indifferentism. It clearly proclaimed the one Catholic Church and rejected absolute autonomy of conscience, affirming the obligation of conforming one's conscience to the divine law.

Archbishop Nicodemo of Bari (a member of the preparatory Commission to which keel I belonged in 1960-62, and conservative in general tendency) welcomed the revised text as substantially acceptable, but wanted a half-dozen points further clarified because of the grave importance of the matter. In particular, he wanted it made clear whether the Council was asserting an objective and absolute right, proper to all men equally, or merely a subjective right of each individual. (Before the Council I myself had held and taught that the right to profess a false religion, even in good faith, could not be more than subjective. I had been converted to the view that it was objective, i.e. based on man's nature, because, in the final issue, man as made by God can only conform his will to God's by following his honestly formed certain conscience, even when it happens to be false. It seemed evident to me that this was clearly what the Council was asserting). The Archbishop was also not satisfied with the limitation of the State's right to inhibit religious liberty to cases in which this was necessary to public order; he wanted inclusion of reasons of the common good in the historical situation (which it seems to me, have been the chief justification claimed for religious persecution in the past, and, if admitted, would regate the main object of the schema).

Archbishop Morcillo of Madrid, a definite conservative, wanted the declaration reduced to a mere judgement on the concrete historical situation. It ought not to be a pronouncement of principles, but a practical solution of the juridical problem created by the present situation in which most States were pluralistic, more closely linked, and religious ecumenism was favoured. The arguments advanced had no permanent validity and conflicted with papal teaching. The State had no competence to judge religious truth, merely to receive the teaching of the Church and make it its own. At this point the speeches became increasingly repetitive or mainly concerned with points of detail.

Aramburu, speeking in the name of some Argentine bishops, was unhappy about the restrictive clause; "nisi vel perturbat pacem publicam vel publicam violat moralitatem vel iura laedat aliorum". Whose public peace? That of the majority? Or of all, including the minority?

Bishop Carli of the tiny diocese of Segni, an arch-conservative, rejected the schema's scriptural arguments as being invalid. No one had even denied that the act of faith must be free, but Christ, Paul and John assumed that those who rejected the gospel were in bad faith, whereas now they were assumed by the schema to be in good faith.

Another Italian bishop, J. Marafini of Veroli-Frosinone, wanted it made clear that the State was not relieved of its duties to religion, and that its incompetence to judge in religious matters did not imply indifferentism; it still had to respect the Natural Law in moral questions.

(At the end of this Congregation, it was announced that the "modi" were being submitted by Fathers on sheets of every kind of paper, some of it of an inferior quality unworthy of preservation in the Council archives. Partly printed forms were therefore going to be distributed through the ushers).

At the 130th (3rd) General Congregation, 17 September, Cardinal Cooray of Colombo, Ceylon, wanted an express statement that religious freedom was limited by objective truth, for no moral or juridical norm had validity unless it was based on objective truth.

(Comment. From this it would seem that he had missed the point of the schema; viz, that a man's right to religious freedom was not based on the objective truth of his religious beliefs, but on his objective nature, itself a truth of the objective order).

Cardinal Florit of Florence was pleased that the revised text based religious freedom on the dignity of the human person, but feared that the exclusive right of the Catholic Church to preach the gospel might appear as a mere appendix. There were two distinct rights: a) the merely natural right which belonged to all without distinction, and b) the supernatural right which belonged exclusively to believers and was much the superior. The council must take account of both. The substantial point of the schema was that man, by nature free, had a right to communicate his beliefs which was subject to no limits other than those of public order. This implied indifference towards religion on the part of the State. But the State was of its nature concerned with the whole of the common good which consisted of many things, including religious truth; and therefore religious freedom was subject to civil limitation on more grounds than mere public order. The State could and should, in the present historical situation, ensure religious liberty within the limits stated in the schema, but on practical grounds, rather than on a given principle.

Cardinal Seper, coming as he did from a country with a recent history of religious repression (Jugoslavia), was more concerned to ensure the reality of religious freedom. It was very important to define the State's role accurately. The problem must not be conceived as a question of equilibrium, but as assertion of a natural right. The reference to conscience must therefore be expunged from the passage dealing with the role of the civil power. "De internis non iudicat praetor" (Roman law adage). All religious discrimination must be strongly resisted. Public order should be based on justice, and therefore the limits which the State could set on religious freedom on this ground should be called "just", not simply "due".

No one, said Cardinal Heenan (in his first intervention as a Cardinal), could be unaware of the importance of this declaration. Many non-Catholics were convinced that we had a double standard in the matter, being *for* freedom when in the minority, *against* it when in the majority. We needed sincerely to face this accusation. Tolerance between Catholics and Protestants was a recent phenomenon. The right to follow conscience was scarcely admitted. *Cuius regio, eius religio*. No one nowadays defended that kind of intolerance. It was absurd to speak of truth or error having rights; rights belonged to persons. Proselytism by non-Catholics was a danger in Catholic countries, but the schema provided adequately for the case in the clause about "public order"; and that kind of proselytism was not approved by Anglicans, Methodists, etc.

Cardinal Conway of Armagh, also making his debut as a Cardinal, was pleased that the freedom was based on the dignity of the human person and was defined as immunity from coercion. They in Ireland had suffered much for 200 years, but now full religious freedom for all was written into the Constitution. He had however a few corrections to suggest. 1) In regard to the education of children, the right included the right of parents to choose schools. The State could rightly demand suitable education for all, but it ought to behave equally towards all schools which fulfilled those conditions and could not justly add a condition: "provided religious instruction is not given". Otherwise the right to choose schools was theoretical, not real. The application of the principle was complex, but it was simple in itself; no discrimination for religious reasons. He therefore proposed an addition to this effect. 2) The statement that the civil power exceeded its limits if it intervened in matters concerning man's relation to God and should therefore restrict itself to matters of this world, was, he maintained, ambiguous. It could be taken to mean that that relationship had nothing in common with the world, whereas all history showed that the religious factor exercised a powerful influence in worldly affairs. States were aware of it. Parliaments began with prayers. The US President was sworn in on the Bible. The Queen of England was crowned with a religious ceremony.

Cardinal Ottaviani's reaction was predictable. The Catholic Church, he said, had a true right to freedom, because she had a divine mission. They were not addressing U.N.O., but making a declaration as a Council of the true Church of God. The present schema contained many controversial statements. It admittedly said that truth and falsehood were not equally worthy of esteem, but one tolerated the false rather than commended it. It was not part of human dignity to teach falsehood, but rather to protect truth, especially among simpler folk. It would be better to distinguish between physical and moral coercion. God did not coerce, yet He obliged; and so too the Church. The scriptural argument consisted of a one-sided selection of favourable texts, the others being omitted. There was no mention of the grave words of Christ against Capharnaum, Bethsaida, Corozain. The witness of the magisterium needed to be completely recast right down to Pius XII's *Ci riesce*.

Bishop Cantero of Saragossa objected that the admitted obligation of obeying one's conscience did not of itself suffice to create a juridical right. The foundation of religious liberty should be sought in the nature of religious assent. Religious acts fall under the social power not qua religious, but qua social. Hence, he concluded, religious liberty was founded in the very psychological and social liberty of man in religious matters. (If this does not sound conclusive, the reason may be that my notes did not keep up with his thought).

Bishop Baraniak of Poznan, Poland, wanted a forthright statement and defence of the full right to Religious Liberty, often, as he said, violated. The Bishops of Poland thought the text basically acceptable. The definition and arguments were better expressed, but emendations were necessary to avoid misinterpretation by men of ill will. Great care was necessary in defining the rights of the State in regard to religion. False and damaging interpretations of "public order" were current.

Bishop Sauvage of Annecy wanted a more explicit and accurate presentation of the foundation of religious liberty, in particular a fuller statement of the social nature of man which was an essential element of his personal dignity.

Cardinal Santos of Manila merely wanted to exclude a possible misunderstanding about the doctrinal foundation of religious liberty. The schema began from the greater modern awareness of the dignity of the human person. In his opinion it should begin from man's duty to seek and worship God. From that it would follow that a man's right to determine his religious allegiance knowingly and willingly, and not under external coercion, was a natural right. It was here that man's dignity lay.

Cardinal Beran, of Prague, was received with the applause due to an illustrious confessor of the faith who had suffered imprisonment both under the Nazis and under the Communists, and his attitude to the declaration, like that of all speakers from behind the Iron Curtain, was firmly based on hard experience. To force anyone to act against his conscience was to sin against God, he said. The moment religious liberty was radically restricted in his country, there followed grave dangers to faith, grave temptations to lie, etc. Hypocrisy in the profession of the faith could be as bad as weakness in the faith. Last century coercion had been used to make Bohemia Catholic. History warned them of the need to declare religious liberty in clear terms. He begged them not to attenuate the force of the declaration, And ended with a hope that the priests and bishops who had been so long in prison for their faith might be freed.

Cardinal Owen McCann of Cape Town considered the schema to be substantially acceptable, but held that it did not sufficiently express the duty of every person to conform his conscience to the truths revealed by God and handed down by the Church. Objectively this revelation was binding on all men and he wanted a sentence added to that effect. The procession of Cardinals awaiting their turn to speak was so long that, for the first time in the history of the Council, I went out for coffee before they were finished with the microphone and so missed hearing Cardinal Sheehan of Baltimore. When I returned, Cardinal Rossi of Sao Paulo was speaking. I gathered little, however, except that he wanted the concept of religious liberty clarified, was concerned about the pastoral consequences, and was dissastified with what the schema said about confessional States.

Cardinal M. Browne, O.P. quondam Pope's Theologian who, as Vice-President of the Theological Commission, commonly gave the impression of speaking as Theologian to the Council, began by saying that he proposed to speak "sub aspectu theologico"! After a brief reference to the factual situation and its practical requirement, he summarized the trend of papal teaching on religious liberty. It had never imposed the faith on any unwilling person, but it had had three things in view: a) that in a mostly Catholic State the faith should be protected; b) that the public authority, while behaving benignly to non-Catholics, should promote the Catholic faith; c) that in a mixed-religion State, the State should behave benignly to the Catholic Church. But in this schema religious liberty was presented as a natural right to profess religion, not in the sense of the true religion but the religion of one's conscience, and that publicly. It was said to be based on the dignity of the human person, and the State was said to be incompetent in regard to religion. Now, in regard to the alleged foundation of religious liberty, several things could be said. Man's dignity consisted in his elevation to the supernatural order, and this required the faith to be protected. Admittedly charity, etc, must be shown to those who held other religious opinions, but such opinions did not have equal rights. There can be no right to spread error. As for the remote foundation of religious liberty, what the schema said was partly true and partly false. The State's function was admittedly to promote the common temporal good, but to the end that the citizens might live well, and that included discerning and embracing the true faith. As for the limits of religious liberty, he asked, was the public diffusion of anti-religion in a Catholic State contrary or not contrary to public morality? Did it or did it not injure the rights of others? Catholic citizens had a right that their faith should not be exposed to danger. God had a right that the religion instituted by Him and embraced in a Catholic State be protected. The question to be asked was: "How ought , rulers of Catholic States to act with a view to the true common good of their own State, having regard also to the needs of other States and of the whole world?".

Cardinal Cardijn, founder of the Y.C.W., was very pleased with the schema. It confirmed the conclusions drawn by the Y.C.W. from their work in every part of the world. The declaration was urgently necessary, because the modern world was daily becoming more unified and open to conflict. It was our great duty to build in collaboration with all men of good will a world founded on truth, justice, liberty and love. Sincere respect for liberty in religious matters was needed. Mistrust made cooperation impossible. Mutual trust made it easy to cooperate in every field in building a more humane world, especially among the young. Pastoral effectiveness supplied another reason, for in the greater part of the world Christians were very few and the means used to spread the faith in the Middle Ages were no longer effective. One could rely only on the power of the Word of God, and on poverty, etc... Religious liberty consisted in the benevolence of peoples. It was not only important for missionary action, but indispensable to sincere and efficacious ecumenism. It had pedagogic value as conducing to that internal liberty by which man became responsible towards God. (Unfortunately he overran his time and had twice to be called to come to a halt, which rather dimmed the lustre of his performance, his "big day", which followed closely on his elevation to the Sacred College).

The next speaker was Archbishop Lefebvre, former missionary bishop who had become General of the Congregation of the Holy Spirit (C.SS.P). He began by asking whether the concept of religious liberty was new or centuries old. The Relator (De Smedt) had said it emerged and evolved gradually from the 18th C. But where? In ecclesiastical tradition, or in Hobbes, Locke, Rousseau? Lamennais etc. had tried to reconcile it with Catholic doctrine and were condemned. Leo XIII said it was contrary to Catholic doctrine. Was this what they were being called upon to subscribe to? It was in the name of man's personal dignity that the Communists called upon men to be atheists. Christ was put to death in the name of public order. It was the Masons that had called upon the Church to declare this liberty. It could not be proved from reason. Liberty could not be understood except in the light of the divine law. Man's dignity came through observance of the divine law, and could come no other way. The divine law required liberty and also set the measure of religious liberty. There was only one true religion. Other cults could at most be said to have a right to a certain civil immunity.

(This is the Lefebvre who, at the time these notes were typed out 1975, had become famous as the founder of an extremely right-wing seminary in Switzerland).

Bishop J. Gran of Oslo was very pleased with the schema in its revised form, because it was now concerned merely with civil liberty and so avoided conflict with Christian principles. It did not attribute a right to error, for only persons had rights, but a right to all to adhere to God freely. He grieved to find some resisting this liberty. Scandal would be caused in Scandinavia if the Council did not speak unambiguously. Their rulers had granted them religious liberty, not because they agreed with the Catholic religion, but because they respected their human dignity. Catholics ought to do the same. It ought to be approved nem. con.

Bishop Anoveros returned to the problem of defining the limits of public order. It would be better to speak of civil liberty in religious matters, rather than of religious liberty. Bishop Muldoon, Auxiliary of Sydney, summarized the course of the debate in the last session and in this, and sided with those who held that the Council could not issue a purely pragmatic declaration which abstracted from theoretic moral principles. In his view the text needed the *relatio*, which however would not be promulgated. Without it, many Catholics and non-Catholics would be misled.

At the 132nd (5th) General Congregation, 21 September, the names of the representatives of the Council who were to accompany the Pope to New York, 4th October, were announced. They were Cardinals Cicognani, Tisserant, Agaganian, Gilroy, Spellman. Caggiano (Argentina) Doi (Japan), Rugambwa (Africa).

Discussion of Religious Liberty was then resumed by Cardinal Dante, formerly papal Master of Ceremonies, who found the schema to contain equivocal statements of very grave consequence, in particular in regard to the limits which the State could legitimately set to religious liberty. They would be interpreted according to the State's attitude to religion. Hence the schema should not set such limits, merely those of the Natural Law.

Cardinal Journet, the Swiss theologian, packed more into his ten minutes than I could jot down even in summary and I missed some of his points. The human person, he said, was a member of two social orders, the temporal and the spiritual, and yet he transcended the political order by his ordination to God. This made him free in relation to the political society and responsible only to God. Even a person of erroneous conscience remained a human person and must be acknowledged as such by the political society. He could not be coerced unless he acted externally against the true public good. It was the duty even of the civil society to manifest explicitly the honour in which its members held God. It could not ignore the religious societies within it. So much for the so called rights. But, in addition to this natural order, the Church had a supernatural and inviolable right to preach the Gospel to every creature. At the time of Constantine, the rulers of the Church turned to the secular arm for the defence of Christianity, but under the influence of the Gospel the distinction between the spiritual and the temporal was gradually worked out. The doctrinal principle according to which temporal things were subordinate to spiritual things was not therefore destroyed, but differently applied, i.e. recourse to the arms of light replaced recourse to the arms of the camps. He concluded by saying that the declaration was in his opinion to be highly approved.

Bishop Koslowieski of Zambia, speaking in the name of some Central African Fathers but not of all, made three pastoral points. 1) The arguments on which the thesis rested were not sufficient and should be revised in the light of Cardinal Urbani's comments. 2) The intention and meaning of the chief terms used should be clearly explained. Religious liberty was restricted by countries which had signed the U.N. declaration. 3) A similar clarification was necessary for the Catholics themselves. Religious liberty was restricted by abuse of authority just as authority was diminished by abuse of liberty. The schema should speak more clearly on the need for a rightly formed conscience.

Bishop Munoz Vega of Ecuador said the difficulty was that the declaration was addressed to the whole world with all its religiously pluralistic States. He felt that attention to this laudable scope had separated the document too much from its theological foundations. It was based on modern studies about Church and State which were not mature enough for a conciliar document. It was impossible to achieve full clarity without establishing the nexus between natural and supernatural law, namely that, in the eyes of God, no religious liberty was to be attributed to a person except with a view to the attainment of his end. Supernatural law presupposed natural law, but this latter did not exist for its own sake, but was subordinated to the supernatural law *in ordine ad finem*.

At this point, the closure was proposed and voted, with Bishop Holland waiting at the microphone with a speech he was never able to deliver. As Agaganian said in proposing the motion on behalf of the Moderators, 62 Fathers had spoken in the five-day debate and it seemed enough. The vast majority of the Fathers rose to their feet in approval. Even those hysterical Americans who had created such a hubbub on the penultimate day of the Third Session because the Presidency Council had ruled that the revised schema was new enough to require discussion before its basic acceptability could be voted, even they could not deny that the Moderators had kept their promise of an immediate and thorough discussion at the beginning of the Fourth Session.

De Smedt of Bruges then gave his *Relatio*, expressing the gratitude of the Commission for a constructive discussion containing many suggestions of great value. All proposed emendations would be carefully studied, etc.

etc. They were dealing with a new problem which called for progress in the explicitation of Catholic doctrine, like that of Catholic social doctrine from *Rerun novarum* to *Pacem in terris*. In the moral order, all individuals and public authorities were morally bound to seek the truth, nor was it ever lawful for them to defend what was false. The Church had a duty and an objective right to preach Christ, The question dealt with in the schema, however, had to be carefully distinguished from such moral questions. It was concerned with the concrete situation in modern civil society.

Agaganian then called upon Secretary-General Felici to read the text of the vote to be taken on the general acceptability of the schema. It read: "Is the revised text of the schema on Religious Liberty agreeable to the Fathers as the basis of a definitive declaration to be yet further perfected in accordance with the Catholic doctrine regarding the true religion and the emendations proposed by the Fathers in the discussion and to be approved in the normal form of the Council". The reply had to be *placet* or *non placet*. The opportunity for amendments (*placet iuxta modum*) would come when the text was voted piecemeal.

The sensation-mongers who spent more time sniffing for rats than listening to the speeches, read a deep significance into the wording of the motion. A rumour began to circulate that the co-ordinating Commission had decided the night before by 14 to 11 not to have a vote (though it was not explained what good that would have done); that the Pope had overruled them, which explained why Tisserant and Agaganian had only arrived at the end of that morning's Mass; and that the text of the motion had probably been drafted jointly by Father Courtney Murray and Bishop Colombo, the Pope's theologian. The one hard fact was the result of the vote. The basic acceptability of the revised schema was approved by 1997 votes to 224. To anyone listening to the discussion it had been a sure thing all along.

There followed the general discussion of the revised text of the schema on the *Church in the Modern World*. This pastoral constitution, said Cardinal Spellman, should be "perlucid", very sincere and at the same time candid and humble. It was necessary that they should both hear and be heard. They needed the help of all mankind. The schema should make it clearer right at the beginning what it was seeking. It did not offer simple solutions, but dialogue with all men of good will. The substance of Christian liberty and obedience must be explained, because many today spoke as if obedience to the Magisterium were against the liberty of the sons of God. The chapter on Peace, in particular, had been well revised. The desire was for a well founded peace. The international institutes were not yet adequate and nations must provide for their own defence. It was not easy to judge the right method of resistance, but if rulers decided after prudent study that military service was necessary, how could individuals be free to refuse? The whole of that section needed to be revised.

This, said Cardinal Landazzuri, was the first conciliar document in which the Church had addressed all mankind on grave problems. It contained much that was good and the new redaction marked a genuine progress. Yet not a few emendations were still needed. Sometimes the wording smacked of the *cathedra*, sometimes it had a popular ring hardly consonant with the dignity of the Council. It was too long, saying many things but not much. It was repetitive, treating e.g. three times of the social nature of man. Its use of the same word in different senses, e.g. "Church", was confusing. But its chief defect was that it was still not clear to whom it was directed; in one place it said all men, yet in another it assumed knowledge of the Trinity. There were only two ways of addressing all men, either by abstracting from revealed doctrine or by explaining it. There were difficulties either way, but the equivocation derived from the constitution itself. It would perhaps be better to issue a declaration in the words of Christ which were still intelligible to all men, and deal with problems in the light of faith. The whole of the first Part needed redrafting.

Cardinal Silva Henriquez of Santiago, Chile, found it too long, but acceptable in general as a basis. The laity needed enlightenment as to their vocation in the world. In regard to the proposed title, a "pastoral constitution", the word "pastoral" had more than one meaning, and in the wide sense all the documents of the Council were pastoral; the term should therefore not be added here. If, as was declared at the Third Session, the Council merely meant to proclaim accepted Catholic doctrines to the world, the matter should be referred to the theological Commission.

Cardinal Jaeger of Paderborn liked it on the whole, but suggested that it should avoid unrealistic optimism, and that a special post-Conciliar Commission should be set up to deal with contemporary theology, as happened after Trent, showing how progress was linked with Catholic tradition.

Cardinal Bea thought it a much better text and a more apt language, but it tended to bore the reader by repetition of the same ideas, especially in the first part. And both the doctrine and the manner of presenting it needed to be polished up. He had had constantly to refer to the French text to find out what the Latin meant.

At the next General Congregation, the 133rd (6th), four Fathers exercised their right to return to the subject of Religious Liberty as speaking in the name of 70 or more other Fathers.

Bishop Wojtyla of Poland said it was not sufficient simply to repeat what was in the civil law. They must declare its relationship to that liberty which was based on the doctrine of the Church derived from reason and revelation.

Bishop Doumith of the Lebanon maintained that the concept of the confessional State as justified without distinction was equivocal. The Christian confessional State did not necessarily imply discrimination against others, whereas in non-Christian States religious liberty belonged only to believers (he presumably meant Moslems) and religion was a source of civil law. Either the schema must distinguish between confessional States, or it had better keep quiet on the subject.

Bishop Grotti of Brazil was admirably succinct; he announced that since what he had meant to say had already been said, he would submit his speech in writing.

Bishop Ancel, Auxiliary of Lyons, speaking for more than 100 Fathers, took rather longer to say something briefly "aliquid brevissime". There had, he said, been many requests for the ontological foundation of religious liberty, some not regarding the argument from the dignity of the person as sufficient in itself, or not seeing how religious liberty linked up with the obligation to seek the truth. His thesis was that it was this very obligation that constituted the ontological foundation of the liberty. Every man, as endowed with reason and will, was bound to order his life according to the demands of the truth, an objective obligation of universal validity. To fulfil it in the manner proper to his nature, man needed to be free from all coercion. Hence far from the obligation being contradictory to the liberty, it was the foundation of the liberty.

* * *

The Council then reverted to the *Church in the Modern World* with a speech from Cardinal Ruffini. Like Cardinal Bea, he found the schema repetitious and the Latin so inept as hardly to deserve the name. He disliked the apology made for the wrinkles which were alleged to have always disfigured the Church. If sons of the Church had disgraced their Mother, she herself had always been a source of endless benefits (eloquently described) to the world.

Cardinal Siri of Genoa complained of the omission of matters which belonged more directly to the mission of the Church to the world. Nothing was said about sin, indifferentism, laicism, or the prevalence of technology over all spiritual values. The Church could not neglect what was proper to her, and he feared that the faithful would be puzzled if she did. He agreed with the comments of Landazzuri, Bea and Ruffini.

In regard to the scope of the document, Cardinal Koenig of Vienna suggested that it should not repeat doctrine in regard to the mission of the Church that was already contained in the constitution *De Ecclesia,* and should limit itself to those things which the Church could contribute to the world in virtue of her own proper mission. In regard to method, it must not cling too closely to the the immediate and transitory present; it must be clearer as to who was speaking to whom and by what right, and must not appear to promise a paradise on earth and solution of all problems.

Cardinal Döpfner, speaking for some German and Scandinavian Fathers, expressed their gratitude for an improved text from which it ought to be possible to produce a good document that Session. It did not however clearly distinguish between what belonged to the supernatural order and what to the natural, nor sufficiently indicate the consequences of sinful actions.

Bishop Jordan of Edmonton, Canada, was pleased to note that the schema had happily avoided the error of many Christians who thought the Church had the answer to all difficulties. On the other hand, it had almost nothing to say about the fruitful use of leisure.

Bishop Aramburu of Tucuman, Argentina, thought it should have begun with a foundation of universally accepted philosophical truths, before tackling the study of problems, as St Thomas did in *Summa contra Gentiles*. Thus man was a rational social creature. As a creature he needed to be referred to his final end, God. And so forth.

Bishop McVinney of Providence, U.S.A., suggested that the cause of our ills was to be found in tepidity. Men were ready to practise virtue only as long as no effort or sacrifice was required. The Council should not take too rosy a view of the world and its ways. It was an amoral world. To the men of today moral principles were for fools only. Everyone had his price and was out to get what he could. Power was in the hands of the few. The maxim was look out for no.1 and keep your nose clean. It was the Church's job to redeem the world. The call was not only for liberty, but for liberty in an "open" Church. Authority was held in contempt, yet there could be no kerygma without the authority of the Church's magisterium. Many had no esteem for the virtue of obedience.

To Bishop J.D. D'Avack the schema smacked of naturalism. There were many mentions of Christ but scarcely of the Christ crucified of St Paul's preaching. True, it was necessary to attract the men of today, but not to deceive them. It could give the impression that they could manage without supernatural grace and the help of the Church.

In similar vein, Bishop Rusch of Innsbruck criticized its tendency to advance philosophical considerations in place of theological. So, e.g. in dealing with man, the "image of God" was treated in a merely philosophic manner, not in the light of Sacred Scripture or the Fathers.

Archbishop G. Sigaud regarded it as a new and suspect way of treating theological matters. One could not serve God and Mammon. The tower of Babel was an attempt to construct a world, but it did not lead to God. The figure of this world was passing away. The schema implied that the progress of knowledge (scientia) was due to non-Christians, but in fact it was Christian Europe that led the way. The Church should be present in the world as a leaven, but not the world in the Church.

At the 134th (7th) General Congregation, 23 September, Cardinal Rugambwa of Tanzania declared himself pleased with the schema, especially because the solidarity of the human race was affirmed in the proemium. It was most urgent that this truth should be affirmed, that peace should be founded on justice and that there should be more international cooperation.

Cardinal Sheehan of Baltimore, while expressing his general approval, regretted the unhappy separation of natural and supernatural facts and truths; they complemented each other and should be dealt with synthetically. A synthesis was very different from a compromise.

Bishop Baudoux of Canada liked the schema's positive way of addressing the world with a healthy optimism.

Archbishop Morcillo, while admitting that it contained many praiseworthy things, clearly did not like it at all. It lacked judgement and norms. The title of "pastoral constitution" was unsuitable. Constitutions were rare in Councils and limited to general and fundamental principles. The schema was often dealing with things as they stood. Moreover, a "constitution" could only be addressed to Catholics. No other document was called "pastoral", because they were all supposed to be pastoral.

Renard of Versailles was also critical. Even the best of human values could be inimical to the faith. The schema lacked sagacity. It should state more clearly that the irruption of Christ into the world was something completely new, beyond the reach of philosophy or humanism.

Bishop Kominek, speaking in the name of 65 Polish Fathers, said they regarded it as an essay in practicality. The constitution *De Ecclesia* was the "lex credendi"; this should be the "lex agendi" which complemented it. It needed some notable corrections. The remarks on atheism should be made in the preamble and in a different way. As to religion and culture, religion was the inspiration of true culture. Whereas the first part was in general acceptable, though needing to be expressed in simple homiletic form, the second part was much more questionable. It went into too much detail about economic and social life without any special competence. It offered fluctuating and useless solutions which smacked of capitalism. And so forth.

At this point the Fathers agreed almost unanimously to a proposition of the Moderators that the discussion should now pass to a consideration of the schema part by part (2111 *placets* to 44 *non placet*). It would deal first with the preamble and Part I (chapters I-IV), and then with Part II.

Cardinal Cardijn offered some general comments on this "praiseworthy constitution". It wanted the Gospel to be considered in the concrete by all men, by the young, the workers and the inhabitants of the Third World. In the existing demographic situation the young constituted one half of mankind, much the most dynamic part, which would have an influence on the future of the world. They could not therefore be overlooked. Moreover, they were more united among themselves. The world in which they lived was troubled by very grave problems and it rested with them whether it would be a better or worse world. The Council should therefore address a special message to the young, not paternally, but virilely addressed to young people conscious of their own responsibility. As for the inhabitants of the Third World, the Church should help them as much as possible, not only with money and techniques, but especially with fraternal education designed to help them help themselves.

At the 155th (8th) General Congregation, the particular examination began in earnest with speeches on the Preamble and introduction.

Cardinal Frings, unable to read his own script, got the Secretary General to read it for him. He instanced cases in which the terms "People of God" and the "world" were used incorrectly or inconsistently and asked that these two notions be rectified and the terms used in the same sense throughout.

Bishop Herman Volk of Mainz said that in interpreting the world a distinction must be drawn between what was mutable and what was not. The problems did not arise only from modern conditions. The equilibrium which was said to have been lost today had never existed. To many the progress was such that they no longer felt the need of God. To others the order was so disrupted that they no longer hoped for help either from God or from man. It was vitally important to speak to the world of Christ. He must not appear as a mere addition.

Bishop Elchinger, Auxiliary of Strasbourg asked from what point of view the schema meant to address the world. Early on it said "to all men", but this intention was less evident in the text. The subject was not "The Modern World", but "The Church in the Modern World". Men paid more attention to deeds than to words. They wanted to learn how in the concrete the Church meant to act, whereas the schema talked only of what the world ought to do. They looked for recognition of their personal dignity, and it was not clear what the Church meant to do in fulfilment of these expectations. The schema must say concretely how the Church intended to cooperate with the world and help the world.

Bishop Himmer of Tournai observed that the workers constituted the greater part of the present world and that of the proximate future; it was with that world that the Church must institute dialogue. From the beginning therefore the schema must have in mind the changes which affect the mind and heart of the workers, especially their access to constant and irreversible progress. This progress ought of its nature to lead to a deeper human development, as outlined in *Mater et Magistra*.

Cardinal Meouchi of the Lebanon, commenting on Part I, regretted that it did not seem to insist on the importance of the Holy Spirit in the people of God as a people, and lacked a Christian anthropology, built upon the image of God.

Cardinal Richaud of Bordeaux, on the other hand, was pleased to note a true balance and profundity of doctrine, except for a surprising and highly regrettable absence of formal reference to the social doctrine of the Church as in *Mater et Magistra*.

Cardinal Seper, coming from a Communist state, was chiefly interested in the section on Atheism. The Council could not be silent about it, because there were movements which regarded atheism as a condition of progress; but whatever the Church said must be coherent. It must not be forgotten that many men today had inherited atheism rather than embraced it. The Council's object was not simply to condemn atheism or to prove the existence of God, but to show how faith not only does not prevent progress but helps it. They should openly acknowledge that many Christians, by clinging to established positions, hindered progress, but the cause was their immobilism and conservatism, not their faith, they should expressly declare that it was God Himself who ordered men to work for a just social order in the world.

The Maronite Archbishop Ziade of Beirut regretted the absence of the Risen Christ from the schema. The Resurrection was mentioned twice only and even then materially. The theological vision of the world began not from the first but from the second creation. The question was that raised in 1 Cor: What was the relation between this world and the world to come. It could not be reborn unless it first died. The grain of wheat must die. Resurrection was the work of God. That consummation was nothing else than Christ Himself resurgent. The new creation had already begun inside of history, not outside. It had a communitarian dimension. The Church was inserted in the world in order that the world might be embraced already in the Church. If they did not bear witness to the risen Christ, their preaching was in vain.

Bishop Cantero of Saragossa had two criticisms to make of Part I. From the psychological point of view, it had both a naturalistic and a clerical ring, an ingenuous optimism and a western outlook. It rejected the intervention of Caesar in the things of God, yet preached the intervention of the Church in the things of Caesar, so giving a handle to political charges. It would bind Catholics to more detailed policies than those of non-Catholics. The proper mission of the Church was concerned with the order of persons rather than of things. Nor did the internal structure of the first part correspond to the logical order of its doctrinal elements. It dealt with actualities, but the *actio* of the Church followed its *esse*, and therefore the first chapter should deal with the function of the Church in the world *simpliciter*, not necessarily *this* world.

The 136th (9th) General Congregation was still concerned with Part I of the Church in the Modern World. Once again we had the French-speaking Maximus IV. He was dissatisfied with the treatment of Atheism and of War. In regard to Atheism, the schema described Marxism without naming it, but condemnation of Marxism was not enough to save men from Atheism. It was necessary to name the causes. Many self-styled atheists were not hostile to the Church. They were seeking a truer presentation of God and a Church in solidarity with the poor. So let egoism and exploitation of men by men be denounced. Many atheists were Lazaruses scandalized by rich Christians. Let it be shown that the true socialism was Christianity. The need was not for condemnation but for a positive gospel.

Neither was Cardinal König of Vienna satisfied with the treatment of atheism. Militant atheism was not the only form. The schema should not only distinguish the various forms and their intimate nature, but their distinctive phenomena, the remedies, and the Church's manner of action. The roots (not found in Asia) were the rupture of the unity of Christians in the 16th C., the illuminism of the 18th, the effort to expel God Himself in the 19th, the unjust social order. The remedies were Christian cooperation in every field in which the faith was not compromised, and deeper understanding among pastors. The Church should not anathematize anyone, but seek a peaceful *modus vivendi*, inviting atheistic governments to draft a document based on the natural law by which all might collaborate for the progress of their country.

Cardinal Florit of Florence wanted more clarity and vigour in the treatment of atheism. The atheistic character of Marxist materialism was not accidental, because for it the only reality was economic. The schema should show mistaken Catholics that the Marxist economic doctrine could not be adopted without its atheism. It should also indicate the causes, and remedies of atheism, which, he said, was diffused among youth under the cloak of science. The Church was judged from outside and from the conduct of many professed Christians. The obstacle to belief in God was His apparent impotence in the face of evil. The schema should deal with this obstacle, showing that God was love of His very nature, and that He sought a free response from man and compelled no one. Hence came evil, but God used it to good purpose. In Christ crucified the value of pain and suffering was revealed.

Cardinal Rossi, speaking in the name of 92 Brazilian bishops, had little fresh to say. He wanted a more precise notion of the People of God, and the World, etc., a better order, and a clearer expression of the "aggiornamento" wanted by John XXIII, a continuous need of the Church. Moreover, what the schema had to say about developing nations should not be limited to Asia, but envisage also Latin America which had many needy inhabitants.

Bishop Klepacz was concerned with possible "doublespeak". The Council had awakened great hopes but also not a little anxiety, stimulated by moral decadence in the midst of material progress. False prophets had battened on this anxiety, using the same words as others but in different senses, e.g. words like truth and justice. Hence, when the Council used such words it should guard against their misuse.

After two further speeches (Ruotolo, De Souza), Bishop N. Elko of Pittsburgh asked that dialectical materialism be expressly named for the pest it was. It would be pusillanimous to treat of it only indirectly. Hitherto only the Popes had spoken; now it was the turn of the universal episcopate. The faithful were expecting not only a mandate but efficacious remedies; viz: correction of the errors of Christians, the duty to know the enemies of God and to defend His name, etc. etc.

Fairly general interest was aroused by the intervention of the newly elected General of the Jesuits, Father Arrupe. He spoke rapidly in an accent which I found difficult to follow, presenting what amounted to a presidential "state of the nation" review, rather than a critique of Part I of the schema. The walls of the city of God were, he said, impenetrable, but outside of them naturalism, diffidence and fear were universal, to be found in all the media. Christians were only a small portion of mankind, but even so their influence was not what it should be, owing largely to dispersion of effort. They could not rely on merely human methods. They must preach Christ crucified. They must examine their pastoral methods. They must be creative rather than merely defensive. They tended to take refuge in abstract truths, whereas they should be establishing concrete foundations and methods of work. It was time for action. He proposed therefore that first-class experts should conduct a concrete and exact investigation of the state of the world, that the main lines of action be defined, that the Pope should assign the main fields of activity. The needs were technical investigation, absolute obedience to the Pope, fraternal charity.

Archbishop Guerry of Cambrai began by recalling that, shortly after the Third Session, Pope Paul had appealed to the world from Bombay to denounce the arms race. That most noble proposal should have found a place in the schema. All it got was a footnote reference. Such a silence was serious. The Pope's appeal suggested a positive solution. (At this point, Cardinal Döpfner, the Moderator of the day, called upon the speaker to confine his remarks to comments on Part I, but he went on to the end of his text).

Bishop Pildain of the Canary Islands, congratulated the Commission for devoting two sections to the gravest problem of our time, the unprecedented wave of atheism. Atheism used three chief means. The first was science; the Council should fight constructively on this ground, setting up suitable centres of higher studies everywhere. The second was the misery of nations due to the unjust distribution of goods consequent upon liberal capitalism, which the Church must solemnly condemn. The third was the luxury of the wealthy, which the Church must castigate.

Bishop J. Corboy of Zambia said the difficulty was that the world expected the Church to explain how it could deal with worldwide problems, whereas the Church could not give absolute answers but only general principles. It would therefore be a mistake to lay down categoric and absolute principles in Part I, because many things were currently evolving or being formulated afresh, and ample liberty should be left to the theologies of the future. The Council should urge theologians to study human activities in the light of faith. The Church's social doctrine was of supreme importance; for the Church could only show herself in the new nations by social action enabling them to help themselves. A profound theology of human activity in general and in particular was necessary and was still lacking. Finally, the general principles asserted in the first part must be more clearly applied in the second part to specific problems; the connection was at present very weak.

Father A. Fernandez, General of the Dominicans, called for a clearer assertion of the one family of nations, a natural community. The unity of creation came from God. From this principle flowed rights and duties for all. All were members of this society, which was prior to the national society. All were first citizens of the world, and their rights as such had priority. This natural unity and brotherhood of the human race was made more evident by our elevation to the supernatural life in Christ our Redeemer. According to revelation, all, from our first parent himself, were elevated to the same supernatural end, sons of the same heavenly Father, brothers and heirs in Christ, citizens and members of God's household. All racial discrimination was thereby excluded. The supernatural was not contrary to the natural but above it. This very clear doctrine was not always evident in the schema. It needed to be purified from ambiguities. Finally, to solve problems it was not enough simply to enunciate principles; it was necessary to harmonize them.

The discussion of Part I was continued at the 137th (10th) General Congregation by Cardinal Batanian, Armenian Patriarch of Cilicia. he liked the method of procedure of Part I, but thought the Introduction was too prolix and needed to be reduced to synthetic form. Among the modern problems mention should have been made of situation ethics, a dangerous deviation which, even if it did not deny the objective moral law, evaded it. He did not like the title "Pastoral Constitution" and suggested "Allocutio Ecclesiae Mundo Huius Temporis".

Bishop Emmanuel Lopez of Spain said that he would like to add a few words about religious liberty, and was not called to order by the Moderator. It was true that faith must always be free; cf. can. 1351; but it did not follow that every sort of religious liberty was good. There was another side to it. No one could be coerced into rejecting the Catholic faith against his will. Everyman had a right to the true faith.

Bishop Sergius Mendez of Mexico said he agreed with Cardinal Shehan of Baltimore on the need for a better treatment of anthropology in the schema. Part I should begin by answering the question: What is man? Until it was answered, evangelization was impossible. Secondly, how did man stand in relation to the Absolute and Transcendent. The anthropological perspective was lacking throughout. There was need of depth analysis; the psychological revolution could not be ignored. The language of psychoanalysis had passed into the language and concepts of modern man. Without knowledge of them dialogue was impossible.

Bishop Paul Leineka of Czechoslovakia briefly revealed the view of life behind the Iron Curtain. A great part of mankind, a third of the world, was under a dictatorship of militant atheism. What he had to say was said from experience, he added, in prison, but from love of his brethren, not from hate. The rulers of that third of the world sought to make all men atheists. The chief problem of the Council should be to supply efficacious remedies, which would have to be supernatural. The first remedy was the Council itself, as an exercise in self-knowledge. Its *modus agendi* must be that of the Saviour. Its sign should be that which Christ gave to his disciples in His New Commandment: love and unity. Those were clearer arguments for the existence of God than miracles. They were, so to speak, the sacrament of the presence of God in us. All our effort must be to demonstrate unity and love to the faithful; it would be the beginning of the death of atheism. The first steps had already been taken in Episcopal Collegiality and ecumenism. The final remedy lay in the Cross. The blood of Martyrs was the seed of the Church. "Sine sanguinis effusione non fit remissio". He had himself seen the crushing of a Church but also the fruit, a foretaste of the triumph of love and unity.

Archbishop Marty of Rheims (who has since become Cardinal Archbishop of Paris) kept to the subject of atheism. He did not like the way it was treated in the schema. The talk should not be about a system, but about the men affected by it. The modern atheist presented himself as a humanist who wanted to achieve salvation within the limits of the terrestrial world. Faith in God seemed to him as an illusion which diminished man. In France, Christians and atheists meet daily in conversation. It was difficult but these meetings always led to greater mutual trust and a better distinct ion between the natural and the supernatural. The foundation of the Secretariate for Unbelievers was very much noted by atheists. The relevant section of the schema should be revised with the aid of that Secretariate.

Archbishop Garrone of Toulouse (now Cardinal Prefect of the Congregation of Catholic Education) felt that the nature and importance of the dogma of creation was not sufficiently highlighted. Though it could be reached by reason, experience showed that it was not easy. The more man probed into nature and dominated it, the less he was awed by it. The dogma of creation should be ever-present to man's mind, otherwise religion itself was in danger. It surprised him to find how little effort was made to emphasize this truth. The doctrine was not expressed accurately enough. The presence of God in created things was a fact, and accounted for their dignity.

Bishop Schick of Germany resumed the point already made in this Congregation by Bishop Mendez, namely, what was man. Like Mendez he claimed that anthropology was the foundation of the solution of the modern problem. What did man say about himself? The mood was one of insecurity and even despair. Part I, n. 11 attempted a reply. It should begin from the words of Genesis. Man's dominion was the corollary of God's creation of him. Only man transcended the world he lived in. Only he conversed with God. Religion belonged therefore to man's essence. But at the same time there was man's dissimilarity in relation to God by reason of his temporal historical existence. Here was the place to introduce sin, disease and death. Sin was contrary to God as an abuse of man's dominion; only the man who kept God's commandments was in order. The sacrament of the Incarnation opened a new way of transcendence. Man's destiny was radically changed in Christ.

With half the world under Communism, said Bishop Michael Rusnak of Toronto, the few words which n. 19 devoted to this problem were quite insufficient. All it amounted to was a vague allusion to human experience and an invitation to atheists to investigate the matter objectively. The section on Atheism should be much longer. It said almost nothing about the heresy of the 20th Century. It should and could deal with Communism, because not only did it deny God, but other basic principles as well. It was necessary to give the Catholic doctrine and to show the world that the communist system was based on both doctrinal and practical oppression. Charity required an all-out denunciation. All religious communities were suppressed in Czechoslovakia in one night in 1950. The list of those currently in prison there was available; so too the present position of priests and laity. It would be an act of charity to make these things known.

There followed speeches by Bishops Soares de Resende, Darmajuwana, Moschera, Kuaricz, Bengsch, Wojtyla, and Romero, which, as far as my notes reveal, had little or nothing to say on Part I which had not already been said. At this point, the number of intending speakers on Part I being exhausted (not to mention the audience), it was announced that on the following day we would pass on to Part II.

The 138th (11th) General Congregation began therefore, on Wednesday 29 September with the reading of the list of Fathers who had intimated their desire to speak on Part II.

Cardinal Ruffini turned his and our attention immediately to Marriage, then in no. 61. The treatment there given to it, he said, was ill-arranged and not very accurate. Pius XI had dealt with it better in *Casti Connubii*, and he asked why it had not been used. The schema was confused about the ends of matrimony. The distinction into primary and secondary was soundly based in Catholic doctrine. In the text, the secondary ends were so extolled as to be compatible with contraception. Chastity was required by the divine law even in marriage, and as St Augustine said: "God does not command the impossible, or if he does, makes it possible by His grace". True conjugal love is rightly praised, but it must be holy.

Cardinal Leger followed with a speech which was in sharp contrast. The new draft, he said, gave a better description of conjugal love, yet it would be little help to modern youth, because it did not cohere with the concept of marriage as instituted for the procreation and education of children. That formula, he said, was incomplete. As far as the human species was concerned, marriage was that institution by which it was conserved and propagated. But it also joined persons and aroused deep feelings which needed to be expressed, without neglect of the good of the species. For persons it was not simply an institution for the procreation and education of children, but principally a community of life. He therefore proposed that it be clearly stated that marriage was an intimate community of life and love, and that the significance which offspring had for love — "proles fastigium amoris", be explained.

Cardinal Suenens, mindful no doubt that his comments on the same subject had (so he claimed) been misunderstood at the previous Session, walked warily. He was glad to note the Council's timely desire for the extension and better coordination of scientific work in the field of marriage.

It was of great importance for humanity to have a better knowledge of the laws of fecundity, etc. There had not yet been enough scientific research, and few Catholics had participated. For our Catholic universities the desire expressed by the Council should almost amount to a command. As he saw it, it implied no moral judgement, since it remained in the merely scientific field. He went on to suggest that, after the manner of the annual renewal of baptismal vows at the Paschal vigil, there should be an annual renewal of marriage vows, e.g. on the feast of the Holy Family, with a suitable ceremony devised by the Liturgical Commission.

Archbishop Colombo of Milan, speaking in the name of 32 Italian bishops (not a very significant number for Italy) was much less critical of the schema than Ruffini had been, its doctrine on marriage, he said, was solidly founded and pastoral. It was very pleasing to note that the ends and "goods" of marriage were situated in a fully human and personal doctrine, so that love was said to be an intrinsic end and the indissolubility of marriage was deduced from the demands of conjugal love. He was pleased also with what was said about responsible parenthood, a principle which clearly included the right to use all honest means which were apt to that end. Some things needed to be made more explicit, e.g. the duty of fostering love. But there was a grave lacuna in regard to the physical act of marriage. Hitherto, both the theologians and the Magisterium had taught that acts opposed to its integrity were always contrary to the law of God. Readers would interpret silence as a change of doctrine. It was therefore necessary to avoid all ambiguity about the integrity of the conjugal act, and especially to show the continuity of the magisterial teaching. On this point, it will be seen, he was as firm as Ruffini.

I was absent during the next three speeches (in quest of coffee and rest) returning only in time to hear Bishop Maiaski of Breslau, alias Wroclau, summoning the Council, in the name of all the bishops of Poland, to proclaim in a loud voice the absolute inviolability of very innocent life not yet born into the world.

Bishop Zoghby of Egypt then introduced the problem of broken families as one crucial to the common good, and in particular the problem of the innocent party. One spouse, perhaps through frailty, had left the other, and the innocent party had come to the bishop. The bishop, he pointed out, could do nothing except urge the need of lifelong continence, which presupposed the most robust faith. They were faced either by a tormented conscience or a life which they regarded as impossible. Was there no solution: Had the Church the right to say to the innocent party: "Look after yourself"': Had she the power to do so. Heroism was never imposed by Christ as binding under pain of loss of salvation, but only to those who would be perfect (Note. Bishop Zogbhy seemed to have overlooked Matt.18,9 ff: "If your eye causes you to sin, pluck it out, etc.) The Eastern Churches had been conscious of their power to solve such cases from the earliest times, as indicated in Matthew's "except it be for fornication". The Church was the judge. The Roman Church had always followed the restrictive sense, whereas the Eastern Churches favoured the innocent spouse. Would that the West would follow suit. (The speech created something of a stir, but there were no catcalls from the audience, or rebukes from the Moderators).

* * *

At this point in the manuscript Monsignor McReavy has inserted the Intervention of Bishop Zoghby which took place during the 138th General Congregation and which he considered to be of particular interest. He also gives a reference to an account of this intervention as found in the Journal Documentation Catholique (7/11/65).

> For the innocent and definitely abandoned party.
>
> "The traditional solution offered by the priest presupposes heroic virtue, a rare faith and an uncommon temperament".
>
> "The solution of perpetual continence is not for the common Christian. Has the Church the right to say she has no other to offer?". She cannot lack sufficient authority to protect the innocent party from the consequences of the other's sin. It does not seem normal that perpetual continence, which belongs to the state of perfection, can be obligatorily imposed as a chastisement on the innocent party because the other has played traitor. The oriental Churches separated from Rome have always been conscious of having this authority and have always used it in favour of the innocent party The marriage bond was certainly made indissoluble by the positive law of Christ, but, as the gospel of Matthew indicates (5, 32, 19,6), "except in case of adultery". It is for the Church to judge the meaning of this clause; if the Church of Rome has always interpreted it in a restrictive sense, it was not so in the East, where the Church interpreted it from the first centuries in favour of possible remarriage of the innocent party.
>
> True, Trent (Sess. 24, can. 7 de Matrimonio) sanctioned the restrictive Roman interpretation, but it is well known that the formula adopted by this Council in this canon was designedly redrafted so as not to exclude the Eastern tradition which followed a practice contrary to that of the Church of Rome. The credit for that goes to the Venetian theologians who were well aware of the Greek tradition based on the interpretation of the Greek Fathers and even certain Western Fathers such as Ambrose of Milan. (Wenger: Trent merely wanted to settle a practical doubt on indissolubility. Lagrange: "She defined that she was not in error in teaching, in line with the evangelical and apostolic doctrine, that adultery cannot dissolve the bond of marriage, but has not fixed the precise sense of every text").
>
> "We know how the Eastern Fathers tried to deter widowers and widows from second marriages, following in that the advice of the

Apostle, but they never wanted to deprive the innocent party unjustly abandoned, of the right to remarry. This tradition, preserved in the East and never rejected during 10 centuries of union, could today be taken up again and adopted by Catholics. The progress of patristic studies has in effect highlighted the doctrine of the Eastern Fathers who were neither less good exegetes nor less good moralists than those of the West. Pastoral concern for sorely tested spouses was differently manifested among Western canonists. They strove by a subtle casuistry bordering on acrobatics to detect all the impediments capable of vitiating the marriage contract....sometimes to the scandal of the faithful... Is not the Oriental tradition a more apt exercise of divine mercy?".

(Precisions of Bishop Zoghby to the press afterwards.

1) The Catholic communities of the East have without exception followed the R.C. discipline and practice. 2) The Fathers and Doctors of the Eastern Church who laid the foundations of the Christian doctrine and formed the great majority of the Fathers of the great ecumenical councils could not have yielded to political influences in interpreting Christ's words in Matthew as they did. To pretend this is to forget what the universal Church owes to their knowledge and sanctity. 3) The Code of Justinian (6th C. could not have influenced Origen, Basil, Chrysostom etc. 4) The Eastern Church adopted this interpretation and practice in favour of the innocent party long centuries before the separation with the Church of Rome. The latter never condemned them during long centuries of union or got them condemned by Ecumenical Councils presided over by representatives of the Bishop of Rome, at which the Churches of the East and West sat together. This is clear proof that the Roman Church had never thought of contesting the legitimacy of the Oriental discipline on this point.)

(Comment of Maximos IV Saigh, Melchite Patriarch of Antioch, op.cit. The contrary practice of the Eastern Church can claim some texts of certain Fathers. But these are contradicted by others, and, in any case, they do not constitute a sufficiently constant and universal tradition to lead the Catholic Church to a change of discipline on this point.)

* * *

Very different was Archbishop Nicodemo of Bari. While admitting that all the problems could not be completely treated, he was anxious lest the treatment of marriage, however brief, should leave gaps . These could be avoided by frequent reference to the magisterium of recent Popes. So too, vague statements which lacked clarity or caution. He instanced the principle whereby parents were left to decide the size of their families according to various subjective criteria. It was ambiguous and could be invoked by spouses to justify contraceptive acts. It was not sufficient for the schema to deal only with children already conceived and keep silent about means of preventing conception.

(Note. It became known that the point of dividing the schema XIII, as it was then known, into two parts was to limit the number of speakers, since only one speech on each part was allowed to any member).

At the 139th (12th) General Congregation 30 September, the discussion on Part II was resumed with Cardinal Journet as the first speaker. The doctrine of the indissolubility of marriage, he said, probably in answer to Zoghby, was the very doctrine of Jesus Christ revealed to us, as was clear from Mark 10, 2-12. "What God has joined together, let no man put asunder". Paul himself taught the same, and in the Lord's name (1 Cor.7). It was evident from these that Matthew's doctrine must be the same, notwithstanding his clause, which could mean that separation was lawful, but not a second marriage. Under the influence of the civil law on divorce, the *Novellae* of Justinian were introduced into the Code of the Eastern Church as a "nomocanon" (Civil-ecclesiastical law) and to justify that practice the Eastern Church invoked the Matthean text about fornication. Since, however, they admitted other grounds of divorce, it would appear that they were following a human custom rather than an evangelical norm. The Church could not change the divine law. Situations which called for a heroic life could be met with God's help.

Cardinal Heenan begged that the vernacular versions of the finally approved Latin text be composed with great skill, and suggested that it would be better styled a "Message" (Nuntius) rather than a "Constitution". Whatever might happen to the Latin text, it was certain that the vernacular versions would be read. The present English version was scarcely better than the Latin. On the morality of contraception the schema observed a deep silence. The Commission was not to blame, since it was awaiting advice from above. But if they kept quiet on this one controversial point, the faithful would feel deceived and non-Catholics would assume that the Council could not decide. He suggested therefore that this chapter on marriage be omitted until the Pope and his special Commission had reached their decision.

Cardinal Rossi, in the name of 70 bishops of Brazil, expressed general satisfaction with the chapter on marriage. Perhaps for the sake of brevity, it had packed a lot into a few words. As for his particular comments and criticisms he would submit quite a few, but in writing. As to the section on legitimate ways of limiting offspring, the indeterminate declaration in the text was not at all sufficient.

Cardinal Conway of Armagh likewise found the chapter on marriage substantially satisfactory, but in need of some additions. He would like to see something said about the benefits that accrued to the institution of marriage when the wife was a true consort and the mother reigned as queen in the society of the family. In the section on indissolubility, the words of our Lord, "What God has joined, etc" should be quoted. As to fecundity, they were all aware of the problems in this matter, but the text did not faithfully express the mind of the mixed Commission. The subcommissions had clearly underlined the means prohibited as illicit, but the words of the text on page 49, "Sciant coniuges..." did not convey any such prohibition. They did not refer to means but to judgements. They should at least add: "by means conformed to the law of God". The magisterium would be diminished by silence. As to the title of the document, he would prefer "Epistola Pastoralis", or "Litterae Synodales ad mundum".

Cardinal Browne, another Irishman, was perplexed by some things said about the place of conjugal love among the ends of marriage. They were presumably talking about *fines operis* (ends intrinsic to the act). The primary end was that which determined the essence of marriage, the secondary ends were mutual aid and remedy of concupiscence. Mutual aid included mutual love, *amor amicitiae,* that love which served the good, not only of the offspring, but also and in a very great degree the good of the spouses, and was confirmed in them by their love for their children. The *fines operantis* could be many and various, but it was urgent that love should dominate and that it should be *amor amicitiae* (disinterested love) and love of *bonum utile* was always pursued and regulated according to the mean of virtue. (Comment: it was to be wondered whether this lecture's pure Thomism registered with many of the Fathers.)

An Indonesian Bishop whose name was almost unpronounceable by a western, viz. Djadjasepoetra, then spoke in the name of the conference of Bishops of Indonesia. Last year, he said, he had called their attention to the fact that whereas Europeans married because they loved, the non-Europeans of his part of the world loved because they were married. The outlook of the schema was too occidental. In his country, the intention to build up a family was the customary motive for marriage and it conduced to true and stable love.

Bishop Tomasek (Czech) speaking in the name of 40 other Fathers, mainly from Africa and Latin America, returned to the subject of fecundity. The threat of hunger menaced even the rich countries, for the standard of life was affected by having more than two or three children. It was a matter of great importance to provide suitable remedies. There was need of a vast international programme of relief, through the medium of UNO or commercial undertakings, long term loans etc. Young couples needed loans to set up worthy families.

Bishop de Silva of Braga said that there were some imperfections in an otherwise acceptable text. In particular the vague statement beginning: "Sciant coniuges...", which left the spouses to decide the size of their family apparently according to subjective criteria. It would have been better to use the words of Pius XI in *Casti Connubi* and of Pius XII.

At this point I went out for coffee, missing De Roo and Urtasun. When I returned Bishop J. Reuss, Auxiliary of Mainz, praised the schema for stressing the importance of conjugal love, and for very wisely abstracting from the problem to be studied by the Pope's special Commission. Yet he felt that the discussion begun the previous day called for some comment. It was the Pope himself that had set up the Commission for the scientific investigation of certain problems (namely birth control). If the answer to those problems was so clear, as Ruffini implied, it was difficult to understand why the Pope had set up his Commission. Until it had completed its work, the schema could not treat the problem as settled. Meanwhile it was doubtful whether the rhetorical manner of speaking corresponded to the modern needs. Conjugal love could not be simply identified with the conjugal act, as it was in the text. The conjugal act was among other conjugal acts, a mutual giving of bodies. Love led to its completion in a manner worthy of human nature, an intimate personal union. Hence it was rightly said in the text that marriage, though ordered to offspring, was not a mere institution for offspring. The responsibility of spouses to form their whole matrimonial life should be clearly urged. True responsibility included generosity. By responsible action man responded to the will of God.

Bishop J. Bednost spoke of the matrimonial crisis. Our urbanised and industrial society did not favour marriage. It presented special difficulties for women, not only in the developing nations but even in the wealthy nations where, out of desire for more consumer goods, women went out to work. Man was a family being by his intimate nature. His whole life, biological, spiritual and social, evolved in the family situation. Free love led to anarchy. Yet the conditions of modern life did not favour the family. The tendency was to transfer the education of children to others, Church, State, etc. The Church must help, but the family needed to collaborate intimately with the Church and school. Family prayer in common strengthened the family from within. Etc. etc.

F. Von Streng, reading a text of the Bishop of Basel, called for clearer denunciation of the evil of abortion. Bishop De Orbegozo of Peru, while agreeing that procreation was not the sole end of marriage, could not accept the quality of ends implied in the schema. As for the passage about taking account of the economic situation, it read like propaganda for the Birth-Control movement.

Now that the end of the Council was beginning to come in sight, many Fathers had been asking what was the programme for the month of October. At the 140th (13th) General Congregation on Friday 1st October, the Secretary General answered their enquiries, as far as was then possible, "nam praevidere futura non semper competit hominibus". On the following Monday, October 4, when the holy Father was setting out for New York to deliver a message of peace to the UNO, the General Congregation Mass would be for that intention. On the next day, October 5, at the end of the General Congregation, the Fathers would wait "in aula S. Petri" the returning Pontiff and hear an address from him, about 12 noon. The order of work would remain unchanged until mid-October, and then, from the 17th to 23rd a short vacation was foreseen, but only from General Congregations, not from work, because during those days the Commissions would be hard at work preparing new texts, and fresh work still remained for all the Fathers because the Pope wanted their advice on certain subjects about which he was to issue some instructions, which subjects would be communicated to the Presidents of the Episcopal Conferences.

Cardinal Gracias, speaking in the name of the Indian Conference of Bishops, of whom, he said, there were about 78 at Rome, then resumed the topic of matrimony as dealt with in the schema. Even in the East, he said, the dignity of marriage was endangered. To find out what outstanding laymen thought of the document, he had submitted the English version to five such persons. They regarded it as a very moving document. However, he suggested, before the final draft of the schema was promulgated, it should be entrusted to laymen to render into the vernacular, otherwise it might perhaps prove inefficacious. It was not strong enough in its reprobation of materialism, which, he said, quoting Lord Halifax, was more ruinous to the family than war. Chapter I (i.e. on marriage) could not however be understood unless chapter III was discussed with it, because the strength of family life depended on economic factors. The schema should stress that the generosity of the rich nations to the poor benefited the rich. Chapter III was deficient on not a few things. How, for example, were private rights to be harmonised with the demands of the government. In his opinion, the less State intervention, the better.

Cardinal Slipij of the Ukrainian Church, long a confessor of the faith in Soviet prisons, commented that this schema on the Church in the Modern World did not treat the world completely. There were more than 300 million Christians behind the Iron Curtain. Little was said about that world. The Church extended outside the limits of Europe and America.

Bishop Daungu of Masaka, for 90 other Fathers, called the attention of the Council to racial discrimination, a great moral problem. The schema mentioned it, but briefly, confusedly and lightly, and mixed it up with other kinds of discrimination as if they were all equally grave. Racial discrimination deprived man of his liberty. It was therefore necessary that the council should speak out strongly about it and without ambiguity, especially because some nations sought to justify it by appeal to the Old Testament. The Council could not treat this matter "quasi per transennam" (sideways).

After Bishop A. Hacault of Canada had raised a hermeneutical point and suggested that the schema should admit the relative goodness of polygamy and then show the superiority of the monogamous Christian marriage, the Moderators suggested that it was perhaps time to move on to chapter II, and the Fathers, as usual, rose promptly to their feet in agreement.

But Bishop P. Schmitt of Metz asserted his right to speak on chapter I, because he had taken the precaution of obtaining 70 supporters. There were factors in the modern world, he said, from which the Church could learn, which conspired to promote the dignity of man, such as the movement for stricter social justice, the greater sense of independence, the sense of the absurdity of war, recognition of the distinction between State and religion, the spirit of scientific research. These facts led to theological considerations, the duty of the Church to thank God for these points of contact with the world, and because in these ways the world collaborated towards salvation. Nothing of this was extraneous to Christian effort.

When I returned from coffee the discussion had moved on to the subject of human culture. Bishop Lebrun of Autun drew the attention of the Fathers to the cultural effect of sport in particular. He stressed its importance in modern life. There was sport in every country, national and international competitions attracted large numbers of spectators. Their number and value was increasing daily. Many people devoted their leisure to it individually or collectively. It affected the modern mentality. Then there were the values of sport to consider: the special contribution it made to the full development of man, the necessary restraint it imposed on mind and body, its favourable effect on the increase of certain qualities, such as team spirit, promptitude of decision, courage, etc. self-discipline. He urged therefore an addition to the schema on this subject.

Father A. Fernandez, O.P. General of the Dominicans, thought the chapter on culture too profuse and not sufficiently exact. The importance of culture was that it was one of the better human goods which could contribute greatly to everything which this document sought to promote. The diffusion of culture was a necessity, because the living together (conviventia) of mankind was impossible as long as many lacked culture. Special care was needed to ensure that the poor had access to culture. Culture was the chief means to the propagation of atheism and also to defeating atheism. That was why the communists concentrated first on the universities, a major peril in Latin America and other young nations. It was essential that this atheistic and materialistic culture be countered.

It would seem that the subject of culture was not attracting a capacity gate, because at this point, the Secretary General interjected: "The Fathers are requested to return to their seats". It was evident that he had an announcement to make, but wanted to give the strollers in the aisles and gossipers in the bars time to get back into their seats.

Meanwhile, M. Pelegrino, then Archbishop Elect of Turin, who has since risen to prominence, did his best to hold his shifting audience with a maiden speech. He liked the chapter and wanted to propose only two very small variations. The first concerned historical research. It had great importance both for culture and for faith. It could not be ignored here. His second point was liberty of research, laudably admitted to be a right of all the "faithful". But who were they? The context dealt with laity. But Bishops and clergy were laity. It must not be thought that there was no danger here. He himself knew a religious was penalised for an opinion now to be found in papal documents. It should therefore be made clear that freedom of research belonged to all. Otherwise the pest of lying and hypocrisy would persist. The clause "clergy or laity" ought therefore to be added. (A courageous maiden speech for an Archbishop Elect!)

The Secretary General was now able to make his announcement to a relatively full house. It was that the Pope had communicated to all the Fathers the text of the message he was sending to UNO. Felici proceeded to read it.

Bishop E. Blanchet, Rector of the Institut Catholique at Paris then resumed the topic of culture, and, though I made no note of it at the time, many Fathers almost certainly returned to the aisles. The speaker thought that the description of modern culture was very insufficient. For example, it had nothing about history which had had such an *essor* recently and such importance, for it was from history that many difficulties against the faith had been raised. No one could say what the life of man would be like, 100 years on. Modern psychology had given men the power to treat their fellow men as things. There was nothing in the text about philosophy, except the name; yet Marxism was a philosophy rather than a science, and so also was existentialism which made man the measure of right and wrong. The general tone was unduly optimistic. It was not a matter of the gentleman's agreement, but of a hard struggle, not only between men, but within man himself; yet there was not a word in the text about the gravity of these struggles. In the immense modern struggle faith had to seek its place. It was the stumbling block of the strong. There was need for pastoral zeal in the scientific life.

Bishop C. Padin of Brazil also thought the description of culture inadequate. It said nothing about the mark of originality which was essential to a culture. The complementary nature of all cultures should also have been declared. The exaggerated value attributed to Greco-Latin classical culture was inadmissible.

When the list of prospective speakers was read out at the beginning of the 141st (14th) General Congregation, Monday 4 October, it appeared that only five more wanted to say their piece on culture. The first was Archbishop Morcillo of Madrid. The first cause of culture was, he said, God the Creator; witness His command in Genesis to man to subject and dominate the earth, which man could only do through his intelligence. The command was given to the human race as a whole. Technological progress had now brought culture to the multitude and socialised it. The Redeemer also played a part in human culture, because the economy of the redemption gathered up all things to the glory of God. Finally Christ's command of charity made all things serve God. But the subject should be handed over to a post-Conciliar Commission. It was not worthy of an ecumenical Council to issue this chapter on such a matter.

Bishop A. Frotz, Auxiliary of Cologne, regretted that the sign of obedience to God the Creator which was an essential element of culture was missing from the text. Man acted not as man but always as male or female. He was not talking, he said, about any emancipation of women, but about the right order founded on the plan of God. The diversity of man and woman ought to be acknowledged here; otherwise we were left with that levelling-out which was inimical to culture. The woman's part should be treated expressly and distinctly.

Bishop Otto Spülbeck of Meissen welcomed the optimism of the schema in regard to the scientific field; it opened the way to dialogue with scientists. But the method raised his doubts. For example, the schema quoted Romans 1,20 about the pagans who knew not God when they could have argued to Him from the visible creation. This raised the question whether that was the right rule and method of scientific research. It was true that Vatican I said it, but in the world of the natural sciences contemplation of the world was not pursued in that spirit. Other methods were also needed. The merely mathematical way of thinking did not reveal, e.g. the contingent nature of a thing, a metaphysical concept.

Bishop Pierre Veuillot, then Coadjutor Archbishop, said that there were two orders of knowledge, both of which tended towards the truth each according to its own way. Science deserved respect for the technical and other progress it had achieved. But the Council should direct its attention to the moral state of science, its materialism, pessimism, atheism. Its very progress was a cause of anxiety, especially ethical anxiety. There was need for a sense of responsibility. There was ground for fear in a liberty that was not referred to its principle. The schema concurred with the optimism of past decades which was not so general now. In addition therefore to acknowledging what science had achieved, the schema should exhort scientists to respect the ultimate end for which it existed.

Bishop Zoghby, as it turned out was not concerned with culture, but with the stir created by his remarks on divorce at the 138th General Congregation and was allowed by the Moderators to clarify his position. In his plea for the innocent party, he said, he had a strictly pastoral object in view, to find a solution of the agonizing situation in which so many found themselves. His speech, he claimed, had carefully affirmed the principle of the indissolubility of marriage and carefully avoided the word "divorce". He regretted that the newspapers had used the word. In the East, the indissolubility of marriage was so firm among Catholics and non-Catholics alike that it could not be questioned. It was like the union of Christ and His Spouse the Church. Divorce among the Orthodox was simply a dispensation of the innocent party in certain cases by application of the principle of "oikonomia" which in no way affected the principle of indissolubility, no more than did an exercise of the Petrine privilege. His suggestion referred merely to a dispensation in favour of the innocent party, *salva indissolubilitate*. He had quoted Matthew only as a ground for this dispensation. He had not thought it incongruous to make such a proposal, having regard to the doctrine of the Eastern Fathers. He had never attacked the fidelity of East and West to the indissolubility taught by the Roman Church. That was the meaning of his recent intervention. As to its timeliness, it was for others to judge.

* * *

Monsignor McReavy provides a note concerning Bishop Zoghby's second intervention during the 141st General Congregation, 4 October 1965, giving a reference to Documentation Catholique 7-11-1965.

> Since certain publications have given too wide proportions to my recent Conciliar intervention in regard to the very frequent and sad case of the innocent abandoned spouse and have spread it round the world, I have sought to speak again in Aula, not to retract or change what I said, but to briefly recall the following: 1) My intervention had a strictly pastoral end, to discover a solution to an agonizing problem of so many young husbands and wives condemned to live alone in forced continence without fault on their part. 2) I clearly affirmed in my intervention the immutable principle of the indissolubility of marriage and deliberately avoided the word divorce... 3) This indissolubility is so anchored in the tradition of East and West, Orthodox and Catholic, that it cannot be questioned in a conciliar intervention... In Orthodox theology, divorce is merely a dispensation granted to the innocent party in well defined cases and out of purely pastoral concern, in virtue of what the Orthodox call the "principle of economy', which means dispensation on condescension. This dispensation does not exclude the principle of the indissolubility of marriage. It is even used in its service, as are the dispensations accorded by the Catholic Church in virtue of the Petrine privilege. 4) All I suggested was a dispensation in favour of the innocent party. Quoting the traditional Catholic interpretation of Matthew, I envisaged the eventual possibility of adding to the motives of dispensation already admitted by the Catholic Church that of fornication and definitive abandonment of one by the other, to banish the danger of perdition which threatens the innocent party. Such a dispensation would not have questioned the indissolubility of marriage, no more than do the others. 5) It was based on the indisputable authority of holy Fathers and Doctors of the Eastern Church. 6) This is the perspective in which the Roman Church has never contested the legitimacy of that Oriental discipline favourable to the remarriage of the innocent party.

* * *

When the debate passed to chapter III, on the economic and social life, Cardinal Siri of Genoa was the first to speak. The schema made some good points, he said, but it was imprudent to speak too definitively of things that were dependent on techniques. The Council should keep to immutable principles. Thus it was right to speak of the responsibility of every man, but, in the matter of worker participation in management, desirable though it was, there were technical aspects, and the question was which way was the more apt. The schema should therefore not descend unduly to details.

Cardinal Benjamin Arriba y Castro of Tarragona questioned the expression "Church of the poor". The social doctrine of the Church was very beautiful, but, he asked, prefacing his question with "num", had it been put into practice in the way that might have been expected. The answer could be read at the beginning of page 7, where there was reference to the hunger of a huge part of mankind. That he said was the real world. Where had the Church's doctrine been put into practice? It was not for the Church to displace the State, etc., but it was her duty to proclaim the principles of social justice. A special institute should, he thought, be created in the Roman curia for social matters.

Cardinal Bueno y Monreal of Seville said that the Church had often been blamed for being too late with her social doctrine. She must not make that mistake again. It was an age of constant change, but the principles of the Gospel were valid in any age or situation. There was too much evidence of the liberal and capitalist mentality in the schema. It had nothing to say on collective production, so widespread today, nor on the fair distribution of the produce or profits. Liberal capitalism stood for maximum profits from minimum costs. He feared that the schema might give a handle to those who promoted class struggle and strikes. The doctrine of private property was not derived from natural law, nor inseparable from Catholic doctrine.

Bishop E. Swanstrom, a New York Auxiliary, assented to all that the schema had to say about hunger, pestilence and other miseries. It was admirably said. But the question remained: how were they to be relieved. At this point I retired for my midmorning coffee and must have been detained, because when I returned to my place, Bishop Hengsback of Essen and Mar Gregorios of South India had had their say, and Bishop Fernandez, Auxiliary of Delhi, was at the microphone. His chief proposal was that a post-Conciliar organ be instituted to ensure that the will and readiness of the Church to work for the relief of those who could not live a truly human life was effectively and permanently actuated. It would be its job to probe the true nature of progress, to take effective steps so that all the underprivileged were directed to positive objectives, to ensure that whatever was given by Christians or non-Christians was given from the right motive, not from a disguised self-love; briefly that it was aimed at men, not things.

Bishop Franic of Split, Jugoslavia, praised the new ideas in the chapter which showed that the Church was ready to adapt herself to the modern situation. The solutions suggested, however, were not yet mature, and the chapter should therefore be remitted to the newly constituted Synod of Bishops which would be an excellent instrument for the purpose. The schema had less to say than *Mater et Magistra* on worker-participation and it was not enough. A man's labour was part of his person and his person could not be sold. This idea was found in the chapter, but not developed. There was not enough recourse to the natural law. The schema shrank from metaphysics, without which they could not proceed.

In the opinion of Bishop Höffner of Munster, who spoke in the name of 80 bishops of German tongue, the chapter had not attained the maturity of *Quadragesimo anno, Mater et Magistra* and *Pacem in terris*. It made many emphatic demands without indicating concrete and realistic means to fulfil them. It breathed a too optimistic ideology of progress to the perfect state, as if everything could be achieved as long as men sincerely wished it; and that was as impossible as the eradication of sin. It did not deal correctly with managers and entrepreneurs whose work was indispensable in bringing workers and capital together. It treated economic conditions which were vastly different according to the state of development, as if they were all the same.

Bishop G. Coderre of St Jean de Quebec, speaking for many Canadian bishops, said that the schema was too much concerned with a situation which was already on the way out, and it was ignorant of processes which were already bringing in a new kind of industrial society, the "post-industrial period", as it were.

Bishop Garcia de Sierra was doubtful whether the Church's mission and competence extended to some of the particularities of the chapter.

At the 142nd (15th) General Congregation, 5 October, discussion of chapter III was resumed with Cardinal Wyszynski of Warsaw as the first speaker. To avoid too abrupt an opening, he suggested that the chapter should begin with a brief historical introduction. The Church had not only now become concerned about the working classes and the introduction could show the record of her concern. To counter the individualistic philosophy behind various economic systems, the schema must expound the sound doctrine of the human person, the new person with a new life in a new world. Progress was to be measured by that of the human person. As to the section on emigrants, the Cardinal said (no doubt with concern for the millions of Polish emigrants) that they were often treated as second rate citizens and that attempts were made to denationalize them. It was a difficult question, but deserved deeper treatment than it received in the schema.

Cardinal Cardijn said that the workers of the world, who were daily increasing in number, should be addressed by the Council in more realistic terms. It was true that in Western Europe, America and Australia their status had improved greatly, but conditions elsewhere were gravely unjust. There was no prepararatory qualification for the job, their work was interrupted without compensation, their unions were forbidden, they lacked housing and proper or sufficient food. Workers should be conscious of their interdependence and collaborate, and the Church should re-assure them and remind the public authorities of their grave responsibility. Pius XI had said that workers were themselves the first apostles of all who labour.

A solemn invitation to all authorities and all associations of workers to coordinate their efforts so as to realise the immense possibilities should be inserted in the schema.

Father G. Mahon (Superior General of Mill Hill Missionaries) said that the world looked to the Church for two things: a clear enunciation of essential principles, and concrete action by the Church as a worldwide body. He had in mind especially the problem of hunger. The schema indicated the principles, but, as it said itself, "bene sentire non sufficit" (To listen carefully is not enough). He proposed, as others had done, the erection of a permanent secretariate for social justice in the world, with four functions; 1) To put to the world the principles contained in the schema, in *Mater et Magistra, Pacem in terris*, and Paul VI's message. During the third Session there were 22 interventions on the subject of world hunger; since when some 35 million had died of hunger. A Secretariate could convince the world of the size of the problem. 2) To supply real and valid aid to missionaries seeking to relieve hunger. It was true that the primary work of the missionary was of another kind, but they could do much in the social field, did they not live lonely and cut off from others. A Secretariate could supply them with technical assistance. 3) It could assist episcopal aid agencies which already did great work, without being itself a charitable organization (opus caritatis). 4) It could call to mind two principles: a) economic progress required cultural progress – "not in bread alone..." b) Nothing was possible without change of heart and mind among men; only so could there be just division and distribution of the world's wealth. He ended by asking the Council to declare its desire for a permanent Secretariate, and that a Votive Mass for social justice and peace be instituted.

Bishop Himmer of Tournai, with an eye rather to the thriving than to the starving peoples of mankind, reflected that in the present period of unprecedented growth, it was important that progress should not be considered to consist in maximum production, but should always be centred in the human person, and in man's fulfilment of the vocation which he had received from the Creator to dominate nature. The tragedy of our times was that in the process of transforming matter man had become forgetful of God, and could never achieve satisfaction that way. The schema should stress the constructive character of the Church's doctrine.

Bishop E. Larrain of Chile, referring to the schema's use of the term "developing nations", said that in Latin America it was a euphemism for regression. It was necessary therefore to indicate what constituted true Christian progress and on what it was founded. Progress was not a mere fact but a right of every individual person and nation. It was correlative to the strict moral obligation of the richer countries to help the poorer. Progress should be something more than mere economic growth. It consisted in the service of man, in growth in perfection, not simply in having more but in being more.

Bishop Echeverria was concerned with international relations. The schema dealt with the huge economic diversity, but was silent about the explosion of the modern social conscience. Men had become aware of their dignity and wanted to end class distinction. Our pragmatic world wanted deeds not words. The Council should erect a practical organ or institution to increase the activity of the Church in the social field.

Bishop Anoveros of Spain found the norms in the schema too abstract. The question of rich and poor nations was so grave that the Council ought to deal with it much more deeply. Was it not time to say that a living wage was a matter of commutative justice.

(After three more speeches, Pastillo, Castellano, De Vito, discussion moved on to chapter IV.)

Chapter IV of the schema was entitled: *De vita communitatis politicae.* The result of the rule allowing only one speech per Father on each of the two parts of the schema was now beginning to show; those who had chosen to speak on chapters I, II, or III of Part II (Family, Culture, Economic-Social life) were now gagged. No cardinal opened the discussion. That distinction fell to J. Marafini, Bishop of Veroli-Frosinone in Italy. He regretted the absence from the schema of a clear declaration on the morality of fiscal laws. There was a widespread idea that they were purely penal laws, for, even though the doctrine that they carried a moral obligation was spreading, it had not yet reached the people. Until all citizens paid their taxes conscientiously, the cure of economic ills was impossible. True, some tax laws were unjust, but not all. The Council should stress the legislator's moral obligation to make just laws, but also stress that the presumption was in his favour.

Bishop E. Beitia of Spain said that the cooperation of Church and State should be a healthy one, otherwise it was worse than separation. Some questioned the classical thesis, some were ready to accept universal pluralism and suppression of privileges. They assumed that the State could not profess the true faith without discrimination against other religions. He maintained that public profession of faith by the State and a concordat relation with the Church were desirable where possible.

Bishop Baraniak of Poland, viewing the matter from the other end of the spectrum, complained that the schema did not sufficiently explain what cooperation with an atheistic State was lawful. Maybe it was not dangerous where the State merely demanded cooperation in production. But the greater part of the world lived under atheistic-materialistic regimes, and it was evident that a Christian could not cooperate with atheistic materialism. The question was whether and how far one could cooperate in things which were honest in themselves but would be used for evil ends.

Archbishop Hurley of Durban, with 70 backers, noted that the word "Status" had been avoided in the Latin version, but appeared in all the vernacular versions, and in an equivocal sense, meaning either the Government or the whole public society. It would be better to avoid the term in documents. The same ambiguity is attached to "respublica". He hoped that the use of the term "societas perfecta" would cease. As for the Church, it was only by analogy that she could be called a "society". Human activity could not be divided into spiritual and temporal, since all human activity belonged to both orders. It was true that the Church did not want to be confused with the civil society, but she sought to influence it. The schema rightly said that the Church did not rest her hopes on privileges obtained from the civil authorities and would indeed be ready in certain circumstances to renounce the exercise of some legitimately acquired rights; but in fact they had been the source of such conflict that liberty was denied. In the past, the Church had insisted too much on her rights. In the future, it would be better to speak of the rights of men.

So, after only these four interventions, the discussion passed on to chapter V *On the Community of Nations and the Promotion of Peace* with Cardinal Alfrink as the opener. He said he admired the dexterity of the new text, but had some changes to suggest in order to avoid false interpretations. The chapter should state clearly that all discord and violence, even when unavoidable, was of its nature in conflict with the spirit of Christ. Even a just war was contrary to the Gospel, because all war was contrary to the spirit of Christ. In the section dealing with the use and possession of modern arms, a distinction of great importance needed to be made between the two. The balance of terror was precarious, and it was therefore rightly said that possession of such arms merely as a deterrent was not illegitimate in itself. He feared however that it would be the source of many difficulties, because the statement could not stand without limitations. The only remedy was abolition, as Pius XII had said. It would be better to use the text of Pius XII and John XXIII. As regards the section on Minor Wars and Acts connected with wars, the two should be clearly separated. The passage on conscientious objection should be retained, because abuses could be guarded against by the civil law itself. Praise should be given to institutes which work for peace. War and peace did not simply happen; they were made by men.

(AT THIS POINT, the acting Secretary-General intervened to say: "At this precise moment, the Supreme Pontiff has arrived at Rome").

Cardinal Owen McCann of Cape Town admitted that the many organizations which had arisen since the war to foster unity among the nations were very laudable, but said it would be opportune to constitute a special Secretariate at the Holy See to coordinate their work. Local organizations must retain their independence, but they needed to cooperate with others of the same kind. Such a Secretariate would work in an inspirational way. There were two worlds, the haves and the have-nots. In some there was a superabundance of food, in others men were dying of famine. Technical means to distribute the fruits of the earth could certainly be found. The problem would not be solved overnight, but to work for that was a matter of social justice. The Secretariate he had proposed would be a moral force in the world.

(The Pope arrived in St Peter's with all his party about 12.50. Cardinal Liénart welcomed him back and he made a brief address in return, saying that the *vox verbi* must now be followed by the vox actionis of all the Church.)

At the 143rd (16th) General Congregation it became clear from the list of speakers that a considerable number of Fathers had reserved their option on Part II to this final chapter V (On the Community of Nations and the Promotion of Peace). The first to speak was Cardinal Liénart (who incidentally had been an officer in the French army of the first world war). The Church had always regarded war as a calamity and sought to make it more humane, but there existed terrible new weapons, such that it would be a crime against God and man to inflict such slaughter as they could cause. Any offensive war was made an unjust war nowadays by the very fact of the use of those weapons. Governments must be attentive to the injustices which breed war and strive to supply a solution. He hoped that the schema, already praise-worthy, might be yet further perfected and its doctrine in no way attenuated.

Cardinal Léger of Montreal followed. Many, he said were hoping that the Council would work for the extirpation of war, and some were demanding that it solemnly condemn modern war and especially the use of nuclear weapons. No. 98 of this schema (approved 28 May 1965 for discussion) meant to reply to these requests, but it could not be left as it was, because of an internal contradiction; it leaned both ways, to those who condemn modern war and to those who held that it could be lawful in certain circumstances. In his view, the situation had changed. War could scarcely be just according to the traditional principles. The classical theory of the morality of war was quasi-unreal. In dealing with the morality of modern war, therefore, the Council should not distinguish or condemn in the abstract. It should state the modern situation and then declare that in practice war has become "alienum a ratione" (cf. *Pacem in terris*). He agreed with the schema on the necessity of an international authority, but would like a stronger statement of the duty of governments to work for that end. Exhortations were not enough. Men must be warned of the various ways in which international unity was held up or damaged. The schema's statement on conscientious objection was good but should derive the motive for it from the Gospel and the Christian spirit. The cooperation of non-Christians as well as of Christians with those who seek peace should be sought.

Cardinal Duval of Algiers, speaking on behalf of the Bishops of North Africa called for stronger words on the obligation to work for peace, and a protest against the ever-growing gap between the haves and the have-nots. Racism also ought to be severely condemned. The horror of modern war was not sufficiently expressed. It was not enough to say that uncontrolled warfare "was not easily exonerated", as in n. 98; total war, whatever the weapons, was to be altogether condemned. A more synthetic manner of expression was needed and a more positive way of urging the new human order that had to be created. There had to be a new way of thinking.

During my coffee break I missed the intervention of Archbishop Garrone and returned to hear the end of that of Bishop Simons, from India, who apparently was in favour of contraception and therapeutic abortion when the common good of the human race demanded them.

Abbot Christopher Butler, O.S.B. said that the practical difficulty was obvious. We all had a *patria*, and *pietas erga patriam* was a virtue, yet we must now give a truly catholic answer, putting aside our particular inconveniences and remembering that there is neither Jew or Greek but that we are all made one in Christ. We must speak for all men, proceeding cautiously lest the balance of the whole be damaged. The statement that possession of nuclear weapons merely for deterrence cannot be said to be illegitimate in itself, should be omitted. The real question was not about mere possession, but preparation for use and for indiscriminate and therefore illicit use. This ought to be said, and likewise that not only the execution but even the intention was gravely criminal, whether for rulers or for subordinates. There was no ground for speaking in that context of cooperation by subjects with criminal superiors. All had a moral relation to the whole human family and to the community of nations which did not yet exist but ought to be created. He did not like the list of reasons for conscientious objection; it was sufficient to declare that some objectors were true prophets. It should be clearly affirmed that not by such aid – "non tali auxilio"– did the Church want to be protected from her adversaries. Christ had not willed to be defended either by the sword or by legions of angels. Let it be clearly stated that bad intentions, even when hypothetical, remained bad.

Bishop Gordon Wheeler, Auxiliary of Middlesbrough, said that n. 94 did well to mention economic aid among the means to international cooperation, but it should stress the need for this aid to be afforded according to the principles laid down by the Popes. Charity required that aid be given in such manner as to raise those aided as much as possible. Sometimes misery was merely increased. Moreover countryfolk must be dissuaded from crowding into great cities. The first necessity was a good agriculture. Great efforts of organization were needed and unselfish help. There must be dialogue with all experts, for, as St Augustine said, charity without knowledge goes astray. The ecumenical movement had changed the whole climate in religious relationships. The same could happen in regard to help to the needy nations. As to war, the Popes had reminded us how irrational was nuclear war. The schema condemned it and then watered down its condemnation. The whole doctrine of "just war" needed rethinking in the light of the need for a world government. (Odd that two English converts, Butler and Wheeler should follow each other).

Bishop L. Castan of Spain recalled that Trent had proposed an international tribunal with suitable force to settle international disputes, but the times were not then propitious. All that the schema had to say was excellent in itself, but it was not logically ordered or well connected. Total war failed to fulfil the three conditions traditionally required to justify war. One of these was that it must be declared by a competent authority. No merely national authority was competent to declare a nuclear war which could harm other nations. The text failed to make it clear that a war was unjust if a single condition was unfulfilled. The schema also had nothing explicit about a purely defensive war, thereby implying that it too was unjust. But that left the way open to tyranny. It was the aggressor that must be condemned. As to conscientious objection, authors differed, and the Council should leave the question to them.

Bishop Marling of the USA mentioned an estimate that a 3% growth of population required a 10% economic growth. That, he said, was impossible for the underdeveloped nations. What could be done in Holland was utterly inapplicable in India. The vast gap between stages of development was the central problem, and nothing bold enough to solve it had yet been proposed. It would be better to exhort the public authorities to investigate all lawful means to a solution. Christ's assurance that our Heavenly Father "knows we have need of these things" did not exempt us from effort to increase our material goods.

When Bishop Charles Grant, Auxiliary of Northampton, came to the microphone, it must surely have been the first occasion when three Fathers from England, spoke in the same General Congregation. His theme was the close connection between extreme want and threats to international peace. Much, as the Bishops knew, was already being done, and more might be done by joint effort with our separated brethren and all men of good will. The Church, however, must make even greater efforts. Between 1950 and 1961, the rich nations had given 13 billion dollars to the poor nations and yet it had proved ineffective. With the aid of a coordinating institution under Cardinal Frings particular institutions had become much more efficacious. A similar Secretariate should direct and coordinate the action of the Church. The same conclusion followed from consideration of the needs of peace. There could be no cure until we all realized that we are one family and formed one society with world authority and real power. The schema seemed, at first sight, to condemn and at the same time to tolerate the balance of terror and increase of nuclear weapons. The words "solely as a deterrent" could be taken to exclude all intention of using them, but they would be understood as meaning that it was lawful to have them as long as the intention was to use them only in self-defence. Yet if such use was wrong, so also was the intention. He proposed therefore either that the words be expunged, or that a clause be added: "excluding all intention of using them". The Council should merely acknowledge the existence of the balance of terror without passing moral judgement on it.

Bishop P. Rusch of Innsbruck complained that n. 98 of the schema did not condemn offensive war, as many had hoped it would, now that the condition of the *moderamen inculpatae tutelae* could no longer be observed with modern weapons, and therefore only defensive war could be justified.

No. 100, admitted the need of a universal authority but failed to indicate effective means to it; in fact, the only way was to limit arms to the universal authority. The action of the Church in the international community would be more effective if she had an instrument which could organize an effective presence for her, a.v. a *Consilium Pacis, in re morali, technica et militari*. Something should also be said about the threat of ideological war.

Bishop P. Brezanoczy, in the name of all the Hungarian bishops, welcomed the schema's dynamic description of peace as an organic thing, not a mere fact. It would seem to follow from this that an institution must be set up, in Rome or elsewhere, which could mobilize the resources of the Church aptly and in time, and the Holy See might have a permanent means of intervening in UNO. It was regrettable that the schema, after condemning total war, appeared to water down its own condemnation. A solemn, clear, universal and absolute condemnation of nuclear war was altogether desirable. It was a violation of the Fifth Commandment. To quote St Augustine: It is better to kill war by words than men by arms.

It was announced at this point that the whole schema *De Pastorali Munere Episcoporum* had been definitively approved by 2167 to 14, and was to be submitted to the Pope who would decide whether and when it was to be promulgated in public session.

At the 144th (17th) General Congregation, 7 October, there was still a lengthy list of Fathers waiting to speak on chapter V. The first was Cardinal Martin of Rouen. He was not happy about the style of the schema. It lacked spirit and might put off the public by its frigidity. As to the distinction between offensive and defensive war, it was possible in theory but altogether precarious in practice. It left us in a vicious circle and so conduced to the mad "defensive" arms race. A spark could start a major conflagration. So too with the terms "just" and "unjust" war; one could no longer use the language of the old Authors, because modern war was not what they were thinking of. Hence, the very notion of war, of any kind of war, as a means of solving international disputes was to be reprobated. To this end, it was necessary that all Christians as such, clergy and people, should take the lead in the cause of peace. "War on War", as Pius XII said. "Iam nunquam bellum", as Paul VI had said the other day (i.e. at New York). Finally, there was the evident necessity of strengthening that superior authority already mentioned by many. Meanwhile Pope Paul had called upon rulers to divert arms expenditure to works of charity.

Cardinal Ottaviani was, as expected, utterly forthright. War must be completely outlawed. No. 98 of the schema was too brief about the means needed to avert wars, and should be expanded. The young and peoples generally must be educated by all the means of social communication. The idea of brotherhood must be fostered more among all men of whatever tongue or race. Fostered too must be the distribution of goods. All totalitarian regimes must be resisted. There must be support for all international authorities and tribunals, support backed by sanctions. Under the name of war, a very vague word, guerilla wars were often promoted by communists, aggression being called "liberation". All such forms of violence must be abolished. So too ideological warfare, a very fertile source of real war. The principles laid down by Pius XII, etc. must be publicized. "Scatter the nations that desire war". He ended with a hope that the world might one day become a single universal republic, a single fatherland, by a confederation such as that of USA and Brazil.

Bishop M. Gaviola of the Philippines noted the deep silence of the schema about the population explosion, even in the section dealing with rapid demographic growth. The Council should openly proclaim the immutable moral principles, because the Birth-Control movement drew its chief arguments from the so called explosion, and had no scruple about the lawfulness or unlawfulness of the means it propagated to control it. The Council should speak clearly about illicit means and resist the scientific theories which threw doubt on the very providence of God. It would be opportune to collect statistics about the practice of birth-control. The imbalance between large population and true progress was to be found in some States, but not everywhere.

Bishop M. Klepacz of Poland, admitting that all were scared of a third world war, called for a close study of international organizations. It was a world of egoism and cupidity. Only physical violence was feared. Economic conditions did not incite men to pursue the best. One third of mankind was hungry. Many were in concentration camps. Sterilization , etc. etc. Only Christ's doctrine, which contained all that was good, could stay the rush to the precipice. War was the supreme catastrophe. The only efficacious remedy was the propagation of peace in the hearts of men. The schema, therefore, must reveal the real situation, must present peace as the fruit of justice, must provide for the defence of the rights of poor and weak nations. "Peace in this way, but not at any price!".

Bishop Cantero of Saragossa was very pleased with chap. V. Its principles and doctrine were more mature than any of the other chapters of this Part. It contained practical realism without casuistry. In the real world, no other formula has yet been found to preserve rights against unjust aggression except the ability to resist. While man remained weak and sinful, defensive weapons would remain necessary. Nowadays, all men and all governments of good will abhor war and knew that nuclear war meant that it was the duty of rulers to do all possible to avoid it. In particular, public opinion in favour of peace must be formed, and there should be more emphasis on this, for if public opinion had been formed, it became that much easier for rulers to preserve peace. Conscientious objection could not be omitted/admitted absolutely.

Archbishop P. Gouyon of Rennes, speaking for 70 Fathers, said that they would all like to forbid war altogether, but history showed that not all would follow suit, and that means subjection to oppression. No people could be denied the right to the means of self defence against aggression, though legitimate defence alone could be justified. Every war was a calamity, but the distinction between a limited war and total war was a valid one. On the other hand, most of the combattants had no part in the negotiations etc. that had led to a war. Alleged just causes were often unjust. War was not a way of judging justice. Every war, even a limited war, risks becoming total. The end did not justify the means. It was not always easy to say who was the first aggressor. Only an international authority was adapted to the defence of violated rights.

Bishop Carli of Segni, Italy, thought the questions in the schema not yet ripe for answering. For example, the question of conscientious objection should either be thoroughly dealt with or prudently omitted. It was the common doctrine that even in this atomic age there could be a just war and therefore outright refusal to serve at all was unlawful. It was also unjustifiable in time of peace, because no violence was required. Military service was necessary to the efficacy of any international authority. However, since there were respectable voices raised against that opinion, he thought it would be better to keep quiet. But if the schema would not keep quiet, it should be complete and logical. As it stood it was illogical. If military service were a manifest violation of the law of God, conscientious objection was obligatory for all, and if it were not a manifest violation, conscientious objection was unlawful.

Archbishop Beck of Liverpool regarded chap. V as being of supreme importance, because all else was possible provided the arms race were stopped. The section on international order, he said, did not take enough account of the chief obstacle, viz, the fragmentation of mankind into 120 sovereign States which admitted no limitation on their autonomy. It was necessary that national sovereignty should give way to the international community. There was need of a serious examination of the way in which history was taught. Taught patriotically it was an obstacle to international cooperation. To create conditions in which war would no longer be a legitimate instrument of justice, there must be an international authority with effective power. The question was what was to be done in the meanwhile, and how long it would take. As long as there was no effective international authority, possession of adequate weapons of self defence was not illegitimate. It was no use omitting this point as some had asked; it was on this that the world wanted advice. In reality, it was not a question of possession but of intention. How far could one go in threats. Could one threaten what the schema called a crime? What was "massive retaliation"? What could the Church offer? What was the morality of bluff and counter-bluff? It was arguable that, until there was an effective international body such that States could disarm without risk, they were in a necessary occasion of sin which had to be tolerated. It was the Council's duty to insist on the necessity of doing everything possible to get out of that occasion. It should also be stressed that a State loses its right to command, if what it commanded was clearly wrong. At this point, although, according to the list read out at the beginning of the Congregation, there were still another 8 awaiting their chance to speak on chap. V, the closure of the debate on the schema was proposed and carried and the revised schema on Missionary Activity was presented for discussion.

After it had been introduced by the Relator of the Commission, Fr Schütte, Father General of the S.V.D., Cardinal Méouchi of the Maronites opened the debate. In general he liked the new version, but offered some observations on the arrangement of the material. It was more of an academic lecture on missiology than a concrete synthesis. For example, it had nothing on the preaching of penance. The rhythm of the apostolate was a sort of explosion, like that of a seed. The proportion of the paragraphs did not correspond to the dignity of the subjects. The preaching of the word ought to be given more space. The Father had not sent His angels but His Son, and therefore we should send as missionaries the best men we possessed. Nowhere did the schema elaborate the parables of which almost all had a missionary sense. More attention should be paid to the part of the laity. The spiritual vocation of the missionary should be more closely traced. A larger part should be assigned to Episcopal Conferences.

Cardinal de Barros Camara of Rio de Janeiro, speaking for 57 Latin American bishops, readily accepted what was said about the Church's obligation to preach the Gospel, but asked for something to be said about the obligation to receive the Gospel, especially after so much had been said about religious liberty. A lot had been said about sociology, but it should be remembered that christian sociology included original sin and redemption. He now wanted to say something in the name of 300 bishops about the activity of non-Catholic missionaries. The criteria and norms regarding proselytism could usefully be included in the projected ecumenical directory.

Cardinal Santos of Manila thanked the Fathers for all the sympathy and help that had been forthcoming on the occasion of the recent volcanic explosion in the Philippines. He expressed his general satisfaction with everything in the schema and merely suggested a few modifications of order.

Cardinal Jäger of Paderborn was also pleased with the schema as a whole. The structure and arrangement of material were excellent. Something should be added in n. 8 about the judgement of God. Not all obeyed the Gospel. Christ was a sign destined to be contradicted, and that was the judgement of God already in operation. The Church shared the passion of its Lord. Also, at the end, something might well be added on the scandal caused by the life of Christians, and the section on ecumenism should be strengthened and developed.

The translation of Bishop Dwyer from Leeds to Birmingham was published officially at noon. I learned it when we emerged from St Peter's and got into our motorcoach. The following day, Friday, Bishop Cleary left for Birmingham to arrange for the enthronement, and Bishop Dwyer left for Leeds to provide for its administration.

At the beginning of the 145th (18th) General Congregation, several of the Fathers who had been gagged by the closure of Schema XIII, claimed their right to speak in the name of 70 Fathers, whose signatures they had perhaps obtained ad hoc.

The first was Bishop Ancel, Auxiliary of Lyons. In no. 100 of chapter V, he said, two things were clearly affirmed: a) that all should renounce the right to war, and b) that this could not be done without the constitution of an international authority with supreme and effective power. Several had opposed these affirmations, implicitly accusing the Church of being anti-patriotic. Others, on the contrary, condemned the doctrine as being hypothetical and inefficacious. He wanted to reply to these charges. First, as to the moral obligation of love of one's country, this love was evident in Christ when He wept over Jerusalem, in St Paul who was ready to be anathema for his brethren. So too a true patriot could and should wish and work for the pre-eminence (praestantia) of his nation, but pre-eminence in cooperating for the common good of the human family. In no way worthy of praise therefore were those nations which sought to dominate over others and get rich at their expense. That was a foolish nationalism. There was nothing unpatriotic in renouncing the right to war. There was no such thing as the right to offensive war, and defence would be better secured by an international authority. The Church did not spurn those who shed their blood in legitimate defence of their country. As long as the world remained, there would always be the need of international forces. As to the alleged, he asked, inefficacy of the Church's doctrine, what, he asked, did the world expect. All that was possible to the Church was to bear witness to the truth. The world did not expect a casuistic lecture but a clear affirmation. A solemn declaration should be inserted to the effect that the hour would come in which, *servatis iuribus nationum*, an international authority ought to be set up with supreme power.

Last year, said Bishop Rupp of Monaco, the schema had passages a) about the strategic unity of Christians and especially Catholics for dialogue with the world, and b) about vindication of the right of migrating which fosters justice and peace. On these things, he complained, the revised schema was silent. It was silent even where the nature of the subject required it to speak, e.g. where it dealt with the Body of Christ. All it had was a vague allusion, non-scriptural, to the unity of mankind. Something could well have been expected about the immense populations of the East which sought land. On this too the schema was silent, but it grew sentimental on other things. He ended by reading a text subscribed by more than 100 Fathers from the various continents.

Bishop A. Faveri of Tivoli, speaking in the name of more than 70 Italian Fathers said that if the Church was to benefit from the Council, she must foster charity even more than in the past. It was the function of the Church assigned to her by Christ. The Constitution on the Church dealt with the principle, but the present document on the Church in the Modern World provided the text in which to deal with the practical application of the principle.

Bishop W. Philbin of Down and Connor said that the schema had one substantial defect. It had attempted to indicate what the Church could contribute to a better ordering of temporal affairs. What in fact it had done was to provide a philosophical disquisition. But that kind of instruction did not constitute the best that the Fathers could do by way of help to the world. What the text offered could be found elsewhere and better. A great opportunity was being missed. The problem was not one of distinguishing good and evil, but the difficulty of doing what was known to be good and avoiding what was known to be evil, the "perficere autem non invenio" of St Paul, a compendium of all human history. St Paul had asked himself who would free him from that infirmity and had answered, "the grace of God". Our one remedy, said the speaker, was Christ, the author of grace. The schema talked like a Pelagian. It implied throughout that all would be well if men would carry out the enclosed instructions. On the contrary it should be preaching the whole Gospel. He did not know that the time was inopportune. St Augustine was attracted to the Gospel not by its principles but by its offer of help to him in his weakness. It was the tragedy of our age; it entertained the noblest aspirations and yet its wars were worse than ever. Many were becoming desperate. Was this not a *praeparatio evangelica*? The document should be a Christian Manifesto, Jesus Christ, yesterday, today and for ever. He proposed that it should either conclude in this fashion, or that the whole should be reduced to that.

Bishop P. Boillon of Verdun was in favour of cutting out all distinctions and aim by declaring war to be unlawful. However, since the danger of aggression remained, public opinion would first have to be educated accordingly. There would have to be humility in the international order so that citizens would admit limitation of national sovereignty, poverty in the international order so that the citizens of the rich nations would accept a diminution of their standard of living for the benefit or others, and gentleness ("dulcedo" which I presume means "douceur") in national affairs. Witness was borne by those who fought against all injustice.

That speech definitely brought to an end the long debate on this verbose Constitution which had not even been proposed when the Council began.

Archbishop Garrone of Toulouse, Relator of the responsible Commission, summed up, mentioning some of the main points raised and either promising to attend to them or explaining why it might be difficult to do so. The Congregation's attention was then brought back to the schema on *Missionary Activity*.

Cardinal Frings, speaking in the name of many missionary bishops expressed great satisfaction with the substance of the revised schema. It rightly emphasized the Church's right and duty to maintain constant missionary activity, which had sometimes been questioned recently. The Church must always remain missionary. But perhaps the schema could demonstrate more positively that this activity of the Church pertained to the salvation of men. He also proposed that something be added about the missionary function of the native clergy themselves.

Cardinal Alfrink also thought the schema was very praiseworthy on the whole. Its conception of missionary activity was, however, too hierarchical. The subject responsible was the whole people of God, though under the leadership of the hierarchy. The *proemium* and chapter I needed to be revised in that sense. One consequence of the restricted concept was that the text dealt only with the vocation of clerics and religious, though no. 24 conceded that layfolk could be missionaries. The whole People of God was anointed by the Holy Spirit for missionary action. The schema was also too silent on non-hierarchical charisma. The section on motives for missionary action made no mention of the fact that the period between the first and second coming of Christ was the time of mission; it should be presented as the primary motive.

Cardinal Journet spoke on the absolute necessity of missionary work. Of Christ the scripture had said that there was no salvation in any other. Hence, though plurality of religions remained a fact, it was in law a very great aberration. Consequently missionary activity was not merely a counsel but an urgent obligation of the new law.

Bishop M. Legarra of Panama, speaking in the name of 77 Bishops or Vicars Apostolic, planters and tillers of the faith in missionary territory, said that among the merits of the text was the place it attributed to the missionary institutes which helped the prelatures on the spot. But they could come and go, and the prelate could find himself a general without an army. Stress should therefore be laid on the responsibility and solidarity of an institute towards the territory where it served. The concept of a prelature was no longer apt to the existing situation.

Bishop S. Mazzoldi of Uganda proposed what he regarded as an important addition to an otherwise very good schema. The work of the missionary would always be resisted as Christ had foretold. There were great areas where there was no freedom for the Gospel. The schema did not deal explicitly with this problem, and it should do so, asserting the full right and liberty of the Church to send her missionaries everywhere, and the duty of the universal Church to help the persecuted.

V. McCauley of Fort Portal, Uganda, observed that the Blessed Virgin Mary was proposed to all as their exemplar, to all except Missionaries. He listed the other schemata where this was done to laity, religious, clerics, priests; yet this schema had nothing to say about the Mother of the Church. It was very important that she should be put before Missionaries also as their model. The schema had only a word to say about the sacrament of Confirmation by which the baptized were more completely bound to the Church and made apostles. It was not enough.

Rudolf Koppmann, a Vicar Apostolic from Africa, regretted the silence of the schema about the presence of evil in the world and the reign of Satan, of which missionaries had first-hand experience. He intended considerately to submit some other minor amendments "in scriptis".

At the 146th (19th) General Congregation, Monday 11 October, Cardinal Ottaviani resumed the discussion. His main criticisms were that not all the biblical testimonies were accurately quoted, not all the doctrinal principles were correctly expressed, and there was no lack of obscure assertions.

Cardinal König was less severe. He liked both the material and the arrangement very much. But it should be more clearly stated that *in our days* almost all of us live together with unbelievers and therefore all of us have a duty to witness to our faith. It was right to search in non-Christian religions for what was *praeparatio evangelica*. There was no salvation except through Christ, but the grace of Christ had a dynamism that extended beyond the boundaries of the visible Church. Yet though one could be saved outside the visible Church, all in the Church had the duty of evangelizing.

M. Queginer, of the Paris Society for Foreign Missions, asked for a clear rejection of the opinion that Christ did not wish the salvation of everyone, but only of a little Church; also a statement of the necessity of increasing the number of men devoted to the missions, and of the importance of the image which the Church presented of herself. For historical reasons the College of Bishops had played very little part in the work of the missions, whereas the Holy See had done practically everything. There should be better coordination and cooperation with the episcopal order, but no excessive centralization.

A. Sapelak of Argentina, in the name of 22 Fathers, asked why missionary activity did not include those nations which are in danger of losing the faith through lack of pastors.

My coffee-break coincided with the interventions of Gonsalvez da Costa and J. Cordeiro of Pakistan.

M. McGrath of Panama said that just as the constitution *De Ecclesia*, after dealing with the Mystery of the Church, went on immediately to deal with the People of God, so here a similar order should be followed. The text did not distinguish the functions of the various members. It did not clearly state that missionary activity was the mission of the whole people of God. There were many references to bishops, but they were inadequate. The hierarchy was constitutive of the Church, even of local churches. It should be put at the beginning as the basis. Mention was made of the government of the universal Church by the College of Bishops under the Pope, but it was not given its proper place as the basis of missionary activity. All bishops have solidarity with the Pope, and all missionaries with them.

The Secretary General, Felici, intervened at this point to read a letter which the Pope had sent to Cardinal Tisserant, chairman of the Presidential Council. The Holy Father said he had been informed that some Fathers meant to raise the question of celibacy, whether it was to be retained or not.

He did not want to interfere with their liberty, but desired to notify them that he did not think it at all expedient to have a public discussion of such a matter which needed to be handled with such prudence. As far as it lay with him, not only was celibacy to be preserved but strengthened. If any Father had some observations to make, let him give them in writing to the President of the Council who would see that he, the Pope, got them and weighed them.

S. Lokuang of China (expelled, of course) said that the notion of "mission" would suffer if, as some proposed, the de-christianized countries, e.g. in S. America, were included.

N. Greise of Indonesia did not think that the schema's concept of missions was apt to inspire vocations.

Bishop J. Corboy of Zambia, in the name of 70 Bishops, said that what the schema said about the mission of the Church, in particular about the hierarchy with whom the faithful collaborate, did not square with the chapter in *De Ecclesia* on the People of God and its essential unity, nor with the decree "On the Apostolate of the Laity".

J. Attipetty of Verapoly, India, wanted explicit mention made of St Thomas, as the principal doctor of theology. He was worried by the danger of relativism.

The 147th General Congregation which took place on Tuesday 12 October, third anniversary of the first General Congregation, began with the reading of a letter to the Pope in reply to his letter on celibacy; it was approved with applause.

Discussion of missionary activity was then resumed.

Cardinal Rugambwa spoke of the lively faith which should animate all missionaries and be fostered in all those faithful who devote themselves to missionary activity. Among its fruits was a true judgement on the problems of this world.

Cardinal Suenens called attention to an odd omission in nn. 23-24 on missionary formation. It had nothing on apostolic formation properly so called, and yet the Pope had specially urged "institutio apostolica" throughout the course, and it was to be found in *De Institutione Sacerdotali*. A methodology was needed in this field. It had not yet been sufficiently thought out. The priest works with the laity as their leader and therefore must learn the art of animating, directing etc, and cooperation with other missionaries. Moreover, the need to press on urgently with the preaching of the gospel was not sufficiently stressed.

Cardinal Zungrana sought to combat the error that the new independent dioceses had no longer needed the aid of outside missionaries. The latter had made their mistakes like any other men, but had done and were still doing a great and necessary work. Very many Fathers would not be there but for them. They were and remained their chief aid in the evangelization of the world.

Bishop de Souza of India, having been called to the microphone, mercifully informed the Fathers that what he had meant to say had already been said better by many others and therefore he would submit his comments in writing. O si sic omnes!

Bishop Guffens, a Belgian Auxiliary, stressed the need for a great increase in the number of teachers on the missions; the Gospel could be preached even in the teaching of the humanities.

Bishop Victor Garaygordobil of Ecuador, while admitting that it would be well if missionaries gave themselves to the work for their whole life, commended nevertheless the modern practice whereby many, including not a few diocesan priests, volunteered for a period. He hoped that many dioceses would undertake particular missions, just as did the missionary institutes.

Bishop J. Sibomana of Rwanda commented at length on the section dealing with the authority of the Bishop. The doctrine on the Bishop should be an integral part of missionary spirituality; his function as centre of the dioceses should be inculcated into future missionaries. Their duty of obedience to their own religious superiors, of course, remained, but along with their obedience to the Bishop. All authority was from God and God was not divided. They should understand that the Bishop for whose service they were sent had authority as such in the ministry. The missionary should be grafted into the diocesan ministry, and the Bishop under whom they worked would be the common father, a true bond between the local clergy and those from elsewhere. The lack of any explicit mention of this integrating element of missionary spirituality should be remedied.

Absence at coffee caused me to miss the next two speakers, J. Martin and J. Gahamanyi. I returned to hear Bishop M. Ntuyahaga of Burundi expatiating on the missionary institutes. They were still needed, but in a new style, as collaborators rather than as directors. The African Churches were living in a new period, a period of transition from missions to new Churches *proprii iuris*. The Council should propose suitable norms for further elaboration by the Episcopal Conferences. The bishops wanted a certain stability in the cooperation of the missionary institutes.

Bishop J. Grotti of Brazil complained that the document did not make it clear how the lay missionaries mentioned were to be formed and trained; and that the little it had to say about secular institutes seemed rather offensive. Why were they to be "under the authority of the Conference"? That of the Bishop would suffice. And to say that they "could be useful"! A dog could be that. They deserved to have more and better things said about them than this. Lay cooperators could be distinguished into two classes, those in institutes and those not. But they were all missionaries, necessary and worthy of praise.

The next speaker was the prestigious General of the Jesuits, Father Arrupe. Effective cooperation in missionary work, he said, required exact knowledge of the condition of the missionary world, and especially of the following. First, the urgency of missionary labour. Two thousand million were living outside the Church and their condition was rapidly changing. Eighty years ago, for example, Japan was scarcely evolved, whereas now it was among the most highly evolved among the nations. There were 90 universities in Tokyo. Secondly the difficulty of the work in such a mixture of cultures and religions, ancient and modern. Missionaries must know and love the nations in which they work. When they returned to the west they found a lack of missionary spirit, especially among adults, but rather infantilism, sentimentalism, a sense of superiority often based on ignorance, a kind of blindness whereby what was nearest seemed greatest, and superficiality. E.g. There were some who after a brief visit made superficial and ignorant pronouncements which not only created false ideas and confusion, but caused harmful reactions in the missions. In conclusion, there was need for informative organs, greater estimation of foreign cultures, more preparation, more realization of our common responsibility.

Bishop Yupin, exiled Bishop of Nanking, observed that the term "mission" had originally meant "ad exteros", but that this was less apt today. The whole Church ought to be missionary, even to those who were "of the household of the faith". In regard to the missionary vocation, he said that signs which would suffice for the priesthood were not enough. The missionary needed to have love for the people to whom he was sent, and to familiarize himself with their language, history, art etc. Like Saint Paul, we must be all things to all men. The Chinese bishops wanted to see seminaries established for China, especially in areas fruitful in vocations, where future missionaries would be formed in Chinese culture and become Chinese so that they might evangelize the Chinese. Laymen already did much and could do more, if, e.g. professional men and technicians in missionary countries lived exemplary lives; some did, but others scandalised. Good laymen were not missionaries in the strict sense, but they were the light and the leaven.

(At this point the Secretary-General called all perambulating Fathers back to their seats: "Ad sedes redeant Patres". Evidently a vote was imminent).

Meanwhile, two more Fathers were able to get their word in. Bishop S. Soares of Mozambique called for a new section on social action. There was need of lay specialists to permeate the people. The statement that the "local church " was a cell of the universal Church was misleading; the Church was never "local", always "superlocal". He added a few more minor criticisms and concluded by suggesting the erection of a "Secretariate of Evangelization".

He was followed by a Korean Father, B. Kinam Ro, who appeared to sympathise with the accusation that the Church was out-of-date, e.g. her antiquated ceremonial. He suggested that this should be updated as soon as possible and that the regulation of details be left to the Conference of Bishops. It would also be a great help if Catholics in missionary areas were seen to be practising their religion. In the Korean war the US Catholic soldiers had given a fine example.

The Moderators now announced that in their view the schema on missionary activity had been discussed long enough, and asked the Fathers to vote, *per schedulas*, as to whether the schema satisfied them as a basis for elaboration and perfection according to the comments of the Fathers. The result, announced at the next General Congregation, was 2070 *placet*, 15 *non placet*.

Nevertheless, there remained a number of speakers who had secured the signatures of 70 supporters and therefore retained their right to speak. The first among them was Bishop Donal Lamont of Rhodesia. He and his supporters accepted the schema in substance, he said. It was not a mere sop to certain persons the Church. It dealt with the missionary activity of the whole Church. It was not an end, but a means whereby the resources of all the faithful were assembled. Missionaries did not want a mere schema or a treatise on missiology, but a solemn promise from all the Bishops to accept the burden which they had inherited from the Apostles. As to the content of the schema, more stress should be laid on the work of Brothers and Sisters in the schools, without which priests could do almost nothing. No race was incapable of evangelization, no race so cultured as not to need it. It was not enough for the Fathers to vote *placet* and leave it at that. As was said of old, "Deus vult". So today, all must arise and gird themselves to the task.

At the 148th (21st) General Congregation, Wednesday 13 October, the names of eleven more Fathers claiming their right to speak on the 70 supporters rule were read out. Not much new was contributed.

Omar Degryse, O.M.I, complained that only here and there did the schema touch on Ecumenism, and yet there was a very close connection between ecumenical and missionary activity. Mention should be made of the many ways in which missionaries could collaborate on the Missions so as to foster eventual unity.

L. Satoshi Nagae of Japan suggested that missionary activity was not sufficiently presented as necessary to the growth to maturity of local Churches. The Council should have an eye not only to the present but also to the future, and not limit its concern to the planting of the faith. The new Churches looked to the old for aid. Mutual interchange could be most useful.

J. Velasco, a missionary bishop exiled from China was critical of the whole theology of the schema. Its principles were vague and its theology new.

A. Pirovano had a useful point to make about missionary institutes. The schema admitted their importance and regarded them as necessary but made no provision for their survival. In the past, bishops had instituted them from their own diocesan clergy, e.g. the Paris Foreign Missionary Society. Canon law had recently detached them from their diocesan incardination, so that now they had no link with their diocese of origin. The new seminaries and colleges that had been set up differed only in being extraneous to any diocese and therefore lacking an apparatus for seeking vocations. The schema should state that dioceses which have missionary institutes should regard them as an ordinary means of providing secular missionaries, proper to them and not extraneous.

Bishop J. De Reaper, Mill Hill, Kenya, wondered why the schema should talk of material needs as though they were sordid. Missionaries were practical men, when they returned to their dioceses they would be asked what the Council had done to ensure better financial cooperation by the well established Churches. Missionaries were sent out by the universal Church and had the right to expect support. They were not mendicants, and yet had to spend much time begging from the rest of the Church. Even missionary bishops had to devote much of their time to writing to possible benefactors. Some other solution ought to be found, such as a proportionate annual donation from every diocese.

After a layman from Togoland had addressed the Fathers in French in the name of the Auditores, Father Schütte, General S.V.D., Relator of the relevant Commission, summed up on its behalf.

Archbishop Marty of Rheims, Relator of the augmented Commission *De Disciplina Cleri et Populi Christiani*, which, after the rejection of the meagre Propositions *De Sacerdotibus*, had with the aid of some coopted theologians (e.g. Lecuyer, Congar) produced an entirely new schema *De Ministerio et Vita Presbyterorum*, now presented it for discussion. (This was the Commission to which I belonged, but contributed very little).

Seven cardinals headed the list of those who wished to speak. The first was the Oriental-Rite Cardinal Méouchi. He liked the new document in the main. It contained spiritual riches. But it reflected the occidental mentality and was tainted by juridicism. Whereas it should make frequent reference to the Holy Spirit, it was more concerned with external organization. Why was the mission of priests restricted to Christians, whereas it should extend to all? It did not sufficiently indicate that presbyteral union are acquired by unity of ministry. In its analysis of vocation it failed to perceive the communitarian foundation; God's call was made through the community and for the community.

In Cardinal Ruffini's view also, the schema was in general deserving of praise, but with a view to perfecting it, he offered a series of textual criticisms, the validity of which could only be judged with the text before one's eyes. He wanted mention of frequent confession and spiritual direction as means to preserving chastity and rousing fervour.

For Cardinal Arriba y Castro of Tarragona it was a schema of primary importance. At the first session he had said that if the Council were not one of sanctity, it would be nothing. A better title might well be: *De Sanctitate Sacerdotali*. As for its doctrine, it said many things opportunely, but some were missing. The virtues which made a holy priest must be acquired in the seminary, or else, as a general rule, they would be acquired nowhere.

Cardinal Quiroga y Palacios of Compostella declared himself very pleased and offered his heartfelt thanks to the Commission. He would observe however that the obligation of holiness derived from the very nature of Holy Order, and that all the reasons advanced in support of this truth applied *a fortiori* to themselves, the bishops; they therefore should set the first example of sanctity. This might opportunely be added. The communion of bishops and priests in intimate fraternity was hierarchical and therefore the overdone insistence on the independence of priests from their bishops should be corrected.

The comments of Cardinal Léger of Montreal were restricted to the principal object of the second part of the schema, priestly sanctity. All priests needed a spirituality which harmonized with their state, and it was to be regretted that the schema only partly met this need. No. 12 did not show how exercise of the priestly ministry provided a stimulus to sanctity. No. 14 proposed evangelical counsels as they were observed in the religious life. He proposed therefore that from the beginning of Part II, priestly sanctity should be presented as union with Christ through exercise of the ministry; it should not begin from the dangers to be avoided, but show how union with the good Shepherd and relations with men can be means to holiness. The virtues proper to priests should be described; they were those of the Good Shepherd, viz, zeal, pastoral solicitude, magnanimity, evangelical concern, respect towards all, especially the poor, disposability. The schema rightly dealt with obedience, poverty and chastity, but not as if they were religious vows. Obedience was a duty of state. Poverty was required because they preached to the poor. Even prayer and devotion to the Blessed Sacrament should be presented as part of the ministry of a preacher of the gospel.

For Cardinal Richaud of Bordeaux on the other hand, the schema was well adapted to sustain the ideal etc. of priests. He feared however that priests might be disappointed if they did not find that intimate notion which moved their heart. Christ was always moved by love of His Father.

The schema as a whole was also "very pleasing" to Cardinal Colombo of Milan, though it could be perfected. The section on the ministry would be more fruitful if it were more clearly linked to the mystery of the Church, the *prima mediatrix* according to the will of Christ; and it should be made clearer that the ministry was derived not merely from canonical mission but from its sacramental connection with the mission of the bishops. Also more emphasis should be put on the ministry of the sacrament of Penance. It was the priest's job to move his flock to frequent Confession. By that sacrament the Christian was united to the actions of Christ and so entered into his paschal mystery. It was not a mere means of remitting sin.

Archbishop Henriquez of Venezuela found the theology of No. 1 somewhat jejune. All things were to be summed up in Christ whose sacrifice had a cosmic dimension. Priests were consecrated to make that sacrifice present. It was through the sacrifice of Christ that they were truly configured with him, and priestly holiness consisted in this configuration. It was true that they participated in the mission of their bishop, but that meant little to a solitary priest in a cut-off place. In the difficulties of life, the priest could best find joy in Christ Priest and Victim, with whom he was himself conjoined as a victim.

Bishop Santini of Italy thought the schema praiseworthy, and that it should help towards a holy life. It should however stress how greatly the renewal of the Church depended on priests who live in the midst of the people in such a way that all may see Christ in them. There was no lack of preaching. What was lacking was the enlightening Spirit flowing from meditation on the word of God. As to the non-churchgoers, the remedy lay in personal contact, meeting them and talking to them, imitating in that the example of Christ. Parish priests should live with their curates; mere economics nowadays demanded it. The example of priests was the chief means to vocations.

Bishop Yubani of Spain found the passage dealing with associations of priests not very practical. It was a matter of great moment which needed developing. It should be the object of any association to foster that spirituality which as founded on the ministry which priests were called to exercise in cooperation with their bishop. Faithful conjunction and cooperation with the bishop greatly conduced to holiness. Priests' associations were a better aid to sanctity in so far as they promoted cooperation with other priests of the diocese and with the bishop.

(Note. Outside the Council, I had worked all the week on a report produced by the Pontifical Commission set up to examine the birth control question, in order to give my opinion on it to our hierarchy, only to learn from Cardinal Heenan (who had given me the job and obtained a copy of the document from Cardinal Cicognani) that the Pope had scrapped it as unworthy. That, incidentally, was my opinion of it. However, I still had to prepare a statement on the contraception issue for a hierarchy meeting).

At the beginning of the 150th General Congregation Friday 15 October, the Secretary General Felici announced some radical changes in the remaining programme of the Session, presumably because most of the remaining work would have to be done in Commission, and there would be less need of General Congregations except for voting. We were therefore to meet on the morrow, despite its being a Saturday, but there would be no General Congregations in the following week, October 18-23. They would be resumed on Monday 25 October to complete the discussions and get really busy on voting amendments, but there would be a further vacation from 30 October to 8 November — "feriae mortuorum, seu aestas Sancti Martini".

Cardinal Döpfner then rose to speak on behalf of 65 German and Scandinavian Fathers. He admitted that great progress had been made in the revised schema, and that its notion of the priest was acceptable not only from the cultic point of view, but in relation to the threefold function of Christ and the path to sanctity. It was a basis for a better document, but it still had grave defects. Its style smacked too much of spiritual reading, whereas it should be more sober and theological. In its doctrinal parts it repeated what was already in the Constitution on the Church. In the second part, it had nothing on the personal life of the priest, or of his relation to temporal property, and he did not like what it said about the evangelical counsels. As to modern problems, he continued, the priests of today lived in a kind of diaspora and suffered more from solitude than formerly. The pastoral situation was utterly changed, so that many old priests no longer felt equal to it. They had much new knowledge to acquire and not infrequently were troubled by doubts of faith. The schema did not meet personal problems of that kind. It had nothing on "pastoralization" of the pastors.

The complaint of Cardinal Tatsuo Doi of Japan was that the new form, though a great improvement on the old, neglected the missionary countries and devoted its attention almost exclusively to priests working in Christian countries.

Cardinal Alfrink, after a word of praise, said he would concentrate on what was missing from the schema. It envisaged the priest in the sacristy and had little applicable to the priest working among the lapsed, among non-Catholics or among unbelievers; yet that was a daily duty nowadays. It had almost nothing on the the priest's mission to throw the light of faith on terrestrial things, merely urging him to keep out of politics. It could be interpreted to mean that the Gospel is an external superstructure. It had almost nothing on communion with the Father through Christ. It seemed to regard activity rather as a danger, whereas the Constitution *De Ecclesia* taught that it was by activity a priest grew in love of God. It failed to mention the need to study various other documents of Vatican II in which there was much that related to the life and ministry of priests. Finally it had nothing on the problems and anxieties of modern priests, but implied that "all was clear and serene".

Cardinal Landazzuri was somewhat more complimentary; not only did he declare his general agreement, like nearly all speakers, but he expressed special joy at what the schema had to say about the spiritual life of the priest. However, while admitting the need to insist on the preaching of the word, he asked that the primacy of the priest's sacrificial function be made clear. (Note. Several criticisms on this point reached our Commission. An attempt, was made to explain that in calling preaching the priest's "primary" function, the reference was to order of time; preaching was the means by which the eucharistic community was brought into being. The word "praecipuum" — "principal" was used to denote his sacrificial function).

Cardinal Suenens began with the familiar opening. The schema was far superior to its predecessors, but did not yet fully meet the need. The doctrine was sound, but often as-it-were intemporal. The priesthood had its own intimate and permanent exigences, but also its existential exigences derived from the concrete modern situation. The characteristic feature of these latter is that many priests always experience difficulty in finding their place in the world and in the Church. In the world they feel alien. They seek dialogue, but modern men do not acknowledge priests. Difficulties arise even from their place in the Church, twixt bishops and layfolk. The schema had provided the principles which supply solutions, but not together. He added three brief criticisms. If the Holy Sacrifice was central to their lives, why was it presented as a mere support. Why was there so little about the Holy Spirit. Why in speaking of the Blessed Virgin Mary was the specific place of Mary in the life of the priest not shown. Moreover, the priest's obedience could not be interpreted as passive submission. He was the animator of the lay apostolate. Cardinal Jägger of Paderborn was mainly complimentary. Never before in a Council had there been a comprehensive decree of this kind. It provided a solid foundation. He proposed however that the points made in *De Ecclesia* about the Holy Spirit should be inserted here. It was the Holy Spirit that made the priest a sharer in the priesthood of Christ.

Cardinal Herrera of Malaga, Spain, was very pleased with the schema. It was apt to our time and practical. What it said about preaching was excellent; the first duty of the priest, along with the bishop, was to preach the word of God. But practical training was often deficient. Deacons should live with priests during their pre-ordination year and preach on Sundays.

Bishop Miranda said it chimed very opportunely with the spirit of Vatican II.

Bishop Franic of Split, Jugoslavia, who had called for poverty in bishops when they were being discussed, was very pleased with what this schema had to say about priests and poverty, but proposed that a promise of poverty should be included in the ordination to the diaconate, and that commendation should be given to community of goods and especially to bishops who lived with their clergy in such community.

Bishop D'Avack of Italy stressed the need to avoid any sharp division between the private prayer and spiritual life of the priest and liturgical worship. Each demanded the other. The private prayer of the priest needed to be offered through Christ in the Mass, and the liturgy was empty without individual spiritual life.

Bishop Nabaa of the Lebanon told the Council about the actual poverty of his priests, some of whom were poorer than the proletariate. A solution must be found and the schema should lay down rules as to who must pay and how much. He was not asking for an income that would provide bourgeois comfort, but merely what was necessary to honest maintenance, with equality for all.

Bishop A. Charue of Namur wanted more stress on the objective sanctity that should follow ordination, and on the covenant of love which Christ wanted to enter into with his priests: "Iam non dicam vos servos". The conclusion should be clearly drawn that priests have cause for joy. More stress should also be laid on the notion and exercise of authentic charity, in both its universalist and communitarian sense.

Bishop S. Brzana, an American Auxiliary, wanted more said about humility, the essential foundation of all virtues, and about the duty of priests to help their fallen brethren.

Bishop Renard of Versailles commented, mainly with appreciation, on what the schema had to say about the relation of priests to their bishop.

Bishop Mancini spoke of the importance of encouraging a higher sense of responsibility among priests; they must not be made or become inert instruments of the bishop.

Bishop A. Tome of Argentina was "vehemently delighted" by the schema, but suggested that penetration of the modern world might require new forms of apostolate, and that it might be well for priests to earn their living like St Paul.

The 151st (24th) General Congregation of Saturday 16 October brought another batch of diocesan Cardinals who apparently felt that this was a topic on which they ought not to remain silent.

Cardinal Lefebvre of Bourges assented in general to the text, but grieved that it made no mention of spiritual paternity. "In the building up of the body of Christ": this above all was the proper function of the priest, to incorporate mankind in Christ. In this fatherhood he reached his summit. What was the ministry of the word for, if not for this. What was the fruit of the Mass and sacraments, if not to unite men to Christ. What was the ministry of governing (regendi) designed for, if not to help men to be formed in the likeness of Christ. It was to this fatherhood that the whole ministry was directed. "I am in labour until Christ be formed in you" (St Paul). It was for this end that priests refrained from marriage.

Cardinal Rugambwa wanted a clearer exposition of what the priest was and of how he stood in relation to the priesthood of Christ and of the bishops; also of his missionary duty, and of the new methods needed to adapt his ministry to our time. His formation should continue without a break after his ordination, lest he become a man of the past.

Cardinal Roy of Quebec agreed with Cardinals Colombo, Léger, Suenens and Döpfner that a still deeper theology of the priesthood was needed. The schema spoke well about the brotherhood of priests in their diocese, but not at sufficient length. It was not silent about the need for cooperation, but spoke as though cooperation between neighbours was sufficient. It was not sufficient in the wider communities of today. A parish could no longer be regarded as a "parva civitas". Other groups on every side exceeded the limits of the parish. Hence there was need of a new arrangement of the whole diocese, with priests who were not attached to parishes. The law had not yet recognized such priests and they themselves felt as though they had no proper place of their own. Their function needed to be clearly acknowledged.

Cardinal Florit of Florence began with more than a word of praise, and then turned his attention to the modern problems of priests, especially the crisis of authority and the difficulty of finding new ways of inserting the priest in the modern world. It was necessary to lay down valid principles which had generic value everywhere. No. 3 failed to make a firm declaration of the union of the priest with the sacrifice of Christ. There was the same lacuna in n. 13, where the value of the Cross for union with Christ was not sufficiently brought out. Christ immolated himself in order that they might be immolated with him. It would also be opportune to make some concrete ruling which would favour the spirit of poverty, e.g. to include a promise of poverty in the rite of ordination. It was a matter of grave obligation for all priests, not because of the presence of poor people in their parishes, but because of the objective value of evangelical poverty by reason of the mystery of the sacrifice.

The problem, according to Cardinal Heenan of Westminster, was so to frame the principles that they might be able to provide useful advice. The pastoral art differed from country to country, but what was common to all ought to be enunciated. Although this was the age of the lay apostolate, it never succeeded without the leadership of zealous priests, acting not just as brother among brothers, but as fathers and leaders. For that, spiritual formation was necessary. He quoted the rule of the Legion of Mary in regard to the spiritual Director. It was not enough to say that priests "should know themselves to have obligations towards brethren who had fallen away". The obligations should be spelled out. Was it not the duty of a priest to warn the bishop or V.G: "Principiis obsta". Too many priests do not want to be regarded as "delators". "Hinc illae lacrimae". The schema did well to commend hospitality among priests and common recreation. They should find their closest friends among their fellow priests. As to the call to the Missions, priests are ready enough to go out and help where it is necessary; but it is reported that in some needy regions there are monks who will not lend a hand, and other Priests spend all their time teaching profane studies to select pupils. If these reports are true, etc...

Cardinal Sheehan of Baltimore had two reservations to add to his general commendation of the schema. Its pastoral scope was laudable, but it did not have a balanced view of the plenitude of the ministry. As a mediator between God and man, the priest had a twofold relationship, to God and to man. His dynamic relation to God was treated only in passing. A priest was consecrated for preaching, divine worship and service of the Church. A more theocentric note was desirable. Too much stress on service of the People of God smacked of the heresy of activity. Secondly, it lacked clarity in regard to the union of priests with their bishop. The docrine of the common priesthood of priests and bishop, found in *De Ecclesia*, should be accurately reproduced in the schema. Every kind of false episcopalism was to be avoided. Both shared the one priesthood of Christ. Priests are subordinated precisely because they shared it less fully.

Cardinal Rossi, speaking in the name of 46 Brazilian bishops deprecated the tone of the schema. It was too exhortatory and consolatory, as though the whole life of the priest was a tribulation and a danger; there should be more about the joys. Moreover, in dealing with the priest's spiritual life, it lacked a unifying principle; priests were called to holiness because of the proximity of their connection with Christ and the Church. Furthermore, it needed to be completed from the Constitution on the Liturgy; active participation was even more obligatory for priests than for layfolk.

Cardinal Bea began by telling the Fathers that they should be very grateful to the Commission. Their priests would be grateful for such a document, the first of its kind in the history of the Church. He would make only one point, and that about the way it dealt with celibacy. What it said in n. 14 about the motives was excellent. Celibacy was rightly said not to be demanded by the nature of the priesthood, but the basis of the surrender of marriage was inherent in it. What therefore was to be said about married priests? Unless he was mistaken, the Council ought to deal with both kinds, and show how priests of either state should be formed, etc. In that way, it would be useful to their oriental brethren. For the rest, there were some faults in the ordering of the material and the style and latinity were defective in many cases.

Bishop J. Klooster of Surabaya, Indonesia, proposed the addition of a clause to the effect that even the evangelical counsels had a foundation in modern psychology. The schema could also well be co-ordinated with others in the same field so as to avoid repetitions and add vigour to the text.

Bishop J. Bank of Hungary's speech was read for him by another Father. On the subject of the ministry of preaching, he said, the schema was quite insufficient. Preaching was in disrepute. New methods must be found. Bishops should require that all the doctrines of the faith should be presented in an adult way, e.g. every three years. As to marriage cases, it was advisable that those whose marriages were invalid only by defect of form should be sanated by the Pope after five years. There should be serious preparation for marriage, annually in every parish. Sponsalia should be obligatory, just as in Religion temporary vows preceded permanent. And the impediment of error should be redefined so that those who have been deceived into marrying could be freed.

After the next two speeches, which I missed through being out for coffee, the Moderators called upon the Fathers to vote "per schedulas" whether they were now satisfied with the schema as a basis for elaboration according to their comments. (The result, announced later, was 1507 yes, to 12 No.)

While the votes were being collected and counted, the discussion was resumed.

Bishop Fernandez Condé said that he approved "totis viribus" the proposed setting up of a "coetus" of priests to advise the bishop, but it would be better called the "senatus et consilium Episcopi", as the chapter of

Canons was. There was need for a complete reorganization of the bishop's advisory body.

Bishop S. Barela, speaking in the name of the bishops of Poland, drew attention to what he called a dangerous omission. The text did admittedly mention that priests were "conjoined with Christ the Priest", but marginally. Was not the priest ordained to offer sacrifice with Christ, and was not the reason of this that he was not merely a minister but also in some sense the victim, who accepted the Cross which God laid upon him? The omission of this doctrine was dangerous, because it could be taken in a modernistic sense. Mention should also be made of the necessity of union with Mary, Mother of the Body of Christ. The schema made only two brief references to her. All priests needed her help in order to grow in virtue, for she was the Mediatrix of all graces. She was not only the mother of the Great High Priest, but spiritual mother of all priests: "Ecce, Mater tua!" She was the source of the unity of the family. Finally it had only three words about the Pope, whereas it should stress the need of love for him, shepherd of all the faithful, hence of all priests, not merely through the bishop, but immediately.

Bishop S. Soares of Beira wanted something deeper and new. The expressions used almost throughout the schema did not show forth the real dignity of the Priesthood. Its nature was known through its relation to Christ. The dignity of the priest, like the dignity of the bishop, derived from his share in the priesthood of Christ. This participation ought therefore to be expressly stated. The priest was more united to the priesthood of Christ ontologically than any other except the bishop. Secondly, it should be made clear that a priest existed not for himself but for the community. Moreover, it should be explicitly stated that the decree applied to all priests, religious as well as secular, for the society of priests is one; a religious priest was first a priest of the Church.

The final speech of the morning which, but for the 70 supporters rule, would have been the final speech of the Council proper, was given by Bishop N. Ndongmo who called for a clearer statement of the truth that the priesthood was constituted by relation to the priesthood of Christ the Head.

Archbishop Marty then summed up on behalf of the responsible Commission.

(On emerging from the General Congregation I was picked up by J. Brewer and taken along with Tom Worden to Enzo's house at Albano to witness and celebrate the final stage in the making of the wine for the English College. When the filtering was completed, we went upstairs to sample the new wine at a typically huge meal of Enzo's. The previous Saturday, 9 October, I had witnessed the end of Enzo's grape harvest, which was followed by a huge repast on the roof of his vineyard-house).

There were no General Congregations during the week 18-23 October. I spent most of the week composing a report on the Birth Control controversy and also on the *Positio de Sacrarum Indulgentiarum Recognitione* which had been prepared by an extra-Conciliar Pontifical Commission and on which the Pope wanted the opinion of the hierarchies (Cardinal Heenan had leant me his copy for the purpose). On the Friday, 22 October, I read my paper on Birth Control to the hierarchy in the College library. I completed my summary of the *Positio* at 7 p.m. on the Sunday, 24 October.

At the 152nd (25th) General Congregation, Monday 25 October, the names of 14 Fathers who claimed right to speak on the schema concerning Priests, in virtue of having 70 or more supporters, was read out. The first, Bishop Roman Arrieta of Costa Rica raised the question of proper distribution of priests. Delay in solving this problem, he said, would affect the salvation of hundreds of thousands. The inequality was very great. In some regions there was a superabundance of pastors, in others the sheep were abandoned to the wolves. The shortage in certain areas was not due to the local hierarchy, but to the expulsion of hierarchies in the last century, which created a vicious circle: true Christian life was not implanted because of lack of priests and there was a lack of priests because of lack of true Christian life. There were many good priests ready to go where they were most needed, but often they were not allowed to go because their bishops thought they were short of priests, having only 1 for 500, whereas elsewhere the figure was 1 for 25,000. There was need of rules for volunteers. Where priests were abundant, a new kind of seminary, directly dependent on the Holy See, should be erected to train them for work in the needy areas. Dioceses which had to turn down good vocations because of lack of room should send them elsewhere. So too where there was not enough work to keep the local clergy busy. Bishop E. de Roo of Canada, speaking in the name of 133 bishops of various nations, said that the ministerial priesthood was definable only in the context of the priesthood of the whole Church, and that was *sui generis*, being not only cultic, but also missionary and dynamic. The salvation of the whole people of the pilgrim Church was founded on the mystery of Christ, Shepherd and head of the flock which he was leading to the Father. Seen in this light the priest was primarily one that was "sent", i.e. "apostolus", to lead the people to the Father. In that way his various functions were united. It was for the shepherd to go ahead of the flock as its head and leader. The schema would be better co-ordinated if it were based on this concept of participation in the mission of Christ the Shepherd.

For Bishop E. Charbonneau the text lacked lucidity and theological depth. It did not allow enough scope for personal initiative. Priestly obedience could not be conceived or expressed outside its ecclesiastical and existential context. It was primarily directed to the good of the Church. and was not to be confused with religious obedience. The priest was a head to lead the people, not a mere executive. He received an authentic grace, participation in the episcopal charism. It followed that priestly obedience did not consist merely in submission, but in the active communion of the bishop and *presbyterium*. This involved both a descending and an ascending movement. It was the bishop's job to provide his priests with all the elements necessary to their pastoral life, one of which was responsibility. The priest was not a mere executor of episcopal decisions. He should share the bishop's pastoral function, even if in second place. Always enjoying a real independence in relation to his bishop, he should be a creator and father. His necessary subordination to the bishop did not in any way prevent him from acting responsibly. This point of obedience needed clarifying in the schema.

Bishop Flores of Spain enlarged on the theme that all priesthood flowed from that of Christ.

Bishop G. Segedi of Jugoslavia was much more down to earth. The only contact that many Christians had with the Church was at funerals; a clause should be added covering this point. He also spoke on the priest and the sick. I missed the next two speakers, Connelly and Garcia, through slipping down to one of the bars for coffee. And the Congregation ended early at 11.50.

At the 153rd (26th) General Congregation, on Tuesday 26 October, the first speaker was Bishop Foley of Lancaster. He began with a word about clerical dress. It could differ, but it seemed necessary that in every region a distinctive dress should be strictly prescribed. As to the ministry of priests, though the schema said many fine things, it was incomplete in one grave respect. It had only a very few generalities about the apostolate. It was a pity that the schema prepared *De Cura Animarum* had been dropped. He proposed therefore that it be clearly indicated that an outstanding part of the priest's ministry was the apostolate by personal contact. Secondly, that some of the outstanding scriptural texts illustrating care of souls be inserted, and also quotations from the classical works on the priestly apostolate, such as St Gregory's *Regula Pastoralis*, St Charles Borromeo, Trent, St Alphonsus Liguori. He instanced St Charles' decree on pastoral visitation, which declared that "the house to house visit of the priest is a necessary practice". Finally he urged that if there was not room for all this in the decree under discussion, a declaration on the subject be issued to the clergy.

Bishop A. Fares of Italy regretted the silence of the schema on the priest as administrator of the sacrament of Penance. He needed to be trained as teacher, physician and judge. The necessity of spiritual direction, and for the priest himself, ought to be indicated, along with daily examination of conscience, sacramental confession every week or fortnight, monthly day of recollection, and a retreat every year or at least every third year.

E. Pechuan of Argentina spoke about the place of Mary in the life of the priest, as mother of the great High Priest and of every priest. Every priest was anointed in her womb, for without her we should have had neither Redeemer nor priesthood. Now that she had been acclaimed "Mother of the Church", *a fortiori* she should be declared to be Mother of Priests, and specifically so named in this Decree.

Bishop E. Compagnone of Anagni thought that the section on the special call of priests to sanctity lacked precision, depth and unity. It was introduced almost as an extra, whereas it was of the nature of the priesthood, based on the fact that Christ bestowed his Holy Spirit on all priests. It was supremely important that priests should pursue sanctity as sharers of the priesthood of Christ. It should be regarded as normal.

I was out at coffee when Bishop Pellegrino spoke on the promotion of studies among priests. It was the last speech on a Council schema, properly so called, after it, Felici made some announcements and the Congregation was concluded.

* * *

When we reached the English College, Derek Worlock was free to inform us at 12 noon that he had been appointed Bishop of Portsmouth, and did so. We preceded immediately to drink his health in the mezzanine flat which he shared with Alan Clark, Father W. O'Brien and me. In the afternoon I had a Commission meeting, my first on the revised text; and once we had broken up into small sub-committees to deal with all the amendments (modi) proposed by the Fathers in the debate just concluded, we really made progress. In the evening, at 7.45, I went to dinner at the house of Mr Cape, assistant to the British minister to the Holy See. Bishop Holland was also invited and we went together. My place at table was next to Princess Aurietta Doria-Pamphili. I was puzzled as to why I had been invited and never really solved the problem. Perhaps it was Mr Cape's idea to confront me with Bishop Simons who had made a sensational speech about contraception and abortion. (We never clashed).

* * *

A General Congregation, the 154th (27th), was held on the following day, 27 October, to proceed with the voting on amendments, etc. Though we were to be treated at the beginning to an address from a parish priest, Thomas Falls of Philadelphia, even Felici could not promise a lively morning. He warned us that there would have to be intervals between the votes, in which nothing was happening. "In silentio et in spe", he joked, "'erit fortitudo nostra". He added that we would just have to get used to it, because the fruit had to be harvested and it was to be hoped that it would be abundant. His own silence was not complete.

In one interval, he said: "I have read in some newspapers and books, i.e. especially those published after a session, a bit of a yarn (narratiuncula) about the Secretary General (i.e. himself). It said that before the public session of 21 November 1964, the Secretary General warned the Fathers not to give a *non placet* vote, because the world would be watching. I never said any such thing. I warned the Fathers against giving an invalid vote, because the world would be watching." (Note: At a public session, the time for amendments was over. Every voter had to vote *placet* or *non placet*; hence a vote *placet iuxta modum* would be null and void).

When the Council reassembled two days later for the 155th (28th) General Congregation (29 October), it was announced that the chief work of the morning was to be seven votes on the schema *De Revelatione* (the revised form of the *De Fontibus Revelationis* which had been rejected in the first session), six votes on the single chapters and one on the text as a whole. The Secretary General also read out a detailed programme for the month of November which comforted us with the information that there would be no more General Congregations until November 9, and they would thenceforth begin at 9.30, instead of 9 a.m., "ob diminutionem laborum", most of the remaining work being that of the Commissions. There would also probably be a break from the 22nd or 23rd November to the end of the month. Nevertheless, some of the Fathers were troubled by the lack of speakers at these Congregations, and so the Pope had arranged that two reports which he had asked all the Episcopal Conferences to deliver to him should be read in the "aula" of the Council.

Accordingly, from the 9th of November after Cardinal Cento had introduced the Position paper which had been prepared by a special Commission on the Revision of Indulgences, the Presidents of the Episcopal Conferences would read their respective reports.

* * *

(On the following day, Saturday, 30 October, all the bishops resident at the English College had departed, except Beck, Restieaux and Grasar; and Beck was due to leave on the Tuesday following. I spent the weekend writing letters, and on the Tuesday, 2nd November, Restieaux and Grasar took me out to Palazzola in Dwyer's car; we had lunch at Nemi. On 4th November, the three of us drove out to Lake Bracciano in perfect autumn weather, had a look at the castle and church, lunched at a lakeside restaurant, drove round to Vicarello, had a forty minute walk, and returned to home by Trevignano. Most of our bishops returned to the College from England and elsewhere on Monday 8 November).

* * *

At the 156th General Congregation, Tuesday 9 November, the *Positio de Sacrarum Indulgentiarum Recognitione*, along with the official *relatio*, was distributed to us all as had been promised. Felici was at pains however to emphasize that, though the Holy Father had granted permission "ut sermo fiat de ea in Aula", it was not a Council document. When the voting on Council Documents had been set in motion therefore, Cardinal Cento read his official *relatio* on the *Positio de Sacrarum Indulgentiarum Recognitione*, and Sessolo read one on behalf of the *S. Cong. S. Paenitentiae*, section *De indulgentiis*. Then Felici read a letter from Pope Paul to Cardinal Tisserant congratulating him (chairman of the Presidential Board) on the approaching conclusion of the Council, and decreeing that, after a solemn public session at which the remaining documents would be promulgated, the Council should be solemnly concluded on the feast of the Immaculate Conception, 8 December, the date on which Vatican I had been solemnly inaugurated. The rest of the Congregation was occupied in taking votes and announcing the results.

The 157th (30th) General Congregation, Wednesday10 November, began with vote on the Apostolate of the Laity decree taken as a whole, which was to be followed by voting on Missionary Activity. Meanwhile the Fathers were to hear the reports of Presidents of Episcopal Conferences on the *Positio de Indulgentiis*. The latter were reminded beforehand by Felici that, in their reports, they were to expound solely the mind of the Conference which they represented. It was not a Council document, nor therefore a discussion. After reading their report, they were to hand in their script to the Secretariate. Any President who did not intend to speak should hand in his script directly.

Maximos IV Saigh, the aged Melchite Patriarch of Antioch opened the bowling with considerable vigour. The Orient, he said, did not know indulgences. They had been introduced into the West on premisses which did not justify the conclusions drawn from them. The Early Church had not meant to interfere with God's justice when it suspended or absolved from canonical penances. It was a practice which tended to substitute for penitential satisfaction. If the Church would not suppress indulgences purely and simply, his Conference asked it to make them more acceptable by suppressing all "days and years", as proposed in the *Positio*, suppressing from partial indulgences all mathematical proportion between merit and satisfaction, were suppressing all idea of total acquittal introducing a theology in which emphasis was laid on the satisfaction made for the faithful by the merits of Christ. Thus the Church would avoid doctrinal differences with the Reformers and disciplinary differences with the Orthodox.

The Maronite Patriarch Paul Méouchi of Lebanon said he would simply hand in his script containing the observations of the Maronites directly to the Secretariate.

The Patriarch Stephanos I Sidarous of Cairo, head of the Coptic Patriarchate of Alexandria, admitted that in Egypt indulgences were a great obstacle to reunion. Nevertheless, he added, their faithful both believed and practised the doctrine of indulgences. The schema of the *Positio* was therefore to be accepted. Their Synod had unanimously approved it.

Cardinal Cerejeira, for the Bishops of Portugal, said that they approved the schema in general, because it manifested a desire for renewal and purification. It could perhaps be improved, but he would hand in his other comments to the Secretariate.

Cardinal Gilroy, for the Australian Conference, simply read out their voting figures on the various chapters of the *Positio*.

Cardinal Sheehan of Baltimore did the same for the U.S.A. Conference. He would hand in the amendments proposed by those bishops who had voted *iuxta modum*. In general, he said, they liked the proposed norms, but very many had openly said that they did not think it opportune to deal at this time with indulgences.

At the 158th (31st) General Congregation, Thursday 11 November, while the first batch of votes was being collected, Felici raised a point of correct terminology. The labours and decrees of the Council would be recalled by future historians and if they followed the precedent of Trent and Vatican I, they would refer to "Sessions". It was therefore worthwhile to determine here and now what were "Congregations" and how many there had been, and what were "Sessions" and how many. The Fathers already knew the answer to the first question, but there was confusion about the second. The word "Session" had been used to denote a period of the Council, and his Secretariate had proposed that it be given this meaning, but the Latinists had objected. So they had used it to denote "series of Congregations", but this conflicted to some extent with the *Ordo* which had given it a juridical sense. However, the four improperly called "Sessions" of the Council would disappear in history. They would become one, i.e. 1962-1965, because, in the intervals when the Fathers were away, the work of the Council had continued in its Commissions, so that the whole period was "conciliar". The "Sessions" properly so called were those Congregations of the Fathers in which the Acts of the Council were done publicly, whether to open or close the Council, or to make public professions of faith, or to decree the promulgation of documents already approved in General Congregation. So far, therefore, there had been seven "Sessions", properly so called:

1) 11 October 1962, Inauguration of the Council by Pope John XXIII; there had been no closure; the 7 December was the 37th General Congregation, at the end of which Pope John came in and addressed some paternal words; 8 December 1962 was a *Capella Papalis*, not a conciliar act.

2) 29 September 1963, the new Pope and Fathers made their profession of Faith.

3) 4 December 1963, promulgation of *Liturgy* and of *Means of Social Communication*.

4) 24 September 1964, profession of Faith of the new Fathers;

5) 21 November 1964, promulgation of *De Ecclesia, De Ecclesiis Orientalibus*, and *De Ecumenismo*.

6) 24 September 1965, profession of Faith of new Fathers.

7) 28 October 1965, promulgation of *De Pastorali Episcoporum Munere*, etc.

(Subsequently the 8th would occur on 18 November, the 9th on 7 December, and the 10th on 8 December 1965 bringing the total number of "Sessions" to ten).

Cardinal Wyszynski then reported the opinion of the Polish Hierarchy on the *Positio de Indulgentiis*. Reform of indulgences was, he said, desired by all and ought not to be deferred. It should harmonize with the rest of the conciliar documents. The *Positio* was to their liking "iuxta modum". They would like an even greater reduction and simplification. They liked the new rule about partial indulgences.

Cardinal Alfrink, for the Hierarchy of Holland, said he would be very brief. There was a fundamental discrepancy between the practice hitherto and the modern theology. The suggested revision was a step forward in so far as it got rid of some exaggerations, etc., but it did not get rid of the discrepancy. The *reatus poenae* was considered as a merely vindictive penalty which was taken away by Indulgences and was therefore connected with a juridical act. The Dutch Bishops wanted the *Positio* brought into line with modern theology.

Cardinal Arriba y Castro for the Spanish Episcopal Conference agreed that there was urgent need of reform and thought that the *Positio* was on the right lines. A new chapter was needed defining how bishops could grant indulgences. All indulgences should be applicable to the dead. There should be a single and universally applicable definition of a plenary.

Cardinal Urbani of Venice, for the Italian Episcopal Conference, expressed their general agreement, but he asked that the Catholic doctrine should be recalled in a preface and an explanation given that indulgences were applied to the dead *per modum suffragii*. It should be expressly stated that effective separation from sin was a necessary previous condition.

Cardinal König, for Germany and Austria, welcomed the move towards revision of the doctrine and practice, but held that it had not gone far enough. Certain points were oversimplified, with hardly any attention to modern thought. Scripture was sometimes misinterpreted. Questions disputed among theologians were presented as not disputed. Hardly any attention was paid to the transition, around the 13th century, from a visible to an invisible penal system. So much for general comment; detailed comments would be submitted in writing. For historical as well as ecumenical reasons the document still needed to be improved.

Cardinal Döpfner, speaking in the name of the Bishops of Germany, said he agreed with all the comments of Cardinal König who spoke for Austria and Germany. As to the object of indulgences, due attention ought to be paid to the transition in the 13th century from a visible ecclesiastical penalty to the invisible temporal punishment incurred *coram Deo*. This transition had consequences in regard to the measure of the remission granted by the Church which were scarcely applicable on the invisible plane. If it was impossible to measure the remission granted in the sacrament of Penance, how could this be done outside it. The temporal punishment entailed a penalty to be paid not only after death but also here in life, e.g. in the inclination to sin which remained. The difficulty was even greater if the link with the charity owed to God were taken into account, for the penalty could not be extinguished without acquisition of the grace necessary to charity. In a word, the measure of the penalty corresponded to the defect of charity. As to the nature of the Church's action, the concept of the "treasury of the Church" had a somewhat material or even commercial ring about it. In truth, it represented God Himself accepting man's efforts in view of the merits of Christ. Viewed intrinsically, it was not properly an exercise of jurisdiction, much less was it a mere act of intercession; it was essentially an interposition of herself by the Church. Hence its efficacy *ex opere operato* in removing the *reatus poenae*; but the effect was subject to limitation by the degree of man's cooperation. Nor was the difficulty avoided by the distinction made between *absolutio* and *solutio* (payment). It was not a disbursement of part of the treasury, but an appeal to the whole. It should not therefore be promulgated in its present form. The Commission should be notably increased to include theologians from every school. Etc.

The 159th (32nd) General Congregation of Friday 12 November was completely devoted to voting. Felici made two announcements of some interest, though for very different reasons.

The Pope had granted that, after December 8th, Cardinals could leave Rome without first seeking his leave, and, added the Secretary General, this certainly applied to the rest of the Fathers. Secondly he had been asked whether the conferences advertized as taking place at the *Domus Mariae* during the current month of November had official status, or had been authorised by the Council Secretariate. The answer to both questions was in the negative. (Note: the *Domus Mariae* group were said to be very "progressive").

After Archbishop Marty had read his *Relatio* on behalf of our Commission, voting began on the *Ministry and Life of Priests*, and 8 votes were taken (*placet, non placet*, or *placet iuxta modum*) on the various sections of the preface and first two chapters. It was of special interest to me, because it was to be our job to deal in committee with all the amendments (*modi*) proposed, and to do so not only with expedition but in a way that would satisfy the Fathers.

A General Congregation 160th (33rd) was held the next day, 13 November, a Saturday, because of the urgent need to press ahead with any voting which allowed for amendments. The only voice heard at it was Felici's and he became self-conscious about it. Some, he observed, were complaining that he had a lot to say. He would prefer to keep quiet all the time, but it was not possible. Voting was already occupying all the available time and would continue to do so the following week, and consequently oral presentation of the *expositiones Patrum* on Indulgences could not be conveniently fitted in. These therefore should be submitted in writing, as many already had been, and would the Fathers please avoid theological disquisitions and keep to the question of discipline, so as to ease the work of the Holy See.

The General Congregations: 161st (34th) Monday 15 November, the 162nd (35th) Tuesday16 November and the 163rd (36th) Wednesday 17 November were consumed in voting, without other notable incident.

Thursday, 18 November, was devoted to a Public Session at which *De Divina Revelatione* and *De Apostolatu Laicorum* were promulgated.

At the 164th (37th) General Congregation Friday 19 November, the tedium of the voting was relieved by the singing of a Subiaco choir. Other choirs which broke the monotony at these speechless General Congregations included the Vienna Boys Choir and the Regensberg Domspatzen choir.

Then followed a vacation from General Congregations lasting from Saturday 20th November to Monday 29th November incl. I attended meetings of our Commission on the 19th, 20th, 22nd and 23rd, each lasting at least three hours, to deal — mainly in sub-committee — with the *modi* (amendments) proposed by the Fathers to our schema on the Ministry and Life of Priests. In the subcommittee to which I was attached there were only five active participants, so that we were able to deal expeditiously with the material assigned to us.

On Tuesday, 30 November the 165th (38th) General Congregation was begun with a Maronite Mass at which the Pope attended. Our Commission had met its date-line, and the amended text of the *Ministry and Life of Priests* was distributed to the Fathers. etc. I met Mgr Willy Onclin (a Louvain contemporary and friend of mine, who was an important member of our Commission) and he told me that he had been up all night correcting the proofs for the printer.

An interesting announcement was made about a mechanical error which had occurred at the recent Public Session in the vote on the *Apostolate of the Laity*. The counting-machine had torn and rejected 35 voting slips which had not therefore been included in the announced list of results. Later examination had however shown that they were all certainly *placet* votes. Hence the true result had been: Present and voting: 2342; *placet* 2340; *non placet* 2. (This, I think, was the nearest to unanimity that the Fathers achieved. Who were the 2, and how did they feel when they heard the result?)

Voting on our Commission's treatment of the amendments which had been proposed to the text of *Ministry and Life of Priests* began at the 166th (39th) General Congregation, Thursday 2 December, and in no case did *non placets* exceed 38.

The 167th (40th) General Congregation, Saturday 4 December, was mainly devoted to the voting on the treatment of the amendments proposed to *The Church in the Modern World*. During it, it was announced that every bishop attending the Council was to receive a gift from the Holy Father of a plain gold episcopal ring (no stone),"ad significandam nostram cum Eo coniunctionem", as Felici put it. And a message from the non-Catholic Observers to the Fathers was read by Felici in their name, in which, as the end of the Council approached, they wished to express their heartfelt gratitude, etc. They had everywhere been received "humaniter". Dialogue had been initiated. The bonds that had been established would remain. That same evening, there was an ecumenical celebration at St Paul's in which the Pope, the Conciliar Fathers and the Observers all participated.

The 168th (41st) and last General Congregation, Monday 6 December 1965, was mainly occupied in the distribution of various texts, the reading of the Bull proclaiming an extraordinary Jubilee, and Archbishop Felici's farewell address from the Ambo. The final vote on the treatment of amendments proposed to *The Church in the Modern World*, i.e. on the schema as a whole, revealed a substantial number of still-dissatisfied Fathers. Present and voting 2373: *placet* 2111, *non placet* 251, *placet iuxta modum* (therefore null) 1; null 10.

At the Solemn Public Session on Tuesday 7 December the four remaining acts of the Council were promulgated; *De Libertate Religiosa; De Activitate Missionali; De Presbyterorum Ministerio et Vita; De Ecclesia in Mundo Huius Temporis.* Since in those days Monsignori were still counted as members of the Pope's household, we had ringside seats just to one side of the Papal Altar, which made the long ceremony much more interesting than it could have been to the majority of the bishops. That night, at 7.30, the Pope gave a special audience to the *Periti*, at which he began by reading a prepared address, but then put it aside and spoke to us much more feelingly and effectively "off the cuff".

The Public Session of Closure, Wednesday 8 December1965, was held outdoors in St Peter's Piazza in the presence of a vast crowd, and was fortunately blessed with perfect weather. Once again special seats about twenty yards to the left of the Pope's throne were assigned to Monsignori, so that we were able to assist throughout the very long ceremony in reasonable comfort and with a splendid view. It was an enormously impressive occasion.

I packed that evening and caught the 1.10 p.m. Alitalia plane to London the following day.

It had been quite an experience.
L.L. McReavy

I completed this typescript copy of the notes which I had scribbled during the Council in November 1975.

Chapter V

The Lectures

Introduction

After the Letters and the Journal a further insight into the Council and its workings can be found in a collection of Lectures and talks listed in the Archive Catalogue as: Speeches delivered by Monsignor Lawrence McReavy mostly to the Lancashire clergy and relating to the progress of the Vatican II sessions.[1] These Lectures, almost identical in content, were also given in various places in the Diocese of Hexham and Newcastle.

In a private memoir Cuthbert Rand noted: "As a *Peritus* of the Council Lawrence was much in demand to give talks about it, and especially during Unity Week". Lawrence McReavy did much through his talks to make known the work of the Council and: "within the College his enthusiasm for the Council counted for a great deal".

Shortly after returning to Ushaw after each Session of the Council, Monsignor McReavy gave the Staff and students an account of its development and progress: "While he was at the Second Vatican Council he learned so much and he told us all about it! He would spend the first "quarter" in Rome, then return home and hold forth about the way the Church was going – hold forth at any time, breakfast, lunch, supper. But seriously, he did much to spread the word by his own acceptance of the conciliar teaching – within Ushaw as well as without. His experience was invaluable and his diaries, cartoons and anecdotes brought the Council to life in the classroom".[2] These lectures were published in the *Ushaw Magazine*.

Monsignor McReavy welcomed every invitation to speak about the Council to Priests, Religious and Laity. Even while on holiday visiting his nephew in Quarr Abbey on the Isle of Wight he did not lose the opportunity to give a talk on the Council to the monastic community. For Lawrence McReavy it was a duty to share with others the privilege he had received in experiencing the life of the Church at an important moment in its history.

I. The Period of Preparation for the Council (1959-1962)

In an address to the students of the Roman Seminary September 10, 1960, Pope John XXIII said: "we expect young seminarians to take a real and enthusiastic part in the great event. This interest must not only be in the

[1] Ushaw Archives: UC/P41/C4 1962 – 1965.

[2] Butters, J., "Further Memories" *Ushaw Magazine* 270 (1989-1990) 119.

preparation of the Council but also a time of intense prayer, personal and in common .... pray, dear sons, pray every day for the Council. You will be the first to breathe its wonderful and unique atmosphere, the first to apply its decrees at the dawn, perhaps, of your priesthood. May you also enjoy its fruits which are to be more abundant because of your prayers".

Monsignor Lawrence McReavy took these words of Pope John XXIII seriously and the students of Ushaw College were to benefit from the talks which he gave to them, beginning during the preparatory period right through to the conclusion of the Council.

Lecture to Divines and Philosophers 20 February 1961

On the Preparation of the Second Ecumenical Council of the Vatican

The First Ecumenical Council of the Vatican was discontinued abruptly, 18 July 1870, without having completed the work which had been assigned to it. Occasionally therefore, since then, it had been surmised that the Vatican Council might be reconvened. Nevertheless, it came as a surprise to the world as a whole when, on 25 January 1959, less than three months after his election to the supreme pontificate, Pope John XXIII announced to the Cardinals who had assembled with him at St Pauls Outside the Walls to celebrate the feast of the conversion of St Paul, that he had decided to convoke an Ecumenical Council.

Since then, another Motu Proprio *Superno Dei Nutu* (At the Bidding of God on High) of June 5, 1960 (AAS 1960 n. 7, p. 433), he has told the world that "the thought of celebrating an Ecumenical Council came to him suddenly, like the flower of an unexpected spring, almost as soon as he had been raised to the papal throne, and he attributed this fact to a divine inspiration." The Cardinals, he tells us, received his announcement with joy, and, a few months later, on the feast of Pentecost, May 17, 1959, he established an Antepreparatory Commission for the Ecumenical Council consisting of selected members of the Roman Curia, under the chairmanship of Cardinal Tardini, to undertake the remote preparation of the work.

A few weeks later, 29 June, 1959, the Pope took the occasion of his first encyclical, *Ad Petri Cathedram*, to define more precisely the object he had in view in convoking the Council.

It was to be celebrated, he said, primarily "to promote an increase of the Catholic faith and correct renovation of the morals of the Christian people, and to adapt ecclesiastical discipline to the needs and conditions of the times. This (he hoped) would provide a wonderful spectacle of truth, unity and charity, which would be accepted by all who behold it, even those who are separated from the Apostolic See, as a warm invitation to seek and attain that unity which Jesus Christ besought of His Heavenly Father with earnest prayers." At the same time, he decreed that the forthcoming Council should be known from its place of assembly as the Second Vatican Council. It is not therefore a mere continuation of the First.

Notes.

Published under title "Acta et documenta Concilio Oecumenico Vaticano II apparando. Series I (Antepreparatoria)" 10 volumes. A volume of 780 pages contains the suggestions coming from England and Germany. (Two more of 810 and 900 for rest of Europe).

For the first Vatican Council, only 224 replies were received from the Episcopate, and they required only a simple volume of 423 pages.

Series II (Praeparatoria) will comprise the work that is now being done by the Preparatory Commissions, and is likely to run to even more volumes than the Antepreparatory. Whatever else the Council produces, it will certainly provide future scholars with a tremendous amount of documentation.

The Antepreparatory Commission wasted no time. On 18 June, 1959 Cardinal Tardini sent out 2700 letters to Bishops, Nuncios and others all over the world asking their advice and proposals as to what should be discussed at the Council. The Universities were asked to contribute studies on the problems which needed to be examined. The deadline for replies was fixed as 30 April, 1960.

By 30 May, 1960, 2000 replies had been received. When these had been classified and summarised in national resumés, they were communicated to the various Congregations of the Roman Curia, which made use of them in drawing up a series of concrete questions for the Pope's approval.

The Pope (as he assures us in *Superno Dei Nutu*) kept in close union with all this antepreparatory activity, and himself carefully studied the proposals of the Bishops and the Roman Curia and the suggestions and studies sent in by the Universities, and thanked God for such a generous response to his request.

Being now in a position to see clearly what matters should be considered by the forthcoming Council for the good of the Church and the salvation of souls, he decided that the time had come to appoint Preparatory Commissions to study the material which would in due course be submitted to the deliberations of the Council.

He decided also that these Commissions should consist of Cardinals, Bishops and ecclesiastics of outstanding virtue and learning, secular and religious, chosen from the various parts of the world, so as to make it clear that the best elements of the universal Catholic Church were engaged.

With the Motu Proprio *Superno Dei Nutu* the project moved from the Antepreparatory to the Preparatory stage. It decreed as follows:

1. That Preparatory Commissions should be set up to study and investigate the matters selected by the Pope, in the light of the proposals made by the Bishops and the Roman Curia.

2. That each Commission could be divided, as the need arises, into various sections or sub-commissions.

3. That each Commission should have its own President and a definite number of members; the President to be a Cardinal, and the members to be chosen from among the Bishops and invited ecclesiastics.

4. That to each Commission should be added a number of Consultors chosen from experts.

5. That each Commission should have its own Secretary.

6. That the President, Members, Consultors and Secretary of each Commission should be chosen by authority of the Pope.

7. That ten Preparatory Commissions should be established though others might be set up, if the Pope thought fit.

The ten Commissions are:

a) The Theological Commission to study questions relating to Sacred Scripture, Sacred Tradition, faith and morals (no English Member);

b) A Commission on Bishops and Government of Dioceses (bishop Dwyer is a Member);

c) A Commission on discipline of clergy and Christian People (no English Member, but there are two English Consultors, myself and Fr W. O'Connel OFM a resident in Rome);

d) A Commission on Religious
(no one from England as far as I know);

e) A Commission on the Sacraments
(no one from England as far as I know);

f) A Commission on Sacred Liturgy (J.B.O'Connell is a Member);

g) A Commission on Studies and Seminaries
(no one from England);

h) A Commission on Oriental Churches (no one from England);

i) A Commission on Missions
(archbishop Matthews is the Secretary);

j) A Commission on the Lay Apostolate (no information).

8. That in addition there shall be a Secretariate on Modern Means of Communication of Ideas (Press, Radio, TV, Films etc) with a President, Members and Consultants likewise chosen by Papal authority. (Bishop Beck is a member and Father Agnellus Andrew is a Consultor).

9. "The better to show our love and goodwill towards those who are graced by the Christian name but separated from this Apostolic See, and to enable them to follow the Council's labours, and more easily find a way to that unity which "Jesus Christ besought from

His Heavenly Father with fervent prayers" there shall be a special Secretariate, presided over by a Cardinal of our choice and constituted in the same way as the other Commissions".

(It has been named the *Secretariate for the Unity of Christians*. Archbishop Heenan and Father Gerard Corr are Members; Msgr H.F Davis and Father M. Bevenot SJ are Consultors).

10. Finally, that a Central Commission should be established, over which the Pope shall preside personally or through a Cardinal designated by him. Its members should not be of the Presidents of the Commissions and Secretariates. Thirty five Cardinals were later named, (among whom were Cardinals Godfrey and Heard) and thirty two bishops were chosen from various parts of the world (among them the Archbishop of Glasgow).

11. That a number of Consultors should be added, selected from Bishops and invited ecclesiastics.

12. That it should have a Prelate as Secretary, who shall be the Secretary General (Archbishop Felici).

13. That the Members, Consultors and Secretary should be chosen by the Pope.

14. That the function of the Central Commission should be to follow most, if need be, arrange in order the labours of the individual commissions, weigh their conclusions and present them to the Pope that he might decide.

In mid-October 1960, all Members and Consultors were notified through their respective Apostolic Delegations or Nunciatures that they were urgently requested to come to Rome in time to assist at a Solemn Audience to be given on 14 November to all the Preparatory Commissions and to attend the first meeting of their particular commission. A list of the questions fixed by the Holy Father for study by our Commission was enclosed with a note to the effect that we could add others within our field.

Unfortunately we were required to take an oath before a delegated person that we would faithfully fulfil our function and observes secrecy on the matters discussed.

By November 12th, 1960, most of the Members and Consultors had assembled in Rome, and received special tickets to enable them to attend a solemn Mass of the Byzantine-Slav Rite concelebrated in St Peter's by a dozen Oriental bishops in the presence of the Pope on Sunday, November 13th. The Pope in his address declared that this Mass was meant to inaugurate the preparatory phase of the Council and to highlight one of its principal aims: the unity of the Church: *Unus Dominus, una fides, unum baptisma.*

The following morning, Monday, November 14th, 1960, all the Commissions assembled in the apse of St Peter's Basilica for the Solemn Audience. The Pope walked up the Basilica to his throne under the Chair.

Thirty-five Cardinals and several hundred bishops were seated on either side of him, and the rest of us occupied tribunes lower down. (Impressive moment. I felt that I was assisting at something unique in the history of Church. Never before had such a large representative body of experts been gathered from all over the globe to prepare a General Council). He spoke for about half an hour, and began by discussing our work as "a holy vigil of intense and pacific labour".

Past Councils, he recalled had been concerned primarily to settle disputed points of doctrine, the *Lex credendi*. In the modern materialist world, it is not so much a question of consulting the Fathers on points of doctrine or discipline, but of giving full value and splendour to the substance of human and Christian thought and life. It is to prepare this work, he said that you have been called from the four corners of the world. Welcome, and God bless you. It is a great work which will require time, patient labour and love, and will command the respectful attention of our separated brethren. The Council, he hoped, would reinvigorate the faith, doctrine and discipline of the Church, its religious and spiritual life, and re-affirm those principles of Christian order which should inspire civil, economic, political and social life.

When the Pope had completed his address, he descended from his throne, greeted the Cardinals individually, saluted the rest of the company with a fatherly gesture and then, mounting his *sedia gestatoria*, was carried down the basilica through the thousands of students from all the Roman colleges and residencies who had been invited to fill the nave. The scene outside St Peter's was Pentecostal in its witness to universality of Church.

Some of the Commissions and Secretariates had already begun their work on the Sunday. Ours did not meet until the Wednesday. I am not free to say what we discussed. But the first job was to divide the material and assign it to Sub-commissions of members, each with a Relator to present a report. It was decided that all the members of our Commission should reassemble in the second week of every alternative month and meet morning and evening for the whole week. They are free to ask any Consultor for his views and the Consultor must send a written answer to be included in the Acta of the Commission. Consultors, however, need not attend personally unless they are individually summoned. I have received the minutes of the week-long sessions already held, and have attended two (November and May) and was impressed by the progress that has already been achieved and by the practical value of the recommendations that have already been precisely formulated.

On several occasions, the Pope has made it clear that nothing is nearer and dearer to his heart than the reunion of East and West. It is not the primary object of the Council, but the Pope's hope and prayer is that it may be one of its fruits. He felt himself inspired by God to summon the Council and, on February 2, 1960, he said: "this morning, in approaching the altar of our private chapel to celebrate Mass, we offered our humble life for the success of the ecumenical Council". He expects us all to offer at least our prayers. The great work is on the move and promises to make of the second Council of the Vatican one of the greatest assemblies in the history of Christendom.

II. The First Session of the Second Vatican Council (1962)

From the *Ushaw Magazine* number 217 (March 1963) pp. 32-34

Monsignor McReavy, since his return from the Second Vatican Council, has kindly written the following note on the events of the October to December session:

The first session of the Second Ecumenical Council of the Vatican will be remembered for three significant interventions of the Holy Father, but for which the Council might have ground slowly to a halt, weighed down by the sheer bulk of the agenda and the constitutional right of every one of the 2500 Fathers to speak his mind on every topic presented for discussion.

Owing to the need for due consultation in appointing the members of the ten conciliar commissions, it was not until the fourth General Congregation, on October 22nd that the first topic, the draft project on the liturgy, was introduced. A fortnight later, at the twelfth General Congregation, some thirty-eight speakers were still awaiting their turn to speak on the second of the eight chapters. Those of us who had to listen for three hours every morning to the daily dose of ten-minute speeches, many of them repetitive, were becoming more and more depressed. It was like being in a tunnel with no visible end to it; nor, at that time, had anyone in the assembly any right to impose an end.

Then, at the thirteenth Congregation, on November 6th came the blessed announcement that the Holy Father had empowered the Presidential Bench of Cardinals to propose the closure of the discussion when they felt that a matter had been adequately debated. The President of that day immediately proposed the closure of the debate on chapter II, and, before he had finished speaking, the whole assembly had risen to its feet in joyous and unanimous approval. Everyone felt an immense sense of relief. The agenda was still huge, but at least they could get on with it. It took only four more congregations to deal with the remaining six chapters on liturgy, and, on November 14th, the Council was able to begin discussion of the draft project *De Fontibus Revelationis*.

This proved to be, in the main, a theological treatise similar in form to those of the textbooks. It soon appeared, however, that this was precisely what many of the Fathers did not want. It was, they said, too technical and scholastic and completely lacked the pastoral and ecumenical approach. It therefore failed to fulfil the Pope's declared purpose in summoning the

Council, which was to present the Church's doctrine, frankly indeed and without compromise but in a form likely to commend it to modern man and, in particular, to our separated brethren.

A five-day debate ensued, in which all the big guns were engaged and the quality of the speeches reached the highest level attained during the whole session. Then, on the sixth day, the assembly was asked to decide by vote whether it wanted to postpone the discussion of this project until it had been revised along the lines suggested. Few expected those in favour of postponement to secure the necessary two thirds majority, nor did they; but they came near enough to make it clear that discussion of the existing *schema*, which by the rules of the Council would have to continue, was likely to be indefinitely prolonged.

The next morning, rumours were circulating that Cardinals Tisserant and Cigognani had been to see the Pope overnight and that there was to be an announcement. There was. It was to the effect that, by decision of the Holy Father, the schema *De Fontibus* was to be revised by a mixed commission under the joint presidency of Cardinals Ottaviani and Bea.

The relatively uncontroversial subject of Social Communications was dealt with in three days, and the *schema* on reunion with the Oriental Churches met with general approval and was passed with a few amendments. But massive opposition was encountered again when, on December 1st, the schema *De Ecclesia* was introduced, and largely for the same reasons as had been urged against the schema *De Fontibus*. Once again, when an interminable debate seemed to be looming ahead, the Holy Father intervened to banish our gathering depression. At the thirty-fifth Congregation, on December 6, it was announced that, by his decision, all the remaining schemata were to be revised and abbreviated before the Council re-assembles on September 8th, 1963. Two days later we came away, tired but much less pessimistic about the duration and effectiveness of the Council.

The subject of the following talk is the First Session of the Council but there is no indication of where or when it was given.

The Ecumenical Council

When the history of the second Ecumenical Council of the Vatican comes to be written, the more discerning historians will, or should, call attention to three significant dates in the first session. They were:

a. The 13th General Congregation, on Tuesday, 6 November, 10.15 a.m. When the debate was interrupted with an announcement that the Presidential bench had received a faculty from the Pope to propose the closure of the discussion, when they thought that the subject had been adequately explored;

b. The 24th General Congregation, 21st of November, when it was announced that by order of the Pope, the schema *De Fontibus* was to be revised by a mixed Commission, even though the vote to this effect on the previous day had not reached the required two thirds majority.

c. The 35th General Congregation, Thursday December 6th, when it was announced that, by order of the Pope, all the schemata were to be revised before the Second Session opened in September 1963.

The significance of these three interventions of the Pope lies in the fact that, without them, the Council might have dragged on indefinitely, or more probably ground to a halt owing to the impracticability of reassembling the bishops year after year for apparently endless discussions.

It is easy to be wise after the event but it must be remembered that none of the bishops attending the Council, nor any of the officials responsible for its preparation had any experience which would have enabled them to determine in advance what was practicable in a Council of such magnitude with a wider agenda than had ever been attempted in the history of the Church.

The first Vatican Council had assembled some 700 bishops, mainly from Europe, to discuss and pronounce primarily on a single subject, the infallibility of the Pope.

The second Vatican Council sent out summons to over 3000 bishops and nearly 2500 attended the opening ceremony, and the number assisting at the daily debates never fell below 2000.

Its agenda covered the whole life and activity of the Church. The Pope, it is true, had stated a single goal, the *aggiornamento* of the Church's doctrine and discipline, i.e. to bring the faith and practice of the Church up to date, to restate the immutable faith in terms intelligible to our age, to revise and adapt our preaching and practice to modern needs.

In 1959, when the bishops and Catholic universities of the world were invited to send in their suggestions on this theme, nearly 2000 replies were received and they contained 6000 suggestions, enough for a dozen General Councils. Needless to say, these were thinned out and synthesised before the preparatory work began. But even so, it required 10 Preparatory Commissions and two Secretariats to cover every aspect of the proposed modernisation, and each one of them had a formidable list of weighty questions to discuss and report upon.

When a commission of experts drawn from all over the world sets itself to draft a report on a question of great moment to the Church, it was not tempted just to skimp its report. On the contrary, the tendency was to seek to cover every aspect of the question and leave nothing unsaid. There was, of course, a certain amount of collaboration between the various commissions to avoid overlapping and duplication of the same material, but not enough. The Theological Commission in particular was chary of allowing anyone else to tread upon its private mat.

The Central Commission was meant to collate and abbreviate the draft reports, and I understand that they did quite a bit of elimination. Even so, the number and length of the *schemata* finally approved for discussion by the Fathers was truly formidable and would have appeared even more so if it had all been published prior to the opening of the Council. Even if the agenda had been much more brief and simple, it would not have been an easy matter to organise a conciliar assembly of 2500 bishops, all equal in authority, into a smoothly working body. It is not therefore surprising that the Council was slow in getting underway.

The opening ceremony, Thursday, 11 October, was immensely impressive. Rain and sunshine, procession, half hour to file into seats, solemn High Mass, the Pope's Profession of Faith, Archbishop Felici made the Profession of faith on behalf of the Bishops. There was a Torchlight procession at night.

Two days later, Saturday 13th of October, the first General Congregation, ran into its first snag which might have been foreseen. The President called on the Bishops to nominate 16 of their number to be members of each of 10 Commissions. This was declared to be impossible! Time was needed to consult. Consequently the Congregation was brought to a close and we were out of the Basilica by 10.15.

Sunday October 14th and Monday 15th were spent in seeking names. Tuesday, 16th of October at the second General Congregation the votes were taken followed by three days off. Saturday 20th of October at the third General Congregation the results were made known, and a pronouncement addressed to the world was issued.

Monday 22nd October, the fourth General Congregation, began the discussion of the first draft project, *De Liturgia*. A fortnight later, at the 12th General Congregation, Monday, November 5th, there were still some 38 speakers waiting their turn to speak on chapter II. By this time, of course, most speakers were merely repeating what others had said, and in spite of constant appeals from the Presidential Bench, they persisted in doing so.

Those of us who had to listen for three hours every morning to this sort of thing were becoming more and more depressed. It was like being in a tunnel with no visible end to it. When one asked why it was allowed to go on, the only answer forthcoming was that every Bishop had a right to speak his mind on every point submitted to the Council. The Presidential Bench had no authority to gag their fellow bishops, etc.

Then came the blessed morning of Tuesday, November 6th, the 13th General Congregation, when, at 10.15, the Secretary General announced that the Presidential Bench had been empowered by the Pope to propose the closure of the debate when they thought the matter had been fully ventilated. The President of the day immediately made use of this power to propose the closure of the debate on chapter II, and asked the Fathers that if they were in favour to indicate their pleasure by standing. Before he could complete his sentence, the whole assembly had risen to its feet. Everyone felt an immense sense of relief. There was a mighty lot still remaining to be done, but at least we could get on with it.

Four more General Congregations were devoted to the remaining six chapters, and on Tuesday November 13th, the 18th General Congregation, the closure of the debate *De Liturgia* was proposed and voted and, the following day, we passed to the debate *De Fontibus.*

It was here that another point of contention arose which, had it not been resolved, would have led to a great deal of fruitless and prolonged discussion. The schema *De Fontibus* had been prepared by the *Theological Commission* (Presided over by Cardinal Ottaviani) with little or no consultation with any others than the professional theologians assembled round and possibly by Cardinal Ottaviani.

They produced a theological treatise similar in form and style to those that can be found in the theological textbooks of the last hundred years. But it soon appeared that this was precisely what many of the Fathers did not want. Their attack was immediate and formidable in the weight of its authority. It was not the orthodoxy of the schema that they questioned and criticised, but its manner of presenting the matter. It was far too technical, scholastic, completely devoid of the ecumenical spirit and lacking the pastoral approach. It was a waste of time to call an Ecumenical Council, if it were merely to subscribe to textbook statements of the Church's doctrine which no one disputed.

The declared purpose of the Pope in calling this Council was to restate the Church's doctrine, without compromise or watering down, but in a way which would commend it to modern man and, in particular, to our separated brethren. The schema *De Fontibus* completely failed to do this, and should therefore be rejected as a basis for discussion and revised in line with the Pope's declared intention by a mixed Commission in which the *Secretariat of Unity* would have a say.

A five-day debate ensued, between the 14th and 20th November, in which all the big guns were engaged and the quality of the speeches reached the highest level attained during this session. The pros and cons were more or less evenly balanced. Those who defended the schema took the line that it was the primary job of the Council to issue a scientifically exact statement of the Church's doctrine. The pastoral or ecumenical slant should and could be added afterwards by those whose job it was to expound the Church's doctrine to the faithful or to explain it to non-Catholics. It was dangerous to attempt any sort of adaptation in a conciliar document. Moreover, it would be improper, if not unlawful, to reject a document which had been approved by the central Commission and by the Pope himself for discussion by the Fathers. (At this point, an anonymous Father called the attention of the Presidential Bench to art. 33 n. 1, of the Order of Procedure.)

After the debate of Monday November 19th, the 22nd General Congregation, there was little further that could be said on either side, and everyone expected a vote to be taken, the only question being what form it would take. If the proposition were whether the Fathers approved of the schema, those who wanted to retain it would have to raise a two thirds vote (i.e. there would have to be two thirds *placet*, as for the schema *De Liturgia*). Anything over a third of *non placets* would suffice to throw it out.

There was quite a stir the following day, Tuesday November 20th, when, at 10.15, the President (Cardinal Frings), said that the Presidential Bench had decided to call a vote on the proposition: "Whether the discussion of the schema is to be discontinued" i.e. sine die.

Placet would mean discontinue, *non placet* would mean retain. In other words, a two thirds vote was required to throw out the schema and postpone discussion of *De Fontibus* until a new schema had been prepared.

Few expected the opponents of the schema to collect two thirds of the votes, nor did they, but they came nearer to it than many expected. The official handout did not give the figures, merely stating (correctly though misleadingly) that the effect of the vote was that the debate on the present schema should continue. The figures appeared however in the evening editions of the secular press (1368 *placet*, 822 *non placet*, 19 null), and everyone was aware that the defenders of the schema had won a purely technical and hollow victory. It could hardly be satisfactory to go on discussing and attempting to amend the statement which a considerable, even if not two thirds majority wanted completely revised.

When I got to my Tribune the following morning (Wednesday November 21st, the 24th General Congregation) I was told by a fellow expert that Cardinals Tisserant and Cicognani had been to see the Pope the night before, to discuss the situation, and that there was to be an announcement. There was. It was to the effect that, by decision of the Pope, the schema was to be revised by a special mixed Commission of Theology and Secretariate of Unity, under the joint presidency of Cardinals Ottaviani and Bea.

We passed, on the Friday November 3rd, the 25th General Congregation, to the relatively innocuous and uncontroversial subject of *Social Communications* (completed in three days), and then to reunion with Oriental Churches (*Ut omnes unum sint*, prepared by the Preparatory Commission for the Oriental Churches, under Cardinal Cicognani), which was welcomed with general approval and passed with few amendments. (Vote on Friday November 30th , the 30th General Congregation, 2068 *placet*, 36 *non placet*).

Saturday December 1st, the 31st General Congregation, saw the opening of the debate on the schema *De Ecclesia*, also prepared by Cardinal Ottaviani's *Theological Commission*. He did not want it to be broached with only a week to go, but the Bench decided that it was worthwhile getting the preliminary opinion of the Fathers as to the general value of the schema.

Once again it was largely adverse and for the same reasons as had been urged against the schema *De Fontibus*. On the third day of the debate, Tuesday, December 4th, one of the Cardinals (Suenens) made an eloquent plea for a general revision of all the schemata during the recess, all of them, he argued, need to be rewritten in a more pastoral and ecumenical fashion, if the Council were to achieve the purpose for which the Pope had called it, and all of them needed to be simplified and abbreviated if the Council were to get through its appointed task within reasonable time.

We know that the Pope can listen to all the debates. It may be that he was listening to this particular speech and found that it expressed his own mind. Anyway, on Thursday December 6th, at the 35th General Congregation, the Secretary-General announced that by order of the Holy Father all schemata were to be revised and abbreviated before the Council resumed its sessions on September 8, 1963.

General impressions.

1. The daily ocular evidence of the Catholicity of the Church: the scene on the steps of St Peter's; all colours, tongues, rites and headgears.

2. The unique opportunity to learn and appreciate the immense diversity of conditions in which the Church operates, and the different methods of meeting them.

3. The wide diversity of points of view, compatible with complete unity of Faith.

III. The Second Session of the Second Vatican Council (1963)

The Second Session of the Council

(*Ushaw Magazine*, 220 (March 1964) 1-10)

There were fewer sensational developments in the second session of the Second Ecumenical Council of the Vatican, largely because the *schemata* discussed had been revised during the interval to suit the pastoral and ecumenical viewpoint which the majority of the Fathers felt to be proper to the general purpose of the Council, and for lack of which the first session had thrown out the schemata submitted on the Sources of Revelation and on the Church. The structure of the Council had also been revised with a view to greater efficiency. At the first session, the General Congregations in St Peter's were controlled, more or less, by a presidential bench of ten cardinals They still sit impressively at a long, scarlet-draped table at the head of the nave and their number has been increased to twelve, but their only real function now is to see that the rules are observed. Effective direction of the debates has been transferred by Pope Paul to a new group of four "Moderators," who sit at a small table in front of the Presidents and take control by turns. They are Cardinals Agagianian, Lercaro, Döpfner and Suenens, and they were probably chosen, not only because they are rather more dynamic, but also because they had identified themselves more openly at the first session with the pastoral and ecumenical aims of the Council.

Otherwise, the procedure is much the same as before. At the General Congregations which last from 9 a.m. to 12.15, Monday to Friday, a *schema* is first submitted to general discussion of its suitability as a basis on which to build the definitive conciliar document, and then, if the Fathers accept it, each chapter is discussed successively in detail. When this process is completed, the schema goes back to the relevant Commission to be revised according to the expressed opinion of the Fathers and, in due course (which almost inevitably means a later session), presented for their *placet*, *non placet*, or *placet iuxta modum*. Thus the *schemata* on the Liturgy and on the Means of Social Communication which had been fully discussed at the first session were voted through, in their revised form, section by section, at this session, and were finally approved, the former with only 19 dissentients (reduced to 4 at the solemn promulgation), the latter with 503 dissentients (reduced to 164).

To judge from the programme, five *schemata* were to have been fully discussed at this second session: the Church, the Blessed Virgin, Bishops and Government of Dioceses, Ecumenism, and the Lay Apostolate. In fact, there was time only for the Church, Bishops and Government of Dioceses, and the first three of the five chapters on Ecumenism. The reason why the target was not achieved was that the debate on the Church, which was generally admitted to be the cardinal topic of the whole Council, was allowed by the Moderators to occupy 23 of the 43 General Congregations.

The *schema* on the Church, which had been revised by a mixed Commission under Cardinals Ottaviani and Bea, met with general approval when it was presented for acceptance in its new form. There was some criticism of the arrangement of the material and a well-supported suggestion that the *schema* on the Blessed Virgin should be attached to that on the Church as a final chapter, but, upon a promise from the Moderators that the material would be re-arranged and that the Fathers would be given an opportunity to vote about the place of the Blessed Virgin, the *schema* was accepted by 2231 votes to 43.

After a liberal amount of sermonizing on the appropriate image of the Church, in chapter I, the debate moved on to the eagerly awaited chapter II, on the hierarchical constitution of the Church and, in particular, the status of the episcopate, which the First Vatican Council, after defining the papal primacy, had been compelled by extraneous factors to leave undetermined. Since it was regarded as one of the primary functions of Vatican II to complete the work of Vatican I on this point, the debate was given a free rein and lasted nearly nine days.

Most of the speeches were concerned with the question of the collegiality of the episcopate. It is, of course, evident that the Bishops form a college with the Pope when he assembles them in an ecumenical council. The question is whether they form a college with him in the government of the universal Church outside of an ecumenical council, and if so, with what practical consequences.

The debate revealed two sharply divided schools of thought. What may be called the "monarchical" school, led by Ruffini and generally supported by Italian Fathers, argued that the monarchical concept of the Church, as expressed in the doctrine of the papal primacy defined at Vatican I, excluded any right to collegial participation by the episcopate in the government of the Church as a whole (a conclusion which will doubtless seem familiar to many who did their theology in the first quarter of this century). The other school appealed rather to the scriptural sources from which the doctrine of the papal primacy is itself derived, and claimed that these clearly show that the Apostles were conscious of forming a college with Peter their head, e.g. when they met to fill the place of Judas, and they acted collegially while such action remained practicable, e.g. when they instituted the diaconate. Nor was this a modern discovery or a revived Gallican thesis. On the contrary, as the Auxiliary Bishop of Bologna demonstrated, in one of the most applauded speeches of the whole session, the doctrine of episcopal collegiality had been defended by some of the most ardent supporters of the papal primacy, Italians at that, and to be found among those who had drafted the primatial definition at Vatican I.

Pius XII himself, as recently as 1957, in the encyclical *Fidei donum*, had reminded the bishops of the world of their collective responsibility, as successors of the Apostles, for the missionary work of the Church, and had called it a function of divine institution.

The only other topic in this chapter to receive comparable attention from speakers was the proposal to restore the diaconate as a permanent office, to which perhaps married men might be ordained. It was strongly supported by many missionary bishops and also by Cardinals Döpfner, Richaud and Suenens, who emphasized that the proposal, as it stood, merely opened the way to those parts of the Church which felt the need of a stable diaconate, and imposed nothing on those that wanted no change. Amid all the fuss about bishops and deacons, simple priests might have been overlooked, had it not been for the intervention of some English-speaking Fathers. Bishop Beck was the first to call attention to the singular reticence of the *schema* on this topic, and to suggest that, before insisting on the hierarchical difference between bishops and priests, it would have been more logical to deal explicitly with the priesthood that is common to both. As Archbishop Conway of Armagh pointed out, the *schema* had 9 pages on bishops, 7 on layfolk, and a mere half-page on priests, and that only to remind them that their priesthood was of second grade. Archbishop Hurley of Durban suggested that, from the pastoral point of view, they are anything but second grade. Indeed, he said, they are "the hands, feet and very voice of the Bishop", so that it depends on them whether a pastoral message from the Bishop reaches the flock as a clap of thunder or a tinkle on the telephone.

Apart however from a few brief interventions of this kind, the debate centred for day after day on episcopal collegiality and, to a lesser extent, the diaconate proposal. Eventually, on the eighth day of the debate, Moderator

Suenens intervened half-way through the morning to observe that there were still enough speakers awaiting their turn to occupy a further three days, and that, since nothing fresh was likely to be said on the main points of dispute, the Moderators proposed to take a vote on these points, not to settle them definitively, but to give the Doctrinal Commission a clearer idea of the balance of opinion among the Fathers than could be gathered from the tally of speeches; the Fathers were assured that they would receive the text of these questions the following day, 16th October, and would be invited to vote on them the day after that.

With this assurance, the Fathers voted almost unanimously to pass on to chapter III. On the following day, however, no questions were distributed and no explanation was offered. Moreover, a number of Fathers exercised their right, as representing three or more others, to have their say on chapter II; among them Bishop Holland of Portsmouth, who proposed that, as a visible mark of episcopal collegiality, a representative central body of bishops elected by the various episcopal conferences should be created as a permanent institution to advise and help the Pope in the government of the universal Church.

When, after six further General Congregations, the discussion of the *schema* on the Church was brought to a close, two issues still remained to be settled: the question of the separate treatment of the Blessed Virgin, and the promised but not yet distributed propositions on chapter II. Our own Hierarchy had campaigned, from the moment of their arrival in Rome, to have the *schema* on the Blessed Virgin included in that on the Church, partly because it was more ecumenical to have it there, but also because the function and prerogatives of Our Lady can best be understood in the context of the Mystical Body of Christ. They had even brought an alternative text which would fit into the context of the Church and had actively sought support from other interested groups of bishops. The Moderators had already promised the assembly that this question would be settled by vote, and, as soon as the debate on the Church came to an end, they invited Cardinals Santos and Konig to put the case for and against separate treatment of the Blessed Virgin. The text of the two speeches was distributed so that the Fathers might study them at their leisure, and, after a weekend of intensive electioneering outside the Council, the vote was taken on. October 29th. It was a close thing, the Fathers voting by a bare majority of 40 (1114 to 1074) to attach *De Beata Virgine* to *De Ecclesia*.

The long-awaited questions on chapter II were distributed on the same day. Rumour had it that the fortnight's delay was due to an objection lodged by Cardinal Ottaviani, President of the Doctrinal Commission, and supported by members of the Presidential Bench, that it was the exclusive right of his Commission to draft and submit texts on the matters concerned for the vote of the Fathers, and that the issue was finally decided in favour of the Moderators at a plenary meeting of the Presidents, Moderators and Secretariate, by a majority of one vote.

In these questions, the Fathers were asked whether they wanted the following five declarations to be made in the *schema* on the Church: 1) that episcopal consecration constitutes the supreme grade of the sacrament of Order; 2) that every bishop legitimately consecrated in the communion of the bishops and of the Roman Pontiff, head and centre of unity, is a member of the body of bishops; 3) that the body or college of bishops succeeds to the college of Apostles in the office of evangelizing, sanctifying and pasturing, and that, along with its head, the Roman Pontiff, and never without this head (whose primatial right over all pastors and faithful remains intact), it has full and supreme power over the whole Church; 4) that the said power belongs by divine law to the college of bishops united to their head; 5) that consideration be given to the opportuneness of restoring the diaconate as a distinct and permanent grade of the sacred ministry, according as it may be useful to the Church in the different regions.

The following day, 30th October, the Fathers voted affirmatively to all five propositions: 1) 2123 *placet* votes to 34 *non placet*; 2) 2049 to 104; 3) 1808 to 376; 4) 1717 to 408; 5) 1588 to 525. The announcement of these results was greeted with a burst of applause, which seemed to indicate that the great majority of the Fathers agreed with the Moderators that this was an excellent method of discovering the balance of their opinion without an otherwise indefinite debate.

When the Council re-assembled on November 5th, the subject for discussion was Bishops and Government of Dioceses. To judge from the atmosphere at the press conferences, this debate stirred little interest outside the Council, except in so far as it re-echoed the previous debate on episcopal collegiality and its effect on the practical relation of the bishops to the Roman Curia. When Cardinal Ruffini reminded the Fathers that, according to the express declaration of the Moderators, the famous vote on collegiality did not settle anything not even the meaning of the term, Cardinal Frings was quick to reply that the Doctrinal Commission could not ignore the morally unanimous will of the Fathers. There was also a minor clash, somewhat blown up in the Press, between Cardinal Frings and Cardinal Ottaviani on the method of procedure of the Holy Office in condemning heterodox or dangerous writings, which drew from Cardinal Ottaviani the protest that the implied allegation of arbitrary judgements showed "nescience" in regard to the facts.

The enthusiasm for collegiality had waned somewhat by the time the discussion had passed to the status and function of the National Conferences of Bishops, to which the Council tends increasingly to refer decisions on the practical application of its decrees and proposals. Most speakers seemed anxious to avoid giving the Conferences any more power over their episcopal members than was absolutely necessary, and determined to preserve the monarchical character of diocesan government. Nor was there much support for the proposal in the *schema* that bishops should have to retire at a fixed age.

The deliberations of the Fathers became noticeably more interesting to the Press when, on November 18th, the *schema* on Ecumenism, to which had been added a fourth chapter on the Jews and a fifth on Religious Liberty, was presented for discussion. To forestall time-wasting criticism by meeting objections in advance, the Moderators first called upon three selected speakers to make explanatory *relationes* to the assembly, Bishop Bukatko on the Oriental Churches, Cardinal Bea on the Jews, and Bishop De Smedt on Religious Liberty. They were expert and eloquent performances, but they did not succeed in stifling critics of the added chapters from arguing that special treatment of the Jews would cause resentment in Arab countries and that Religious Liberty ought to be left to the promised *schema* on the Church and the Modern World. To avoid delay, therefore, the Moderators proposed that the Fathers should leave the question of the added chapters to a later date and vote simply on the acceptability of the three chapters on Ecumenism. They accepted them and proceeded to discuss them in detail.

The debate was neither exciting, nor illuminating, nor, in spite of efforts by the Moderators to hustle it along, expeditious. When however, on November 27th, Cardinal Döpfner intervened to announce that 41 speakers were still awaiting their turn to enlarge on chapter II, and suggested that, to judge from the number of repetitions, meditations and examinations of conscience, it was time to pass to chapter III, the Fathers readily agreed. This gave Bishop Dwyer, who had his name down for chapter III, the opportunity to call attention to some of the hard facts of the ecumenical dialogue which the more starry-eyed optimists were inclined to overlook. It was not simply a question of explaining our doctrine to non-Catholics with charity, as some seemed to think. We could be on the best of terms with them and make our position crystal clear, without diminishing the gulf that divides us. Nevertheless, as Archbishop Heenan had already assured the assembly on November 20th, the English Hierarchy were eager to pursue the road mapped out by the Council and would patiently persevere in it.

The discussion came to an end on December 2nd, without the Fathers having had the promised opportunity to decide on the acceptability of the two added chapters. There must have been some complaints about this behind the scenes, because Cardinal Bea, President of the Ecumenical Commission, intervened to assure the Fathers that the only reason was lack of time. The Council was due to be prorogued by the Pope in a solemn Public Session on December 4th, and that left only one more free day. It was not enough for adequate discussion of the disputed chapters. He guaranteed however that they would come up for discussion when the Council resumed its deliberations next September.

The session was to have ended with an announcement to the pastors of the world, and the text had been distributed with a request that the Fathers should send in their votes before the weekend. But it was a poor effort, according to many, and when no less than 600 votes were found to carry reservations, the project was abandoned. Fortunately, the splendour of the solemn Public Session compensated for this minor set-back and went some way towards reviving our optimism. We were told that all the remaining *schemata* are to be drastically pruned to their "puncta centralia". Even so, it would seem that only a miracle could enable them all to be discussed, emended and voted through in a single further session; a miracle, or a liberal application of the gag.

IV. The Third Session of the Second Vatican Council (1964)

The Third Session of the Council appears to have occupied McReavy's attention rather more fully than the first two Sessions and this is also reflected in the number of Lectures devoted to this Session.

Each Thursday afternoon throughout the Sessions of the Council a Press Conference was given under the auspices of the Information Office of the Hierarchy of England and Wales. The following text of the Press Conference given by Monsignor Lawrence McReavy, on the 19th November 1964, differs from the other Lectures in this section in that it was given while the Third Session was in course.

The Press Conference

Rome, 19th November 1964

The distinctive feature of this third session of the Council has been the sheer volume and diversity of the subject-matter discussed and voted upon by the Fathers. It is safe to say that never in the history of the Church have so many bishops debated and decided so many matters of grave moment in so short a time.

In 48 General Congregations (including tomorrow's), they have discussed, in whole or in part, no less than 13 schemata, namely, the two new chapters added to the Constitution on the Church (the eschatological aspect, and the Blessed Virgin Mary); the new preface and section on care of souls added to the decree on the *Pastoral Function of Bishops; Religious Liberty; the Jews; Divine Revelation; the Lay Apostolate; the Priestly Life and Ministry; the Oriental Churches; the Church in the Modern World; Missionary Activity; Renewal and Adaptation of the Religious Life; the Training of Priests; Christian Education*; and *the Sacrament of Matrimony*.

At the same time, while following or taking part in these debates, the Fathers have been called upon to express their will by vote on many of these documents, chapter by chapter, and in some cases section by section. In particular, the great Constitution on the Church, cardinal document of the whole Council, required no less than fifty-six ballots to get it through the first stage, and then, since the Fathers were free to add modifications to their final vote on each chapter as a whole and these were considered and in some cases incorporated by the Doctrinal Commission in the definitive version, a further eight votes were needed to approve the decisions of the Commission, plus a final vote, today, on the Constitution as a whole.

Moreover, in many cases, the Fathers had to hear and study explanatory reports from the Commissions designed to help them in making their decisions. For example, four lengthy reports preceded the voting on the controversial chapter III which deals with the Hierarchical Constitution of the Church. The explanation of all this intensive industry is not, of course, to be found in the spontaneous energy of the Fathers. Eager though most of them are to complete the work of the Council, they would almost certainly have liked more time to study the documents and reports piled upon them in an almost daily stream. The pressure came from the Co-ordinating Commission, aided and abetted by the Moderators.

Cardinal Tisserant, in his opening address to the first Congregation of this session, 15th September, expressed the desire of the Co-ordinating Commission to conclude the Council in this session and its belief that it could be done. It was for this end that all schemata not hitherto presented to the assembly had been drastically reduced to propositions during the interval following the second session, all except the schema on the *Lay Apostolate*. Further, in order to expedite the debates, any Father who desired to speak had to give five days' notice, plus a summary, and the Moderators were empowered to require Fathers whose points were similar to choose a common spokesman. And at the 9th Congregation (25th September) the Moderators issued a time-table of the submission of summaries which, when interpreted in the light of the rule of five days previous notice, implied that the plan was, if possible, to complete the debates by about 23rd October, leaving the rest of the session for revision and voting.

For a while the debates were kept to schedule. The plan, if there was one, began to creak during the debate on the *Lay Apostolate* which was allowed to run on, somewhat repetitiously, for five Congregations (6th to 12th October), partly, it was surmised, because the only remaining schema due for full debate (*The Church in the Modern World*) was not yet ready for presentation. To allow even more time, two of the schemata of Propositions, the *Priestly Life and Ministry* and the *Oriental Churches*, were introduced ahead of schedule and discussed. When, however, the first of these, after a two-day debate, was sent back by the Fathers for revision and amplification into a full-length schema, it became evident that the original plan of finishing the Council in this session could not possibly be achieved. To judge from subsequent events, a new plan was then devised with the limited object of ensuring that all the remaining schemata would at least be presented and discussed sufficiently to enable the relevant Commissions to revise their texts in a manner likely to win the approval of the Fathers at a fourth session. This has allowed these schemata to receive a fuller degree of discussion than would have been possible under the original plan. So, for example, twelve Congregations were devoted to the debate on *The Church in the Modern World*, and an average of two and a half to the rest. The schema of Propositions on *The Missionary Activity of the Church*, like that on the *Priestly Life and Ministry*, was sent back, by 1601 votes to 311, for revision and amplification.

Even if these revised documents are eventually submitted to fresh discussion, a short fourth session, a few weeks, should now suffice to complete the work of the Council. Had the same degree of pressure that has characterized this third session been applied from the first, three sessions would have been ample. But there would have been reasonable ground for complaint and regret.

Reflections on the Third Session of Vatican II

(*Ushaw Magazine*, March 1965 n. 223 pp. 7-15)

The distinctive feature of the third session, 14 September to 21 November 1964, was hustle; that and the unprecedented mass of documents which the Fathers were called upon to digest, discuss and vote upon. It was like the last-minute run around a house in process of being vacated, when most of the big stuff has been dealt with, but a multitude of smaller items remain to be cleared up. The reason was that the governing body had begun the session with the firm purpose of making it the last. Already, with this object in view, all *schemata* not yet presented to the assembly, except *The Church in the Modern World* and *The Lay Apostolate*, had been reduced to brief series of propositions on which the Fathers were to be asked to vote after a summary discussion; and to limit the number of speakers, five-days notice had to be given of any intended intervention.

The list of final dates for notice of intended speeches on the various *schemata* revealed that a provisional time-table was in existence, which, had it been kept to, would have concluded the debates by 23 October approximately, leaving a month for the revision and final approval of the documents.

For the first few weeks the debates were kept to schedule easily enough, because the Moderators can always be sure of an affirmative vote when they propose the closure of a discussion; the Fathers surge to their feet with an audible swish of mantellettas. In this way, the assembly dealt expeditiously with the discussion of two added chapters on *The Church*, some sections on the care of souls to be inserted in *The Pastoral Duties of Bishops* (discussed in the second session), the declarations on *Religious Liberty* and on *The Church's Relation to Non-Christians* (formerly *The Jews*), both left over from the second-session debate on Ecumenism, from which they were now detached, the completely revised constitution on *Divine Revelation* (replacing *The Sources of Revelation*, thrown out at the first session), and, with some sharp criticism, *The Lay Apostolate*.

To this point, everything was going roughly according to the time-table. It was when the brief series of propositions on *The Priestly Life and Ministry* was introduced on 13 October (ahead of time, because *The Church in the Modern World* was not quite ready) that the plan to finish the Council broke down. The Fathers, conscious of the time and space they had devoted to the office and duties of bishops, would not allow their beloved priests to be dismissed in a few laconic and mainly juridical platitudes, and, after a two-day debate, they sent the document back to be re-written as a full-length theological treatise. A fourth session was thereby made inevitable.

From then on, the powers-that-be were satisfied to ensure that all the remaining documents would at least be presented and discussed sufficiently to enable them to be amended according to the mind of the Fathers before the fourth session. In this they succeeded. The propositions on *The Oriental Churches* were accepted, debated, amended and voted with such expedition that the decree was able to be promulgated with *The Church* and *Ecumenism* at the final solemn assembly. *The Church in the Modern World* (to my mind, a windy and, on some points, dangerously inexact manifesto) was inconclusively debated for nearly 13 Congregations, and, one hears, is likely to be radically revised before the fourth session. The propositions on *The Missionary Activity of the Church* were sent back, like those on *Priests*, for complete revision. The propositions on *Renewal of the Religious Life* and on *The Formation of Priests*, as well as the *Declaration on Christian Education* were accepted in general and summarily discussed, but remain to be voted upon, after amendment, in the fourth session. The *votum* on *The Sacrament of Marriage* (really on the reform of marriage law) was passed for the consideration of the Pope, in or before the general reform of Church law. In principle, therefore, the fourth session should be mainly devoted to voting on documents amended in the light of previous discussion. In practice, there is likely to be extensive discussion of the two that were sent back, especially of the revised draft on *The Church in the Modern World*, which all regard as of crucial importance.

The journalists, who incidentally do not attend the debates, gave full publicity to the alleged "uproar" created in the assembly by the postponement of the vote on *Religious Liberty*. It would be more exact to say that it created a considerable stir, largely because it was the culmination of a series of delays. The document had made its first appearance at the second session, when, along with *The Jews*, it was an appendix to *Ecumenism*. Because both appendices were highly controversial, the Moderators induced the Fathers to accept the chapters on Ecumenism for discussion, promising them a vote on the acceptability of the appendices before the end of the session. Through lack of time, they never got it. However, as we have seen, the document was duly presented early in the third session, was accepted and debated, and went back to the Church Unity Commission for amendment accordingly.

Rumour has it that the amended version was ready for voting as early as 23 October, but that the Theology Commission then claimed the right to examine it and took an unconscionable time doing so. What is certain is that it did not reach the Secretariate for printing until Wednesday, 11 November. Printed over the weekend, it was distributed in St Peter's on Tuesday, 17 November, with notice that it was to be voted on the Thursday. On the Wednesday, it was announced that a number of Fathers had protested that this did not give them time to study what was virtually a new document, as indeed it was in structure, and that the Presidential Bench (whose sole job it is to apply the rule-book) had decided to take a preliminary vote, the next day, as to whether to proceed with the voting. On the next day, however, Tisserant announced on behalf of the Presidential Bench that they had changed their minds and that, owing to lack of time for due study, the vote would not be taken that session. No explanation for their change of mind was given, though it has since been reported that the Tribunal of the Council had ruled that the proposed preliminary vote was out of order, it being the duty of the Presidential Bench to interpret and apply the rules.

Anyway, the immediate result was that a number of Fathers, mainly American, after discussing the position in the aisles, organized a petition to the Holy Father and obtained a very large number of signatures. Cardinals Meyer, Ritter and Leger took the petition immediately afterwards to the Pope, urging him most strongly to order a vote. That evening, we are told, the Pope discussed the matter at a meeting of his cardinals and decided that he ought not to overrule the interpretation given by the Presidential Bench to art. 35 of the Rule-Book, i.e. that the Fathers have a right to *adequate time* to examine an amended text before being summoned to vote upon it. This decision, announced on the Friday, did not allay the annoyance of those who had thought the declaration to be as good as approved, but its proper object should be those, if any, who deliberately delayed the handing in of the amended document to the Secretariate. It will certainly be passed next session.

Some were also said to be critical of the Pope's action in adding 19 further amendments to the amended version of *Ecumenism* before it was put to the vote of the Fathers at the final general congregation, Friday, 20 November. Since no act of the Council has any force until he approves it, it was at least courteous on his part to insert the amendments he felt to be necessary, before rather than after the Fathers had voted. At the final general congregation, the vote was 2054 for, 64 against: at the solemn public session, the following day, when it was promulgated, the vote was 2137 for, 11 against.

Even the most ardent ecumenists would however admit that the chief and most consoling fruit of the session, and indeed of the whole Council, was the promulgation of the great Constitution on *The Church*. It had had quite a chequered history. The first draft, presented towards the end of the first session, in November 1962, had been rejected after a week's debate as too scholastic and juridical in structure and tone. Those Fathers who had come to the Council responsive to Pope John's call for an *aggiornamento* of the life and practice of the Church and to his primarily pastoral and ecumenical vision, and who had already discovered in the debate on *The Sources of Revelation* that they were in a majority, called for a new and deeper insight into the biblical notion of the Church, as an indispensable pre-requisite to its renewal. Their desires were met by a mixed Commission (Theology, and Unity of Christians), appointed by Pope John to re-write it during the interval, and when the new version was presented at the beginning of the second session, it was found generally acceptable for discussion.

The debate dominated the second session, occupying 23 out of the 43 general congregations. It was rightly regarded as the key document of the Council, both as the long-awaited complement of Vatican I (which had meant to deal with the nature and constitution of the Church after defining the papal primacy, but had been prevented by the Italian invasion of the Papal States), and as the necessary basis of all other proposed reforms.

The first two chapters were found to have struck the right note. Following the Bible, the first chapter, on the Mystery of the Church, gropes for symbols to convey the inner but hidden reality of the Church, as Kingdom of God, the one fold, God's field, God's House, family, temple, spouse, the People of God and the Mystical Body of Christ.

The second chapter develops in detail the fruitful theme of the People of God, which best links the Old Testament with the New, explains the whole of salvation history, and reminds us that, until its consummation at the Second Coming of Christ, the Church, though redeemed, is in pilgrimage, like the Israelites on their erring way from the bondage of Egypt to the Promised Land, and like them ever in need of reformation and renewal. It excludes the kind of ecclesiastical triumphalism castigated by the Bishop of Bruges in a memorable speech.

The main debate, however, in that second session had centred round chapter III, on the hierarchical structure of the Church, because it was here especially that Vatican I's doctrine of the papal primacy needed to be complemented by a balancing doctrine on the office of bishops. The chief issues, on which at first there seemed to be a sharp difference of opinion, were as to whether the body or "college" of bishops succeeds to the universal pastoral mission given by Christ to the college of Apostles, so that under and along with its head, the successor of Peter, and without prejudice to his primacy, it has full and supreme power over the universal Church even outside a General Council; and whether every bishop validly consecrated in communion with the head and members of the college is thereby constituted a member of it. After a nine-days debate during which the defenders of these two propositions were at pains to emphasize that it was not a question of a college of equals, because the papal primacy over it was not in dispute, some test questions put by the Moderators as "feelers" showed that the vast majority of the Fathers inclined to the collegial view of episcopal authority in the Church. This cardinal issue regarding the hierarchical structure of the Church was therefore as good as settled in the middle of the second session.

Nevertheless, the constitution on the Church continued to permeate the whole of the third session. True, it took only a few days to complete the discussion of the two added chapters for which the Fathers had called, on the eschatological destiny of the pilgrim Church, and on the place of the Mother of God in the mystery of Christ and the Church; but the voting on the complete document, section by section, continued right through the session. To make absolutely sure of the mind of the Fathers, the controversial chapter III was divided for this purpose into 39 sections. Altogether, 56 separate ballots were needed to get the constitution through this first stage of approval, and then, because the Fathers were free to add *modi* (modifications) to their vote on each chapter taken as a whole, a further 8 votes were taken to secure approval of the treatment accorded by the Commission to these modifications, plus the vote on the constitution as a whole (19 November), repeated before its promulgation at the Solemn Public Session on 21 November. And after all this fuss and bother and controversy, running right through three sessions, the final verdict of the Fathers was 2151 for, 5 against. A clear guarantee, surely, that the seal of the Holy Spirit is on the "new look" which the Council has given to the old Church, and an assurance that it remains the same Church.

Less important in itself, but hardly less significant as a sign of the times was the promulgation of the decree on Ecumenism. As one of the Fathers remarked when the initial draft was under discussion in the second session (18 November to 2 December, 1963), ours may come to be known as the ecumenical century. It was in 1908 that the Church Unity Octave began, and ever since then the movement has gained steadily in momentum among Catholics and non-Catholics alike. The groundwork had therefore been well laid long before the Council was even thought of, and doubtless for this reason the document had a relatively easy passage through the ordeal of conciliar debate. There were, of course, differences of opinion as to the right means to the goal, but no dispute about the need for a more positive and active approach to the problem of Christian reunion.

As the decree emphasizes, our divisions are plainly contrary to the will of Christ, who prayed the night before He died, not only that we might be one, but that our unity might witness to His divine mission. Needless to say, we have always known this. What is new in the decree is the Church's solemn and sincere commitment to the ecumenical approach to the old problem. It urges us to seek to build on what we have in common and reminds us how much and precious that is, notably our brotherhood in Christ through incorporation in Him by baptism, and our common veneration for the Bible as God's saving message to mankind. Brothers should remember and respect their brotherhood even when they are estranged.

This is not to make light of our differences, which are real enough and on some points grave. But the decree proposes that we should first seek to narrow the area of our differences by making sure, through friendly and equal discussion between qualified representatives, that they are not based on misunderstanding of each other's true position, and then endeavour patiently to resolve those that still remain through continued dialogue, aided by earnest prayer, public witness to our common faith in God and Christ, collaboration in all good works, and, above all, self-renewal and conversion to full Christian living.

The amended version of the decree which went through all the prescribed stages of voting in this third session differs from the initial draft mainly in the greater extent to which the detailed application of the proposals concerning joint prayer, common action and dialogue is left to the discretion of the local hierarchy. On this it is insistent: among Catholics, the movement must remain firmly under hierarchical control. But that the Catholic bishops of the whole world are henceforth committed to the ecumenical movement is surely clear from the moral unanimity of the final vote: 11 dissentients among 2148 voting Fathers. Not only has the third session of the Council given us a new vision of the Church, it has charted its course towards the long-desired reunion of all Christians in the one fold under the one shepherd.

A following talk was given to the clergy of the Lancaster Diocese at Preston and Carlisle.

Highlights of the Third Session of Vatican II

The distinctive feature of the third session was the hustle. The coordinating Commission began with the idea that the Council could be brought to an end, and when, half-way through, it became evident that, for all their driving, this could not be accomplished, they at least made sure that every remaining document was presented and summarily discussed. In the event, only three documents reached the final stage of promulgation, *De Ecclesia, De Oecumenismo,* and *De Ecclesiis Orientalibus*.

Unquestionably, the chief fruit of the session and indeed of the whole Council is and will remain its impressive dogmatic Constitution on the Church, promulgated on 21 November 1964 with only five dissentients. From the first it had been universally regarded as the key document, both because it provides the long-awaited complement of Vatican I, and because the *aggiornamento* for which the Council was primarily summoned could only be achieved through a deeper insight into the very nature of the Church.

A whole century-and-a-half of theological probing, especially in Germany, from Moehler (died in 1838), through Scheeben and Koster to *Mystici Corporis* (an answer to Koster) and beyond, had prepared the way for this deeper insight but there was little evidence of it in the first draft presented at the first session (November 1962) and rejected by the Fathers as too scholastic and juridical. At the second session (1963), a completely revised document, the work of a mixed Commission, which viewed the Church first as Mystery and as People of God, before dealing with its structure, was presented and debated through 23 of the 43 Congregations of the session.

The most controversial chapter proved to be that on the *Hierarchical Structure of the Church*, which raised the disputed questions of the sacramentality of the episcopate, its collegiality and relation to the government of the universal Church, and the restoration of a permanent diaconate.

The debate on these questions dragged on for nine days and would have lasted much longer, but for the shrewd device of the five famous propositions by which the Moderators discovered the general feeling of the Fathers without having to listen to them all individually. It was also decided to add a chapter on the eschatological nature of the Church on earth and to append *De B.M.V.* as a final chapter.

Revised accordingly, the schema came back at the beginning of the third session for discussion of the two added chapters and for the voting on all eight chapters severally. The voting continued right through the session, because every section on which there might be difference of opinion was separately voted, the controversial chapter III being divided for this purpose into 39 sections. Altogether, 56 ballots were required to get the Constitution through this first stage of approval, and then, since the Fathers were free to add "modi" to their vote on each chapter as a whole, a further 8 votes were need to approve the treatment accorded to these "modi", plus the vote on the whole schema (November 29), repeated at the solemn promulgation on November 21. And after all this fuss and bother, the final verdict was 2151 to 5, a clear guarantee that the seal of the Holy Spirit is on the new look which the Council has given to the old Church, and an assurance that it remains the same Church. In my non-expert opinion, it is a magnificent document.

I cannot say the same about the schema on *The Church in the Modern World*, which occupied 12 Congregations of the Session. Conceived only after the Council was well under way, it missed the two year process of elaboration in a Preparatory Commission and had to be hastily put together between the 2nd and 3rd Sessions by a mixed Commission (Theological and Lay Apostolate) working mainly through the group of experts, Haring and Co, who attracted the irony of Archbishop Heenan in his much publicized speech. The governing idea is sound enough: that the Church, immersed as she is in the world, cannot be indifferent to the problems and anxieties of the world but must confront them realistically and offer Christian solutions, where such are available. And the first three chapters approach this mission with some relevant and constructive considerations, on the relation of the Church to the world, on the "signs of the times", on the wholeness of man's vocation to save his soul and build a better world through his engagement in it, on the dedication of the Church to the service of mankind, on the way in which Christians should behave in the world, with understanding, charity, fraternal communion in a spirit of detachment, respectful dialogue with all men of good will. But if, as was said in the introductory report, the object of the schema is to lay the basis of such a dialogue, the esoteric, airy-fairy terms in which much of the first three chapters are couched should have been avoided, in favour of a simpler language intelligible to the ordinary man.

Then, when, in chapter IV, it proceeds to deal with the crucial problems of the modern world, and, in particular, with those of contraception and nuclear war, it is too imprecise to provide clear and practical norms of action. The section on conjugal life (n. 21), for example, omitting the distinction between primary and secondary ends on which our doctrine has hitherto been based, concentrates rather on the unquestionable importance of a pure and faithful conjugal love, observing, quite rightly, that "marriage is not a mere instrument of procreation". But when we look for a ruling on contraception, this is what we get: "Such however is the nature of conjugal love that marriage is of its nature ordered to the procreation and education of children. Hence, the true cultivation of conjugal love and the whole pattern of family life deriving from it have as their consequence that spouses should be generously disposed to cooperate with the love of their Creator and Saviour who enlarges and enriches His family through them." As to the number of their children, that is for them to decide with prayerful responsibility, according to the gifts of God and the norm of true love.

Every one of these statements is individually acceptable. The trouble is that they are equally acceptable to those who, favouring the Lambeth line, urge that spouses whose married life as a whole is generously life-directed, as far as the gifts of God and the norm of true love will permit, cannot be accused of sinning against the law of marriage, if, in exceptional circumstances, they resort to contraception. In other words, it leaves the current controversy unsettled, and apparently of set purpose.

Significantly, there is no mention of the Church's traditional doctrine, as emphatically proclaimed in *Casti Connubii*, not even a footnote reference. True, the *Adnexa*, a separate document which we we were given to understand expresses the full mind of the Commission, says explicitly: "*Every* deliberate human intervention which vitiates the personal activity (opus) proper to the conjugal act is contrary to the divine law and ordinance of marriage, nor can such a manner of acting be reconciled with the integrity of conjugal love", and adds a reference to *Casti Connubii*, but this document was not presented for discussion and its text could not therefore be voted upon. However, my latest information is that the special Commission appointed by the Pope to study this question does not intend to evade the issue.

On the nuclear deterrent, the schema makes the unexceptionable points that true peace cannot be based on parity of deterrents, and that differences should be solved by conventions rather than by force. But then, after admitting that when all means of peaceful solution have been exhausted, it can be lawful to repel unjust aggression by force, it adds: "The use, however, of nuclear weapons whose effects are greater than can be estimated and therefore cannot be reasonably controlled by men exceeds all just proportion and is therefore to be judged most criminal before God and man. Hence, every honest effort must be made, not only to have nuclear war solemnly proscribed by all nations and assemblies as a monstrous crime, but also that nuclear weapons and others of similar dire force be altogether extirpated and suppressed". It concludes that since war becomes ever more unreasonable as a means of repairing injustice, the Council denounces the arms race, and summons all nations to collaborate for a just peace, e.g. through the setting up of an international community with the instruments necessary to the avoidance of war and the promotion of peace.

All very fine-sounding! But, as Archbishop Beck observed, it makes questionable statements about the controllability of nuclear weapons, and says nothing to solve the current dilemma of war-hating countries who cannot unilaterally abandon their nuclear weapons without sacrificing their only effective deterrent against nuclear attack. To be realistic, it should at least distinguish between a "countervalue" strategy, which could never be justified, and a "counterforce" strategy which could be, at least in principle.

Finally a word about the annoyance created, especially among the Americans, by the postponement of the vote on religious liberty. Note, "annoyance", not, as the journalists put it, "uproar". Apart from the drone of speeches and the occasional illicit outbreak of clapping, the only sound ever heard in St Peter's is a buzz of conversation. What happened was this. The subject should have come up for discussion in the second session, when it formed an appendix to the schema on Ecumenism, as did *De Iudaeis*, but owing to the strong opposition manifested to these appendices during the debate on the schema "in genere", a vote was taken on the acceptability of the chapters on Ecumenism as a basis for detailed discussion, and the Fathers were promised a vote about the acceptability of the appendices before the end of the session. To the annoyance of many, they never got it, though Bea insisted that the only reason was time (only a day remained) and promised that the two subjects would come up early in the third session. They did, as detached declarations, and they were accepted, debated and sent back to the Commission for amendment accordingly.

Rumour had it that the unity Commission had the amended version ready for voting by October 23, but that the Theology Commission then claimed the right to study it and dragged its feet. Anyway, according to Archbishop Fellici, the Council's secretariate did not receive it for printing until the Wednesday of the second last week. Printed at the weekend, it was distributed to the Fathers on the final Tuesday, with notice that it was to be voted on the Thursday.

The minority opposition objected that this did not give them time to study what was virtually a new document (it was, in structure). On the Wednesday, Tisserant announced this objection and said that, on the Thursday, there would be a preliminary vote as to whether or not to proceed to the voting. The minority, realising that this amounted in effect to a rejection of their demand for time, appealed to the rule-book. On the Thursday, Tisserant announced that the Presidential Commission had upheld the appeal and that there would be no vote until next Session. The Americans, confident that it was as good as through, were very annoyed and before the end of the morning they had collected over 800 signatures to a petition to the Pope, and a deputation sought audience with the Pope immediately afterwards. The Pope discussed the matter with his cardinals and decided that, since the ruling was in order, he would not countermand it. This decision, communicated on the Friday, did not abate the resentment of those who felt frustrated, but its proper object should have been those who had delayed the presentation of the document to so late a date. It will be passed by a comfortable majority when it comes up at the next Session.

* * *

The following talk was given shortly after the conclusion of the Third Session of the Council at Bishop Auckland Town Hall on January 18th, 1965.

Dear Brothers and Sisters in Jesus Christ.

Two months ago, I was in St Peter's, Rome, when the Vatican Council approved the final draft of its decree on Ecumenism by the massive majority of 2137 votes to 11.

I was resident, as I have been throughout the Council, at the English College, which, for the two centuries before the Reformation, was a hospice for English pilgrims visiting Rome, and where one can still see on the walls of its present chapel memorial tablets of pilgrims who died there in those days. One of them bears the name of a Dean of Auckland. Every time I see it, as a Durham man born and bred, I am reminded of the thousand years in which all Christians of this country were one household in the faith, united in creed, worship and communion.

The Vatican Council's decree on Ecumenism likewise recalls this fact of our long common history and sees in it both a witness to our affinity and a challenge to fresh effort to recover the unity we have so sadly lost.

Reunion of all Christians is indeed one of the principal objects of the Council, as it was of the good Pope John who called it together. Our divisions are plainly contrary to the will of Christ who, on the night before He died, prayed to His Father: "That they all may be one, as thou, Father, in me, and I in thee; that they also may be one in us; that the world may believe that thou hast sent me (Jn 18, 21). As our unity was meant to be a witness to Christ's divine mission, so our disunity is a scandal to the world. It implies, says St Paul, that Christ Himself is divided. Fidelity to Christ requires therefore that we do our best to end it.

In a sense, this duty to achieve union has always been recognized by Christians, even in the days when the chief means to it on either side was to suppress or discredit the other. The Catholic Church in Council has now emphatically committed all its members to a new way, that of ecumenism. What is new about ecumenism is the completely different spirit, method and approach with which it tackles the old problem. Instead of seeking to blame or discredit those Christians from whom we differ, it invites us to build on what we already have in common, and that is a great deal. All who have faith in Christ as Lord and Saviour and are baptised in the name of the Father and of the Son and of the Holy Ghost are incorporated in Christ as members of his body and Sons of his eternal Father, and therefore brothers in the Lord. Our present unhappy estrangement cannot alter this basic relationship. A further link is to be found in our common love and veneration for the Bible as the word of God to men; for though we may differ sometimes as to its meaning or as to the authority of the Church to expound it, we agree at least in seeking in it the key to God's saving plan for mankind, and we share a common desire to preach the gospel to every creature and to apply it in our own daily lives.

Ecumenism requires us therefore to behave to our fellow Christians as to brothers, to respect the sincerely held convictions of those from whom we are temporarily estranged, to avoid all harsh or untrue expressions, judgements and actions, and to appreciate genuine Christian values wherever we find them, whatever the denomination.

This is not to make light of our differences. However honestly held, they are real and on some points grave. They cannot be ignored or swept under the carpet as though they did not matter. That would be a false irenism, a peace-at-any-price policy which could never produce a true and lasting union, and for which genuine ecumenism has no place.

What ecumenism proposes is that we should first seek to narrow the area of our differences by making sure, through friendly and equal exchange between our qualified representatives, that we each fully understand what the other actually holds and are not merely divided by faulty communication. And even though we should still be left with some points of radical disagreement, we should try to solve them, not by scoring points in bitter controversy, but by sympathetic and inexhaustibly patient dialogue, which seeks, not victory but the fulness of truth. Humanly speaking, full and final agreement may seem impossible, but with God all things are possible, and His grace will not be denied us, if we use the means available.

What are these means? The first is earnest and constant prayer. We must ardently want reunion and pray for it unceasingly, in public and in private, jointly and severally, without ever abandoning hope. The second is public witness to our common faith in God, one in three Persons, and in Jesus Christ our Lord and Saviour.

The third is friendly collaboration in all good works, for example, in the social application of Gospel principles, in the campaign against world hunger, illiteracy, maldistribution and inadequate housing, in the struggle for a firm and lasting peace based on justice. Finally, perhaps the most important means is our own self-renewal and reformation according to Christ, both as individuals and as communions.

In the judgement of the Vatican Council, true ecumenism is impossible without a change of heart and holiness of life. The first call is to full Christian living. Our object is to come together in Christ, and to grow together in Him by faith, hope and charity.

The more (to quote St Paul) we "put on Christ", both as individuals and as communions, the closer shall we draw together. Our final reunion may be long delayed and demand immense patience. But Christian faith, as our Lord assures us, can move mountains, Christian hope is not confounded, and in Christian charity lies the bond of perfection, even the perfection of unity.

V. The Fourth Session of the Second Vatican Council (1965)

The Final Session of Vatican II

(*Ushaw Magazine*, March 1966 n. 226 pp. 1-11)

On Wednesday, 8th December 1965, during a solemn ceremony celebrated before a vast crowd assembled in the warm, almost summery sunshine of St Peter's great *piazza*, Pope Paul VI brought to a close what may prove to have been the last ecumenical Council in the history of the Church. I suggest this, not because of any presentiment of imminent doom, or because the number of bishops is increasing at a rate which must soon make it impossible to assemble them all in what could meaningfully be called a Council, but because the Church appears to have found what may prove to be an adequate substitute.

I refer to the "Synod of Bishops" which the Holy Father set up, at the first General Congregation of this fourth and final session, as a permanent central institution representative of all the bishops of the world and a practical expression of their collegiality. By convoking this synod in general assembly, the Pope will henceforth be able to seek and discover the mind and will of the whole episcopal college through the accredited and duly briefed representatives of the various episcopal conferences. The synod could therefore well serve all the purposes for which it has hitherto been necessary or useful to call a General Council. Nor would the consequent change from an institution in which every bishop was theoretically entitled to speak his mind *coram Ecclesia* to one in which he could only intervene through chosen spokesmen be an altogether novel development. It was substantially introduced in the first session of Vatican II, when the Fathers decided that a topic could be closed to further discussion by majority vote and that thereafter the right to speak should be limited to those who spoke on behalf of at least seventy other Fathers, a restriction that was in fact frequently applied in later periods of pressure.

But whether or not Vatican II proves to be unique in being the last of a long line, it was certainly unique among General Councils in its purpose and outlook.

Called by Pope John, not to define a disputed doctrine, but to review the whole life, worship, institutions and discipline of the Church, with an eye to making them more pastorally effective, and the image of the Church herself more attractive to separated Christians, the Council had first to communicate these ends to its members as the criteria by which they should judge the draft documents prepared for them to discuss and elaborate. To judge from initial reactions, many had come to the Council unconvinced of the need of a wholesale pastoral review, or with little realization of what changes it might entail.

The critical moment came half-way through the first session, when the Fathers were called upon to discuss a draft document *On the Sources of Revelation* which, by espousing a particular opinion on an issue which Trent had deliberately left open, tended to widen the gap between the Catholic and Protestant positions, and for no apparent good reason. The ecumenically minded Fathers reacted strongly and came so near to getting the two-thirds majority vote required to reject the draft, that Pope John intervened overnight and ordered it to be sent back for revision by a mixed commission comprising the Secretariate for Christian Unity. From that date, 20th November, 1962, the Fathers of mainly pastoral and ecumenical bent became aware of their numerical strength and they never afterwards relaxed their grip. Their numbers grew and they gave dramatic evidence of their power in the last week of the first session, when they rejected the initial draft *On the Church*, because it failed to take a new look at the Church from the biblical, pastoral and ecumenical viewpoints; and Pope John sealed their ascendancy when, that same week, he ordered all the remaining drafts to be drastically pruned and revised along these lines.

Thereafter, the course of the Council through its three remaining sessions was almost predictable. No draft document presented in the *Aula* stood much chance of being accepted as a basis for discussion and elaboration unless it bore evidence of due attention to Sacred Scripture, pastoral preoccupation, and genuine concern for Christian reunion. Clear indications that these were the decisive criteria can be found, in varying measure, in all the sixteen documents which the Council eventually promulgated, two at the end of the second session (*Liturgy*, *Means of Social Communication*), three at the end of the third (*The Church*, the *Oriental*

Churches, Ecumenism), and eleven in the course of the final session. Since I have already dealt with the earlier sessions in previous articles, I shall limit my further reflections to the products of the final session.

Despite the size of its programme, the final session was, for me at least, the most relaxed of them all. Even though copy-hungry commentators continued to make the most of whatever unresolved tensions they detected and to predict last-ditch resistances, I never saw any real ground for doubting that the eleven remaining documents would go through. The opposition on certain issues was indeed active and vocal, but all previous confrontations had shown it to be restricted to a relatively small minority whose views were inevitably destined to be overridden by the inexorable march of the vote-taking. The majority of the Fathers never spoke in the assembly (thank God!), but one knew roughly from experience how they would vote.

In any case, five of the eleven documents were already as good as through, since they had obtained affirmative votes at the third session and needed only to receive the assembly's approval of the treatment accorded in Commission to the amendments submitted with the votes. All five comfortably surmounted this final hurdle during the first week of the session and were promulgated in due course at a solemn Public Session held on 25th October.

They were: (1) The *Decree on the Pastoral Function of Bishops in the Church*, which seeks to give practical effect to the collegial concept of church government by enhancing the status of episcopal conferences and pastoral competence of diocesan bishops *vis-a-vis* the Roman curia. The final vote in General Congregation was 2167 to 14, and in the Public Session of promulgation, 2319 to 2. (2) The *Decree on the Adapted Renewal of the Religious Life*, a blueprint for the revision of religious constitutions and canon law. Final vote: in General Congregation, 2126 to 13; at promulgation, 2321 to 4. (3) The *Decree on Priestly Training*, an outline sketch which puts the emphasis on the practical formation of true pastors of souls, steeped in the word of God and equipped to make effective pastoral use of the revised liturgy. Final vote: in General Congregation, 2196 to 15; at promulgation, 2318 to 3. (4) The *Declaration on Christian Education*, a somewhat abstract pronouncement, rushed through with regrettable haste during the over-packed final week of the third session. Final vote: in General Congregation, 1912 to 183; at promulgation, 2290 to 35. (5) The *Declaration on the Relation of the Church to Non-Christian Religions*, which began as a chapter on the Jews in the original draft on Ecumenism and had a rough passage through second and third sessions, largely owing to political apprehensions on the part of Arab bishops. Final vote; in General Congregation, 1763 to 250; at promulgation, 2221 to 88. A triumph for the patience of Cardinal Bea.

Two further documents, the *Constitution on Divine Revelation* and the *Decree on the Lay Apostolate*, had been fully debated at the third session and had been revised accordingly, but still had to go through the two stages of the voting process. Neither of them created any stir during its double journey through the *Aula*. The former, by ecumenically avoiding the two-source position which had led to the rejection of the original draft in 1962, while at the same time stressing the indispensability of Tradition to the full and certain knowledge of the revelation made through Scripture, succeeded in pleasing both sides, as can be seen from the final voting figures: 2081 to 27 in General Congregation, and 2344 to 6 at the Public Session of promulgation. The object of the document on the lay apostolate (to give practical effect to the new view of the laity's status and vocation in the Church, already approved in the constitution on the Church) had never been in dispute. Any difference of opinion was restricted to the methods to be adopted, and rumour had it that there was indeed quite a battle going on behind the scenes to prevent the lay apostolate from being identified with "Catholic Action". A satisfactory compromise must have been reached, because the final voting figures were 2201 to 2 in General Congregation, and 2305 to 2 at the promulgation (the only instance in which the opposition, both of them, refused to budge!). These two documents were promulgated at a special Public Session held on 18th November.

The main interest of the final session was thus centred on the four documents which, when it began, had still to survive the whole conciliar process from acceptance as a workable basis to the final approval of the treatment of amendments (*expensio modorum*). These, in the order of presentation, were the drafts on religious liberty, the Church in the modern world, missionary activity, and the ministry and life of priests. Judging from the previous endurance records of the Fathers, I had estimated that the process of accepting and discussing these four drafts could not drag on much beyond four weeks. In the event, it was completed at a leisurely pace on the last day of the fifth week. But it took (or perhaps it would be more correct to say that the authorities decided in advance to allot) a further eight weeks to get the documents revised in Commission, voted in General Congregation, amended in Commission and approved in General Congregation. Some attempt was made to relieve the tedium of these voting Congregations by introducing extraneous diversions. So, for a few days, we were treated to reports by the spokesmen of several hierarchies on their reaction to a proposed reform of indulgences, and at least twice a visiting choir which had performed at the opening Mass stayed on to entertain us with choice pieces of polyphony. But, on the whole, this final period was a dull anticlimax, happily relieved by the three separate weeks of vacation from general assembly that had to be interposed to enable the Commissions to complete their task of revision and amendment.

The *Declaration on Religious Liberty*, it will be remembered, had had a very chequered career. It first appeared as one of two chapters tacked on to the original draft on Ecumenism (the other chapter dealing with the Jews), when that document was presented during the second session. When it became clear that most opposition was centred round these two chapters, they were withdrawn from the vote on the general acceptability of the whole document, in order to speed acceptance and discussion of the chapters dealing directly with Ecumenism, but with a promise that a vote would be taken on the acceptability of the two withheld chapters before the end of the session. The promise was not kept owing to lack of time. Revised as separate "declarations", both texts were introduced, accepted and discussed during the third session, but so much time was taken by the Commission responsible for revising the text on religious liberty in line with the discussion, that once again its eager supporters were frustrated in their desire to carry it even through the first stage of voting. Its opponents had objected, with some reason, that in its revised form it was equivalently a new document which they needed time to study, and their objection was upheld as warranted by the rule-book.

When, revised again, it was presented for fresh discussion at the beginning of the fourth session, the main task of its supporters was to drive home to the opposition what precisely it maintained and, even more importantly, what it did not maintain. It did not, and does not, proclaim, as the opposition seemed to suspect, that every man has a God-given right to profess, propagate and do what is objectively contrary to God's will. This is to put the principle round the wrong way. What in fact it asserts is that every man has an objective right, inherent in his very nature as a responsible and social person, to worship God individually and socially according to his honestly formed conscience, because, in the final issue, that is the only way in which God's will reaches him and therefore there is no other way in which man, as objectively made by God, can seek to conform his will to God's in the manner proper to a responsible person. Consequently, no human authority can justly impede individuals or groups in the exercise of their religious liberty, except in the measure necessary to public order. A preliminary indication of the balance of opinion in the *Aula* was obtained immediately after the closure of the discussion (21st September), when, to the question whether the draft was acceptable as the basis of a declaration to be perfected in line with Catholic doctrine concerning the true religion and the duly approved amendments proposed, there were 1997 affirmative votes to 224 negative. Nevertheless, the alarmists continued to predict a battle to the death on the part of the Iberian and other Latin Fathers which might even yet torpedo the declaration. Had the said Fathers voted solidly, this might have happened, for they numbered many hundreds. In the event, the final vote in General Congregation was 1954 in favour, 249 against, which became 2308 to a mere 70 when the vote was repeated at the Public Session of promulgation. It would appear therefore that even the so-called "Latins" were eventually converted.

Then came the *Pastoral Constitution on the Church in the World of Today* which had been discussed to the point of agreed closure during the third session, but had since been so thoroughly revised that a further discussion was deemed expedient. Not projected until the end of the first session, this document still creaked from the effects of its hasty preparation and its completely novel and ill-defined theme of dialogue with the modern world, and though the latest version was agreed to be an improvement, the general verdict was that much tinkering remained to be done. It was criticized as repetitive, uncertain as to whom it was addressing, unrealistically optimistic in its view of the world, obscure, evasive of the real issues, failing to distinguish clearly between the natural and super-natural orders, and written in inept Latin. Nevertheless, it was accepted as a workable basis for detailed discussion and the Fathers agreed to discuss it in two parts and to allow no one to speak more than once on each part.

Despite this restriction, however, the discussion dragged on through some fourteen General Congregations, with occasional highlights, but a considerable measure of tedium. The draft then went back, on 8th October, for a long hibernation in the responsible Commission. When it re-appeared for voting on 15th November, it had been considerably recast and, to my mind at least, notably improved. The voting occupied three days, a team of readers taking turns to read out each section before it was put to the vote. The amendments proposed by those who voted *placet iuxta modum* were reported to number forty-thousand, and even after these had been collated by the Commission to a much smaller number, they nevertheless sufficed to fill two large volumes for the Fathers to study. It was not surprising, therefore, that the members of the Commission, not to mention the Vatican Press operatives, had to work day and night in order to get the expensio modorum ready for approval in twelve votes on 4th December. That there was still considerable dissatisfaction with the amended text was made clear on 6th December, when the vote on the document as a whole resulted in 2111 for, 251 against. As usual, however, many of the dissentients bowed to the opinion of the majority when the vote was taken again at the Public Session of promulgation, on 7th December, and produced the figures: *placet* 2309, *non placet* 75.

The *Decree of the Missionary Activity of the Church* which came up for discussion on 7th October had a much easier passage. The draft "propositions" on this subject which were presented at the third session were rightly rejected by the assembly as an inadequate and unworthy treatment of a matter which, in view of the essentially missionary character of the Church, must always be regarded as of primary importance. The completely new and extended draft prepared for the fourth session provided a good basis for a satisfactory decree and, after a relaxed debate spread over five General Congregations, was approved for elaboration by the Commission in the light of the comments made by the Fathers, with only fifteen dissentients. The duly elaborated text was voted through on 10th-12th November, the treatment of amendments was approved on 30th November, with a final vote super integrum of 2162 to 18, and at the promulgation on 7th December, the verdict was 2394 to 5. The large contingent of missionary Fathers must have gone away in much happier frame of mind than they did the previous year.

No sinister significance should be attached by the clergy to the fact that the draft *Decree on the Ministry and Life of Priests* was the last document to be discussed by the conciliar Fathers. Rather was it to the credit of the Fathers. It was a consequence of their forthright decision to reject as unworthy the few measly propositions concerning priests which had emerged from the pruning process after the first session and had been optimistically offered for their approval during the third session, and of their demand for a comprehensive treatment of the subject which they could offer to their "providi cooperatores" without a blush. Their reaction to the completely new draft must have been highly gratifying to its compilers. "In genere, valde placet" was a recurrent opening comment, and even the criticisms, prefaced by "attamen", which commonly followed, were mainly constructive suggestions. Indeed, there were only twelve dissentient votes when, after a three-day debate, the usual motion was put as to whether the draft could suitably be passed to the Commission for further elaboration in the light of the animadversions of the Fathers.

The duly elaborated text was read and voted, section by section, on 12th-13th November, and, on 2nd December, after the proposed amendments had been considered in Commission, the Fathers approved the treatment accorded to them and signified their satisfaction with the amended document as a whole by an affirmative vote of 2243 to 11, which, when the decree was promulgated on 7th December, became 2390 to a mere 4. Cardinal Döpfner had suggested in the debate that the document read too much like "lectio spiritualis".

In a sense, however, that is the purpose many of the Fathers wanted it to serve, and, in my opinion, it makes good spiritual reading. I should however declare an interest, because the responsible Commission was the one to which I was attached. It is much too early to judge whether or how far Vatican II has achieved the task for which it was summoned by Pope John. An accurate balance-sheet may not be possible in our lifetime. I think it fair to say, however, that the sixteen documents which the Council produced have at least chartered the future course of the Church's life and ministry in accordance with the Pope's vision. That, in effect, is the most it could ever have hoped to do. The rest inevitably depends on the manner in which the whole People of God, bishops, clergy, religious and laity, guided and aided by the Holy Spirit whose presence in the Council was almost palpable, implement its decrees and proposals in the years to come, beginning promptly and earnestly from now.

VI. General Talks on the Council (1966)

The following is the text of a talk was given at Darlington and again at Sunderland during the Unity octave of January 1966, a few weeks after his return from Rome after the conclusion of the Second Vatican Council (December 8th, 1965). A similar talk was given in Newcastle on November 11th, 1966.

The Significance and Achievements of the Vatican Council

The Second Ecumenical Council of the Vatican which completed its labours on December 8th last, after 168 General Congregations and 10 public sessions spread over four years, was unique in the history of the Church. The aim which inspired Pope John to assemble it was not, as in previous general councils, from Nicaea in 325 to Vatican I in 1870, to define a doctrine or settle a dispute, but to effect what he called an "aggiornamento" in the life of the Church, a.v. to bring the Church up to date in her institutions and manner of presenting herself and her doctrine to the world. By that means he hoped to pave the way to the eventual reunion of all Christians, a cause which had become very dear to his great heart during his 20 years as a papal representative in Bulgaria and Turkey where he had daily experience of the side effects of this disunion.

It would be an exaggeration to say that the 10 Preparatory Commissions and two Secretariates which he set up in 1960 to draft the agenda of the council were guided and inspired by his vision throughout their two years of labour. Snowed under with suggestions from over 2000 bishops in every country of the world, they produced between them for the consideration of the Council Fathers over 70 draft documents covering every aspect of the life and worship of the Church. I worked on one of those Preparatory Commissions and can testify that our concentration on our individual trees tended to make us lose sight of the wood. Even when the council assembled for its first 10 weeks session in October 1962, it took many of the Fathers quite a while to realise that the draft prepared for their discussion contributed little to the pastoral and ecumenical reforms they were meant to promote.

The one exception, perhaps, was the first draft presented, the document on liturgical worship, and this, after all, was the fruit of 50 years of preparation. Ever since the beginning of the century, with the full support of the Popes, a liturgical movement had been working for a reform of the liturgy which, by devising more appropriate forms and making greater use of the vernacular would promote more active and meaningful participation by the laity in the daily worship of the Church. This essentially pastoral object and inspired the draft document on liturgy. The discussion was long-winded, and much time and labour were required to get the eventual constitution through the various stages of revision and amendment, but when it was finally approved and promulgated on December 4, 1963, there were only four dissentients. It was the first, and one of the chief fruits of the Council, one which, in my opinion, helps to bring us closer to our fellow Christians. Certainly it does not widen the gulf.

The turning point of the Council – the "crunch" – was reached when the draft document on the *Sources of Revelation* came up for discussion, midway through the first session. On a point of theological dispute, on which previous councils had avoided taking sides, it favoured the view that revelation is contained partly in Scripture, partly in tradition, thereby implicitly excluding the equally tenable view, more acceptable to our separated brethren, that it is contained in Scripture as understood and expounded by tradition. The ecumenically minded Fathers reacted strongly and came so close to getting the two thirds majority required for rejection of the draft that Pope John intervened and ordered it to be sent back for complete revision by a mixed Commission which included the Secretariate for Unity. The form in which this document was finally approved in the fourth session, by 2344 votes to 6, will, I am sure, be much more acceptable to non-Catholic Christians.

This date, 20 November 1962, settled the future course of the Council. It made the pastorally ecumenically minded Fathers aware of their numerical strength and they never afterwards relaxed their grip. They reasserted it dramatically when the key document on *The Church* came up for debate in the last week of the session.

They found it too juridical, too much like a chunk out of the textbook, and they said so quite bluntly. Instead they wanted the Church to take a fresh look at herself and primarily from the biblical, pastoral and ecumenical viewpoints. Indeed, Cardinal Suenens called for a complete revision of all the remaining documents along these lines, and two days later, on the second last day of the session, Pope John decided that this was to be done by the council Commissions in the interval between the first and second sessions. In addition, the unwieldy mass of material was to be radically pruned and streamlined.

From that moment, the course of the council through its three remaining sessions (1963-1964-1965) was almost predictable. No document presented for debate would hope to win approval unless it was pastoral in spirit, and helpful (or at least not an impediment) to the cause of Christian reunion. In all, the council produced 16 documents of varying importance and quality, too many, evidently, for me even to summarise. I must therefore limit myself to the few that are of special interest to this gathering.

The key document of the whole council was the Dogmatic Constitution on *The Church*. The completely new draft produced in time for the second session (1963) was found to be much more acceptable in structure and tone, and, after a detailed and occasionally intense discussion that lasted half that session, it was revised, amended and voted through in the course of the third session (1964). To my mind, it marks a notable step forward. Instead of concentrating on the external framework of the Church, it probes into its inner reality, presenting it primarily as the sacrament or sign and instrument of man's union with God in Christ and of the unity of the whole human race, and mystery which the Bible itself can only convey in symbols and images, such as the kingdom of God, the one fold, God's field, house, family, Temple, spouse, the mystical body of Christ, the people of God.

A whole chapter is devoted to this concept of the Church as the People of God, which makes the Old Testament so meaningful to the New, illumines the whole of salvation history, and helps us to remember that the Church, redeemed as the Israelites were from the house of bondage, is still, like them, a Pilgrim on the way to the promised land, given to backsliding and ever in need of reformation and renewal.

At the level of hierarchical structure, the constitution rounds off the incomplete doctrine of Vatican I by affirming the collegial nature of the Church's government i.e. that the whole body of bishops throughout the world, as successors to the universal pastoral mission of the College of Apostles, have joint responsibility and authority, with and under the Pope, in the government of the whole Church.

Other important chapters stress the universal vocation to holiness and the full involvement of the laity in the apostolate (to which a separate decree was later devoted). The whole picture should, I feel, prove much more congenial to our separated brothers in Christ than that which has sometimes emerged in the past from Catholic treatises on the Church.

The decree on Ecumenism, which was likewise debated in the second session and amended and voted through in the third, also marks a considerable advance in our way of thinking, away from the Cold War mentality of the post-Reformation era. Instead of harping on our differences, it urges us to appreciate and build upon the great deal we have in common with our fellow Christians, notably our brotherhood in Christ and our common incorporation in Him by baptism, our common faith in Him as Lord and Saviour, our common veneration of the Bible as the vehicle of God's saving message to mankind. Our differences, grave as they are, may be partly due to misunderstanding, and with God's grace they can be resolved through patient dialogue, earnest prayer, public witness to our common faith in God and Christ, collaboration in good works, and, above all, self renewal and conversion to full Christian living. The more we "put on Christ", the closer we shall grow together.

The same spirit of Christian hope and charity, the same positive appreciation of values characterizes the Council's declaration on the relation of the Church to non-Christian religions. This document was originally concerned only with the Jews, and it had a stormy passage, but it got through eventually by 2221 votes to 88.

The Council's declaration on Religious Liberty also had a difficult passage. A vocal minority, which proved in the event to be much less numerous than many imagined, took it to mean that every man had a God-given right to believe, teach and do wrong, as long as it seemed right to him. This is to put the principal round the wrong way. What in fact it asserts is that every man has a right to worship God individually and socially according to his honestly formed conscience, because, in the final issue, this is the only way in which man, as God has made him, can seek to do God's will as a responsible person; and therefore that no human authority can justly impede individuals or groups in the exercise of their religious liberty except in the measure necessary to the preservation of public order. It was interesting to note that, as the debate proceeded, many speakers were more concerned about possible abuse by civil governments of this pretext of preserving public order than about abuse of religious liberty. You may have read reports that the so-called "Iberian block" of Spanish, Portuguese and Latin American bishops would resist this declaration to the bitter end. It is sufficient to answer to quote the final voting figures: 2308 for, 70 against. The "Iberian block" alone numbers several hundred bishops.

My final word must be on the Pastoral Constitution on *The Church in the Modern World*, which, after several extensive revisions and a host of amendments, finally was approved by 2309 votes to 75. This too, I feel, is of ecumenical value, because in it the Church, for the first time in Council history, addresses herself not just to her own members, or even to Christians generally, but to mankind as a whole and seeks to enter into dialogue with all who will genuinely respond beginning with a survey of the modern situation, it reflects on the vocation of man and human society as seen in the light of Christian faith, and points the way to the solution of some of the grave modern problems. As a first essay of its kind, it naturally had its teething troubles, and it remains far from perfect; but at least it bears witness to the outward looking which characterised this council, its ready appreciation of positive values wherever found, and its willingness to collaborate with all men of goodwill.

Handwritten addition

"One of the greatest events in the history of the Church" — Paul VI.

History will give its verdict. It will take many years before the changes bear fruit and much depends on how earnestly bishops, priests and faithful cooperate.

Unique in many respects. In sheer size of the assembly, in the number and variety of themes discussed, in benefiting from the presence and cooperative criticism of delegate observers from other Christian churches, in the breadth and universality of the Council's outlook and address.

It has certainly sharpened the Church's sense of involvement in the problems that vex the modern world, war, hunger, illiteracy, over population and pledged her to active cooperation with all men of good will. It has charted the path of the Church perhaps for centuries to come.

Chapter VI

The Summaries: Position Papers

After his arrival in Rome on October 8th and in the interval before the work of the Council got underway Lawrence McReavy found that he had a lot of free time on his hands. He records "The weather is warm and humid, with frequent showers; so I prefer to stay in and study the schemata and brush up my theology". *(L2)*

What began as a useful way of occupying his free time became an important task of providing summaries of the Council documents and discussions for the Bishops of England and Wales. These summaries were not merely of a secretarial nature, they were what today would be called "position papers". This voluntary and generous undertaking by Monsignor McReavy was to become quite burdensome. These papers show, as their content reveals, that McReavy made a significant contribution to the work of the English bishops.

On Friday October 19, he records: "I worked from 8 a.m. to 1 p.m. drafting a summary of the schema *De Liturgia* which Monsignor Worlock multicopied for all the bishops. Several, including the Cardinal, expressed appreciation. It helped me to feel that I was doing something useful". *(L3)*

Salient Points In The "Schema De Sacra Liturgia"

by Monsignor L. McReavy

Chapter I. General Principles

i) Liturgical Training and Active Participation

9. The Church sets great value on the full, conscious and active participation of all the faithful in liturgical worship, as the primary and necessary source of a truly Christian spirit. But, first, pastors themselves must be thoroughly imbued with the liturgical spirit.

10-12. There must be properly trained professors of liturgy in the seminaries; liturgy must be treated as a principal subject; the spiritual life of the seminarists must be given a liturgical formation, and their whole "ratio vitae" must be informed with the liturgical spirit.

13-14. The pastoral clergy must be helped to understand, live and communicate the liturgical life, and it is one of their chief duties to instruct and encourage the faithful in active participation, not only by their words but also by their example.

ii) Restoration of the Sacred Liturgy

There should be a general revision of the liturgy, to exclude unsuitable accretions and make the significance of the sacred rites more clear. A revision of the liturgical books should be carried through within a few years by worldwide experts. The revised rubrics should provide for lay participation. Any revision should be preceded by careful research, theological, historical and pastoral. No innovations that are not truly useful, and no notable differences between the rites of neighbouring regions. Devotion to S.Scripture as the fountain of the liturgy is to be fostered.

Without prejudice to the substantial unity of the Roman rite, the liturgy should be adapted to the native genius and traditions of the various regions.

Episcopal Conferences should have wider faculties, especially in regard to administration of sacraments and sacramentals, processions, liturgical language, sacred music and art, "actis a Sancta Sede recognitis".

The liturgy has great didactic value, and moreover the prayers, chants and actions are meant to elicit from the faithful a "rationabile obsequium". Hence, rites should be simple, clear, brief and intelligible to the faithful.

Though Latin is to be retained, there should be wider use of the vernacular in the lessons and admonitions and in some of the prayers and chants; the limits to be proposed to the Holy See by the Episcopal Conferences of the various regions.

Scripture readings should be fuller, more varied and more apt; there should be more scriptural preaching, rubrically indicated, and more liturgical catechesis and admonitions.

Liturgical actions are done in the name of the whole Church, and therefore common celebration of rites which naturally call for the participation of the faithful is to be preferred to private; and the congregation is to be encouraged to participate actively by acclamations, responses, antiphons, chants and bodily movements. But no changes may be introduced by private authority, and every participant must keep to the part assigned to him. Servers, lectors, commentators and choristers must be imbued with the spirit of the liturgy and properly trained in their parts. There must be no "acceptio personarum privatarum".

The liturgical life of a diocese should be centred round its Bishop and Cathedral, and this aspect should be cultivated even at the parish level, where a sense of community should be inculcated, especially in the Sunday Mass. Hence, no baptisms, confirmations, first communions, marriages or funerals outside the proper parish, without reasonable cause.

To promote liturgical pastoral action a liturgical Commission should be set up by the Conference of Bishops in every country, even in every diocese, though sometimes it may be better to group a few dioceses. Also Commissions of sacred music and sacred art.

Chapter II. The Holy Eucharist

There should be a revision of the Ordo Missae to facilitate understanding and active participation.

The Mass should contain a fuller course of Scriptural lessons, spread over several years. Homily strongly recommended.

The "Common Prayer" of the faithful should be restored, after the Gospel and homily.

A fitting use should be made of the vernacular, especially in the lessons, Common Prayer, and some chants.

There should be communion under both kinds in certain cases, e.g. the Ordination Mass.

Concelebration at the Chrism Mass, and, if provision cannot otherwise be made for private celebration, at gatherings of priests; the Ordinary to be the judge, the rite to be that of the Pontificale, with, certain adaptations, and with communion under both kinds.

Chapter III. Sacraments And Sacramentals

As signs, these have an instructive function and therefore the thing signified (which, in some cases, has been obscured by accretions) should be made easily perceptible.

The new *Editio Typica* of the Roman Ritual should clearly indicate the parts which can be in the vernacular in regional rituals, these latter to be prepared as soon as possible by the Bishops Conferences on the basis the Roman Ritual, and approved by the Holy See.

Baptism

A catechumenate of adults should be introduced, with successive rites during instruction.

The rite of adult baptism should be revised, with a proper Mass. That of infants should take account of the realities and clarify the part of parents and god-parents.

There should be a short form for cases of necessity.

Instead of the *Suppletio Caeremoniarum*, there should be a new rite of reception; likewise for validly baptized converts.

Blessing of baptismal water by short form during the rite, for just cause.

Confirmation

Revision of the rite so as to bring out its connection with baptism. Leave to confer it within Mass. Previous renewal of baptismal promises.

Penance

Revision of the rite so as to express its effect more clearly.

Extreme Unction

To be renamed "Unctio Infirmorum", as being the sacrament of the gravely ill rather than of the dying. Normally to be conferred between confession and communion. Number of anointings and form of prayers to be revised to suit different conditions of invalids. Occasional repetition during a long illness.

Ordination

A revised rite, with initial allocutions in vernacular.

Matrimony

A thorough revision, to signify the sacramental grace more clearly. Retention of local customs. Rites to be drafted by Bishops' Conferences with approval of Holy See.

Normally *intra Missam*, after Gospel. The oratio to be "super utrumque coniugem" and in vernacular. If *extra Missam*, the Epistle and Gospel of the Mass should be read.

Sacramentals

Thorough revision to facilitate participation and meet modern needs. Very few blessings to be reserved, and only in favour of Bishops.

A more uniform, sober and worthy rite of Religious Clothing and Profession, which can take place *intra Missam*.

Exsequial rite to give a clearer expression to the paschal sense of Christian death. Complete revision of infant burial.

Chapter IV. Divine Office

Lauds and Vespers are to be the two poles of the daily office. Compline to be clearly a final prayer. Matins to be adapted for recitation at any hour. Little Hours meant as a sanctification of the daily tasks.

Psalms to be spread over more than the week. Hymns to be purged of mythology and bogus piety.

Scripture lessons to cover a greater amount of the Bible. A wider measure of readings from the Fathers. Historical accuracy to be respected in Vitae Sanctorum.

Morning and evening prayers, drawn from the Sacramentaries, to be inserted in ferial Lauds and Vespers. Vespers to include daily Preces for various needs. Little Hours to end with a Pater in place of the prayer of the day.

Pastors should endeavour to have Vespers in common on Sundays, etc.

Clerics must continue to say office in Latin. Others can be allowed the vernacular, and those who recite with them fulfill their obligation.

Chapter V. The Liturgical Year

To be revised so as to foster pious celebration of the mysteries of Redemption, especially the paschal mystery. More emphasis on Sunday as the *Dies Domini*, and on the Feasts of Our Lord.

The twofold character of Lent (to prepare for or recall Baptism, and to do penance) to be given clearer emphasis in the Liturgy. Penitential practice to be revived, with universal Good Friday fast.

Universal celebration of Saints' Feasts to be limited to those of universal import. Church favours a fixed Easter and is ready to co-operate with a permanent civil calendar.

Chapter VI. Sacred Furnishings

Bishops Conferences to have the faculty of introducing or substituting new materials, and, with approval of Holy See, new forms.

Chapter VII. Sacred Music

An inestimable artistic treasure, but primarily a handmaid of the liturgy. Hence there should be forms which the faithful can use, and some vernacular chants. Whatever the solemnity, the faithful should always be able to share in the singing.

Musical training in the Seminaries, along with sound liturgical formation.

Faithful to be taught to alternate their voice with that of the priest or choir.

Gregorian to retain its principal place and the editio typica to be completed.

Popular chants to be encouraged and given a place even in liturgical actions, short, orthodox, easy.

New instruments to be authorised, provided not played automatically.

Chapter VIII. Sacred Art

There is no specifically "Church" art. Every style admissible, provided suited to its sacred purpose. But Ordinaries must exclude any works repugnant to faith or morals, or so distorted or mediocre as to give offence.

In passing judgement, Ordinaries must take expert advice. There should be commissions of sacred art at every level, diocesan, provincial, national and international. Bishops should foster the training of craftsmen.

Canons and statutes in regard to sacred buildings and furnishings must be brought into line with the restored Liturgy.

The debate on the Liturgy began at the Fourth General Congregation on Monday October 22nd. After the Eighth General Congregation on Saturday October 27th McReavy wrote that the debate "ploughed away along the interminable furrow of the Proemium and Caput I of the schema De Liturgia. *Most of the speakers had nothing fresh to say, and usually spent the first minutes of their ten minute allowance admitting it, but it did not prevent their reading their script to the bitter end." (L6)*

"Thursday, November 1 – Friday, November 2 – Saturday, November 3: Free Days. I spent them in summarising and collating the debate on the Preface and chapter I of De Liturgia. *Polycopied and distributed to Bishops, who were very grateful". (Diary entry)*

"I have spent the All Saints-All Souls break analysing the debate on chapter I for the benefit of our bishops, reducing a manuscript of notes to six pages of typescript which Worlock is going to roneo". (L6)

Analysis of the Debate "De Liturgia" to the End of Chapter I

By Monsignor L. McReavy

I. Opinion As to the General Value of the Schema, or Chapter I

(1) Approval

Approval of the schema as a whole was expressed by Cardinals Frings and Döpfner (who both called for the publication of the original text, and regarded the schema as moderate and pastoral); Montini (because the basic principle throughout was the good of the faithful); Lercaro (because it sought to promote active participation); Rugambwa, claiming support of the Bishops of East Africa and Madagascar (because it corresponded with the expectations of the faithful); Ritter, claiming support of most U.S.Bishops (because to reject it was equivalent to rejecting the essential principle of adaptation to modern conditions); Volk (because it provided for communal participation in a clearly intelligible liturgy and this was necessary to full Christian experience, perfect worship, and the personal dignity which modern man had largely lost); Acejo, who also called for the publication of the original text (because the guiding principles of salus populi and adaptation had been wisely followed). Frings, Döpfner and Acejo wanted deletion of the NOTA on title-page.

Approval of chapter I was expressed by Cardinal Léger, who wanted prompt implementation, in order to open up the hidden mysteries of the liturgy to all; by Cardinal Gracias (because it expressed what many had long desired); by Bp Beckers, for the Episcopal Conference of Holland (deserves highest praise; some imperfections, but no need for wholesale revision); by Bp Kemerer of the Argentine, claiming 25 signatures (excellent); by Bp Kobayashi, for all the Bishops of Japan (especially pleased with n. 24); by Bp Weber, exiled from China, who wanted it accepted as it stood, without time wasting over details, in order to get prompt action.

(2) Modified Approval

Cardinal Godfrey: "Generatim placet", but it should have begun with a precise definition of liturgy and taken more account of the pious exercises which count for so much in lives of faithful; omit n. 26. Card. Ricketts: To be approved in general, especially n. 22, but limits of episcopal adaptation should be more clearly defined.

Card. Bea: The time might not yet be ripe for certain developments, but the Council should refrain from closing doors that might conduce to the salvation of souls. Patriarch Maximus IV: Excellent on the whole, but n. 24 too absolute. Bp McGrath (Auxil. Panama): General contents and style good, but should be revised by theologians to secure accuracy and better connection.

(3) Criticism, Without Any General Expression of Approval

Apostolic Delegate U.S.A.: Poetical, inexact, inferior to *Mediator Dei*. Archbp. Dante: The Council should limit itself to basic principles and general norms. Card. Ottaviani: The doctrinal parts need complete theological overhaul, to correct misleading expressions and exaggerations. Card. Ruffini: Many faulty or obscure expressions. Card. Browne (for Card.D'Alton) proposed several textual emendations. Bp Parente found it verbose and, in some expressions, incorrect or inept. Card. Siri and Bp Olaechea-Loizaga wanted revision of the doctrinal propositions by a mixed commission of liturgists and theologians.

Bps Flores and Garcia (Spain) called for clearer definition of the distinction between liturgy and pious exercises.

Bps Hervas y Benet (Spain) and Carraro of Verona wanted exposition of the liturgical principles and their doctrinal basis.

II. On the Need for Adaptation to Modern Conditions

Ritter: Imperative, because of the gulf separating modern man from the 16th century situation, because of the clamorous call from all parts of the world, and because indispensable to active participation. Léger: Necessary not only on the Missions, but in most former Christian nations.

Ancel (Auxil. Lyons): Ditto. Most regions are infected by Naturalism and Materialism which deaden the mens christiana. In these, many can only be reached through the liturgy, and only if its meaning is made clear; but adaptations must be authentically liturgical.

Gracias welcomed the wider faculties for adaptation in nn. 21-22.

Ricketts welcomed n. 22, but wanted clear definition of limits of episcopal adaptation.

Siri felt it necessary to admit the need of adaptation, because of the wide diversity of local conditions, but wanted a cautionary clause added to 20, 21 and 22, to keep adaptations to the necessary or very useful, under control of Holy See, proponentibus Episc. Confs.

Abbot Prou admitted adaptation was necessary, but feared that wide episcopal faculties might lead to disruption of Roman Rite.

Bp Lokuang (Formosa): Indult concessions to China in this matter should now become law.

De Sousa (India): Bishops Conferences should have wider faculties for adaptation, with leave to experiment for ten years before seeking final confirmation of Holy See.

Spuelbeck (E.Germ): Adaptation is a matter of life and death for East Germany.

Avalos (Paraguay): Structural accommodation is necessary to restore to many rites their lost significance.

III. On the Use of Vernacular in the Mass

(1) Definite Approval, At Least Ad Normam Art. 24

In addition to those who expressed approval of chapter I as a whole, specific approval of n. 24 was expressed by Döpfner, Urganelli and Descuffy (Turkey). The following also seemed satisfied with it:

Montini: Retain Latin for the sacrificial parts of the Mass, but use vernacular in the didactic.

Likewise Cooray (Ceylon).

Feltin: Permit vernacular in all parts addressed to the people, except in solemn Mass.

Gracias: Very content with n. 24. Fitting to use vernacular in didactic parts. Many cannot read, and even those who can prefer to hear. Abaun (Spain): agreed with Gracias.

Meyer (Chicago): Art. 24 norma optima est. Provides the needed via media and corresponds to the expectations of the faithful.

Beckers (for Dutch Bps): Most want a via media; and all that is proposed is a faculty, not an obligation. Hervas y Benet: via media. Respect and foster Latin, but be liberal to vernacular within limits proposed by Episc. Confs. and approved by Holy See.

Le Cordier: Art. 24 meets the hopes and needs of the faithful. Mother Church should talk to her children in their tongue. Fides ex auditu.

Isnard (Brazil, claiming to speak for 20 others): Missa catechumenorum in vernacular because all catechesis must be in an intelligible tongue.

Thiandoum (Dakar, claiming to speak for other Bps in Africa): Parts addressed to the people should be in vernacular.

Léger (Montreal) and Kobayashi (for Bps of Japan) wanted to substitute "statuere" for "proponere". The latter emphasized that to Japanese Latin is "western", "foreign", a hindrance to conversion.

A number wanted much more than contemplated by art. 24.

Patriarch Maximus IV: Art. 24 is too absolute about the maintenance of Latin. The original liturgical principle was the language of the assembly, intelligibility. In the East, every language can still be liturgical. Why should Latin (adopted when it was vernacular) be sacrosanct? For "proponere", read "statuere".

Koslowiecki: Would retain Latin in his own diocese for purely practical reasons (variety of vernaculars), but objected to Latin being given a privileged status.

Bau (Argentine): Wider use of vernacular, not only in liturgy of Word, but also in eucharistic liturgy, in the measure proposed by Ep.Confs., with approval of Holy See. More conformed to the rational dignity of the faithful that they be able to understand. Dead Latin no longer an apt instrument of the dialogue of God and People.

McGrath (Panama) approved Bau.

Kemerer (Argentine, with 25 signatures) agreed with Léger that "statuere" should be substituted for "proponere".

Morrow (India): Change art. 24. Allow liturgy to be in Latin or vernacular, as desired by the Episcopal Conferences, with approval of Holy See. Latin is not sacred. Mass should not be an esoteric rite. Conscious participation is scarcely possible except in vernacular.

Weber (exile from China): Concede a vernacular liturgy. Charity, not Latin, is bond of unity.

Spuelbeck: Vernacular a pastoral necessity in E.Germany, where liturgy is the only remaining means of instructing. For "proponere read "statuere".

Kandela. (Syria): The Syrian Bps were ready to sacrifice Aramaic, our Lord's own language, for Arabic, where necessary. Why not the same with Latin. Whatever is said aloud by priest, or in dialogue, must be in vernacular.

Simons: Latin is still needed for scholarly study, but for nothing else.

Franic: Art. 24. must not revoke the 1000 year use of palaeoslavic in Croatia.

(2) Reluctance, Or Definite Opposition, to Vernacular in Mass

Spellman. No vernacular in Mass. Changes make things difficult for pastors of big city parishes and disturb the faithful.

Suarez (Catanzaro). Keep to Latin, the link between liturgy and faith.

McIntyre. Keep the Mass as it is. The clarity of Latin is necessary to the immutability of doctrine.

Godfrey. Vernacular useful in some sacraments and sacramentals, but not desirable to make any change in the Mass. Not, therefore absolutely opposed to any use of vernacular in Mass, provided that Episc. Confs. reach an agreed, acceptable and peaceful solution, actis a SS. recognitis.

Bacci. National languages should not be introduced into Mass, anywhere. Understanding can be better communicated by catechesis. Let the Council reserve the question to the Holy See.

Siri. Some use of the vernacular may be necessary, but not more than is necessary or very useful, under control of Holy See, proponentibus Confs. Episc.

Gonsalvez del Amara. Latin in the Mass, except for Epistle and Gospel.

Parente. Caution necessary. Latin accentuates the sense of mystery.

Staffa. Preserve Latin entirely, at least in regions under the common law. Vernacular would involve loss of liturgical music, and require constant revision.

Gawlina. Keep Latin, but allow popular vernacular chants at Mass. Flores. Refer art. 24 to decision of Pope, with episcopal advice.

Carli. Retain "proponere", and reserve definitive judgement to the Holy See.

Mansilla-Reoyo (Spain). Latin should be permanently preserved in the West.

Cotantini. (Italy). Keep Latin even in. the didactic parts. Pastoral needs can be met in other ways, especially thorough catechesis.

Abbot Reetz. (Beuron). Ante-Mass in vernacular would relegate Gregorian chant to monastic museums. Not necessary for all to understand, provided all join in their own way, and understand why, if not what is being said.

Calewaert (Ghent): Allow vernacular in Lessons, Oratio Communis, and some chants. Retain Latin in responses, Kyrie, Gloria, Credo, Sanctus, Agnus Dei. But substitute simpler chants for Introit, Gradual, Offertory and Communion, which can be sung in vernacular.

Rolim de Mbura (Brazil): Vernacular not necessary to active participation.

De Vito (India): Keep Latin. Impossible to choose between a variety of vernaculars. Better to have translations and comments read aloud.

Saboia-Bandcira (Brazil): Vernacular would encourage laicism.

Battaglia (Italy): To "servetur Latina", add "cum amore".

D'Agostino; Keep Latin in West. Every Catholic should be able proudly to say: "civis Romanus sum".

Peruzzo (Italy. "sum senex"). History and Guéranger show that vernacularists have always ended up as schismatics.

III. On the Use of Vernacular in the Mass

(1) In Favour

Cardinals Doi and Feltin.

Gracias welcomed the wider faculties in nn. 21-22.

Beckers (for Dutch Bps.): No one disputes the power of the Pope to reserve the ordering of the liturgy to himself alone as from 16th C. But there is nothing to prevent the Council, with the Pope, conceding wider faculties. A mere question of what is expedient.

Isnard (Brazil): The "ius proponendi" already belongs to all, even layfolk. What is being granted by the schema?

De Sousa (India) Ditto. Episc. Confs. should have the "ius statuendi". Missionary Bps are better judges than the Roman curia. They are of age, and include wiser heads which will restrain the hot-heads.

Kemerer (with 25 signatures), Kobayashi (for Bps of Japan), Spuelbock also proposed "statuere" for "proponere".

Thiandoum (Dakar): Episcopal Confs. should have the faculty to introduce vernacular where they think necessary.

(2) Against

Those (see under III) who want to retain "proponere", or reserve to Holy See.

Abbot Prou who feared that wider faculties would disrupt the Roman Rite.

(3) Practical Difficulties

Del Campo: The Episcopal Conference is not yet a juridical institution with legislative power, and mature consideration is needed before making it so.

Borromeo (Italy) and Gonzaga and Rolim de Moura (Brazil): Faculties must be limited to National episcopal conferences, to avoid confusion.

Meyer: A bishop cannot be subject to a National Commission (as implied in n. 34), but only to the Pope.

The Council bulletin for ninth General Congregation on Monday October 29th stated that the "discussions of the first chapter of the project on the liturgy have revealed a unanimous and harmonious concept of the Fathers on the nature and ends of the liturgy. All have stressed that the liturgy continues in time the work of Redemption, pre-announced by God in the Old Testament and fulfilled by Christ in the New Testament."

On November 11th McReavy wrote that "we have had a strenuous but valuable week of debates on the Sacred Liturgy schemata". (L7)

Analysis of Main Points of Controversy In Chapter II, De Liturgia

By Mgr. L.L. McReavy

Revision of the Ordo Missae (Art. 37)

(1) Opposed, or reluctant and cautious

Spellman. "maxima prudentia".
Ottaviani. A "res sanctissima" which we should hesitate to touch.
McIntyre. No change.
Fares (Italy). Do not touch the Canon.
Saboia-Bandeira (Brazil). No change affecting structure of Mass.
Barrachina-Estevan. Ditto.

(2) More or less in favour

Rusch (Innsbruck). Restore Offertory of Faithful.

Devoto (Argentine). Restore Celebration Facing People (ditto Da Cunha Marelim of Brazil). Make the Ordo simple and clear, with less signs of cross, etc.

Satoshi-Nagae (Japan). Allow vernacular in chant of both Ordinary and Proper, in Oratio Communis, and in Pater. Japanese cannot even pronounce Latin.

Hallinan (U.S.). Clarify and simplify so as to facilitate participation and instruction through liturgy.

Pao-Zin-Tou (Formosa). Keep the Canon the same everywhere, except perhaps for vernacular Pater and Agnus. Episcopal changes should be outside the Ordo properly so called. Shorten the pre-Canon, lengthen the post-Canon, e.g. by moving the Gloria to after Communion.

Duschak (Philippines). In *congregational* Mass, the Missa Catechumenorum must evidently be in vernacular; but even the Canon should be refashioned after the model of the Last Supper, the celebrant using Christ's words, and, like Him, speaking aloud and in vernacular.

Laszlo (Austria). Revision needed for active participation, to bring out the biblical sense of the sacred actions, to meet pastoral needs.

Ferrari (Italy). Wanted — a low Mass designed for community use.

Jenny (France). Keep the Ordo, but with emendations necessary to clarify the meaning of the various rites.

Vicina Araguiz (for Bps of Chile). The liturgy of the Word should not be from the altar, but from e.g. an ambo, and in vernacular.

Dwyer (Leeds). Limit revision to Mass of Catechumens, keeping rest as it is and in Latin. Any change in first part, including vernacular, should be same for all who use Roman rite. If Africa and Far East have special needs, let them have their own Rites, but keep Roman Rite intact and uniform for all countries in Europe, or of European origin.

Communion Under Both Kinds (Art. 42)

(1) Opposed, or unready to concede as much as Art. 42

Ruffini. The reasons for the Tridentine prohibition are even stronger in these days of frequent Communion. At most, refer decision to Pope. Perhaps it could be allowed in Ordination Mass.

Godfrey. No change in present discipline. If any is to be made, impose strict limits for whole western Church. Wide divergence and confusion, if decisions were left to Episcopal Conferences.

Ottaviani. Surprising that it has survived rejection by most of Central Commission. Dangerous and impractical.

Florit (Florence). Only in concelebration.

Pereira (Mozambique). Only in Ordination Mass, never to laity.

McQuaid (for Bps of Ireland) Impossible even "in casibus bene determinatis."

Cambiaghi (Italy). Limit to priestly Ordination.

Jop (Poland). Delete art. 42. Impossible in practice.

Inglesias Navarri (Spain). No reason for change, exc. perhaps in Ordination.

Da Cunha Marelim (Brazil). Never to laity.

Aramburu (Argentine). Ditto. At least reserve decision to Holy See.

Melas and Fares (Italy). No change, even in Ordination.

(2) Ready to concede art. 42, or even more

Alfrink. Christ instituted Eucharist as a festive repast of two elements: "manducate" et "bibite". Hence, though Communion under one kind is complete in essence, it is incomplete in external form. Impractical to make the external form general, but desirable to exhibit it on certain carefully defined occasions. Ecumenical value.

Bea. "Omnino placet art 42".

Jubany (Spain). No one wants it to be general, but pastoral reasons for taxatively determined cases, e.g. Ordination, Religious Profession, Concelebration.

Przyklenk (Brazil). It expresses the indoles communitaria of Eucharist. No danger now to faith. Practical difficulties are exaggerated, witness the Easterns. Allow at First Communion, Ordination, Religious Profession and Nuptial Mass.

Jaeger (Paderborn). Allow clearly defined cases, e.g. Priestly Ordination, Solemn Profession, Nuptial Mass, Baptism of Adults, Reception of convert.

Weber (Strasbourg). Desired by many Bps. Safe. No obligation imposed. Add Blessing of Abbot, Religious Profession, Nuptial Mass.

Edelby (Edessa). It is the genuine original form, apostolic, not the exception. Latins should get rid of their complex about it.

Boillon (Verdun). Approve Viaticum sub specie vini for those who cannot swallow solids.

Beakers (for Bps of Holland and Indonesia) and Perraudin (for Bps of Ruanda Urundi) approved art. 42, but called for deletion of clause "sublato fidei periculo".

Zak (Austria). Ditto. He claimed that the objections were largely irrelevant because they assumed more than a limited set of cases.

Muldoon (Australia) was mainly anxious that the limits be defined, and suggested: "Only on Priestly Ordination, Religious Profession, and Nuptial Mass".

Seitz (Vietnam). Full assent.

I. Concelebration. (Art. 44)

(1) Opposed, or unwilling to go as far as art. 44

Ruffini. Better for a large gathering of priests to celebrate on alternate days.

Godfrey. No objection in case of priests assisting at the Chrism Mass. Doubtful whether opportune at gatherings of priests. Stipend difficulties.

Ottaviani. Against. It would deprive faithful of many individual Masses.

McQuaid (for Bps of Ireland). No change. Reasons rarely verified.

Inglesias Navarri (Spain). No reasons for common-law change, though it might perhaps be conceded as a privilege to monasteries.

Melas (Italy). Only in *Missa Coenae.*

Fares (Italy). Limit to monasteries.

L.L. McReavy going into St Peter's.

Bishop Cunningham and L.L. McReavy
on the steps of St Peter's on 12th November 1963.

Final meeting of Preparatory Commission.

McReavy says that he thought that with the completion of the work of this Preparatory Commission his particpation in the work of the Council was completed. Later in the year, shortly before the beginning of the Council, he was appointed a Peritus.

L.L. McReavy in the tribune for the Experts during the Council.

L.L. McReavy during the Council.

L.L. McReavy during the Council.

Watercolour of the bishops going into the Council painted by L.L. McReavy.

Funeral of L.L. McReavy celebrated by Archbishop Derek Worlock.

Funeral of L.L. McReavy celebrated by Archbishop Derek Worlock.

The Bishops of England and Wales for whom L.L.McReavy wrote Position Papers.

(2) Ready to approve art. 44 or even more

Léger. Extend art. 44 to other cases: iudicio Ordinarii in every instance. Positively advisable for conventual Mass, provided individual Masses are not required for good of faithful.

Gracias. Approved 44, but the two cases should be exemplative rather than taxative.

Bueno Monreal (Seville). Ditto.

Bea. approved implicitly.

Pereira (Mozambique). *Missa in Coena* rather than *Chrismatis*, but add "other extraordinary cases, iudicio Ordinarii".

Kleiner (Abbot Gen.Cist.). Approved, especially in regard to conventual Mass. Active participation for a priest means concelebration.

Sansierra (Argentine). Approved, but suitable also for Bps at Provincial Synod, and Bps and Pope at Ecumenical Council.

Koenig (Vienna). Agreed with Bea that this door should not be closed. No obligation is placed on Bps.

Cambiaghi (Italy). Approved cases in art. 44, but added sick priests in hospital.

Khoury (Lebanon) and Edelby (Edessa). Commend rather than tolerate, and add *Missae Coenae.*

Van Cawelaert (Congo) 260 African Bps approve art. 44 with Léger's emendations.

Cousineau (Haiti). Also followed Léger.

De Vito (India) Approved. But *Missa Coenae* for *Chrismatis.*

Perraudin (for Bps of Ruanda Urundi). Approve as it stands.

Bookers (for Bps of Holland and Indonesia). Ditto.

Seitz (Vietnam). Ditto.

Theas (Lourdes) Warm approval for reasons given by others, but also to solve Lourdes Mass problem.

Zauner (Austria). Extend art. 44 to the cases mentioned in the original schema. Those who composed it were men of experience and prudence, not youthful revolutionaries, and they were morally unanimous.

At the Eighteenth General Congregation on November 13th the debate on the Liturgy was closed. It had occupied fifteen sessions.

The Sources of Revelation

In his Diary McReavy made the following entries:

"Wednesday, November 14. Ottaviani introduced De Fontibus, *which came immediately under attack.*

Thursday, November 15. Dictated my summary of the first day debate De Fontibus Revelationis *to Miss Breen (of the Grail) who had it typed and duplicated for distribution to the bishops by supper time."*

"De Fontibus Revelationis, *which has brought a clash of personalities and a sharp division between northern and southern Europe as to the appropriate way of presenting the Gospel to our age, and controlling error without suppressing scholarly research". (L8)*

Summary of the Debate on the Schema "De Fontibus Revelationis"

14th November 1962

A. In Favour of the Schema as a Basis of Discussion

Cardinal Ottaviani.

1) The circulation of substitute schemata cannot easily be reconciled with Canon 222, according to which it is for the Pope alone to determine the matters to be dealt with in an Ecumenical Council. It is disrespectful to the Pope. If the Fathers have emendations to make they should make them on this schema approved by the Pope for discussion, not on any other.

2) Some say that it lacks the pastoral tone. But the primary object of the Council is to propound doctrine. The pastoral tone can be added by others later. But the pronouncements of the Council must be brief and lucid, issued not in the manner of a sermon or pastoral or encyclical, but as a text of unchangeable doctrine.

3) Some say that it is not abreast of the new theology, but fashions in theology come and go.

4) It is to be hoped therefore that the Fathers will respect this fruit of the labours of the Preparatory and Central Commissions.

Cardinal Ottaviani's report was then read for him as follows:

The principal function of the Council is to protect and promote Catholic doctrine formulated in its most exact terms, without receding from the sense in which the Church has always interpreted the divine deposit. One should not look for new statements (renovatio) but an increase of doctrine. The Pope said it is for the Council to propound the sacred deposit in a more efficacious way. Its primary object is doctrinal. Its acts should not read like homilies. The doctrinal magisterium of an Ecumenical Council involves a solemn judgement on what is to be believed and done, and has the infallibility with which Christ endowed his Church. It is not expedient that the Church should cease from rejecting errors.

The Schemata were prepared according to the vota of the Bishops and are truly consonant with their mind. They were drafted by a Commission of Experts from different countries, and have their unanimous approval. They were also checked by the Central Commission. It is not a disciplinary but a dogmatic constitution. The doctrine of a Council is irreformable and it cannot afford to pander to current but ephemeral terminology. If here and there errors are condemned it is because doctrine must be protected from current errors.

Cardinal Ruffini.

This is a question of supreme importance. The very "centrum concilii". The schema pleases me on the whole (universim placet). It was prepared by the Theological Commission and checked very exactly by the Central Commission. Why should it be thoroughly revised? It is the schema approved by the Pope for discussion by the Council. By what authority would any other be discussed? And if the second schema were rejected, another would have to be prepared and so on and on. It should therefore be put to free debate. It is not perfect. I myself have emendations to propose, but that is the object of the debate, to perfect the schema, and, if need be, complete it.

Cardinal Siri (Claiming to have consulted the full conference of Italian Bishops).

1) Though the schema needs to be emended it is useful and indeed necessary to discuss it as it stands. The matters dealt with are so fundamental that we cannot proceed until we have full certainty on some of its points.

2) Some of the doctrines of Vatican I have been questioned by the Modernists and therefore it is fitting that the same matter be dealt with again at least by way of positive expression of reaffirmation.

3) Many are distressed that the dignity, value and certitude of Sacred Scripture are not always preserved and look for guidance from this Council. It is right to meet their legitimate hope.

4) There are, however, points in the schema which need clarifying. It does not preserve due proportion between Scripture and Tradition, and it is not always clear from the schema how the text is superior to any human text.

Quiroga Y Palacios. (Santiago di Compostella)

Was difficult to understand, but accepted the schema. It presents doctrines in the way required nowadays though some expressions and distinctions need clarifying for our separated brethren.

Morcillo (Saragossa) – claiming the signatures of many Spanish Bishops.

It is true that this schema represents only one school of thought, but the same is true of the others. Hence the Spanish Bishops propose that the present schema be discussed with a view to making it better. It is ecumenical in spirit and tries to present Catholic doctrine clearly. It provides a valid basis for discussion and it is better to adopt it than to try to find a substitute.

B. Against the Schema as a Basis of Discussion

Lienart. Non placet.

1) Because its whole tenor is quite inadequate to the matter in question. It speaks of two Sources (*Fontes revelationis*) and it is true that there are two ways in which revelation comes to us. But it has nothing to say about that other source which is the Verbum Dei. Our Lord taught us first by his own mouth and then through the Apostles. Before that God spoke through Moses and the Prophets. The schema should therefore have dealt first with the Verbum Dei.

2) Because the subject is treated in a frigid scholastic way, whereas it should have been expressed in terms which would show our separated brethren that we share their devotion to the Verbum Dei.

3) Because, whatever the value of the reasonings advanced, it is better in a supernatural matter like revelation to rely primarily on the "fidei documenta" i.e. the inspired authors. They are more sure than our reasonings.

Conclusion: The schema should therefore be thoroughly revised.

Frings. Non placet.

1) Because of the language of this schema and especially the second schema. The first duty of a pastor is to preach the truth. The same truth can be preached either in an attractive or repellent manner. At Vatican I the schema of Franzelin was rejected because its tone was too professorial. It is the voice of the "Mater et Magistra", indeed of the Good Shepherd that is needed. The schema lacks that pastoral note so dear to Pope John.

2) Because of the way it treats two doctrines:

a) The doctrine of two Sources. That is a new way of speaking, foreign to the Fathers, to St Thomas Aquinas and to all Ecumenical Councils. It was understood during the nineteenth century in the period of Historicism. The one and only source is the revelation of the Word of God, about which there is nothing in the schema. This is not likely to conciliate separated brethren.

b) The way the doctrine on inerrancy is expressed is too frigid and approximates to the doctrine of verbal inspiration. There are two theological opinions still in the field, the one proceeds in a deductive manner from the definition of Trent; the other also starts from the definition of Trent but in addition has regard to the text as it stands in context. It is not the custom for Councils to settle disputes between Catholic theologians, but only to condemn heresies.

3) Because of the excessive size of the schema. How can the Council hope to deal with such a mass of material? Some things must be omitted, some abbreviated, some run together, and the schema reduced to a quarter of its size, like the one mentioned by Ottaviani.

Léger. (Montreal)

The whole scheme needs revising. It contains some good articles but its mentality is no help to the Church.

1) It is imprudent to decide or even speak with such certitude on questions disputed among experts e.g. the relation between Scripture and tradition.

2) The Church will suffer if biblical theology is handicapped. There is a danger that the schema may unjustly create diffidence among exegetes.

3) The schema is based on fear of error. That is its mentality. But, though errors must be repelled, the Church should be able to speak serenely on any subject. The positive approach pleases both Catholics and non-Catholics.

4) The opinion it advances is only one of the opinions in the Church and the different schools do not themselves talk in terms of conflict.

Koenig. Non placet.

1) On the relation between Scripture and tradition there is no unanimity among theologians.

2) On the question of inerrancy — what about the "Obiter dicta"? The schema goes beyond the Encyclical which allowed free discussion. It is sufficient for the protection of the Faith to state the principles.

Alfrink.

The schema is out of harmony with the allocution of John XXIII, who said it was not our job to repeat the well-known teachings of theologians. It repeats at length what all the manuals contain, without adding anything from more recent studies. There was no need to call a Council to study this. The Pope wants an expression suited to our time.

It may be objected that chapter IV deals with the errors of our time, but the schema fails to clarify doctrines which have not yet been sufficiently explained, and this is the more to be regretted because the correct understanding of these doctrines is a necessary step towards reunion.

I propose therefore, that the schema be abbreviated and amended or a new schema substituted in line with the Pope's desires. In saying whether this is the kind of constitution we want, are we not doing what the Pope wants us to do?

Suenens.

Non placet, for the reasons already given. It lacks brevity. The rest of the speech was devoted to proposals for shortening debates in general.

Ritter (St Louis, U.S.A.)

The schema should be rejected and another substituted.

1) It has no evident usefulness. It contains nothing new, no adaptation or efficacy for contemporary man. Mere repetition of Trent and Vatican I is useless.

2) It is full of ambiguity. It should indicate the prepared solutions of difficulties.

3) It is pessimistic and negative in spirit. It throws suspicion on a large number of recent biblical studies. Scholars expect support and positive enlightenment. We should help rather than repress them. If there is no solution the schema should say so. If there are errors it should show that they are errors. As it is it will result only in tedium and fear of Scripture.

Cardinal Bea. Non placet.

1) It does not correspond to the scope set by Pope John, who wanted "the whole and pure truth of God so presented that men would understand it and freely assent to it'! As pastors we want to satisfy the needs of all, not merely of some. Such was the programme proposed by the Holy Father. The scope of the Council therefore is not to discuss some doctrines or repeat former doctrines, but to present them attractively in the way our times demand.

2) The schema is quite devoid of pastoral character. It envisages not the man of today, but the theological schools — and even a single school.

3) There is nothing in the first part about the fact of revelation, yet the modern atheistic world needs to be reminded of this fact. There is no need for the Council to discuss the four Evangelists or the Vulgate version or the notion of inspiration which can be found in any treatise.

4) The schema condemns collective inspiration which is taught by only one or two, but this is not the question. The question is how the inspired writer was influenced by the collectivity.

5) It is hardly necessary to say that reunion was not considered at all. Yet our doctrine should be presented in a way that will make it clear to our separated brethren.

6) Finally the schema has much to say about exegetes. Only once have I noted the work of modern exegetes praised. The schema speaks of them with a certain suspicion and fear without touching on their problems. The whole thing needs thorough revision to make it brief, clearer, more pastoral and ecumenical.

Patriarch Maximus IV (Of Antioch of the Melchites).

The choice of subject in an Ecumenical Council is not determined by its objective value but by its value relatively to the time.

1) I doubt whether the schema does what the Bishops and Universities want. An Ecumenical Council should remain aloof from the questions of the schools.

2) There is no need of new definitions of Faith. Specialists are still disputing. It is not for us to impose definitive solutions.

3) Even doctrines that are certain are presented here belligerently.

4) The schema fails from the ecumenical point of view and should be rejected all together.

Manek. (In the name of all the Bishops of Indonesia and with their signatures).

The schema is unsatisfactory and not suitable for discussion without thorough revision.

1) It contains much that is superfluous and unsuitable to an Ecumenical Council e.g. matters treated in the manuals.

2) It condemns the teachings of reputable authors, and a Council should not do that without necessity.

3) As it stands it would create a new obstacle to the dialogue with our separated brethren of whom it takes no account.

4) It sanctions the opinion which teaches two sources, whereas Trent acknowledged only one. In regard to inspiration, it sanctions the scholastic opinion which is at most theologically certain. It is superficial on the question of the historical truth of the Gospels.

Summary of the Debate "De Fontibus"

By Monsignor L.L. McReavy

November 16th-17th.

A. Placet (with welcome)

Cardinal Cerejaire (Lisbon)

A satisfactory basis of discussion. The Constitution can only produce pastoral and ecumenical fruits if its doctrine is firm, integral and unambiguous.

Cardinal McIntyre (Los Angeles)

It offers a clear compendium of Catholic doctrine such as we need today, when all sorts of loose theories are circulating.

Cardinal Santos (Manila)

Satisfactory, and can be emended, supplemented, etc. if necessary. It is for the Council to provide the definite, integral and sound doctrine i.e. the pabulum which must be explained pastorally by others, ourselves included. Adaptation to modern needs is a question of means. The doctrine itself needs no adaptation.

Fares (Catanzaro)
As it stands it provides an apt basis for discussion, even though it needs clarifying in parts.

Battaglia (Faenza)
Commendable for clarity and proper use of words. The objections raised against it are not valid. Nothing is more ecumenical than truth, integral and exact. The scholastic form is proper to a theological statement.

Cardinal Garibi (Mexico)
Satisfactory, even though there is room for emendation. The Council must declare the true doctrine clearly, if only to counter the many new doctrines circulating.

Saiz (Spain)
Most suitable and should be retained even though it certainly needs many emendations.

Rosales (Philippines)
Clear and orderly. It is necessary to give the whole truth without ambiguity.

B. Placet (acceptance)

Cardinal Camara (Rio)
We cannot reject the official schema without first examining it in debate. Voting will show how much emendation is necessary.

Cardinal Caggiano (Buenos Aires)
It would be a grave responsibility to reject the schema drafted by a world-wide Commission, on the basis of suggestions from the world-wide episcopate. Placet iuxta modum. A more pastoral tone is needed.

Cardinal Urbani. (Venice)
Accept it and emend the form. It contains much that is useful in these days of imprudent biblical speculation. The form is too scholastic and should be made more pastoral. Express the principles but omit reference to controverted questions. Warn against dangers, but show sympathy to scholars.

Cardinal Browne.
Satisfactory in substance. Most of the objections raised (he listed eleven) could be settled in debate. The Two-fold Source doctrine is the ordinary teaching of the Church today and is in accordance with the mind of St Thomas.

Tabera Araoz (Spain).

A sound basis for discussion, though not without defects. It should keep within the limits of accepted Catholic doctrine and present it sincerely and "suaviter".

Florit (Florence)

Continue discussion of the present schema. We agree on the substance of our doctrine. It is a question of method, of presentation. It can be improved, but its ambiguity is due to charity rather than astuteness. The whole force of the Gospels is being sapped by Formgeschichte.

Cardinal de la Torre (Ecuador)

It is not true that all Latin America wants the substitute schema. Ecuador at least wants to discuss and emend this one.

Parente.

It is not perfect, but it is worthy of discussion. The substance i.e. the principles, must be settled in debate. Points of form can be settled by vote, and the schema made more attractive. The doctrine of Two Sources is a common one since Trent.

(Cardinal Frings intervened shortly afterwards to say that no-one doubts that revealed truth is derived from Scripture and Tradition, but essentially there is only one Source with two streams emanating from it.).

Butorac (Yugoslavia)

Accept, and emend it where necessary, even "radicitus".

C. Non placet

Cardinal Lefebvre (Bourges)

It does not comply with the Pope's pastoral proposals. It is too negative, rigid and scholastic and makes too little effort to attract. It needs substantial and fundamental revision.

Cardinal Silva Enriques. (Chile) — Claiming to speak for other Latin American Bishops.

It is too scholastic, unecumenical and likely to cause dissension among Catholics . It speaks like a judge rather than a pastor. Dangers to Faith can best be be avoided by showing the splendour of the truth positively and charitably. The precise meaning of inerrancy is a question for experts.

Bengsch (Berlin)

Unsatisfactory because of the intention behind it and its way of speaking. Opinions still in dispute are condemned as errors. It fails to deal with the problem of the salvation of the countless millions who died before revelation, or all the unevangelised or unbaptised.

Reuss (Auxiliary Mainz)

The problems here contained cannot and must not be solved in haste, The Council should therefore proceed with a schema on another subject while this one is being revised.

Gargitter (Bressanone)

Many of its points should be omitted. If it has to deal with errors it should do so paternally and it should be much more sympathetic and helpful to scholars in their difficult task. Otherwise it will suppress not only errors but scientific progress and discussion with non-Catholics.

Guerry (Cambrai) — With the consent of all the Bishops of France.

The implication that those who want a fresh presentation are prepared to sacrifice the truth to pastoral needs is quite unwarranted and must be quashed. It is not our doctrine that has to be adapted, but its presentation. We cannot convert the world by merely repeating formulae. Indeed our own minds need adaptation.

Palacios (Mexico)

It should be revised and abbreviated to suit its pastoral purpose. The freedom of scholars should not be limited unnecessarily.

Butler (Downside)

Expert representatives of the two schools of thought should first meet and work out an agreed statement if possible. Otherwise reject this schema.

Cardinal Döpfner (Munich)

Reject and replace with a schema prepared by experts of the two schools, nominated by the Pope. In the Preparatory Theological Commission one side prevailed unduly and paid more regard to fear of error than to the problems of the scholars. In the Central Commission many objections were raised to the schema, but very few changes were made in the final version. Emendations were not dealt with individually.

(Ottaviani intervened, claiming that Döpfner was misinformed. There were differences of opinion in the Theological Commission but they were settled by debate and vote. More than one school was represented on the Commission, e.g. Cerfaux. The Central Commission did not proceed in summary fashion. Finally it is improper to reject the schema that has been passed by majority vote.).

The President at the written request of a Father then called attention to Article 33, paragraph 1. of the Ordo, which says:

"Quivis Pater verba facere potest de unoquoque proposito schemate vel admittendo, vel reiiciendo, vel emendando..."

Charue (Namur)

The "non placet" of Cardinal Suenens is shared by all the Bishops of Belgium and others of Belgian origin in the Congo. We want something more attractive, positive, biblical and ecumenical. The Supreme Authority needs to be asserted through a Holy Office, but it is not for a General Council to play the part of a Holy Office. We should show prudence and serenity in reconciling Christian doctrine with scientific truths. Problems should be investigated not denied. The schema fails to distinguish between the two kinds of Formgeschichte. Finally do not put obstacles in the way of sincere research.

Hakim (Melchites)

The scholastic form and structure of this schema is quite alien to us of the Oriental Church.

At the twenty-fifth General Congregation on November 23rd the debate on the schema on Social Communications was opened.

In his Diary McReavy made the following entry: "Thursday, November 22. Worked from 8 to 1.15 on a summary of the 50 page schema on the Means of Social Communication. After lunch, with Msgr Davis to San Clemente where a French guest expert gave a guided tour. After tea, dictated my summary of above schema to Miss Breen for duplication."

McReavy wrote to Monsignor Paul Grant:"Thursday being a free day, I spent the whole morning (8 to 1.15 without a break) doing a marginal summary of the 50 page schema on Means of Social Communication, which we were to begin discussing on the Friday. After tea, I dictated it to one of the Grail-girls, who had it polycopied that night, and delivered early next morning". (L9)

Summary of the Schema On Instruments of Social Communication

by Monsignor L.L.McReavy

Preface

The Church has a special interest in the new means of mass communication, press, cinema, radio and television. Rightly used they have cultural value for individuals and society and help to spread the Kingdom of God. But the Church knows that they can be, and often are, misused to the common harm. The Council therefore lays down certain general norms.

Part I. The Doctrine of the Church

Chapter 1. The Right and Duty of the Church

The rights and duties of the Church in this matter derive from her Divine Commission to teach all nations the truths of Faith and the natural law. This entitles her to use modern means of social communication and to teach men how to use them. In every age she has used the most apt means and guarded against their misuse. She has the right to free use of the modern means and it would be a crime if the State or anyone should exclude her or the Holy See or individual Churches. Her right to teach extends to the particular relevance of the use of these means. Men of good will are therefore urged to co-operate with her, confident that it will be for the good of all.

Chapter 2. The Observance of the Objective Moral Order

The objective moral order must prevail over all other considerations, economic, political or social, because it alone covers man's whole nature, conduces to his perfection and provides universally valid principles for use of means of communication.

There are three criteria to be jointly considered:

(i) The power of these means to compel attention and to hold it immoderately.

(ii) The moral principle of the matter communicated.

(iii) The particular circumstances of any particular communication e.g. its sources or the age or spiritual or intellectual level of those to whom it is addressed.

Three questions also arise:

(a) The right of information. In modern life information is a social necessity and therefore a social right, but the information must be conveyed integrally without mutilation or slant and in an honest and seemly way.

(b) Social freedom. All social expression is subject to the moral law. It should conduce to human perfection and should take account of the maturity and responsibility of those to whom it is addressed.

(c) Treatment of Moral Evil. Description or representation of evil can serve an honest purpose, but care must be taken to avoid irreverence, lasciviousness or allurement to evil.

Chapter 3. The Duties of Individual Associations and of the Secular Power

A grave responsibility rests on those who control these instruments or co-operate in their use, to ensure that public opinion is correctly formed by these means. Readers, listeners and viewers must beware of what will do them harm or give scandal to others and must withhold support from those who present or propagate evil, paying timely regard to the judgement of competent authority.

The young especially should be urged to practise discretion and moderation and a prudent selection in these things and should learn by discussion with teachers, parents and priests to pass a correct judgement on what they see or hear or read. But the main responsibility lies with those who are proximately engaged i.e. journalists, producers, actors, etc. Their prime consideration must always be the common religious and cultural good. They themselves therefore must first form a correct view of human life and they should belong to a professional association which has sound principles. The duty of the Civil Authorities is to defend true and just freedom to information; to foster religious culture and the arts; to protect the rights of the readers, listeners, etc.; to support the best efforts in social communication, especially those which have no commercial backing; and to be vigilant against immoral or anti-social pursuits.

Part II. The Action or Apostolate of the Church

Chapter 1. The Propagation of Christian Truth and Instruction

Pastors and Faithful should make diligent use of the means of social communication in the apostolate.

(i) Preparation of those who are at the receiving end.

Anything which seeks to promote efficient instruction should be actively supported, e.g. Associations for decency of press, stage, books, etc.

(ii) Use of modern means of Communication in the Apostolate.

This is a matter of urgent necessity. It is for the Bishops to judge whether it is better for the Church to have its own instruments, or to use those supplied by society or private individuals. What is important is that the Church should have effective means of putting its message across.

(iii) The Training of Priests and Laymen for this kind of Apostolate.

Bishops and Religious Superiors should select suitable men for training. There should be many more schools and Institutes in which laymen engaged in journalism, cinema, radio or T.V. could obtain an integral Christian formation especially in social doctrine and special care should be devoted to the formation of critics.

Chapter 2. On Helping to Spread the Truth

The difficulties and costs are formidable, but it is vital to overcome them. The money must be found. The Faithful therefore are urged to subscribe manfully, indeed it is their duty to support Catholic papers, cinemas, radio and T.V. stations, and there should be annual days devoted to encouraging this co-operation.

Part III. Ecclesiastical Discipline and Ordinance

Chapter 1. Ecclesiastical Discipline

(i) In regard to Catholic Undertakings.

(a) Those which belong to the Church must obey the rules and instructions of the Ecclesiastical Authority.

(b) Those which will be identified with the Church owing to their name, etc. need ecclesiastical approval of their name and activity and this can be temporary and withdrawn for a just cause.

(ii) In regard to Clerics and Religious.

(a) Clerics and Religious engaged as Directors or Ecclesiastical Advisors in journalism, radio, etc. must be nominated by, or have express leave from the competent Ecclesiastical Authority (this to be conditional on their adequate training) and they must comply with the norms and prescriptions of the same.

(b) Ordinaries and Religious Superiors must ensure that adequate knowledge of the use of these instruments is available to those whose formation requires it.

(iii) The Faithful in General, are urged to rely on the guidance of the Church in regard to press, cinema, radio, T.V., and if they are engaged in promoting or directing such activities to comply with the doctrine of the Church and co-operate with the Offices set up by the Hierarchy.

Chapter 2. The Organs of Ecclesiastical Authority

(i) The Offices of the Holy See set up by Pius XII and made permanent by John XXIII should have its competence extended to all instruments of social communication, the Press included.

(ii) Every Bishop in his own Diocese has a right and duty to direct the proper use of these instruments, to exercise vigilance over undertakings of this kind and to regulate for any matter affecting the public apostolate even when they are directed by exempt Religious. Diocesan or Regional Offices are helpful to this end.

(iii) In every nation there must be national offices for cinema, radio, T.V. and press governed by a group of Bishops or a delegated Bishop to co-ordinate their activities, and staffed chiefly by expert laymen under a Priest Director chosen by the Bishops. The chief duties of these Offices are to form the conscience of the Faithful in the use of these instruments, to keep them informed of the moral quality of films, books and transmissions and to mould public opinion by prompt issue of correct, news and denial of false news and to promote useful ventures, etc. But they must refrain from any form of business or commerce.

(iv) International Catholic Associations should be promoted by National Offices for mutual consolidation and to deal with questions needing international solutions. Such Associations are immediately dependent on the Holy See.

Part IV. Particular Instruments of Social Communication

Chapter 1. The Press, i.e. any form of printed periodical or publication

The Church's concern is especially directed nowadays to newspapers, illustrated magazines and above all the Catholic papers.

(i) Newspapers. Newsmen have got to seek a love of truth and respect for the moral law and the dignity of man. News should be presented in a way suited to its importance, not only lies but conspiracies of silence and slanted reporting must be avoided. In dealing with religious news, editors should seek expert advice.

(ii) Illustrateds. They are too often sensual and salacious and commonly omit anything related to God and the spiritual life.

(iii) Periodicals of Comment, etc. Editors of these incur a grave responsibility especially if they are likely to fall into the hands of the young or are addressed to them.

(iv) All Owners and Editors have a grave moral duty to present true news and honest pictures. Writers should seek out the truth and report it correctly with justice and charity. Reporters and photographers should not reveal secrets if the common good or respect for the human person requires otherwise. Sellers should supply only what is good and suitable to the age of their readers.

(v) The Faithful should avoid bad publications and those who sell them and support the good. Children should be trained to discern and choose the good. The National Press Office should promote instructions to these ends.

(vi) The Duty of the Secular Authority is to maintain conditions in which the Press can enjoy legitimate liberty in forming public opinion. But in the interest of the common good it should suppress evil use of the Press.

(vii) The Catholic Papers. Since a generically honest Press is not enough to inspire a truly Christian spirit a Catholic Press either directly dependent on Ecclesiastical Authority or run by Catholics is needed. The Church has a right to it and Bishops should see that it exists in their dioceses, but it must be of good standard well supported by clergy and people, able to compete in quality with other papers. For this purpose the National Office should join an International Catholic Association to which all Catholic Papers and Agencies are federated.

Chapter 2. Cinema

(i) Film producers, writers and cinema managers should enter a free agreement to observe a moral code, so that they will not be tempted by gain to make or show bad films. In making films which raise religious or moral issues, they should seek the advice of the Catholic Film Office. Honest producers and distributors should combine to promote by various means the making and showing of good films. They should be careful not to endanger the morals of their actors, especially if they are young. In every nation a reasoned moral judgement on every film should be issued by the National Office in good time and with the widest publicity and made by a Board of reliable laymen nominated by the Bishops. All the Faithful should take great care to learn and respect these verdicts. In chapters 3 and 4 similar recommendations are made for Radio, Television, etc.

At the twenty-seventh General Congregation on November 26th the debate on Social Communications was closed. The debate on the schema for reconciliation between the Church and separated Eastern Christians was opened.

"We moved on immediately to a schema prepared by the Oriental Commission on Reunion with the Oriental dissidents. We had been warned of this, so I stayed up till 11.30 on Saturday night doing a marginal summary which was dictated and polycopied on Sunday, ready for today's debate. It is a much more interesting subject and I think it is a good schema, though several have already objected to its placing. They say it should have come after the Theological Commission's schema De Ecclesia *(which incidentally is the next subject). The old guard have already shown signs of wanting to torpedo any approach to the Orientals that is not couched in exactly the same terms as we have fruitlessly used these past ten centuries". (L9)*

Summary of the Schema On the Unity of the Church: Omnes Unum Sint

By Monsignor L.L. McReavy

United by God's predilection and vocation but separated by sin, we are reborn in Baptism to new unity with Christ and one another, being made one Body in Christ. This Body of Christ is the Church, which until the second coming of Christ is twofold:

a) Triumphant in Heaven.

b) Growing to full stature on earth in the human social frame-work of rulers and ruled.

Christ provided for this need of hierarchy by building His visible, terrestial Church on the Apostles, with Peter as their Head. Their authority descends to their successors. Neither Peter nor his successors have in any way supplanted Christ. Christ remains Head in the full sense. Peter (the Pope) is Head only vicariously and in the government of the visible Church.

Christ willed His Church to be one, not only in heaven, but on earth, with a visible temporal unity through submission to the Episcopate and its Head, the Pope. Hence the Church deplores the schisms that have risen here, and declares that there is only one Church even here on earth, and that it is the Church governed by Peter's successor. No church on earth separated from this See can truly belong in the same way to the invisible heavenly Church, still worse is the error which would subject the Church to any civil power.

It would be wrong, however, to confuse unity in Head with uniformity in Body. One body can have diverse members and be the better for it. Hence the Church respects regional diversity especially that of the Oriental churches, under a single co-ordinating Authority.

Bona-fide members of separated churches are not entirely alien to the true Church. Nevertheless they are deprived of many means of salvation, especially the magisterium, and certainly division does great harm to the cause of Christ. But division has not broken all the spiritual bonds of the past. We share a common patrimony with our Eastern brethren by which we are still brothers. Mindful of this the Church has never ceased to work for the union of all peoples in Christ by prayer, Councils, solution of doubts, creeds, etc. Nor have the Popes ever abandoned their efforts. This world-wide Synod, therefore, exhorts all Christians to join prayer and effort for unity:

1. Supernatural means

The first need is prayer for God's help. Without it the difficulties are such as to make us despair. With it all things are possible, for the prayer of Faith can move mountains. Hence this Synod prescribes private and public prayer for these intentions and recommends the universal adoption of the Pentecost Novena and the Unity Octave, also prayer to Mary, the Protectress of Christian Unity, who is also beloved to the Oriental church. It would also help considerably if more Catholics lived up to their Faith.

2. Theological means

East and West have different approaches to the Divine truths. We should not cling unduly to our own forms of expression as long as truth is correctly understood and expounded. More attention and respect should be paid to the Oriental mind, and more stress should be placed on our common beliefs by recourse to the Scriptural and Patristic sources of our common patrimony. Theologians should avoid harsh words, and prefer the positive to the apologetic approach, especially in Ecclesiology. But there must be no false irenism, or watering down of Catholic doctrine.

3. Liturgical means

This Synod respects the attachment of Orientals to their honourable liturgies. It wishes them to be retained and cultivated and will never force anyone to abandon his own Rite. Sacred Rites are living expressions of Catholic dogmas. Orientals need not therefore fear that they would not be at home in the Catholic Church.

4. Canonical or Disciplinary means

The same applies to all their legitimate customs. This Synod affirms their right to be governed according to their own rules.

5. Psychological means

We must learn to see and love each other as brothers in Christ, redeemed by His Precious Blood; and to show it in the way we write about the faith, liturgy and history of our dissident brethren. The spirit of truth is charitable. God alone who reads the heart is Judge. Historical truth can and must be established both objectively and peacefully. The history of schism reveals faults on both sides.

There must be unity in what is necessary, but in all else we should sustain each other in charity. Since mutual ignorance is one of the causes of our long disunion, there is need for fraternal discussion with our separated brethren. The Bishops should foster this opportunely.

Christian civilisation is today in peril and its values can be defended only by a united Authority. To this therefore the Synod summons all Christians. Many of our brethren are in need. Our charity should embrace them all without exception of persons. Mindful of the soothing effect of gratitude, this Synod urges all to pray, grateful for how much we owe to the now dissident Eastern Church with its glorious roll of Fathers and its seven great Councils.

6. Practical means

In this same spirit the Synod recommends effective means of realising the one fold willed by Christ. Bishops should not be content to invigilate over ecumenical action but should positively promote it. This is especially the duty of Uniate Oriental Bishops.

Every Diocese and Religious Order should have its group of Oriental experts; clerical students should be duly instructed in correct ecumenical methods. There should be special Institutes for Oriental clerics where the whole of theology can be stated from the Oriental viewpoint. In other

Faculties there should be enough instruction for mutual knowledge, and provision should be made to admit dissident clerics.

All the Faithful without exception have a responsibility in this matter and occasional "Days for the East" should be organised to remind them of it.

Praise is due to the many Associations which already labour for Christian Unity, but this Synod urges them to combine their efforts. There should be a mixed Council or Congregation at Rome to direct this work. The loyalty to the Holy See of Catholic Orientals would be increased if they had a greater part in the Government of the Church and if the representatives of the Holy See were drawn from all nations.

7. The Conditions of Unity with Orientals

a) Nothing but what is necessary to unity will be demanded.

Those who have been in schism in good faith need only make a simple profession of Faith, no abjuration will be required except from those who have separated themselves by their own act.

b) The reconciled communities would be able to retain their own discipline.

c) Since the Sacred Orders of Orientals are valid, they will be able to exercise them upon return to the Church.

d) The present state of Oriental affairs in the Catholic Church is not immutably fixed. Discipline and Hierarchical Order can be altered where necessary.

Friday, November 15th: "Mild, some cloud, but no rain. The 68th General Congregation was a dull affair. Four Fathers exercised their right to resume discussion of chapter III, and those who then spoke on chapter IV had very little to add and were not numerous enough to last the rest of the morning. The debate on De Episcopis *thus petered out at 11.45 and we were released with the announcement that the discussion of* De Oecumenismo *would begin on Monday morning.*

4.30 p.m., I went with Grasar and Pearson to the English Press Conference on Ecumenism, given by Cardinal Heenan, aided by Msgr F. Davis and Father Charles Davis. There was a large attendance, though questions were slow in coming at first, they eventually more than filled the allotted period, and at the end, I heard the Chicago Daily News reporter, behind me, vote it a very good conference. I devoted the rest of the evening to a votum on the relation of De Oecumenismo *to the crushing law of Canon 1258 re Communio in sacris. (Diary 1963)*

The Conciliar Debate on "De Oecumenismo" in General

By Mgr. L.L.McReavy

I. The Title of the Schema

Among those who discussed the appropriateness of the title, opinion was almost equally divided.

Ruffini claimed that it was used here in its non-Catholic sense, and should either be dropped, or, if it were kept, its Catholic sense should be stated and the sense in which it is taken here should be explained.

So too Dueno Y Monreal: the word "ecumenism" should not be used, because of its different meanings.

Dacci likewise wanted the title changed, and not to "Catholic Ecumenism", because that could be taken to mean "interconfessionalism".

Sapelak complained that the title implied that ecumenism was a new development in the Church.

Sidarous (Egypt) accepted the title but wanted a better definition to preclude false irenism.

Konig wanted the different meanings explained, because a community's understanding of ecumenism depends on its ecclesiology; the distinctive Catholic concept of unity should be made clear.

Carli: the title of the schema should be *De Oecumenismo Catholico*.

Morcillo: chap. I should be headed :"Catholic Principles of Oecumenism".

II. Special Treatment of Orientals, i.e. separately from Protestants

This was wanted by Tappouni, because the relation of Orientals to the Church is radically different; by Ruffini because Protestant sects have far less in common with us and are so divided among themselves; and by Sapelak, because lumping Orientals with Protestants obscures the dignity of the Oriental Churches and their sacramental priesthood.

III. The Relevance of Chapter IV "De Iudaeis"

It will be remembered that the relevance of this chapter to Ecumenism was defended expertly and at length by Cardinal Bea in his "relatio".

He was supported by Ritter, because, whether or not it pertains to ecumenism strictly, it clearly pertains to the aim of the Council; by Meyer, because the Jewish question is intimately connected with both theoretical and practical Ecumenism; and by Jelmini (for the Swiss Bishops), who however wanted the inclusion also of Moslems and all who believe in God.

The great majority of those who discussed the point wanted the chapter either omitted, or made inclusive of non-Christian religions; though only the final vote will reveal whether they really represent majority opinion.

Thus Tappouni: a Council is for Christians, and if it has to deal with non-Christians it should do so without discrimination; so too the Secretariat for Unity of Christians; inclusion of the chapter will cause political upset.

Ruffini: other non-Christians are more open to conversion.

Bueno Y Monreal: The Jews should be considered, with other non-Christians, in a section devoted to the relation of the Church to those outside the People of God.

Doi-Tatsuo: the chapter should be entitled — "The Relation of Catholics to Jews and other Non-Christians".

Sidarouss: this is no place to speak of the Jews, and it could do harm.

Maximos IV: out of place in the context of Christian unity, or else include non-Christians generally; anti-Semitism could be condemned in a note.

Léger: should not be here, because ecumenism refers to Christian unity.

Gori: discrimination between Jews and other non-Christians will cause trouble.

Batanian: not here.

Dacci: good in itself, but out of context.

So too Lorcillo.

Florrit: put it in "De Ecclesia" because of the special relation of the Jews to the Church.

Da Veiga: If Jews, then Islam, Hinduism, etc. as well.

Pont: remit to future Secretariat for non-Christian religions.

IV. The Appropriateness of Chapter V, on Religious Liberty

Opinion was fairly equally divided among the few who spoke.

Ritter and Meyer welcomed its inclusion as intimately connected with ecumenism and necessary to any dialogue. So too Jacq.

Mendez wanted it first in the schema, as a fundamental principle, not a corollary.

Pont agreed that it was a necessary condition for dialogue, but wanted more time for reflection.

Léger; it should be in a separate schema, because it concerns all religions.

Dacci: good but out of place.

Florit: put it in schema XVII.

Likewise Hervas, because it pertains primarily to the rights of the human person.

V. Methodology of the Dialogue

Not much light has so far been thrown on this by the debate.

Some, like Carli and Nicodemo, apparently take it to mean telling the truth to heretics with charity; which may be a discreet way of declaring disbelief in ecumenism.

Similarly Rohero: proclaim the necessity to salvation of belonging to the Catholic Church, and expressly insist that only good faith can save those who remain outside it.

Abed (Lebanon), on the contrary, holds that we must begin by acknowledging their good faith and not imply that they have no saving habitation outside the House of Peter.

Morcillo agrees on the need for fidelity to the truth, but hopes that mutual knowledge through dialogue will eventually break down prejudice and increase cooperation.

Baudoux likewise relies on a true supernatural conversation, guided by the Holy Spirit, seeking agreement in faith, but without any relativism.

Mazur: no extenuation of Catholic doctrine, but need of great patience and magnanimity in collaborating with God's universal salvific will.

Volk sees the dialogue as a concrete manifestation of the catholicity of the Church, embracing all that is good and true in christianity; a total expression of the Church's doctrine and practice; unity in multiplicity rather than in uniformity.

Jelmini; the dialogue requires not only a change of heart, but also a readiness to adapt human, ecclesiastical and Latin structures in the Church.

The most "advanced" and specific programme was that of Huyghe: the first condition is conversion of all Christians, ourselves included, and no smugness; the second condition is common action, in the form of:

a) common prayer,

b) ecumenical collections for the poor and needy,

c) theological reflection together on evangelical renewal,

d) common pastoral action to the non-Christian world.

Flusin: avoid speaking as though those who were born in heresy or schism are to blame for it, and be ready to work with those who want corporate, not individual, reunion.

Pont: begin by begging and offering forgiveness sincerely.

Jaeger: make sure you have theologians with a thorough knowledge of their doctrine as well as our own.

Diade (Lebanon): we can all benefit by the traditions of other churches, and should stress what is common rather than what divides.

Florit: common elements are a mark of division rather than union, and therefore we should seek to instil in non-Catholics a holy inquietude by showing them what they lack.

Some speakers are apparently waiting to be told by the proposed Directorium how to conduct the dialogue, but meanwhile are in favour of it.

In his Diary McReavy noted that on Saturday and Sunday, (October 5/6) he worked on a summary of the first week's debate, which was duplicated for the English and Welsh bishops. The American Press Office had begun to produce a full and accurate daily summary of the debates, and arrangements had been made to supply copies daily to other English-speaking hierarchies. These daily reports and the notes on points of dogma arising from the debates supplied by Dr Patsy Redmond led McReavy to observe: "I felt much less under pressure than at the first Session".

"Patsy Redmond is among the guests here. He came out with Bishop Dwyer on holiday, and his theological knowledge has been quite useful in the formal discussions which we have been having in the Common Room (Hierarchy and Periti) on dogmatic questions arising out of the schema De Ecclesia. *I am quite out of my depth, or rather, I sit in as a disciple, and have found the discussions very helpful". (L12)*

McReavy spent the All Saints-All Souls break preparing observations on the text concerning Bishops and Diocesan administration: "Friday to Monday inclusive was declared a mid-term break and most of the bishops went off on various 3 to 4 day jaunts, I had been given the job of preparing comments on De Episcopis, *so that kept me busy for three of the four days". (L16)*

De Episcopis et De Diocesium Regimine

Comments by Mgr. L.L. McReavy

There is no need to add to Bishop Dwyer's excellent explanatory digest of the matter to be debated in General Congregation, but there are two minor points which may be worth noting.

a) Art. 19 of the schema requires that, if all who have the right to attend the National Episcopal Conference cannot in fact do so, the Statutes of the Conference shall provide means to ensure that the mind and wishes of all the bishops shall be made known ("ut mens et vota omnium Praesulum innotescant"). This appears in the summary (n. 19) as "means of notifying all of the mind and decisions of the Conference".

b) Art. 23 requires any bishop who intends to act contrary to a N.C. decision to give written notification of his reasons to the Conference, through its President, in advance. The summary (n. 23) omits this qualification.

1. The "first fundamental principle" of the schema, i.e. that Diocesan Bishops should have by law all the faculties necessary to the apt and expeditious exercise of their ordinary pastoral function, is far from being a revolutionary new idea. This was precisely the intention of those who drew up the 1918 Code of Canon Law, and, strange though it may now seem, they were under the impression that they had effectively implemented it by the

powers they conceded to bishops in the Code, and that there would be no further need of lists of delegated faculties from the Roman Curia.

Within a year or two of the promulgation of the Code, the ordinary powers of the bishops had been shown by experience to be so inadequate that new formulae of quinquennial faculties had to be devised, and even these have not saved the bishops from the need of constant recourse to Rome, even in certain routine cases.

The schema re-affirms the general principle once again, but some may think it unfortunate that, by going no further than this, it effectively limits the scope of debate. As Carli explains in his brief history of the preparation of the schema (Relatio, p. 19), the Coordinating Commision decided (Jan. 1963) that all detailed proposals made by the Preparatory Commission in regard to what extra powers should be granted to bishops by law, and even the four general criteria to be followed in this widening of ordinary power (schema, p. 29; Dwyer, n. 3) should be relegated to the Appendix Prior and thus excluded from debate in General Congregation, (Cf. footnote to p. 27 of schema). The liberty of the Fathers is therefore limited to sending in written suggestions to the Secretary General for transmission to the Code-Reform Commission, an extra-Conciliar body. One can only hope that this Commission will not repeat the mistake of the makers of the Code in accepting the principle of adequate ordinary episcopal power, but failing to give adequate effect to it.

The same applies to detailed suggestions of the Fathers in regard to the relations of bishops to the Roman Curia, which, by being relegated to Appendix Altera, have likewise been removed from the scope of public debate.

2. Appendix Prior, p. 35, VIII, art. 27, extends a bishop's faculty to permit the reading of prohibited books, but, since this is outside the scope of debate, and there is nothing in the text to be debated which touches on the general question of the prohibition of books by curial decree, composition of the Index, etc., it would appear that the Fathers are to be denied the opportunity of expressing their mind on this thorny subject openly and forcefully in public debate. The Preparatory Commission on Discipline of Clergy and People prepared a schema on this question, but it was withdrawn by the Coordinating Commission and referred to the Code-Reform Commission, thus by-passing the Council. Incidentally, the same happened to some other schemata of practical interest to the bishops in their general administration, e.g. those dealing with reform of procedural law, and with a completely new approach to Crimes and Penalties.

3. Chap. II of the schema makes important proposals in regard to Coadjutors and Auxiliaries which would notably increase their power. In particular, a Coadjutor would henceforth have right of succession, together

with full V.G. powers, which his bishop would not be able to restrict by reservation.

In view of these proposals, it may be felt that the question of the method of selecting and appointing Coadjutors and Auxiliaries, has become one of considerable interest to the Fathers. The schema, however, makes no proposals in regard to any modification of the present law and practice, and therefore offers no scope for open debate. Carli (Relatio, p. 15) adds that "if the Fathers think that something should be expressly said on this subject, they are free to put their proposals to the Holy See". They always were free to do so; the question is whether they should be free to raise the subject in the Council.

Carli (Relatio, p. 16) also maintains that the proposals in regard to Coadjutors etc., do not blur the monarchical concept of the Diocesan Bishop, because such appointments are meant in future to be an extreme remedy, i.e. only for aged or infirm bishops who cannot be induced to resign and for large dioceses which cannot be divided. There seems reason to doubt whether they will be as exceptional in practice as they are meant to be in principle.

4. The change in the status of Coadjutors and Auxiliaries is likely to affect the status of the V.G. The schema avoids answering questions which arise from its proposals, e.g. whether. the Coadjutor will be a V.G. formaliter as well as materialiter, whether his power will be proper or vicarious, whether he will count as a local Ordinary. It is content merely to define his relations with the bishop and with the V.G.

It is interesting to note (p. 12 of the schema, note 4) that some Fathers have suggested a reform of the juridical concept of the V.G., which would enable the bishop to appoint, in addition or even instead of a V.G., one or more "vicarii episcopales", with ordinary jurisdiction for only a part of the diocese, or only a particular matter. This seems worth discussing.

5. It is also worth noting that, for reasons stated by Carli (Relatio, p. 16) the majority of the Preparatory Commission wanted to propose that an Auxiliary be made equivalent in law to a V.G., sede plena, and to an Administrator Apostolic, sede vacante, and that superior Commissions rejected this. Hence Art. 12 (which leaves an Auxiliary's powers to be determined by his papal Letter of Appointment, plus any episcopal delegation) and Art. 15, para. 2 ("optandum ut nominetur Vicarius Capitularis") are a sort of compromise solution which invites judgement from the Fathers.

6. The reasons for and against resignation by aged or infirm bishops are clearly stated by Carli (Relatio, p. 17-18). The original proposal by the Preparatory Commission that, in case of permanent ill-health or upon reaching the age of 75, whether or not a bishop offered his resignation, the Pope should decide whether or not he should resign, — was tempered by

superior Commissions to the present mild Art.16, which reduces it to an earnest request and omits mention of any particular age-limit. The question arises whether, if resignation is in general desirable in such cases, Art.16 will be an effective method of obtaining it.

7. National Conferences.

Art. 18 requires a National Conference "in unaquaque Natione". What is a "Nation"? If England and Wales, why not the United Kingdom?

The schema says little or nothing about the government and procedure of National Conferences, leaving everything to be determined by the statutes of each conference. There is however a safe-guard in that these need the approval of the Holy See.

8. In regard to the force of N.C. decisions, Carli (Relatio, p. 19-20) defends the proposed Articles 22-24 on the ground that, under them, bishops will still retain their freedom to act according to their conscience "in almost all matters", because it is only "in a few clearly defined cases" that he will be juridically obliged to carry out a two-thirds decision. Some may feel that the cases covered by the four categories of Art.24 are likely to be neither few nor very clearly defined. If, however it be remembered that, even in these cases, a two-thirds decision will not bind rigorously until it has been confirmed by the Holy See, it will be appreciated that the number of such obligations is not likely to be high; many points on which there is a two-thirds vote at a National Conference meeting are, it seems, unlikely to be referred to the Holy See for confirmation.

9. Papal reservation of appointment to parishes.

One might have expected this to be treated under Government of Dioceses. In fact, it is dealt within the schema *De Cura Animarum*, p. 71, n. 19, where it is proposed that the Holy See will no longer reserve any benefices carrying care of souls, except Consistorial benefices (e.g. Episcopal Sees).

The weekend of November 16th and 17th Monsignor McReavy records: "Saturday and Sunday I spent working on a combination of the week's debates with comments for the benefit of our bishops: it is being poly-copied at this moment by our secretariate". (L17)

A Survey of the Debate "De Pastorali Munere Episcoporum"

by Monsignor L. McReavy

I. Regarding Exempt Religious Working in A Diocese

Card. Browne — The whole matter of exempt religious should be left to the Code-Reform Commission, as being too complex for settlement in the Aula.

Corboy (Rhodesia) — The apostolate of religious cannot realistically be separated from their religious life, as in the schema. They are intimately connected. The justification of exemption is to be found rather in the fact that the vocation and apostolate of religious is not territorially circumscribed.

Himmer (Tournai) — In dealing with the apostolate of religious in a diocese, the schema should expressly mention schools, so as to secure coordination of all Catholic schools.

Rossi (Brazil, for 98 Bishops) — It should clearly state that pastoral works are solely the responsibility of the Bishop. Disagreements between Bishops and religious should be referred to a conference of Bishops and religious.

Staverman (Indonesia) — The schema should deal first with all clergy engaged in care of souls, without distinguishing between seculars and religious; as it is, such religious are presented as being of second rank.

Renard — Ditto, A better comprehensive term would be the "presbyterium dioecesanum".

Guilly (Georgetown) — Religious are auxiliaries, not directly of the individual Bishops, but of the College of Bishops, through the Pope. Exemption enables them to help the whole College, through the Pope, to the benefit of the universal Church.

D'Souza (India) — Collegiality should mean a greater sense of unity. Without a fraternal spirit of mutual trust, no mere laws will solve the problems of exemption.

II. On the Relation of Bishops to Their Clergy and People

Card. Léger — Imperative that Bishops should get to know modern man, whose whole outlook is rapidly changing; should adapt their teaching method and language accordingly; should revise their method of governing, so as to ensure dialogue and communication between Bishop and faithful; should modernise their external appearance.

Guyot (Coutances) — Clarify the continuity between the doctrine on the priesthood and that on the episcopate from the point of view of sacramentality, and urge the establishment of a stable structure of pastoral dialogue between Bishop and clergy, so as to promote mutual confidence and consultation for the general good of the diocese.

Renard (Versailles) — The priesthood is essentially one, and hence Bishop and priests complementary; Bishops should value the experience and advice of their priests.

Proano (Equador) — Ditto; indeed Bishops should be grateful for candid criticism and exercise a virile responsibility.

Urtasun (Avignon) — A relation of mutually trustful contact between a Bishop and his priests is of great value. There should also be cooperation with religious women and brothers in a "pastorale d'ensemble".

Iriarte (Argentine) — A profound change is called for in a Bishop's "style de vie", more efficient use of his time and activity, a plainer manner of speaking, use of the advice of his priests and faithful, simplicity of dress and dwelling.

III. Various

Card. Richaud — Too many things which should be discussed in the Aula, to establish general principles, are being reserved to the Code-Reform Commission, The law on removal of P.P's is inadequate and subjects a Bishop to the judgement of his clergy. Appeal should not be to the P.P. consultors but, as in marriage cases, to the Archbishop.

Carli — The statement that Bishops enter the College by consecration is inexact. Bishops must exist before they can form a community, and hence their relation to their diocese antecedes their relation to the whole Church. Even the Pope only becomes such through being made Bishop of Rome.

Rupp (Monaco) — More detail is required in regard to a Bishop's duty to the constantly migrating population characteristic of today.

Baraniak (Poland) — Ditto.

Card. Confalonieri — The problem of emigrants should be studied by episcopal conferences and they should make apt provision according to the norms laid down by the Holy See.

Otcenasek (Czech) — Add a passage on the need to introduce religious sociology into seminaries and curial offices.

Foley (Lancaster) — Restoration of religious practice requires intimate contact between pastors and people.

Proano (Equador) — Knowledge of one's flock should be sociological, not just individual.

Ruiz (Mexico) and Himmer (Tournai) — Ditto.

Kaiser (Peru) — Better distribution of clergy is urgently required, if whole areas are not to be lost to the faith.

Lucey (San Antonio) — If the faith is languid in many places it is because Bishops and clergy fail to provide adequate catechesis.

Greco (Louisiana) – Mention and stress the importance of the Confraternity of Christian Doctrine.

Moralejo (Valencia) – In the appointment of Bishops, the competent episcopal conference should have a say, and the priests and even faithful of the diocese concerned should be heard.

Staverman (Indonesia) – It is not enough to urge "mercy" towards fallen priests unless a way is offered of exercising it. The present rigidity is unjustifiable.

Guerry (Cambrai) – The Bishop's teaching function needs to be presented in a new form. Public declarations on questions of current interest, in the manner of Pius XII, manifest the presence and solicitude of the Church to the world and relate the Gospel to everyday life. But for this the Bishop must first acquire accurate knowledge of the facts from experts, lay included, and must exercise supernatural prudence, devoid of political partisanship, charity, humility, courage and clarity.

Bednorz (Poland) – The need is for team work by priests animated by the missionary spirit.

Miranda (Mexico) – Each Bishop should co-ordinate all work for vocations in his diocese, to eliminate competition and enable boys and girls to understand objectively the nature and object of the various forms of vocation.

November 20th 1963: "Wednesday 4 p.m. to 5.30. Discussion in our Bishops' Common Room, at which I presented and expounded a votum which I had prepared De Communicatione in sacris". *(L19)*

De Oecumenismo
A Note on "Communicatio in Sacris" As Understood in the Schema

By Monsignor L.L. McReavy

The Existing Law:

Canon 1258: para. 1: "Haud licitum est fidelibus quovis modo active assistere seu partem habere sacris acatholicorum,".

Para. 2: "Tolerari potest praesentia passiva seu mere materialis, civilis officii vel honoris causa, ob gravem rationem ab Episcopo in casu dubii probandam, in acatholicorum funeribus, nuptiis similibusque solemniis, dummodo perversionis et scandali periculum absit."

De Oecumenismo, art. 7: "... In quibusdam peculiaribus rerum adiunctis, cuiusmodi sunt supplicationes quae "pro unitate" indicuntur atque in oecumenicis conventibus, licitum, immo et opportunum est catholicos viros cum fratribus separatis in oratione consociari. Communes precationes in eiusmodi adiunctis, remota quavis communicatione in cultu officiali, habendae sunt et perefficax medium supplicationis pro unitate et genuina significatio vinculorum quibus catholici cum fratribus separatis coniunguntur."

1. At first sight, art. 7 may seem to involve a substantial change in the law and even, some may suggests a change in the moral doctrine underlying it. The law of can. 1258 was completely negative. By its terms, all active participation in sacris acatholicorum is forbidden, and in such absolute terms ("quovis modo") that the late Canon Mahoney regarded it as intrinsically evil and therefore forbidden by the divine natural law, no less than by the ecclesiastical law. Even passive or merely material assistance is merely said to be "tolerable" (a.v. not positively permitted), and only at funerals, weddings and suchlike functions, and for a grave cause.

The proposed new law, on the contrary, in addition to including a positive permission and indeed recommendation of prayer in common in certain cases, appears to narrow the field of prohibition by substituting the more precise phrase "cultus officialis (acatholicorum)" for "sacra acatholicorum". Is there any doctrinal significance in this change?

2. Clearly there is a marked change in the manner of approach. The proposed new law is certainly inspired by a very different spirit from that which motivated can. 1258. The mind of the Code legislator was dominated by consideration of the dangers to faith involved in any form of religious communication with non-Catholics; whereas the attitude of *De Oecumenismo* appears to be that the benefits to the Church as a whole outweigh any dangers involved to individuals. Nevertheless, if the text of the schema is compared, not simply with the bare text of can. 1258, but with the interpretation commonly given to this canon by moral theologians, it will be seen, I suggest, that the proposed new law does not differ really from the old in what it forbids.

Moral theologians have not normally been very clear in their definition of "sacra acatholicorum". It is a wide term and they usually give it a wide definition: "res ad religionem vel cultum pertinentes". But they have generally narrowed the scope of the strict prohibition of can. 1258, para. 1, by distinguishing between public or representative religious acts of non-Catholics and their private or non-representative religious acts. Noldin, for example, defined their public religious acts as those which they perform as "religious communities (coetus)", e.g. those which they perform in their churches; and their private religious acts as those which they perform as private persons (Theol. Moralis, 1924 edition, II, n. 34); in other words, we may say, those which they perform merely as creatures of God. The moral conclusions based on this distinction have hitherto been:

a) ACTIVE participation in the PUBLIC religious acts of non-Catholics is never lawful. It is in this sense that can. 1258, para. 1, is commonly taken. If, as Mahoney held, active participation in such services indicates, necessarily and of its very nature, approval of the sect concerned as a divinely authorized form of religion, then clearly the canon would merely be repeating the divine natural prohibition. But even if, as I believe, active participation in the public services of non-Catholics does not intrinsically involve approval of heresy or schism (i.e. that approval can be eliminated in certain circumstances), nevertheless it so commonly carries this implication that the Church forbids it in any form — "quovis modo".

b) Passive or merely material participation in the public religious acts of non-Catholics can be tolerated, ad normam can. 1258, para. 2.

c) Active participation in the PRIVATE religious acts of non-Catholics can be justified on the principle of double effect, when the benefits to be derived are such as to compensate for any moral dangers involved (danger of indifferentism, scandal of the weak, etc.). Moralists generally have excluded this form of communication from the scope of can. 1258.

3. If, as seems likely, the phrase "cultus officialis" in the schema is identifiable with "public religious acts" as explained above, it will be seen that there is no substantial change in the law or in the moral doctrine underlying it. The "communes precationes" permitted and even recommended in certain circumstances are reduced, by virtue of the exceptive clause — "remota quavis communicatione in cultu" — to the category of "private religious acts of non-Catholics", participation in which, if not hitherto encouraged, has not generally been regarded as formally forbidden. Hence, all that the decree really adds is an assurance that, in ecumenical contacts, the benefits of such participation outweigh the dangers hitherto so strongly, perhaps unduly, stressed.

The question of the collegiality of the bishops was a major issue discussed during the Council's second Session.

Episcopal Participation in the Government of the Church

By Mgr. L. McReavy

Pope Paul VI to the Curia: "If the Council expresses a desire to see representatives of the episcopate assisting the Supreme Head of the Church in the care and responsibility of the government of the Church, certainly the Curia will not resist."

De Episcopis, art. 5: "Some Bishops of the various nations, to be designated by their National Episcopal Conference, should be nominated by the Apostolic See as Members or Consultors of the Sacred Congregations of the Roman Curia, by which, at fixed times, they should be convoked for the greater furtherance of the common good and the more efficacious averting of common dangers."

I. Opinions of the Conciliar Fathers

(1) Inadequacy of Art. 5

Gouyon (France): Art. 5 (above-quoted) provides a first step in collegiality, but, to be effective, it will have to insist that the episcopal Members of the Curia participate in all major decisions, ordinary as well as extraordinary, and that periti, chosen by the Episcopal Conferences and non-resident in Rome, assist.

McCann (for Bishops of S.Africa and S.Rhodesia) also thought art. 5 insufficient, because the episcopal Members would not be able to attend regularly enough in the Curia.

Browne of Galway said it might be dangerous to have residential Bishops in the Curia.

Ferreira of Portugal also thought art. 5 inadequate because, if collegiality is of the essence of the Church, it should always be operative. Likewise De Souza (India).

(2) Need for a new chapter

Cardinal Liénart called for the insertion in the schema of a new chapter on the mutual relations of the Pope and the College of Bishops.

So also Cardinals Koenig, Alfrink, De Barros Camara (for 110 Brazil Bishops), and Bishops Hermaniuk (Canadian Ukrainians) and Hodges (for some other U.S. Bishops).

(3) A permanent representative central organ was considered by many to be the best way of giving concrete, expression to episcopal collegiality in the government of the Church.

Thus Liénart, Alfrink, Bea, Simons, Moralejo, Maximus IV, Ritter, Florit, Gouyon, McCann, Browne of Galway, Ferreira, Van der Burgt (for 30 Bishops of Indonesia).

Gargitter: Either this, or stable commissions of Bishops for certain matters.

Doctrinal reasons advanced for Central Organ

Liénart: It would manifest the unity of the Church, provide better for adaptation to local circumstances, help towards reunion, especially with Orientals.

Alfrink: A central organ of Bishops working with and under the Pope would not be the same thing as the "Corpus Episcoporum", nor a representative parliament, but it would be a sign of collegiality and instrument of its exercise, a manifestation of unity, a source of greater trust. If collegiality is of divine origin, then the College precedes the Curia, the order being Pope, College, Curia, and the Curia becomes the executive instrument of Pope and College.

Bea: Because the Church is a living body in which all members are called to collaborate according to their proper function; this would enable the Bishops to do so.

Simons: Owing to the diversity of peoples, languages and cultures in the world, Christ entrusted the government of His Church not merely to the Pope, but to the whole body of Bishops under the primacy of the Pope.

Moralejo: The Body of Bishops should have some say in regard to legislation that affects the universal Church.

Maximus IV: The body that assists the Pope in his universal pastorate should not consist of cardinals who are priests of Roman churches, but should be representative of the universal Church.

Florit: A central Congregation of Bishops, superior to the existing Congregations, should be established as a concrete expression and explanation of collegiality, even though it could never be collegial in the strict sense, since it would depend on the Pope for its existence and functioning.

McCann: There should be a representative consultative body of Bishops, meeting once a year with the Pope and the heads of the Congregations, to consider major problems, aggiornamento, and execution of the Council's decrees. It would speed up the Council if many disciplinary and practical questions were left to this body.

Browne of Galway: It could consist of those residential Bishops who are Cardinals and of others named by the Pope, but should be a real senate, meeting regularly to help the Pope in his legislative function.

Van der Burgt: A College of Bishops, mainly elected by the episcopal Conferences, is the only effective way of combining sane decentralisation with strong unity. If established now, it could relieve the Council of much of its work.

Frings: The vote on collegiality, even if it is only indicative of the mind of the Fathers, was almost unanimous, and therefore cannot be ignored by the Theological Commission, as Cardinal Browne seemed to imply. The conciliar commissions are the instruments of the General Congregations and exist to carry out the expressed will of the Fathers.

So also Archbishop De Souza.

Criticism of proposals based on the principle of collegiality

Ruffini: There is need for further study of the notion of collegiality. The vote was never meant to decide the question.

So also Cardinal Browne, who thought that collegiality could never be admitted in the strict juridical sense, and objected that the suggested College of Bishops co-ruling with, or even under, the Pope would clearly diminish his authority and therefore be contrary to Vatican I.

Ottaviani: The five propositions were put by the Moderators without being previously submitted for examination to the Doctrinal Commission which is competent in matters of dogma. If they had been, the text would have been perfected and equivocations excluded. To say that the College of Bishops succeeded to the College of Apostles is to beg the question. Apart from the Council of Jerusalem, the Apostles never acted as a College, and an eminent Scripture scholar has assured me that collegiality cannot be deduced from Scripture. Those who favour this notion wish at least a reduction of the exercise of the Pope's primacy.

Lefebvre, Gen. C.S.Sp.: Juridical collegiality cannot be proved. If it could, the Church would have erred for 20 centuries in not using it. Only moral collegiality with moral bonds is justifiable.

Practical arguments for Central Organ of Bishops; Defects of existing set-up.

Simons: The present curial organisation is not adapted to the exercise of universal jurisdiction, because it is unaware of local conditions, and is not representative of the pastors of the universal Church; indeed it is often a barrier between the Pope and the Bishops.

De Souza: The Curia was useful in the past in protecting Bishops against meddlesome civil rulers, but is out of date. Bishops are better able to judge local needs, and should be free to provide for them, in all except major reserved cases.

Frings: A clear distinction should be drawn between administrative and judicial functions and applied even to the Holy Office, whose methods no longer harmonise with modern conditions; no one should be judged and condemned without a hearing, or without a chance to correct himself or his book. (Ottaviani indignantly rejected this charge as based on "nescience"). The Curia was warmly defended by Batanian (former pupil of Ruffini), Mason of the Sudan, and Del Pino. The last-named thought that even Art. 5 went too far in suggesting that Episcopal Conferences should designate Bishops for nomination by the Pope as members of the Curia. It should be left to the Pope or his Delegates.

The Practical Problem of integrating a Central Organ of Bishops into the existing Structure

Lercaro: Nothing prevents the Pope from enabling the College of Bishops to exercise its supreme (not delegated) and full power over the universal Church habitually through a representative organ, provided that the final judgement of its opportuneness is his, that he remains free to act independently, and that he uses it only for major issues, as he did with the Consistory until the 16th Century (the existing Consistory's lack of function is one of the chief defects of the present curial organisation). But the problem of integration is complex and cannot be solved merely by creating a new organ. All sorts of problems arise in regard to the present set-up (College of Cardinals, administrative and judicial functions, etc.) which only the Pope is competent to solve. The matter should therefore be withdrawn from the schema and the Fathers should limit themselves to making proposals to the Pope, not based on a mere 3-day debate, but on the studies of a special Conciliar Commission designated before the end of this Session.

Rugambwa: The African Bishops hope for prompt creation of an episcopal council for universal Church government. Inter-nationalisation of the Curia touches only the fringes of the problem. A new structure of the central organs of the Church is necessary to meet modern needs. It is not a mere question of representation, but of functionality. These central organs are the means by which supreme power over the universal Church is exercised, and this supreme power is exercised in two ways, by the Pope ex sese, and by the Body of Bishops in union with the Pope. The Pope himself invites us to propose the main lines of a new structure. It is, however, too great and complex a matter to be dealt with in the present Decree. It should be discussed as a separate question, under the direction of the Moderators, before we move on to the next subject, and the opinions of the Fathers should be passed to a special Commission, to work out a text in form of a petition to the Pope.

II. Comment

The objection made by Cardinal Browne and others that collegiality has not yet been defined and that it cannot be reconciled, in its strict juridical sense, with the primacy of the Pope, seems to me to be irrelevant. Not a single defender of the thesis of episcopal participation in the government of the universal Church has even suggested that Christ committed the government of the Church to a College in the strict juridical sense (i.e. one in which a majority vote is decisive). They have merely argued that the Bishops form a college, that they have a certain collegial responsibility for the universal Church with and under the Pope, that this is not effectively manifested or exercised by the present Curial organisation,, and that it could best be done by a representative central organ. As far as I can gather, all alike admit that the extent of the power of this organ would depend entirely on the Pope's decision. It can hardly therefore be said to be an attack on his primacy. On the other hand, the point made by Lercaro and to some extent by Rugambwa (both of them favourable to the proposed central organ of Bishops) that the integration of such a Council into the existing structure of central government raises problems that cannot be settled in general debate, or by mere vote of the Fathers, and that a special study, followed by a special intervention of the Pope, is required, seems valid enough.

Are Episcopal Faculties in Any Sense Papal Concessions?

Art. 3 does not expressly say that they are. After safe-guarding the Pope's right to reserve cases to himself, it adds that residential Bishops should have by common law all the faculties which are needed for the more apt and expeditious exercise of their ordinary and immediate jurisdiction under the jurisdictional primacy of the Pope; and therefore that they should have wider faculties than hitherto, including, among others, those listed in the Appendix.

Several Fathers, however, dislike this wording. Here are some of their criticisms:

Bazelaire (France): These faculties pertain ordinarily to the episcopal office, and therefore, though the Pope has the right to reserve them as far as necessary, once the necessity ceases, it is improper to speak of their restitution as an "amplification" of episcopal power, as though they were gratuitous concessions.

Correa (Columbia): The powers of Bishops should be treated as flowing from the very nature of the episcopal office, not as mere concessions or privileges. Save for reserves made by the Pope, the Bishops have all the powers required for their function and mission. Similarly Alfrink, who suggested a list of reservations rather than of faculties.

Ritter (Cardinal, for many U.S. Bishops): By divine law, residential Bishops possess all powers required for the effective exercise of their ordinary and immediate jurisdiction. When therefore the Pope withdraws reservations which he has made by virtue of his primatial power, he does not grant faculties but restore powers.

Garcia (Spain): Bishops have full power in their dioceses, excepting only what the Pope reserves. A list of these reservations should be drawn up.

Frings likewise: The first Appendix should be a list of reservations, not faculties.

Schoiswohl (Austria): Civil governments cannot be expected to respect the Church if she preaches the principle of subsidiarity but does not practise it. Bishops should exercise fully the powers they have by divine law. The term "faculties" should be used only for powers given by positive law, and thus capable of reservation.

Martinez (Spain): Episcopal powers should be treated more theologically and not presented as concessions.

Bea (Cardinal) approached the subject via the principle of subsidiarity, which he holds to be intrinsic to the notion of the Mystical Body, in which all are called to fulfil their proper function. Bishops are not mere Vicars of the Pope, but essential members of the living Body of the Church. The good of the whole Church requires that every Bishop should himself fulfil his proper role, with due respect for papal restrictions, for these likewise are for the good of the Church. His conclusion was that Bishops can do all that is incumbent on them by virtue of their consecration, excepting only those things that the Pope has reserved.

Cardinal König and Bishop Gargitter likewise called for episcopal powers to be determined according to the principle of subsidiarity, i.e. that the higher authority should not substitute itself for the lesser authority in matters in which the lesser can well act for itself.

Criticisms of the Above Opinions

Ruffini (Cardinal): Bishops do not succeed to all the prerogatives of the Apostles. Some powers are proper to them; others they have in virtue of their participation in the jurisdiction of the Pope.

Del Pine (Spain): Some of the statements made on the powers of Bishops imply that they are all popes.

Souto (Spain): Rather than complain about faculties being presented as concessions, we should be grateful to the Pope and the Congregations for amplifying our powers.

Comment

It is a valid theological principle that a divinely instituted office, such as that of a Bishop, carries with it by divine law all the power necessary to its proper and effective fulfilment. Moreover, even though the same divine law entitles the higher authority of the Pope to restrict the lesser authority of Bishops in the measure necessary or really useful to the common good, the valid sociological principle of subsidiarity requires that such restrictions shall not exceed the necessary minimum.

Nevertheless, there is point in Ruffini's qualification, that some episcopal powers are only obtained by participation in the Pope's supreme jurisdiction, those namely (and they are many) by which Bishops are enabled to dispense from universal laws; moreover, it is largely these powers that many want amplified.

The Pope, by virtue of his supreme jurisdiction, can and does rightfully make many laws binding on the universal Church. The obligation of a law can be relaxed only by the will of its maker, or by those to whom he has conceded the power to dispense. Hence, all faculties which enable Bishops to dispense from universal laws are, in their essence, concessions from the Pope.

It can be argued that, since universal laws of human origin can seldom if ever be equitably adapted to a worldwide community as heterogenous as the Church, the just and proper government of its various parts requires that local Ordinaries shall have power to relax such laws in individual cases for a just cause; for if every case had to be referred to the Supreme Authority, more hardship would be caused to individual subjects than is either necessary to or even compatible with the common good. The conclusion, however, of this argument (if it be admitted), is not that Bishops have by divine commission the power to dispense from universal laws in particular cases, but that the maker of these laws, the Pope, should concede to local Ordinaries the degree of dispensing power that is necessary to meet just local and personal needs. At most, one might say that Bishops have a right not to be denied by the supreme authority the measure of dispensing power which is required for the apt and expeditious exercise of their ordinary pastoral office.

Report on the Schema Decreti "De Clericis"

Prepared by Monsignor L.L.McReavy
for the Hierarchy Meeting July 1963

The subject-matter of this schema was originally handled in a series of projects drawn up by the Preparatory Commission on Discipline of Clergy and People, entitled: *De Clericorum Vitae Sanctitate, De Obligationibus Parochorum, De Officiis et Beneficiis Ecclesiasticis, deque Bonorum Ecclesiasticorum Administralione*. Largely on the basis of this material, the Conciliar Commisssion of the same name, on instructions from the Coordinating Commission, drafted a schema *De Clericis* comprising three chapters (entitled as here in the published version), plus an *Exhortatio de Distributione Cleri*. The work was done by the "viciniores" of the Commission and submitted in April of this year. The published version has retained the three chapters in an improved and more orderly form, but has transferred the proposals *De Distributione Cleri* to another schema.

Chapter I. *De Vitae Sacerdotalis Perfectione* calls for little comment

The principles (1-3) are unexceptionable. i.e. that sanctity is demanded alike by the priestly character, received in Ordination, and by the priestly ministry. Among the duties (n. 4) by which sanctity is fostered and nourished, attention is called to the following:

Under 4 (d), for "amore confratrum", it might have been better to read: "amicali consortio confratrum". It is when love is expressed in companionship that it most effectively serves as a spiritual aid. Its value is indicated in n. 7, but might well have been included here under the aids to holiness.

Novel and valuable features of this list of aids are — 4(e) on the need for priests to practise charity to fallen priests; 4(g) on cultivation of the social graces, politeness, cleanliness, etc. (hitherto the law considered it sufficient to have these brought to the attention of seminarists — can. 1369, it 2).

5. The warning to priests not to domineer over their flocks is new.

6. The aids to sanctity are largely as in c. 125-126, but two points need noting:

a) Re Priests' Retreats. Can. 126 requires them "tertio saltem quoque anno". The schema submitted proposed that they be annual for the first five years and thereafter at least every alternate year. The approved schema requires them to be annual, except for express exemption by Ordinary.

b) Omission of the Visit to the Blessed Sacrament, listed in c.125, seems odd. The original version of the schema read; "necnon ardentissima pietate ergo Christum Dominum, praecipue in SS. Eucharistia."

7. is partly contained in can. 134, but emphasizes the need for clerical reunions.

9. is already in Can. 1353.

11. makes can. 128 more explicit.

12. Encourages sick priests to seek leave to say Mass at home, or to enjoy other indults. Why then should it be thought necessary to make desirable privileges of this kind dependent on indults? Would it not be better to increase the Bishop's ordinary power, which is at present limited by can. 822, para. 4 and 1194 to giving permission "in aliquo extraordinario casu et per modum actus."

13. The general requirement of a timely will (favouring pious causes) is new. Can. 1301 merely required beneficiaries to ensure by testament that sacred furnishings reached their proper destination.

Chapter II. *De Studio et Scientia Pastorali*

This chapter marks a considerable development on can. 129 which leaned to the side of caution in regard to profane and modern knowledge. It ordered clerics "not to give up their studies after ordination to the priesthood, especially their sacred studies, and in those to keep to the traditional and commonly received doctrine of the Church, avoiding profane neologisms and pseudo-science."

The schema insists that study is for the priest a "duty of state", second only to prayer (16); that he needs to acquire and retain a sound and up-to-date knowledge, sacred and profane (15); that he must develop his seminary knowledge with an eye to contemporary problems and needs (17); that it is not enough for him to be a know-all, but must learn to see everything in the light of faith (18); that his knowledge must be based on Scripture and Tradition, but that it must be adapted to modern needs by consultation of approved modern theologians and exegetes.

The measures recommended in 21-25 will strain the resources of many dioceses – a special pastoral course for newly-ordained priests; short refresher courses, the first after 3 years, and then every 3 or 5 years (Footnote 20 observes that some dioceses have substituted annual courses of pastoral revision for the junior clergy exams of can. 130). National or regional pastoral institutes for deeper study of pastoral methodology, etc., with a pastoral library accessible to the clergy. A diocesan director of pastoral studies.

Chapter III. *De Recto Bonorum Usu*

It may seem strange that this chapter, which deals with administration of Church property, should come in a schema *De Clericis,* because administration is not a function proper to the clerical state, but only to certain ecclesiastical offices.

Hence, the Preparatory Commission dealt with administration in a separate schema, *De Officiis et Beneficiis Ecclesiasticis, deque Bonorum Eccl. administratione*. But, as the title of this chapter indicates, the Council wants to deal with the subject.

But, as the title of this chapter indicates, it prefers to deal with administration of ecclesiastical property in the wider context of the Right Use of property in general by clerics, their own as well as that of the Church.

It begins therefore in n. 28 by recalling that the natural and traditional destination of all property which belongs to the Church or the exercise of an ecclesiastical office is to serve the ends of the Church, not to enrich the clergy or their relatives.

The ancient axiom was "Bona Ecclesiae, bona pauperum". The clergy were regarded as sharing in them *titulo paupertatis,* because, by devoting themselves wholly to the service of God, they had made themselves poor. This is the principle behind the rule of can. 1473, which allows beneficiaries free use only of that amount of their beneficial revenue which they need for honest maintenance, and obliges them to devote the rest to poor and pious causes. Only Cardinals have hitherto been exempted (by can. 239, 198) from this prohibition of self-enrichment out of revenue derived from an ecclesiastical office.

29. Abolishes the beneficial system (in which beneficium tended to predominate over officium) and requires that henceforth the emphasis of the law shall be on ecclesiastical offices, defined as all functions stably

conferred for a spiritual purpose. (Details are left to the Commission for Revision of the Code).

30. Equitable provision must be made for all who fulfil any function in the Church. All priests must be assigned a remuneration which befits their dignity and enables them to practise charity to the needy; the rate must be fair to all in similar circumstances, but must also take account of years of service and importance or dignity of function. A fitting pension is to be provided for those who retire after a fixed period. (75 is suggested in another schema as the age at which any priest can be called upon to retire).

31. Schemes of social assistance and insurance for sick and aged priests are to be devised. As a precaution against avoidable illness, all priests are to be medically examined at least once a year. (The Holy Office Monitum, referred to in footnote 12, forbade priests to go to psychoanalysts, except with Ordinary's permission.)

32. To meet these and other needs, a Common Diocesan Fund is to be formed.

33. Of the 8 sources here indicated, (b) and (c) are worthy of special note.

(b) is "that part of the revenue accruing to clerics from the exercise of a sacred office, which exceeds the fair remuneration assigned to them by diocesan law, and is not needed for the fulfilment of Mass obligations or other burdens attached to their office." This extends the principle of c.1473, and transfers the benefit from "poor and pious causes" to the diocesan common fund.

Source (c) is money collected by taxing income received by clerics from the legitimate exercise of an activity not connected with a sacred office. Note. Several members and periti doubted whether the Church has a right to tax income derived by a priest from profane exercise of a natural gift or skill, and whether in any case it would be practical. They suggest that it would be better to remind priests of their special and grave obligation to contribute to the needs of the Church from their personal resources, however derived, and propose a revised version of 33 (c) to that effect.

35. The second part is new. If necessary to the good of the diocese, the Bp can order the joint administration of several or all secular offices by a Council nominated by himself.

36. merely enlarges on c.1524.

37. requires a directory or manual of administration for all administrators, and that books of administration shall be uniform throughout each country.

38. Qualified laymen should have a share in all important business.

39. Bishops and administrators are urged to exercise charity from the ecclesiastical resources they administer. Canon 1535 allowed this, but in such negative terms as almost to discourage charity — "facere ne praesumant, nisi iusta interveniente causa." The more positive note is welcome.

* * *

Three Letters to the Right Reverend Monsignor Worlock, at Archbishop's House, Westminster, London, concerning an Analysis of the schema Propositionum De Sacerdotibus *prepared at the request of Archbishop Heenan by Monsignor Lawrence McReavy.*

Ushaw College
Durham
27th June 1964

Dear Monsignor Worlock,

As you will be aware, His Grace has asked me to prepare a *Relatio* on Schema VIII. *De Sacerdotibus*. The Commission on Discipline sent me the final polycopied typescript, bound in a printed cover, entitled: *Propositiones e Schemate 184. De Sacerdotibus Desumptae ac Relatio Generalis de Labora a Commissionibus Peractis*; but I have not yet received a printed version of Schema VIII.

In case there should be some difference of wording between the two, I should be grateful if you would arrange for a copy of the printed version to be sent to me.

With all good wishes,
Yours sincerely,
L.L.McReavy

* * *

Ushaw College
Durham
3rd July 1964

Dear Monsignor,

I enclose the *relatio* which Archbishop Heenan asked me to prepare, and send to you for duplication on the — schema *Propositionum De Sacerdotibus*.

It is perhaps on the long side, but, at the meeting on July 23rd, it will be possible to take certain things as read, and concentrate on the main points, keeping well within the 15 minutes maximum allowed.

Yours sincerely,
L.L. McReavy

* * *

Ushaw College
Durham
6th July, 1964

Dear Monsignor,

Thank you very much for your letter of the 3rd July, which has crossed with mine sending you a copy of the full schema. I doubt very much whether there is anything you would wish to change in the light of this and I will take steps to see that copies of your paper are duplicated and available to the Bishops for their meeting on 23rd July.

I am very grateful to you for the trouble which you have taken and look forward to seeing you then.

With all good wishes,
Yours very sincerely,
L.L. McReavy

* * *

Confidential Meeting of the Conciliar Fathers and Periti of England and Wales Archbishop's House,Westminster 23rd July, 1964.

To Consider Agenda For Third Session:

1. Revelation. Schema not yet received. (Bishop Holland)
2. The Church. Schema not yet received. Abbot Butler to report on background.
3. Bishops. Bishop Holland to present Relatio.
4. Eastern Church. Bishop Hornyak to present Relatio.
5. Foreign Missions. Schema not yet received. (Fr. G. Mahon.)
6. Ecumenism. The Archbishop of Westminster to report.
7. Religious. The Archbishop of Liverpool's Relatio is tabled.
8. The Priesthood. Monsignor McReavy's Relatio is tabled.
9. Lay Apostolate. The Bishop of Menevia's Relatio is tabled.
10. Matrimony. Monsignor Whitty to present Relatio.
11. Seminary Training. The Bishop of Brentwood's Relatio is tabled.
12. Schools. The Bishop of Brentwood's Relatio is tabled.
13. Church In The World Today. Schema not yet received. Mgr. Worlock to report on background.

* * *

Schema Propositionum "De Sacerdotibus"

An Analysis by Mgr. L.L. McReavy

Genealogy of These Ten Propositions

Only four of the schemata submitted by the Preparatory Commission on Discipline eventually reached the Conciliar Commission of the same name, the rest having been remitted to the extra-conciliar Code-Reform Commission or to other Commissions.

These four were: 1) *De clericorum vitae sanctitate*; 2) *De officiis et beneficiis clericorum*; 3) *De distributione cleri*; 4) *De fidelium associationibus*.

In February 1963, the fourth was transferred to the schema *De laicis*. The first three were collated into a single new schema entitled *De clericis*, comprising three chapters (*De vitae sacerdotalis perfectione*; *De studio et scientiae pastorali*; *De recto usu bonorum*) and an Exhortation *De distributione cleri*. The printed version of this schema was issued in May 1963.

In the light of the 464 comments received from 237 Fathers, a revised version was produced during October — November 1963, which substituted the title *De sacerdotibus* (because in fact the schema deals only with priests), and changed the title of chapter 1 to *De vita spirituali sacerdotum* (because it deals with the priestly obligation of tending to perfection, rather than with any special state of perfection peculiar to priests, — the Commission having preferred not to take sides on the disputed question whether there is such a state). This chapter 1 was thoroughly revised to make it more theological than juridical, but the Commission left the theological nature of the priesthood to the schema *De Ecclesia* (where, as was noted, it has so far received scant attention).

Finally, in January 1964, the Coordinating Commission ordered the as-yet-unpublished schema *De sacerdotibus* to be reduced to its essential points in the form of propositions. The present ten propositions were extracted from it. It is to be regretted that the text of the revised schema has not been included in the present booklet for comparison, especially as the Commission seems to expect that, if the propositions are approved, both they and the schema will be referred to the appropriate post-conciliar Commission for implementation.

Comparison of These Ten Propositions with the Revised Schema

Propositions 1-3 seek to summarize chap. 1 *De vita spirituali sacerdotum*. Briefly paraphrased, they make the following points:

Proposition 1. Pursuit of holiness is of *special obligation* for priests, because, in virtue of their ordination, they belong to God by *an extra title* which requires them to show forth the priesthood of Christ in their episcopal or priestly ministy, and to work as His representatives for the good of His whole Body, reflecting His sanctity and innocence in their lives.

Proposition 2. Priests should find their *chief means of sanctification in the exercise of their divine commission*, in union with their Bishop; imitating the divine Victim they offer in the Holy Sacrifice, practising what they preach, feeding God's flock and, like the Good Shepherd, giving their lives for their sheep. Yet they should not allow apostolic labours to displace *the traditional aids to holiness*, e.g. mental prayer, for these are as necessary today as ever.

Proposition 3. They should lead exemplary lives of *evangelical detachment* from worldly things and *complete dedication* to the work of salvation. United by fraternal charity to their fellow-priests in prayer, work and recreation, they should as far as possible cultivate *life in common*. They should also practise the *evangelical counsels*, being poor in spirit and alien to vanity, cherishing chastity, and showing filial obedience to superiors in the spirit as well as in the letter.

Comment

All the main points of chapter I are here contained. But the following points, made more explicitly in the schema, are perhaps worthy of note:

1) The ministry in which priests are to find their chief means of sanctification is threefold. They are sacrificers and sanctifiers, preachers and teachers of the word of God, pastors of the flock of Christ.

2) To be effective preachers and teachers, they must first steep themselves in the Scriptures, the works of the Fathers and theologians and the lives of the saints, and then communicate the fruits of their meditation.

3) As pastors, called to minister rather than to be ministered to, they should never domineer, but seek to form their faithful into co-workers, to foster vocations, know their sheep, win the godless, cultivate the appropriate gifts of mind and body, e.g. courtesy, simplicity, cleanliness, politeness.

4) The schema lists the other traditional aids, besides mental prayer, viz: spiritual reading, visit to the Blessed Sacrament, devotion to Our Lady, daily examen, days of recollection, frequent confession and use of spiritual direction, annual retreat. It omits specific mention of the Rosary, because the Oriental Churches have their own devotions.

5) It also urges priests to shoulder joyfully the crosses of the apostolate (failure, tribulations), and to face death with tranquil acceptance in Christian faith and hope.

Propositions 4-5 summarize chapter 2, *De studio et scientia pastorali.*

Proposition 4. Lifelong study of the sacred sciences and of those other sciences that are specially useful in the apostolate is *an essential duty of state* for priests.

Proposition 5. To facilitate this, suitable aids should be provided; e.g. a Director of Studies; pastoral centres and courses in the theory and practice of catechetics, liturgy and sociology; libraries where the appropriate books and periodicals are readily available.

The schema adds the following detailed recommendations:

1) Special pastoral courses of practical application for newly ordained.

2) Short refresher-courses at suitable centres, e.g. after three years, and then every third or fifth year up to an age fixed by the Ordinary.

3) Regional and national courses at which experience can be shared and action co-ordinated.

4) National or regional institutes for specialized study and exchange of ideas.

Proposition 6. Summarizes the Exhortation *De distributione cleri*.

It declares that, though the ancient (for "pervertere" read "pervetere") system of incardination and excardination is to remain, the rules should be revised to facilitate better distribution of diocesan priests and special pastoral activities at the regional, national or international level, or for particular social groups; and that, for these purposes, international seminaries, personal dioceses or prelatures, etc., should be set up.

The schema adds the following:

1) A survey of the need for greater mobility of the clergy.

2) A call to priests to be ready to go, with the permission or exhortation of their Bishop, to areas where priests are lacking.

3) A reminder to layfolk of their duty to help, not only by prayer and alms, but also, if possible, by direct apostolic activity.

4) A request to the Code-Reform Commission to sanction prelatures, with or without territory, whose priests, after special training, will be available for service whereever there is a lack of priests qualified for special apostolates.

Propositions 7-10 summarize chapter III, *De recto uso bonorum*.

Briefly paraphrased, they recommend the following:

Proposition 7. Not only church property, properly so-called, but whatever clerics acquire in the exercise of an ecclesiastical office is traditionally and of its nature intended to provide for divine worship, maintenance of the clergy, and apostolic or charitable works, especially to the poor.

Proposition 8. The beneficial system should be abandoned and priority in law given to ecclesiastical offices, understood widely to include all stably conferred functions for a spiritual end.

Proposition 9. Bishops are to provide by diocesan statute for the honest maintenance and decent pension of all ecclesiastical office-holders, in such manner that the amount of money received by each is basically the same for all in the same circumstances, befits their condition, and enables them to practise charity to the needy.

Proposition 10. To meet this and other diocesan needs, every diocese should do its best to build up a common fund, primarily from the offerings of the faithful, but also from other sources to be juridically determined; and it is to be desired that the richer dioceses will help the poorer.

Comment

1) The principle stated in Proposition 7 is historically and canonically sound. Originally, the clergy shared in that part of the *massa communis* which was destined for the poor, on the ground that they had made themselves poor by devoting all their energies to the service of God; and even when this arrangement was replaced by the beneficial system, the principle was maintained that no beneficiary, except a Cardinal, could enrich himself or family out of beneficial revenue, but must devote to poor and pious causes whatever was superfluous to his honest maintenance (can. 1473).

The schema *De Sacerdotibus* underlines this principle, stressing that it is never lawful for a priest to turn an ecclesiastical office into an occasion of personal profit or devote revenue received in it to the enlargement of his own or his family's estate. It reminds priests that, in making their will, it is their duty to leave to the Church or the poor money acquired "occasione sacri ministerii", and urges them to do so even out of their own patrimony.

2) Proposition 8 is taken by Archbishop Marty (Relatio, p. 13) to mean that ownership of what has hitherto been counted beneficial revenue shall be juridically vested in the office, and that, after the office-holder has been assigned the amount necessary to his honest maintenance, the rest shall be devoted to the proper ends of the office. This, it will be noted, was the principle established for missions in this country by the Westminister Provincial Synods (Conc. II, Decr. VIII,I).

3) In regard to the equality of remuneration, advocated in Proposition 9, the schema provides for a certain elasticity: "...in definienda remunerationis copia, ratio habenda est aequitatis pro clericis in iisdem adiunctis versantibus; item gravitatis munerum; denique antiquitatis clericorum in officiis adimplendis". As to the "congrua pensio", it says: "sacerdotibus post certum tempus officium relinquentibus decora pensione semper providendum erit".

4) In regard to the sources of the massa communis, the schema lists the other sources which, according to Proposition 10, are to be "juridically determined".

They are —

b) From that part of the revenue received in an office by clerics, which exceeds the fair amount assigned by diocesan law, and is not necessary to the fulfilment of Masses or other special obligations of the office.

c) From offerings made by priests from a salary paid to them for a profane job done by leave, or from their own patrimony.

d) From goods given to the diocese without express destination.

e) From a part of the revenue from diocesan property, if ample.

f) From charitable contributions received from richer dioceses.

g) From taxes imposed by the Ordinary on richer parishes and shrines.

h) From the revenue of any institution in the diocese which depends on the Bishop and has more than it needs.

5) In addition to certain recommendations already contained in the law, the schema requires that the art of good administration be taught in the seminary according to a Manual, uniform for the whole nation; and that lay experts be used.

* * *

Ushaw College
Durham
6th March 1965

Dear Monsignor,

The new text is a great improvement on the old, and I should not much mind if it were introduced and passed as it stands. It condemned in clear terms what is intrinsically evil in any war, uses the necessary qualifications in its condemnation of the abuses and crimes likely to be entailed by any future use of nuclear weapons, and avoids exaggerations.

As far as my inexpert eye will allow me to judge, it nowhere talks scientific nonsense. Dr P.E. Hodgson would be able to satisfy you on this point.

Some minor comments.

G.6, 11.29-30. "...crimen contra ipsum hominem". Why not "contra Deus et hominem". The essence of a sin is that it is a transgression of the law of God.

G.8, 11.8-12. It is good to see an admission that it is not intrinsically evil to make nuclear weapons, and I hope that this admission, even though only contained in an "annotatio", will be retained. I have never been able to construct a logical defence for the contrary claim made by our unilateralists.

G.8, 11.47-48. I find this a rather weak statement of the obligation of governments to work honestly and untiringly for reciprocal disarmament. Both Pius XII and *Pacem in terris* were clearer and more forceful on this point. See my booklet *Peace and War* (copy sent under separate cover), pp. 53-551

G.8, 1150. "occisio innocentium". With a perhaps pedantic passion for accuracy I should like the insertion of the word "directa". Indirect killing of some innocent persons has always been an almost unavoidable effect of all wars, past and present.

G.9, 11.5-15, does not deal expressly with the correct treatment of armed partisans operating in occupied territory, a difficult phenomenon of modern war (cf. my *Peace and War*, p. 40). Nor with the question of forced labour (ibid. p. 40-41). However, the text merely says "praesertim", and it would be difficult to summarize the requirements of the moral law on these two matters in two succinct phrases, as is done for the other cases mentioned.

G.9, 1.5. I would add to the list: "mendaciorum propagatio". It is one of the major impediments to peace nowadays.

Yours sincerely
L.L.McReavy

P.S. I hope to God that the Holy Father does not postpone his decision on contraception, or leave the matter to be fought out in St Peter's. More and more harm is done with every day of delay.

* * *

Ushaw College
Durham
10th March, 1965

Dear Monsignor,

Very many thanks for your letter. I was delighted to have your opinion of the new text and when I go back to Rome once more, later this month, I will do my best to meet the other points which you have raised. You will have seen that the Pope's Commission of Doctors is meeting in Rome in a few days time. Much must depend on whether they are able to give any sort of agreed advice. I think that if they do so there is the possibility that the Pope may say something before the Summer is out. Otherwise it seems inevitable that the problem will be handed back to the Commission and to the Fathers in Council. At least I shall be glad to find out what has happened when next I return to Rome.

With all good wishes,
Yours ever,
L.L. McReavy

* * *

From Monsignor McReavy's Journal: "There were no General Congregations during the week 18-23 October, 1965. I spent most of the week composing a report on the Birth-Control controversy and also on the Positio de Sacrarum Indulgentiarum Recognitione *which had been prepared by an extra-Conciliar Pontifical Commission and on which the Pope wanted the opinion of the hierarchies (Cardinal Heenan had leant me his copy for the purpose). On the Friday, 22 October, I read my paper on Birth Control to the hierarchy in the College library. I completed my summary of the Positio at 7 p.m. on the Sunday, 24 October".*

* * *

The Controversy on Artificial Birth Prevention

Paper read to the Hierarchy of England and Wales
by Monsignor L.L. McReavy

Until this last decade, the universal and unquestioned teaching of Catholic moral theologians was that any positive intervention designed to prevent the marriage act from resulting in conception or birth was intrinsically and gravely evil. This, said Vermeersch in the 1919 edition of his *De Castitate*, eleven years before *Casti Connubii*, was so clear from Catholic tradition, beginning from the Fathers and continued in the unanimous opinion of theologians and the ordinary magisterium of the Church, as to need no formal reprobation of the contrary error.

The contrary practice was of course immemorial, the chief methods mentioned by earlier writers, always with grave condemnation, being previous sterility potions, coitus interruptus and abortion. There is an echo of this in the *Catechismus Romanus* (of the Council of Trent); "Quare fit ut illorum scelus sit gravissimum qui matrimonio iuncti medicamentis vel conceptum impediunt vel partum abigunt". Artificial birth-prevention did not, however, become a major moral issue until the 19th century, when fertility ceased to be generally regarded as an unmixed blessing and when the use of contraceptive instruments was made practicable by the vulcanization of rubber, circ. 1840.

It is not therefore surprising that recorded replies of the Holy See on the subject date only from 1822. Even then, the first three replies recorded in Denzinger (1822, 1842 and 1851) deal only with coitus interruptus, and only from the point of view of the wife's co-operation and the confessor's duty. It is taken as self-evident that the husband's act is gravely wrong. The first reference to contraceptive instruments is found in a Holy Office reply (April 1853) which declared that "incomplete use of marriage, whether onanistically or condomistically (i.e. using the wicked instrument called a "condom') is intrinsically evil, and that a wife may not knowingly yield herself passively in condomistic intercourse, for she would be co-operating in an intrinsically unlawful thing". The first reference to use of the infertile period came in a reply of the S. Penitentiary, June 1880, which cautiously ruled that spouses using their marriage "on days when conception is more difficult" were "not to be disturbed"; and added: "the confessor may cautiously suggest it to those he has failed to deter from the execrable crime of onanism". Subsequent replies of the same Congregation (March 1886, April 1916, June 1916) dealt with the duty of a confessor to question seriously suspected onanists and to absolve only those who were resolved to amend, and with the co-operation of a wife whose husband seeks to have intercourse onanistically, sodomitically or with an instrument; co-operation can be lawful in the first case, never in the second or third.

It is clear therefore that when Pius XI made his formal pronouncement on the subject in *Casti Connubii* (Dec. 1930), in evident reply to the 1930 Lambeth Conference declaration made a few months earlier, he was merely confirming a hitherto unquestioned Christian position. Far from stunning the episcopate into "frozen silence", his statement caused little or no stir among either the bishops or the faithful. They would have been stunned if he had said anything to the contrary. The whole passage (pp. 25-29 in CTS version) deserves attention, but the core of it is this; "Since therefore, openly departing from the uninterrupted Christian tradition, some recently have judged it possible solemnly to declare another doctrine regarding this question, the Catholic Church, to whom God has entrusted the defence of the integrity and purity of morals, standing erect in the midst of the moral ruin that surrounds her, in order that she may preserve the chastity of the nuptial union from being defiled by this foul stain, raises her voice in token of her divine ambassadorship and through our mouth proclaims anew; any use whatever of matrimony exercised in such a way that the act is deliberately frustrated in its natural power to generate life is an offence against the law of God and of nature, and those who indulge in such are branded with the guilt of a grave sin."

This solemn declaration of the Supreme Pastor clearly cannot be dismissed as an *obiter dictum*. It was made by him with a deep sense of his responsibility as spokesman for the "divine ambassadorship of the Church" in her God-given function of defender of the moral law, to "proclaim anew" what she had always held to be that law. So solemn are its terms that Vermeersch and Cappello both regarded it as *ex cathedra*. Others, such as Creusen, saw it rather as an authentic declaration of a doctrine guaranteed as infallible by the ordinary and universal magisterium. Even after the recent questioning, Ford, Kelly and Schillebeeckx still consider it irrevocable. Baum and Drinkwater object that the ordinary and universal magisterium supposes acceptance by the bishops, not merely from, obedience but from personal persuasion after mature reflexion, and claim that, in fact, the response of the bishops was merely 30 years of frozen silence. This implies that, in 1930, the Pope thrust a new doctrine on them which they had not previously accepted freely, an implication which surely cannot be sustained. It was a doctrine which even the Anglican bishops had accepted and proclaimed down to, and including, the 1920 Lambeth Conference.

It seems morally certain that Pius XI himself was satisfied that he was merely proclaiming the ordinary and universal teaching of the Church, and meant to do so in his official capacity as her spokesman. At the beginning of the encyclical, he had affirmed his intention of correcting "certain pernicious and growing errors" and, indeed, "in our office as Christ's Vicar upon earth and Supreme Shepherd and Teacher". Then, as we. have seen, when he came to deal with this particular error, he. again invoked his title to speak for the Church. Finally, in the concluding section of the letter, he appealed to the Church's divine warrant as "the teacher of truth in those things also which concern the right regulation of moral conduct, even though some knowledge of the same is not beyond human reason", and he protested against the notion that the faithful need only obey the Church "in those. matters which she has decreed by solemn definition." If ever an attempt was made by a Pope to declare authentically the ordinary and universal teaching of the Church on a moral issue, this surely was a prime example. I personally know of no clearer instance.

This was likewise the conclusion of his successor, Pius XII. In his carefully worded address to the Midwives (1951), after repeating the ruling of *Casti Connubii* on contraception, he added; "This prescription is in full vigour today, as it was yesterday and will be tomorrow and always, because it is no mere precept of human law, but the expression of a law that is natural and divine." He applied it in explaining the Holy Office declaration of 1940 that "direct sterilization, perpetual or temporary, of man or woman, is unlawful and indeed prohibited by the law of nature", defining direct sterilization as that "which seeks to render procreation impossible, whether this be intended as a means or as an end". In 1958 (to haematologists) he explained that an intervention which causes sterility can be justified on the principle of totality, provided it is done for an equally immediate therapeutic effect which is alone directly intended and is sufficient in value to compensate for the unwanted sterilizing effect; but when the intervention is directly designed to deprive the organism of its procreative power, it stands condemned by reason of its directly contraceptive purpose.

These also were the criteria that Pius XII applied to the use of anovulant pills. If, he said, a woman takes them, not with a view to preventing conception, but as a remedy for a malady, the resultant temporary sterilization is indirect and justifiable on the principle of double effect; but to arrest ovulation in order to preclude conception and thereby preserve the uterus and organism from the consequences of a pregnancy is direct and therefore unlawful sterilization. He never dealt expressly with the use of anovulants to regularize the cycle, but it is not excluded by his principle, because, in that case, the directly intended object is not to sterilize intercourse, but simply to make use of natural sterility practicable. Indeed, in 1951 (to the Family Front), he expressed a hope that medical science would eventually provide a sure basis for the practice of rhythm.

Some recent critics of the rulings of Pius XII, e.g. L. Janssens, and W. Van der Marck, O.P., seek to evade them by accepting the view of those doctors who restrict the term "sterilization" to interventions which mutilate the generative organs or destroy the function. This, they argue, cannot be said of the use of anovulants, since it merely suspends fertility, or induces "ovarian repose". But this is to assume either that the moral sense of the term must coincide with the medical sense, or that Pius XII mistakenly thought that the pill caused an organic lesion. There is no ground for either assumption. It was already well known that no organic lesion was involved. He was dealing with the plain fact that the suspension of ovulation withholds from conjugal intercourse an element essential to its fecundity and thus renders it sterile in the ordinary sense of the word, for as long as the treatment lasts. To use the pill directly for this purpose, he said, was direct sterilization in the sense of the Holy Office decree. If he erred, it was on a point of morality, not bio-chemistry.

So much for the weight of authority behind the traditional position. It is so great and significant theologically that, in the opinion expressed by one hierarchy to the papal commission, any ambiguity in the re-affirmation of the accepted doctrine which might be construed as a retreat from it, would have grave consequences throughout the whole ambit of the Catholic magisterium in regard to faith and morals. One has only to think of the millions who must have been refused the sacraments and led thereby to abandon the practice of their religion on this one ground. If the Church could have misled the faithful on so grave a matter, with such grave consequences and for so long a period, what value or reliability could be attached to her moral teaching generally?

The Grounds of the Traditional Position

Pius XI, in *Casti Connubii*, indicated rather than demonstrated the grounds of the Church's doctrine: Holy Scripture, unanimous Christian tradition, and the natural moral law. All of these have recently been attacked.

1) The Bible has only one direct reference to a contraceptive act, i.e. the Onan story. Many exegetes hold however that Onan was struck dead for evading his levirate duty to raise issue to his deceased brother, rather than for the act by which he did so. It is not a modern view. St Francis of Sales mentions it as held by some heretics of his time, and answers that the Bible describes the deed itself as detestable. Besides, according to Deuteronomy, if Onan's sin was mere evasion of his levirate duty, he should at most have had his shoe removed and his face spat upon by the widow. However, a still more cogent argument for the inviolability of the marriage act could perhaps be derived from the sacred character and purpose attributed to the sex function in Genesis I and II.

2) The strength of the argument from tradition lies, not in any abundance of patristic strictures against contraceptive practices, but in the fact that whenever they are mentioned they are condemned. According to a recent work of research (Noonan, *Contraception: A History of its Treatment* by the Catholic Theologians and Canonists, Harvard Univ. Press, 1965) two clear principles are constant in the ecclesiastical tradition from Augustine to Pius XII, condemnation of onanism and of temporary sterilization. Cf. also Daly, "Natural Law and Morality Today" (art.) pp. 162-5.

3) For the argument from the Natural Law, again cf. Fr. Cahal Daly's article, "Natural Law Morality Today" (offprint from Christus Rex). He deals with most of the current objections to, or misconceptions regarding,

the natural moral law, notably the assumption that all its precepts and prohibitions should be obvious to everybody. On the contrary, as Vatican I declared, divine revelation and the guidance of the Church are morally necessary to enable fallen man to deduce them fully and accurately. This was shown in the general reaction to the Pope's ruling that the unborn child could never be killed directly, even to save the life of the mother. What is clear is that, in a divinely ordered creation, there is a right order of means to ends, and consequently that any use of a human faculty which is in intrinsic conflict with the end it was designed to serve or the means by which the end was meant to be achieved, as discerned by right reason, is objectively out of order and therefore wrong. Now, it is obvious that, at the structural level, every feature of the anatomy and functioning of the sex faculty was designed directly and immediately for that mutual act of male and female which constitutes the first and only voluntary stage in the process of reproduction — the introduction of the male sperm into the female genital tract, where, if nature supplies the complementary ovum, conception may occur. It does not, of itself, effect generation, but it is intrinsically orientated to it. This then, according to the traditional argument, is its primary intrinsic purpose, built in to its very structure. To be used ordinately, it must be used in a manner which respects this orientation.

It is, of course, obvious that it serves other purposes, in particular, as Genesis itself indicates, it enables the couple to express with their whole being, body and soul, that intimate personal love and mutual self-giving which should unite them as parents and contribute to their full personal development. These other purposes provide legitimate motives for conjugal intercourse, as the Church has always held in allowing marriage of the sterile and use of marriage when sterile; but just as they do not explain its intrinsic finality, so neither can they justify its exercise in a way which, by positive intervention, defeats its natural orientation. It is this that specifies the act of sexual union and distinguishes it from all other human actions. It is essentially an act of giving and receiving the seed of new life, that part of the total generative process which God has enabled and invited man and wife to supply. To rob it of this character by direct intervention, before, during or after its use, is to belie its nature; it is *contra naturam*, a counterfeit.

To quote Pius XII (Midwives address): "Nature puts at man's disposal the whole chain of causes which will result in the appearance of a new human life; it is for him to release this vital force and for nature to develop its course and bring it to completion. When once man has done his part and set in motion the marvellous process which will produce new life, it is his bounden duty to let it take its course. He must not arrest or frustrate its natural development". For an answer to the charge that this is mere "biologism", cf. Daly, p. 166. Man is body-soul. Both must be respected. They cannot be separated.

Application to Oral Contraception

If it is intrinsically evil to deprive the conjugal act of its procreative potentiality by positive intervention, it is morally irrelevant whether this occurs before, during or after the act. A morally evil end necessarily vitiates any means directly employed to achieve it. "The end is present in the means, is willed or is refused in the choosing of the means" (Daly, p. 167). When pills capable of inducing a temporary sterility are taken with directly contraceptive intent, it is not the sterilizing effect that renders their use immoral, for the same pills could be licitly used with the same effect for a directly therapeutic purpose. What is wrong is the contraceptive purpose for which temporary sterility is procured. It is therefore no answer to appeal, as do Janssens, etc., to the fact that anovulants do not impair the integrity of the conjugal act as an expression of love. One could argue on those lines to the liceity of a post-coital spermicidal douche, or a diaphragm.

Nor can one argue *a pari* from the liceity of exclusive use of the sterile period to the liceity of inducing sterility by anovulants, as Janssens also seeks to do. There is no parity. Periodic continence, even though the motive is to avoid conception, does not sterilize any act of intercourse; it simply makes use of natural sterility. The *finis operantis* is admittedly the same — avoidance of conception, but that can be lawful for a sufficient reason. It has been further objected that the liceity of such intercourse cannot be derived from its procreative orientation because it is not procreative, and therefore must be based exclusively on its aptness to express mutual self-giving, which is thus shown to be a sufficient independent end. But this is to misunderstand the meaning of procreative orientation and to argue as if it meant that the conjugal act, performed naturally in the fertile periods, were itself procreative. It is not. It is never in itself more than a preliminary to procreation, and it retains this character even in the sterile periods, when it is naturally performed.

Finally, the short answer to any attempts to justify the use of directly contraceptive interventions is that, once respect for the procreative orientation of the act ceases to be absolutely obligatory, there is no point at which one can logically stop, short of a completely existentialist and situationalist attitude to sex morality, which would justify any use of the function found in the concrete to be conducive to personal fulfilment. In fact, most advocates of a change seem committed to some form of situation ethics.

On the Primacy of the Procreative End

Canon 1013: "Matrimonii finis primarius est procreatio atque educatio prolis; secundarius mutuum adiutorium et remedium concupiscentiae."

The official doctrine, as here stated, has never denied that marriage is divinely ordered to the personal good of the spouses, as well as to the common good of the human race. This is clear from Genesis 2 ("It is not good for man to be alone...helper like unto himself...two in one flesh"). It was clearly stated in the *Catechismus Romanus*, quoted by *Casti Connubii*. It is implicit in the term "mutuum adiutorium". However, it is not regarded as conflicting with the primacy of the procreative end. Cf. Daly, p. 168.

When this primacy was questioned in the 1940s by Doms and Krempel, the Rota was instructed by Pius XII to study the question. It did so in a judicial sentence of 1944, and shortly afterwards, 1 April 1944, the Holy Office declared it inadmissible to hold that the secondary ends are not essentially subordinate to the primary end.

Pius XII (Midwives, 1951) emphasized that this was not meant to belittle the personal values of the conjugal union to the spouses. "It is as human beings, not as irrational animals, that they are appointed to be authors of their progeny... To reduce the communal life of man and wife and their marital relations to nothing more than an organic function for transmitting life-germs would be to convert the home... into a mere biological laboratory" (hence, he said, the rejection of artificial insemination).

The marital act is a personal action, a simultaneous and direct co-operation of husband and wife, which, because of the very nature of the agents and the distinctive character of the act, is the expression of that mutual self-giving which makes them "one flesh". But, "though all this is true and willed by God, it must not be dissociated from the primary end of matrimony which is to serve the cause of new human life..." Had nature's sole or even chief objective been the joy and delight that husband and wife would take in giving themselves to each other, in possessing each other; had nature intended the marital act merely to make their personal experience as enjoyable as possible, and not rather to stimulate them in the service of human life, then the Creator would have devised and shaped that act according to another plan. As it is, the act is completely subordinated and ordered to the one great purpose: "generatio et educatio prolis."

It is, however, perfectly tenable that a better terminology could be devised to denote the precise inter-relation of the two ends. There would seem to be good ground for the claim that, in many vernaculars, the term "secondary" does not convey the intended sense of "essentially subordinated to the primary", but has rather the derogatory sense of "unimportant" or even "dispensable". It would be perfectly in line with the traditional doctrine to declare that marriage and conjugal intercourse are intrinsically ordered to a two-fold end, procreation (with education) and the expression of mutual love and self-giving. This latter is already implicit in the notion of "mutuum adiutorium", which, no less than procreation, is a *finis operis*, i.e. an intrinsic end of marriage and marital intercourse. But, by the same token, since both ends are intrinsic, they are inseparable. In particular, both must be respected in the performance of the conjugal act. There must be no positive intervention designed to deprive it of its procreative orientation, and it must never be allowed to degenerate into an animal act devoid of love. "The good of offspring", said St Augustine (De Genesi ad litteram, IX, vii, 12) "consists in this, that children be begotten with love, nourished with tenderness and reared with religious care."

Confidential Points From the Debate "De Beata Maria Virgine"

by Monsignor L.L. McReavy

I. On "Mary Mediatrix"

Ruffini — The title is universally accepted, but the firm foundation on which it rests needs to be clearly indicated. The objection that Christ is the only Mediator is weak; only Christ is "Magister", "Sanctus", and yet etc.

Léger — The title is difficult to explain accurately and differently understood; better to omit it.

Bea — Ditto, because of the danger of misunderstanding by Catholics and difficulties with non-Catholics.

Djajasepoetra (Indonesian) — Omit the doctrine and, if the title is to be retained, merely list it with the others.

Ruotolo — Placet, because it speaks clearly of Mary Mediatrix and yet avoids contraverted opinions.

Rendeiro — Begged in the name of 82 Bishops that the text about Mary's mediation be retained; its omission would bewilder the faithful who believe that all graces come through Mary.

Van Lierde — Pastoral experience shows the fruitfulness of the doctrine of the New Eve, which is well understood by the faithful.

Ancel — Would personally have preferred to avoid the term but acquiesced in the text because it had been carefully phrased to secure a desirable unanimity. It gives the common doctrine, and shows that it derogates in no way from the unique mediation of Christ.

Alfrink — Our Lady certainly has a special function, well described in n. 53 and unquestioned, but we must distinguish between the title and the doctrine which it expresses. The title needs multiple explanations, because it is used in a sense absolutely different from that in which Christ is called Mediator. Its retention in the text would give it a certain authority. Its omission would not affect the doctrine, and would be ecumenically helpful.

II. On Mary "Mater Ecclesiae"

Wyszynski (for the Polish Bishops) — Mary's Spiritual motherhood should be put in first place, and she should be proclaimed "Mater Ecclesiae".

Marques (Mexico) — Also wanted explicit proclamation of the generally accepted doctrine of Mary's spiritual motherhood in the economy of grace.

Hervas (Spain) — The chapter should be entitled *De Beata Maria Virgine Matre Ecclesiae*; this is the reason why many wanted it joined to the schema *De Ecclesia*; it has solid theological foundation, Pope Paul has twice used it, and its omission will seem like rejection.

Van Lierde — Two titles have been suggested: *De Maria Sanctissima Matre Ecclesiae* and *...omnium credentium Matre*; for the first, it can be said that she preceded the Church in time, graces and functions, concurred in its birth, and cooperates as its supereminent member in the birth of faithful to the Church; the second title is more ecumenical.

De Uriarte — It is de fide that Mary is Mother of God made man; it is certain, but not de fide that she is Mater Ecclesiae.

Monte (Servite Gen) — Unlike St Augustine, the schema is afraid to call Mary "Mater membrorum Christi".

Garcia (for many Spanish Bishops) — Declare her "Mater Ecclesiae"; the Pope wants it and it is a traditional title.

Mendez (Mexico) — The title "Mater Ecclesiae" has a correct sense and is implied in the text, but it is alien to the Greek tradition, being first used in the West by Berengarius. Leo XIII was the first Pope to use it. If she is mother of our mother the Church, she is our grand-mother. The Mexican Bishops want a declaration of her spiritual motherhood, but not the title "Mater Ecclesiae".

Casten (Spain, for 80 Bishops) — Regretted the absence of the title "Mater Ecclesiae" and asked that it be restored. Mary fulfils the three conditions: sponsa sponsi, mater filiorum, sedula curatrix.

III. General Comments On The Schema

Léger — Better than the previous one.

Döpfner — In genere placet.

Henriquez — Placet; well balanced; but to avoid ambiguity, scriptural terms should be used only in their literal sense.

Marques — Very praiseworthy on the whole.

Ruotolo — Placet.

Suenens — Placet, apart from two defects: a) a certain minimalism; Our Lady is presented too much as a figure of past history and not enough is said about her present influence and association in the work of salvation. Right to avoid controversy, but it fails to present what is taught by the magisterium and accepted by the faithful; b) one grave omission: no mention of the intimate link between her motherhood and the apostolate.

Rendeiro (Portugal) — In genere placet, but certain negative expressions should be replaced by positive.

Fernandez (Gen. O.P.) — Placet quoad substantiam, but the warning to preachers in n. 55, not to make Mary equal to Christ, is insulting and uncalled for.

Signora — Placet, but it should come back after chapter I.

Mendez (for 50 bishops) — keep the text as it is, with small exceptions, so as to avoid division.

Ruffini — Mary's association with Christ in the work of redemption is unduly played down.

Léger — More sobriety, clarity and accuracy of expression is desirable, and it should deal expressly with the right ordering of cult of Mary.

Bea — In several places, it fails to observe the initial intention of leaving open questions unsettled.

Mingo — It is silent about truths which the Church teaches openly.

Sapelak — It is silent about her chief function, patrocinium et auxilium.

Gawlina — It should present Mary as the most absolute examples of Christian perfection.

Jeger — It should show her connection with the Holy Spirit.

Kempf — Her connection with the Church should be more fully explained.

The Cardinal had also handed on to me a 93-page report on the revision of the present system of indulgences, prepared by an extra-conciliar pontifical Commission. I have put in about four days of work on that, reducing it to about six pages of typescript, so that our hierarchy will more easily be able to answer the questions which it puts to them.

I have had no Saturday off this week, or even Sunday. I finished my summary a few minutes ago, 7 p.m. Sunday evening, after a full day's servile work. (L34)

Positio De Sacrarum Indulgentiarum Recognitione

Summary by Mgr. L. L. McReavy

This extra-conciliar document of 93 pages, drawn up by a special Pontifical Commission, consists of three parts; the theology of indulgences, the Commission's schema of a revised discipline, and a commentary on the schema with questions to be answered. For convenience, these latter two parts will be run together.

Part I. The theological principles concerning indulgences and the historical evolution of the system.

Part I makes the following points: —

1. *The just man in this life can make satisfaction for others.*

It is *de fide* that penitential satisfaction can be made in this life for the temporal punishment still owing for sin after its guilt has been remitted

(Trent; Denz. Schon. 1580, 1713); and it is clear from St Paul's doctrine of the Mystical Body (Rom.12, 5; 1 Cor. 12, 25-6; 7,14; Col. 1, 24, and Gal. 6, 1..2) and implicit in the doctrine of Communion of Saints that vicarious satisfaction is not only possible but pleasing to God. It can be made for the Holy Souls by way of suffrage (2 Mach. 12, 43; Trent, Denz. 1820).

2. *The Church has a treasury of the satisfactions of Christ and the Saints.*

The existence of this treasury, inexhaustible by reason of the infinity of the satisfaction made by Christ, is vouched for by the magisterium (Denz. 1025-7, 1447-8, 1467, 2641).

3. *The Church can dispense this treasury.*

Implicit in her power to remit sins (in. 20, 23) — accessorium sequitur principale, and in her power to bind and loose (Mt. 16, 19; 18, 18).

4. Though there are early examples of equivalent indulgences, e.g. the remission granted to those who had lapsed under persecution, in consideration of a "libellus pacis" obtained from an imprisoned confessor of the faith, the theology and discipline, as we know it today, was not substantially evolved until 13th C.

In the 14th C. came the multiplication, on ever easier conditions, of indulgences expressed in the days, months and years of the old penitential tariffs, which had ceased to be imposed and had no determined meaning. The fact that the good work was commonly an alms led to abuses. Trent had nothing to say about the doctrine, being concerned only to repress abuses (Denz. 1835). The time is now opportune to revise the discipline, as part of *aggiornamento.*

5. *Nature of an indulgence.*

An indulgence is a remission of the temporal punishment still due to sin, after its guilt has been remitted through contrition, which the legitimate ecclesiastical authority grants from the treasury of the Church, on the fulfilment of certain conditions, to the living *per modum solutionis* (i.e. enabling them to pay their debt, though some theologians regard it as "absolution" by the power of the Keys), to the dead, who are no longer the Church's subjects, *per modum suffragii.* It is valid before God (Denz. 1416, 1468-72, 2640).

6. *Conditions*

a) On the part of the grantor: legitimate authority and just cause.

b) On the part of the recipient: baptism, intention, fulfilment of prescribed work, state of grace, at least at end of fulfilment.

Utility

Not comparable to good works considered as earning an eternal reward, but serve as a reminder of the need to make satisfaction and of many basic truths of faith.

PARTS II AND III. Schema of revised discipline, and commentary.

The schema retains the discipline in its substance, but simplifies it drastically, especially in regard to indulgenced objects, clears away the tangled growth of Decreta Authentica, and introduces an entirely new notion of partial indulgences.

Chapter I. Partial Indulgences

1. A partial indulgence, attached to a prayer or pious work, is to be called simply that, with no determined number of days or years.
2. By it the ecclesiastical authority grants from the treasury of the Church as much again of remission of temporal punishment before God, as the person himself gains already by the satisfactory value of the prayer or work to which the indulgence is attached.

Comment

This new rule for partials is regarded as the cardinal point of the whole revision. In place of the former undetermined measure of days etc. (undetermined because the Church had never defined what penitential discipline was envisaged), it substitutes a measure which, though known only to God, is objectively determined. It is linked to the degree of charity, which is the basis of the satisfactory value of our good works. It puts the stress on right intention and fervour in the indulgenced act. The old system tended to encourage choice of good works according to the size or the indulgence; the new makes the size of the indulgence proportionate to the satisfactory value of the concrete work. i.e. to the penitential effort and degree of perfection with which the individual does the work. It removes all the former inequalities and incongruities. It is easily explicable to the faithful. Nor is any break with former theology involved, for, under the new norm as under the old, the effect still depends formaliter on the Church's action, the effort and devotion of the person being merely the material measure of the remission she grants.

Quaeritur

1. Placetne nova norma pro indulgentia partiali?
2. Any comment on the formula used to express the new norm?

Chapter II. Plenary Indulgences

1. Only one plenary can be gained per day.
2. To gain a plenary, one must do the indulgenced work and fulfil the three conditions of Confession, Communion and prayer for Pope within the appointed time.
3. These can be fulfilled on the day of the work or during the week before or after.
4. But a separate Communion is required for every plenary.
5. A person who does the work but fails to fulfil the conditions within the prescribed time, gains a partial indulgence.
6. There will be special norms for a Jubilee Year. Other indulgences will remain obtainable during it.

Comment

All the Commission agreed that plenaries should be less numerous, and not more than one a day obtainable. Rules 2-4 provide a uniform and easily remembered set of conditions for every case. The existing discipline usually requires four conditions, but there are many exceptions which no one can memorise. Commutation by a confessor for the impeded, as in can. 935, will remain.

Quaeritur

1. Do you agree to ("placetne") the rule — "only one plenary a day", or would you prefer a stricter rule, e.g. once a week?
2. Given the rule — "only one plenary a day" — should it be further decreed that a person can gain only one (or two) a month for himself, on a day to be chosen by him, as far as possible among feasts of first class, and only for the Holy Souls on the other days?
3. Do you agree to the rules about conditions (three, to be fulfilled in every case by everyone, saving commutation "pro impeditis", but able to be fulfilled on the day of the work, or during the week before or after, and a separate Communion for each plenary)?
4. Do you agree to the rule granting a partial to those who fail to gain a plenary because of failure to fulfil the conditions?
5. Any other comments?

Chapter III. Personal Indulgences

1. The chief works that pertain to the apostolate and are works of mercy and charity shall be indulgenced.
2. The Rosary of Our Lady is to have precedence over other rosaries even in regard to indulgences.

3. Pious associations, whatever their origin or nature, shall be assigned about 10 plenaries a year, some common to all associations, on the more solemn feasts of Our Lord and Our Lady, others special to each association. Partial indulgences shall also be attached to the works proper to each association. Since the above indulgences are attached to prayers or works, and not to the use of insignia, they shall henceforth be classed as personal.

4. The *summaria* (indulgence-lists) of religious orders and congregations shall be revised.

5. At the final sermon of a Lenten or Advent series, retreat, or mission, all priest-preachers shall be able to impart a blessing, with a crucifix and single Sign of the Cross, carrying a plenary indulgence obtainable by all who have attended the final sermon and a third of those that preceded it.

Comment

These five norms were unanimously accepted by the Commission. Hitherto the indulgences of most associations could only be obtained by wearing always, day and night, a scapular, or cord, etc., of a particular type and specially blessed. In future such insignia will be ornaments, not bonds, and members will gain the indulgences merely by fulfilling the indulgenced works.

Ad 4. The "summaria" of religious are at present both prolix and marked by inequalities, both between religious institutes and between them and the general faithful.

Ad 5. There will be no need of a special apostolic faculty, and, to avoid confusion, it will no longer be called a "papal" blessing. The formula — "Benedictio Dei Omnipotentis, etc." may, but need not, be used.

Quaeritur

1. Do you agree to the proposed norm for the revision of indulgences granted to associations, whereby they are to be equitably reduced and become "personal" by being detached from insignia?

2. Any comments on the rest of the above norms?

Chapter IV. Real Indulgences (i.e. attached to things)

1. All who habitually and devoutly carry one or more duly blessed objects of piety (crucifix, cross, rosary, scapular, girdle, cincture, medal) gain a daily partial indulgence and a plenary once a year on the usual conditions.

2. All other indulgences now attached to things (scapulars, girdles, cinctures, medals) become personal by virtue of chap. III, n. 3. The insignia proper to each association will remain as signs of membership.

3. All priests are competent, not only to bless pious objects, but also to attach the indulgences mentioned in n. 1. The blessing of a crucifix carries with it also the indulgence of the Way of the Cross for those prevented from

making it, and the indulgence *in articulo mortis*. This latter can, however, be gained with an unblessed cross, if it would otherwise be unobtainable, *servatis ceteris de iure servandis*.

4. Those who piously carry or reverently keep at home one or more pious objects (crucifix, cross, rosary, medal, small statue), blessed by the Pope or by any bishop, can gain in addition to the common indulgences of no. 1, another plenary on SS. Peter and Paul, on the usual conditions, and also a plenary *in articulo mortis, servatis ceteris de iure servandis*.

Comment

After long discussion, rule 1 was accepted by the great majority, and the other three almost unanimously. No. 1 is the chief norm, the others being complementary. It adopts a midway course designed to eliminate the defects of the present system (pages of minutiae about the material, form, blessing and manner of wearing pious objects), without causing the *admiratio fidelium* that would result from the total abolition of real indulgences, proposed by one member. This, it was felt, would be to throw out the baby with the bath-water. Use of pious objects is based on the same theological reason as sacraments and sacred images. Moreover, they are a constant reminder to the faithful of the presence of the Church in their daily lives. The new rules, taken in conjunction with chap. I, n. 2 and chap. III, n. 3, while retaining the use of indulgenced objects, avoid the defects of the present system. In future, the indulgences will not be simply attached to the objects, but will be related to the action of the person who devoutly uses them. The indulgences remain "real" in the sense that an object is required, but personal devotion is necessary and is the measure of the remission granted. The one partial indulgence per day relates to all the devout acts of the day and thus can earn as much remission as the multiple indulgences of the present system. The indulgences are the same for every blessed object.

Quaeritur

1. Do you agree to the norm whereby, with the removal of all existing diversities, duly blessed pious objects shall enjoy the same indulgences, i.e. a daily partial and an annual plenary, obtainable by those who habitually and devoutly carry one or more objects of piety?

2. Do you agree to the norm whereby all priests receive the faculty to bless common objects of piety, as explained in n. 3.?

3. Do you agree that, when there is no formula or the prescribed one cannot for a reasonable cause be recited, objects may be blessed with a single sign of the cross and the words "In the name of the Father, etc. Amen"?

4. Any other comments on real indulgences?

Chapter V. Local Indulgences

1. The rules concerning a plenary are extended even to "toties quoties" plenaries, not excepting the Portiuncula and Way of the Cross.

2. A "plenary indulgence toties quoties" shall in future be called simply an "indulgence toties quoties". Those who do the prescribed work will be able to gain one plenary on any one day, on the usual conditions, and a partial for every repetition of the prescribed prayers, even without leaving the church.

3. Existing local indulgences, granted in perpetuity, shall not in general be subjected to revision or reduction, saving the above rules about plenaries. Fresh concessions or renewals shall be made with moderation.

4. Privileged altars, local or personal, are suppressed. But the Church intends to make the fullest suffrage for the faithful departed in the sacrifice of the Mass, and exhorts her children to beg of God's mercy "omnibus in Christo quiescentibus locum refrigerii, lucis et pacis".

Comment

Ad 4. It is difficult to explain to the faithful what the plenary indulgence of a privileged Mass does for the soul involved, which the Mass itself is not already capable of doing. What is clear is that both work only *per modum suffragii*. Since, therefore, under the new discipline, the Church intends to attach her fullest suffrage to Masses for the dead, the Holy Souls are no worse off. Moreover, appreciation of the Mass itself is increased.

Quaeritur

1. Do you agree to the norm of one plenary only a day being applied even to so-called "toties quoties" plenaries?

2. Do you agree with the provision of n. 4 regarding privileged altars and regarding the fullest suffrage of the Church in Masses for the dead?

3. Any other comments on local indulgences?

Chapter VII

The Diary of the Council. A Time-line of the Council

Over a period of several decades Monsignor McReavy used school *Exercise Books* with a green cover, familiar to generations of boys and students at Ushaw, to keep a brief record of events, meetings, journeys, appointments and visits, and other items of personal interest.[1] The entries rarely provide information in the narrative form commonly associated with a Diary. Consequently the parts of his diaries covering the Second Vatican Council were for the most part jottings. The true Diary of the Council is the Journal in which he gives an account of the General Congregations.

The primary value of the Exercise Book Diaries is that they provide a time-line with which to follow Monsignor McReavy's day to day life during the period of the Council. There are a few revealing remarks which do not occur in his letters or the Journal. These are mainly personal and often concerning his health: "Feeling exhausted. Long siesta in afternoon". (November 11, 1962). "Felt giddy on way up to tea, and again on Monday at Mass. Exhausted." (October 25, 1964) and on the following day he noted: "Still feeling physically and mentally exhausted, and rather wobbly on my feet." This and similar information was confided only to his Diary.

The Diary

The First Session

October 11th – December 8th 1962

Tuesday, October 2, 1962

Received Brief from the Secretariate of State (signed Cicognani) informing me that Holy Father had named me a "Peritus Conciliaris" with accompanying booklet ("Ordo") explaining my duties. 2 p.m. rang the Bishop who said I should treat it as a command. Rang Norman Richardson (travel agent) and by 3.30 was booked for the Alitalia flight (Monday 8th 12.45). Wired Vice-Rector of English College asking him to fix accommodation for me somewhere.

Days spent in clearing up *Clergy Review* work and preparing for departure.

[1] Ushaw Archives: UC/P41/F5 1934 – 1987. Nine Books.

Sunday, October 7

Departed Durham 10.58, arrived King's Cross for 4.39, met by Father Peter Anglin and drove in car to Clitherow House. Dinner at Grill. John Marshall and wife came.

Monday, October 8

Driven to airport by Father Handley. Received by Alitalia P.R. woman and shepherded to the plane in advance with Archbishop Grimshaw and other Bishops (including Ripon). 1 p.m. plane. Same privileged reception on arrival at Rome. Met by Mgr Alan Clark who regretted to inform me that there was no room for me at the English College, but that he had got me a room off the Piazza Navona. To Rome by air coach (no room in College car). To English College. Father Ashdowne drove me to Piazza Navona building, but finding that the room was completely unfurnished brought me back to College where I was given Bishop of Northampton's room for the night. I did not sleep till 4 a.m. through worrying about where I was to stay.

Tuesday, October 9

Was relieved to learn after breakfast that I could have the room of a student who had just declared his intention of leaving on Friday next and that till then Peter Cookson (Ushaw boy) would let me have his room. Went to the Secretariate of the Council to enquire about taking my oath, which the rest of the *Periti* had taken in St Peter's the previous evening. Lunch at Mgr Lefebvre's flat.

Wednesday, October 10

Went with Mgr Davis to get photographs for our Council Tessera (Passport). Thunderstorm at night.

Thursday, October 11

Solemn Opening of the Council.

Still raining, when, at 7:20 a.m., in choir robes, drove to St Peter's. Rain stopped on the way. Went straight into St Peter's and found a place in the middle Tribune on Gospel side. Had to wait over an hour before the procession of bishops came, six abreast, through the great West door. Out at 1.30. Lunch 2.20. After supper went out with Mgr Worlock in car driven by Mgr Clarke to see the illuminations. Could not get to St Peter's, where there was a great torchlight procession, but drove round the Capitol, illuminated by torches.

Friday, October 12

Went to Secretariate and received my Tessera and copy of volume I of Schemata. Moved to my new room on the top floor.

Saturday, October 13

First General Congregation.

Went in alto piano. (For account of this and succeeding General Congregations, see the separate manuscript record).

Sunday, October 14

Feast with students in honour of St Edward. Heavy rain.

Monday, October 15

Bought an umbrella.

Tuesday, October 16

End of scirocco. Sunshine. Second General Congregation.

Wednesday, October 17

Free day. Study. Went to Herder's bookshop. Evening, to Belgian College to see Mgr Anné and Bishop Calewaert.

Thursday, October 18

In lovely weather drove with Bishop Dwyer and Father O'Brien in Dwyer's car to Palazolla, via Frascati, Monte Porzio and the Latin Vale. Sumptuous lunch at Albergo just below Villa. Then to Villa, where most of the other bishops had gathered. Visited the new swimming pool and the sforza. Tea on terrace. Home about 6.30.

Friday, October 19

Worked from 8 to 1 on summary of schema *De Liturgia* which was Polycopied for the bishops. Afternoon, the preliminary pencil sketch of the Theatre of Marcellus.

Saturday, October 20

Third General Congregation. Walked to St Peter's with Mgr Davis to save car expense. Afternoon, finished painting of the Theatre of Marcellus.

Sunday, October 21

Afternoon. Sketch of Fabrician Bridge.

Monday to Wednesday, October 22-24

General Congregations.

Monday, October 22

Afternoon, finished Fabrician Bridge.

Tuesday, October 23

Drove with Bishop Dwyer to Baths of Caracalla.

Thursday, October 25

Drove with Bishop Dwyer to Albano (Church of Our Lady of Galloro). Lunch at the De Sanctis Trattoria overlooking Lake Nemi. Bishop MacEachern and another Canadian Bishop came in while we were lunching. Then via Velletri and Latin Vale to Palazolla for Tea.

Friday, October 26

Afternoon, did a preliminary sketch of Castel Sant Angelo.

Monday, October 29

Ordination Feast in Refectory of College.

Thursday, November 1 – Friday, November 2 – Saturday, November 3

Free Days. I spent them in summarising and collating the debate on the Preface and chapter I of *De Liturgia*. Polycopied and distributed to Bishops, who were very grateful.

Friday, November 2

With Mgr Davis to San Lorenzo.

Saturday, November 3

The Scots and Irish hierarchies joined the English and Welsh hierarchies at the English College for Tea and a meeting. Over 50 bishops present.

Sunday, November 4

Attended, in choir robes, the Capella Papale in St Peters, for the fourth anniversary of the Pope's coronation. Solemn Mass in Ambrosian rite by Cardinal Montini.

Monday, Tuesday, Wednesday.

General Congregations.

Thursday, November 8.

Worked on summaries.

Friday and Saturday, November 9/10.

General Congregations.

Sunday, November 11

Feeling exhausted. Long siesta in afternoon.

Monday, November 12

Loss of appetite.

Tuesday, November 13

End of *De Liturgia*. Did some work in evening.

Wednesday, November 14

Ottaviani introduced *De Fontibus*, which came immediately under attack.

Thursday, November 15

Dictated my summary of the first day debate *De Fontibus Revelationis* to Miss Breen (of the Grail) who had it typed and duplicated for distribution to the bishops by supper time.

Friday, Saturday.

(No entries).

Sunday, November 18

Evening, attended reception given to *Periti* at the Gregorian University.

Monday, November 19

Highlight of the five-day debate on *De Fontibus Revelationis*. Evening, went to North American College to hear a lecture on Form-criticism by Father Barnabas Ahern, C.P., a first-class performance. Chief critic was Archbishop Vagnuzzi, Apostolic delegate to U.S.

Tuesday, November 20

After five more speeches *De Fontibus*, the Presidential Bench put to the vote the question "An interumpenda sit disceptatio de schemata De Fontibus". The debate continued, and the result of the vote was announced at the end of the morning: *Placet* 1368; *non placet* (i.e. continue) 822, null 19. Since 1368 did not comprise two thirds of the 2209 voting, it was announced that discussion of the present schema would continue.

Wednesday, November 21

24th General Congregation began with announcement that the Pope had decided that the schema *De Fontibus* should be revised by a special mixed Commission (Theology and Unity) under Ottaviani and Bea.

Thursday, November 22

Worked from 8 to 1.15 on a summary of the 50 page schema on the *Means of Social Communication*. After lunch, with Mgr Davis to San Clemente where a French guest expert gave a guided tour. After tea, dictated my summary of above schema to Miss Breen for duplication.

Friday, Saturday, November 23/24

(No entry).

Sunday, November 25

After tea, went with bishops (with Cardinal and Worlock in Cardinal's car) to Vatican in hope of being admitted to audience, but Nassali-Rocca who met us in the Long Gallery said firmly to the Cardinal "Vescovi soli". We non-bishops (Mgr Davies, Canon O'Connell, etc) had to wait in the Throne room (Cardinal's banqueting hall) until the bishops came out of audience. They ended it with an "Ad Multos Annos" begun unexpectedly by Bishop Wall, and they said it was rather a flop. The Pope commented: "Ad Multos Annos. Yes, as long as I remain fit and well. No one wants a sick Pope". He was already unwell and audiences were discontinued a day or so later.

Monday, November 26

27th General Congregation completed the debate on *Means of Communication* and passed to *Ut Unum Sint* (Reunion with Oriental Churches).

Tuesday, November 27

Secretary General announced that Pope had acceded to request of many bishops that next Session should be postponed to September 8th.

Thursday, November 29

Lunch at Tre Scalini (Piazza Navona) with Bishop of Hexham and Hexham students. After tea, attended an "At Home" at residence of Mr Cape, First Secretary to Legation to Holy See.

Friday, November 30

Close of debate on *Ut Omnes Unum Sint*.

Saturday, December 1

Secretary General announced that Pope was better and hoped to resume public blessings shortly. Vote taken on *Ut Omnes Unum Sint*. Ottaviani and Franic then introduced the schema *De Ecclesia*.

Sunday, December 2

Very cold wind. 11 a.m. visited the Scavi under St Peter's with some of the bishops, conducted by Miss Derex (of Holland).

Monday, December 3

Attended reception at residence of Sir Peter Scarlett, British Minister to the Holy See. Met Hans Küng.

Tuesday, December 4

5 p.m. attended first meeting of Conciliar Commission on Discipline of Clergy and People. Only Periti present. After the new secretary had

explained our task, Cardinal Ciriaci gave us an address and then shook hands with us individually.

Wednesday, December 5

General Congregation concluded at 11.55 to enable us all to assemble in Piazza for Pope's (resumed) blessing at midday.

Thursday, December 6

Felt dizzy during Coffee break in St Peter's. Definitely unwell after tea. Took Beecham's powders and went early to bed.

Friday, December 7

Unable to attend last General Congregation of the Session. Stayed in my room all day.

Saturday, December 8

Unable to go to St Peter's for closing Mass and Pope's Blessing. Lunch with students at 12.45 and then Mgr Clark drove me and Mgr Davis to airport for the 2 p.m. plane. Reached London airport shortly after 4 p.m. Heavy rain. Caught the 5.50 train to Maidstone. Called at the Presbytery and Father Twomey drove me home. Feeling very much under the weather.

Sunday, December 9

Said 10 o'clock Mass and rested at home for remainder of day. Monaghan came at night and we showed the film stills of the Council in the projector.

Monday, December 10

8 a.m. Mass. Took a Beechams just before leaving for 11am train. 1 p.m. from King's Cross. 550 into Durham. Met by A. Smith with College car. Warm welcome, but everyone disturbed by my wan appearance. Early to bed.

The Second Session

September 29th – December 4th 1963

Friday, September 27

Left Maidstone by 9 a.m. train. Caught the 1 p.m. plane to Rome with about six of the bishops and reached Rome English College at 2.50 where I was given a newly prepared room in a mezzanine flat recently constructed at the far end of the Cortile. Dr P Redmond who had come out on holiday with Bishop Dwyer was in residence in the College.

Saturday, September 28

Shopped. In the evening, called on Anné at the Belgian College and met Bishop Calewaert of Bruges. Momentary encounter with Cardinal Suenens at entrance.

Sunday, September 29

Inaugural Public Session in St Peter's. Went in robes and was given a good seat in pen reserved to Prelates at the right of papal altar, next to Monsignors Worlock and Cosgrove. Pope spoke for a full hour.

Monday to Friday, September 30 to October 4

Debate on *De Ecclesia*. The Bishops persuaded Dr Redmond to stay on as a dogmatic theologian.

Saturday to Sunday, October 5/6

Worked on a summary of the first weeks debate, which was duplicated for our bishops. Since the Americans had begun to produce a full and accurate daily summary of the debates, and arrangements had been made to supply copies daily to our hierarchy, and Dr Redmond was available to supply notes on points of dogma arising from the debates, I felt much less under pressure than at the first Session.

Monday to Friday, October 7/11

Continuation of the debate on *De Ecclesia*, especially on chapter II (Hierarchical Constitution of Church) which occupied nine General Congregations, mainly on Collegiality and Pope and the proposed restoration of diaconate. Best speech was by Bishop Betazzi, newly consecrated Auxiliary Bishop of Bologna, on Collegiality (Friday, October 11).

Saturday, October 12

Lovely day. Took underground train from Colosseo to Ostia Antica where I was met at the entrance gate by Bishop Dwyer and P Redmond who had followed by car. We spent two hours walking round the Roman town in hot sunshine, had lunch at a restaurant facing the Castello of Ostia, and then drove via Ostia Lido down the coast and back to Rome by another route.

Sunday, October 13

Feast of St Edward. Big dinner in College refectory. Felt heavy for rest of the day.

Monday to Friday, October 14/18

Continuation of the debate on *De Ecclesia*.

Tuesday, October 15

First meeting of Subcommission of Commission on Discipline, to which I had been appointed some days earlier. Our job, to revise *De Clericis* chapter II, *De Studio et activita pastorali* in line with emendations sent in by the Fathers during the interval between the Sessions. Four members (Bishop Janssens of Hildersheim (Chairman), Bishop of Luxembourg, Bishop of Liège and an Italian Bishop) and four *Periti* (self, Nabuco, an Italian, and Father Heston who did not turn up). Secretary, Father Sigmond OP, Rector of the Angelicum. We made excellent progress, with the minimum of fuss. Same day, Fathers voted end of debate on chapter II *De Ecclesia* after Moderator Suenens had announced that they would be given the text next day of propositions on the draft points arising and would be called upon to vote on them the day after that (Thursday), so as to give the Doctrinal Commission a better idea of the variety of opinion.

Wednesday, October 16

The promised text of propositions for vote failed to appear (no explanation offered) and a number of speakers claimed right to give their speeches on chapter II. We then moved on to chapter III.

Friday, October 18

4.30 p.m. Participated as one of the panel of an English Press Conference on Liturgy; principal speaker Archbishop Grimshaw, aided by Canon O'Connell.

Saturday, October 19

11.15 a.m. by hired car with Bishop Pearson and Mgr F. Davis to Fiuggi, via Palestrina and Genzzano where we lunched. Pearson remained at Fiuggi, and Davis and I returned via Anagni.

Sunday, October 20

Suffering from bad eyestrain which had begun before I left England. Consecration at St Peter's of Monsignor Igino Cardinale, our new Apostolic Delegate, attended by most of our hierarchy, but not by me. 11 a.m. visited Castel Sant Angelo and climbed to roof. In the evening, made a holy hour (one hour 40 mins) at S. Lorenzo in Damaso where the Rector and students of the English College operated.

Monday, October 21

Cardinal Ottaviani prefaced his speech at the 52nd General Congregation with an objection against three *Periti* whom, he said, had distributed a votum on the non-celibate diaconate in St Peter's. Caught a chill in the evening and went to bed early after taking a Beechams.

Tuesday, October 22

4.30 p.m. second meeting of our Subcommission, at which we completed the task assigned to us. Returned to English College in time to attend the reception of the East African Bishops at the College.

Wednesday, October 23

Debate on chapter III *De Ecclesia* still dragging on. Everyone wondering why the Moderators do not intervene.

Thursday, October 24

De Liturgia, chapter IV was voted through as a whole, but with 552 *iuxta modum*. Debate on chapter III *De Ecclesia* voted closed. Then, at the request of the moderators Cardinals Santos and Ruffini put the case for separate treatment of BMV and Cardinal König for insertion in *De Ecclesia*. Text of speeches to be issued tomorrow for study over the weekend.

Friday, October 25

Eight Fathers exercised right to speak on chapter III *De Ecclesia* and then we moved to chapter IV. Bishop Dwyer and Beck flew back to England for a break.

Saturday, October 26

Worked in library to 11 a.m. on Right to Marry. Then, Revv. Bernard and Leo Sharratt, accompanied by Dr Redmond, discovered me, and I went with them to St Peter's and back.

Worked again in the evening on the Right to Marry, in the hope of presenting a votum on the subject, if and when the subject of mixed marriages might come up for discussion.

Sunday, October 27

Attended the Ordination in College Chapel by Cardinal Heard of nine priests, including three Ushawmen (Sharratt, Tully and Cookson) and then went to lunch with Cookson family at convent of Sisters of the Atonement, on the Janiculum. Taxi back to College and then at 4 p.m., by coach, robed, with bishops to St Peter's for the Beatification Ceremony (veneration of relics) of B. Dominic Barberi. Admitted to special bench reserved to English hierarchy just to right of Pope's priedieu. Walked home.

Monday, October 28

9 a.m. Commemoration of election of late Pope John XXIII instead of General Congregation. Mass celebrated by Pope Paul at the Conciliar altar. Eloquent address in French by Cardinal Suenens. I attended in robes, but in usual Tribune. 4.30 p.m. went to lecture by Father Courtney Murray SJ on Religious Toleration.

Tuesday, October 29

The vote was taken on BMV, the Fathers deciding by a bare majority of 40 (1114 to 1074) to attach it to *De Ecclesia*. There had been considerable activity over the weekend by the opponents and several statements of the case for separate BMV had been circulated. *Il Tempo* accused English bishops of seeking to attenuate defined doctrines such as the Assumption and Immaculate Conception. Mgr Worlock made a protest at *Il Tempo* Offices and finally obtained a printed "dementi" which withdrew the charge in response to a "prezziossima chiarificazioni" from the English Bishops!

The long awaited propositions of the Moderators on chapter II *De Ecclesia* were distributed during the Congregation. A small informal meeting was held in our Common Room at teatime to discuss how the Bishops should vote. Redmond and I entertained Fathers Bernard and Leo Sharratt to dinner at the trattoria da Pancrazio.

A small informal meeting in Common Room at teatime discussed what vote should be given on the five propositions. Some doubts were expressed whether Episcopus = summus gradus Sacramenti Ordinis. 7 p.m. Redmond and I entertained the two Fathers Sharratt (Bernard and Leo) to dinner at the Trattoria da Pancrazio, an underground vault in the ruins of the Theatre of Pompey.

Wednesday, October 30

58th General Congregation. The five propositions were carried, all by large majorities. 1. 2123 *placet* to 34 *non placet*. 2. 2049 to 104. 3. 1808 to 336. 4. 1717 to 408 5. 1588 to 525 (diaconate). At the end of the General Congregation the Fathers voted to close the discussion *De Ecclesia*, subject to right of those who invoked article 57; and it was announced that the next subject would be *De Episcopis*. A very satisfactory morning's work. Rumour has been circulating that the long delay in putting the above five propositions (said to be wanted by those members of the Theology Commission who were being blocked by the Ottaviani faction) was due to doubts raised by the Presidents Bench whether the Moderators were competent to discuss this; and that the issue was finally settled at a joint meeting by a majority of one vote. The Bishop of Coutances (apparently) confirmed this at lunch today. In the evening most of the Bishops and 30 students went to Saints John and Paul for a Pontifical High Mass (Heenan) and Sermon (Alfred Wilson CP) in honour of the Beatification of Dominic Barberi. The Pope has written a letter to the Archbishop of Westminster, for general release, on the same subject. I spent the evening studying the schema *De Episcopis*.

Thursday, October 31

59th General Congregation. The relatio on chapters VI and VII *De Liturgia* was made and the Fathers were asked by Moderator Döpfner if, instead of voting on the individual emendations, they were content to vote on the chapter as a whole. They indicated their affirmative "surgendo" and at the end of the Congregation it was announced as passed by large majority.

Döpfner observed that there had been constant complaints about the protracted debates, yet, despite yesterday's vote to end debate *De Ecclesia*, more than 25 still wanted to speak by virtue of article 57. He begged them to keep strictly within the limits of the subject, to avoid all repetition; notified them that they would be warned at 6 mins and gonged at eight, and reminded them that written observations would be given the same attention as spoken. We just managed to get through by the end of morning. Archbishop Roberts came to supper. He is staying with "Bob Kaiser". Worlock went to *Il Tempo* to protest against the charge that the British draft *De BMV* sought to "attenuate" Immaculate Conception and Assumption. The editor agreed to see Abbot Butler.

Friday, November 1

All Saints. Raining. House is half empty. Bishops Dwyer, Beck, Rudderham and Petit are in England. Bishops Restieaux and Pearson at Nice. Bishops Grasar and Foley at Assisi. Archbishop Grimshaw and secretary at Villa above Palazzola. Bishop Holland on Retreat at Frascati. Heenan and Brunner have colds. *Il Tempo* this morning prints an implicit retraction which it calls a "preziossima chiarificazione" of the English draft on BMV, both as regards its intention and contents.

Saturday, November 2

All Souls. Dry but scirocco. Worked on schema *De Episcopis*.

Sunday, November 3

Beautiful sunny day, with pleasant breeze. 10.30 with Bishop Cashman, P. Redmond and M. Ashdowne (driver) in car down through Campagna, Pontine Marshes, coffee at Latina, to Terracina and thence along beautiful precipitous coast to Formio, where we lunched at Ristorante della Quercia, overlooking the harbour. Excellent lunch: Antipasto, Sole, fruit, local wine. Then through the gap in the Aurunci to Cassino, up to the Abbey. Then back by the Autostrada, arriving at College 7pm.

Monday, November 4

Worked all morning on comments on *De Episcopis*.

Tuesday, November 5

60th General Congregation began *De Episcopis* in genere. Some good speeches, especially from the French Bishops who complained that the schema failed to give practical expression to the theological principles enunciated in *De Ecclesia*. Hot sticky scirocco, oppressive even in St Peter's. 12 noon. Announcement that Mgr Tickell had been named Episcopus Castrorum. 4 p.m. Conciliar meeting of Hierarchy, at which I presented and expounded a votum calling attention to specific points in the schema *De Episcopis*. 5 p.m. Reception for Canadian Bishops.

Wednesday, November 6

Still hot scirocco. Death of Archbishop Mannix. Discussion of *De Episcopis* "in genere" ended by general agreement. Moderator then put question whether Fathers wanted to accept it as a *basis* for discussion. Past, with about 400 odd dissents. Maximus IV Saigh ended the debate with a demand that the Curia should be replaced by an Episcopal Body, on which only those Cardinals who have Sees should participate. Ruffini led off with an objection that the Collegiality of the Bishops had not been finally decided, and that, in any case, its meaning had not been determined. Most of those who followed continued however to call for a version of *De Episcopis* which gave practical application to Collegiality.

Fulton Sheen, Bishops of Lourdes and Quimper, Agnellus Andrew and Vernon Sproxton (BBC) came to lunch. Exhausting weather. Dragged my steps throughout a 20 min walk to far end of Piazza Navona and back. Tom Driberg came to supper and listened to a long theological discussion, started by a question on Anglican orders, in which Charles Davis expressed some (to me) novel views.

Thursday, November 7

Heavy rain during the night. Sunny with scirocco. Bishop Foley (temporarily, for Vicar General's funeral) and P. Redmond (permanently) left for England.

62nd General Congregation. Discussion of chapter I *De Episcopis*. Several speakers spoke warmly in praise of Curia e.g. Batanian, Del Pino and Mazon (but next day, Ruffini, in expressing gratitude in Aula to Batanian, mentioned that he was a former pupil of his).

Friday, November 8

63rd General Congregation. Felici announced presence of Archbishop Carinci (aged 101) who wished to thank Fathers for their messages of previous day, and to wish them as long a life as his and even longer. An interesting detail. Frings, in evident answer to Ruffini's speech of Wednesday, asked whether the almost unanimous consensus of the Fathers re Collegiality counted for nothing. It was not for Conciliar Commissions to review again what the Council had decided, but to carry out the will of the Fathers. The appendix on relations of Bishops to Curia should be brought back into the text, so that particular effect could be given to the vague general principles in it. The distinction between adonii et judici should be extended to all Congregations, Holy Office included. The ratio agendi of the Holy Office was to be adapted to modern conditions. Even in the Holy Office, no one should be judged or condemned without being heard and given a chance to correct self or book.

Ottaviani (two speeches later) in a very angry voice begged leave to preface his comments with a strong protest ("altissimi") against the charges made against the Holy Office whose head is the Pope, made, he said, ex nescientia procedurae, and of the amount of previous consultations. The most constructive speech of the morning was made by Cardinal Lercaro who, dealing with the Collegiality of the Bishops and their power over the whole church, observed that there was nothing to stop its more frequent exercise through some representative central organ. This however raised problems. It had to be integrated with existing structures (Cardinals, Curia, Administration etc) and only the Pope could do this. The Pope had expressed a desire for proposals to be made, and it was not a matter that could be settled in a two day debate. The whole matter should be removed from the schema. The Fathers should make their proposals, but only after the matter had been studied by a special commission after the Session. Rugambwa followed with similar suggestions.

In the evening, I went to Press Conference by Bishop Dwyer on the schema *De Episcopis*. Quite competent. But I was told by P. Keegan and later by Desmond Fisher that the American Press Conference given every day at 3 p.m. has ours beaten to a frazzle for liveliness, frankness and a general efficiency. Bishops Rudderham and Petit have returned from England.

Saturday, November 9

Weather still very warm. Worked all day on a collation of last week's debates about expressions of Episcopal Collegiality in a representative central Council assisting the Pope in government of Church, and on question whether episcopal faculties are regularly regarded as concessions.

Sunday, November 10

Weather still very warm. No rain. Did not go to the Pope's Taking Possession of Lateran, partly because too much work to do, partly because doubtful whether I'd get a good enough place. (I later gathered that I would have done, and that it was an excellent Ceremony). After lunch, watched the Italy v Russia match on TV. Evening, worked until 7pm on Collation of Debates with comments.

Monday, November 11

Warm and sunny, like a summer's day. Archbishop Murphy and Bishop Ellis returned to England, the former because of constant stomach trouble.

64th General Congregation enlivened by an impassioned protest from De Vito of Lucknow against any suggestion of resignation. Fathers are to vote tomorrow whether to transmit chapter V of *De Episcopis* to Code Reform Commission.

After lunch, went for a long walk with Bishop Dwyer round the centre of Rome.

Tuesday, November 12

Still warm and sunny. At the 65th General Congregation the Fathers voted to remit chapter V of *De Episcopis* to Code Reform Commission. *Placet* 2025; *non placet* 141. Suenens made a strong plea for a prescription regarding resignation by aged and infirm Bishops; a law is required, salvo iudicio in casiis particularibus. Hervas proposed abolition of Coadjutors cum iure. Some wanted less Titulars, less Auxiliaries, others wanted them to be given a clearer juridical status. Some want to solve the problem of aged bishops by appointing Coadjutors with all the power of an Administrator Apostolic, so that the old man retains role and honours, but all responsibility and rights pass to Administrator. Then fathers voted to end discussion of chapter II, and we passed to chapter III. National Conferences: McIntyre and Gracias spoke against giving them juridical status. Meyer — no juridical obligation except when absolutely required, and demanded by Pope or General Council — otherwise of a new form of centralisation. Ritter was strong on uniformity and satisfied with the schema, because discussions obligatory only when confirmed by Pope. Landazurri-Ricketts wanted less Provincial Councils.

4 p.m. Hierarchy Conciliar meeting on Liturgy and on Ecumenism. 5.30 to 7 p.m. Reception at College for French, Belgian and Dutch Hierarchies, plus the one Bishop of Denmark.

At supper, Van Vilsen, a Dutch Dominican Bishop (Kronstadt, South Africa), defended the Pill and claimed that good Dutch Catholics were using it without scruple.

Wednesday, November 13

Still equally warm and sunny. 66th General Congregation began with a magnificent Mass in the Byzantine Russian Rite (Liturgy of St John Chrysostom), beautifully sung, especially the Deacon who had a magnificent bass voice. Debate all the morning on Episcopal Conferences, most speakers being anxious that they should not be able to impose a juridical obligation. Afternoon, booked my return flight for Thursday, December 5, 1.15 p.m. and ordered two copies of photo of Bishop Cunningham and self on steps of St Peter's (November 12th).

Thursday, November 14

Rain during the night, and still falling lightly when we left for St Peter's. There we received copies of Paul VI's Apostolic Letter *Summi Dei Verbum* commemorating fourth centenary since establishment of Seminaries by Trent. The Vote was taken separately on the two chapters of *De Instrumentis Communicationis Socialis*, both of which were passed.

25 speakers on chapter III of *De Episcopis* were announced, but after 10 had spoken, the Moderators proposed closure and it was accepted. Those who still wished to speak, vi article 57, could do so tomorrow, if they

repeated their request, but they were asked to use discretion, because in the past, most such speeches had been mere repetitions (applause).

Chapter IV was therefore introduced (on Divisions and Boundaries of Dioceses) and six speakers were heard. Criteria were suggested and discussed. One thought it inexpedient to divide a homogenius conurbation, another thought it impossible for a Bishop to be pastor of a city of 7, 8, or 900,000 and suggested Episcopi Suburbani to govern various zones. Another thought 20,000 enough, and was against suppression of small dioceses; whereas an Italian (Sorrentino), himself Bishop of a very small diocese wanted firm action to reduce the number of tiny dioceses in Italy, over 300, some with only 20 to 30 parishes, of which some had only 20 to 30 families.

Friday, November 15

Mild, some cloud, but no rain. The 68th General Congregation was a dull affair. Four Fathers exercised their right to resume discussion of chapter III, and those who then spoke on chapter IV had very little to add and were not numerous enough to last the rest of the morning. The debate on *De Episcopis* thus petered out at 11.45 and we were released with the announcement that the discussion of *De Oecumenismo* would begin on Monday morning.

4.30 p.m., I went with Grasar and Pearson to the English Press Conference on Ecumenism, given by Cardinal Heenan, aided by Mgr F. Davis and Father Charles Davis. There was a large attendance, though questions were slow in coming at first, they eventually more than filled the allotted period, and at the end, I heard the Chicago Daily News reporter, behind me, vote it a very good conference. I devoted the rest of the evening to a votum on the relation of *De Oecumenismo* to the crushing law of Canon 1258 re Communio in sacris.

Saturday, November 16

Bright and sunny and quite warm. A May day morning. Typed out my votum and then went for a stroll prior to making for Tre Scalini, where Bishop Cunningham entertained the Hexham students and dinner (1 p.m.). Hors d'oeuvre, cannelloni (I took minestrone), Pollo Romano (others lamb or steak) ice cream or fruit or dolci.

Evening. To the Columban Father's house where we were hospitably entertained (the two Davis, self and Father O'Brien). Returned feeling very well indeed. The shock had cured the gastric heaviness from which I had been suffering all week and longer. Everyone (the newspapers included) is talking about the meeting to be held today by the Pope in the Vatican, allegedly to smooth out differences between the various factions among the senior members of the Council (Presidents, Moderators). It is said, e.g., that Ottaviani has been holding up the printing of the chapter on Religious Liberty (said to have been passed by vote of the Theology Commission earlier in the week) which is to be added to the schema *De Oecumenismo*.

Sunday, November 17

Some rain. Still warm. The bishops met at 10 a.m. to discuss what immediate steps might be taken in implementing the liturgical reforms and concerns especially regarding the vernacular. Grimshaw is anxious to keep the lead among the English speaking nations. Nothing much in the way of rumour about yesterday's meeting at the Vatican, except a rumour that the resumption of the Council may be postponed to 1965 to let things settle down. After tea, went for a walk to the Piazza del Populo. Holy Hour 7 to 8.

Monday, November 18

Definitely autumn. Sharp at first and some haze.

First debate on *De Oecumenismo*. Only eight speeches, because of other business. Some criticism of the title, and from the Orientals, sharp criticism of the inclusion of a special chapter *De Judaeis*. Went to American Press Conference in afternoon.

Tuesday, November 19

Sharp but pleasant. Most of the 70th General Congregation was taken up by Malabar Mass, and three Relationes on *De Oecumenismo*. (Bukatko on *De Orientalibus*, Bea on *De Judaeis*, and De Smedt on *De Libertate Religiosa*). Nine speakers, mostly favourable to schema. After lunch, with Dwyer in car to Aventine, where we visited Santa Sabina and strolled around. Tickle and Foley back from England. Evening. Gonzi of Malta came to talk to our Bishops.

Wednesday, November 20

Warm again. (70 degrees in St Peter's Square at midday).

Debate in general favourable. Archbishop Heenan made his best speech yet, and received the only round of applause of the morning. Cardinal Bacci complained that, on October 20th, when the five famous propositions were announced as to be put to the vote, he sought leave to speak and was denied it by the Moderators, and had felt bound in conscience to appeal to the Pope. Later in the debate, Cardinal Agananian (Moderator of the day) explained what had happened. Bacci had come to the table and complained about a defect of latinity. The moderators had referred to the "ius primatiale" of the Pope. Bacci wanted the genitive "ius primatus". The Moderators decided that the text was clear enough, that "primatialis" meant the same as "primatus" and that this sense in any case was evident from context. They decided therefore that there was no ground for further delay.

4 p.m. conciliar discussion — mainly about the clause "... gravis communicatione in cultu officiali", I wanted it clarified. Butler was deputed to intervene on the point, but he prefers to expunge the clause altogether and substitute according to the judgement of local Bishops' Conference.

5.30 to 7. Reception for US Hierarchy. Good turn up but would have been more if there had not been a day's strike on public transport, which made taxis harder to get.

Tom Burns came to supper and afterwards there was a warm discussion between him and Bishops Beck, Petit and Heenan about some recent examples of slanted or positively invented reporting in *The Universe*.

Thursday, November 21

Bright sunshine. Warm and pleasant. 34 speakers de schema in genere were announced (Felici cutting short the list with "et satis"), but after seven had spoken, the Moderators proposed closure of de schema in genere (agreed standing) and asked the Fathers to vote (by paper) whether they accepted the first three chapters as the basis for discussion. (Same question will be put later on chapter IV, and on chapter V). We then proceeded to the debate on chapter I and got through five speakers. Chapter III *De Liturgia* was voted through.

Evening 6 p.m. Attended, *vice* Archbishop Heenan, an international meeting of Periti (about 20) at the Spanish College to discuss *De Oecumenismo*. The chief participants were Lucas Fischer (Swiss professor) and Professor Nisiotis and the Archbishop of Saragossa (Morciar) was chairman. Fischer maintained that the schema did not provide a basis for ecumenical discussion since it began from the point of view of Catholic ecclesiology instead of beginning from Christ. Nisiotis agreed. The schema viewed non-Catholic Churches merely from the stand point of the elements which they had in common with the Catholic Church, and therefore presented a false picture of things. A sharp breeze (tramontana) in the evening.

Friday, November 22

Sunny but sharp.

The schema *De Liturgia* as a whole was voted through. *Placet* 2158; *non placet* 19; *iuxta modum*, therefore null 1. *The first completed achievement of the Council!*

Lunch. Yves Nolet came as my guest. After lunch, I walked to St Cecilia's and back.

4.30 went with the Bishops to tea with Irish Hierarchy at the Irish College – followed by a discussion on joint consultation in implementing the liturgical changes.

Supper. Guests included Patrick Smith (BBC Rome correspondent). Robert Kaiser (*Time*) and Nichol (*Times*), Desmond Fisher (*Catholic Herald*) and the managing director of the *Catholic Herald*. Towards the end of supper, Patrick Smith was called to the phone and came back with the news that President Kennedy had been shot dead. Archbishop Heenan conveyed the news to the table and there was universal consternation. Italian TV at once abandoned all its programmes except for occasional bulletins and a special program on the President's life. Heenan immediately sent a telegram to the

Vice-President, Mrs Kennedy and Cardinal Spellman. The heating went on for the first time at the College.

Saturday, November 23

Sunny but cool. Worked most of the morning on a collation of the debate in genere on *De Oecumenismo*. Only about eight of us in for dinner. Rested in afternoon and did little work in the evening.

Sunday, November 24

Weather as before. After High Mass, typed out my collation of last week's debate.

1 p.m. Lunch in honour of Cardinale, the new Apostolic Delegate, attended by Sir Peter Scarlett and Mr Cape, and all the Hierarchy (who had held a hierarchy meeting from 10.15 to 12.30). Festa. After lunch, went for a walk with Bishop Dwyer.

Monday, November 25

Moved on two chapter II of *De Oecumenismo*. After three Cardinals had spoken, Tisserant intervened to complain that "hodie, fere empti aditum huius aulae" leaflets had been distributed, bearing names of Fathers who invited other Fathers to join with them in voting *non placet* to the Decree *De Communicationibus*, which had already been approved by a large majority in Aula. He deplored it as contrary to the dignity of the Council (he said leaflets were distributed to us as we got out of our buses, and before we went through the barrier below the steps of St Peter's). The final vote de integro schem. Social Communications was taken: Voters 2112. *Placet* 1598; *non placet* 503, null 11.

5 p.m. Attended, in robes, Requiem for Kennedy at Lateran. About 35 Cardinals and 1000 Bishops turned up. Phils' concert after supper.

Tuesday, November 26

Scirocco moist. A few speakers claimed right to speak on chapter I including Leven of Texas, who made a rather immoderate attack on those who speak as though all were well in Catholic countries and venturing to lecture bishops on non-Catholic countries. Then on with chapter II. Not much progress.

4.30 Thunderstorm. Attended a meeting of the Commission on Discipline, under Cardinal Castaldo of Naples. We got through the matter of subcommission in a half-an-hour, and then I came away accompanied by Nabuco, who had barely arrived. Reception at the College for the German, Austrian, Polish and East European Hierarchies (Frings Döpfner, König, Wyszynski).

Wednesday, November 27

Heavy rain at 8 a.m. Thunder and lightning , and again when we emerged from St Peter's. A *good debate. HUSTLE.* 41 speakers for chapter II were read out, but after only seven had spoken, Moderator Döpfner intervened to say that, judging from the number of repetitions, meditations and examinations of conscience, this subject was exhausted, and that the fathers were asked to indicate "surgendo" whether they wanted to proceed to chapter III. Almost unanimously they did, and annual list of 24 speakers was read out.

Cardinal Bacci, after proposing that "et auctoritate" should be added to the sentence "Cuius (Romanae Sedis) est praesidere in caritate" devoted the rest of his speech justifying his attempt to have "ius primatiale" changed to "ius primatus" in the five propositions voted upon during *De Ecclesia*. It was a theological and thereby linguistic point, to remove all ambiguity, and in any case linguistics are important in doctrine, witness the iota at Nicaea. Moderator Suenens firstly remarked at the end of Bacci's speech that, in the opinion of the moderators "nulla aequivicatio est in hac re in mente Patrum".

A rousing and realistic speech from Bishop Dwyer, who pointed out that "veritas in caritate" was not enough for dialogue. We have long had caritas – friendly relations – and as the Archbishop of Wales had said recently, Anglicans reject our doctrines, not because they don't understand them, but because they understand them and think them erroneous.

Thursday, November 28

Damp but warm. Nothing very threatening in the morning's debate. Yesterday's progress on to Chapter III was held up, because 15 speakers exercised their right to resume discussion of Chapter II. Cardinal Frings raised the question of Mixed Marriages. It should be made clear that in every Mixed Marriage the Catholic was bound "gravissima obligatione" to ensure that all children be brought up in the Catholic faith; if the non-Catholic did not agree, let him not be forced. At the least pro foro interno et sacramenti, the Church should declare that in future mixed marriages are valid, as they were in Germany until the decree which imposed the law of the present Code.

1 p.m. Gave a lunch to 9 Ushawmen (eight English College and one – Spence – from Scots College) at Scoglio De Frisio in Via Merulana, opposite Sant'Alfonso Church. They had laid the table for a Thanksgiving Day dinner and seven of us opted for it. The main dish was gargantuan (turkey and all the trimmings), and followed by pumpkin pie (21.000 lire).

Friday, November 29

Bright and breezy. Springlike. Debate continued on Chapter III, but first a lot of announcements by Felici regarding the *Sessio Publica* (nothing is being defined as of faith in the two documents to be solemnly passed

— Liturgy and Social Communications and in future if anything is ever defined it will be made perfectly clear), regarding the unofficial dates of next Session: September 14 to November 20.

The final revised text of *De Liturgia* was distributed, and the text of a message to priests of the whole world — to be voted on Monday, December 2. The results of election of new members. Butler was elected to the Theological Commission and Bishop Wall to the Commission De Seminariis. Most of the debate centred around reunion with Orientals. With Dwyer by car to the Janiculum, where we had a very pleasant walk, with lovely views of Rome.

Saturday, November 30

9-11 a.m. Attended, in choir robes, the Episcopal Consecration of Monsignor Tickle (Ordinary of the Forces) in the College Chapel, by Cardinal Heard, assisted by Archbishop Heenan and Bishop Grasar, in the presence of the British Hierarchy and many other celebrities. Reception afterwards in the Salone and Gallery (champagne and sandwiches). 6.45 To the Vatican, with Mgrs Clark and Worlock in the College car, for the Papal Audience to Periti (7.15) in the Sala Clementina. Monsignor Colombo read an address to the Holy Father, who then read an address to us (over 200) stressing the volume of work for the Council. He then walked along the front row, giving his ring to as many as could get near him.

Sunday, December 1

Weather still fine. Hierarchy met 10.15-12.30 to discuss liturgical changes. 1.30 Consecration Dinner with Cardinal Cicognani as chief guest. Afterwards, drove with Bishop Dwyer to the Pincian Gardens for a stroll. Lovely weather. No need of an overcoat. Visited the Sacred Heart convent next to San'Trinità dei Monti to see their picture of Our Lady (1840) and bought copies. The Americans are said to be annoyed at the apparent unwillingness of the Council authorities to let the Fathers vote as to whether chapter IV (*De Judaeis*) and chapter V (*De Libertate Religiosa*) are to be kept in the schema *De Oecumenismo*. Rumours that Cardinals Meyer and Ritter had decided to raise the subject but had received a hint that it would not be welcomed.

Monday, December 2

Bright and sunny. Feast of the College Martyrs.

79th and last General Congregation of the Session. Mass by Archbishop Ngô-Dinh-Thuc, brother of late President Diem of Vietnam, who offered it for his 2 dead brothers, on the 30th day after their murder.

Felici explained the inter-Session work. The Commissions will work hard on the *Animadversiones Patrum*, and the Fathers can send in fresh ones up to January 30th. Owing to the large number of Animadversiones (over 600) sent in regarding the proposed *Nuntius* from Council, it would be impossible to send it out now; and therefore must be postponed. Only 15 speakers were announced and one of them withdrew. When the debate finished, Bea summed up, and then Bishop Hengsbach gave a relatio *De Apostolatu Laicorum*, which it had been hoped to discuss in this Session. The Moderator then thanked everyone and the Session ended.

1 p.m. Photo in Cortile of Hierarchy, visitors and students, followed by feast in refectory and coffee and liqueurs in the gallery. 6 p.m. Reception at the Legation. 8 p.m. Film: "The World of Harold Lloyd"

Tuesday, December 3

Solemn Commemoration of Fourth Centenary of the Council of Trent. Dialogued Low Mass coram Papa by Cardinal Secretary of State, a long Latin discourse on Trent and its effects by Cardinal Urbani, Patriarch of Venice, a French address to the Holy Father (mainly on Ecumenism) by Jean Guitton, and a short Italian speech by Signor Veronese. Then Felici read out the list of Faculties granted, as from December 8, to the Bishops, Resident and Titular. All rather boring. Weather fine and warm.

12.30 with Bishop Brunner, Mgr O'Mahoney and Father B. Loftus to the Ristorante Da Pancrazio for lunch. Drowsy afterwards.

Wednesday, December 4

Solemn Public Session to close second Session of the Council. 8.30 a.m. In robes, with the Bishops, by coach to St Peter's. Walked up the nave and found a good seat, next to Mgr Worlock, in the benches reserved to Prelates at the right of the Papal throne. An impressive and not too prolonged ceremony. Dialogued Low Mass. Solemn voting on the Constitution *De Sacra Liturgia* (passed with only four dissentients) and on the Decree on Means of Social Communications (164 *non placet*). At the end of the Pope's address, he announced his intention of paying a visit to the Holy Land early in the New Year. (Applause). Out into the sunshine a little after 12.30. After tea, went to Gammarrelli's to buy sash, piping and buttons. Raining. Started to sort out my papers etc. Father Hoersy SJ and Father Molinari SJ came to supper and afterwards, in the Common Room, they were challenged about indisciplined Jesuits, notably Rahner. They admitted that the General had been too unwell these last two or three years to exercise effective control. Molinari said of Rahner that he posed more questions (in an obscure way,) than he attempted to answer.

Thursday, December 5

Packed until 10.30. Then discovered that my plane ticket was made out for BEA 1.15 p.m. November 5 instead of Alitalia 1.15 December 5. Temporary panic. Fortunately Bishop Tickle rang up the airline offices and discovered that my name was on the passenger list correctly.

11.45. In car, driven by Mgr Clark, with Bishop of Middlesborough, to Beda to pick up Bishop Cunningham. Near Ostia Antica, found Bishops

Grasar, Parker and Restieaux standing by the side of the road, their hired car having broken down. An American in a C.D. car was returning from taking Bishop McDevitt to the airport came to their aid. I transferred to his car with Bishop Parker and we arrived in good time. No excess baggage was charged to our party. The plane took off at 1.20 but when it had climbed over the Mediterranean, with sundry things that, we thought, indicated trouble with the landing gear, the captain announced that, owing to a mechanical fault, we were returning to Rome airport. Rather tense for a while, but the trouble cannot have been landing gear, because we made a smooth landing and a number of cars with technicians came out and tinkered with various things in the pilot's cabin, and again taking on fresh fuel, we took off at 2.15 and reached London about 3.40, English time. Caught the 5.20 to Maidstone and arrived home by taxi about 6.30.

Friday, December 6

Received letter from Monsignor Grant informing me of the sudden death of Reverend Leo Sharratt, in sleep, in night of Wednesday to Thursday.

Saturday, December 7

7.30 p.m. Assisted at reception into Church, at St Francis' Maidstone, of Tony Brown, Kate's fiancé.

Monday, December 9

Returned to Ushaw, to learn that Leo Sharratt had been buried that morning.

December 10 – 25

This time (unlike First Session) I was fit enough to resume duties at once. I also prepared a talk on the second Session of the Council and gave it on different nights, first to Divines and then to Philosophers. Further, I managed to devise four Conference cases for Shrewsbury and dispatched them on Christmas eve.

The Third Session

September 14th – November 21st 1964

Tuesday, September 1

10.32 Dover. Nearly strained my arms carrying my heavy case and sack from taxi to the boat. 12.50 boat. Ceinture at Paris to Gare de Lyon, where I had to lump my bags along a very long platform to change trains. A good dinner on the train and dozed fitfully through the night in a first-class carriage with six occupants.

Wednesday, September 2

Arrived Pisa at 10.30, booked a room in Hotel Nettuno on the Arno and drove there in a carrozza. Lunch, siesta then visited the Campo dei Miracoli.

Thursday, September 3

Painted a sketch of the leaning Tower, with Cathedral in background. Very hot.

Friday, September 4

Coach to Lucca, where I painted church of San Frediano.

Saturday, September 5

Scirocco. Long walk in search of subject, driven home by shower and then in late afternoon did a sketch of an old tower on the Lungarno

Sunday, September 6

Scirocco. Painted view in Piazza dei Cavalieri. Showers in the afternoon.

Monday, September 7

Read and packed until 11.45 when taxi to station arrived. 12.10 train to Empoli, changed, arrived at Siena 2.15 p.m. An Italian with whom I talked on the train gave me a lift in his car and booked me into the Hotel Italia, just outside the gates.

Tuesday, September 8

Perfect weather. Morning, sketch of the Duomo. Afternoon, hurried sketch of the tower in the Campo.

Wednesday, September 9

Very hot. Morning, sketch of San Domenico; afternoon, sketch of landscape from the walls.

Thursday, September 10

Morning, sketch of the Porta Romana. Evening, sketch of the parish church where I was saying Mass.

Friday, September 11

Sketch of the Campo. Did the drawing from a postcard in the shade near the Duomo, and after lunch did the painting. Not very successful. The photo perspective was faulty.

Saturday, September 12

12.20 train to Rome, via Chiusi. The train from Chiusi was packed even in the first-class and it was only by kindness of a traveller that I had a seat for part of the journey. Arrived Rome 4:30 p.m. and got a taxi to the College. Tea, a bath, and then unpacked in my old room in the Mezzanine flat.

Sunday, September 13

Hot weather. Walk with Dwyer in morning, and again with him in afternoon to Saint Peter's.

Monday, September 14

Solemn opening of Third Session. 8.15 coach to St Peter's. Good seat in the Prelates' part to the right of papal altar. Pope concelebrated with 24 bishops in a very impressively simple ritual. After lunch, to Villa with Archbishop Grimshaw's car. Sketched courtyard.

Tuesday, September 15

First General Congregation. After lunch, to Villa with Archbishop Grimshaw and Father O'Brien. Finished sketch of courtyard, which I gave to Bishop Tickle.

Wednesday, September 16

After lunch, declined an invitation to go in Archbishop Grimshaw's car to Villa, had a nap, tea and then a short walk. After supper, Father O'Leary gave a talk in Bishops' Common Room on the latest opinions re contraception; Tom Burns wrote that they already have several books on same line.

Thursday, September 17

After lunch, with Bishop Dwyer in his car to the Foro Italico and then to top of Monte Mario but couldn't find a place to walk. After tea, conciliar meeting on schema *De Ecclesia.*

Saturday, September 19

11.15 a.m. to Palazzola in Archbishop Grimshaw's car. Lunch with many of the Bishops. Painted front view of Villa (later gave it to Rector), had tea on sforza where the students were playing the B.E.A. at cricket.

Sunday, September 20

Worked till lunch. 3 — 5.30 at Pamphili to watch cricket between touring Australian amateurs and the Roman Sports Association. News of death in England of Monsignor Lamb, Vice-Rector of the Beda College.

Monday, September 21

After lunch, did preliminary sketch of S. Giorgio in Velabro. Charles Davis arrived.

Tuesday, September 22

Finished sketch of San Giorgio.

Wednesday, September 23

After lunch, did preliminary sketch of triumph of Apollo Sostenes.

Thursday, September 24

After lunch, finished sketch of Triumph. Evening, conciliar meeting of Hierarchy on future schemate.

Friday, September 25

(no entry)

Saturday, September 26

11 a.m., in Bishop Tickle's car with Bishops Foley and Dwyer to airport where Dwyer left for England to attend Dinn's funeral, and on to Villa for lunch. Returned in Archbishop Grimshaw's car at 6 p.m.

Sunday, September 27

(no entry)

Monday, September 28

Rain. Big traffic jam after the General Congregation. Coach reached College at 1.25 p.m.

Tuesday, September 29

After lunch, preliminary sketch of San Nicola in Carcere.

Wednesday, September 30

After lunch, finished sketch of San Nicola in Carcere. Evening began reading P. Fitzpatrick's Manuscript on contraception.

Thursday, October 1

Conciliar meeting of Hierarchy. Father Davis reported on the revised schema *De Revelatione*. Monsignor Worlock on the schema *De Ecclesia in Mundo Huius Temporis*. Bishop Pearson on the reaction of National Board of Catholic Women to reports of change in Church's doctrine on Contraception. According to Worlock, the final vote of the Commission was that the schema should include the Church's doctrine on Contraception. It is not in the schema.

Friday, October 2

(no entry)

Saturday, October 3

After lunch, to Pamphili to watch cricket knock-out competition. Ditto on Sunday afternoon.

Monday, October 5

(no entry)

Tuesday, October 6

(no entry)

Wednesday, October 7

Heard in the bar at St Peter's that the Pope has instructed the Felici to form a committee to study the question of Mixed-marriages. Cautious, and that the Felici had named Onclin as Secretary (confirmed to me by Onclin). After lunch, did sketch of Saints John and Paul.

Thursday, October 8

Conciliar meeting of Hierarchy about the schema *De Ecclesia in Mundo Huius Temporis*.

Saturday-Sunday, October 10-11

A quiet weekend. Heavy rain on Saturday.

Tuesday, October 12

100th General Congregation. Address to Fathers by Pat Keegan.

Saturday-Sunday, October 17-18

Stayed indoors. Did a sketch of Via Appia Antica from Father O'Brien's photo.

Wednesday, October 21

Dinner at Grand Hotel with Father Houghton (host) and Bishops Wheeler and Grant.

Saturday-Sunday, October 24-25

Wet weekend. Wrote animadversions on *De Ministerio et Vita Sacerdotalis* and delivered them by hand at Congregation of Council. Felt giddy on way up to tea, and again on Monday at Mass. Exhausted.

Monday, October 26

Evening collected my Third Session medal at Santa Marta and booked my return flight to London for Friday, November 20th, 14.25. Still feeling physically and mentally exhausted, and rather wobbly on my feet.

Saturday, October 31 to Tuesday, November 3

Long Weekend. Mixed weather. Went with Archbishop Grimshaw to the villetta above Palazzola. Lunch at De Sanctis. Archbishop ate hardly anything.

Wednesday, November 5

Commission meeting at Congregation of Council 4.30

Saturday, November 7

A General Congregation, to pay for the long weekend.

Monday, November 9

Commission meeting at Congregation of Council 4.30. Discussed revised version of *De Ministerio et Vita Sacerdotalis.*

Tuesday, November 10

After the General Congregation, I entertained 14 students to lunch at the Soglio di Frisio restaurant. Costing 44,000 lire, with 4000 sconto. Paid 41,000. At 6 p.m. Father Häring addressed the Bishops, but we priests were not invited.

Wednesday, November 11

Went to reception at home of Mr Cape, First Secretary of the Legation. 6-7 p.m.

Thursday, November 12

Commission meeting at 4.30. Approve final version of *De Ministerio et Vita Sacerdotalis.*

Friday, November 13

Byzantine Mass concelebrated by Maximus IV and other Patriarchs, coram Papa, who, at the end, gave his tiara for relief of world hunger. No General Congregation.

Saturday, November 14

General Congregation to make up for yesterday's omission. Dinner with Bishop Cunningham and Hexham students at the Tre Scalini. Father Mahon, General of the Mill Hill Fathers, attended.

Sunday, November 15

Did a sarcastic cartoon about recent pronouncements in the Council debate on *De Ecclesia in Mundo Huius Tempore.* Supper at the Columban Fathers.

Wednesday, November 18

Tisserant announced that many Fathers had asked for congruum tempus to study the revised schema *De Libertate Religiosa* (discussed previous day, Tuesday, November 17), because it is a new text which, vi art. 35, should first be examined. The Presidency had decided that there should be a vote tomorrow (Thursday).

Thursday, November 19

De Ecclesia final vote. Only 10 dissidents. Tisserant announced that the Presidential Council had reviewed their decision and ruled that, after the Fathers had heard the Relatio of de Smedt on religious liberty, they would not proceed to vote on it in this session. Their comments should be sent in to the Commission before January 31, 1965.

Sensation. Cardinals Meyer and Rittter and other American bishops immediately organised a counter-petition to Pope and had gathered over 800 names before the end of the Congregation. After the Congregation they sought audience with the Pope, who that evening called a meeting of the Cardinals and decided that he could not reverse the Presidents' decision, since it was according to the rulebook.

Friday, November 20

Last General Congregation of this Session. Final votes on *De Oecumenismo* and *De Ecclesiis Orientalibus*. Tisserant — Many Fathers "magno dolore afflicti sunt" by yesterday's decision not to proceed to voting on Religious Liberty. Announced Pope's decision, as above.

I came away at 12, as Heenan finished speaking on mixed-marriages, caught a bus to the College, had early lunch 12.42 -1.10 with the Vice-Rector (J. Brewer) who then drove me to the airport where I caught the 2.25 plane. Reached London on time and caught the 5.22 to Maidstone, reaching home by 6.30. Kate's new baby — Damian.

Monday, November 23

Returned to Ushaw.

The Fourth Session

September 14th — December 8th 1965

Wednesday, September 8

Heavy rain. Breakfasted at our digs and then in a taxi with mother to the Abbey where I concelebrated at the solemn Mass at which Leo made his Solemn Profession. Lunch with the monks. Tea in the parlour. Taxi back to digs, where the landlady made supper for us. Kathleen and Alban called later.

Thursday, September 9

Bright and sunny. Sat in deckchairs and had a picnic lunch on promenade and then got the 1 p.m. boat and 1.40 boat train. Packed train for Waterloo. Back to Maidstone about 6 p.m. Mother bore up splendidly.

Saturday, September 11

Harry arrived for the weekend. Left on Monday.

Monday, September 13

Dennis Dockery drove me in his car to London airport. There met Archbishop Beck and Gray and the Anglican Bishop of Ripon. VIP treatment, drinks and then special car to the Alitalia plane to Rome. Met at Rome airport by Monsignor Alston, Rector, who drove us to the English College, where I settled into the same room as in the two previous sessions on the mezzanine. After tea, went to the Secretariate to collect schemata and had a stroll in the Via della Conciliazione. Warm but not unpleasantly.

Tuesday, September 14

Solemn Public Session in Saint Peter's to inaugurate *Fourth Period of Council*. 8:30 a.m., in robes, to our usual seats at right of papal altar. Pope's address (40 min) referred to the new *Synod of Bishops*. 4.40 p.m. by bus with bishops to Santa Croce in robes. Stood around outside until, about 6 p.m., slow penitential procession with hymns to the Lateran, Pope bringing up the rear carrying reliquary of true Cross. Long-winded sermon by Cardinal Traglia. Blessing by Pope with true Cross. Huge crowd. Traffic jam. Got back to College at 8:30 p.m.

Wednesday, September 15

First General Congregation (128th). New Liturgy for Congregation Mass, fresh texts of Scripture for Epistle and Gospel every day. Gospel enthroned in Introit procession and therefore no prayers at foot of altar. Reading of Motu Proprio *Apostolica Sollicitudo* creating the Synod of Bishops. Pope left at 10.40 a.m.. Tisserant then exhorted the Fathers to avoid vain repetition and to abstain from applause. Agaganian greeted Fathers on behalf of Moderators. Felici read telegram of congratulations from Patriarch Athanagoras to Paul VI.

Finally the schema *De Libertate Religiosa* was introduced and we had speeches from Spellman, Frings, Ruffini (plure optime, attamen), Siri (libertas est in genere defendenda, sed magis defendenda est lex divina). Arriba y Castro, Urbani, Cushing, Alfrink (8 Cardinals).

Thursday, September 16

129th General Congregation. Debate on Religious Liberty continued (5 Cardinals 11 bishops).

Friday, September 17

130th General Congregation. Debate on Religious Liberty. Cardinal Heenan and Conway intervened (6 Cardinals, 12 bishops).

Saturday, September 18

To Anzio with Bishop Cleary and Father O'Brien in latter's car. Bishop bathed. Pleasant lunch in a homely Trattoria. On to Nettuno to visit the home of Maria Goretti.

Monday, September 20

131st General Congregation. Debate on Religious Liberty continued (9 Cardinals, 4 bishops).

Voting began on *De Divina Revelatione.*

Tuesday, September 21

132nd General Congregation. After four more speeches (4 Cardinals, 2 Bishops), debate on Religious Liberty was closed. De Smedt summed up and the Moderators proposed a novel motion: "whether the amended text satisfied the Fathers as the basis of a declaration to be further prepared according to Catholic doctrine "de vera religione" and the emendations proposed by the Fathers in debate and approved in accord with the Ordo Concilii?" *Placet* or *non placet,* per schedulas. Rumour that the Pope had prescribed the taking of this vote. Result: 1997 to 224.

De Ecclesia in Mundo Huius Tempore in genere debate began (4 Cardinals). Announcement of Pope's visit to UNO. 5.30 p.m. to North American College for Monsignor R. Sennott's Jubilee Mass and Dinner, given by Cardinal Cushing (who spoke lengthily and repetitively at the Mass), very sumptuous banquet.

Wednesday, September 22

133rd General Congregation. *De Ecclesia in Mundo Huius Tempore* in genere for more speakers (with 70 supporters) on Religious Liberty. Then four Cardinals and eight bishops on *De Ecclesia in Mundo Huius Tempore.* 5.30pm Hierarchy meeting in Library. Report on foundation of "St Paul's Conference of English-speaking Bishops". After the meeting, Father Vin Lang and his mother came by arrangement to my room for drinks before going out with Bishop Holland to dine at Da Pancrazio (6 in all).

Thursday, September 23

134th General Congregation. *De Ecclesia in Mundo Huius Tempore* in genere, continued, 2 Cardinals, 6 Bishops, (but further speeches in genere

1 Cardinal, 1 Bishop). (Voting began on *De Apostolatu Laicorum*). Fathers voted end of disceptatio in genere and then voted per schedulas that the disceptatio in specie should be a) circa proemium et primam partem b) circa secundam partem.

Friday, September 24

Concelebrated with Dwyer on anniversary of his consecration, along with Bishops Holland and Cleary and Mgr F Davis. My first Concelebration.

135th General Congregation. *De Ecclesia in Mundo Huius Tempore* Proemium and Part I. 5 Cardinals, 6 Bishops.

Saturday, September 25

To Anzio again with Bishop Cleary and Father O'Brien. Painted sketch of harbour. Lunch at Anzio.

Sunday, September 26

Thunder and heavy showers. Pope and bishops went to Gypsy Congress at Pomezio. Supper at Scoglio di Frisio — as guest of Father Vin Lang. Concelebrated every day from Sunday onwards.

Monday, September 27

136th General Congregation. Feally excluded from Tribune of Fathers General. Debate on *De Ecclesia in Mundo Huius Tempore* Part I. Continued. 4 Cardinals, 9 Bishops.

Tuesday, September 28

137th General Congregation. Ditto continued, 1 Cardinal, 14 Bishops, and then, "exhausto numero oratorum" transitus ad partem secundam (cras). Met Father Joseph Dunne in the Piazza, out on a conducted tour.

Wednesday, September 29

138th General Congregation. *De Ecclesia in Mundo Huius Tempore* Part II. Speeches arranged in order of chapters. (Voting began on Modi of *De Pastorali Munere Episcoporum*). Chapter I. 4 Cardinals, 6 Bishops. Zoghby's outburst on divorce as cure for broken marriages. Conciliar Meeting. Then attended reception at British Minister's

Thursday, September 30

139th General Congregation. *De Ecclesia in Mundo Huius Tempore* Part II. Chapter I. 5 Cardinals (including Heenan and Conway). 9 Bishops. Drove with Bishop Rudderham and Father O'Brien to see the new church of St John Bosco.

Friday, October 1

140th General Congregation. *De Ecclesia in Mundo Huius Tempore* Part II. Chapter I. 2 Cardinals, 2 Bishops. Closure of chapter I but 1 further Bishop. Chapter II 7 Bishops.

Evening. Dinner with Father Joseph Dunne at Maestro di Stefano's

Saturday, October 2

Went with Bishop Cleary and Father O'Brien to beach near Anzio. Nice lunch at same friendly Trattoria as on first trip.

Sunday, October 3

Lunch at Maestro di Stefano's with Bishops Rudderham, Grasar and Cleary and Father O'Brien.

Monday, October 4

141st General Congregation. *De Ecclesia in Mundo Huius Tempore* Part II. (Pope flew to New York). 6 Bishops on chapter II and chapter III 3 Cardinals, 8 Bishops. Afternoon, watched TV of Pope's arrival in New York. Holy Hour 4.45-5.45. 8-9 p.m. watched TV of his speech.

Tuesday, October 5

142nd General Congregation. *De Ecclesia in Mundo Huius Tempore* Chapter III. 2 Cardinals, 7 Bishops (including Father Mahon. Chapter IV 4 Bishops. Chapter V 2 Cardinals.

12.50 Pope arrived at St Peter's direct from airport and addressed us. Liénart welcomed him back on behalf of Fathers. 10.30-11.15 watched recording of Pope in Yankee Stadium.

Wednesday, October 6

143rd General Congregation. *De Ecclesia in Mundo Huius Tempore* Part II. Chapter V (Voting *De integro Pastorali Munere* and *De Accom. Vitae Relig.*) 3 Cardinals, 9 Bishops (including Suenens on birth control and abortion). Final vote on *De Pastorali Munere* 2167 to 14.

Thursday, October 7

144th General Congregation. *De Ecclesia in Mundo Huius Tempore* Part II. Chapter V continued. Cardinals Martin and Ottaviani (applauded) 6 Bishops (including Beck). Closure and transition to *De Activitate Missionali* but resumed by 5 (with 70 supporters) at next General Congregation. *De Activitate Missionali* 5 Cardinals spoke. Voting on Adaptation of Religious Life. 12 a.m. Publication of Dwyer's translation to Birmingham.

Friday, October 8

Bishops Cleary and Dwyer left for England.

145th General Congregation. 5 more speakers on *De Ecclesia in Mundo Huius Tempore* (4 on part II chapter V, Philbin on substantial defect in whole schema). *De Activitate Missionali* 3 Cardinals, 4 Bishops.

Saturday, October 9

To Enzio's to watch the grape harvest. Binge on roof of his vineyard house. Then to his Albano house to watch his grape stripping process.

Monday, October 11

146th General Congregation. *De Activitate Missionali* 2 Cardinals, 9 Bishops. Felici read letter from Pope to Cardinal Tisserant ruling that the issue of clerical celibacy was *not to be raised* in debate *De Presbyterorum Ministerio et Vita*. Vote super *De Accom. Renov. Vitae Religiosae*. 2126 to 13.

Tuesday, October 12

147th General Congregation. *De Activitate Missionali* 3 Cardinals, 13 Bishops (including Arrupe SJ General). Closure and Quaestio indicativa: Utrum placeat tamquam basis 2070 *placet*, 15 *non placet*, but *debate prolonged* by speakers with 70 supporters.

Wednesday, October 13

148th General Congregation. 10 further speeches on *De Activitate Missionali*. Marty (Relator)

Introduced our schema *De Presbyterorum Ministerio et Vita*.

Thursday, October 14

149th General Congregation. *De Presbyterorum Ministerio et Vita*. Seven cardinals spoke and five others. After I had worked all the week on the report of the Pontifical Commission on Birth Control, lent to me by Cardinal Heenan, he told me that he had been informed that the Pope had rejected it as unworthy. I agree. But I still have to prepare a statement on the birth-control controversy for our Hierarchy.

Friday, October 15

150th General Congregation. *De Presbyterorum Ministerio et Vita*. Seven cardinals spoke and nine others.

Saturday, October 16

151st General Congregation. *De Presbyterorum Ministerio et Vita*. Eight Cardinals, including Heenan, spoke and eight others. Closure and Question: acceptable as a basis: 1507 to 12.

12.30 To Enzo's Albano place to see wine filtering and ate a huge meal.

Vacatio from General Congregations during the 18- 23 October. Worked on my paper on Birth-Control controversy and also on the *Positio de Sacr. Indulgentiarum Regognitione* (Heenan's copy).

Thursday, October 21

Lunch with the Bishop of Hexham and his students.

Friday, October 22

Read my paper on the Birth-Control controversy to our hierarchy in college library, answered questions 10 a.m. to 12. Then went to lunch at Alfredo's in Trastevere with Monsignor L. Anné and Yves Nolet. Evening went to concerts at Angelicum Regensburg Domspatzen.

Saturday-Sunday, October 23-24

Worked on "Positio" on Indulgences and finished a six page summary and comment on 7 p.m. Sunday.

Monday, October 25

152nd General Congregation. *De Presbyterorum Ministerio et Vita* resumed by seven speakers with 70 supporters. Relatio *De Libertate Religiosa.* Congregation ended at 11.50.

Tuesday, October 26

153rd General Congregation. Debate *De Presbyterorum Ministerio et Vita* four more speakers. Vote on Religious Liberty

12 noon Worlock's appointment Portsmouth announced.

4.30 first meeting of our Commission (for me at least).

7.45 with Bishop Holland to Cape's for supper. Other guests were Bishop Fernandez of Delhi, Canon Pawley, Princess Aurietta and Frank Doria, Bishop Simons of Indore, Bishop of Aberdeen, Vice Rector of Scots College.

Wednesday, October 27

154th General Congregation. No more speeches. Voting on *De Lib. Religiosa.*

Thursday, October 28 Sessio Publica

Promulgation of *De Pastorali Epsicop. Munere*; *De institutione Sacerdotalis*; *De Accom. Vitae Relig.*; *De Educatione Christiana*; *De Habitutine Ecclesiae.*

Friday, October 29

155th General Congregation.

Vacatio from General Congregation October 29 to November 9

Tuesday, November 2

With Restieaux and Grasar by car to Palazzola. Lunch at Nemi.

Thursday, November 4

After lunch, to sea, at Fusana in Bishop Pearson's car. Back for tea.

Friday, November 5

Overslept! Awoke at 7.40. Breakfast and said Mass at nine

Drove with Bishops Restieaux and Grasar to Bracciano. Looked at Castle. Lunch at lakeside. Drove round by Vicorello, had a walk. On to Trevignano and back to Rome by 5pm.

Saturday, November 6

Lunch at La Campana with Bishops Parker, Rudderham, Grasar and Father O'Brien.

Sunday, November 7

Ordination of three priests in College Chapel. Met Vincent Avery. Arnold Lunes to lunch.

Monday, November 8

Most of the bishops now back.

Tuesday, November 9

Cardinal Heenan joined our concelebrating group (for eight or nine days)

156th General Congregation. Six votes *de modis De Apostolatu Laicorum*. To fill the interval, Positio *De Indulgentiarum* introduced by Cardinal Cento. Letter from Pope to Tisserant announcing Public Session on December 7 and to close Council on December 8.

Wednesday, November 10

157th General Congregation. Votes *de modis* super integrum *De Apostolatu Laicorum*. Voting on revised text of *De Activitate Missionali*. Presidents of Episcopal conferences began giving reports on the *Positio De Indulgentiarum*. (Maximos IV very critical, Meouchi (in scriptis), Sidarous, Gilroy and Sheehan for US.

Evening took Vincent Avery to supper at La Carbonara

Thursday, November 11

158th General Congregation. Reading and voting on revised text of *De Activitate Missionali*. Reports on Indulgences from Wyszynski, Alfrink, Ariba y Castro, König and Döpfner (who gave the Poschmann and Rahner view). Announcement by Felici. The word "Sessio" is properly applicable only to Public Sessions in which Acta are promulgated, or the Council is opened or closed, or a profession of faith is made, or documents are promulgated. There have been seven hitherto, and there will be three more (18 November, 7 and 8 December).

Friday, November 12

159th General Congregation. Reading and eight votes on *De Ministerio et Vita Presbyterorum.* (Revised text). Felici, in answer to question, said Conferences at Domus Mariae this month have no official status nor are they authorised by the Secretariate.

Evening, entertained to supper at La Carbonara by Grasar.

Saturday, November 13

160th General Congregation. Meeting and voting revised text *De Ministerio et Vita Presbyterorum.*

Felici, some complain that the Secretary General speaks too much. I would prefer to keep silent. I never speak "propria auctoritate".

Monday, November 15

161st General Congregation. Reading and voting revised *De Ecclesia in Mundo Huius Temporis.*

Tuesday, November 16

162nd General Congregation. Reading and voting revised *De Ecclesia in Mundo Huius Temporis.*

Wednesday, November 17

163rd General Congregation. Reading and voting revised *De Ecclesia in Mundo Huius Temporis.*

Thursday, November 18

Public Session. Promulgation of *De Divina Revelatione, De Apostolatu Laicorum.*

Friday, November 19

164th General Congregation. Voting modi *De Libertate Religiosa.*

Vacatio from General Congregations November 20-30

Attended meetings of our Commission: Friday, November 19 4.30 to 7.30; Saturday, November 20 9-12.15; Monday, November 22 4-7.15; Tuesday, November 23 4-7.15 (completed)

Wednesday, November 24

4.30 Attended talk on the experimental seminary of Louvain by Rector at Villa Miani. Went with Beck and Dwyer.

Friday, November 26

4.30 attended talk by Prof Noonan on lessons drawn from history of Church's attitude to Contraception.

Monday, November 29

Lunch for hierarchy and periti at the Spanish sisters hotel in the Via Ibena. Very sumptuous.

Tuesday, November 30

165th General Congregation. Voting on modi *De Activitate Missionali.*

Thursday, December 2

166th General Congregation. Voting on *De Ministerio et Vita Presbyterorum.*

Friday, December 3

Mgr Davis lecture on Newman at the Gregorianum.

Saturday, December 4

167th General Congregation.
12 votes on modi *De Ecclesia in Mundo Huius Temporis.*
5 p.m. Sacra Celebratio at St Paul's, of Pope, Fathers and Observers (I did not go).

Monday, December 6

168th and Last General Congregation. Vote *De Ecclesia in Mundo Huius Temporis.*

Tuesday, December 7

Public Session. Promulgation of *De Libertate Religiosa; De Activitate Missionali; De Ministerio et Vita Presbyterorum; De Ecclesia in Mundo Huius Temporis.*
7.30 Papal audience to Periti.
Supper with secretaries at trattoria near Piazza Navona.

Wednesday, December 8

Public session of closure in St Peter's Piazza. Good seat about 20 yards to side of Pope's throne. Lovely warm day. Packed in evening.

Thursday, December 9

1.10 Alitalia plane to London. Reached Maidstone at 6 p.m.

Saturday, December 11

Tony drove me to station. 1 p.m. from King's Cross. President and Vice-President met me at Durham. Ushaw 6 p.m. Reception with drinks in front parlour 6-6.30.

Conclusion

The home-coming reception at Ushaw marked the completion of Monsignor Lawrence Leslie McReavy's participation in the work of the Second Vatican Council. He was so conscious of the privilege that he had received that he was anxious to share his experience with others. For several years after his return from the Council he gave many talks and conferences on the Council and its work. Lawrence Leslie McReavy was a man of the Council and he upheld its teaching and embodied its spirit until the end of his long life at Ushaw.

Clearly the documents in this volume retell the story of the Council according to their literary form: the Letters differ in style to the Journal, the Lectures are different to the Diary and taken with the other documents they might be grouped together and described as similar to the colours of a prism dispersing the light of the Council. To a degree repetition is unavoidable. But whoever reads through the chapters of this collection of Monsignor McReavy's writings will acquire a good knowledge of the Council and its workings. This means that Lawrence McReavy's enthusiasm for the Council will continue to live on.

In the *Ushaw Magazine* for the Academic Year 1991 published shortly before Lawrence McReavy's death there appeared an Article entitled *The Spirit of Childhood* in which L.L.McReavy speaks about humility. Since this present volume is primarily concerned with presenting the writings of one of Ushaw's "Great Men", the last paragraph of this Article provides a fitting conclusion and tribute to one who was above all, a holy and humble priest:

> If the world is ever to be a happier place to live in, men must endeavour to recapture the simplicity of the child. The child does not overestimate itself or its rights and lives in ceaseless indignation at fancied injustices; it has absolute trust in the father and mother God has given it; to them it reveals with simple candour all its needs and wants, and there makes an end of it. That is what you and I must do. I say "must" do, because a childlike and humble spirit is not only necessary to sanctity, but to salvation.

Index